Contents

TEST YOURSELF

PLANNING YOUR FUTURE

How to Prepare for the Armed Forces Test

ASVAB

Armed Services Vocational Aptitude Battery

Compiled by the Editorial Department
of Barron's Educational Series, Inc.

BARRON'S EDUCATIONAL SERIES, INC.

New York / London / Toronto / Sydney

The publisher acknowledges gratefully the following for permission to adapt material:

Barkus, Philip. HOW TO PREPARE FOR THE POSTAL CLERK-CARRIER EXAMINATION. Barron's Educational Series, Woodbury, N.Y. 1972

Bright, Delores H. HOW TO PREPARE FOR THE PROFESSIONAL AND ADMINISTRATIVE CAREER EXAMINATION. Barron's Educational Series. Woodbury, N.Y. 1977

Edwards, Gabrielle I. BIOLOGY THE EASY WAY. Barron's Educational Series, Woodbury, N.Y. 1984

Farley, Eugene J. and Farley, Alice R. GETTING READY FOR THE HIGH SCHOOL EQUIVALENCY EXAMINATION. Barron's Educational Series, Woodbury, N.Y. 1973

General Motors Corporation. WHAT MAKES AUTOS RUN. Detroit.

General Motors Corporation. MECHANICAL PRINCIPLES AND THE AUTOMOBILE. Detroit.

Lehrman, Robert L., PHYSICS THE EASY WAY. Barron's Educational Series, Woodbury, N.Y. 1984

Macmillan Publishing Company for permission to adapt material on pages 224 to 233 from GAS ENGINE MANUAL, Third Edition. Reprinted with permission of Macmillan Publishing Company from GAS ENGINE MANUAL, Third Edition by Edwin P. Anderson, revised by Charles G. Facklam. Copyright © 1962, 1965, 1977 by Howard W. Sams. Co., Inc. Copyright © 1985 by G.K. Hall & Co.

Miller, Rex. ELECTRONICS THE EASY WAY. Barron's Educational Series, Woodbury, N.Y. 1984

Rockowitz, Murray. HIGH SCHOOL EQUIVALENCY EXAMINATION. Barron's Educational Series, Woodbury, N.Y. 1984

South-Western Publishing Company for permission to reprint material on pages 320 to 322 from ENERGY: ELECTRICITY/ELECTRONICS. Adapted from ENERGY: ELECTRICITY/ ELECTRONICS by Rex Miller and Fred W. Culpepper, Jr., published by South-Western Publishing Co. Reprinted with permission.

U.S. Military Entrance Processing Command. ASVAB YOUR FUTURE IS NOW. North Chicago, IL. 1983

U.S. Military Entrance Processing Command. HOW TO USE YOUR ASVAB RESULTS. North Chicago, IL. 1983

All inquiries should be addressed to:
Barron's Educational Series, Inc.
250 Wireless Boulevard
Hauppauge, New York 11788

International Standard Book No. 0-8120-3670-0

Library of Congress Cataloging-in-Publication Data

How to prepare for the Armed Forces test—ASVAB, Armed
  Services Vocational Aptitude Battery.

  1. Armed Services Vocational Aptitude Battery.
I. Barron's Educational Services, Inc. Editorial Dept.
II. Title: ASVAB, Armed Services Vocational Aptitude
Battery.
U408.5.H69   1986   355'.0076   86-10958
  ISBN 0-8120-3670-0

PRINTED IN THE UNITED STATES OF AMERICA

89   987

How To Use This Book Effectively

To obtain maximum benefit from this book, we recommend the following approach:

1. Read the sections, "All About the ASVAB" and "Test-Taking Techniques" which appear on pages 1 and 7.

2. Take Model Examination One. This test, which is in the format used on the actual ASVAB, will give you a clear idea of what the examination is like. Take the test, following all the instructions given, including the time limits. After you complete the test, check your answers and record your scores on the Progress Chart on page 455. Your scores will enable you to see your strengths and weaknesses. You have thus diagnosed the problems you have and can now plan your study time.

3. Use the guide on page 456 to plan your studies. Concentrate your study efforts in your weak areas but review other topics as well. Chapters 4 through 11 provide comprehensive review material.

4. Take Model Examination Two. Before you take it, reread the section "Test-Taking Techniques" on pages 7 to 9. After you finish this examination, check your answers, review the explained answers, and complete the Progress Chart on page 455. Then restudy the appropriate chapters in accordance with the advice given in the study guide.

5. Take Model Examination Three. After you have finished this examination, follow the same procedure that you followed after finishing Model Examination Two. Your scores should have improved with each test as you became familiar with the material and reviewed material in your weak subjects.

6. Analyze your job opportunities by studying the *academic composites* and *occupational composites* charts on pages 457 and 458.

1 All About the ASVAB

What Is It?

The Armed Services Vocational Aptitude Battery, the ASVAB, is a group of 10 subtests that measures your ability in separate career areas and provides an indication of your academic ability.

The Test Format

Subtest	Minutes	Questions	Description
1. General Science	11	25	A subtest of knowledge measuring the physical and biological sciences.
2. Arithmetic Reasoning	36	30	A subtest measuring ability to solve arithmetic word problems.
3. Word Knowledge	11	35	A subtest measuring ability to select the correct meaning of words presented in context and to identify the best synonym for a given word.
4. Paragraph Comprehension	13	15	A subtest measuring ability to obtain information from written passages.
5. Numerical Operations	3	50	A *speeded* subtest measuring ability to perform arithmetic computations.
6. Coding Speed	7	84	A *speeded* subtest measuring ability to use a key in assigning code numbers to words.
7. Auto and Shop Information	11	25	A *speeded* subtest measuring knowledge of automobiles, tools, and shop terminology and practices.
8. Mathematics Knowledge	24	25	A subtest measuring knowledge of high school mathematics principles.
9. Mechanical Comprehension	19	25	A subtest measuring knowledge of mechanical and physical principles and ability to visualize how illustrated objects work.
10. Electronics Information	9	20	A subtest of knowledge of electricity and electronics.

Testing Time	144	minutes
Administrative Time	36	minutes
TOTAL TESTING TIME	180	minutes
TOTAL NUMBER OF ITEMS	334	

Your scores on these tests are combined into scores on the following composites:

Verbal
Math
Perceptual Speed
Mechanical
Trade Technical
Academic Ability

Why Should I Take It?

An aptitude battery helps you measure your potential. It can give you a good indication of where your talents lie. By looking at your composite scores and your own personal interests, you can make more intelligent career decisions. For example, the ASVAB:

1. Predicts success in military training schools.
2. Predicts eligibility for various branches of the service. It is required for enlistment in the U.S. Army, Navy, Air Force, and Marine Corps. (While the Coast Guard has its own exam, it will accept ASVAB results.) Each branch of the military has its own standard of eligibility, so that a person who scores low on the ASVAB may be eligible for one branch of the service, but may not be eligible for another.

   Once a person is in a branch, the branch can determine career field or job specialty by minimum score requirements. Anyone who achieves an appropriate score in a desired area may get a particular job, as long as the job is available.
3. Predicts success in secondary and post secondary courses and selected civilian career fields.

The Armed Services Vocational Aptitude Battery is the result of more than 35 years of military service research. It was specifically designed to identify individual aptitudes. If you are a senior trying to decide what to do after high school, your test scores can help identify fields that you might explore. No matter what your age or inclination, the ASVAB can be valuable to you because it can tell you more about yourself.

The ASVAB is not a "PASS" or "FAIL" test. Your scores will only show how well you did in comparison to a representative sample of other students in the United States who took the same tests. You have a lot to gain and nothing to lose when you take the ASVAB.

When and Where Can I Take It?

The ASVAB is administered year-round, and is normally administered at field stations throughout the United States, as well as by mobile teams. Officials of the Military Enlistment Processing Command proctor the examination.

How Do I Apply?

Ask your guidance counselor to make arrangements for you, or contact the nearest recruiter of the service of your choice. There is no cost for this examination since the Department of Defense wants to tell you about military service opportunities and assist you in career exploration.

Am I Obligated to Join the Military?

No! Taking the ASVAB does not obligate you to the military in any way. You are free to use your test results in whatever manner you wish. Additionally, ASVAB results will *not* be used to enter your name in any draft registration system.

You will, however, be required to sign a statement authorizing the release of your test scores to representatives of all the military services, and, like the majority of high school students, if you are an upperclassman, you will probably be contacted by a service member sometime before you graduate. You should expect this whether or not you ever take the ASVAB.

Nevertheless, be sure to find out about the many job opportunities with the military services (Air Force, Army, Marine Corps, and Navy) and the U.S. Coast Guard.

Hundreds of thousands of students enter one of the military services each year. Your ASVAB test scores are good for enlistment purposes for two years after you take the test. Phone or ask a service recruiter to determine whether you would qualify to enter that service (assuming that you meet other qualifications for enlistment such as age, physical requirements, etc.)

What Do My Test Scores Mean?

Who Sees Them?

The ASVAB is used by the Armed Services for recruiting purposes and by your counselor for guidance counseling. Therefore, your test scores will be provided to your counselor and to the recruiting services and the Coast Guard.

The personal information you will provide at the time of testing will be maintained on a computer tape and on microfiche records for not more than 2 years. Your test scores, age, sex, school, etc., may be kept for a longer period of time for research purposes to assist in evaluating and updating test materials. However, all personal identifying information (name, social security number, street address, and telephone number) will be erased from research records after 2 years.

Your personal identity information and related test information will not be released to any agency outside of the Department of Defense except the U.S. Coast Guard, which is under the jurisdiction of the Department of Transportation, and your school system. This information will not be used for any purpose other than recruiting by the Armed Services, counseling in your school, and research on test development and personnel measurement. Information on your test scores which is provided to your school will be handled and disposed of in accordance with the policies of the governing state or local school system.

How Can I Use Them?

Since ASVAB is a vocational aptitude test, its primary value is in relating your test scores to jobs in the vocational-technical career fields. Whether or not you plan on going on to college, you should be aware of the range of jobs in the trades, what skills and training they require, and how much they can pay. (Some technical careers pay surprisingly very well.) See pages 455 to 457 for a look at how your test scores can help you analyze your job opportunities and potential.

The Nature of the Test

What to Expect

When you go to the examining station to take the ASVAB, you will be given a booklet with 10 short tests, each consisting of *practice questions* and *actual test questions*. You will also be given a *separate answer sheet* on which to mark your answers, a special pencil to use, and some scratch paper for doing any figuring you may want to do.

At the examining station, you will be given complete instructions as to what to do in taking the tests and how much time you have to work on each test. After you have been given the instructions, you will be allowed to practice by answering some sample questions. Finally, you will be given plenty of opportunity to ask questions before you start, so that you will understand exactly what you are supposed to do on the tests.

How to Take It

In 9 of the 10 ASVAB tests, there are four possible answers, labeled A, B, C, and D, for each question. The other test (Test 6) has five possible answers, labeled A, B, C, D, and E. Only one answer in each question is correct or best. Your job is to read each question carefully and decide which of the answers given is the best. Then you record your choice on the separate answer sheet by blackening out the space which has the same number and letter as your choice.

In all cases, you are to choose the best answer and mark your answer sheet in the space for it. You must not make any stray marks on the answer sheet because the scoring machine might record those marks as wrong answers. You also should not make any marks in the ASVAB test booklet.

In most of the tests, you will have enough time to try every question, and you should try every one. There are two tests (Tests 5 and 6) which you may not finish in the time allowed. Do not worry about them. Most people don't finish them, but be sure to work as quickly and accurately as you can. Do not go on to the next page until the examiner tells you to.

Some tests will be easier for you than others, but do the best you can on each. All are important. Your score on each test of the ASVAB will be based on the number of answers you mark correctly. *Wrong answers will not count against you*.

Sample Questions

Part 1   General Science

This test has questions about general science, including biology, chemistry, earth science, and physics, as usually covered in high school courses.

1. Water is an example of a
 1-A solid.
 1-B gas.
 1-C liquid.
 1-D crystal.

2. Which of the following foods contains the most iron?
 2-A liver
 2-B cucumbers
 2-C eggs
 2-D candy

3. An eclipse of the sun throws the shadow of the
 3-A earth on the moon.
 3-B moon on the earth.
 3-C moon on the sun.
 3-D earth on the sun.

4. Lack of iodine is often related to which of the following diseases?
 4-A beriberi
 4-B scurvey
 4-C rickets
 4-D goiter

Part 2   Arithmetic Reasoning

This is a test of your ability to solve arithmetic problems. Use your scratch paper for any figuring you wish to do.

5. A person buys a sandwich for 50¢, soda for 25¢, and pie for 40¢. What is the total cost?
 5-A $1.00
 5-B $1.05
 5-C $1.15
 5-D $1.25

6. If 12 workers are needed to run 4 machines, how many workers are needed to run 20 machines?
 6-A 24
 6-B 48
 6-C 60
 6-D 80

7. It cost a couple $13.50 to go out for the evening. Sixty percent of this was for theater tickets. What was the cost for each ticket?
 7-A $3.95
 7-B $4.05
 7-C $5.40
 7-D $8.10

8. A pole 24 feet high has a shadow 8 feet long. A nearby pole is 72 feet high. How long is its shadow?
 8-A 16 feet
 8-B 24 feet
 8-C 32 feet
 8-D 56 feet

Part 3   Word Knowledge

This test has questions about the meaning of words. Each question has an underlined word. You are to decide which of the four possible answers most nearly means the same as the underlined word, then blacken the appropriate space on your answer sheet.

9. *Small* most nearly means
   9-A sturdy,
   9-B round.
   9-C cheap.
   9-D little.

10. The accountant *dis-covered* an error.
    10-A searched
    10-B found
    10-C enlarged
    10-D entered

11. The wind is *variable* today.
    11-A shifting
    11-B chilling
    11-C steady
    11-D mild

12. *Cease* most nearly means
    12-A start.
    12-B change
    12-C continue.
    12-D stop.

Part 4   Paragraph Comprehension

This is a test of your ability to understand what you read. In this section you will find one or more paragraphs of reading material followed by incomplete statements or questions. You are to read the paragraph and select one of four lettered choices which best completes the statement or answers the question. When you have selected your answer, blacken in the correct numbered letter on your answer sheet.

13. The duty of the lighthouse keeper is to keep the light burning no matter what happens, so that ships will be warned of the presence of dangerous rocks. If a shipwreck should occur near the lighthouse, even though he would like to aid in the rescue of its crew and passengers, the lighthouse keeper must
    13-A stay at his light.
    13-B rush to their aid.
    13-C turn out the light.
    13-D quickly sound the siren.

14. From a building designer's standpoint, three things that make a home livable are the client, the building site, and the amount of money the client has to spend.
    According to the passage, to make a home livable
    14-A the prospective piece of land makes little difference.
    14-B it can be built on any piece of land.
    14-C the design must fit the owner's income and site.
    14-D the design must fit the designer's income.

Part 5   Numerical Operations

This is a test to see how rapidly and accurately you can do simple arithmetic problems. For each problem, decide which answer is correct, then blacken the space on your answer sheet which has the same number and letter as your choice. This is one of the two speed tests on the ASVAB which you probably will not finish. The objective is to do as many questions as you can without making mistakes.

15. $2 + 3 =$
    15-A 1
    15-B 4
    15-C 5
    15-D 6

16. $6 - 5 =$
    16-A 1
    16-B 2
    16-C 3
    16-D 4

17. $60 \div 15 =$
    17-A 3
    17-B 4
    17-C 5
    17-D 6

18. $15 \div 3 =$
    18-A 2
    18-B 3
    18-C 5
    18-D 6

Part 6   Coding Speed

This is a test to see how quickly and accurately you can assign code numbers. At the top of each set of questions there is a code number "key." The key is a group of words with a code number for each word.

Each question in the test is a word taken from the key at the top. From among the possible answers listed for each question, you are to find the one which is the correct code number for that word. Then blacken the square for that answer on your answer sheet.

Key

bargain . . 8385	house . . . 2859	owner . . . 6227
chin 8930	knife 7150	point 4703
game 6456	music . . . 1117	sofa 9645
	sunshine . 7489	

Answers

		A	B	C	D	E
19.	game	6456	7150	8385	8930	9645
20.	knife	1117	6456	7150	7489	8385
21.	bargain	2859	6227	7489	8385	9645
22.	chin	2859	4703	8385	8930	9645
23.	house	1117	2859	6227	7150	7489
24.	sofa	7150	7489	8385	8930	9645
25.	owner	4703	6227	6456	7150	8930

Part 7   Auto & Shop Information

This test has questions about automobiles, shop practices, and the use of tools.

26. The most commonly used fuel for running automobile engines is
    26-A kerosene.
    26-B benzene.
    26-C crude oil.
    26-D gasoline.

27. Carburetors are usually adjusted with a
    27-A file.
    27-B chisel.
    27-C hammer.
    27-D screwdriver.

28. A chisel is used for
    28-A cutting.
    28-B prying.
    28-C twisting.
    28-D grinding.

29. The saw shown above is used mainly to cut
    29-A across the grain of the wood
    29-B along the grain of the wood
    29-C plywood.
    29-D odd-shaped holes in wood.

Part 8   Mathematics Knowledge

This is a test of your ability to solve problems using high school mathematics. Use your scratch paper for any figuring you wish to do.

30. If $a + 6 = 7$ then a is equal to
    30-A 0
    30-B 1
    30-C −1
    30-D 7/6

31. What is the area of this square?
    31-A 1 square foot
    31-B 5 square feet
    31-C 10 square feet
    31-D 25 square feet

32. Angle B is 90 degrees. Which line in the triangle is the longest?
    32-A AB
    32-B AC
    32-C neither
    32-D can't be determined from the information given

33. If $3X = -5$, then $X =$
    33-A 3/5
    33-B −5/3
    33-C −3/5
    33-D −2

Part 9   Mechanical Comprehension

This test has questions about general mechanical and physical principles. An understanding of these principles comes from observing the physical world, working with or operating mechanical devices, or reading and studying.

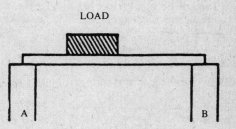

34. Which post holds up the greater part of the load?
    34-A Post A
    34-B Post B
    34-C Both equal
    34-D Not clear

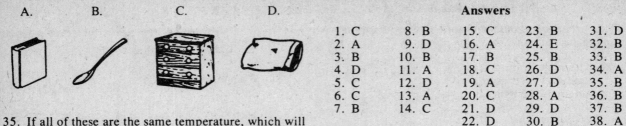

A.   B.   C.   D.

35. If all of these are the same temperature, which will feel coldest?
    35-A A
    35-B B
    35-C C
    35-D D

Part 10   Electronics Information

This is a test of your knowledge of electrical, radio, and electronics information. This information can be learned through working on radios, electrical equipment, reading books, or taking courses.

36. The safest way to run an extension cord to a lamp is
    36-A under a rug.
    36-B along a
           baseboard.
    36-C under a sofa.
    36-D behind a sofa.

37. Which of the following has the *least* resistance?

    37-A rubber
    37-B silver
    37-C wood
    37-D iron

A.   B.

C.   D.

38. Which of the above is the symbol for a transformer?

    38-A A
    38-B B
    38-C C
    38-D D

2 Test-Taking Techniques

Many people incorrectly believe that the amount of time spent studying is the most important factor in test preparation. Efficient study habits are part of the key to successful test preparation. Of course, all else being equal, the amount of time you devote to your studies is a critical factor. But spending time reading is not necessarily studying. If you want to retain what you read, you must develop a system. For example, a person who devotes 60 minutes a day to uninterrupted study in a quiet, private area will generally retain more than someone who puts in twice that time by studying five or six times a day for 15 to 20 minutes at a time.

Rules for Studying More Effectively

We have listed a number of rules for you to follow to increase study time efficiency. If you abide by these rules, you will get the most out of this book.

1. **MAKE SURE YOU UNDERSTAND THE MEANING OF EVERY WORD YOU READ.** Your ability to understand what you read is the most important skill needed to pass any test. Therefore, starting now, every time you see a word that you don't fully understand, make certain that you write it down and make note of where you saw it. Then, when you have a chance, look up the meaning of the word in the dictionary. When you think you know what the word means, go back to the reading material which contained the word, and make certain that you fully understand the meaning of the word.

   Keep a list of all words you don't know, and periodically review them. Also, try to use these words whenever you can in conversation. If you do this faithfully, you will quickly build an extensive vocabulary which will be helpful to you not only when you take this examination, but for the rest of your life.

2. **STUDY UNINTERRUPTEDLY FOR AT LEAST 30 MINUTES.** Unless you can study for at least an uninterrupted period of 30 minutes, you should not bother to study at all. It is essential that you concentrate for extended periods of time. When you take the practice examinations, do a complete examination in one sitting, just as you must do at the actual examination.

3. **SIMULATE EXAMINATION CONDITIONS WHEN STUDYING.** As much as possible, study under the same conditions as those of the examination. Eliminate as many outside interferences as you can.

4. **ALWAYS FOLLOW THE RECOMMENDED TECHNIQUE FOR ANSWERING MULTIPLE CHOICE QUESTIONS.** In this chapter we provide an invaluable technique for answering multiple-choice questions.

5. **ALWAYS TIME YOURSELF WHEN DOING PRACTICE QUESTIONS.** Running out of time on a multiple-choice examination is a tragic error that is easily avoided. Learn, through practice, to move to the next question after a reasonable period of time spent on any one question. Therefore, when you are doing practice questions, always time yourself so that you will stay within the recommended time limits.

6. **CONCENTRATE YOUR STUDY TIME IN THE AREAS OF YOUR GREATEST WEAKNESS.** Model Examination One will give you an idea of the most difficult question types for you. Though you should spend most of your time improving yourself in these areas, do not ignore the other types of questions.

7. **EXERCISE REGULARLY AND STAY IN GOOD PHYSICAL CONDITION.** Students who are in good physical condition have an advantage over those who are not. It is a well-established principle that good physical health improves the ability of the mind to function smoothly and efficiently.

8. **ESTABLISH A SCHEDULE FOR STUDYING, AND STICK TO IT.** Do not put off studying to those times when you have nothing else to do. Schedule your study time, and try not to let anything else interfere with that schedule.

Strategies for Handling Multiple-Choice Questions

The remainder of this chapter outlines a very specific test-taking strategy valuable for a multiple-choice examination. Study the technique, practice it; then study it again until you have mastered it.

1. **READ THE DIRECTIONS.** Do *not* assume that you know what the directions are without reading them. Make sure you read and understand them. Note particularly whether there are differing directions from one section of the examination to another.

2. **TAKE A CLOSE LOOK AT THE ANSWER SHEET** The answer sheets on your practice examinations are typical of the one you will see on your exam. However, do *not* take anything for granted. Review the directions on the answer sheet carefully, and familiarize yourself with its format.

3. **BE CAREFUL WHEN MARKING YOUR ANSWERS.** Be sure to mark your answers in accordance with the directions on the answer sheet.

Be extremely careful that:
- you mark only one answer for each question,
- you do not make extraneous markings on your answer sheet,
- you completely darken the allotted space for the answer you choose,
- you erase completely any answer that you wish to change.

4. MAKE ABSOLUTELY CERTAIN YOU ARE MARKING THE ANSWER TO THE RIGHT QUESTION. Many multiple-choice tests have been failed because of carelessness in this area. All it takes is one mistake. If you put down one answer in the wrong space, you will probably continue the mistake for a number of questions until you realize your error. We recommend that you use the following procedure when marking your answer sheet.
- Select your answer, blacken that choice on the answer form, and ask yourself what question number you are working on.
- If you select "C" as the answer for question eleven, blacken choice "C" on the answer form, and say to yourself, "C is the answer to question eleven."
- Then find the space on your answer sheet for question eleven, and again say "C is the answer to question eleven" as you mark the answer.

While this might seem rather elementary and repetitive, after a while it becomes automatic. If followed properly, it guarantees that you will not fail the examination because of a careless mistake.

5. MAKE CERTAIN THAT YOU UNDERSTAND WHAT THE QUESTION IS ASKING. Read the stem of the question (the part before the choices) very carefully to make certain that you know what the examiner is asking. In fact, it is wise to read it twice—unless you are working on one of the "speeded" subtests.

6. ALWAYS READ ALL THE CHOICES BEFORE YOU SELECT AN ANSWER. Don't make the mistake of falling into the trap that the best distractor, or wrong answer, comes before the correct choice! Read all choices!

7. BE AWARE OF KEY WORDS THAT OFTEN TIP OFF THE CORRECT AND INCORRECT ANSWERS.
Absolute Words—*Usually a Wrong Choice*
(They are generally too broad and difficult to defend)

never	always	only
none	all	any
nothing	everyone	
nobody	everybody	

Limiting Words—*Usually a Correct Choice*

usually	sometimes	many
generally	some	often
few	possible	
occasionally		

8. NEVER MAKE A CHOICE BASED ON FRE QUENCY OF PREVIOUS ANSWERS. Some students pay attention to the pattern of answers when taking an exam. Always answer the question, without regard to what the previous choices have been.

9. ELIMINATE CHOICES YOU KNOW ARE WRONG. As you read through the choices, eliminate any choice you know is wrong. If you eliminate all but one of the choices, the remaining choice should be the answer. Read the choice one more time to satisfy yourself, and blacken its letter designation (if you still feel it is the best answer) on the answer sheet. (See the procedure given above under Strategy 4.) If you were not able to narrow the choices to one, many times, the second time you read the remaining choices, the answer is clear.

10. SKIP OVER QUESTIONS THAT GIVE YOU TROUBLE. The first time through the examination be certain not to dwell too long on any one question. Simply skip the question after blackening the number on the answer sheet (to keep your answers from getting out of sequence), and go to the next question. Do not guess at this point if you do not know the answer.

11. RETURN TO THE QUESTIONS YOU SKIPPED IN A SUBTEST AFTER YOU FINISH THAT PORTION OF THE EXAMINATION. Once you have answered all of the questions you were sure of in a subtest of the examination, check the time remaining. If time permits, return to each question you did not answer and re-read the stem and the choices. If the answer is still not clear and you are running out of time, then make an "educated guess" among those choices. When making an "educated guess," follow the guidelines that are presented in Strategy 13.

12. NEVER LEAVE QUESTIONS UNANSWERED SINCE THERE IS NO PENALTY FOR WRONG ANSWERS.

13. RULES FOR MAKING AN "EDUCATED GUESS." Your chances of picking the correct answer to questions you are not sure of will be significantly increased if you use the following rules:
- Never consider answer choices that you have already eliminated. (See Strategy 9.)
- Be aware of key words that give you clues as to which answer might be right or wrong. (See Strategy 7.)
- If two choices have a conflicting meaning, one of them is probably the correct answer. And, if two choices are too close in meaning, probably neither is correct.
- If all else fails and you have to make an outright guess at more than one question, guess the same lettered choice for each such question. The odds are that you will pick up some valuable points.

14. **BE VERY RELUCTANT TO CHANGE ANSWERS.** Unless you have a very good reason, do not change an answer once you have chosen it. Studies have shown that all too often people change their answer from the right one to the wrong one.

DIAGNOSE YOUR PROBLEM

3   MODEL EXAMINATION ONE

ANSWER SHEET—FIRST MODEL EXAM

PART 1 GENERAL SCIENCE

1. Ⓐ Ⓑ Ⓒ Ⓓ	6. Ⓐ Ⓑ Ⓒ Ⓓ	11. Ⓐ Ⓑ Ⓒ Ⓓ	16. Ⓐ Ⓑ Ⓒ Ⓓ	21. Ⓐ Ⓑ Ⓒ Ⓓ
2. Ⓐ Ⓑ Ⓒ Ⓓ	7. Ⓐ Ⓑ Ⓒ Ⓓ	12. Ⓐ Ⓑ Ⓒ Ⓓ	17. Ⓐ Ⓑ Ⓒ Ⓓ	22. Ⓐ Ⓑ Ⓒ Ⓓ
3. Ⓐ Ⓑ Ⓒ Ⓓ	8. Ⓐ Ⓑ Ⓒ Ⓓ	13. Ⓐ Ⓑ Ⓒ Ⓓ	18. Ⓐ Ⓑ Ⓒ Ⓓ	23. Ⓐ Ⓑ Ⓒ Ⓓ
4. Ⓐ Ⓑ Ⓒ Ⓓ	9. Ⓐ Ⓑ Ⓒ Ⓓ	14. Ⓐ Ⓑ Ⓒ Ⓓ	19. Ⓐ Ⓑ Ⓒ Ⓓ	24. Ⓐ Ⓑ Ⓒ Ⓓ
5. Ⓐ Ⓑ Ⓒ Ⓓ	10. Ⓐ Ⓑ Ⓒ Ⓓ	15. Ⓐ Ⓑ Ⓒ Ⓓ	20. Ⓐ Ⓑ Ⓒ Ⓓ	25. Ⓐ Ⓑ Ⓒ Ⓓ

PART 2 ARITHMETIC REASONING

1. Ⓐ Ⓑ Ⓒ Ⓓ	7. Ⓐ Ⓑ Ⓒ Ⓓ	13. Ⓐ Ⓑ Ⓒ Ⓓ	19. Ⓐ Ⓑ Ⓒ Ⓓ	25. Ⓐ Ⓑ Ⓒ Ⓓ
2. Ⓐ Ⓑ Ⓒ Ⓓ	8. Ⓐ Ⓑ Ⓒ Ⓓ	14. Ⓐ Ⓑ Ⓒ Ⓓ	20. Ⓐ Ⓑ Ⓒ Ⓓ	26. Ⓐ Ⓑ Ⓒ Ⓓ
3. Ⓐ Ⓑ Ⓒ Ⓓ	9. Ⓐ Ⓑ Ⓒ Ⓓ	15. Ⓐ Ⓑ Ⓒ Ⓓ	21. Ⓐ Ⓑ Ⓒ Ⓓ	27. Ⓐ Ⓑ Ⓒ Ⓓ
4. Ⓐ Ⓑ Ⓒ Ⓓ	10. Ⓐ Ⓑ Ⓒ Ⓓ	16. Ⓐ Ⓑ Ⓒ Ⓓ	22. Ⓐ Ⓑ Ⓒ Ⓓ	28. Ⓐ Ⓑ Ⓒ Ⓓ
5. Ⓐ Ⓑ Ⓒ Ⓓ	11. Ⓐ Ⓑ Ⓒ Ⓓ	17. Ⓐ Ⓑ Ⓒ Ⓓ	23. Ⓐ Ⓑ Ⓒ Ⓓ	29. Ⓐ Ⓑ Ⓒ Ⓓ
6. Ⓐ Ⓑ Ⓒ Ⓓ	12. Ⓐ Ⓑ Ⓒ Ⓓ	18. Ⓐ Ⓑ Ⓒ Ⓓ	24. Ⓐ Ⓑ Ⓒ Ⓓ	30. Ⓐ Ⓑ Ⓒ Ⓓ

PART 3 WORD KNOWLEDGE

1. Ⓐ Ⓑ Ⓒ Ⓓ	8. Ⓐ Ⓑ Ⓒ Ⓓ	15. Ⓐ Ⓑ Ⓒ Ⓓ	22. Ⓐ Ⓑ Ⓒ Ⓓ	29. Ⓐ Ⓑ Ⓒ Ⓓ
2. Ⓐ Ⓑ Ⓒ Ⓓ	9. Ⓐ Ⓑ Ⓒ Ⓓ	16. Ⓐ Ⓑ Ⓒ Ⓓ	23. Ⓐ Ⓑ Ⓒ Ⓓ	30. Ⓐ Ⓑ Ⓒ Ⓓ
3. Ⓐ Ⓑ Ⓒ Ⓓ	10. Ⓐ Ⓑ Ⓒ Ⓓ	17. Ⓐ Ⓑ Ⓒ Ⓓ	24. Ⓐ Ⓑ Ⓒ Ⓓ	31. Ⓐ Ⓑ Ⓒ Ⓓ
4. Ⓐ Ⓑ Ⓒ Ⓓ	11. Ⓐ Ⓑ Ⓒ Ⓓ	18. Ⓐ Ⓑ Ⓒ Ⓓ	25. Ⓐ Ⓑ Ⓒ Ⓓ	32. Ⓐ Ⓑ Ⓒ Ⓓ
5. Ⓐ Ⓑ Ⓒ Ⓓ	12. Ⓐ Ⓑ Ⓒ Ⓓ	19. Ⓐ Ⓑ Ⓒ Ⓓ	26. Ⓐ Ⓑ Ⓒ Ⓓ	33. Ⓐ Ⓑ Ⓒ Ⓓ
6. Ⓐ Ⓑ Ⓒ Ⓓ	13. Ⓐ Ⓑ Ⓒ Ⓓ	20. Ⓐ Ⓑ Ⓒ Ⓓ	27. Ⓐ Ⓑ Ⓒ Ⓓ	34. Ⓐ Ⓑ Ⓒ Ⓓ
7. Ⓐ Ⓑ Ⓒ Ⓓ	14. Ⓐ Ⓑ Ⓒ Ⓓ	21. Ⓐ Ⓑ Ⓒ Ⓓ	28. Ⓐ Ⓑ Ⓒ Ⓓ	35. Ⓐ Ⓑ Ⓒ Ⓓ

PART 4 PARAGRAPH COMPREHENSION

1. Ⓐ Ⓑ Ⓒ Ⓓ	5. Ⓐ Ⓑ Ⓒ Ⓓ	9. Ⓐ Ⓑ Ⓒ Ⓓ	13. Ⓐ Ⓑ Ⓒ Ⓓ
2. Ⓐ Ⓑ Ⓒ Ⓓ	6. Ⓐ Ⓑ Ⓒ Ⓓ	10. Ⓐ Ⓑ Ⓒ Ⓓ	14. Ⓐ Ⓑ Ⓒ Ⓓ
3. Ⓐ Ⓑ Ⓒ Ⓓ	7. Ⓐ Ⓑ Ⓒ Ⓓ	11. Ⓐ Ⓑ Ⓒ Ⓓ	15. Ⓐ Ⓑ Ⓒ Ⓓ
4. Ⓐ Ⓑ Ⓒ Ⓓ	8. Ⓐ Ⓑ Ⓒ Ⓓ	12. Ⓐ Ⓑ Ⓒ Ⓓ	

PART 5 NUMERICAL OPERATIONS

1. Ⓐ Ⓑ Ⓒ Ⓓ   11. Ⓐ Ⓑ Ⓒ Ⓓ   21. Ⓐ Ⓑ Ⓒ Ⓓ   31. Ⓐ Ⓑ Ⓒ Ⓓ   41. Ⓐ Ⓑ Ⓒ Ⓓ

2. Ⓐ Ⓑ Ⓒ Ⓓ   12. Ⓐ Ⓑ Ⓒ Ⓓ   22. Ⓐ Ⓑ Ⓒ Ⓓ   32. Ⓐ Ⓑ Ⓒ Ⓓ   42. Ⓐ Ⓑ Ⓒ Ⓓ

3. Ⓐ Ⓑ Ⓒ Ⓓ   13. Ⓐ Ⓑ Ⓒ Ⓓ   23. Ⓐ Ⓑ Ⓒ Ⓓ   33. Ⓐ Ⓑ Ⓒ Ⓓ   43. Ⓐ Ⓑ Ⓒ Ⓓ

4. Ⓐ Ⓑ Ⓒ Ⓓ   14. Ⓐ Ⓑ Ⓒ Ⓓ   24. Ⓐ Ⓑ Ⓒ Ⓓ   34. Ⓐ Ⓑ Ⓒ Ⓓ   44. Ⓐ Ⓑ Ⓒ Ⓓ

5. Ⓐ Ⓑ Ⓒ Ⓓ   15. Ⓐ Ⓑ Ⓒ Ⓓ   25. Ⓐ Ⓑ Ⓒ Ⓓ   35. Ⓐ Ⓑ Ⓒ Ⓓ   45. Ⓐ Ⓑ Ⓒ Ⓓ

6. Ⓐ Ⓑ Ⓒ Ⓓ   16. Ⓐ Ⓑ Ⓒ Ⓓ   26. Ⓐ Ⓑ Ⓒ Ⓓ   36. Ⓐ Ⓑ Ⓒ Ⓓ   46. Ⓐ Ⓑ Ⓒ Ⓓ

7. Ⓐ Ⓑ Ⓒ Ⓓ   17. Ⓐ Ⓑ Ⓒ Ⓓ   27. Ⓐ Ⓑ Ⓒ Ⓓ   37. Ⓐ Ⓑ Ⓒ Ⓓ   47. Ⓐ Ⓑ Ⓒ Ⓓ

8. Ⓐ Ⓑ Ⓒ Ⓓ   18. Ⓐ Ⓑ Ⓒ Ⓓ   28. Ⓐ Ⓑ Ⓒ Ⓓ   38. Ⓐ Ⓑ Ⓒ Ⓓ   48. Ⓐ Ⓑ Ⓒ Ⓓ

9. Ⓐ Ⓑ Ⓒ Ⓓ   19. Ⓐ Ⓑ Ⓒ Ⓓ   29. Ⓐ Ⓑ Ⓒ Ⓓ   39. Ⓐ Ⓑ Ⓒ Ⓓ   49. Ⓐ Ⓑ Ⓒ Ⓓ

10. Ⓐ Ⓑ Ⓒ Ⓓ   20. Ⓐ Ⓑ Ⓒ Ⓓ   30. Ⓐ Ⓑ Ⓒ Ⓓ   40. Ⓐ Ⓑ Ⓒ Ⓓ   50. Ⓐ Ⓑ Ⓒ Ⓓ

PART 6 CODING SPEED

1. Ⓐ Ⓑ Ⓒ Ⓓ Ⓔ   15. Ⓐ Ⓑ Ⓒ Ⓓ Ⓔ   29. Ⓐ Ⓑ Ⓒ Ⓓ Ⓔ   43. Ⓐ Ⓑ Ⓒ Ⓓ Ⓔ   57. Ⓐ Ⓑ Ⓒ Ⓓ Ⓔ   71. Ⓐ Ⓑ Ⓒ Ⓓ Ⓔ

2. Ⓐ Ⓑ Ⓒ Ⓓ Ⓔ   16. Ⓐ Ⓑ Ⓒ Ⓓ Ⓔ   30. Ⓐ Ⓑ Ⓒ Ⓓ Ⓔ   44. Ⓐ Ⓑ Ⓒ Ⓓ Ⓔ   58. Ⓐ Ⓑ Ⓒ Ⓓ Ⓔ   72. Ⓐ Ⓑ Ⓒ Ⓓ Ⓔ

3. Ⓐ Ⓑ Ⓒ Ⓓ Ⓔ   17. Ⓐ Ⓑ Ⓒ Ⓓ Ⓔ   31. Ⓐ Ⓑ Ⓒ Ⓓ Ⓔ   45. Ⓐ Ⓑ Ⓒ Ⓓ Ⓔ   59. Ⓐ Ⓑ Ⓒ Ⓓ Ⓔ   73. Ⓐ Ⓑ Ⓒ Ⓓ Ⓔ

4. Ⓐ Ⓑ Ⓒ Ⓓ Ⓔ   18. Ⓐ Ⓑ Ⓒ Ⓓ Ⓔ   32. Ⓐ Ⓑ Ⓒ Ⓓ Ⓔ   46. Ⓐ Ⓑ Ⓒ Ⓓ Ⓔ   60. Ⓐ Ⓑ Ⓒ Ⓓ Ⓔ   74. Ⓐ Ⓑ Ⓒ Ⓓ Ⓔ

5. Ⓐ Ⓑ Ⓒ Ⓓ Ⓔ   19. Ⓐ Ⓑ Ⓒ Ⓓ Ⓔ   33. Ⓐ Ⓑ Ⓒ Ⓓ Ⓔ   47. Ⓐ Ⓑ Ⓒ Ⓓ Ⓔ   61. Ⓐ Ⓑ Ⓒ Ⓓ Ⓔ   75. Ⓐ Ⓑ Ⓒ Ⓓ Ⓔ

6. Ⓐ Ⓑ Ⓒ Ⓓ Ⓔ   20. Ⓐ Ⓑ Ⓒ Ⓓ Ⓔ   34. Ⓐ Ⓑ Ⓒ Ⓓ Ⓔ   48. Ⓐ Ⓑ Ⓒ Ⓓ Ⓔ   62. Ⓐ Ⓑ Ⓒ Ⓓ Ⓔ   76. Ⓐ Ⓑ Ⓒ Ⓓ Ⓔ

7. Ⓐ Ⓑ Ⓒ Ⓓ Ⓔ   21. Ⓐ Ⓑ Ⓒ Ⓓ Ⓔ   35. Ⓐ Ⓑ Ⓒ Ⓓ Ⓔ   49. Ⓐ Ⓑ Ⓒ Ⓓ Ⓔ   63. Ⓐ Ⓑ Ⓒ Ⓓ Ⓔ   77. Ⓐ Ⓑ Ⓒ Ⓓ Ⓔ

8. Ⓐ Ⓑ Ⓒ Ⓓ Ⓔ   22. Ⓐ Ⓑ Ⓒ Ⓓ Ⓔ   36. Ⓐ Ⓑ Ⓒ Ⓓ Ⓔ   50. Ⓐ Ⓑ Ⓒ Ⓓ Ⓔ   64. Ⓐ Ⓑ Ⓒ Ⓓ Ⓔ   78. Ⓐ Ⓑ Ⓒ Ⓓ Ⓔ

9. Ⓐ Ⓑ Ⓒ Ⓓ Ⓔ   23. Ⓐ Ⓑ Ⓒ Ⓓ Ⓔ   37. Ⓐ Ⓑ Ⓒ Ⓓ Ⓔ   51. Ⓐ Ⓑ Ⓒ Ⓓ Ⓔ   65. Ⓐ Ⓑ Ⓒ Ⓓ Ⓔ   79. Ⓐ Ⓑ Ⓒ Ⓓ Ⓔ

10. Ⓐ Ⓑ Ⓒ Ⓓ Ⓔ   24. Ⓐ Ⓑ Ⓒ Ⓓ Ⓔ   38. Ⓐ Ⓑ Ⓒ Ⓓ Ⓔ   52. Ⓐ Ⓑ Ⓒ Ⓓ Ⓔ   66. Ⓐ Ⓑ Ⓒ Ⓓ Ⓔ   80. Ⓐ Ⓑ Ⓒ Ⓓ Ⓔ

11. Ⓐ Ⓑ Ⓒ Ⓓ Ⓔ   25. Ⓐ Ⓑ Ⓒ Ⓓ Ⓔ   39. Ⓐ Ⓑ Ⓒ Ⓓ Ⓔ   53. Ⓐ Ⓑ Ⓒ Ⓓ Ⓔ   67. Ⓐ Ⓑ Ⓒ Ⓓ Ⓔ   81. Ⓐ Ⓑ Ⓒ Ⓓ Ⓔ

12. Ⓐ Ⓑ Ⓒ Ⓓ Ⓔ   26. Ⓐ Ⓑ Ⓒ Ⓓ Ⓔ   40. Ⓐ Ⓑ Ⓒ Ⓓ Ⓔ   54. Ⓐ Ⓑ Ⓒ Ⓓ Ⓔ   68. Ⓐ Ⓑ Ⓒ Ⓓ Ⓔ   82. Ⓐ Ⓑ Ⓒ Ⓓ Ⓔ

13. Ⓐ Ⓑ Ⓒ Ⓓ Ⓔ   27. Ⓐ Ⓑ Ⓒ Ⓓ Ⓔ   41. Ⓐ Ⓑ Ⓒ Ⓓ Ⓔ   55. Ⓐ Ⓑ Ⓒ Ⓓ Ⓔ   69. Ⓐ Ⓑ Ⓒ Ⓓ Ⓔ   83. Ⓐ Ⓑ Ⓒ Ⓓ Ⓔ

14. Ⓐ Ⓑ Ⓒ Ⓓ Ⓔ   28. Ⓐ Ⓑ Ⓒ Ⓓ Ⓔ   42. Ⓐ Ⓑ Ⓒ Ⓓ Ⓔ   56. Ⓐ Ⓑ Ⓒ Ⓓ Ⓔ   70. Ⓐ Ⓑ Ⓒ Ⓓ Ⓔ   84. Ⓐ Ⓑ Ⓒ Ⓓ Ⓔ

PART 7 AUTO & SHOP INFORMATION

1. Ⓐ Ⓑ Ⓒ Ⓓ	6. Ⓐ Ⓑ Ⓒ Ⓓ	11. Ⓐ Ⓑ Ⓒ Ⓓ	16. Ⓐ Ⓑ Ⓒ Ⓓ	21. Ⓐ Ⓑ Ⓒ Ⓓ
2. Ⓐ Ⓑ Ⓒ Ⓓ	7. Ⓐ Ⓑ Ⓒ Ⓓ	12. Ⓐ Ⓑ Ⓒ Ⓓ	17. Ⓐ Ⓑ Ⓒ Ⓓ	22. Ⓐ Ⓑ Ⓒ Ⓓ
3. Ⓐ Ⓑ Ⓒ Ⓓ	8. Ⓐ Ⓑ Ⓒ Ⓓ	13. Ⓐ Ⓑ Ⓒ Ⓓ	18. Ⓐ Ⓑ Ⓒ Ⓓ	23. Ⓐ Ⓑ Ⓒ Ⓓ
4. Ⓐ Ⓑ Ⓒ Ⓓ	9. Ⓐ Ⓑ Ⓒ Ⓓ	14. Ⓐ Ⓑ Ⓒ Ⓓ	19. Ⓐ Ⓑ Ⓒ Ⓓ	24. Ⓐ Ⓑ Ⓒ Ⓓ
5. Ⓐ Ⓑ Ⓒ Ⓓ	10. Ⓐ Ⓑ Ⓒ Ⓓ	15. Ⓐ Ⓑ Ⓒ Ⓓ	20. Ⓐ Ⓑ Ⓒ Ⓓ	25. Ⓐ Ⓑ Ⓒ Ⓓ

PART 8 MATHEMATICS KNOWLEDGE

1. Ⓐ Ⓑ Ⓒ Ⓓ	6. Ⓐ Ⓑ Ⓒ Ⓓ	11. Ⓐ Ⓑ Ⓒ Ⓓ	16. Ⓐ Ⓑ Ⓒ Ⓓ	21. Ⓐ Ⓑ Ⓒ Ⓓ
2. Ⓐ Ⓑ Ⓒ Ⓓ	7. Ⓐ Ⓑ Ⓒ Ⓓ	12. Ⓐ Ⓑ Ⓒ Ⓓ	17. Ⓐ Ⓑ Ⓒ Ⓓ	22. Ⓐ Ⓑ Ⓒ Ⓓ
3. Ⓐ Ⓑ Ⓒ Ⓓ	8. Ⓐ Ⓑ Ⓒ Ⓓ	13. Ⓐ Ⓑ Ⓒ Ⓓ	18. Ⓐ Ⓑ Ⓒ Ⓓ	23. Ⓐ Ⓑ Ⓒ Ⓓ
4. Ⓐ Ⓑ Ⓒ Ⓓ	9. Ⓐ Ⓑ Ⓒ Ⓓ	14. Ⓐ Ⓑ Ⓒ Ⓓ	19. Ⓐ Ⓑ Ⓒ Ⓓ	24. Ⓐ Ⓑ Ⓒ Ⓓ
5. Ⓐ Ⓑ Ⓒ Ⓓ	10. Ⓐ Ⓑ Ⓒ Ⓓ	15. Ⓐ Ⓑ Ⓒ Ⓓ	20. Ⓐ Ⓑ Ⓒ Ⓓ	25. Ⓐ Ⓑ Ⓒ Ⓓ

PART 9 MECHANICAL COMPREHENSION

1. Ⓐ Ⓑ Ⓒ Ⓓ	6. Ⓐ Ⓑ Ⓒ Ⓓ	11. Ⓐ Ⓑ Ⓒ Ⓓ	16. Ⓐ Ⓑ Ⓒ Ⓓ	21. Ⓐ Ⓑ Ⓒ Ⓓ
2. Ⓐ Ⓑ Ⓒ Ⓓ	7. Ⓐ Ⓑ Ⓒ Ⓓ	12. Ⓐ Ⓑ Ⓒ Ⓓ	17. Ⓐ Ⓑ Ⓒ Ⓓ	22. Ⓐ Ⓑ Ⓒ Ⓓ
3. Ⓐ Ⓑ Ⓒ Ⓓ	8. Ⓐ Ⓑ Ⓒ Ⓓ	13. Ⓐ Ⓑ Ⓒ Ⓓ	18. Ⓐ Ⓑ Ⓒ Ⓓ	23. Ⓐ Ⓑ Ⓒ Ⓓ
4. Ⓐ Ⓑ Ⓒ Ⓓ	9. Ⓐ Ⓑ Ⓒ Ⓓ	14. Ⓐ Ⓑ Ⓒ Ⓓ	19. Ⓐ Ⓑ Ⓒ Ⓓ	24. Ⓐ Ⓑ Ⓒ Ⓓ
5. Ⓐ Ⓑ Ⓒ Ⓓ	10. Ⓐ Ⓑ Ⓒ Ⓓ	15. Ⓐ Ⓑ Ⓒ Ⓓ	20. Ⓐ Ⓑ Ⓒ Ⓓ	25. Ⓐ Ⓑ Ⓒ Ⓓ

PART 10 ELECTRONICS INFORMATION

1. Ⓐ Ⓑ Ⓒ Ⓓ	6. Ⓐ Ⓑ Ⓒ Ⓓ	11. Ⓐ Ⓑ Ⓒ Ⓓ	16. Ⓐ Ⓑ Ⓒ Ⓓ
2. Ⓐ Ⓑ Ⓒ Ⓓ	7. Ⓐ Ⓑ Ⓒ Ⓓ	12. Ⓐ Ⓑ Ⓒ Ⓓ	17. Ⓐ Ⓑ Ⓒ Ⓓ
3. Ⓐ Ⓑ Ⓒ Ⓓ	8. Ⓐ Ⓑ Ⓒ Ⓓ	13. Ⓐ Ⓑ Ⓒ Ⓓ	18. Ⓐ Ⓑ Ⓒ Ⓓ
4. Ⓐ Ⓑ Ⓒ Ⓓ	9. Ⓐ Ⓑ Ⓒ Ⓓ	14. Ⓐ Ⓑ Ⓒ Ⓓ	19. Ⓐ Ⓑ Ⓒ Ⓓ
5. Ⓐ Ⓑ Ⓒ Ⓓ	10. Ⓐ Ⓑ Ⓒ Ⓓ	15. Ⓐ Ⓑ Ⓒ Ⓓ	20. Ⓐ Ⓑ Ⓒ Ⓓ

1

GENERAL SCIENCE

Directions

This test has questions about science. Pick the best answer for each question, then blacken the space on your separate answer form which has the same number and letter as your choice.

Here is a sample question.

1. An example of a chemical change is

    1-A   melting ice.
    1-B   breaking glass.
    1-C   rusting metal.
    1-D   making sawdust from wood.

The correct answer is rusting metal, so you would blacken the space for 1-C on your answer form.

Your score on this test will be based on the number of questions you answer correctly. You should try to answer every question. Do not spend too much time on any one question.

When you begin, be sure to start with question number 1 in Part 1, and number 1 in Part 1 on your answer form.

Do not turn this page until told to do so.

GENERAL SCIENCE

Time: 11 minutes; 25 questions

1. A ringing bell, placed in a vacuum under a glass bell jar, will

   1-A   have the pitch of its sound raised.
   1-B   crack the thick glass of the bell jar.
   1-C   undergo no change.
   1-D   be inaudible.

2. The light year is used to measure

   2-A   intensity of light.
   2-B   distance.
   2-C   time.
   2-D   brightness.

3. If a piece of corundum weighs 4 ounces in the air, but appears to weigh only 3 ounces when submerged in water, its specific gravity is

   3-A   one-fourth.
   3-B   one.
   3-C   three.
   3-D   four.

4. Which kind of time does a sundial keep?

   4-A   legal
   4-B   standard
   4-C   solar
   4-D   sonic

5. Of the following, the best conductor of heat is

   5-A   asbestos.
   5-B   copper.
   5-C   brass.
   5-D   glass.

6. Ecology may best be described as the study of

   6-A   methods of fighting pollution.
   6-B   erosion of land.
   6-C   changes in plants.
   6-D   the relationship between the environment and living things.

7. When a candle burns, the chief products are

   7-A   carbon monoxide and nitrogen.
   7-B   carbon dioxide and nitrogen.
   7-C   carbon monoxide and water.
   7-D   carbon dioxide and water.

8. Of the following, the one that yields the most energy per ounce, as a result of normal metabolism, is

   8-A   protein.
   8-B   sugar.
   8-C   starch.
   8-D   fat.

9. The half-life of radium is 1,620 years. What fraction of a radium sample will remain after 3,240 years?

   9-A $1/16$
   9-B $1/8$
   9-C $1/4$
   9-D $1/2$

10. Which is a chemical property of water?

    10-A   It freezes.
    10-B   It evaporates.
    10-C   It condenses.
    10-D   It decomposes into gases.

11. Which of the following statements correctly refers to the process of photosynthesis?

    11-A   Light is necessary for the process to occur.
    11-B   Oxygen is necessary for the process to occur.
    11-C   Carbon dioxide is given off during this process.
    11-D   The process is carried on by all protozoa.

12. The relative humidity of the air when dew forms is

    12-A   100 percent.
    12-B   75 percent.
    12-C   50 percent.
    12-D   25 percent.

13. To start a fire with the aid of the sun, one should use a

    13-A   concave lens.
    13-B   flat mirror.
    13-C   magnifying lens.
    13-D   concave mirror.

14. The change from daylight to darkness is caused by the

    14-A   inclination of the earth's axis.
    14-B   force of gravitation.
    14-C   rotation of the earth.
    14-D   revolution of the earth.

15. A substance that is readily absorbed through the walls of the stomach is

    15-A   starch.
    15-B   alcohol.
    15-C   amino acids.
    15-D   ascorbic acid.

16. The positively charged particle in the nucleus of an atom is a(n)

    16-A   proton.
    16-B   isotope.
    16-C   neutron.
    16-D   electron.

17. Which one is unrelated to the other three?

    17-A   Pluto
    17-B   Moon
    17-C   Neptune
    17-D   Uranus

18. Sulfur is mined chiefly for the production of

    18-A   sulfa drugs.
    18-B   sulfanilamide.
    18-C   sulfuric acid.
    18-D   superphosphates.

19. To which organism is the whale most closely related?

    19-A   tuna
    19-B   turtle
    19-C   dinosaur
    19-D   horse

20. A beam of parallel rays of light is reflected from a plane mirror. After reflection, the rays will be

    20-A   absorbed.
    20-B   converged.
    20-C   diffused.
    20-D   parallel.

21. How much voltage is needed to produce a current of 0.5 ampere in a circuit that has a resistance of 24 ohms?

    21-A   6 volts
    21-B   12 volts
    21-C   24 volts
    21-D   36 volts

22. Aeration of water will produce

    22-A   a loss of oxygen.
    22-B   a loss of methane.
    22-C   a gain of carbon dioxide.
    22-D   a gain of carbon dioxide and loss of oxygen.

23. What is the correct formula for "dry ice"?

    23-A HO_2
    23-B H_2O_2
    23-C CO
    23-D CO_2

24. If a person lifts a 50-pound package to the top of a 25-foot ladder, how many foot-pounds of work are performed?

    24-A   75 foot-pounds
    24-B   500 foot-pounds
    24-C   1,000 foot-pounds
    24-D   1,250 foot-pounds

25. What chemical reaction is represented by the following equation?

$$2H_2S \rightarrow 2H_2 \uparrow + S_2 \uparrow$$

    25-A   composition
    25-B   decomposition
    25-C   replacement
    25-D   double replacement

ARITHMETIC REASONING

Directions

This test has questions about arithmetic. Each question is followed by four possible answers. Decide which answer is correct. Then, on your answer form, blacken the space which has the same number and letter as your choice. Use your scratch paper for any figuring you wish to do.

Here is a sample question.

1. If 1 quart of milk costs $0.80, what is the cost of 2 quarts?

    1-A $2.00
    1-B $1.60
    1-C $1.20
    1-D $1.00

The cost of 2 quarts is $1.60; therefore, the answer 1-B is correct.

Your score on this test will be based on the number of questions you answer correctly. You should try to answer every question. Do not spend too much time on any one question.

Notice that Part 2 begins with question number 1. When you begin, be sure to mark your first answer next to number 1 on your answer form.

Do not turn this page until told to do so.

ARITHMETIC REASONING

Time: 36 minutes; 30 questions

1. The Parkers bought a table that was marked $400. On the installment plan, they made a down payment equal to 25% of the marked price, plus 12 monthly payments of $30 each. How much more than the marked price did they pay by buying it this way?

   1-A $25
   1-B $50
   1-C $60
   1-D $460

2. A scientist planted 120 seeds, of which 90 sprouted. What percent of the seeds failed to sprout?

   2-A   25%
   2-B   24%
   2-C   30%
   2-D   75%

3. An airplane traveled 1,000 miles in 2 hours and 30 minutes. What was the average rate of speed, in miles per hour, for the trip?

   3-A   200 miles per hour
   3-B   300 miles per hour
   3-C   400 miles per hour
   3-D   500 miles per hour

4. What is the value of this expression?

   $$\frac{0.05 \times 4}{0.1}$$

   4-A   20
   4-B   2
   4-C   0.2
   4-D   0.02

5. Joan Smith's bank balance was $2,674. Her bank balance changed as follows over the next four-month period:
   −$348, +$765, +$802, −$518
   What was her bank balance at the end of the four-month period?

   5-A $5,107
   5-B $4,241
   5-C $3,475
   5-D $3,375

6. A canteen sold 12½ gallons of milk at 35 cents a pint. How much did the canteen receive for the milk?

   6-A $33.60
   6-B $34
   6-C $35
   6-D $32.20

7. A square measures 9 feet on a side. If each side of the square is increased by 3 feet, how many square feet are added to the area?

   7-A   144
   7-B   81
   7-C   60
   7-D   63

8. What is the average of ¼ and ⅙?

   8-A $5/24$
   8-B $7/24$
   8-C $5/12$
   8-D $1/5$

9. Joe Gray's salary was increased from $260 per week to $290 per week. What was the increase in his salary, to the nearest percent?

   9-A   12%
   9-B   11%
   9-C   10%
   9-D   9%

10. If 1 pound, 12 ounces of fish costs $2.24, what is the cost of the fish per pound?

    10-A $1.20
    10-B $1.28
    10-C $1.24
    10-D $1.40

11. A front lawn measures 25 feet in length, and 15 feet in width. The back lawn of the same house measures 50 feet in length and 30 feet in width. What is the ratio of the area of the front lawn to the area of the back lawn?

    11-A   1:2
    11-B   2:3
    11-C   3:4
    11-D   1:4

12. The price of a car was increased from $6,400 to $7,200. What was the percent of increase?

    12-A   10%
    12-B   11⅑%
    12-C   12½%
    12-D   15%

13. What is the next term in this series: 3½; 2¼; 13¼; 12; _____?

    13-A   1¼
    13-B   10¾
    13-C   23
    13-D   14½

14. A movie house opens at 10:00 A.M. and closes at 11:30 P.M. If a complete showing of a movie takes 2 hours and 15 minutes, how many complete showings are given at the movie house each day?

    14-A   5
    14-B   6
    14-C   7
    14-D   8

15. At a concert, orchestra seats sell for $20 each, and balcony seats sell for $10 each. If 324 orchestra seats were occupied, and the box office collected $10,000, how many balcony seats were sold?

    15-A   375
    15-B   352
    15-C   330
    15-D   310

16. In a certain city, taxicab fare is $0.80 for the first ¼ mile, and $0.20 for each additional ¼ mile. How far, in miles, can a passenger travel for $5.00?

    16-A   5 miles
    16-B   4¼ miles
    16-C   5½ miles
    16-D   5¾ miles

17. A scale drawing of a building plot has a scale of 1 inch to 40 feet. How many inches on the drawing represent a distance of 175 feet on the plot?

    17-A   4⅛ inches
    17-B   4⅜ inches
    17-C   4½ inches
    17-D   4¾ inches

18. The wholesale list price of a watch was $50. A dealer bought a shipment of watches at a discount of 20% and sold the watches at 10% above the wholesale list price. What was her profit on each watch?

    18-A $8
    18-B $10
    18-C $12
    18-D $15

19. The minute hand of the clock is missing. but the hour hand is on the 11-minute mark. What time was it when the clock broke?

    19-A   5 minutes after 11
    19-B   11 minutes after 12
    19-C   12 minutes after 2
    19-D   20 minutes after 1

20. During a season a professional basketball player tried 320 shots and made 272 of them. What percent of the shots tried were successful?

    20-A   85%
    20-B   80%
    20-C   75%
    20-D   70%

21. A painter and a helper spend 3 days painting a house. The painter receives twice as much as the helper. If the two men receive $375 for the job, how much does the painter receive?

    21-A $175
    21-B $200
    21-C $225
    21-D $250

22. What is the difference between a 50% discount and a discount of 33⅓%?

    22-A   0.17
    22-B   ⅓
    22-C   0.25
    22-D   ⅙

23. What is the value of $3a^2 - 2a + 5$, when $a = 4$?

    23-A   43
    23-B   45
    23-C   61
    23-D   21

24. This table gives the annual premiums for a life insurance policy, based on the age of the holder when the policy is taken out.

Age in Years	Premium per $1,000
22	$18
30	$22
38	$28
46	$38

Over 20 years, how much is saved by taking out a $1,000 policy at age 30, rather than at age 46?

24-A $16
24-B $32
24-C $320
24-D $400

25. A chair was marked for sale at $240. This sale price was 25% less than the original price. What was the original price?

25-A $300
25-B $280
25-C $320
25-D $60

26. What is the quotient when 0.675 is divided by 0.9?

26-A 7.5
26-B 0.075
26-C 75
26-D 0.75

27. On May 15, an electric meter read 5,472 kilowatt hours. The following month, on June 15, the meter read 5,687 kilowatt hours. The utility charges the following rates for electric service.

First 10 kilowatt hours—$2.48
Next 45 kilowatt hours—$0.16 per kilowatt hour
Next 55 kilowatt hours—$0.12 per kilowatt hour
Over 110 kilowatt hours—$0.07 per kilowatt hour
What was the total charge for the kilowatt hours consumed during the month from May 15 to June 15?

27-A $22.53
27-B $23.63
27-C $22.63
27-D $24.43

28. What is the difference between the square of 49 and the square of 31?

28-A 18
28-B $1\frac{1}{2}$
28-C 1,440
28-D 2,056

29. An auditorium contains x rows, with y seats in each row. What is the number of seats in the auditorium?

29-A xy
29-B $x + y$
29-C $x - y$
29-D $y - x$

30. When a certain number is divided by 15, the quotient is 8, and the remainder is 7. What is the number?

30-A 127
30-B $8\frac{1}{2}$
30-C $3\frac{3}{5}$
30-D 77

WORD KNOWLEDGE

Directions

This test has questions about the meanings of words. Each question has an underlined boldface word. You are to decide which one of the four words in the choices most nearly means the same as the underlined boldface word, then mark the space on your answer form which has the same number and letter as your choice.

Now look at the sample question below.

1. It was a **small** table.

    1-A   sturdy
    1-B   round
    1-C   cheap
    1-D   little

The question is which of the four words means the same as the boldface word—the word **small.**

Little means the same as small so the D answer is the best one.

Your score on this test will be based on the number of questions you answer correctly. You should try to answer every question. Do not spend too much time on any one question.

When you begin, be sure to start with question number 1 in Part 3 of your test booklet and number 1 in Part 3 on your answer form.

Do not turn this page until told to do so.

WORD KNOWLEDGE

Time: 11 minutes; 35 questions

1. **Subsume** means most nearly

   1-A understate
   1-B absorb
   1-C include
   1-D belong

2. **Consensus** means most nearly

   2-A accord
   2-B abridgment
   2-C presumption
   2-D quota

3. **Altercation** means most nearly

   3-A defeat
   3-B concurrence
   3-C controversy
   3-D vexation

4. **Irresolute** means most nearly

   4-A wavering
   4-B insubordinate
   4-C impudent
   4-D unobservant

5. **Laconic** means most nearly

   5-A slothful
   5-B concise
   5-C punctual
   5-D melancholy

6. **Audition** means most nearly

   6-A reception
   6-B contest
   6-C hearing
   6-D display

7. **Novices** means most nearly

   7-A volunteers
   7-B experts
   7-C beginners
   7-D amateurs

8. **Conciliatory** means most nearly

   8-A pacific
   8-B contentious
   8-C obligatory
   8-D offensive

9. To **counteract** means most nearly

   9-A to undermine
   9-B to censure
   9-C to preserve
   9-D to neutralize

10. **Precedent** means most nearly

    10-A example
    10-B theory
    10-C law
    10-D conformity

11. **Diaphanous** means most nearly

    11-A transparent
    11-B opaque
    11-C diaphragmatic
    11-D diffusive

12. **Deferred** means most nearly

    12-A reversed
    12-B accelerated
    12-C forbidden
    12-D delayed

13. To **accentuate** means most nearly

    13-A to modify
    13-B to hasten
    13-C to sustain
    13-D to intensify

14. **Authentic** means most nearly

    14-A detailed
    14-B reliable
    14-C valuable
    14-D practical

15. **Unanimity** means most nearly

    15-A emphasis
    15-B namelessness
    15-C disagreement
    15-D concurrence

16. **Notorious** means most nearly

    16-A condemned
    16-B unpleasant
    16-C vexatious
    16-D well-known

17. **Previous** means most nearly

    17-A abandoned
    17-B former
    17-C timely
    17-D younger

18. **Flexible** means most nearly

    18-A breakable
    18-B flammable
    18-C pliable
    18-D weak

19. **Option** means most nearly

    19-A use
    19-B choice
    19-C value
    19-D preference

20. To **verify** means most nearly

    20-A examine
    20-B explain
    20-C confirm
    20-D guarantee

21. **Pert** means most nearly

    21-A ill
    21-B lazy
    21-C slow
    21-D saucy

22. **Aesthetic** means most nearly

    22-A sentient
    22-B sensitive
    22-C tasteful
    22-D inartistic

23. **Decimation** means most nearly

    23-A killing
    23-B annihilation
    23-C armistice
    23-D brawl

24. **Indignant** means most nearly

    24-A angry
    24-B poor
    24-C indigent
    24-D lazy

25. **Cliché** means most nearly

    25-A commonplace
    25-B banality
    25-C hackney
    25-D platitude

26. **Harmony** means most nearly

    26-A rhythm
    26-B pleasure
    26-C discord
    26-D agreement

27. **Indolent** means most nearly

    27-A moderate
    27-B hopeless
    27-C lazy
    27-D idle

28. **Respiration** means most nearly

    28-A recovery
    28-B breathing
    28-C pulsation
    28-D sweating

29. **Vigilant** means most nearly

    29-A sensible
    29-B watchful
    29-C suspicious
    29-D restless

30. **Incidental** means most nearly

    30-A independent
    30-B needless
    30-C infrequent
    30-D casual

31. To **succumb** means most nearly

    31-A to aid
    31-B to oppose
    31-C to yield
    31-D to check

32. **Feasible** means most nearly

    32-A capable
    32-B harmful
    32-C beneficial
    32-D practicable

33. **Versatile** means most nearly

    33-A well-known
    33-B up-to-date
    33-C many-sided
    33-D ambidextrous

34. **Imperturbability** means most nearly

    34-A obstinacy
    34-B serenity
    34-C sagacity
    34-D confusion

35. **Strident** means most nearly

    35-A swaggering
    35-B domineering
    35-C angry
    35-D harsh

4

PARAGRAPH COMPREHENSION

Directions

This is a test of your ability to understand what you read. In this section you will find one or more paragraphs of reading material followed by incomplete statements or questions. You are to read the paragraph and select one of four lettered choices which best completes the statement or answers the question. When you have selected your answer, blacken in the correct numbered letter on your answer sheet.

Now look at the sample question below.

In certain areas water is so scarce that every attempt is made to conserve it. For instance, on one oasis in the Sahara Desert the amount of water necessary for each date palm tree has been carefully determined.

2. How much water is each tree given?

    2-A   no water at all
    2-B   exactly the amount required
    2-C   water only if it is healthy
    2-D   water on alternate days

The amount of water each tree requires has been carefully determined so the answer 2-B is correct.

Your score on this test will be based on the number of questions you answer correctly. You should try to answer every question. Do not spend too much time on any one question.

When you begin, be sure to start with question number 1 in Part 4 of your test booklet and number 1 in Part 4 on your answer form.

Do not turn this page until told to do so.

PARAGRAPH COMPREHENSION

Time: 13 minutes; 15 questions

1. Twenty-five percent of all household burglaries can be attributed to unlocked windows or doors. Crime is the result of opportunity plus desire. To prevent crime, it is each individual's responsibility to

   1-A   provide the opportunity.
   1-B   provide the desire.
   1-C   prevent the opportunity.
   1-D   prevent the desire.

From a building designer's standpoint, three things that make a home livable are the client, the building site, and the amount of money the client has to spend.

2. According to the passage, to make a home livable

   2-A   the prospective piece of land makes little difference.
   2-B   it can be built on any piece of land.
   2-C   the design must fit the owner's income and site.
   2-D   the design must fit the designer's income.

Family camping has been described as the "biggest single growth industry in the booming travel/leisure market." Camping ranges from backpacking to living in rolling homes with complete creature comforts. It is both an end in itself and a magic carpet to a wide variety of other forms of outdoor recreation.

3. It can be inferred from the passage that the LEAST luxurious form of camping is

   3-A   backpacking
   3-B   travel trailers
   3-C   truck campers
   3-D   motor homes

Most drivers try to drive safely. A major part of safe driving is the right speed. But what is the "right" speed? Is it 20 miles per hour, or 35, or 60? That question is hard to answer. On some city streets and in heavy traffic, twenty miles per hour could be too fast. On a superhighway, 35 miles per hour could be too slow. Of course, a good driver must follow the speed limit, but he must also use good judgment. The "right" speed will vary by the amount of cars, surface of the road, and how well you can see.

4. The general theme of this passage is that a good driver:

   4-A   drives at 35 miles an hour.
   4-B   adjusts to different driving conditions.
   4-C   always drives at the same speed.
   4-D   always follows the speed limit.

Gardening can be an easygoing hobby, a scientific pursuit, an opportunity for exercise and fresh air, a serious source of food to help balance the family budget, a means of expression in art and beauty, an applied experiment in green plant growth, or all of these things together.

5. All of the following are made possible by gardening according to the passage EXCEPT

   5-A   relaxation.
   5-B   exercise.
   5-C   experimentation.
   5-D   hard work.

About three fourths of the surface of the earth is water. Of the 336 million cubic miles of water, most (97.2%) is found in the oceans and is salty. Glaciers hold another two per cent of the total. Less than one per cent (.8%) is available as fresh water for people to use. And much of that is not near the people who need it.

6. The amount of fresh water available for people use is:

   6-A   97.2%
   6-B   .8%
   6-C   2%
   6-D   75%

Early settlers in the United States made the most of the herring fishing season. When spring came the fish arrived in great numbers in the rivers. No nets or hooks were needed. Men used what was called a *pinfold*. This was a large circular pen built in shallow water. It was made by driving stakes closely together in the floor of the river.

7. A *pinfold* was made with:

   7-A   hooks and nets.
   7-B   only nets.

7-C   stakes driven into the river bottom.
7-D   fishing rods.

The powers of the United States government are divided. One part of government, the Congress, makes the laws. Another part, the President and the different heads of departments, put the laws into effect. The third part, the courts, must try cases when laws are broken. The idea behind this is to prevent one part or branch of government from getting all the power.

8. As a result of the divided powers of government

8-A   Congress rules the United States.
8-B   the President rules the United States.
8-C   power is shared.
8-D   no branch has power.

A narcotic is a drug which, in proper doses, relieves pain and induces profound sleep, but which, in poisonous doses, induces stupor, coma, or convulsions. Narcotics tend to be habit-forming and, in many instances, repeated doses lead to addiction.

9. A proper dose of a narcotic induces

9-A   coma.
9-B   convulsions.
9-C   deep sleep.
9-D   stupor.

Because nitrogen, phosphorous, and potassium are used by plants in large amounts, these nutrients are likely to be deficient in the soil. When you buy a fertilizer, therefore, you generally buy it for its content of these materials.

10. Unfertilized soil naturally deficient in nitrogen, phosphoric oxide, and potash probably lacks these nutrients because

10-A   they are not soluble.
10-B   manufacturers do not recommend them to gardeners.
10-C   they are rare elements never found in the earth.
10-D   plants use them up in large quantities.

Where does pollution come from? It comes from a wide variety of sources, including furnaces, smokestacks, incinerators, power-generating stations, industrial plants, dirt and dust caused by tearing down old buildings and putting up new ones, ordinary street dirt, restaurants that emit smoke and odors, cars, buses, trucks, planes, and steamships. Sixty percent of pollution is caused by motor vehicle exhausts, while another thirty percent is due to industry.

11. Most air pollution in that city is caused by

11-A   industry and incinerators.
11-B   cars, trucks, and buses.
11-C   airplanes.
11-D   smokestacks of buildings.

The use of sunglasses as an aid to vision is important. For the most part, the eye is a "daytime" instrument. It requires light to work properly. However, too much bright light and glare can create discomfort. As a result the eyes blink, squint, get tears, or have have trouble seeing well. Sunglasses help by keeping much of this bright light and glare from reaching the eyes.

12. The main purpose of sunglasses is to

12-A   hide the eyes.
12-B   screen out harmful rays of the sun.
12-C   remove the need for regular glasses.
12-D   protect the eyes from dirt.

Would you like to be good at a trade? Would you like to know a skill that pays well? One sure way to skill, good pay, and regular work is to train on the job. This is called apprentice training. While it is not the only way to learn, apprentice training has good points. You can earn while you learn. You know the skill "from the ground up." You can advance on the job.

13. Apprentice training is described by discussing:

13-A   both sides.
13-B   the good side.
13-C   the bad side.
13-D   a specific trade.

14. When you work at a job covered by social security, you and your employer contribute equal amounts. Your portion of the tax is taken from your wages or pay check before you receive it. This is called a *deduction*.

14-A   Total tax rate is retirement rate plus insurance rate.
14-B   Insurance rates are higher than retirement rates.
14-C   Money taken from your pay is called a deduction.
14-D   Only your employer contributes to social security.

Nucleic acids are found in all living organisms from viruses to man. They received their name because of their discovery in the nuclei of white blood cells and fish sperm by Miescher in 1869. However, it is now well established that nucleic acids occur outside of the cell nucleus as well.

15. Nucleic acids are found
    15-A   only in cells of man.
    15-B   only in viruses.
    15-C   in all living cells.
    15-D   only in white blood cells.

NUMERICAL OPERATIONS

Directions

This is a test to see how rapidly and accurately you can do arithmetic problems. Each problem is followed by four answers, only one of which is correct. Decide which answer is correct, then blacken the space on your answer form which has the same number and letter as your choice.

Now look at the sample problem below.

1. 4 + 3 =

    1-A   1
    1-B   12
    1-C   7
    1-D   2

The answer to the problem is 7, so you would blacken the space for 1-C on your answer form.

This is a speed test, so work as fast as you can without making mistakes. Do each problem as it comes. If you finish before time is up, go back and check your work. Part 5 of this model test begins with question 1. Thus, the first answer should be recorded next to 1 on your answer form.

Do not turn this page until told to do so.

NUMERICAL OPERATIONS

Time: 3 minutes; 50 questions

1. $6 - 3 =$

1-A   18
1-B   9
1-C   3
1-D   2

2. $3 \times 4 =$

2-A   9
2-B   12
2-C   15
2-D   18

3. $10 - 1 =$

3-A   11
3-B   10
3-C   9
3-D   8

4. $4 \div 2 =$

4-A   0
4-B   1
4-C   2
4-D   3

5. $8 + 1 =$

5-A   9
5-B   8
5-C   7
5-D   1

6. $5 \times 0 =$

6-A   6
6-B   5
6-C   1
6-D   0

7. $2 + 7 =$

7-A   8
7-B   9
7-C   10
7-D   11

8. $7 + 1 =$

8-A   9
8-B   8
8-C   7
8-D   6

9. $2 - 1 =$

9-A   0
9-B   1
9-C   2
9-D   3

10. $9 - 5 =$

10-A   7
10-B   6
10-C   5
10-D   4

11. $6 + 5 =$

11-A   12
11-B   11
11-C   10
11-D   9

12. $10 \times 2 =$

12-A   20
12-B   15
12-C   10
12-D   5

13. $18 \div 3 =$

13-A   12
13-B   9
13-C   6
13-D   3

14. $8 \times 2 =$

14-A   16
14-B   14
14-C   12
14-D   10

15. $9 - 9 =$

15-A   6
15-B   3
15-C   1
15-D   0

16. $5 + 2 =$

16-A   11
16-B   9
16-C   7
16-D   5

17. 12 − 5 =

    17-A 7
    17-B 8
    17-C 9
    17-D 10

18. 3 + 2 =

    18-A 8
    18-B 1
    18-C 6
    18-D 5

19. 7 × 2 =

    19-A 20
    19-B 18
    19-C 16
    19-D 14

20. 5 − 2 =

    20-A 10
    20-B 7
    20-C 6
    20-D 3

21. 6 + 7 =

    21-A 11
    21-B 12
    21-C 13
    21-D 14

22. 6 ÷ 3 =

    22-A 2
    22-B 3
    22-C 8
    22-D 9

23. 4 − 0 =

    23-A 4
    23-B 2
    23-C 1
    23-D 0

24. 8 ÷ 8 =

    24-A 16
    24-B 4
    24-C 1
    24-D 0

25. 10 − 3 =

    25-A 13
    25-B 8
    25-C 7
    25-D 6

26. 2 × 2 =

    26-A 0
    26-B 1
    26-C 2
    26-D 4

27. 3 ÷ 3 =

    27-A 0
    27-B 1
    27-C 6
    27-D 9

28. 4 + 8 =

    28-A 13
    28-B 12
    28-C 11
    28-D 10

29. 7 × 5 =

    29-A 45
    29-B 40
    29-C 35
    29-D 30

30. 5 + 1 =

    30-A 0
    30-B 4
    30-C 5
    30-D 6

31. 1 + 7 =

    31-A 9
    31-B 8
    31-C 6
    31-D 1

32. 10 ÷ 5 =

    32-A 2
    32-B 3
    32-C 4
    32-D 5

33. 14 ÷ 2 =

    33-A 12
    33-B 9
    33-C 7
    33-D 3

34. 9 + 7 =

    34-A 15
    34-B 16
    34-C 14
    34-D 13

35. $6 - 2 =$

    35-A 5
    35-B 10
    35-C 3
    35-D 4

36. $8 + 7 =$

    36-A 15
    36-B 19
    36-C 18
    36-D 17

37. $5 \times 4 =$

    37-A 11
    37-B 15
    37-C 20
    37-D 9

38. $7 - 4 =$

    38-A 11
    38-B 5
    38-C 3
    38-D 2

39. $4 \times 3 =$

    39-A 7
    39-B 6
    39-C 14
    39-D 12

40. $2 \times 6 =$

    40-A 10
    40-B 12
    40-C 14
    40-D 16

41. $3 + 8 =$

    41-A 24
    41-B 16
    41-C 14
    41-D 11

42. $10 - 7 =$

    42-A 3
    42-B 2
    42-C 16
    42-D 5

43. $24 \div 4 =$

    43-A 12
    43-B 8
    43-C 6
    43-D 4

44. $3 + 11 =$

    44-A 8
    44-B 10
    44-C 12
    44-D 14

45. $8 \div 2 =$

    45-A 0
    45-B 2
    45-C 6
    45-D 4

46. $7 \times 3 =$

    46-A 21
    46-B 23
    46-C 24
    46-D 27

47. $4 + 4 =$

    47-A 12
    47-B 8
    47-C 12
    47-D 16

48. $0 \div 2 =$

    48-A 1
    48-B 0
    48-C 2
    48-D 20

49. $7 - 3 =$

    49-A 10
    49-B 5
    49-C 4
    49-D 2

50. $5 + 9 =$

    50-A 34
    50-B 24
    50-C 14
    50-D 4

CODING SPEED

Directions

This is a test to see how quickly and accurately you can assign code numbers. At the top of each set of questions there is a code number "key." The key is a group of words with a code number for each word.

Each question in the test is a word taken from the key at the top. From among the possible answers listed for each question, you are to find the one which is the correct code number for that word. Then blacken the square for that answer on your answer sheet.

The sample questions below have already been answered for you. Make sure you understand them. Then try to answer the 84 questions following them as best you can.

Sample Question

Key

green .. 2715	man ... 3451	salt 4586
hat 1413	room ... 2864	tree 5972

Answers

	A	B	C	D	E
room	1413	2715	2864	3451	4586
green	2715	2864	3451	4586	5972
tree	2715	2864	3451	4596	5972
hat	1413	2715	2864	3451	4586
room	1413	2864	3451	4586	5972

Notice that each of the questions is one of the words in the key. To the right of each question are possible answers listed under the letters A, B, C, D, and E. By looking at the key you see that the code number for the first word, "room," is 2864. 2864 is listed under the letter C so C is the correct answer. The correct answers for the other four questions are A, E, A, and B.

Do not turn this page until told to do so.

CODING SPEED

Time: 7 minutes; 84 questions

Key

advance 9302	cube ... 7127	mayor .. 3639
aim 5682	direct .. 6359	obey ... 1945
brown .. 4472	false ... 9589	shoulder 8879
	wrap ... 4372	

Answers

	A	B	C	D	E
1. brown	1945	4472	7127	8879	9302
2. cube	1945	3639	5682	7127	9302
3. aim	4372	5682	6359	8879	9589
4. mayor	1945	3639	4372	4472	6359
5. false	1945	4472	5682	6359	9589
6. aim	3639	4372	5682	7127	9302
7. advance	1945	3639	5682	8879	9302
8. obey	1945	4472	5682	7127	8879
9. wrap	3639	4372	7127	8879	9589
10. shoulder	1945	3639	4472	8879	9302
11. obey	1945	4372	5682	7127	9589
12. direct	4372	5682	6359	7127	9302

Key

extra ... 5963	guilty ... 7149	private . 9324
film 8471	index .. 2584	rich 8362
food ... 9859	learn ... 6225	trial 29 53
	wound . 1586	

Answers

	A	B	C	D	E
13. extra	1586	2584	2953	5963	9859
14. guilty	2584	5963	6225	7149	8471
15. learn	1586	2584	5963	6225	7149
16. food	1586	6225	8362	9324	9859
17. index	2584	6225	8471	9324	9859
18. private	2584	7149	8362	8471	9324
19. trial	2584	2953	5963	7149	8471
20. learn	2584	6225	8471	9324	9859
21. film	1586	2953	5963	6225	8471
22. rich	2584	5963	7149	8362	8471
23. wound	1586	2584	5963	6225	7149
24. extra	2584	5963	8362	9324	9859

Key

bread .. 9338	human . 8102	thing ... 5014
commit . 5680	object .. 4795	tree 1797
fresh .. 8221	purse .. 7244	union .. 9413
	view ... 3035	

Answers

	A	B	C	D	E
25. tree	1797	5014	7244	8102	8221
26. union	3035	4795	5014	7244	9413
27. object	1797	3035	4795	8102	9338
28. bread	4795	5680	8221	9338	9413
29. fresh	1797	4795	5014	8102	8221
30. thing	3035	5014	5680	7244	9413
31. commit	1797	3035	4795	5680	8221
32. bread	3035	4795	5014	9338	9413
33. view	3035	4795	7244	8221	9338
34. tree	1797	5014	7244	8102	9413
35. purse	5680	7244	8221	9338	9413
36. human	3035	4795	5680	8102	9413

Key

bend ... 7442	lamp ... 8741	ring 9111
dirt 3107	order .. 5246	sit 3252
fact 1929	problem 2618	talk 4586
	winter .. 8659	

Answers

	A	B	C	D	E
37. lamp	1929	3107	5246	8741	9111
38. ring	2618	3107	4586	8659	9111
39. winter	3107	3252	5246	8659	8741
40. order	2618	3107	4586	5246	8659
41. sit	1929	2618	3252	5246	7442
42. bend	2618	4586	5246	7442	9111
43. fact	1929	3107	3252	4586	7442
44. talk	2618	3252	4586	5246	8659
45. sit	1929	3107	3252	7442	8741
46. ring	3252	4586	7442	8659	9111
47. dirt	3107	3252	4586	5246	7442
48. problem	1929	2618	7442	8659	8741

Key

atom ... 1340	good ... 9272	number 3529
band ... 6986	hid 9397	stream . 4618
degree . 5989	lay 2445	summer 4121
	wool ... 7315	

Answers

	A	B	C	D	E
49. band	1340	5989	6986	9272	9397
50. wool	2445	4121	4618	7315	9272
51. number	1340	2445	3529	5989	9397
52. lay	1340	2445	7315	9272	9397

		A	B	C	D	E
53.	atom	1340	3529	4121	5989	7315
54.	degree	2445	4618	5989	7315	9397
55.	lay	1340	2445	4121	7315	9272
56.	stream	3529	4618	5989	7315	9397
57.	hid	1340	2445	4121	6986	9397
58.	number	2445	3529	4618	5989	9272
59.	good	1340	2445	4618	6986	9272
60.	summer	1340	4121	4618	5989	9397

Key

```
agile..6427   humid..4903   pit...6656
beacon.8585   jar....3059   rest..7350
data...9130   overt..9845   stun..7689
              wilt...1317
```

Answers

		A	B	C	D	E
61.	pit	6656	7350	8585	9130	9845
62.	rest	1317	6656	7350	7689	8585
63.	beacon	3059	6427	7689	8585	9845
64.	data	3059	4903	8585	9130	9845
65.	jar	1317	3059	6427	7350	7689
66.	overt	7350	7689	8585	9130	9845
67.	agile	4903	6427	6656	7350	9130
68.	wilt	1317	6427	7350	8585	9845

		A	B	C	D	E
69.	humid	3059	4903	6427	7350	9130
70.	pit	3059	6656	8585	9130	9845
71.	stun	1317	4903	6427	7689	9845
72.	humid	3059	4903	6427	6656	9130

Key

```
cabin ..8822   hall ....7891   man ...3451
coat ...6403   hat ....1413   room...2864
green ..2715   kite ....9379   salt ....4586
               tree....5972
```

Answers

		A	B	C	D	E
73.	room	1413	2715	2864	3451	4586
74.	green	2715	2864	3451	4586	5972
75.	tree	2715	2864	3451	4596	5972
76.	hat	1413	2715	2864	3451	4586
77.	room	1413	2864	3451	4586	5972
78.	kite	2864	3451	4586	6403	9379
79.	hall	2715	4586	5972	7891	8822
80.	cabin	1413	2864	3451	6403	8822
81.	coat	1413	2715	4586	6403	7891
82.	man	3451	4586	5972	7891	9379
83.	salt	1413	2715	4586	5972	8822
84.	kite	3451	6403	7891	8822	9379

7

AUTO AND SHOP INFORMATION

Directions

This test has questions about automobiles. Pick the best answer for each question, then blacken the space on your separate answer form which has the same number and letter as your choice.

Here is a sample question.

1. The most commonly used fuel for running automobile engines is

   1-A   kerosene.
   1-B   benzine.
   1-C   crude oil.
   1-D   gasoline.

Gasoline is the most commonly used fuel, so 1-D is the correct answer.

Your score on this test will be based on the number of questions you answer correctly. You should try to answer every question. Do not spend too much time on any one question.

When you are told to begin, be sure to start with question number 1 in Part 7 of your test booklet and number 1 in Part 7 on your separate answer form.

Do not turn this page until told to do so.

AUTO AND SHOP INFORMATION

Time: 11 minutes; 25 questions

1. Underinflating a tire will cause excessive wear on

   1-A the center of the tread.
   1-B both outside edges of the tread.
   1-C the bead.
   1-D the sidewalls.

2. Wheelbase is measured from

   2-A bumper to bumper.
   2-B left front wheel to right front wheel.
   2-C center of front wheel to center of rear wheel.
   2-D fender to fender.

3. A center bolt is used

   3-A on all coil springs.
   3-B to align a leaf spring with the axle housing.
   3-C to prevent leaf springs from moving sideways.
   3-D to prevent the front end from wandering.

4. Syncromesh units are used in standard transmissions because they

   4-A are stronger.
   4-B eliminate grinding of the gears.
   4-C cost less.
   4-D give an overdrive effect.

5. The vacuum modulator in an automatic transmission

   5-A allows the transmission only to downshift.
   5-B controls the shifts of the transmission while sensing engine load.
   5-C creates a vacuum to shift the clutches.
   5-D modulates vacuum for ignition spark advance when overheating.

6. A clutch pedal must have free play so that

   6-A the clutch grabs early.
   6-B the clutch grabs late.
   6-C there is clearance between the disc and the flywheel.
   6-D there is clearance between the clutch fingers and the throwout bearing.

7. A limited slip differential is used to

   7-A allow a car to climb hills faster.
   7-B give better traction on ice.
   7-C keep the rear end cooler.
   7-D give a softer ride.

8. What are the two main functions of the ignition system?

   8-A to provide a primary arc and a secondary spark
   8-B to provide a spark and a means to decrease it
   8-C to provide a high voltage spark and the means to time the engine
   8-D to provide a path for the wires and the spark plugs

9. In an ignition system using a resistor in the primary circuit the resistor is located between the

   9-A battery and the ignition switch.
   9-B ignition switch and the coil.
   9-C coil and the distributor points.
   9-D distributor points and the condenser.

10. The magnetic field within an alternator is provided by the

    10-A rotor.
    10-B stator.
    10-C diodes.
    10-D heat sink.

11. If a horn sounds continuously but the horn relay is good, the most likely cause is

    11-A a short in the horn.
    11-B a grounded horn.
    11-C an open wire at the horn button.
    11-D a grounded wire at the horn button.

12. The purpose of the rubber cups in the brake wheel cylinders is to

    12-A push out the brake shoes.
    12-B prevent brake fluid from leaking out of the cylinder.
    12-C maintain the springs in position.
    12-D absorb the shock of the brake application.

13. The metering valve in a hydraulic brake system

   13-A   holds off pressure to the front brakes.
   13-B   holds off pressure to the rear brakes.
   13-C   equalizes pressure to all four wheel brakes.
   13-D   warns the driver of brake system failure.

14. The order in which the events occur in the four-stroke cycle engine are

   14-A   intake, compression, exhaust, power.
   14-B   intake, compression, power, exhaust.
   14-C   intake, power, exhaust, compression.
   14-D   intake, power, compression, exhaust.

15. If the piston and rod assembly is to be removed from an engine block, any ridge at the top of a cylinder

   15-A   should be removed using a ridge reamer.
   15-B   should be drilled out.
   15-C   should be filed down with a single cut file.
   15-D   does not interfere with the removal of the assembly.

16. To complete the four-stroke cycle the engine camshaft must make

   16-A   one revolution.
   16-B   four revolutions.
   16-C   two revolutions.
   16-D   one-half revolution.

17. The mitre box is used for cutting

   17-A   angles from 90° to 45°.
   17-B   rafters.
   17-C   joists.
   17-D   logs.

18. The coping saw is for cutting

   18-A   wood at any curve or angle desired.
   18-B   steel at any curve or angle desired.
   18-C   straight lines along a board.
   18-D   cross cutting along a straight line.

19. Another name for the wrecking bar is

   19-A   lever.
   19-B   crow bar.
   19-C   slot maker.
   19-D   plumb bob.

20. If a low compression reading in one or more cylinders is substantially increased when oil is squirted into the cylinder, this would indicate that the

   20-A   valves are bad.
   20-B   head gasket is blown.
   20-C   piston is broken.
   20-D   rings are worn.

21. Which type of pump is used to circulate coolant through the cooling system of an engine?

   21-A   diaphragm pump
   21-B   gear pump
   21-C   centrifugal pump
   21-D   piston or plunger pump

22. The screwdriver with a cross or X on the end is called

   22-A   a phillips head.
   22-B   a standard type screwdriver.
   22-C   a wrench.
   22-D   plumb bob.

23. A chisel is used to cut wood by striking it with a

   23-A   screwdriver.
   23-B   hammer.
   23-C   fist.
   23-D   level.

24. A device with glass tubes that have air bubbles in them is used to indicate when a door or window is

   24-A   nailed in place.
   24-B   warped.
   24-C   screwed in place.
   24-D   level.

25. If you wanted to cut circular holes in wood or metal, which of the following tools would you use?

   25-A   Coping Saw
   25-B   Cross-cut Saw
   25-C   Hole Saw
   25-D   Mitre Box

MATHEMATICS KNOWLEDGE

Directions

This is a test of your ability to solve general mathematical problems. Each problem is followed by four answer choices. Select the correct response from the choices given. Then mark the space on your answer form that has the same number and letter as your choice. Use scratch paper to do any figuring that you wish.

Now look at this sample problem.

1. $4 \times 2 =$

    1-A   10
    1-B   8
    1-C   6
    1-D   4

The correct answer is 8, so 1-B is the correct response.

Your score on this test will be based on the number of questions you answer correctly. You should try to answer every question. Do not spend too much time on any one question.

Start with question number 1 in Part 8. Mark your answer for this question next to number 1, Part 8, on your answer form.

Do not turn this page until told to do so.

MATHEMATICS KNOWLEDGE

Time: 24 minutes; 25 questions

1. Which of the following is the smallest prime number greater than 200?

   1-A   201
   1-B   205
   1-C   211
   1-D   214

2. If 40% is equal to the fraction $x/30$, what is the value of x?

   2-A   0.4
   2-B   15
   2-C   1,200
   2-D   12

3. The expression "5 factorial" equals

   3-A   125.
   3-B   120.
   3-C   25.
   3-D   10.

4. What is the result of subtracting $3x^2 - 5x - 1$ from $8x^2 + 2x - 9$?

   4-A $5x^2 - 3x - 10$
   4-B $-5x^2 - 3x - 10$
   4-C $5x^2 + 7x - 8$
   4-D $-5x^2 - 7x + 8$

5. What is the meaning of the statement $-30 < -5$?

   5-A   30 is greater than 5
   5-B   30 is less than minus 5
   5-C   minus 30 is less than minus 5
   5-D   minus 30 is greater than minus 5

6. Solve for x: $8x - 2 - 5x = 8$

   6-A $x = 1.3$
   6-B $x = 2\frac{1}{2}$
   6-C $x = 3\frac{1}{3}$
   6-D $x = -7$

7. A woman has $500 in a bank account. Every week, she writes out a check for $50. If she doesn't make any new deposits, what will her bank account hold x weeks from now?

   7-A $500 + 50x$
   7-B $500 - 50x$
   7-C $550 - x
   7-D $500 + $50 + x

8. When the temperature is 20 degrees Celsius (C), what is it on the Fahrenheit (F) scale? (Use the following formula.)

$$F = \left(\frac{9}{5} \times C\right) + 32$$

   8-A $93\frac{3}{5}$ degrees
   8-B   78 degrees
   8-C $62\frac{3}{5}$ degrees
   8-D   68 degrees

9. The perimeter of a rectangle is 38″. If the length is 3″ more than the width, find the width.

   9-A $17\frac{1}{2}$″
   9-B   8″
   9-C   11″
   9-D $14\frac{1}{2}$″

10. Find the square root of 85 correct to the nearest tenth.

   10-A   9.1
   10-B   9.2
   10-C   9.3
   10-D   9.4

11. If $5x = 30$, then x is equal to

   11-A   150.
   11-B   25.
   11-C   6.
   11-D   0.6.

12. What is the product of $(a - 5)$ and $(a + 3)$?

   12-A $a^2 - 15$
   12-B $a^2 + 2a - 15$
   12-C $a^2 - 2a - 15$
   12-D $a^2 - 2$

13. Solve for z: $3z - 5 + 2z = 25 - 5z$

   13-A $z = 0$
   13-B $z = 3$
   13-C $z = -3$
   13-D   no solution

14. A park commissioner designs a new playground in the shape of a pentagon. If he plans to have a fountain at every corner of the park, how many fountains will there be?

14-A   4
14-B   5
14-C   6
14-D   7

15. If one of the angles of a right triangle is 30 degrees, what are the other two angles?

15-A   30 degrees, 120 degrees
15-B   60 degrees, 45 degrees
15-C   60 degrees, 90 degrees
15-D   45 degrees, 90 degrees

16. What is the value of x in the equation $\frac{x}{2} = 7$?

16-A $x = 14$
16-B $x = 3\frac{1}{2}$
16-C $x = 9$
16-D $x = 5$

17. Divide $15a^3b^2c$ by $5abc$.

17-A $10abc$
17-B $3abc$
17-C $5a^2b^2$
17-D $3a^2b$

18. Two circles have the same center. If their radii are 7″ and 10″, find the area that is part of the larger circle, but not the smaller one.

18-A   3 square inches
18-B   17 square inches
18-C   51 Pi square inches
18-D   70 Pi square inches

19. My average grade on a set of five tests was 88%. I can remember only that the first four grades were 78%, 86%, 96%, and 94%. What was my fifth grade?

19-A   88
19-B   86
19-C   84
19-D   82

20. How many cubic yards of concrete are needed to make a cement floor that is 9′ by 12′ by 6″ thick?

20-A   2
20-B   18
20-C   54
20-D   648

21. A wildlife preserve is laid out in the shape of a perfect circle, whose radius is 14 miles. The lions' territory in this preserve is shaped like a wedge and has a fence around it. Two inner sides of the fence meet at a 90-degree angle in the center of the preserve. How much territory do the lions have?

21-A   140 square miles
21-B   3½ square miles
21-C   210 square miles
21-D   154 square miles

22. Find the value of $(-3)^4 + (-2)^4 + (-1)^4$

22-A   98
22-B   −98
22-C   −21
22-D   21

23. A cyclindrical can has a radius of 7″ and a height of 15″. How many gallons of milk can it hold? (There are 231 cubic inches in a gallon.)

23-A   15 gallons
23-B   14 gallons
23-C   140 gallons
23-D   10 gallons

24. A 10-foot-high ladder is resting against an 8-foot-high wall in a tennis court. If the top of the ladder is exactly even with the top of the wall, how far is the base of the ladder from the wall?

24-A   18 feet
24-B   6 feet
24-C   12 feet
24-D   9 feet

25. Ten ounces of liquid contain 20% fruit juice and 80% water. The mixture is diluted by adding 40 additional ounces of water. What is the percent of fruit juice in the new solution?

25-A   4%
25-B   10%
25-C   20%
25-D   40%

9

MECHANICAL COMPREHENSION

Directions

This test has questions about general mechanical and physical principles. Pick the best answer for each question, then blacken the space on your separate answer form which has the same number and letter as your choice.

Here is a sample question.

17. The follower is at its highest position between points

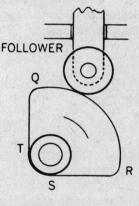

17-A   Q and R.
17-B   R and S.
17-C   S and T.
17-D   T and Q.

The correct answer is between Q and R, so you would blacken the space for 17-A on your answer form.

Your score on this test will be based on the number of questions you answer correctly. You should try to answer every question. Do not spend too much time on any one question.

When you are told to begin, be sure to start with question number 1 in Part 9 of your test booklet and number 1 in Part 9 of your separate answer form.

Do not turn this page until told to do so.

MECHANICAL COMPREHENSION

Time: 19 minutes; 25 questions

1. A ½" open end wrench will fit the head of one of the following N.F. cap screws.

   1-A ½"
   1-B ¼"
   1-C ⅜"
   1-D ⁵⁄₁₆"

2. Two parts are securely held together by a nut, bolt and lock washer. The correct position for the lock washer is

   2-A between the two parts.
   2-B under the nut.
   2-C directly under the head of the bolt.
   2-D over a flat washer.

3. The following tools should be used to disconnect a gas line from a carburetor.

   3-A open end and flare nut wrench
   3-B open end wrench and plier
   3-C two open end wrenches
   3-D pipe wrench and box wrench

4. Each line on the thimble of a micrometer represents

   4-A 0.100".
   4-B one inch.
   4-C 0.025".
   4-D 0.001".

5. A brake spoon is used to

   5-A adjust drum brakes.
   5-B adjust disc brakes.
   5-C remove cotter pins.
   5-D clean the backing plate.

6. The following instrument is used to test battery electrolyte specific gravity.

   6-A voltmeter
   6-B ammeter
   6-C ohmmeter
   6-D hydrometer

7. A starter armature is being tested on a growler. If the hacksaw blade vibrates when placed on the core of the armature, it indicates that the

   7-A field coils are grounded.
   7-B solenoid disc is burned.
   7-C armature is open.
   7-D armature is shorted.

8. The device used to check the runout of a disc brake rotor is a

   8-A torque wrench.
   8-B dial indicator.
   8-C micrometer.
   8-D feeler gauge.

9. Which gage is used to check engine crankshaft endplay?

   9-A depth gage
   9-B plastigage
   9-C feeler gage
   9-D micrometer

10. An ohmmeter test of an electronic ignition pick-up coil indicates an infinite reading. What does this reading indicate?

   10-A normal
   10-B shorted
   10-C open
   10-D grounded

11. A transmission

   11-A controls speed of the engine.
   11-B sacrifices speed for power.
   11-C transmits power at an angle.
   11-D sacrifices power for speed.

12. If a rear axle ratio is 4 to 1,

   12-A the pinion gear has 4 times the number of teeth as the ring gear.
   12-B the ring gear has 4 times the number of teeth as the pinion gear.
   12-C the rear tire is 4 times larger than the brake drum.
   12-D the side gear has 4 times the number of teeth as the spider gear.

13. The motive power of the automotive cranking motor is created by the

   13-A field poles attracting the laminated iron core of the armature.
   13-B repelling force of like poles being formed in the armature opposite the field poles.
   13-C starter neutral safety switch.
   13-D starter drive.

14. Compressing air in a closed container

    14-A   increases the volume and lowers the temperature.

    14-B   lowers the temperature and decreases the volume.

    14-C   increases both temperature and volume.

    14-D   decreases the volume and increases the temperature.

15. The greatest amount of mechanical advantage of power is attained when an 11 tooth gear drives a

    15-A   29 tooth gear.
    15-B   11 tooth gear.
    15-C   47 tooth gear.
    15-D   15 tooth gear.

16. If the transmission ratio is 3.29 to 1, and the differential ratio is 3.85 to 1, then the final ratio is

    16-A   7.14 to 1.
    16-B   0.56 to 1.
    16-C   12.67 to 1.
    16-D   none of these.

17. The pliers is an example of a

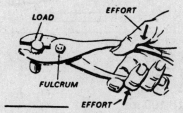

    17-A   first class lever.
    17-B   second class lever.
    17-C   third class lever.
    17-D   first and second class lever.

18. The follower is at its highest position between points

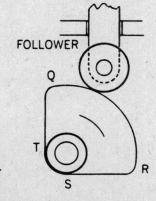

    18-A   Q and R.
    18-B   R and S.
    18-C   S and T.
    18-D   T and Q.

19. If pulley A is the driver and turns in direction 1, which pulley turns fastest?

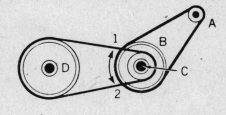

    19-A   A
    19-B   B
    19-C   C
    19-D   D

20. Which shaft or shafts are turning in the same direction as shaft X?

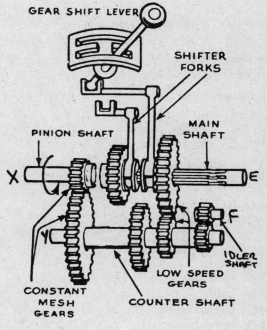

    20-A   Y
    20-B   Y and E
    20-C   F
    20-D   E and F

21. The human arm is an example of a

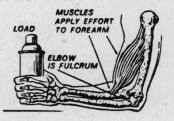

    21-A   first class lever.
    21-B   second class lever.
    21-C   third class lever.
    21-D   second and third class lever.

22. If arm H is held fixed as gear B turns in direction 2, gear

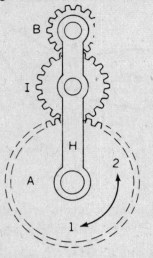

22-A   A must turn in direction 1.
22-B   A must turn in direction 2.
22-C   I must turn in direction 2.
22-D   A must be held fixed.

23. Gearset Y is

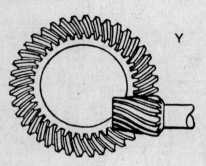

23-A   rack and pinion.
23-B   spur.
23-C   hypoid bevel.
23-D   spiral bevel.

24. If the force on piston X is 10 lbs, then the output force of piston Y will be

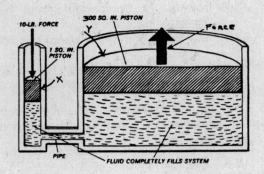

24-A   300 lbs.
24-B   30 lbs.
24-C   10 lbs.
24-D   3000 lbs.

25. How much effort must be placed at point A to lift the weight at B?

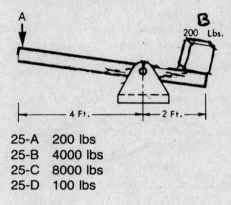

25-A   200 lbs
25-B   4000 lbs
25-C   8000 lbs
25-D   100 lbs

ELECTRONICS INFORMATION

Directions

This is a test of your knowledge of electrical, radio, and electronics information. You are to select the correct response from the choices given. Then mark the space on your answer form which has the same number and letter as your choice.

Now look at the sample question below.

1. What does the abbreviation AC stand for?

    1-A   additional charge
    1-B   alternating coil
    1-C   alternating current
    1-D   ampere current

The correct answer is alternating current, so 1-C is the correct response.

Your score on this test will be based on the number of questions you answer correctly. You should try to answer every question. Do not spend too much time on any one question.

When you are told to begin, be sure to start with question number 1 in Part 10 of your test booklet and number 1 in Part 10 on your separate answer form.

Do not turn this page until told to do so.

ELECTRONICS INFORMATION

Time: 9 minutes; 20 questions

1. Flux is placed inside electrical solder in order to

   1-A   clean the connections during soldering and prevent oxidation.
   1-B   raise the melting point of silver.
   1-C   increase the conductivity of the connection.
   1-D   act as an insulator within the connection.

2. A cold solder connection is

   2-A   clean and shiny in appearance.
   2-B   dull and brittle in appearance.
   2-C   a connection that is properly soldered.
   2-D   a connection achieved with a low wattage iron.

3. A current reading of 1mA is equivalent to

   3-A   0.1 ampere.
   3-B   0.001 ampere.
   3-C   1 ampere.
   3-D   10 amperes.

4. An ohmmeter is used to check the condition of a fuse. If the fuse is good, the meter reading should be

   4-A   100K ohms.
   4-B   120 volts.
   4-C   zero.
   4-D   infinity.

5. Which of the following metals has the highest conductivity?

   5-A   silver
   5-B   copper
   5-C   aluminum
   5-D   zinc

6. Stranded wire is used in extension cords primarily because

   6-A   it costs less than solid wire.
   6-B   it is flexible.
   6-C   it is a better conductor than solid wire.
   6-D   it is only type of wire available in that gage.

7. A toaster is connected to 120 volts and draws 10 amperes when in use. How much power does this appliance consume?

   7-A   12 watts
   7-B   120 watts
   7-C   110 watts
   7-D   1200 watts

8. How many cells does a 12-volt carbon-zinc car battery contain?

   8-A   12
   8-B   8
   8-C   6
   8-D   1

9. The property of a circuit that opposes any change in current is

   9-A   inductance.
   9-B   capacitance.
   9-C   resistance.
   9-D   reactance.

10. Of the choices listed below, which component is an example of a transducer?

    10-A   resistor
    10-B   switch
    10-C   diode
    10-D   speaker

11. The period of a sine wave is determined by

    11-A   its amplitude.
    11-B   the distance between the crests of the wave.
    11-C   the number of hertz in one second.
    11-D   the time it takes to complete one hertz.

12. What is the effective value of an AC signal of 141 volts peak value?

    12-A   141 volts
    12-B   100 volts
    12-C   120 volts
    12-D   56.5 volts

13. The frequency response of the human ear is in the range of

   13-A   16 to 16,000 Hz.
   13-B   20,000 to 30,000 Hz.
   13-C   50 KHz to 1 MHz.
   13-D   1 MHz to 1000 MHz.

14. One kilowatt is equivalent to

   14-A   1 watt.
   14-B   10 watts.
   14-C   1000 watts.
   14-D   1000 volts.

15. What is the total resistance in this circuit?

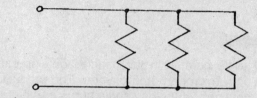

Each resistor = 900 ohms

   15-A   100 ohms
   15-B   300 ohms
   15-C   900 ohms
   15-D   1000 ohms

16.

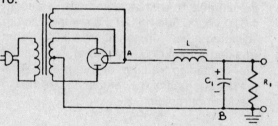

In the above schematic of a DC power supply, an oscilloscope connected at points A and B would display what type of wave form?

   16-A   square wave
   16-B   sine wave
   16-C   pulsating DC
   16-D   sawtooth wave

17. Referring to the schematic in question 16, what is the purpose of C_1?

   17-A   to bleed R_1
   17-B   to increase the output voltage
   17-C   to change the incoming AC to DC
   17-D   to filter the AC ripple voltage

18. Which is the correct schematic symbol for a tuning capacitor?

   18-A
   18-B
   18-C
   18-D

19.

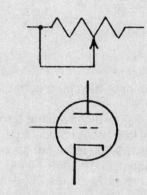

Which choice represents the equivalent solid state component of the vacuum tube drawn above?

   19-A   semiconductor rectifier
   19-B   silicon controlled rectifier
   19-C   zener diode
   19-D   transistor

20.

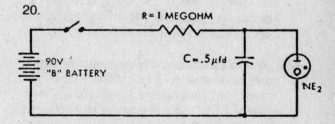

Which choice best describes the operation of the circuit drawn in the above schematic?

   20-A   The lamp will light constantly when the switch is closed.
   20-B   The lamp will light only when the switch is open.
   20-C   The lamp will flash when the switch is closed.
   20-D   The lamp will not light with the switch open or closed.

ANSWERS AND ANSWERS EXPLAINED

1

GENERAL SCIENCE

Answers

1-D	5-B	9-C	13-C	17-B	20-D	23-D
2-B	6-D	10-D	14-C	18-C	21-B	24-D
3-D	7-D	11-A	15-B	19-D	22-B	25-B
4-C	8-D	12-A	16-A			

Answers Explained

1-D   Sound cannot travel through a vacuum.

2-B   A light year is a convenient term to measure great distances. Since light travels at the rate of 186,000 miles per second, a light year is equal to 186,000 miles, times 60, times 60, times 24, times 365—a vast distance!

3-D   Specific gravity equals

$$\frac{\text{Weight of substance in air}}{\text{Loss of weight of substance in water}}$$

Since the weight of the corundum in air is 4 ounces, and its weight in water is 3 ounces, the loss of weight in water is 1 ounce. Hence, the specific gravity of corundum is 4 ounces divided by 1 ounce, or 4.

4-C   A sundial consists of a tilted rod which casts a shadow on a clockface. Solar noon is indicated when the rod casts the shortest shadow when the sun is at the highest point in the sky.

5-B   Of the metals listed, copper is the best conductor of heat. Asbestos and glass are very poor conductors of heat, which is why they are used as insulation materials.

6-D   Ecology is the study of the relations of living things with each other and with their environment. The incorrect choices are factors relating to ecology, but they do not describe ecology.

7-D   The paraffin in the candle contains carbon, hydrogen, and oxygen. The products obtained when the candle burns are, therefore, the oxides of carbon (carbon dioxide) and hydrogen (water).

8-D   Fat has many carbon molecules in its composition.

9-C   The half-life of a radioactive element is the time it takes for one-half of a given mass of the element to change to something else. In 1,620 years, one-half of the sample radium "disintegrates." In another 1,620 years (making a total of 3,240 years), one-half of the remaining radium disintegrates. This leaves one-half of the remaining one-half in the form of radium.

$$\tfrac{1}{2} \text{ of } \tfrac{1}{2} = \tfrac{1}{4}$$

10-D   When water disintegrates, it becomes molecules of hydrogen and oxygen. It no longer has the properties of water. This is an example of matter undergoing a chemical change. The other changes listed as choices are examples of physical change.

11-A   Light is needed by plants in order to carry on the process of photosynthesis—the manufacture of carbohydrates. During this process green plants absorb carbon dioxide and give off oxygen. Protozoa are one-celled organisms.

12-A   The dew point is the condition when air becomes saturated with moisture.

13-C To start a fire with the aid of the sun, it is necessary to concentrate, or converge, the rays of sunlight to a focal point. This is done with a convex lens, which is also a magnifying glass.

14-C The rotation of the earth on its axis exposes different parts of the earth to the sun's rays for different parts of each day.

15-B Alcohol does not have to be digested. The other substances are not broken down, nor are they ready for absorption, until they reach the small intestine.

16-A An atom contains several types of particles. Its central core, the nucleus, consists of positively charged particles, called protons, and uncharged particles, called neutrons. Surrounding the nucleus and orbiting it are negatively charged particles called electrons. Isotopes are atoms that contain the same number of protons as other atoms of the same element, but have different numbers of neutrons.

17-B The moon is a satellite. The others are planets.

18-C Sulfuric acid is one of the most important acids used by industry.

19-D The whale and the horse are mammals. They have a four-chambered heart, mammary glands, and lungs. They bear live off-spring, not eggs.

20-D In a beam of parallel rays, each ray strikes the mirror at a different point. Since the mirror has a plane surface, the rays are all parallel after reflection.

21-B According to Ohm's law, the voltage (V) needed to produce a current (C) is equal to the current times the resistance (R) that it meets: (V = CR). In this case, the needed voltage would be

$$
\begin{array}{r}
24 \ \text{(ohms, a measure of resistance)} \\
\times \ 0.5 \ \text{(ampere, a measure of current)} \\
\hline
12.0 \ \text{(volts, a measure of electric potential)}
\end{array}
$$

22-B During aeration of water, methane and carbon dioxides are liberated (eliminated) from the water, and oxygen is absorbed from the air.

23-D "Dry ice" is solid carbon dioxide (CO_2), made by cooling this gas to -80 degrees Celsius. In this case, CO_2 goes directly from a gaseous state to a solid.

24-D The scientific measure of work is the foot-pound, which is the force of one pound acting through a distance of one foot. To measure work (W) in a specific task, multiply the force (F) in pounds by the distance (D) in feet. Thus, in this example

$$F \times D = W$$
$$50 \times 25 = 1{,}250 \text{ foot-pounds of work}$$

25-B Chemical reactions may be classified under four main types. In composition (direct combination), two or more elements or compounds combine to form a more complex substance. Decomposition (the reverse of composition) occurs when a complex compound breaks down to simpler compounds or basic elements. Replacement takes place when one substance in a compound is freed and another takes its place. Double (or ionic) replacement occurs when ions in a solution combine to form a new product which then leaves the solution.

2

ARITHMETIC REASONING

Answers

1-C	6-C	11-D	15-B	19-C	23-B	27-B
2-A	7-D	12-C	16-C	20-A	24-C	28-C
3-C	8-A	13-C	17-B	21-D	25-C	29-A
4-B	9-A	14-B	18-D	22-D	26-D	30-A
5-D	10-B					

Answers Explained

1-C The down payment was 25% (or ¼) of the total payment.

$400 × ¼ = $100

$30 × 12 = $360 (sum of monthly payments)

$360 + $100 = $460 (cost on installment plan)

$460 − $400 = $60 (extra cost on installment)

2-A The number of seeds that failed to sprout was

$$120 − 90 = 30$$

The percentage of seeds that failed to sprout was

$$\frac{30}{120} = \frac{1}{4} = 25\%$$

3-C To find the average rate of speed, divide the distance covered (1,000 miles) by the time spent traveling (2½ or 2.5 hours). Clear the decimal in the divisor.

$$\frac{1,000}{2.5} = \frac{10,000}{25} = 400 \text{ miles per hour}$$

4-B Solve by multiplying first, and then dividing. Clear the decimal in the divisor.

$$\frac{0.05 × 4}{0.1} = \frac{0.20}{0.1} = \frac{0.2}{0.1} = \frac{2}{1} = 2$$

5-D Find the sum of the deposits and the sum of the withdrawals.

$765 + $802 = $1,567 (deposits)

$348 + $518 = $866 (withdrawals)

Find the difference between deposits and withdrawals.

$1,567 − $866 = $701 (overall gain)

Add this gain to the original balance.

$701 + $2,674 = $3,375 (new balance)

6-C Change 12½ gallons into pints. (8 pints = 1 gallon)

12½ × 8 =

$$\frac{25}{2} × 8 = 100 \text{ (pints)}$$

Multiply the cost of 1 pint by 100.

$0.35 × 100 = $35

7-D Multiply one side of a square by itself to find the area. Thus

9′ × 9′ = 81 square feet

By adding 3 feet to each side of the 9-foot square, you produce a 12-foot square. Thus

12′ × 12′ = 144 square feet

Find the difference between the areas of the two squares.

144 − 81 = 63 square feet

8-A First, change both fractions to a common denominator (12) and add them.

$$\frac{1}{4} = \frac{3}{12} \qquad \frac{1}{6} = \frac{2}{12}$$

$$\frac{3}{12} + \frac{2}{12} = \frac{5}{12}$$

To get the average, divide the sum by 2.

$$\frac{5}{12} ÷ 2 = \frac{5}{12} × \frac{1}{2} = \frac{5}{24}$$

9-A First find the salary increase.

$290 − $260 = $30 (amount of increase)

To find the percent of increase, use the original salary as the base and carry the division out to three decimal places.

$$\frac{\text{(increase)}}{\text{(original salary)}} = \frac{\$30}{\$260} = \frac{3.000}{26} = 0.115$$

Rounded to the nearest hundredth, 0.115 is 0.12.

$$0.12 = 12\%$$

10-B Express the total weight of the fish in ounces.

$$1 \text{ pound} = 16 \text{ ounces}$$
$$16 \text{ ounces} + 12 \text{ ounces} = 28 \text{ ounces}$$

Find the cost of one ounce, and multiply it by 16 to find the cost of 1 pound.

$$\$2.24 \div 28 = \$0.08$$
$$\$0.08 \times 16 = \$1.28$$

11-D Find the area of each lawn.

$$25' \times 15' = 375 \text{ square feet (front lawn)}$$
$$50' \times 30' = 1{,}500 \text{ square feet (back lawn)}$$

To find the ratio, divide one area by the other.

$$\frac{\text{(front lawn)}}{\text{(back lawn)}} = \frac{375}{1{,}500} = \frac{1}{4}$$

The ratio of the front lawn to the back lawn is 1:4.

12-C Find the amount of price increase.

$$\$7{,}200 - \$6{,}400 = \$800$$

To find the rate of increase, use the original price as your base.

$$\frac{\text{(increase)}}{\text{(original price)}} = \frac{\$800}{\$6{,}400} = \frac{1}{8}$$
$$\tfrac{1}{8} = 12\tfrac{1}{2}\% \text{ (rate of increase)}$$

13-C Find the relationship between each pair of numbers in the series. Thus

$(3\tfrac{1}{2};\ 2\tfrac{1}{4})$	$3\tfrac{1}{2} - 1\tfrac{1}{4} = 2\tfrac{1}{4}$
$(2\tfrac{1}{4};\ 13\tfrac{1}{4})$	$2\tfrac{1}{4} + 11 = 13\tfrac{1}{4}$
$(13\tfrac{1}{4};\ 12)$	$13\tfrac{1}{4} - 1\tfrac{1}{4} = 12$

The pattern so far is: $-1\tfrac{1}{4}, +11, -1\tfrac{1}{4}$
To continue the series, add 11 to the fourth number in the series: $12 + 11 = 23$

14-B Find the number of hours the movie house is open.
From 10:00 A.M. to 10:00 P.M. is 12 hours
From 10:00 P.M. to 11:30 P.M. is 1½ hours

$$12 + 1\tfrac{1}{2} = 13\tfrac{1}{2} \text{ (hours)}$$

Divide this total by the length of time for a complete showing of the movie (2 hours and 15 minutes, or 2¼ hours).

$$13\tfrac{1}{2} \div 2\tfrac{1}{4} =$$
$$\frac{27}{2} \div \frac{9}{4} =$$
$$\frac{27}{2} \times \frac{4}{9} = 6 \text{ (showings)}$$

15-B Find the amount taken in for orchestra seats.

$$324 \times \$20 = \$6{,}480$$

Out of $10,000, the remaining amount came from balcony seats.

$$\$10{,}000 - \$6{,}480 = \$3{,}520$$

Divide this amount by $10 to find the number of balcony seat tickets that were sold.

$$\$3{,}520 \div \$10 = 352 \text{ (balcony seats)}$$

16-C Since the first ¼ mile costs $0.80, this leaves $4.20 for the balance of the trip. At $0.20 for each additional ¼ mile, find the number of ¼ miles that $4.20 will cover. (Clear the decimal in the divisor.)

$$\$4.20 \div \$0.20 =$$
$$4.2 \div 0.2 =$$
$$42 \div 2 = 21 \text{ (additional ¼ miles)}$$

Add the first ¼ mile (at $0.80) to this total.

$$21 + 1 = 22 \text{ (¼ miles)}$$

Change the ¼ miles to miles.

$$22 \div 4 = 5\tfrac{1}{2} \text{ (miles for \$5)}$$

17-B Divide the distance by the number of feet (40) to an inch.

$$175' \div 40' = 4^{15}/_{40} = 4\tfrac{3}{8} \text{ (inches)}$$

18-D Find the discounted price paid by the dealer.

$$\$50 \times 20\% =$$
$$\$50 \times 0.2 = \$10 \text{ (discount)}$$
$$\$50 - \$10 = \$40 \text{ (price paid by dealer)}$$

Then find the dealer's selling price, based on an increase over the original wholesale list price.

$$\$50 \times 10\% =$$
$$\$50 \times 0.1 = \$5 \text{ (increase over list price)}$$
$$\$50 + \$5 = \$55 \text{ (dealer's selling price)}$$

Finally, find the dealer's profit.

$$\$55 - \$40 = \$15 \text{ (dealer's profit)}$$

19-C When the hour hand is on the 10-minute mark, it is actually on the number 2 (for 2 o'clock). The hour hand advances to a new minute-mark every 12 minutes of actual time. Thus, when the hour hand stopped at the 11-minute mark, it was 12 minutes after 2.

20-A Divide the number of successful shots by the total number of shots the player tried. Change your answer to a percent.

$$\frac{272}{320} = \frac{34}{40} = \frac{17}{20}$$
$$\frac{17}{20} = 0.85 = 85\%$$

21-D Let x equal the amount the helper receives. Let $2x$ equal the amount the painter receives. Write an equation to show that, together, they receive $375 for painting the house.

$$2x + x = \$375$$

Combine similar terms, and then divide both sides of the equation by the number with x. (This is to undo the multiplication.)

$$3x = \$375$$
$$x = \$125 \text{ (the helper's wages)}$$
$$2x = \$250 \text{ (what the painter receives)}$$

22-D Find the difference between the two percents.

$$\begin{array}{r} 50\ \% \\ -33\tfrac{1}{3}\% \end{array} \text{ (or) } \begin{array}{r} 49\tfrac{3}{3}\% \\ -33\tfrac{1}{3}\% \\ \hline 16\tfrac{2}{3}\% \end{array}$$

Divide the answer by 100% to change it to a simple fraction.

$$16\tfrac{2}{3}\% \div 100\% = \frac{50}{3} \div \frac{100}{1}$$
$$= \frac{50}{3} \times \frac{1}{100}$$
$$= \frac{50}{300} = \frac{1}{6}$$

23-B To solve, substitute the number value for the letter and do the arithmetic operations.

$$3a^2 - 2a + 5 =$$
$$(3 \times a^2) - (2 \times a) + 5 =$$
$$(3 \times 4^2) - (2 \times 4) + 5 =$$
$$(3 \times 16) - (2 \times 4) + 5 =$$
$$48 - 8 + 5 =$$
$$40 + 5 = 45$$

24-C Find the annual difference between the premium paid by someone who is 30 and the premium paid by someone who is 46.

$$\$38 - \$22 = \$16$$

Multiply the answer by 20 to find the total amount saved over 20 years by taking out a policy at an earlier age.

$$\$16 \times 20 = \$320 \text{ (saved)}$$

25-C On sale, the chair is 25% less than the original price. In other words, the sale price is a fraction of the original price.

$$100\% - 25\% = 75\% \text{ (or } \tfrac{3}{4}) \text{ of the original price}$$

If x equals the original price, then the sale price can be written as an equation.

$$\tfrac{3}{4}\,x = \$240$$

To solve for x, divide each side of the equation by $\tfrac{3}{4}$. (This is to undo the multiplication.)

$$\frac{3}{4}x \div \frac{3}{4} = \$240 \div \frac{3}{4}$$
$$\frac{3}{4}x \times \frac{4}{3} = \$240 \times \frac{4}{3}$$
$$x = \$320 \text{ (original price)}$$

26-D The quotient is the answer in division. (Clear the decimal in the divisor before doing the arithmetic.)

$$\frac{0.675}{0.9} = \frac{6.75}{9} = 0.75 \text{ (quotient)}$$

27-B For the month between May 15 and June 15, the meter showed that the electric usage was

$$5,687 - 5,472 = 215 \text{ (kilowatt hours)}$$

The first 10 kilowatt hours cost	$2.48
The next 45 kilowatt hours cost $0.16 per kilowatt hour	$7.20
The next 55 kilowatt hours cost $0.12 per kilowatt hour	$6.60

All usage over the first 110 kilowatt hours was charged at a lower rate.

Thus, 215 − 110, or 105 kilowatt hours cost $0.07 per kilowatt hour	$7.35
TOTAL bill for the month	$23.63

28-C To square a number, multiply it by itself.

$$49^2 = 49 \times 49 = 2,401$$
$$31^2 = 31 \times 31 = -\ 961$$
$$1,440 \text{ (difference)}$$

29-A To find the number of seats in the auditorium, multiply the number of rows (x) by the number of seats in each row (y). This is expressed as xy.

30-A One way of checking a division example is to multiply the quotient (the answer) by the divisor. After multiplying, add the remainder (if there was one in the division answer). Thus

$$\begin{array}{r} 15 \text{ (divisor)} \\ \times\ 8 \text{ (quotient)} \\ \hline 120 \\ +\ 7 \text{ (remainder, after division)} \\ \hline 127 \text{ (original number)} \end{array}$$

3

WORD KNOWLEDGE

Answers

1-C	6-C	11-A	16-D	21-D	26-D	31-C
2-A	7-C	12-D	17-B	22-C	27-D	32-D
3-C	8-A	13-D	18-C	23-A	28-B	33-C
4-A	9-D	14-B	19-B	24-A	29-B	34-B
5-B	10-A	15-D	20-C	25-D	30-D	35-D

Answers Explained

1-C To **subsume** means to include within a larger class or order.

2-A **Consensus,** like accord, means agreement.

3-C **Altercation,** like controversy, means a disagreement.

4-A **Irresolute,** like wavering, means to hesitate between choices.

5-B **Laconic,** like concise, means to express much in a few words.

6-C **Audition,** like hearing, means an opportunity to be heard.

7-C **Novice** designates one who has no training or experience in a specific field or activity and is hence a beginner.

8-A Pacific, like **conciliatory,** implies trying to preserve or obtain peace.

9-D To neutralize, like to **counteract,** means to render ineffective.

10-A **Precedent,** like example, refers to an individual instance (e.g., act, statement, case) taken as representative of a type.

11-A **Diaphanous** ("dia-" is a Greek prefix meaning "through, across"), like transparent, describes material that light rays can pass through.

12-D **Deferred,** like delayed, means postponed.

13-D To **accentuate,** like intensify, means to emphasize or increase in degree.

14-B **Authentic** (from the Greek, "warranted"), like reliable, means entitled to acceptance or belief.

15-D **Unanimity,** like concurrence, means complete accord.

16-D **Notorious** and well-known are almost synonymous in meaning: being or constituting something commonly known.

17-B Former means preceding in time and is synonymous with **previous.**

18-C Both pliable and **flexible** mean to be easily bent or yielding, usually without breaking.

19-B The opportunity to choose is equivalent to freedom to select or exercise an **option.**

20-C To confirm, like **verify,** means to make certain, to corroborate or authenticate.

21-D Saucy, like **pert,** means bold or impudent.

22-C Tasteful, similar to **aesthetic** (from the Greek, "perceptive"), means having the ability to appreciate what is beautiful.

23-A **Decimation** means to kill a large part of.

24-A Angry, like **indignant** (from the Latin, "deeming unworthy"), implies deep and strong feelings aroused by injury, injustice, or wrong.

25-D Platitude, like **cliché** (originally, to pattern in clay), refers to a remark or an idea that has become trite—lost its original freshness and impressive force.

26-D Agreement means **harmony** among people, thoughts, or ideas.

27-D Lazy, like **indolent,** applies to one who is not active.

28-B Breathing, like **respiration,** means inhalation and exhalation of air.

29-B Watchful, like **vigilant,** means alert.

30-D Casual, similar to **incidental,** means happening by chance or without definite intention.

31-C To **succumb** is to cease to resist or contend before a superior force, hence to yield.

32-D **Feasible** describes that which is likely to come about, and is hence practicable.

33-C Many-sided, like **versatile** (from the Latin, "turning about"), means capable of turning with ease from one task to another.

34-B **Imperturbability** or calmness is almost synonymous with serenity.

35-D **Strident** (from the Latin, "creaking") means having an irritating or unpleasant, hence harsh, sound.

4

PARAGRAPH COMPREHENSION

Answers

1-C	4-B	6-B	8-C	10-D	12-B	14-C
2-C	5-D	7-C	9-C	11-B	13-B	15-C
3-A						

Answers Explained

1-C Each individual must prevent the opportunity for crime to occur to prevent crimes.

2-C The design must fit the owner's income and building site.

3-A The selection describes a range of camping from backpacking to rolling homes with complete creature comforts so backpacking can be inferred to be the least luxurious.

4-B According to the selection, the "right" speed varies depending on the amount of cars, road surface and how well you can see so a driver should adjust to different driving conditions.

5-D Hard work is the only term in the list not mentioned in the passage.

6-B The selection states that less than one percent (.8%) is available as fresh water for people to use.

7-C A pinfold is described in the passage as a large circular pen made by driving stakes closely together in the floor of the river.

8-C The division of powers prevents one part or branch of government from getting all the power so power is shared.

9-C The passage states that in a proper dose a narcotic relieves pain and induces profound sleep.

10-C The passage mentions that nitrogen, phosphorous and potassium are used by plants in large amounts.

11-B The passage mentions that 60 percent of pollution is caused by motor vehicle exhausts, so the choice is B—cars, trucks, and buses.

12-B Since too much bright light can create discomfort for the eyes and create difficulties for seeing well, the main purpose of sunglasses is to screen out harmful rays.

13-B The selection mentions only the good points of apprentice training, none of the negative points.

14-C The selection does not deal with insurance rates, tax rates or retirement rates. It defines what a deduction from your paycheck is.

15-C The first sentence states that nucleic acids are found in the simplest living things to the most complex.

5

NUMERICAL OPERATIONS

Answers

1-C	9-B	16-C	23-A	30-D	37-C	44-D
2-B	10-D	17-A	24-C	31-B	38-C	45-D
3-C	11-B	18-D	25-C	32-A	39-D	46-A
4-C	12-A	19-D	26-D	33-C	40-B	47-B
5-A	13-C	20-D	27-B	34-B	41-D	48-B
6-D	14-A	21-C	28-B	35-D	42-A	49-C
7-B	15-D	22-A	29-C	36-A	43-C	50-C
8-B						

Answers Explained

There is no analysis of the answers for this part of the test. See Review Section on Mathematical Knowledge for general information.

6

CODING SPEED

Answers

1. B	13. D	25. A	37. D	49. C	61. A	73. C
2. D	14. D	26. E	38. E	50. D	62. C	74. A
3. B	15. D	27. C	39. D	51. C	63. D	75. E
4. B	16. E	28. D	40. D	52. B	64. D	76. A
5. E	17. A	29. E	41. C	53. A	65. B	77. B
6. C	18. E	30. B	42. D	54. C	66. E	78. E
7. E	19. B	31. D	43. A	55. B	67. B	79. D
8. A	20. B	32. D	44. C	56. B	68. A	80. E
9. B	21. E	33. A	45. C	57. E	69. B	81. D
10. D	22. D	34. A	46. E	58. B	70. B	82. A
11. A	23. A	35. B	47. A	59. E	71. D	83. C
12. C	24. B	36. D	48. B	60. B	72. B	84. E

7

AUTO AND SHOP INFORMATION

Answers

1-B	5-B	9-B	13-A	17-A	20-D	23-B
2-C	6-D	10-A	14-B	18-A	21-C	24-D
3-B	7-B	11-D	15-A	19-B	22-A	25-C
4-B	8-C	12-B	16-A			

Answers Explained

1-B When a tire is underinflated, the center area of the tread moves upward as the side-walls flex. This abnormal action places stress on the tire, causing wear to both outside edges.

2-C The vehicle "track" measurement is taken from the center of the left wheel to the center of the right wheel.

3-B The round head of the leaf spring center bolt fits into a hole in the axle housing. If a center bolt breaks, the axle housing shifts and the rear wheels do not follow the front wheels correctly. "U" bolts clamp the spring to the axle housing and prevent sideways movement.

4-B A syncromesh unit is designed to bring two gears to the same speed before engagement. A syncromesh unit does not change gear ratios.

5-B The modulator is a vacuum operated device that is connected to a source of manifold vacuum. As vacuum changes in response to engine load, the modulator will be actuated and send a signal to the valve body resulting in a different shift point. For example, when vacuum is low, as it normally is when the engine is accelerated, the modulator reacts and causes the transmission to shift at a higher vehicle speed. The higher shift point allows the engine to develop more torque, whch increases engine power.

6-D Too much clearance will cause the clutch to grab early. Hard shifting and clashing gears are problems associated with too much free play. Insufficient clearance will cause the clutch to grab late. A slipping clutch usually results from "no free play."

7-B The limited slip differential transmits power to the driving wheel that has traction. In a conventional differential if one wheel begins to slip, the vehicle will not move. All power remains with the slipping drive wheel.

8-C The ignition circuit must transform 12 volts to more than 20,000 volts. It must also deliver this high voltage spark to the spark plugs at the correct time.

9-B The purpose of the resistor is to lower and control voltage to the ignition coil. Since power for the coil comes from the ignition switch, the resistor is connected between the switch and the coil.

10-A Electricity is produced in the stator. Diodes change voltage from AC to DC.

11-D Under normal operating conditions, whenever the horn button is depressed, a circuit in the relay is grounded and the horn sounds. If the wire to the button becomes permanently grounded, due to an insulation breakdown, the horn will blow continuously.

12-B Wheel cylinder pistons push the brake shoes outward toward the drum when the brakes are applied. Spring tension keeps the springs in place inside the cylinder.

13-A The metering valve is used on a disc/drum type brake system. Its purpose is to hold off hydraulic pressure to the front disc brakes until the rear wheel cylinders overcome the tension of the brake shoe return springs. Disc brakes do not use return springs. The pads ride very close to the disc and make contact with the friction surface of the disc as soon as hydraulic pressure is applied.

14-B   Air/fuel mixture is delivered to the cylinder on the intake stroke, compressed on the compression stroke, and ignited on the power stroke. Burnt gasses are pushed out of the cylinder on the exhaust stroke.

15-A   In normal engine operation a ridge forms at the top of a cylinder bore. To properly remove a piston it is necessary to cut away this ridge. Failure to remove the ridge can result in damage to the piston. The ridge reamer is designed to remove the ridge without damaging the cylinder bore. Filing can ruin a cylinder wall.

16-A   To complete the four-stroke cycle, the engine crankshaft must turn two times. The crankshaft makes two revolutions for each turn of the camshaft.

17-A   The mitre box is used to cut angles from 45° to 90° in some cases where the angle is adjustable in a metal mitre. In the case of a wooden mitre box there are just two angles, 90° and 45°, cut in the sides of the box to hold the saw.

18-A   The coping saw is used in carpentry to cut moldings to fit at corners. It can also be used to cut wood at any curve or angle desired.

19-B   Another name for the crow bar is the pry bar and also the wrecking bar. It has many uses and different names in different parts of the country.

20-D   To properly perform a wet compression test oil is squirted into the combustion chamber. If the rings are worn, oil will temporarily fill the space between the piston and cylinder wall and compression will increase. Oil in the cylinder will not increase compression if a valve is burnt or the head gasket is blown.

21-C   A mechanical fuel pump uses a diaphragm. Gears are used in an oil pump.

22-A   The screwdriver with a straight end is the standard type. The screwdriver with a cross or X on the end is referred to as a phillips head. It comes in four different end sizes to fit different screw heads.

23-B   In order to use a chisel to cut wood it is usually necessary to strike it with some type of object to drive the cutting edge along the wood. This is usually done with a hammer.

24-D   The level is made up of at least two glass tubes with air bubbles trapped in the tubes. As the level is moved the air bubbles move. When the bubbles are aligned in between the two marks on each tube the level is said to be level.

25-C   The best way to cut circular holes in metal or wood is to use the hole saw. It has the blades shaped to cut the size you need. Just select the diameter you want and place the saw blade in the electric drill and drill.

8

MATHEMATICS KNOWLEDGE

Answers

1-C	5-C	9-B	13-B	17-D	20-A	23-D
2-D	6-C	10-B	14-B	18-C	21-D	24-B
3-B	7-B	11-C	15-C	19-B	22-A	25-A
4-C	8-D	12-C	16-A			

Answers Explained

1-C A prime number is a number larger than 1 that has only itself and 1 as factors. (It can be evenly divided only by itself and 1.) 201 is divisible by 3. 205 is divisible by 5. 211, however, is a prime number.

2-D Change 40% to a decimal, and write an equation to solve for x.

$$0.4 = \frac{x}{30}$$

Multiply both sides by 30. You are undoing the division.

$$0.4 \times 30 = \frac{x}{30} \times 30$$

$0.4 \times 30 = x$ (Be careful with the decimal.)

$$12.0 = x$$
$$x = 12$$

3-B The product of all integers from 1 to x is called the "x factorial." The product of all numbers from 1 to 5 is "5 factorial." Thus

$$(5)(4)(3)(2)(1) =$$
$$20\,(3)(2)(1) =$$
$$60\,(2)(1) =$$
$$120\,(1) = 120$$

The expression "5 factorial" is equal to 120.

4-C To subtract one polynomial from another, you change the signs of the terms in the subtrahend. First write the example as a subtraction in arithmetic.

(From) $8x^2 + 2x - 9$
(Take) $\underline{3x^2 - 5x - 1}$

Then change the signs of the terms in the bottom row (the subtrahend), and combine terms that are alike.

$8x^2 + 2x - 9$
$\underline{-3x^2 + 5x + 1}$
$5x^2 + 7x - 8$

5-C In deciding whether a number is greater or less than another, it helps to use a number line.

$$\overset{\displaystyle |\;\;|\;\;|\;\;|\;\;|\;\;|\;\;|\;\;|\;\;|\;\;|\;\;|\;\;|\;\;|}{{-30}\; {-25}\; {-20}\; {-15}\; {-10}\; {-5}\; 0\; 5\; 10\; 15\; 20\; 25\; 30}$$

On the number line above, -5 is to the left of 0 and is, therefore, less than 0. But -30 is to the left of -5. This makes -30 less than -5. The $(<)$ sign is a symbol of inequality, meaning "less than." The statement $(-30 < -5)$ means "minus 30 is less than minus 5."

6-C To solve for x, combine all similar terms, and set the equation equal to zero.
$$(8x - 5x) + (-2 - 8) = 0$$
Do the operations inside the parentheses.
$$3x - 10 = 0$$
Next, add 10 to each side. You are undoing the subtraction.
$$3x - 10 + 10 = 0 + 10$$
$$3x = 10$$
Finally, divide each side by 3 to find the value of x. You are undoing the multiplication.

$$\frac{3x}{3} = \frac{10}{3}$$
$$x = 3\frac{1}{3}$$

7-B In x weeks, she will make out checks for x times \$50, or \$50x. To find out how much she still has after writing those checks, she would subtract \$50x from \$500. Thus her bank account will hold
$$\$500 - \$50x$$

8-D Use the formula
$$F = \left(\frac{9}{5} \times C\right) + 32$$

Substitute 20 degrees for C.
$$F = \left(\frac{9}{5} \times 20\right) + 32$$
$$F = 36 + 32 = 68 \text{ degrees}$$

9-B The perimeter of a rectangle is the sum of its four sides. If x equals its width, then $x + 3$ equals the length. (The length is 3 inches more than the width.) From this, you can write an equation to find the perimeter. (Use the formula $2w + 2l = P$.)
$$x + x + (x + 3) + (x + 3) = 38$$
To solve for x, combine similar terms.
$$4x + 6 = 38$$
$$4x = 38 - 6$$
$$4x = 32$$
$$x = 8 \text{ (inches)}$$

10-B One way to solve this is to square each of the suggested answers, to see which is closest to 85. Thus

9.1	9.2	9.3	9.4
$\times$ 9.1	$\times$ 9.2	$\times$ 9.3	$\times$ 9.4
9 1	1 8 4	2 7 9	3 7 6
8 1 9	8 2 8	8 3 7	8 4 6
8 2.8 1	8 4.6 4	8 6.4 9	8 8.3 6

The squares of 9.2 and 9.3 are near 85. Find the difference between the square of each of these numbers and 85.

(9.2)	85.00	(9.3)	86.49
	− 84.64		− 85.00
	0.36		1.49

The square of 9.2 is closer to 85 than the square of 9.3. Therefore, the square root of 85, to the nearest tenth, is 9.2.

11-C The statement $5x = 30$ means "5 times a certain number is equal to 30." To find the number, divide each side by 5. This is to undo the multiplication.
$$\frac{5x}{5} = \frac{30}{5}$$
$$x = 6$$

12-C Set this up as a multiplication example in arithmetic. Remember that when you multiply terms with unlike signs, the product has a minus sign.

$$
\begin{array}{r}
a - 5 \\
\times\ a + 3 \\
\hline
3a - 15 \\
a^2 - 5a \\
\hline
a^2 - 2a - 15
\end{array}
$$

13-B Begin by combining like terms.
$$3z - 5 + 2z = 25 - 5z$$
$$5z - 5 = 25 - 5z$$

Next add $5z$ to each side, to eliminate the $-5z$ from the right side.
$$5z - 5 + 5z = 25 - 5z + 5z$$
$$10z - 5 = 25$$
Now add 5 to each side to undo the remaining subtraction.
$$10z - 5 + 5 = 25 + 5$$
$$10z = 30$$
$$z = 3$$

14-B A pentagon is a five-sided figure. If the park commissioner places a fountain at every corner of the park, there will be 5 fountains.

15-C Every right triangle contains an angle of 90 degrees. This particular right triangle also has an angle of 30 degrees. To find the third angle, subtract the sum of these two angles from 180 degrees.
$$180 - (30 + 90) =$$
$$180 - 120 =$$
$$60 = \text{degrees in third angle}$$
The other two angles are 60 and 90 degrees.

16-A To solve for x in this equation, multiply both sides by 2. This is to undo the division.
$$2 \times \frac{x}{2} = 2 \times 7$$
$$x = 14$$

17-D Divide only similar terms. First divide numbers, then letters. When dividing powers of a letter, just subtract the exponents.
$$\frac{15a^3b^2c}{5abc} = \frac{15}{5} \times \frac{a^3}{a} \times \frac{b^2}{b} \times \frac{c}{c} = 3a^2b$$

18-C The formula for the area of a circle is Pi $\times$ R^2. Find the area of the larger circle first.
$$\text{Pi} \times 10^2 = 100 \text{ Pi square inches}$$
Then find the area of the smaller circle.
$$\text{Pi} \times 7^2 = 49 \text{ Pi square inches}$$
To find the part of the larger circle that the smaller one doesn't touch, subtract the two areas.
$$100 - 49 = 51 \text{ Pi square inches}$$

19-B The easiest way to solve this is to form an equation, using x as the unknown grade.
$$\frac{78 + 86 + 96 + 94 + x}{5} = 88$$
$$\frac{354 + x}{5} = 88$$

Multiply both sides by 5. This is to undo the division.

$$5 \times \frac{354 + x}{5} = 88 \times 5$$

Simplify both sides of the equation.

$$354 + x = 440$$
$$x = 440 - 354$$
$$x = 86 \text{ (grade)}$$

20-A First change all measurements to yards.

9' = 3 yds   12' = 4 yds   6" = ⅙ yd

To find the volume of the concrete, multiply the length times the width times the height.

$$3 \times 4 \times \frac{1}{6} =$$
$$12 \times \frac{1}{6} = 2 \text{ cubic yards}$$

21-D First find the area of the entire wildlife preserve. Since it is a circle, use the formula for the area of a circle. (Area equals Pi times the square of the radius.)

$$A = Pi \times R^2$$
$$= \frac{22}{7} \times (14)^2 \quad = \frac{22}{7} \times 196$$
$$= 22 \times 28$$
$$= 616 \text{ square feet}$$

The lions' territory is a wedge formed by a 90-degree angle at the center of the circle. Since a circle has 360 degrees, we can find the part of the preserve inhabited by lions.

$$\frac{90}{360} = \frac{1}{4}$$

Next find what this equals in square miles.

$$\frac{1}{4} \times \frac{616}{1} = 154 \text{ square miles}$$

22-A Solve by doing each arithmetic operation and combining answers. Remember that the product of 2 negative or 2 positive numbers is a positive number. The product of a negative and a positive number is negative.

$$(-3)^4 = (-3)(-3)(-3)(-3) = 81$$
$$(-2)^4 = (-2)(-2)(-2)(-2) = 16$$
$$(-1)^4 = (-1)(-1)(-1)(-1) = \frac{1}{98}$$

23-D To find the volume (V) of a cylinder, multiply Pi times the square of the radius (r) times the height (h).

$$V = Pi \times r^2 \times h$$
$$V = \frac{22}{7} \times \frac{7}{1} \times \frac{7}{1} \times \frac{15}{1}$$
$$V = 154 \times 15$$
$$V = 2,310 \text{ cubic inches (volume)}$$

To find the number of gallons this cylinder will hold, divide its volume by 231.

$$2,310 \div 231 = 10 \text{ gallons}$$

24-B The wall, the ladder, and the ground in the tennis court form a right triangle. The ladder is on a slant, and is opposite the right angle formed by the wall and the ground. In this position, the ladder is the "hypotenuse" of the right triangle. In geometry, the Pythagorean Theorem states that the square of the hypotenuse (c^2) equals the sum of the squares of the other two sides ($a^2 + b^2$). Thus,

$$a^2 + b^2 = c^2$$
$$8^2 + x^2 = 10^2$$

Solve by doing the arithmetic operations, and by clearing one side of the equation for x^2.

$$64 + x^2 = 100$$
$$x^2 = 100 - 64$$
$$x^2 = 36$$

Then find the square root of x^2 and of 36.

$$x = 6$$

The base of the ladder is 6 feet from the wall.

25-A First find how many ounces of the original mixture were fruit juice.

$$10 \times 20\% = 10 \times .2 = 2 \text{ ounces}$$

Next find the total number of ounces in the new mixture.

$$10 + 40 = 50 \text{ ounces}$$

Then find what part of the new mixture is fruit juice, and convert it to a percent.

$$\frac{2}{50} = \frac{1}{25} = \frac{4}{100} = 4\%$$

9

MECHANICAL COMPREHENSION

Answers

1-D	5-A	9-C	13-B	17-A	20-D	23-C
2-B	6-D	10-C	14-D	18-A	21-C	24-D
3-A	7-D	11-B	15-C	19-A	22-B	25-D
4-D	8-B	12-B	16-C			

Answers Explained

1-D A ¾″ wrench fits the head of a ½″ cap screw. A $^7/_{16}$″ wrench fits a ¼″ screw. A $^9/_{16}$″ wrench fits a ⅜″ screw. N.F. indicates a fine thread cap screw.

2-B The lock washer prevents the nut from loosening.

3-A The open end wrench is used to hold the carburetor fitting while the flare nut wrench is turned to loosen the flare nut on the tubing. A flare nut wrench will not "round-off" the flare nut.

4-D One complete turn of the thimble equals 0.025″.

5-A The brake spoon is used to turn the star wheel adjuster. Turning the adjuster with the spoon decreases the clearance between the brake shoes and drum. Disc type brakes are not adjustable.

6-D The voltmeter is used to test battery voltage.

7-D "Opens" in an armature are found by using the meter on the growler.

8-B A micrometer is used to check rotor thickness and thickness variation.

9-C A feeler gage is used to measure the clearance between the crankshaft and the main thrust bearing. This clearance determines the end play of the crankshaft. Plastigage is used to measure crankshaft bearing oil clearance. A micrometer is used to measure crankshaft journal diameter.

10-C An infinite reading indicates an open or incomplete circuit. A short would be indicated by a lower than normal reading.

11-B A transmission uses gear reduction to increase engine torque or turning force. During the time torque is increasing, speed decreases.

12-B The pinion (connects to the driveshaft) is the driving gear. The ring (drives axles) is the driven gear. To calculate the gear ratio, divide the drive into the driven gear.

13-B When a starter is energized, the magnetic fields created in the armature and field coils produce the turning effect on the armature shaft. The starter drive engages the flywheel ring gear and cranks over the engine whenever the starter is energized.

14-D The diesel engine is an example of this principle. As a piston moves up on its compression stroke, air in the cylinder is compressed. Ignition takes place when the fuel is injected into the cylinder. The temperature of the compressed air provides the heat for combustion. A diesel engine does not use a spark plug.

15-C The greater the difference between the teeth of two meshed gears, the greater the torque increases.

16-C To calculate the final ratio of a transmission and differential, multiply the ratio of the transmission by the ratio of the differential. $3.29 \times 3.85 = 12.67$

17-A   The fulcrum is positioned between the effort and the load on a first-class lever.

18-A   The pivot shaft is at T and S. The lobe (high spot) of the cam is between Q and R.

19-A   The smallest pulley will turn fastest. When a series of pulleys is connected by drive belts, the smallest diameter pulley will rotate at the highest speed.

20-D   A pair of meshed gears will always turn in opposite directions. X and Y are turning in opposite directions. Since E and F are meshed with Y, both are turning in the direction of X.

21-C   On a third-class lever, the fulcrum is placed at one end, the load is at the other end and the effect is between the fulcrum and the load.

22-B   Two meshed gears will turn in opposite directions. When an idler gear (I is the idler) is placed between the two, both will turn in the same direction. The idler gear turns in direction 1.

23-C   The center line of the small gear or pinion is below the center line of the larger ring gear.

24-D   Pascal's law states "pressure at any point in a body of fluid is the same in every direction." When a 10-lb force is placed on piston X, which measures 1 sq in, the same force is placed on every square inch of piston Y. Since Y is 300 sq in, then $10 \times 300 =$ 3000-lb force.

25-D   To calculate the effort needed to lift the load of 200 lbs, use this formula. The effort multiplied by the effort arm equals the load multiplied by the load arm or:

$E \times e = L \times w$ E = effort needed to lift the load

$E \times 4 = 200 \times 2$ e = length of the effort arm

$E \times 4 = 400$ L = load

          w = load arm

$E = \dfrac{400}{4}$

$E = 100$ lbs

10

ELECTRONICS INFORMATION

Answers

1-A	4-C	7-D	10-D	13-A	16-C	19-D
2-B	5-A	8-B	11-D	14-C	17-D	20-C
3-B	6-B	9-A	12-B	15-B	18-B	

Answers Explained

1-A Flux is the component in solder that, when liquid, removes the impurities present in the connection and helps prevent oxidation. After it has cooled, the remaining flux present *around* or between connections acts as an insulator. Tin increases the conductivity of the connection and it is the combination of tin and lead that results in a combined lower melting point for solder that is desired in electrical work.

2-B A connection that is clean and shiny in appearance would be an example of a properly soldered connection. The wattage of the iron used has no effect on the resulting solder connection. The soldering procedure determines what the connection will look like.

3-B 0.1 ampere is equal to 100 mA.
1 ampere is equal to 1,000 mA.
10 amperes is equal to 10,000 mA.

4-C A good fuse will allow current to flow through it, or indicate continuity on a continuity check using an ohmmeter. If there is continuity, or if the fuse is good, the meter will read zero, or very low resistance. Choices A and D indicate a resistance reading that is very high. Choice B is not a reading to be found on an ohmmeter scale but rather during a voltage check.

5-A The material with the highest conductivity is silver, followed in order of conductivity by copper, aluminum, and zinc.

6-B Stranded wire and solid wire of the same gage do not differ in conductivity. Both are available in numerous gages, including the gage used in extension cords.

However, solid wire of the gage needed for an extension cord is not nearly as flexible as stranded wire. Because an extension cord is often moved, stranded wire is preferable.

7-D The formula to calculate power consumption is POWER = CURRENT × VOLTAGE, or P = I × E. Substituting the values given

$$P = I \times E$$
$$P = 10 \text{ amperes} \times 120 \text{ volts}$$
$$P = 1200 \text{ watts}$$

8-B A carbon-zinc cell has a voltage of approximately 1.5 volts. In a 12-volt carbon-zinc battery there would be 8 cells or 1.5 volts × 8 = 12 volts.

9-A The circuit property that opposes any change in current is defined as inductance. Capacitance is the circuit property that opposes any change in voltage. Resistance is the opposition to the flow of electrons and reactance is the opposition to the flow of an alternating current as a result of inductance or capacitance present in a circuit.

10-D A transducer is a component that converts one form of energy into another form of energy. A speaker converts the electrical energy at audio frequencies in the final stage of a radio receiver into sound energy. A resistor is used in a circuit to limit current flow and drop voltage or consume energy. A diode is used to block energy or rectify an AC signal and a switch is a mechanical means of turning current on and off.

11-D The time it takes to complete one sine wave is known as the period of a wave. The distance between the crests of a wave is equal to one hertz, and the number of hertz completed in one second is known as the frequency. The amplitude of the wave is the distance between the ground line and the highest point of the wave in both the positive and negative.

12-B   The correct choice is B. To convert from AC peak value to AC effective value the formula is

$$E_{eff.} = 0.707 \times E_{peak}$$
$$E_{eff.} = 0.707 \times 141 \text{ volts}$$
$$E_{eff.} = 100 \text{ volts}$$

13-A   The term frequency response is used to denote the range of frequencies that a device, or in this case the human ear, is sensitive to. Sound or audio frequencies fall into the range of 16-16,000 Hz.

14-C   The term "kilo" represents a quantity of a thousand. Therefore one kilowatt is equal to one thousand watts. Watts and voltage are not interchangeable terms. Watts is a unit of measurement for power, and volts is a unit of measurement for voltage.

15-B   The formula for parallel resistors is

$R_T = \dfrac{R}{n}$ Where R is equal to the value of one resistor and n is equal to the number of resistors that are of the same value in parallel. Substituting values into the equation:

$R_T = \dfrac{900}{3}$ ohms

$R_T = 300$ ohms

16-C   The given schematic is of a full wave DC power supply. At points A & B before the filter capacitor C_1 the waveform is that of a pulsating DC. A sine wave could not be displayed because a sine wave indicates a voltage that alternates between positive and negative values. At points A & B the voltage present has been rectified to full wave DC by the duo-diode tube. This resultant waveform is known as pulsating DC. A sawtooth or square wave, although both are examples of pulsating DC, are waveforms resulting from the introduction of other components after the rectification stage.

17-D   The capacitor, C_1, is used to smooth out the AC ripple voltage from the output of the power supply. Choice A is incorrect, as a resistor is used to bleed a capacitor, not vice versa. R_1 is used as an output load resistor. Choice B is incorrect because a capacitor cannot amplify and choice C is incorrect because a capacitor cannot rectify a signal; that is the purpose of the duo-diode tube.

18-B   Choices C & D are schematics of resistors. C is a fixed resistor. D is a potentiometer or variable resistor. Choice A is a fixed capacitor symbol. In choice B the arrow through the fixed capacitor symbol denotes variability. As a tuning capacitor is a variable capacitor, this is the correct choice.

19-D   The schematic symbol drawn is of a triode tube. Its equivalent solid state component is the transistor. In the triode tube, the elements of plate, cathode and grid correspond to the elements of collector, emitter and base respectively in the transistor.

20-C   When the switch is closed, the capacitor will charge through the resistor. When the voltage across the capacitor reaches the voltage necessary for the neon bulb to light, the lamp will glow. As the lamp glows, the capacitor discharges, resulting in a cycle of charge-discharge. This cycle will cause the neon bulb to flash.

CORRECT YOUR WEAKNESSES

Before You Begin

The material in this section is a review of some of the basic concepts and terms taught in high school science courses. As you read these pages, concentrate on any topics you may not have studied in high school. Then try to find a textbook or one of Barron's review books on the particular field of science you feel you want to study more intensely.

Otherwise, divide your time equally among all four branches of science (biology, earth science, chemistry, and physics). Pay special attention to terms in *italics* and to terms that are defined in clusters, or groups. Often, exam questions ask you to distinguish among words that are related to the same concept, but have different meanings (for example, between *evaporation* and *condensation* or between the *proton* and *neutron* in the nucleus of an atom).

Introduction   Science can be divided into life, physical, and earth sciences. *Biology* is the general term for the study of life. It covers topics dealing with human health and medicine, and is closely related to the study of *botany* (the study of plants) and *zoology* (the study of animals). *Earth science* covers conditions affecting the earth (weather, climate, relation of people to their environment.) *Chemistry* is a physical science that investigates the composition, structure, and properties of matter. It is also concerned with changes in matter and the energy released during those changes. *Physics*, like chemistry, is a physical science that deals with matter and energy. However, in physics, more attention is given to mechanical and electrical forces in areas such as light, sound, heat, motion, and magnetism.

The Scientific Method   Each of the sciences uses a way of solving problems that is known as the *scientific method*. It involves several steps:

1. *Observation*. In a sense, the true scientist is always involved in this step. It requires the accurate sighting and recording of a particular occurrence. The accuracy of one observation is proved when a number of independent observers agree that they see the same set of circumstances occurring under the same conditions many times.
2. *Hypothesis*. A temporary set of conclusions drawn from a set of observations is known as a hypothesis. It is usually a very general statement, and suggests the need for a particular experiment.
3. *Experiment*. To test a specific hypothesis, scientists perform experiments. The purpose of the experiments is to answer questions about data truthfully and carefully. Reliable experiments require controlled conditions.
4. *Theory*. When a hypothesis is supported by data obtained from experiments, the hypothesis becomes a theory.
5. *Law,* or *principle*. When a theory stands up under the test of time and repeated experiments, it may be called a "law" or principle.

Biology

Basic Concepts in Biology   There are several basic principles, or concepts, that biologists must constantly deal with. *Homeostasis* refers to the balanced, internal environment of a human cell and of the human organism as a whole. To stay alive, cells must regulate their internal and external fluids according to temperature, acid-base balance and the amount and content of salts and other vital substances.

Unity is shared by all living species insofar as they have certain biological, chemical, and other characteristics in common: there is the unity of the basic living substance (*protoplasm*). All living cells arise from pre-existing living cells. All cells synthesize and use *enzymes*. (An enzyme is a substance which speeds up the reaction of chemicals without itself being changed.) The genetic (hereditary) information of all cells is carried by *DNA* molecules. DNA gives cells the ability to *replicate* (make exact copies of themselves).

Metabolism is a term that relates to all the biochemical activities carried on by cells, tissues, organs, and systems—activities that are necessary for life.

Adaptation refers to a trait that aids the survival of an individual or a species in a given environment.

The basic unit of classification among living things is the *species*. A species is a group of similar organisms that can mate and produce fertile offspring.

Life Functions   To satisfy all the conditions necessary for life, all living systems must be able to perform certain biochemical and biophysical activities which together are known as *life functions*.

1. *Nutrition* includes all those activities through which a living organism obtains *nutrients* (food molecules) from the environment and prepares them for use as fuel and for growth. Included in nutrition are the processes of *ingestion*, *digestion*, and *assimilation*. Ingestion is the process of taking in or procuring food. Digestion refers to the chemical changes that take place in the body so that nutrients can be converted into forms that a cell can use. Assimilation involves changing nutrients into protoplasm.
2. *Circulation* is the movement of fluid and its dissolved materials throughout the body of an organism or within a single cell.
3. *Respiration* consists of *breathing* and *cellular respiration*. Breathing refers to the pumping of air into and out of the lungs of air-breathing animals, or the movement of water over the gills of fish. During breathing, oxygen flows into air sacs in the lungs and diffuses into the blood. Carbon dioxide moves out of the blood into the lungs and out of the body through the nose and mouth. Cellular respiration is a combination of processes that release energy from glucose (sugar).
4. *Excretion* removes waste products of cellular respiration from the body. The lungs, the skin, and the kidneys are excretory organs in humans. They remove carbon dioxide, water, and urea from the blood and other body tissues.
5. *Synthesis* involves those biochemical processes in cells by which small molecules are built into larger ones. As a result of synthesis, *amino acids*, the building blocks of proteins, are changed into enzymes, hormones, and protoplasm. (A *hormone* is a chemical "messenger" produced by the endocrine gland. It helps to control and coordinate the activities of the body.)
6. *Regulation* includes all processes that control and coordinate the many activities of a living thing. Chemical activities inside of cells are controlled by enzymes, vitamins, minerals, and hormones. The *nervous* and *endocrine systems* of higher animals coordinate body activities. The growth and development of plants is regulated by *auxins* and other growth-control substances.
7. *Growth* describes the increase of cell size and increase of cell numbers. The increase of cell numbers occurs when cells divide in response to a sequence of events known as *mitosis*.
8. *Reproduction* is the process by which new individuals are produced by parent organisms. There are two major kinds of reproduction: *asexual* and *sexual*. Asexual repro-

duction involves only one parent. The parent may divide and become two new cells, thus ending the parent generation. Or the new individual may arise from part of the parent cell; in such a case, the parent remains. In either case replication of the *chromosomes* is involved. (Chromosomes are small rod-shaped bodies in cells. They contain the genes of heredity.) Sexual reproduction requires the participation of two parents, each producing special reproductive cells know as *sex cells*, or *gametes*.

The Basic Chemistry of Cells

The cell is like a "chemical factory" that uses some of the elements present in the nonliving environment. Thus, in the living material of the cell, we find carbon, hydrogen, oxygen, and nitrogen in the greatest amounts, with smaller quantities of sulfur, phosphorus, magnesium, iodine, iron, calcium, sodium, chlorine, and potassium. In the cell, these elements are present in both *organic* and *inorganic compounds*. (A *compound* is a chemical union of two or more substances.)

An inorganic compound is one that does not have the elements carbon and hydrogen in its chemical combination. Inorganic compounds in living cells include water, mineral salts, and inorganic acids.

An organic compound has the elements carbon and hydrogen. Examples are *carbohydrates*, *lipids*, *proteins*, and *nucleic acids*.

1. Carbohydrates are composed of carbon, oxygen, and hydrogen. The hydrogen and oxygen atoms are usually present in the ratio of 2:1. For example *glucose* (a sugar) has 12 atoms of hydrogen and 6 atoms of oxygen (as well as 6 carbon atoms), $C_6H_{12}O_6$. Carbohydrates are used by cells primarily as sources of energy.
2. Lipids include fats and fat-like substances. Like carbohydrates, a lipid molecule contains carbon, hydrogen, and oxygen. But the ratio of hydrogen to oxgyen is much greater than 2:1. Most lipid molecules provide twice as much energy per gram as do carbohydrate molecules.
3. Proteins are composed of carbon, hydrogen, oxygen, and nitrogen. Some proteins also contain sulfur. All proteins are built from amino acids, which are essential to life. Some proteins are involved in complex biochemical activities. Others contribute to the structure of cells.
4. Nucleic acids are essential to the continuance of life. They pass hereditary information from one generation to another. This makes possible the continuance of life within each species of living things. *Deoxyribonucleic acid* (DNA) molecules are the particular type of nucleic acid out of which genes are made. *Genes* carry hereditary traits from parent to offspring.

Cells are always engaged in chemical activity. The major difference between living things and nonliving matter is that living systems carry out vital chemical activities on a controlled and continuous basis. The control of chemical processes in cells requires the work of enzymes. Enzymes are thus *organic catalysts*. (A catalyst, in this sense, is a molecule that controls the rate of a chemical reaction but is not, itself, used up in the process.)

Plant Life

The green *plant kingdom* includes species ranging from single cells to *multicellular* ("many-celled") plants. In multicellular plants, different cells are programmed to carry out special tasks. This is called cell *specialization*, and it goes hand-in-hand with a "*division of labor*." According to this division, groups of cells work together to perform some special life function to benefit the entire organism.

Lower plant species such as the single-celled *algae* can live in fresh or salt water. But most species of plants (the higher forms) are "anchored" in one place. Higher plants are sometimes referred to as *terrestrial* (land-dwelling).

The bodies of these higher plants have parts known as *roots*, *stems*, and *leaves*. Roots anchor plants in the soil and absorb water and dissolved materials from the ground. Stems have three major functions: (1) they conduct water upward from the roots to the leaves and conduct dissolved food materials downward from the leaves to the roots; (2) they produce and support leaves and flowers; (3) they provide a means for storing food.

The most important function of green leaves is to carry out *photosynthesis*. This is the food-making process by which inorganic materials are changed into organic nutrients. Green leaves have a pigment called *chlorophyll*. In the presence of that pigment, leaves use the energy of sunlight to make carbohydrates from carbon dioxide (CO_2) and water. These carbohydrates are the food used by plants—and by the animals that eat the plants. During photosynthesis, the oxygen (O_2) needed by animals is released into the atmosphere.

Animal Life   All animals are multicellular. One of the simplest forms of animal life is the sponge, which lives in water, attached to rocks. All animals are composed of cells without walls. They *ingest* (take in) food, digest it, and distribute it to cells that make up their body. Most animals can move. Some lower forms of animals reproduce by *budding*. (A new organism grows from cells of the parent, breaks off, and then continues its own existence.) Some forms reproduce through unfertilized eggs, while others reproduce sexually, using sperm and egg. About 90 percent are *invertebrates*—animals without backbones.

Vertebrates are animals with a true backbone made of cartilage or bone. They have a noticeable development of the head, where a brain is enclosed in a *cranium*. Blood is pumped through a closed *circulatory system* by means of a heart with two types of chambers: an *atrium* and a *ventricle*. Most vertebrates (except humans) have a tail. Another characteristic of vertebrates is a mouth that is closed by a movable lower jaw.

Humans   *Humans* belong to a special order of vertebrates, called *primates*. What distinguishes primates from other vertebrates? Scientists believe that at one time all primates lived in trees. Over evolutionary time, species such as chimpanzees and humans left the trees and adapted successfully to life on land. Certain characteristics of their "tree-life" remain, however. They have (a) hands able to grasp objects; (b) a well-developed sense of sight (primates can see in three dimensions, which enables them to see branches they are going to grasp); (c) a larger brain with more surface for nerve cells. Primates also have teeth capable of chewing a variety of foods.

Humans are special primates, set apart from others in their species by special characteristics. They have *bipedalism* (the ability to walk on two legs, instead of four). They can adapt to living in almost any environment. And they have the power of speech, along with the ability to remember and to make associations between ideas. It is this that is the basis of culture and history.

The human organism has key systems:

- the *skeletal system* (carries the body and supports the organs)
- the *muscular system* (about 40 percent of body weight, it enables the body to move)
- the *nervous system* (permits communication between the organism and its environment)
- the *endocrine system* (includes glands that regulate growth, blood pressure, etc.)
- the *respiratory system* (allows the body to inhale air and exhale carbon dioxide)
- the *circulatory system* (includes the heart and blood vessels)
- the *lymphatic system* (brings oxygen to cells and removes waste products from them)
- the *digestive system* (processes and distributes nutrients)
- the *excretory system* (removes wastes from the body)
- the *reproductive system* (allows humans to reproduce)

The human body has five major *senses*—sight, hearing, taste, smell, and touch—that transmit information about the environment to the nervous system, and eventually to the brain. Two of these senses show the "division of labor" in the body.

1. The human *eyeball* rests in a bony socket of the skull, and is attached to it by three pairs of small muscles. The colored portion of the front of the eye is the *iris;* in its center is a hole called the *pupil*. Behind the pupil is the *lens*, which flattens or thickens to focus on an object. Light enters the eye through the pupil. It passes through the *cornea* and *lens* (which turns the image upside down and reverses it from left to right), and sets up a barrage of signals in the *retina*. These signals pass through the *optic nerve* to the brain where the image is corrected and "recognized."

2. The *human ear* is made up of three divisions: the *outer ear*, the *middle ear*, and the *inner ear*. The outer ear catches sound waves and transports them to the *eardrum*, causing it to vibrate. Three bones in the middle ear—the *hammer*, *anvil*, and *stirrup*—transmit these vibrations to the *cochlea* in the inner ear. The fluid-filled cochlea is lined with hair cells which transmit the vibrations to the *auditory nerve* and, eventually, to the brain. (The air-filled middle ear is connected by the *Eustachian tube* to the throat. Thus, when you yawn or swallow, you help equalize the air pressure in the middle ear.)

Nutrition   *Nutrition* is the sum of all the methods by which an organism satisfies the needs of its body cells for energy, fuel, and regulation. Substances that contribute to the nutritional needs of cells are *nutrients* or (for animals) "food." Nutrients that are needed in large amounts are called *macronutrients:* carbohydrates, proteins, and fats. *Micronutrients*— vitamins and minerals—are needed in smaller amounts. *Malnutrition* results either from eating too little food or from eating an imbalanced diet. A *balanced diet* includes choices from the four major food groups: (a) milk, or dairy products, (b) meat or meat substitutes, (c) vegetables and fruits, (d) breads, cereals and other grain products.

Carbohydrates include starches and sugars. Their primary function is to serve as fuel for the body cells. When body cells receive more simple sugar than they can use, some of the excess sugar is stored in the liver and muscles as *glycogen* ("animal starch"). However, if the quantity of carbohydrates taken in is much too large, the body converts them to fat which is stored under the skin and around the body's organs. Food sources of carbohydrates include potatoes, fruit, cereal grains, beans, baked goods, milk, etc.

Proteins are the most abundant of the organic compounds in body cells. Proteins compose hair, nails and other *fibrous structures* in the body. They form part of certain hormones, are vital to the formation of DNA molecules, and help to build the body's resistance to disease. Food sources of proteins include meat, fish, eggs, milk, cheese, beans, nuts, etc.

Fats are also fuel foods. Certain fats are essential to the structure and function of body cells and to the building of cell membranes. Fats also aid in transporting fat-soluble vitamins. Foods rich in fats include butter, bacon, egg yolk, cream, and some cheeses. Fat-rich foods add to the caloric content of the human diet. A *Calorie* is the unit of heat necessary to raise 1 liter of water 1 degree Celsius. One gram of fat provides 9 Calories. One gram of protein or carbohydrates provides 4 Calories.

Vitamins are organic compounds necessary for the proper functioning of the body. The following table summarizes the source and value of some major vitamins:

Vitamin	Necessary for	Some Food Sources
A	Healthy eyes and skin	Fish liver oil, butter, yellow fruits and vegetables
C (Ascorbic acid)	Healthy teeth, gums, and bones; resistance to infection	Citrus fruits, cabbage, green leafy vegetables

Vitamin	Necessary for	Some Food Sources
D	Strong bones and teeth; regulation of calcium and phosphorus metabolism	fish liver oil, egg yolk, salmon
E	Prevention of oxidation by red blood cells; good muscle tone	Wheat germ, green leafy vegetables
K	Clotting of blood	Green vegetables, tomatoes
B (Thiamin, Niacin)	Growth; good digestion and appetite; normal nerve functions	Yeast, wheat germ, liver, bread, green vegetables
B (Ribo-flavin)	Health of skin and mouth; growth; healthy eyes	Same as for thiamin and niacin; meat

Minerals are inorganic compounds. *Calcium* regulates muscle activity and, together with *phosphorus*, is used in building bones and teeth. (Both calcium and phosphorus are found in dairy products. Calcium is also found in grains and green leafy vegetables.) *Sodium* functions in the regulation of body temperature: large amounts of the body's salts are excreted by the sweat glands. Nerve cells could not carry impulses, nor could muscles contract, without the assistance of sodium and *potassium*. (Potassium is found in beans, peas, and fruit.)

Other minerals include: *fluorine*, which helps resist tooth decay; *iodine* (found in fish and salts), which aids in metabolism; *magnesium* (found in green leafy vegetables), which is also good for metabolism and for healthy bones and teeth; and *iron* (found in liver, egg yolk, red meats, and grains), which is necessary for *hemoglobin*—a chemical that unites with oxygen in the blood.

Fiber in the human diet comes only from plant sources. Fiber is not a nutrient, but it is important for stimulating the normal action of the intestines in the elimination of wastes. Raw fruits and vegetables, whole cereals and bread, and fruits with seeds (figs, strawberries, and raspberries) are excellent sources of fiber.

Diseases A *disease* is a disorder that prevents the body organs from working as they should. In general, diseases can be classified as *noninfectious* or *infectious*. Among the noninfectious causes of disease are malnutrition, poisoning, radiation, and the malfunctioning of the endocrine system. Infectious diseases can be caused by *germs* (bacteria), fungi, parasitic worms, and *viruses*. Viruses are inorganic, but they grow within living cells. Most infectious diseases are *contagious*—that is, they are spread by body contact or by droplet infection.

The human body has many powerful defenses against disease. The skin itself kills most germs that land on it. So does the saliva in our mouths, the acid in our stomachs, the mucus membrane in our nose and throat. If any germs do get past these defenses, our body releases chemicals to surround and destroy the germs. White blood cells, cells in the lymph vessels, and *antibodies* are also part of this defense. Antibodies are "tailor-made" by the body to fight specific germs.

Our communities can do a great deal to help prevent disease. One strategy is to require that all children be immunized against disease. *Immunization* is the injection of a *vaccine*—a weak agent of the disease—into a person's body. This stimulates the body to produce anti-bodies that will be ready to fight germs if they invade the body. Successful methods of immunization have been developed against smallpox, polio, measles, typhus, and other contagious diseases..

Another safeguard is to protect our water supply against contamination. There are several techniques. *Settling* is the process by which water is held in large tanks until suspended solids settle out. In *filtering*, water is allowed to trickle through sand beds several feet deep. This removes 90 to 95 percent of all bacteria as well as fine particles of solid matter. *Aeration* is the process by which water is sprayed into the air. This technique kills some bacteria and allows more air to dissolve into the water. In *chlorination*, some form of chlorine is added to the water to kill any remaining germs.

There are several ways to preserve food—some of them ancient, some very recent: drying, salting, smoking, fast freezing, pickling, and sterilization by heat. Canning sterilizes food and seals it so that no germs can get in. To prevent the spread of disease through milk, dairies *pasteurize* it: They chill milk immediately after collecting it to kill some of the bacteria, and then heat it to a required temperature for a period of time. This kills all the disease-causing germs.

Ecology

Ecology   Ecology is the newest branch of earth science and is very dependent on knowl-edge of biology and chemistry. The interconnection of plant, animal, and human life is becoming more widely appreciated. Ecology, for example, focuses on the effects of chemical waste products on our air, sea, and land.

One of the most important concepts in ecology is that of an *ecosystem*, the system by which a particular living *community* of plant and animal *populations* interacts with its non-living environment. There is no size requirement for an ecosystem: It may be a forest, a pond, an unused city lot, or a crack in the sidewalk. The structure of an ecosystem is the same whether its location is on land or water. What really defines an ecosystem is a set of inter-acting forces:

1. The *air* is made up of 21 percent oxygen, 78 percent nitrogen, .03 percent carbon dioxide, and other inert gases.
2. The *soil* is the source of minerals that supply plants with compounds of nitrogen, zinc, calcium, phosphorus, and other minerals.
3. The *green plants* in an ecosystem are its *producers*, so-called because they make their own food.
4. *Primary consumers* in an ecosystem are its *herbivores* (plant-eaters). These include crickets, grasshoppers, and cattle, for example.
5. *Secondary consumers* (so-called because they feed on the herbivores) are flesh-eaters, such as snakes, frogs, and coyotes. These are called *carnivores*.
6. *Tertiary consumers* are those that feed on the herbivores and carnivores.
7. *Scavengers,* such as earthworms and vultures, feed upon dead organic matter.
8. *Decomposers* are those bacteria and other organisms that break down dead organic matter, thus releasing minerals that are returned to the soil. Without the decomposers, valuable minerals would remain trapped in dead organic matter.

The source of all energy in an ecosystem is the sun. Green plants use the sun's light (its energy) to make their own food. This energy is then transferred from plants to the animals that consume them. Animals use energy to do work and, in the process, give off body heat which radiates into the atmosphere. The cycles of *photosynthesis* (energy trapping) and *respiration* (energy release and use) must continue if the ecosystem is to continue. The flow of energy in the ecosystem can be studied by way of this *food chain* showing the transfer of energy from a producer, lettuce, to a tertiary consumer, the hawk. (Not all food chains are this simple.)

$$\text{Lettuce} \rightarrow \text{Rabbit} \rightarrow \text{Snake} \rightarrow \text{Hawk}$$

Ecosystems that have become permanent in a broad geographical area are known as *biomes*. The earth is divided into several biomes:

1. The *arctic tundra* includes vast stretches of treeless plains around the Arctic Ocean. Here the temperature is the limiting factor in the ecosystem: It ranges from 60° F in the summer to −130° F in the winter. The ground is permanently frozen a few feet below the surface.
2. In the *taiga*, coniferous (evergreen) forests survive long severe winters. Canada has a large taiga.
3. The *deciduous* (leaf-shedding) *forests* of the world are in regions with relatively temperate (mild) climates.
4. *Deserts* form in regions where the annual rainfall is less than 6.5 centimeters—or where rain is irregular, and the rate of evaporation is very high. The Sahara and Gobi Deserts are examples.
5. *Grasslands regions* occur where rainfall is low and irregular. In the United States, the Great Plains is a grasslands region; grasslands in the Soviet Union are called steppes.
6. *Tropical rainforests* are characterized by high temperatures and constant rainfall. This type of biome is found in Central and South America.
7. Oceans and seas form the *marine biome*, the thickest known layer of living things. Here, the depth of water determines where life flourishes.

Earth Science

The term *earth science* includes several related sciences such as *geology* (the study of the earth), *oceanography* (the study of the seas and oceans), *meteorology* (the study of weather and climate), and *astronomy* (the study of the earth as part of the universe).

Geology Geology deals with the formation and composition of the earth. It relates to and borrows from other sciences such as chemistry, physics, and biology. Geologists determine the strength and behavior of rock formations and their reaction to stress. Such knowledge is essential for the design and construction of large-scale buildings, dams, bridges, and tunnels; for the prediction of earthquakes; and for the location and mining of petroleum, coal, and other minerals.

How were the hills and valleys of the earth's surface formed? Glacier National Park in Montana is an outdoor textbook on this question. For millions of years thick beds of ooze in this area solidified into limestone. Later, *sediments* (fragments of rocks and organic matter) covered the limestone and became mudstone. These, in turn, were overlaid with other sediments that also became limestone.

About 70 million years ago, in what is now Montana, terrific stresses in the earth's crust acted on the deeply buried mudstones, sandstones, and limestones. As the tensions and strain became acute, the rock was warped and finally broken. The western part, 1,000 meters thick, slid over the eastern part. The pressures continued for millions of years until a gigantic 500-kilometer-long section of the earth's crust was moved more than 60 kilometers to the east. This section, with strata more than 1 billion years old, actually capped "younger" rock.

The same process created other mountain systems throughout the world. However, few overthrusts have been as great as this, the Lewis Overthrust of Glacier National Park. The carving of the park's rugged landscape was principally the work of *glaciers* (slow-moving masses of ice) during the last 3 million years. The moving ice deepened the main valleys and cut back the base of the cliffs. As the ice melted, the *strata* (layers) of earth's oldest sediments appeared as streaks on the sides of the 300-meter-high *precipices* (overhanging cliffs) in the park.

On a geologic time scale, these different types of change in the earth's surface fall into four periods or eras:

1. The *prepaleozoic* era, characterized chiefly by volcanic activity and the formation of great mountain ranges;
2. The *paleozoic* era, with periodic submergence and emergence of continents and mountains;
3. The *mesozoic* era, characterized by uplift (the elevation of land in a particular place), erosion, and more volcanic activity;
4. The *cenozoic* era, with the rise and fall of coastal lands, general erosion, and the retreat of the glaciers.

The movement of the earth's seemingly "solid" crust is part of the theory of "*continental drift.*" Recent evidence seems to support the idea that at one time all the continents as we know them were joined in one large land mass, "Pangaea." Gradually—according to the theory—this continent split into two land masses, with North America, Europe and Asia in one mass, and the rest of today's continents in the other. Separations continued. The similarities in the Atlantic coastlines of Africa and South America suggest that they were once united. And recently, the fossil remains of a large reptile (Lystrosaurus) that was once common in Africa have been found in Antarctica. This suggests that these two continents were also once joined.

How old is the earth? Methods that have been used to determine the geologic age of earth include measuring *salinity, erosion, sedimentary layers*, and *radioactivity*. The salinity technique assumes that all oceans were originally fresh water. However, as rivers washed over the land, picking up minerals, they began to deposit accumulated salts in the oceans. The rate of this process can be calculated. Thus, the time for all oceans to reach their present degrees of salinity can be approximately figured.

The sedimentary layers method and the erosion method are opposites. The erosion method figures the rate at which a rock formation was worn away by wind or water. With sedimentary layers, the figuring is based on the present thickness of the layer and the assumed rate of its buildup through past deposits. These methods and the salinity technique have led geologists to place the age of the earth somewhere between 100 million and 1.5 billion years.

The most recently developed technique uses the *radioactivity* or "half-life" of an element. By analyzing particular elements such as uranium, strontium, and thorium and by studying their decay products, geologists can figure the age of rock samples. Since each element has a specific *half-life* (the time needed for half the atoms in a mass to disintegrate), scientists using this method figure the age of the earth to be about 3.5 billion years.

The *radioactive dating technique* is helping *paleontologists* to establish the geologic age of *fossils*. Fossils are forms of plant and animal life preserved in rock. Since carbon is part of every organic compound, knowledge of the half-life of carbon-14 is effective in establishing when a particular fossil was actually a living plant or animal.

Oceanography

Using various related sciences, oceanography studies the oceans and seas. Although oceans cover more than three fourths of the earth's surface, only a small portion of this vast area is used by humans. Examination of the ocean floor, marine life, and mineral content of the water is important for the future development of essential materials, food, and medicines.

There are four major oceans on earth: the Pacific, Atlantic, Indian, and Arctic. Together, these bodies of water hold 97% of all water on earth. In the simplest terms, an ocean may be divided into the *shoreline*, the *water* itself, and the *seabed*, or bottom. However, these classifications need further division into zones (levels), as shown in this table.

MARINE ZONES

Zone	Average Depth	Average Temperature	Comment
Shore (between high, low tides)	Varies	Varies by season	Wave action, light for photosynthesis
Water (1) shore to continental shelf	0–200 meters	5–25° C	Waves, currents, greatest amount of plant and animal life
(2) downward slope from continental shelf	200–2,500 meters	5–15° C	Currents, almost dark, fewer marine animals, no plants
(3) deeper plain	2,500–6,500 meters	3–4° C	Dark, limited animal life, no plants
(4) deepest trenches or canyons	6,500–11,500 meters	1–3° C	Dark, very limited animal life, no plants

Generally, animal life and plant life typical of one zone are not found in a different zone. However, there are exceptions; there are no exact boundaries between zones to prevent a sea creature from moving from one level to another. Knowledge of the deeper levels and the ocean bottom is still incomplete.

An important influence of the ocean on human life comes from *tides*. Tides are the alternate rising and falling of water level in the oceans and other large bodies of water. They are the result of the gravitational pull of the sun and the moon on the freely moving waters of the earth. Since the moon is much closer to the earth than is the sun, the moon has a much greater effect on tides. Tides affect the movement of ships, especially when in port in shallow waters.

Astronomy   Although astronomy is often considered part of physics, it is also related to earth science. The *rotation* of the earth on its *axis* (an imaginary line running through the earth from North to South Pole) causes day and night. The *revolution* of the earth around the sun affects the seasons of earth's year. The earth itself is part of a *solar system* with eight other planets, and is part of a *universe* of many stars and suns.

Planet	Average distance from the sun (million miles)	Rank by size	Time for revolution	Number of moons
Mercury	36.0	8	88 days	0
Venus	67.1	6	224 days	0
Earth	93.0	5	365¼ days	1
Mars	141.7	7	687 days	2
Jupiter	483.4	1	12 years	12
Saturn	886.1	2	30 years	9
Uranus	1,783.0	3	84 years	5
Neptune	2,793.0	4	165 years	2
Pluto	3,666.0	?	248 years	?

Occasionally, earth's moon goes into *eclipse*. An eclipse occurs when one astronomical body cuts off light from another. A *lunar eclipse* occurs when the earth comes directly between the sun and the moon, thus causing the earth's shadow (*umbra*) to fall directly on the moon. Since the moon shines only in light reflected from the sun, this position of the earth puts the moon into eclipse.

In a total *solar eclipse*, the moon is directly between the earth and the sun, so that the umbra of the moon falls on the earth. However, the moon is much smaller than the earth. Thus the path of the moon's shadow that sweeps across the earth during a solar eclipse is very narrow. The shadow's maximum width is about 170 miles.

Two astronomical bodies that interest humans are the *comet* and *meteor*. Comets are mostly gaseous bodies that can be seen from earth for periods ranging from a few days to months at a time. The *comet head* contains a small bright nucleus that astronomers think may contain ice, frozen gases, and other particles. When a comet approaches the sun, these gases and particles stream off in the form of a *tail*, sometimes as long as 100,000,000 miles. (Halley's comet is predicted to appear in 1986.)

A meteor is a small piece of extraterrestrial matter that becomes visible when it enters earth's atmosphere. In the friction that attends this entry, a meteor heats up intensely and usually disintegrates before it can reach the ground. Those meteors large enough to reach ground are called *meteorites*. The glow of a meteor's appearance has led it to be called (incorrectly) a "*shooting*" or "*falling star.*"

Meteorology Meteorology is the study of *weather* and *climate*. Weather is the condition of the atmosphere at any given time and place. Climate is the average of weather conditions in a particular place over a period of time. The services of *meteorologists* in predicting the weather are critical to farmers, travelers, and people in many different kinds of business.

Weather is the description of several atmospheric conditions interacting with one another. These conditions—*temperature, air pressure, winds, humidity,* etc.—are themselves influenced by other factors.

1. The temperature of a place is affected by the angle of the sun's rays, the length of its daylight period, its altitude, and its closeness to bodies of water. Water heats and cools more slowly than land and affects the air above it in the same way. Therefore, breezes blowing off the water tend to moderate the temperature of air over faster-heating and faster-cooling land.
2. The pressure of the air depends on its temperature and humidity. Warm air is lighter than cold air, and moist air is lighter than dry air. Thus moist warm air has very low pressure. Changes in atmospheric pressure are measured on a *barometer*. When meteorologists at the weather bureau see a "falling" barometer, they predict rain.

3. Wind is the movement of air from one place to another. Winds are caused by differences in air pressure. Winds always move from areas of higher pressure (cold, dry air)
to areas of lower pressure (warm, moist air). Sometimes the difference in pressure
between two areas is great enough to cause *hurricanes* or *tornadoes*. A hurricane is a
wind of 74 miles or more per hour. A tornado is a wind with a funnel-shaped cloud
that touches the ground.

4. Humidity refers to the amount of moisture in the air. When the air is warm and dry,
moisture on the earth's surface tends to *evaporate* (turn into vapor). When the air is
completely filled with moisture (when it is *saturated*), a drop in the temperature will
cause the moisture in the air to *condense* (form droplets) and *precipitate* (fall) as rain,
snow, sleet, hail, etc.

Chemistry

Chemistry is a physical science that investigates the composition, structure and properties of
matter. Chemistry is also concerned with changes in matter and the *energy* involved during
those changes.

Matter   *Matter* is defined as anything that occupies space and that has *mass*. Mass is the
amount of matter that a particular substance possesses. Depending on the pull of gravity at
one location, a substance may be heavier or lighter than at another place, but its mass always
remains the same. For example, an astronaut who weighs 168 pounds on earth weighs about
28 pounds in space, but still has the same mass.

Matter occurs in one of three *states*, or conditions: A substance may be a *solid*, a *liquid*,
or a *gas*. A solid has both a definite size and shape (for example, an ice cube before it melts).
A liquid has a definite volume, but it takes the shape of the container it's in. (For example, an
ice cube is a solid with a definite shape. If it melts in a cup, the liquid water then takes on the
shape of the cup.) A gas has neither definite shape nor definite volume. Often, the state of
matter that a particular substance is in can be changed by the addition or removal of *heat
energy*. For example, water that is cooled sufficiently will freeze; heated sufficiently, it will
turn into a gas.

Matter can be subdivided in another way: It may be either an *element*, a *compound*, or a
mixture. An element is a substance that is made up of only one kind of atom. For example,
gold, iron, sulfur, oxygen are all elements and each contains only one kind of atom. (There
are more than 100 elements known to science.) A compound is a substance composed of two
or more kinds of atoms joined together in a definite pattern. For example, water (H_2O)
always occurs in the relationship of two atoms of hydrogen to one atom of oxygen. A mixture
is an indefinite blending of two or more substances. Sometimes the substances are very
evenly distributed (for example, food coloring in water). Other times, the mixture is uneven
(for example, raisins in cookie dough).

Matter undergoes two types of change: *physical change* and *chemical change*. In a
physical change, the appearance of a substance may change, but its chemical composition
remains the same (for example, broken glass, split wood, melted ice). A chemical change
involves a change in the chemical makeup of a substance (for example, burning wood) and is
always accompanied by either the release or absorption of energy. To start paper burning, for
example, you have to apply some form of heat to it.

In describing the state of matter and its changes we speak of the *physical* and *chemical
properties* of matter. The physical properties of a substance are those we can observe with
our senses: its color, taste, melting point, hardness, etc. The chemical properties of a sub-

stance are those that describe its reactions with other substances (for example, iron rusts in the presence of oxygen, gold does not, etc.). The smallest particle of a substance that has all the physical and chemical properties of the substance is called a *molecule*.

Energy   *Energy* is usually defined as the ability to do work. Energy may appear in a variety of forms—as *light, heat, sound, mechanical energy, electrical energy,* and *chemical energy.* Energy can be converted from one form to another. For example: (1) Heat from burning fuel is used to vaporize water (change it to steam); (2) this steam energy is used to turn turbine wheels to produce mechanical energy; (3) the turbine turns a generator to produce electricity; (4) this electricity is then available in homes for use as light, heat, or the operation of appliances.

Two general classifications of energy are *potential energy* and *kinetic energy*. Potential energy is said to be due to the position of an object. Kinetic energy is energy of motion. The difference between the two can be illustrated by a boulder on the slope of a mountain. While it remains there, the boulder has high potential energy due to its position above the valley floor. If it falls, however, its potential energy is converted into kinetic energy.

What is the relationship between matter and energy? The *Law of Conservation of Mass and Energy* states that matter and energy are neither created nor lost during chemical reactions. The law also states that matter and energy are interchangeable under special conditions. Albert Einstein's formula for this interchange is

$$E = mc^2$$
$$Energy = Mass \times (speed\ of\ light)^2$$

Symbols and Equations in Chemistry   Chemistry requires the understanding of *symbols* and *equations*. Symbols are short forms for expressing an idea or a term. Symbols in chemistry include the following examples:

Symbol	Meaning
→	Yields, or leads to (Arrows are also used in chemical equations, where they perform the work done by the equal sign in mathematics)
↑	Forms a gas
↓	Forms a *precipitate* (something that settles to the bottom of a liquid)

Element	Symbol	Element	Symbol
Magnesium	Mg	Gold	Au
Phosphorus	P	Barium	Ba
Sulfur	S	Arsenic	As
Mercury	Hg	Iron	Fe
Sodium	Na	Chlorine	Cl

An equation resembles a sentence. A sentence is made up of words. A chemical equation is made up of formulas of molecules. A formula may be of a compound—H_2O, NaCl, for example—or an element, Mg, O_2, etc. A *chemical equation* shows what happens when chemical elements or compounds interact. For example, you can read the following as a sentence:

$$2H_2 + O_2 \rightarrow 2H_2O$$

Translated, this chemical equation reads, "Four atoms (or two molecules) of the element hydrogen and one molecule or two atoms of the element oxygen combine to yield two molecules of a compound called H_2O, which is water." The basic features of a chemical equation are:

1. A chemical equation shows a *chemical change*. Either a new chemical compound is formed, or a compound is separated into its elements.
2. The equation must *balance:* The total quantities to the left of the arrow ($\rightarrow$) must equal the total quantities to the right of the arrow. In the following equation, you have 2 hydrogen (H_2) and 2 chlorine (Cl_2) molecules yielding only one molecule of hydrogen chloride (HCl). This is, therefore, an *imbalanced equation:*

$$H_2 + Cl_2 \rightarrow HCl$$

If you place a 2 before the compound HCl, you make the 2 hydrogen and 2 chlorine atoms on the left equal the two hydrogen and two chlorine atoms contained in two hydrogen chloride molecules on the right. Thus, this equation is balanced:

$$H_2 + Cl_2 \rightarrow 2HCl$$

Measurements in Chemistry   The *metric system* of measurement is the one used by scientists all over the world. Some basic units and prefixes used with the units of the metric system are as follows:

Length

10 millimeters (mm) = 1 centimeter (cm)
100 cm = 1 meter (m)
1,000 m = 1 kilometer (km)

A unit of length used especially in expressing the length of light waves is the *angstrom*, abbreviated Å and equal to 10^{-8} cm.

Volume

1,000 milliliters (ml) = 1 liter (l)
1,000 cubic centimeters (cm^3) = 1 liter
1 ml = 1 cm^3

Mass

1,000 milligrams (mg) = 1 gram (g)
1,000 g = 1 kilogram (kg)

Sometimes, you will want the metric system instead of the customary American notation:

2.54 cm = 1 inch
1 meter = 39.37 inches (10% longer than 1 yard)
28.35 grams = 1 ounce
454 grams = 1 pound
1 kilogram = 2.2 pounds
.946 liter = 1 quart
1 liter (5% larger than a quart) = 1.06 quarts

Prefix	Multiples	Scientific Notation	Abbreviation
mega-	1,000,000	10^6	m
kilo-	1,000	10^3	k
hecto-	100	10^2	h
deci-	.1	10^{-1}	d
centi-	.01	10^{-2}	c
milli-	.001	10^{-3}	m
nano-	.000,000,001	10^{-9}	n

Temperature is measurable on three different scales — *Celsius* (or *centigrade*), *Fahrenheit*, and *Kelvin* (or *absolute*). Their respective freezing and boiling points are:

	Celsius	Fahrenheit	Kelvin
Boiling point of water	100°	212°	373°
Freezing point of water	0°	32°	273°

There are formulas for converting from one system to another:

Example: What is the Fahrenheit value of 30°C?

$$°F = \frac{9}{5}°C + 32°$$

$$°F = \frac{9}{5} (30°) + 32°$$

$$°F = 54° + 32° = 86° F$$

Thus,   30° C = 86° F

Similarly, the formula for converting from Celsius to Fahrenheit is:

$$°C = \frac{5}{9} (°F - 32°)$$

The formula for converting from Kelvin to Celsius is somewhat simpler:

$$°K = °C + 273°$$

Sometimes, when working with very "long" numbers, you may want to use the *scientific notation system*. This system uses exponents to shorten the form of expressing numbers with many places in them. For example:

1. With very large numbers, such as 3,630,000, move the decimal point to the left. When only one digit remains to the left of the decimal point (3.630000), count the number of places you have moved (in this case, six places). Indicate this number of moves as the exponent of 10 (10^6). Then write the short form of your original number as 3.63×10^6.
2. With very small numbers, such as .000000123, move the decimal point to the right. When the first digit is to the left of the decimal (0000001.23), count the number of places you have moved (in this case, seven places). Indicate this number of moves as the negative exponent of 10 (10^{-7}). Then write the short form of your original number as 1.23×10^{-7}.

Atoms and Molecules   An *atom* is the smallest unit of an element that retains the general properties of that element. The core of the atom, the *nucleus,* is very dense and very small by comparison with the rest of the atom. It contains *protons* (positively charged particles) and *neutrons* (particles with no charge). Outside the nucleus are the atom's *electrons* (negatively charged particles). An atom has the same number of electrons as its protons. These electrons are arranged in ''shell'' layers around the nucleus. It's as though an atom were a marble inside a baseball inside a basketball, etc. Atoms tend to borrow, lend, or share electrons from these outer shells. These are called *valence electrons*.

On the basis of their atomic structure, atoms are considered *metals* if they lend electrons, *nonmetals* if they borrow electrons, and *inert* if they neither borrow nor lend. The *atomic number* of an atom is the number of protons in its nucleus. All atoms of the same element have the same atomic number and each element's atomic number is different from all other elements. The *atomic mass* is the number of protons and neutrons in an atom's nucleus. An atom containing the same number of protons as other atoms of the same element, but having a different number of neutrons, is called an *isotope* of that element.

A *molecule* is the smallest particle of an element or compound that retains the characteristics of the original substance. A molecule of water is a *triatomic* (''three-atom'') *molecule* since two hydrogen atoms and one oxygen atom must combine to form the substance water. When atoms do combine to form molecules there is a *chemical bonding*. When such a bonding takes place, there is an exchange of energy.

Gases   Of all the gases that occur in the atmosphere, the most important is *oxygen*. Although oxygen makes up only 21% of the atmosphere, it is equal in weight to all other elements on earth combined. About 50% of the earth's crust (including earth's waters and atmosphere) is oxygen. Most living things require it.

Properties of Oxygen   Physically, oxygen is colorless, tasteless, odorless, and slightly heavier than air. It supports the combustion of other substances but does not burn itself. When oxygen combines slowly with an element (so that no noticeable heat and light are given off), we call the process *slow oxidation*. A common example is rusting iron. (A substance loses electrons in oxidation, and gains them in *reduction*.) When the combination of oxygen with an element is so rapid that the released energy can be seen as light and felt as heat, the process is called *rapid oxidation* or normal burning. Oxygen occurs as molecules containing two oxygen atoms, O_2.

Ozone is a form of oxygen having three atoms in its molecular structure (O_3). Ozone is found in the upper atmosphere and can be formed in the lower atmosphere in the presence of high-voltage electricity.

Properties of Hydrogen   Physically, pure hydrogen is colorless, tasteless, and odorless. It is 1/14 as heavy as air and diffuses (moves from place to place) more rapidly than any other gas. Its chemical properties include burning in air or oxygen, giving off large amounts of heat. Hydrogen molecules also contain two atoms, H_2.

Hydrogen is the lightest of all known elements. The most abundant element in the universe, hydrogen is the major fuel in fusion reactions of the sun. Its ability to burn well makes it an important part of many fuels.

● General characteristics of gases. Most gases behave according to these ''laws'':

1. The particles of a gas move in continuous, random, straight-line motion.
2. As the temperature of a gas increases, its kinetic energy increases, and this increases its random motion. As its temperature decreases, the kinetic energy of a gas decreases until it reaches the point where it liquifies.

3. If the pressure on a gas remains the same, its volume will increase with temperature, and vice versa.
4. If the temperature of a gas remains the same, its volume will decrease as pressure on it increases, and vice versa.
5. If the volume of a gas remains the same, its pressure will increase with temperature, and vice versa.

Liquids   A *liquid expands* (grows larger in volume) and *contracts* (grows smaller in volume) very slightly with a temperature change. Nevertheless, the molecules of a liquid are always in motion. If a particular molecule gains enough kinetic energy near the surface of a liquid, it can overcome the attraction of other molecules in the liquid and escape into a gaseous state. When this occurs, the average temperature of the remaining liquid molecules becomes lower than before the "escape."

In an enclosed area (when the temperature of a gas remains the same), opposing changes tend to take place at the same time: Liquid molecules escape into the gaseous stage *(evaporation)*, and gas molecules return to the liquid stage *(condensation)*. When these opposite changes take place at the same rate, we have what is called *equilibrium*.

When liquid is heated in an open container, equilibrium disappears and liquid molecules begin to pass rapidly into a gaseous stage. When this conversion begins to occur within the liquid as well as at its surface, we have reached the liquid's *boiling point*. The temperature at which a gaseous substance cannot return to the liquid phase is called its *critical temperature*.

Water   Water is so often involved in chemistry that it is important to know how to obtain it chemically and how it is used in science. The method of obtaining pure water in the laboratory is by *distillation*: Water is heated (causing it to evaporate) and then cooled (causing it to condense).

Properties and Uses of Water   Water has been used in the definition of various standards:

1. For weight—1 ml (cm^3) of water at 4° C is 1 gram
2. For heat—(a) the heat needed to raise one gram of water one degree on the Celsius scale = 1 Calorie (cal)
    (b) the heat needed to raise one pound of water one degree on the Fahrenheit scale = 1 British thermal unit (BTU)
3. Degree of heat—the freezing point of water = 0° C or 32° F
    —the boiling point of water = 100° C or 212° F

Water forms compounds that are classified as *bases* or *acids*. Metal oxides (compounds of oxygen and a metal) react with water to form bases, which have the following properties:

1. Bases can conduct electricity in a water solution. The degree of conduction depends on the "*ionization*" of a base—that is, its number of charged particles.
2. Bases react with acids to neutralize each other and form a *salt* and water.
3. They react with fats to form soaps.
4. They cause litmus paper to change from red to blue. (This is a test for the presence of a base.)

Examples of bases include:

$$2Na + 2H_2O \rightarrow 2NaOH + H_2 \text{ (sodium hydroxide)}$$
$$CaO + H_2O \rightarrow Ca(OH)_2 \qquad \text{(calcium hydroxide)}$$

Nonmetal oxides react with water to form acids, which have the following properties:

1. Water solutions of acids conduct electricity. This conduction depends on an acid's ionization.
2. Some acids react with some metals and liberate hydrogen.
3. Acids react with bases to neutralize each other and form a salt and water.
4. Acids react with carbonates to release carbon dioxide.
5. They cause litmus paper to change to a pink-red color. (This is a test for the presence of an acid.)
6. Acids are corrosive.

Examples of acids include:

$$SO_3 + H_2O \rightarrow H_2SO_4 \quad \text{(sulfuric acid)}$$
$$P_2O_5 + 3H_2O \rightarrow 2H_3PO_4 \text{ (phosphoric acid)}$$

Water is often referred to as "the universal solvent" because of the number of common substances that dissolve in water. When substances are dissolved in water to the point that no more will dissolve at that temperature, the solution is said to be *saturated*. The substance dissolved is called the *solute*. The medium in which it is dissolved is called the *solvent*. When a small amount of solute is dispersed throughout the solvent, it is called a *dilute solution*. When a large amount of solute is dissolved in the solvent, it is called a *concentrated solution*.

Some substances form geometric ("building-block") patterns as they slowly come out of a solution (as they lose water). The process is called *crystallization*.

Solids   Particles at the *solid* stage have the most fixed position and maintain a collective shape. The temperature at which particles of a solid begin to break free from fixed positions and slide over each other is called its *melting point*. At certain pressures, some solids vaporize directly, without passing through the liquid stage. This is called *sublimation*. Solid carbon dioxide and solid iodine have this property.

Chemical Reactions   One of the major interests in chemistry is the study of how different substances react with one another. Generally there are four basic types of *reaction*:

1. *Combination (synthesis)* is the formation of a compound from the union of its elements. For example:

$$C + O_2 \rightarrow CO_2 \text{ (carbon dioxide)}$$

2. *Decomposition (analysis)* is the breakdown of a compound to release its components as individual elements or simpler compounds. For example:

$$2H_2O \rightarrow 2H_2 \uparrow + O_2 \uparrow \text{ (electrolysis of water)}$$

3. *Single replacement (single displacement)* occurs when one substance replaces another in a compound. For example:

$$Fe + CuSO_4 \rightarrow FeSO_4 + Cu$$
(iron and copper sulfate) $\rightarrow$ (iron sulfate and copper)

4. In *double replacement (double displacement)* there is an actual exchange of "partners" to form new compounds. For example:

$$AgNO_3 + NaCl \rightarrow AgCl + NaNO_3$$
(silver nitrate and sodium chloride) $\rightarrow$ (silver chloride and sodium nitrate)

In general the *probability* that a specific chemical reaction will take place depends on the amount of heat needed to produce the reaction. The higher the amount of *heat of formation*, the greater the *stability* ("permanence") of a compound, and vice versa.

How long does it take for a chemical reaction to occur? The measurement of a *reaction rate* is based on the rate of formation of a product or the disappearance of a reactant (reacting substance). There are five important factors that control this rate:

1. The nature of the reactants. Some elements and compounds react very rapidly with each other.
2. The exposed surface areas of the reactants. Most reactions depend on the reactants coming into contact. Thus, the more exposure they have to each other at one time, the faster the reaction.
3. The concentrations. The reaction rate is usually proportional to the degree of concentration of the reactants.
4. The temperature. A temperature increase of 10° C above room temperature usually causes a reaction rate to double or triple.
5. The presence of a *catalyst*. A catalyst is a substance that speeds up or slows down a reaction, without being (permanently) changed itself.

Some reactions involve products that continuously interact with the original reactants. That is, reactants and their products interact in both directions. This is shown as follows:

$$A + B \rightleftarrows C + D$$

The double arrow indicates that substances C and D can react to form A and B, while A and B react to form C and D. Such a reaction is said to reach an *equilibrium* when the forward reaction rate is equal to the reverse reaction rate. The symbol K_e, the "*equilibrium constant*," is a symbol for the point at which equilibrium occurs.

Key Elements and Their Families

1. *Sulfur*. After oxygen, the most important element is sulfur. Sulfur is found in a free state in volcanic regions of Japan, Mexico, and Sicily. It can also be produced in the laboratory. Sulfur is used in making sprays to control plant disease and harmful insects. It is used in the manufacture of rubber, to *vulcanize* rubber (give it extra hardness). Sulfur is used in the preparation of medicines and gunpowder. It is also used in making *sulfuric acid, hydrogen sulfide,* and *sulfur dioxide*.

   Sulfuric acid (H_2SO_4) is called the "king of chemicals" because of its widespread industrial use. Some of these uses include:
   a. making other acids;
   b. freeing iron and steel metals of scale and rust;
   c. washing objectionable colors from gasoline made by the "cracking" process;
   d. acting as a dehydrating agent in the manufacture of explosives, dyes, and drugs.
   Hydrogen sulfide (H_2S) is used widely in laboratory tests (many sulfides precipitate with distinct colors) and in making paints. Sulfur dioxide (SO_2) is used as a bleach.

2. *Halogens*. *Fluorine* (F_2), the most active nonmetal, is a yellowish, poisonous, highly corrosive element. When it is added at 1 ppm (part per million) to water, it hardens tooth enamel and reduces tooth decay. *Chlorine* (Cl_2) is used to purify water supplies, to act as a bleaching agent, and to prepare hydrochloric acid (which is used in the manufacture of other chemicals). *Bromine* (Br_2) is used to keep anti-knock gasolines free of lead deposits. *Iodine* (I_2) is most widely known for its use as an antiseptic in tincture of iodine.

3. *Nitrogen.* The most common member of this family is *nitrogen* (N_2) itself. It is colorless, odorless, tasteless, rather inactive, and makes up about four fifths of the air in our atmosphere. Nitrogen-fixing bacteria found in the roots of beans, peas, clover, and similar plants "fix" nitrogen. This means they use nitrogen from the air to form compounds that plants can use. Two important compounds of nitrogen are *nitric acid* and *ammonia*.

    Nitric acid (HNO_3) is useful in making dyes, celluloid film, and lacquers for cars. Nitric acid is also used in the manufacture of powerful explosives—for example, "TNT" and "nitroglycerine." Ammonia (NH_3) is one of the oldest known compounds of nitrogen. It is a colorless, pungent gas, extremely soluble in water. A water solution of ammonia is used as a cleanser. Another use of ammonia is as a fertilizer.

4. *Phosphorus* (P), a nonmetallic element, is yellow to white, waxy, and extremely poisonous. Because phosphorus ignites spontaneously when exposed to air, it is stored under water. The principal use of phosphorus is in compounds which act as fertilizers, detergents, insecticides, soft drinks, and pharmaceuticals. Phosphorous compounds are essential to the diet. (They are important for our bones and teeth.) Phosphorous is a component of *adenosene triphosphate* (ATP), a fundamental energy source in living things.

Metals   Some physical properties of *metals* are: (1) they have metallic luster; (2) they can conduct heat and electricity; (3) they can be pounded into sheets (metals are *malleable*) or drawn into wires (metals are *ductile*); (4) they are not soluble in any ordinary solvent without undergoing a chemical change. A general chemical property of metals is that they are *electropositive* (charged with positive electricity).

    The outstanding properties of *aluminum* (Al) are: it is very light, has high strength, can resist oxidation, and can conduct an electric current. Aluminum is prepared from *bauxite ore*.

    Magnesium (Mg), the eighth most abundant metal in the earth's crust, is found in plant chlorophyll. (Magnesium is necessary to the diet of humans and other animals.) It is light, rigid, and inexpensive, and is used in the manufacture of aircraft fuselages, cameras, and optical instruments.

    Copper (Cu) has been known to humans since the Bronze Age. It is reddish, malleable, ductile, and is an excellent conductor of electricity. It is used in manufacturing wires, utensils, coins, etc. It also is important to the human diet.

    Iron (Fe), a malleable, ductile, silver-grey metal, is abundant in the universe. (It is found in many stars, including the sun.) A good conductor of heat and electricity, iron is attracted by a magnet and is easily magnetized. It rusts very easily. Iron is extracted from ores in a blast furnace, after which it can be mixed with other substances to form steel. It is also important in the human diet.

    Alloys are mixtures of two or more metals. *Bronze* (an alloy of copper and tin) and *brass* (an alloy of copper and zinc) are examples. Certain properties of metals are affected when they are mixed in an alloy. An alloy is usually harder than the metals which compose it, but its melting point is usually lower than that of its components.

Carbon and Organic Chemistry   The element *carbon* (C) is present in all living things. It occurs in both crystalline and amorphous (noncrystal) forms.

1. Crystalline *diamonds,* found in South Africa and other regions, are the hardest form of carbon. They are brilliant, both reflecting and refracting light. Diamonds are used as gems and in the making of drills, saws, etc.

2. *Graphite* (a crystal) is prepared from hard coal in an electric furnace. It is soft, gray, and greasy, and forms a good electrical conductor. It is used as a lubricant, in making lead pencils, and in the construction of atomic reactors.
3. *Charcoal* is formed from the destructive distillation of soft wood. It burns with a glow but no flame. Charcoal is used as a fuel.
4. *Coke* is formed from the destructive distillation of soft coal. It burns with little smoke or flame and is used as a fuel.
5. *Anthracite coal*, almost pure carbon, burns with little smoke and is used as a fuel.

Carbon dioxide (CO_2) is a widely distributed gas. The usual laboratory preparation of carbon dioxide consists of reacting calcium carbonate (marble chips) with hydrochloric acid. There are several important uses for carbon dioxide:

1. It is used to make carbonated beverages.
2. Solid carbon dioxide (at $-78°$ C), or ''dry ice,'' is used as a refrigerant.
3. Fire extinguishers make use of carbon dioxide because of its weight and its property of not supporting ordinary combustion.
4. Plants use carbon dioxide in photosynthesis.

Organic chemistry is the chemistry that deals with the compounds of carbon. Carbon bonds to other carbons as well as to hydrogens, halogens, oxygen, and other elements. The number of organic compounds is in the neighborhood of a million—including dyes, plastic, textile fabrics, medicines, and drugs. Compounds with carbons include methane, alcohol, amino acids, and *carbohydrates*. Carbohydrates are made up of carbon, hydrogen, and oxygen, and are essential to the human diet.

Physics

Physics includes many topics that have been standard for years: *light, heat, mechanics, sound, electricity, magnetism*. Some of these topics have subdivisions. For example, mechanics includes the study of motion, forces, and statics (objects at rest). *Thermodynamics* deals with relations of heat and energy. Today, the study of the actions of particles within the nucleus of an atom has become especially important.

Measuring Force   A *force* is a ''push'' or a ''pull.'' If you hold a 5-pound bag of sugar in your hand, you are exerting a 5-pound force (a pull) on the bag to keep it from falling. In Physics, it is possible to draw this effort symbolically—but not by showing a hand with a bag of sugar! Instead, you draw a diagram of two things: (1) the amount of pull; and (2) the direction of the pull.

To represent the amount of pull, make up a *scale* for one unit of the pull (in this case, one pound). Then draw five connected units (for the five pounds) in the direction of the pull (toward the bottom of the paper, representing the ground). When we deal with both the *magnitude* (size) of the pull and its *direction*, we are working with a *vector quantity*.

Sometimes, two or more forces work on an object. These are called *concurrent forces*. Scientists are interested in finding the combined effect (the *resultant*) of these forces. There are several ways to do this:

1. If both forces are exerted in exactly the same direction, add the forces. For example, if a ''3-*newton*'' force and a ''4-*newton*'' force act on an object in the same direction, their resultant is 7 newtons. A newton (N) is a unit of measure in Physics.

2. If the two forces act in opposite directions (at an angle of 180 degrees), subtract them. With a 3-newton force and a 4-newton force pulling in opposite directions, the resultant is a 1-newton force, exerted in the direction of the larger force (the 4-newton force).

3. If the two forces are pulling at an angle to one another, the solution requires a few steps. Suppose that a 3-newton force and a 4-newton force with a 60-degree angle between them are acting on an object: What is their resultant?

   (a) Select a scale for one unit of the force. (Let ¼ inch equal 1 newton.)

   (b) Draw the vector *AB* for the 3-newton force (¾ inch).

   (c) Using the same scale, draw the vector *AC* for the 4-newton force (1 inch). Start it from the same point as the first vector. Keep an angle of 60 degrees between both vectors.

   (d) Using *AB* and *AC* as the first two sides, draw the parallelogram *ACDB*.

   (e) Draw the diagonal *AD* and lay off ¼-inch units on it. In this example, the diagonal will be a little more than 6 of these units. Since each unit equals 1 newton, we can estimate that the resultant for a 3-newton force and a 4-newton force at a 60-degree angle to each other is about 6.1 newtons.

Sometimes the direction of a vector is given in terms of "north," "south," "east," or "west." In other examples, the direction of one vector is given by relating it to another vector (for example, "85 degrees apart"). If you find two vectors forming a right angle (90 degrees), you can treat the example as one involving a right triangle, and solve it by using the Pythagorean Theorem *(see the section on Mathematics in this General Review)*. In such a case, the resultant you are looking for would be the hypotenuse of the right triangle.

If two equal and opposite parallel forces are applied to an object, their resultant force is zero. (Try pressing one hand against an open door while you press the other hand against the opposite side of the door. So long as you exert an equal force through both hands, the door won't move.)

If an object can rotate, we call the force that produces this rotation the *torque,* or the *moment of a force.* The magnitude of the moment of a force is equal to the product of the force and what is called the *length of the moment arm.* The length of the moment arm is the perpendicular distance from the *fulcrum* to the direction of the force. A fulcrum is a stationary point about which an object rotates. For example, the earth's axis is its fulcrum. A hinge is the fulcrum for a door.

Speed and Velocity *Speed* is the distance covered per unit of time. Speed is a *scalar quantity*—it describes magnitude only, e.g., miles per hour. The *velocity* (v) of an object is its speed in a given direction. Thus velocity is a vector quantity—it has magnitude and direction. Velocity changes if either the speed, or the direction of motion, or both, change.

Sometimes we can think of the motion of an object as a *combination of velocities.* For example, if you walk 4 miles per hour from the last car of the train toward the front while the train is going 60 miles per hour, your velocity is 64 miles per hour in the direction of the train's motion.

Uniform motion is motion in which the velocity is constant. If the velocity changes, the motion is said to be accelerated. *Acceleration* (a) is the rate of change of velocity. Acceleration is a vector quantity. The formula for finding acceleration is

$$\text{acceleration} = \frac{\text{change in velocity}}{\text{time required for change}}$$

An example of how acceleration is expressed would be "four feet per second per second," which can be written as 4 ft/sec^2.

Uniformly accelerated motion is motion with constant acceleration. If an object is allowed to *fall freely* near the surface of the earth (to fall with its initial velocity at zero and with no forces other than gravity acting on it), the acceleration of the object remains constant and is independent of the mass of the object. The letter g is used universally for this acceleration. Usually, $g = 32$ ft/sec^2.

For all types of motion, the general formula is

$$\text{average speed} = \frac{\text{distance covered}}{\text{time required}}$$

Newton's Laws   *Newton's first law of motion.* This law states that if the net force acting on an object is zero, the velocity of the object does not change—that is, its speed and direction of motion remain constant. The term *net force* means the same as resultant force. This law can be stated in other ways: When a body is at rest, or moving with constant speed in a straight line, the resultant of all the forces acting on the body is zero.

An object at rest tends to remain at rest. An object in motion tends to remain in motion unless acted on by an unbalanced force. For example, passengers in a car lurch forward when the driver suddenly applies the brakes.

Newton's second law (F = ma). According to this law, if the net force acting on an object is not zero, the object will be accelerated in the direction of the force. Its acceleration will be proportional to the net force and inversely proportional to the mass of the object. For example, a push that is enough to give a 3,000-pound car an acceleration of 4 ft/sec^2 will be able to give a 6,000-pound van an acceleration of 2 ft/sec^2.

Think of net force as being used to overcome the *inertia* of an object. The greater the *mass* of an object, the greater the force needed to produce a given acceleration. (Mass is the measure of an object's inertia. Inertia is the property by which an object resists being accelerated.)

Newton's third law. This law states that when one object exerts a force on a second object, the second object exerts an equal and opposite force on the first object. (This is sometimes stated: Action equals reaction.) This law is the principle underlying the operation of rockets and jet aircraft. As the hot gases are pushed out from the rear, they exert a forward push on the object from which they escape.

When an object moves with constant speed around a circle, the object's velocity is constantly changing, because its direction is constantly changing. Because the velocity is changing, the object is accelerated. This acceleration is produced by the *centripetal force*— the force which keeps an object moving around a circle in a circular path.

Newton's law of universal gravitation. According to this law, two objects attract each other with a force that is proportional to the product of their masses and inversely proportional to the square of the distance between them. The earth's attraction for objects is known as *gravity.* Gravity accounts for the *weight* of an object on earth—the earth's pull on an object. It is an attracting (force) that acts on every part of an object—a tree, for example. The attraction of the earth for a tree is actually a set of parallel forces. The resultant goes through a point in the tree known as its *center of gravity.* (We can increase the *stability* of objects by building them with a low center of gravity and with as big a base as possible.)

Work   In Physics we talk about *work* done on an object, or work done by an object or by a force. When a force moves an object, the force does work on the object. If a 20-pound force is used to pull an object 3 feet along a flat surface, we say 60 foot-pounds of work was done on the object. Thus, work is equal to the product of the force (in this case, a 20-pound force) and the distance the object moves in the direction of the force (in this case, 3 feet). The *units of work* obtained by multiplying a unit of force by a unit of distance may be expressed in terms of the *foot-pound* (ft-lb), the *joule (newton-meter),* or the *erg.*

Energy   In elementary physics, *energy* is defined as the ability to do work. *Potential energy* is defined as the energy possessed by an object because of its position or condition (for example, a ripe apple at the end of a tree branch). *Kinetic energy* is the energy possessed by an object in motion (for example, a bicycle in motion). When an object does work, it has less energy left after the work. In mechanics, work is done on an object for various reasons:

1. to give it potential energy;
2. to give it kinetic energy;
3. to overcome *friction* (friction is a force which always opposes motion or a tendency to motion);
4. to accomplish a combination of the three reasons just given.

Principle of *conservation of energy.* Energy cannot be created or destroyed but may be changed from one form into another. As a consequence of Einstein's theory of relativity, mass can be considered a form of energy. When mass is converted to forms of energy such as heat, the following formula applies (*m* is the mass converted, and *c* is the speed of light):

$$\text{energy produced} = mc^2$$

Units of energy are the same as units of work. When *m* is expressed in grams and *c* is expressed in meters per second (3×10^{10} cm/sec) the energy will be expressed in ergs. When *m* is expressed in kilograms and *c* is expressed in meters per second (3×10^8 m/sec), the energy is expressed in joules.

Power is the rate of doing work. Since work is calculated by multiplying the force by the distance that the force moves, we have the following formula:

$$\text{power} = \frac{\text{force} \times \text{distance}}{\text{time}}$$

Units of power are expressed as *foot-pounds per second, horsepower* (hp), or *watts:*

$$1 \text{ hp} = 550 \text{ ft-lb/sec}$$
$$1 \text{ hp} = 746 \text{ watts}$$
$$1 \text{ watt} = 1 \text{ joule/sec}$$

Simple Machines   Probably the most direct way of doing useful work on an object is to take hold of it and lift or move it. When this is difficult, we turn to *machines* to help us. A machine is the device which will transfer a force from one point of application to another for some practical advantage. There are six simple machines: *lever, pulley, wheel and axle, inclined plane, screw,* and *wedge.* The force which we apply to a machine in order to do the work is known as the *effort* (F_E). The force which we have to overcome is known as the *resistance,* (F_R).

1. A lever is a rigid bar that is free to turn about a fixed point known as the *fulcrum* or *pivot.* Crowbars, bottle openers, and oars on a boat are examples of levers. So is a see-saw.

    What is the principle on which a lever operates? When a lever is perfectly balanced on its fulcrum, the force (effort) on one arm matches the force on the other. If a box (or other form of load) is placed on one end of such a lever, but not the other, the balance is upset. To restore the balance (actually, to lift the load) we exert a compensating force on the end without the box (the effort arm). To calculate this compensating force, we determine the length of each arm from the fulcrum to the end, and apply this equation:

$$\text{effort} \times \text{effort arm} = \text{load} \times \text{load arm}$$

Example: Assume that a lever 10 feet long has a carton (load) weighing 35 pounds on one end (the load arm). If the fulcrum is 3 feet from the end of the load arm, how much effort is needed on the effort arm to raise the carton?

$$E \times EA = L \times LA$$
$$E \times 7 = 35 \times 3$$
$$7E = 105$$
$$E = 15 \text{ pounds of effort}$$

2. A pulley is useful for lifting heavy objects a considerable distance. It consists of a wheel mounted in a frame in such a way that the wheel can turn readily on its axis. The wheel rim is usually grooved, to guide the rope (or wire, or string) used with it.
3. In a wheel and axle, the wheel is rigidly attached to an axle which turns with it. Applications of the wheel-and-axle machine include the steering wheel of an automobile and a doorknob.
4. When heavy objects have to be raised to a platform or put into a truck, it is often convenient to slide these objects up along a board. The board in this case is an inclined plane—a flat surface, one end of which is kept higher than the other. The effort to pull or push the object "up" along the plane is usually applied parallel to the plane.
5. A screw may be defined as a cylinder around which an inclined plane (a "thread") winds in spiral fashion. A screw can be used to connect one object to another.
6. A wedge may be thought of as a double inclined plane. It is used in devices like an axe to split wood. It is easy to use when its length is large compared to its thickness.

Fluid Pressure and the Atmosphere

The term *fluid* refers to both gases and liquids. A liquid has definite volume, but takes the shape of its container, with its top surface tending to be horizontal. (A gas has neither definite shape nor volume, and expands to fill any container into which it is put.)

Fluids push against the container in which they are placed. *Pressure* (p) is the force per unit area. Liquid pressure is independent of the size or shape of the container. It depends only on the depth (or "height," h) and the *density* (d) of the liquid. (The density of a substance is the mass per unit volume.) Thus the formula for finding water pressure in a container is

$$p = hd$$

There are several principles that derive from the nature of water pressure:

1. *Pascal's principle* states two ideas about pressure applied to a confined fluid (a fluid enclosed on all sides): (a) such pressure is transferred throughout the liquid without any loss; and (b) this pressure acts perpendicularly on all the surfaces of the liquid's container, regardless of their size.

    Imagine a water-filled, U-shaped container, one of whose arms is wider than the other. Each arm of the "U" is sealed by a *piston*. (A piston is a cylinder that slides inside another cylinder—something like a cork that moves easily in and out of the neck of a bottle.) If you exert a small force against the piston in the smaller arm of the "U," the resulting pressure travels through the water in both arms and acts on the underside of the larger piston. The resulting force in this second piston is then larger than the force applied to the first one.

2. *Archimedes' principle* states that the apparent loss in weight of an object immersed in a fluid equals the weight of the displaced fluid. For example, an object weighing 50 grams is placed in water, where it weighs 30 grams. Since the apparent loss of weight is 20 grams, we know that the weight of the displaced water is 20 grams.

3. *Bernoulli's principle* states that if the speed of a fluid is increased, its pressure is decreased. This principle is made use of in the design of airplane wings to give the plane "lift." The wing is designed so that the air will move faster over the top of the wing than across the bottom. As a result, the pressure of the air on the top of the wing is less than on the bottom. This makes the upward push on the wing greater than the downward push, and keeps the plane aloft.

Heat Energy   One way of defining *temperature* is to say it is the degree of hotness or coldness of an object. If we think of *kinetic energy,* however, we get a different definition.

The molecules of a substance are in constant random motion. If we heat a gas, its molecules move faster—that is, when the temperature of a gas goes up, the average speed of its molecules increases. When the speed of the motion of a molecule increases, its kinetic energy increases, too. This leads to thinking of temperature as a measure of the average kinetic energy per molecule of a substance. Thus, a substance has *internal energy* as a result of its kinetic energy.

When a "hot" substance is brought into contact with a "cold" substance, the hot piece gets colder and the cold piece gets hotter. Thus we define *heat* as the form of energy which flows between two substances because they are at different temperatures.

Expansion and Contraction   When heated, most solids, liquids, and gases *expand* (increase in volume); when cooled, most solids, liquids, and gases *contract* (decrease in volume). Solids differ among themselves in their degree of expansion. For example, brass expands more than iron. And different liquids expand by different amounts when subjected to the same temperature change. Gases are more uniform in their expansion and contraction.

Water behaves peculiarly in this respect. As water is cooled from 100° C, it contracts until the temperature reaches 4° C. If it is cooled further the water will expand—until it freezes at 0° C. Thus, water is densest at 4° C.

Heat Engines   *Heat engines* are used to convert heat to *mechanical energy.* Examples of heat engines include the *gasoline engine, diesel engine, steam engine,* and the *steam turbine.* In these engines, hot gases are allowed to expand; as they expand they do work.

If the fuel is burned inside the cylinder of the engine itself, the engine is known as an *internal combustion engine.* The gasoline engine and the diesel engines are internal combustion engines. If the fuel is burned in a separate chamber outside the engine proper, the engine is known as an *external combustion engine.* Steam engines and steam turbines are examples of external combustion engines. In these, the fuel—which may be coal—is burned in a separate furnace and is used to heat water in a boiler. Steam from this process is then directed into the engine.

Methods of Heat Transfer   The three methods of heat transfer are *conduction, convection,* and *radiation.* Heat conduction is the process of transferring heat by the flow of "free" electrons through a medium. (Conduction also involves the bombardment of cool molecules by heated molecules.) For example, if we heat one end of a copper rod, the other end gets hot, too. Metals are good conductors of heat (and also good conductors of electricity). Silver is the best. Copper and aluminum are also very good. Liquids, gases, and nonmetallic solids are poor conductors of heat. Poor conductors are known as *insulators.*

Heat convection is the process of transferring heat in a fluid, which involves the motion of the heated portion toward the cooler portion of the fluid. The heated portion expands, rises, and is replaced by cooler fluid, thus giving rise to so-called *convection currents*. Radiators heat rooms chiefly by convection.

Heat radiation is a process of transferring heat by a *wave motion* similar to light. Radiation can occur through space and through a material medium. The higher the temperature of an object, the greater the amount of heat it radiates.

The *vacuum bottle (thermos bottle)* is designed with the three methods of heat transfer in mind. The bottle is made of glass—a good insulator. The stopper is made of cork or plastic—also good insulators. The space between the walls is evacuated, minimizing heat transfer by conduction or convection. And the inside surfaces (facing the vacuum) are shiny, reflecting radiation that might come from either side. This minimizes heat transfer by radiation.

Energy Sources

For heating buildings and operating machines, humans have depended almost solely on *fossil fuels* such as coal and oil. *Waterfalls* can be used in the regions where they are located. (Waterfalls and fossil fuels ultimately owe their energy to the sun.) In some parts of the earth, huge *solar reflectors* trap the sun's radiant energy. The constant motion of the *tides* might also be a source of energy.

Some people think the hope of the future lies in *nuclear energy*—energy that is released when certain changes take place in the nucleus of an atom. We have already learned to obtain nuclear energy resulting from the splitting or *fission* of the nuclei of heavy elements such as uranium. Only small quantities of such fissionable materials are available. Nuclear energy can also be obtained by the combining or *fusion* of the nuclei of light atoms, such as hydrogen. If this can be done in a controllable manner, a practically endless supply of energy will be available, because *hydrogen*, the necessary "fuel," is obtainable from the oceans in almost unlimited quantity.

Wave Motion and Sound

Wave motion in a medium is a method of transferring energy through a medium by means of a *distortion* (disturbance) of the medium; the distortion travels away from the place where it was produced. The medium itself moves only a little bit. For example, a pebble dropped into still water disturbs it. The water near the pebble does not move far, but the disturbance travels away from that spot. Energy lost by the pebble is carried by the wave, so that if there is a cork floating on the water in the path of the wave, the cork will be lifted by the wave. The cork gets some of the energy that the pebble lost. We can set up a succession of waves in the water by pushing a finger rhythmically through the surface of the water. Similarly, a vibrating tuning fork produces waves in air.

Two basic waves are the *longitudinal wave* and the *transverse wave*. A longitudinal wave is a wave in which the particles of the medium vibrate in the same direction as the path which the wave travels. The waves produced by a tuning fork are examples of a longitudinal wave; so are sound waves. A transverse wave is a wave in which the vibrations of the medium are at right angles to the direction in which the wave is traveling. A water wave is approximately transverse.

There are several important measurements related to wave motion. A *wavelength* can be measured as the distance between any two successive peaks of the wave. As we watch a wave moving past a given spot of the medium, we see peak after peak of the wave. The time required for two successive waves to pass a spot is known as the *period* of the wave. The *frequency* of the wave is the number of complete waves (periods) per second. Out of all these measurements comes a key equation:

$$\text{speed of wave} = \text{frequency of wave} \times \text{wavelength}$$

Sound   In physics, when we speak about *sound*, we usually mean the *sound wave*. Sound waves are longitudinal waves in gases, liquids, or solids. Sound cannot be transmitted through a vacuum. If a sound wave begins in the air and then hits a solid, the frequency of the wave will be the same in the new medium (the solid) as in the air, but the new speed—and therefore the new wavelength—will be different. The *speed of sound* in air is approximately 1090 ft/sec or 331 meters/sec at 0° C. In general, sound travels faster in liquids and solids than in air.

Musical Sounds   Sounds produced by regular vibration of the air are said to be *musical*. (Irregular vibrations of the air are classified as unpleasant sounds, or *"noise."*) The *range of frequencies* in musical sounds is 20 to 20,000 cycles per second (**Hertz**). Longitudinal waves that are higher than those which people can hear are called *ultrasonic* frequencies. (Ultrasonic frequencies are used in *sonar* for such purposes as submarine detection.) The term *supersonic* refers to speed greater than the speed of sound. *Mach* 1 means a speed equal to that of sound; *Mach* 2 is twice the speed of sound; etc. Some airplanes travel at supersonic speed.

   Musical sounds have three basic characteristics: *pitch*, *loudness*, and *quality* (timbre). Pitch refers to frequency: the higher the frequency of a sound wave, the higher the pitch. Loudness depends on the amplitude of the wave reaching the ear. The quality of sound depends on the number of different overtones reaching the ear at the same moment.

   When a sound wave reaches another medium, part of the wave is usually reflected. Where there is reflected sound, a distinct *echo* is heard if the reflected sound reaches the ear at least $\frac{1}{10}$ second after the sound traveling directly from the vibrating source to the ear. The *"Doppler effect"* refers to the way we perceive pitch when the source of a sound is traveling toward or away from us. (This is something a jogger might notice as a car approaches on an otherwise empty road.) As the source of the sound approaches us, the pitch we hear grows higher than the actual frequency produced by the source of the sound. As the source of the sound moves away, the pitch appears to get lower than it actually is.

Light and Illumination   In many ways, *light* coming from the sun behaves like a wave. How can we explain a wave traveling through a vacuum? Electric fields and magnetic fields can exist in a vacuum. Light is considered to be one type of *electromagnetic wave*, along with X-rays and radio waves. The wavelength of light is rather short—about 5×10^{-5} cm. The exact wavelength depends on the color of the light. (The *quantum theory of light*, however, says that light is emitted and absorbed in little lumps or bundles of energy called *photons*.)

   Illumination. A *luminous body* is one that emits light of its own (for example, the sun). An *incandescent object* is one that emits light because it has been heated (for example, the filament in our electric light bulb). An *illuminated object* is one that is visible by the light that it reflects (for example, the moon).

Reflection   In discussing illumination, the term *ray* is used to represent the direction in which the light is traveling. (Light is considered to travel in a straight line.) When light hits a surface, some of it is reflected. We call the light that travels toward the surface the *incident light*, and the light that is reflected the *reflected light*. The angle of the incident light equals the angle of the reflected light. When parallel light rays strike a smooth surface, they are reflected as parallel rays.

   In a *plane mirror* (a perfectly flat mirror), a ray of light striking the mirror is reflected without being changed. In a *convex mirror* (one in which the center bulges outward), the light rays are spread apart by reflection and the reflected image seems smaller than the object. In a *concave mirror* (one in which the center "caves" in), the light rays are focused by reflection and—at a close distance—the reflected image seems larger than the object.

Refraction   *Refraction* is the bending of a wave as it passes from one medium into another. Refraction occurs because of the different speeds at which the wave travels through the two media. The medium in which a light wave travels more slowly is known as the optically denser medium. The medium in which light travels faster is known as the optically rarer medium. Light travels faster in air than in liquids and solids. Light travels faster in water than in glass. A ray of light passing obliquely into a denser medium is bent toward the *"normal"* (that is, toward a perpendicular with the surface of the medium). A ray of light entering a rarer medium obliquely is bent away from the normal.

Lenses   A *lens* is a device shaped to *converge* (focus) or *diverge* (spread) a beam of light through it. Lenses are fashioned to be thin, spherical, transparent, and are usually glass. A *convex lens* is thicker at the middle than at the edge; it is a converging lens. A *concave* lens is thinner in the middle than at the edge; it is a diverging lens. Convex lenses form images similar to concave mirrors; concave lenses form images similar to convex mirrors. There is another important difference. Lenses let light through and refract it; mirrors reflect light.

Optical Instruments   The *camera* and the eye have many points of similarity. The camera has a *shutter* to admit the light, corresponding to the eyelid. Light goes through a camera's *convex lens* to the sensitive *film*. In the eye, light goes through the pupil and lens, falling on the retina where the image is formed. The image on both the film and the retina is real, reduced in size, and inverted.

The *astronomical telescope* is used by scientists who want to see very distant objects invisible to the naked eye. The *microscope* is used for examining small things close at hand. Both the microscope and the astronomical telescope employ a *magnifying eyepiece*. A *projector* is used to throw an enlarged picture on a screen.

Color and Light   If light goes through a (three-dimensional) glass *prism*, the emerging rays are bent away considerably from its original direction. If we use so-called *white light* (such as from an incandescent tungsten filament bulb), the light is dispersed (broken) into its component colors. The order of colors, from the one bent the least to the one bent the most is: red, orange, yellow, green, blue, indigo, violet. We call this array of colors the *spectrum of visible light*. *Infrared light* has a greater wavelength than red; *ultraviolet light* has a shorter wavelength than violet. Both of these are invisible to the human eye.

The color of an opaque object is determined by the color of the light that it reflects. A red object, for example, reflects mostly red; it absorbs the rest. If an object reflects no light it is said to be black. If an object reflects all the light it is said to be white.

Electricity   Nearly all the *mass* of an *atom* is concentrated in the *nucleus*, which ordinarily contains *protons* and (except in the case of the hydrogen atom) *neutrons*. The atom's *electrons* form "shells" around the nucleus. A proton has a positive charge equal to the negative charge of an electron, but its mass is approximately 1,836 times as much as the mass of the electron. A neutron is electrically neutral; its mass is slightly greater than that of the proton. An *ion* is a charged atom or group of atoms.

"Charging" an object usually results in a gain or loss of electrons. In a solid, the positive charges do not move readily. A gain of electrons results in making an object more negative; a loss of electrons results in making it more positive. A neutral object usually acquires the same kind of *charge* as that of the charged object it touches.

An *electric field* is said to exist wherever an electric force acts on an electric charge. If a positive charge is released in an electric field, the positive charge will move in the direction of the electric field. A negative charge released in an electric field will move in the direction opposite to that of the field. The *potential difference* between two points in an electric field is the work-per-unit charge required to move a charge between the points. The unit of potential difference is the *volt*. The common flashlight cell supplies 1½ volts. A home outlet supplies 115 volts.

Electric Current   *Current* is the rate of flow of electric charge. Generally, we speak of *direct current* (DC) and *alternating current* (AC).

Direct current is a flow of current in one direction at a constant rate. To create a *circuit* for such flow, batteries, dynamos, and generators have two terminals—one, positive; the other, negative. The positive terminal has a deficiency of electrons; the negative terminal has an excess of electrons. Work had to be done to push electrons onto the negative terminal against the repulsion of electrons already there. (According to *Couloumb's law*, particles with the same charge repel one another; unlike particles are attracted to one another.) In this case, the potential difference is the work-per-unit charge that was done to get the terminals charged. This charge is now potentially available for doing work outside the battery (for example, operating a desk lamp).

Resistance of a device is its opposition to the flow of electric charges. Electric energy is converted to heat because of this opposition. *Conductance* is the reciprocal of resistance. The higher the conductance of a device (as with something made of copper or silver), the lower the resistance. According to *Ohm's law*, the current in a circuit is directly proportional to the potential difference that is applied to the circuit and inversely proportional to the resistance of the circuit.

As its name suggests, *alternating current* is a current that goes through a cycle: (a) it increases from zero to a certain maximum in one direction; (b) it decreases to zero; (c) it increases to a maximum in the opposite direction; (d) it decreases to zero. The number of repetitions of this cycle per second is the frequency of the current; in the United States this frequency is 60 cycles per second. *AC* current can do some things better than *DC* current. It can be transmitted more easily over long distances, and its voltage can be changed more easily. Only *DC* current can be used for charging batteries, for electroplating, and for operating some electronic circuits.

In today's computer age, *semiconductors* have become very important. A semiconductor is a material whose conductivity is very small by comparison with conductors like copper, but greater than that of insulators like glass. Common semiconductors are germanium and silicon. In practice a small precise amount of an impurity is added to the pure semiconductor, to give it desired characteristics (for example, the ability to control precisely the flow of electrons).

Magnets   A *magnet* attracts iron and steel. A *magnetic substance* is one that can be attracted by a magnet. Magnetic materials include iron and alloys of iron. Examples of nonmagnetic substances are glass and wood. A *magnetized substance* is a magnetic substance which has been made into a magnet. A *magnetic pole* is the region of a magnet where its strength is concentrated. Every magnet has at least two poles, North and South. The *North pole* (N-pole) of a suspended magnet points toward the earth's magnetic pole in the northern hemisphere. (Magnetic poles do not coincide with the earth's geographic poles.) The *law of magnets* states that like poles repel; unlike poles attract. The *magnetic field* is the region around the magnet where its influence can be detected as a force on another substance. The direction of the field at any point is the direction in which the N-pole of a *compass* would point. A magnetic field can be used to produce an electric current.

Chemical Energy   Another important source of electric energy is *chemical energy*. A *voltaic cell* converts chemical energy into electrical energy. It consists of two dissimilar *electrodes* immersed in an *electrolyte* which acts on at least one of them. An electrolyte may be a liquid which conducts electricity by the motion of ions (such as would occur in a solution of salt in water). The electrodes are conductors. The electrode which is positively charged is called the *anode*. The electrode which is negatively charged is called the *cathode*.

A *primary cell* is a voltaic cell whose electrodes are consumed in an irreversible way when the cell is used. The *dry cell* used in a flashlight is a primary cell. A *secondary cell* is a voltaic cell whose electrodes can be used over and over again, with periodic recharging. The automobile battery is an example of a secondary cell.

Tips for Studying

The material in this section is a review of basic terms and problem-solving methods taught in high school mathematics courses. You will find samples of math problems most often asked on the ASVAB exam, with an explanation of how to solve each. (You may find that you know one or several other ways for working out a problem.) Before you study the topics in this section, look over the following suggestions for how to do good work in mathematics.

A. Develop the habit of careful reading. As you read a problem, look for answers to these questions:
1. What is given? (the facts in the problem)
2. What is unknown? (the answer to be found)
3. What do I use? (the best method or steps for solving the problem)

B. Pay careful attention to each word, number, and symbol. In mathematics, directions and problems are compressed into very few words. Sometimes, the principal direction is expressed as a symbol.

Example: What is the value of $6 - 3$? (The minus sign tells you to subtract.)

C. The reading of mathematics also requires close attention to relationships. How does one fact or idea lead to another? Which facts or ideas are connected? Take the following example:

> Mr. Brown and his partner worked for 5 hours on Monday. For his wages, Mr. Brown received $10 an hour. How much did he earn on Monday?

To solve this problem, you can ignore the day of the week and the fact that there was a partner present. Just multiply the number of hours Mr. Brown worked (5) by the amount he received each hour ($10).

$$5 \times \$10 = \$50 \text{ (Mr. Brown's earnings)}$$

Laws and Operations

The numbers 5 and 10 are *whole numbers*. So are 0, 1, 2, 3, 4, and so on. (By contrast, ¾ is a fraction, and 6¾ is a mixed number—a whole number plus a fraction.) In mathematics, when we combine two or more whole numbers, we perform an *operation* on them. There are two such basic operations: *addition* and *multiplication*. In addition, we combine individual numbers ($23 + 4$) to find an answer called the *sum*. In multiplication, we combine groups of numbers for an answer called the *product*. For example, three times four (3×4) means three groups of four; their product is 12.

Subtraction and *division* are really *opposite*, or *inverse*, *operations* of addition and multiplication. Subtraction is performed to undo addition, and division must be performed to undo multiplication. The answer in subtraction is called the *remainder;* in division, it is called the *quotient*. Consider these examples.

BASIC OPERATIONS
Addition
$23 + 4 = 27$ (sum)
Multiplication
$4 \times 3 = 12$ (product)

INVERSE OPERATIONS
Subtraction
$27 - 4 = 23$ (remainder)
Division
$12 \div 4 = 3$ (quotient)

Sometimes, parentheses are used in a math problem to indicate which operation must be done first. For example, in the problem $3 + (5 \times 2)$, you would first multiply 5×2, then add 3. Look at the different results you get when you work without the parentheses, and then with them.

$$
\begin{array}{ll}
3 + 5 \times 2 = & 3 + (5 \times 2) = \\
8 \times 2 = 16 & 3 + 10 \quad = 13
\end{array}
$$

Even though we read a problem from left to right, there is an order in which we must perform arithmetic operations:

1. First, do all work within parentheses.
2. Next, do all multiplications and divisions. Do these in left-to-right order.
3. Finally, do additions and subtractions.

In the following example, notice the order in which arithmetic operations are carried out.

$$
\begin{array}{lll}
(10 - 6) \times 5 - (15 \div 5) = & \text{(first do operations inside the parentheses)} \\
4 \times 5 - \quad\quad 3 = & \text{(next do multiplication)} \\
20 - \quad\quad 3 = 17 & \text{(then do subtraction)}
\end{array}
$$

Occasionally, you are asked to *round off* answers to the nearest ten, hundred, or thousand, etc. We do this in everyday speech when we say that a pair of shoes priced at $37.50 cost "about $40." There is a rule for rounding off numbers. First, look at these labels and the way that the number 195,426,874 is written below them.

millions thousands hundreds

1 9 5, 4 2 6,   8 7 4

If you are asked to round off 195,426,874 to the nearest hundred, you would first find the number in the highest hundreds place (8), and then look at the number to its right (7). If the number to the right is 5, 6, 7, 8, or 9, you round off the hundreds to the next higher number— (9) and replace the 74 with 00. It's the same as saying that 874 is about 900. Your answer would be 195,426,900.

Suppose your original amount was 195,426,834. In that case, when you check the number to the right of 8, you would find 3. Since 3 is below 5, you would leave the 8 and replace the 34 with 00. Your answer would be 195,426,800.

Whole numbers are sometimes classified as either *prime* or *composite numbers*. A prime number is one that can be divided evenly by itself and 1—but not by any other whole number.

Examples: 2, 3, 5, 7, 11, 15

A composite number is one that can be divided evenly by itself, by 1, and by at least one other whole number.

Examples: 4, 6, 8, 10, 15, 27

When a whole number has other divisors besides 1 and itself, we call these other divisors *factors*. In other words, factors are numbers that we multiply to form a composite (whole) number.

Sometimes you will be asked "to factor" a number—for example, 6. The factors of 6 are the numbers that you multiply to produce 6. Since 3 times 2 equals 6, the factors of 6 are 3 and 2.

There is a short way of writing *repeated factors* in multiplication. For example, we may write 5×5 as 5^2. The small 2 written to the right and slightly above the 5 is called an *exponent*. It tells us that 5 is used twice as a factor. You can read 5^2 as either "5 to the second power," or more briefly, "5 squared." Note that 5^2 does not represent "5×2." The expression 2^3 means "2 to the third power," or "2 cubed," and represents $2 \times 2 \times 2$.

Don't confuse these expressions of repeated factors with the term *factorial*. When you see "6 factorial," for example, it means "find the product of every number between 1 and 6." Thus, 6 factorial means $6 \times 5 \times 4 \times 3 \times 2 \times 1$. (The symbol for 6 factorial is 6!)

You may also be asked to find the *reciprocal* of a number. To find the reciprocal of 5, look for the number that you multiply by 5 to get 1. The easiest way to work this out is to divide 1 by 5. You can express the answer either as $\frac{1}{5}$ or as 0.2 (see the following sections on fractions and decimals). Remember that the product of a number and its reciprocal is always 1: the reciprocal of $\frac{1}{4}$ is 4; the reciprocal of $\frac{2}{4}$ is 2.

Finally, there is a popular type of question involving a *series* or *sequence* of numbers. You are given several numbers arranged in a pattern, and are asked to find the number that comes next. The way to solve this is to figure out the pattern. Try the following two examples:

> A.   2, 4, 6, 8, ?
> B.   3, 9, 4, 8, ?

Each number in sequence A is 2 higher than the number to its left. Thus, the missing term is 10. By testing the relationships between numbers in series B, you find the following pattern:

> $3 (+ 6) = 9$ The first step is "add 6."
> $9 (- 5) = 4$ The next step is "subtract 5."
> $4 (+ 4) = 8$ The next step is "add 4."

To continue the pattern, the next step will have to be "subtract 3." Thus, the missing number is 5.

Fractions

Many problems in arithmetic have to do with fractions. (Decimals and percents are other ways of writing fractions.) There are at least four ways to think about fractions.

1. A fraction is a part of a whole. The fraction $\frac{2}{3}$ means that something has been divided into 3 parts, and we are working with 2 of them. The number written above the fraction line (2) is the *numerator*, and the number below it (3) is called the *denominator*.
2. A fraction is the result of a multiplication. The fraction $\frac{3}{4}$ means 3 times $\frac{1}{4}$.
3. A fraction is an expression of division. Thus $\frac{2}{5}$ is the quotient (result) when 2 is divided by 5. This can also be written as $2 \div 5$.
4. A fraction is an expression of a *ratio*. A ratio is a comparison between two quantities. For example, the ratio of 6 inches to 1 foot is $\frac{6}{12}$, since there are 12 inches in a foot.

Using Arithmetic Operations with Fractions

There are special rules and some shortcuts, too, for multiplying, dividing, adding, and subtracting fractions and mixed numbers. (A *mixed number* is one that is made up of a whole number and a fraction—for example, $3\frac{2}{7}$.)

Multiplying Fractions   The general rule for multiplying two or more fractions is to multiply the numerators by one another, and then multiply the denominators by one another.

Example: $\frac{1}{2} \times \frac{3}{4} \times \frac{5}{8} = \frac{15}{64}$ (numerators)

(denominators)

Explanation: $1 \times 3 \times 5 = 15;$ $2 \times 4 \times 8 = 64$

Sometimes, the product you get when you multiply two fractions can be expressed in simpler terms. When you express a fraction in its *lowest terms,* you put it in a form in which the numerator and denominator no longer have a common factor.

Example: Reduce $\frac{24}{36}$ to lowest terms.

Step 1. Find a number which is a factor of both 24 and 36. Both numbers can be divided by 4.

Step 2. Divide 24 and then 36 by 4.

$24 \div 4 = 6$

$36 \div 4 = 9$

Thus, $\frac{24}{36} = \frac{6}{9}$

Step 3. Check again. Is there a number which is a factor of both 6 and 9? Yes, both numbers can be divided by 3. Divide 6 and then 9 by 3.

$6 \div 3 = 2$

$9 \div 3 = 3$

Thus, $\frac{6}{9} = \frac{2}{3}$

Answer: $\frac{24}{36}$ can be reduced to its lowest terms, $\frac{2}{3}$

When the numerator of a fraction is larger than its denominator, it is called an *improper fraction.* An improper fraction can be changed to a mixed number.

Example: Change $\frac{37}{5}$ to a mixed number.

Since a fraction is also an expression of division, $^{37}/_5$ means $37 \div 5$. If 37 is divided by 5, the quotient is 7, and the remainder is 2. Thus

$$\frac{37}{5} = 7\frac{2}{5}$$

Cancellation is a shortcut you can use when multiplying (or dividing) fractions. Suppose you want to multiply $^8/_9$ times $^3/_{16}$. If you immediately multiply the numerators by each other, and the denominators by each other, you get an answer you have to reduce to lowest terms.

$$\frac{8}{9} \times \frac{3}{16} = \frac{24}{144} = \frac{1}{6}$$

An easier way to handle the problem is to see if there is any number you can divide evenly into both a numerator and a denominator of the original example. In this case, there is. You can divide 8 into both itself and 16.

Step 1. $\frac{\overset{1}{8}}{9} \times \frac{3}{\underset{2}{16}} =$

You can also divide 3 into the numerator 3 and the denominator 9. Solve the problem by multiplying the new numerators, and then the new denominators.

Step 2. $\frac{\overset{1}{8}}{\underset{3}{9}} \times \frac{\overset{1}{3}}{\underset{2}{16}} = \frac{1}{6}$

Dividing Fractions Division of fractions looks similar to their multiplication, but there is an important extra step. Suppose you are asked to divide ½ by 3. All division is an effort to undo multiplication. So the question really is, "Where did we get ½?" In the Algebra section of this review, you will find ways to look for a missing number, usually called "x." One such way leads to the following rule.

To divide with fractions (that is, to find how the first term was produced), always *invert* the second term, and change the division sign to a times sign. In other words, write the second term upside down and then treat the problem as a multiplication of fractions. This is also called multiplying the first fraction by the reciprocal of the second fraction.

$$\frac{1}{2} \div 3 \quad = \frac{1}{2} \times \frac{1}{3} \quad = \frac{1}{6}$$

When multiplying or dividing with a mixed number, change the mixed number to an improper fraction before working out the problem.

Example: $2\frac{2}{3} \times \frac{5}{7} =$

$$\frac{8}{3} \times \frac{5}{7} = \frac{40}{21} \quad = 1\frac{19}{21}$$

Adding and Subtracting Fractions To add or subtract fractions, follow two basic rules:

(a) Add or subtract only those fractions which have the same denominator.

(b) Add or subtract only the numerators of the fractions. Keep the same denominator.

If two fractions you want to add or subtract do not have a *common denominator,* find a way to change them so that both denominators are the same. This is easy if one of the denominators divides evenly into the other. To add ⅚ and ¹/₁₂, you can work with the fact that 6 goes into 12 evenly. You can change the ⅚ to ¹⁰/₁₂, a fraction with the same value.

Step 1. Write the fraction you have to change. Next to it, write the new denominator you want to use.

$$\frac{5}{6} = \frac{?}{12}$$

Step 2. To find the missing numerator: (a) divide the original denominator into the new denominator (6 into 12 = 2), then (b) multiply your answer by the original numerator (2 × 5 = 10). Your new fraction is ¹⁰/₁₂. By changing ⅚ to ¹⁰/₁₂, you can now add it to ¹/₁₂.

$$\frac{10}{12} + \frac{1}{12} = \frac{11}{12}$$

If you cannot divide one of the denominators into the other, then you have to find a number that both will go into. If you are working with three fractions, you have to find a number that all three denominators can divide evenly.

Suppose you are asked to add ¼, ⅕, and ⅙. One rule for finding a common denominator for several fractions is to take the largest denominator and start multiplying it by 2, 3, etc., until you find a number that the other denominators will also divide evenly. In this case, 6 is the largest denominator. If you multiply 6 times 2, you get 12—a number that 5 does not divide evenly. You have to keep trying until you reach 60—the first product that all three denominators divide evenly. Thus

$$\frac{1}{4} = \frac{15}{60}$$

$$\frac{1}{5} = \frac{12}{60}$$

$$+ \frac{1}{6} = \frac{10}{60}$$

By adding the converted fractions, you find that $\frac{1}{4} + \frac{1}{5} + \frac{1}{6} = \frac{37}{60}$.
To add mixed numbers, follow these three steps:

Step 1. Add the whole numbers.

Step 2. Add the fractions. If the sum of these is an improper fraction, change the sum to a mixed number.

Step 3. Add the sum of the whole numbers to the sum of the fractions.

Example: $3\frac{2}{3} + 12\frac{2}{3}$.

Step 1. $3 + 12 = 15$

Step 2. $\frac{2}{3} + \frac{2}{3} = \frac{4}{3}\quad = 1\frac{1}{3}$

Step 3. $15 + 1\frac{1}{3} = 16\frac{1}{3}$

In subtracting mixed numbers, you may have to "borrow" as you do in subtracting whole numbers. For example, if you want to subtract $6\frac{3}{4}$ from $9\frac{1}{4}$, you realize you cannot take $\frac{3}{4}$ from $\frac{1}{4}$. (Try to get $.75 out of a quarter!) Thus, you borrow 1 from 9, and rewrite the example.

$$9\frac{1}{4} = 8\frac{4}{4} + \frac{1}{4} = \quad 8\frac{5}{4}$$
$$-\,6\frac{3}{4} = \qquad\qquad\quad -\,6\frac{3}{4}$$
$$\overline{\qquad\qquad\qquad 2\frac{2}{4} = 2\frac{1}{2}}$$

Decimals

Changing Fractions to Decimals   To change a fraction to a decimal, divide the numerator by the denominator. Place a decimal point to the right of the numerator, and add a zero for each decimal place you want in your answer.

Example: $\frac{2}{5} = 5\overline{)2.0}^{\,0.4}$ So $\frac{2}{5} = 0.4$

Here's a short list of common fractions, converted to decimals.

$$\frac{1}{2} = .50 \qquad \frac{1}{3} = .33\frac{1}{3}$$
$$\frac{1}{4} = .25 \qquad \frac{3}{4} = .75$$
$$\frac{1}{5} = .20 \qquad \frac{3}{5} = .60$$
$$\frac{4}{5} = .80 \qquad \frac{1}{8} = .12\frac{1}{2}\ (\text{or }.125)$$

Decimal Fractions   *Decimal fractions* are special fractions whose denominators are always powers of ten. *Powers of ten* are easy to remember. The exponent tells you how many zeros there are in the power of ten. Thus

$$10^1 = 10 \qquad\quad = 10 \times 1$$
$$10^2 = 100 \qquad = 10 \times 10$$
$$10^3 = 1{,}000 \qquad = 10 \times 10 \times 10$$

You can tell the denominator of a decimal fraction by counting the places in the number to the right of its decimal point. When it is written as a fraction, the denominator has the same number of zeros as this number of places. That is, it has the same power of ten. Thus

$$0.7 = \frac{7}{10^1} \text{ or } \frac{7}{10} \qquad \text{(seven tenths)}$$

$$0.07 = \frac{7}{10^2} \text{ or } \frac{7}{100} \qquad \text{(seven hundredths)}$$

$$0.007 = \frac{7}{10^3} \text{ or } \frac{7}{1,000} \qquad \text{(seven thousandths)}$$

$$0.0007 = \frac{7}{10^4} \text{ or } \frac{7}{10,000} \qquad \text{(seven ten-thousandths)}$$

Here's a shortcut for multiplying a decimal by a power of ten. Suppose you want to multiply .16 by 10^3.

Step 1. Count the number of zeros in the power of ten.

$$10^3 = 1,000 \qquad \text{(3 zeros)}$$

Step 2. Move the decimal in .16 to the right. Move it as many places as this number of zeros. Sometimes, you have to add one or more zeros so that you can move the correct number of places.

$$10^3 \times .16 \ = 10^3 \times \ .160 = 160$$

Other examples: $10^2 \times 2.1 \ = 10^2 \times \ 2.10 = 210$
$10^4 \times .43 \ = 10^4 \times .4300 = 4300$

To divide a decimal by a power of ten, count the number of zeros in the power of ten, and move that many places to the left of the decimal.

Examples: $158.7 \div 10^1 = 158.7 \div 10 \ = 15.87$
$.32 \div 10^2 = 00.32 \div 100 = .0032$

Adding and Subtracting Decimals   To add or subtract decimals, line up the numbers so that the decimal points are directly under one another. Then add or subtract as you would with whole numbers. Write zeros at the end of decimals if you find it easier to work with place-holders.

Examples: Add 3.12 + 14.3 + 205.6 + 0.0324, and subtract their sum from 1,000.55. Remember to put the decimal point in the answers.

```
       3.1200              1,000.5500
      14.3000           −     223.0524
     205.6000              777.4976 (remainder)
  +    0.0324
     223.0524 (sum)
```

Multiplying Decimals   Multiply two decimals as though they were whole numbers. Then use these steps to find out where to put the decimal point in your answer.

Step 1. Add the decimal places in both numbers, counting from the decimal point to the right.

Step 2. Count off this same number of places from right to left in the answer.

Step 3. Insert a decimal point where you finish counting off. Add extra zeros, if you need them, to fill out the correct number of places.

Examples: $.02 \times .12 = .0024$
$30 \times 1.5 = 45.0$

Dividing Decimals   To divide a decimal by a whole number, divide the numbers as though they were both whole numbers. Then place a decimal point in the answer directly above the decimal in the problem.

Example: 5.117 ÷ 17

$$\begin{array}{r} 0.301 \\ 17\overline{)5.117} \\ \underline{5\ 1} \\ 17 \\ \underline{17} \end{array}$$

To divide one decimal by another, begin by making the divisor a whole number. Do this by moving the decimal in the divisor all the way to the right. Count the number of places you move it. Then move the decimal in the other number (the dividend) the same number of places.

Example: $\dfrac{1.8}{0.2} = \dfrac{18}{2} = 9$

Percents

A *percent* is a way to express a fraction. It simply means hundredths. To use a percent in solving a problem, change it to a fraction or a decimal.

To change a percent to a fraction, drop the percent sign and multiply by $\frac{1}{100}$.

Examples: 5%   means $5 \times \dfrac{1}{100}$ or $\dfrac{5}{100}$

20%   means $20 \times \dfrac{1}{100}$ or $\dfrac{20}{100}$

100% means $100 \times \dfrac{1}{100}$ or $\dfrac{100}{100}$

To change a percent to a decimal, drop the percent sign and move the decimal point two places to the left. Add extra zeros, if you need them, to fill out the correct number of places. If the percent is given as a fraction, first change the fraction to a decimal.

Examples: 3% = .03   1.2% = .012
           75% = .75   ¼% = .25% = .0025
           15% = .15   100% = 1.00   (or 1)

To change a decimal to a percent, move the decimal point two places to the right and add the percent sign.

Examples: .23 = 23%   .05 = 5%
          .5 = 50%   .66⅔ = 66⅔%

Arithmetic Problems Using Percent   An arithmetic problem using percent usually falls into one of three categories:

 1. Find a number when you are told it is a certain percent of another number. This involves multiplication.

    Example: What is the amount of the discount on a hat marked $49.95 and discounted at 20%?
    Step 1.   Change the rate of discount to a fraction or decimal. 20% = .2
    Step 2.   Multiply the marked price by the rate of discount.
                    $49.95 × .2 = $9.99 (discount)

2. Find what percent one number is of another. This involves division.

Example: A baseball team played 20 games and won 17 of them. What percent of its games did it win?

Step 1.　Express the games won by the team as a part of the total games they played. In other words, state the relationship between the two numbers by writing a fraction (a ratio).

$$\frac{17}{20}$$

Step 2.　Convert this fraction to a percent. Divide the numerator by the denominator. (Add a decimal point and zeros to carry the answer out two places.)

$$\frac{17.00}{20} = 0.85$$

Step 3.　Multiply the quotient by 100 to convert to percent.
0.85 × 100 = 85% (games won)

3. Find a whole number when you know only a part of it and the percent that the part represents. This involves division.

Example: A family pays $5,000 a year in premiums for home insurance. If the rate of insurance is 12½%, how much is the insurance policy worth?

Step 1.　Change the percent to a decimal.
12½% = 0.125 (rate of insurance)

Step 2.　Divide the premium by the rate of insurance.

$$\$5,000 \div 0.125 = 125\overline{)\begin{array}{c}\$40,000 \\ \$5,000,000\end{array}} \\ \underline{5\ 00}$$

The home insurance policy is worth $40,000.

A percent problem you frequently meet has to do with interest earned on a sum of money, the *principal*. A formula for finding interest is: principal (p) × rate of interest (r) × the period of time (t) = interest (i). *Time* is always time in years.

$$i = p \times r \times t$$

Example: How much interest will there be on $5,000 for 6 months at 5%?

Step 1.　Change the rate of interest to a fraction: 5% = ⁵⁄₁₀₀ (or ¹⁄₂₀)

Step 2.　Express the time in terms of years. There are 12 months in a year, so 6 months is ⁶⁄₁₂, or ½, of a year.

Step 3.　Apply the formula for finding interest.

$$i = p \times r \times t$$

$$i = \frac{\$5,000}{1} \times \frac{1}{20} \times \frac{1}{2}$$

$$i = \frac{\overset{\$2,500}{\cancel{\$5,000}}}{1} \times \frac{1}{20} \times \frac{1}{\underset{1}{\cancel{2}}}$$

$$i = \frac{\overset{\$125}{\overset{\cancel{\$2,500}}{\cancel{\$5,000}}}}{1} \times \frac{1}{\underset{1}{\cancel{20}}} \times \frac{1}{\underset{1}{\cancel{2}}} = \$125$$

The interest on $5,000 for 6 months will be $125.

Algebra

Algebra is a way to reduce a problem to a small set of symbols. When we can state a problem with a few symbols, letters, and numbers, it seems easier to solve. The solution we are looking for is often an *"unknown"* quantity, and we speak of "finding the unknowns."

Take an example. We know that if a sweater is priced at $20, we have to pay $20 to buy one. If we want three sweaters, we pay three times that amount, or $60. How do we find the answer, $60? We multiply two numbers to find a third number. Using the style of algebra, we can express this operation briefly. Let p equal the price of one sweater, and let c (the "unknown") equal the cost of three sweaters. Here's an algebraic expression for how we find c.

$$c = 3 \times p \quad \text{(or)} \quad c = 3p$$

In this expression, the letters c and p are called *literal numbers*, meaning they are letters that stand for numbers. Another word for such letters is *variables*, meaning that the numbers they stand for can change. (If the price of the sweater is discounted to $18, then p will equal $18, and c will equal $54.)

Arithmetic Operations in Algebra
All four arithmetic operations are possible in algebra: both basic operations (addition and multiplication), and inverse operations (subtraction and division). We can express these operations algebraically:

1. The sum of two numbers x and y, is
$$x + y$$
2. The difference between two numbers, x and y, is
$$x - y$$
3. The product of two numbers, x and y, is
$$(x) \times (y) \quad \text{(or)} \quad x \cdot y \quad \text{(or)} \quad xy$$
4. The quotient of two numbers, x and y, is
$$x \div y \quad \text{(or)} \quad \frac{x}{y}$$

Equations
An *equation* is a statement that two quantities are equal. This is clear when the quantities are expressed in numbers. Thus

$$3 + 7 = 10 \qquad 7 \cdot 8 = 56$$
$$5 - 3 = 2 \qquad 18 \div 2 = 9$$

But in algebra, equations always include variables, or unknowns. Usually, you will be asked to "solve the equation" by finding the unknown number value. In this sense, the *solution* to an equation is the number which proves that the equation is true. (You show that it's true by substituting the number for the variable.) But how do you find the number?

Suppose you heard someone say, "I can't afford to buy a car for $8,000. That would leave me with only $5,000 in my bank account." How would we express his (or her) statement in algebra? (Remember, the "unknown" is the unstated amount, x, now in the bank account.) Here's one way of writing the expression:

$$x - \$8,000 = \$5,000$$

How do we solve for x?

Step 1. Think about what the expression now means: A certain number, minus $8,000, equals $5,000.

Step 2. Think of how you want to express the solution:
$$x = \text{(the amount in the bank)}$$

Step 3. Think of how the statement of your solution will differ from the equation you begin with: $8,000 will no longer be on the same side of the equal sign as x.

Step 4. Now think about how to "get rid of" or "clear" the $8,000 from the side that shows x. Notice that the sign with $8,000 is a minus sign. If you add $8,000 to the left side of the equation, the two 8,000s will cancel each other. But remember that in a true equation, everything on the left side of the equal sign must have the same value as everything on the right side. If you add $8,000 to the left, you have to add it to the right. Thus

$$x - \$8,000 = \$5,000$$
$$x - \$8,000 + \$8,000 = \$5,000 + \$8,000$$
$$x = \$13,000 \text{ (amount in bank)}$$

How is the equation solved? By performing an inverse operation on both sides of the equation.

Thus, to solve for x, we go through three steps:

Step 1. We decide to "clear for x" by removing all other operations from the side of the equation where x is found.

Step 2. We remove an operation from one side of the equal sign by performing its inverse (opposite) operation on the same side.

Step 3. We then perform the same operation on the other side of the equal sign. (That is, if we subtract 3 from one side, we subtract 3 from the other side.)

Examples of Using Inverse Operations to Solve Equations

1. The inverse of addition is subtraction.

$$\text{Solve: } x + 7 = 50$$
$$x + 7 - 7 = 50 - 7$$
$$x = 43 \text{ (solution of equation)}$$

2. The inverse of subtraction is addition.

$$\text{Solve: } x - 3 = 4$$
$$x - 3 + 3 = 4 + 3$$
$$x = 7 \text{ (solution)}$$

3. The inverse of multiplication is division.

$$\text{Solve: } 0.05x = 4$$
$$\frac{0.05x}{0.05} = \frac{4}{0.05}$$
$$x = 80 \text{ (solution)}$$

(0.05 ÷ 0.05 = 1. When you divide 4 by 0.05, you have to clear the decimal from the divisor, first. Thus 0.05 becomes 5, and 4 becomes 400.)

4. The inverse of division is multiplication.

$$\text{Solve: } \frac{x}{2} = 7$$
$$2\left(\frac{x}{2}\right) = 7 \times 2$$
$$x = 14 \text{ (solution)}$$

Inverse Operations with More Complex Equations   Sometimes, an equation shows x as part of more than one operation. There may also be negative terms (terms with a minus sign). The same basic steps are involved in finding the solution, but may have to be repeated. Remember, the goal is always to isolate x on one side of the equation.

Example: Solve: $3x + 7 = -11$

Step 1. Perform the inverse operation of $+ 7$.
$$3x + 7 - 7 = -11 - 7$$
$$3x = -18$$

Step 2. Perform the inverse operation of 3x $(3 \cdot x)$.

$$\frac{3x}{3} = \frac{-18}{3}$$
$$x = -6 \text{ (solution)}$$

(Remember that in multiplication and division, if the signs of both terms are plus or minus, the answer is signed by a plus sign. If the two terms are different, the answer is signed by a minus sign.)

Sometimes, x appears on both sides of the original equation. In that case, the first step is to remove x from one side (or, "collect all xs on one side") of the equal sign.

Example: Solve: $-7x = 24 - x$

Step 1. Perform the inverse operation of $- x$.
$$-7x + x = 24 - x + x$$
$$-6x = 24$$

Step 2. Perform the inverse operation of $(- 6) x$.

$$\frac{-6x}{-6} = \frac{24}{-6}$$
$$x = -4 \text{ (solution)}$$

Algebraic Expressions   An *algebraic expression* is any collection of numbers and variables. This collection may have more than one variable. For example, $3x + 4y$ is an algebraic expression meaning "3 times one unknown number (x), plus 4 times another unknown number (y)."

Arithmetic Operations with Algebraic Expressions

1. To add or subtract algebraic expressions, remember that only *similar,* or *"like"* terms can be combined. (Terms are similar if they have the same variable, raised to the same power.) Thus, we can subtract $3x$ from $5x$ to get $2x$, but we cannot get x^3 by adding x and x^2, or get $9zh$ out of $4z$ and $5h$.

    Example: Add: $3x + 2y - 4z + 2x - 5y$.
    $$3x + 2x = 5x \text{ (partial sum)}$$
    $$2y - 5y = -3y \text{ (partial sum)}$$
    Therefore, $5x - 3y - 4z$ is the sum.

2. To multiply algebraic expressions, follow these steps.
    Step 1. Multiply the numbers of similar terms.
    Step 2. Multiply the letters of similar terms. When multiplying one power of x by another power of x, just add the exponents.

    Example: $(2x^2) (3x^5)$
    Step 1. $2 \times 3 = 6$ (partial product)
    Step 2. $x^2 \times x^5 = x^7$ (partial product)
    Thus, the product is $6x^7$

Sometimes, you are asked to multiply more complex algebraic expressions. The rules are basically the same.

Example: In $x^2y(3x - 5y)$, the parentheses tell you that x^2y is the multiplier for both $3x$ and $-5y$.

Step 1. $x^2y \times 3x = 3x^3y$ (partial product)
Step 2. $x^2y \times -5y = -5x^2y^2$ (partial product)
    The product is $3x^3y - 5x^2y^2$

Example: In $(a + 2)(2a - 3)$, think of $(a + 2)$ as a two-place multiplier. An easy way to do this example is to set it up as an ordinary multiplication in arithmetic.

$$\begin{array}{r}
2a - 3 \\
\times\ a + 2 \\
\hline
4a - 6 \\
2a^2 - 3a \\
\hline
2a^2 + a - 6
\end{array}$$

$4a - 6$ Multiply $(2a - 3)$ by 2
$2a^2 - 3a$ Multiply $(2a - 3)$ by a
$2a^2 + a - 6$ Product

3. To divide algebraic expressions, follow these steps:
Step 1. Divide the numbers of similar terms.
Step 2. Divide the letters of similar terms. When dividing one power of x by another power of x, subtract the exponents.

Example: $$x^5 \div x^3 = x^2$$

Example:

$$\frac{8x^3}{4x} = \frac{\overset{2}{\cancel{8}}}{\underset{1}{\cancel{4}}} \times \frac{\overset{x^2}{\cancel{x^3}}}{\underset{1}{\cancel{x}}} = 2 \times x^2 = 2x^2$$

Sometimes, a divisor goes into several terms.

Example: $$\frac{\overset{3x^2}{\cancel{24x^3}} - \overset{1}{\cancel{8x}}}{\underset{1}{\cancel{8x}}} = 3x^2 - 1$$

Evaluating Algebraic Expressions   To evaluate an algebraic expression means to replace the letters with numbers, and then simplify (add, multiply, etc.).

Example: Evaluate the expression $(a + 2b)$ if $a = 3$ and $b = 2$.

$$\begin{aligned}
a &+ 2b \\
&= 3 + 2(2) \\
&= 3 + 4 \\
&= 7
\end{aligned}$$

Factoring in Algebra   Sometimes, you are given the answer to a multiplication example in algebra, and are asked to find the original multipliers. This is called *factoring*.

1. Factor the difference of two squares. In this case, your example contains the square of one number, minus the square of another number. (The **square** of a number is the product you get when you multiply a number by itself. The *square root* of a number is the number that was multiplied by itself to produce the square.)

Example: $x^2 - 9$

Step 1. Find the square root of x^2 and place it to the left, within each of two "empty" parentheses. The square root of x^2 is x.

$$(x \quad) (x \quad)$$

Step 2. Find the square root of 9 and place it to the right, within each of these parentheses. The square root of 9 is 3.

$$(x \quad 3) (x \quad 3)$$

Step 3. Place a plus sign between one pair of terms, and a minus sign between the other pair of terms.

$$(x + 3) (x - 3)$$

The factors of $x^2 - 9$ are $(x + 3)$, $(x - 3)$.

2. Factor a *trinomial*. A trinomial is an algebraic expression that has three—and only three—terms separated by plus or minus signs. Its factors are always two pairs of terms. The terms in each pair are separated by a plus or minus sign.

Example: Factor $x^2 - 11x + 30$.

Step 1. Find the factors of the first term in the trinomial. The factors of x^2 are x and x.

$$(x \quad) (x \quad)$$

Step 2. Look at the last term in the trinomial. It has a plus sign. This means that both factors of the trinomial are either plus or minus. Which one? Since the middle term $(- 11x)$ has a minus sign, both factors must have minus signs.

$$(x - \quad) (x - \quad)$$

Step 3. Find the factors of 30. There are several numbers you can multiply to get 30: 30×1, 10×3, etc. But the two multipliers you use must also combine somehow to give you 11, the middle term. When 5 and 6 are multiplied, they give you 30. When they are added, they give you 11. We know the factors have minus signs. So the factors of 30 are actually $- 6$ and -5.

$$(x - 6) (x - 5)$$

The factors of $(x^2 - 11x + 30)$ are: $(x - 6) (x - 5)$

Solving Quadratic Equations

In a *quadratic equation*, the exponent is never higher than 2 $(x^2, b^2, c^2,$ etc.). Examples of quadratic equations include:

$$x^2 + x - 6 = 0$$
$$3x^2 = 5x - 7$$
$$x^2 - 4 = 0$$
$$64 = x^2$$

How do we solve equations like this? Basically, we factor them, and then set each factor equal to zero. After that, it's easy to solve for x. Let's take it step *by* step.

Example: Solve: $x^2 = 3x + 10$

Step 1. Place all terms on one side of the equal sign, leaving the equation equal to 0. (Remember inverse operations.)

$$x^2 - 3x - 10 = 0$$

Step 2. Factor this equation.

$$(x - 5) (x + 2) = 0$$

Step 3. Set each factor equal to zero, and solve the equations.

$$x - 5 = 0 \qquad x + 2 = 0$$
$$x = + 5 \qquad x = - 2$$

Step 4. To check its accuracy, substitute each answer in the original equation.

$$x^2 = 3x + 10 \qquad\qquad x^2 = 3x + 10$$
$$(5)^2 = 3(5) + 10 \qquad (-2)^2 = 3(-2) + 10$$
$$25 = 15 + 10 \qquad\qquad 4 = -6 + 10$$
$$25 = 25 \text{ (proof)} \qquad\quad 4 = 4 \text{ (proof)}$$

The solution of the quadratic equation is x = 5, − 2.

Inequalities   Not everything in algebra is an equation! An *inequality* is a statement that two quantities are not equal to each other. With an inequality, one of these two things must be true:

    1. The first quantity is greater than the second.
OR 2. The first quantity is less than the second.

A number line helps to show how this is true.

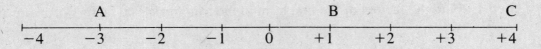

On the number line, A is to the left of B, and B is to the left of C. Whenever one variable is to the left of another on a number line, it is less than the other. Thus, −3 is less than +1, and +1 is less than +4. We can make a few general statements.

    1. Any negative number is less than zero.
    2. Zero is less than any positive number.
    3. Any negative number is less than any positive number.

There are symbols for statements of inequality.

Symbols	Meanings
$6 \neq 7$	6 does not equal 7
$7 > 6$	7 is greater than 6
$6 < 7$	6 is less than 7
$x \geq 8$	x is greater than or equal to 8
$x \leq 8$	x is less than or equal to 8

Solving Inequalities   The rules for solving inequalities are similar to those used for solving equations.

Example: Solve: $x - 3 < 8$

    Step 1. "Clear" for x by transferring − 3 to the other side of the inequality symbol. Do this by performing an inverse operation.

$$x - 3 + 3 < 8 + 3$$
$$x < 11 \quad \text{(solution)}$$

The solution means that any number less than 11 will make the original statement of inequality true. You can prove that by substituting numbers less than 11 for x. Try letting $x = 10$.

$$x - 3 < 8$$
$$10 - 3 < 8$$
$$7 < 8 \text{ This is certainly true!}$$

Geometry

Geometry has to do with the world around us. Some knowledge of geometry is necessary for everyone. Both arithmetic and algebra are used in solving geometry problems. Many geometry problems involve measurement, and use familiar words such as line, or point. An important term in geometry is *angle*.

Angles   An angle is formed by two lines meeting at a point. The point is called the *vertex* of the angle. You can name an angle in three ways.

1. By the point at the vertex (for example, angle B).
2. By the letter names of the lines that meet to form the angle, with the vertex in the middle (for example, angle ABC).
3. By a number inside the angle on a diagram (for example, angle # 2).

Angles are measured in *degrees* (°). Just as a foot is broken into 12 inches, a degree is broken into minutes (′) and seconds (″). (Don't confuse these with time!)

1. A *straight line* is an angle of 180 degrees.
2. A *right angle* is an angle of 90 degrees.
3. An *obtuse angle* is an angle of more than 90 degrees, but less than 180 degrees.
4. An *acute angle* is an angle of more than 0 degrees and less than 90 degrees.
5. *Complementary angles* are two angles whose sum is 90 degrees.
6. *Supplementary angles* are two angles whose sum is 180 degrees.

Lines   *Parallel lines* are two lines which are equally distant from one another at every point along the lines.
Perpendicular lines are two lines which meet to form a right angle.

Polygons   A *polygon* is composed of three or more lines, connected so that an area is closed in. There are several types of polygons.

1. A *triangle* has three sides.
2. A *quadrilateral* has four sides.
3. A *pentagon* has five sides.
4. A *hexagon* has six sides.
5. An *octagon* has eight sides.
6. A *decagon* has ten sides.

Triangles   There are several ways to classify a triangle, but all triangles contain 180 degrees.

1. An *equilateral triangle* is one in which all three sides are equal, and all three angles are equal—60 degrees each.
2. An *isosceles triangle* is one in which two sides are equal. (The angles opposite these sides are also equal.)
3. A *scalene triangle* is one in which all the sides and all the angles are unequal.
4. An *acute triangle* is one in which all three angles are acute (less than a right angle).
5. An *obtuse triangle* is one in which one angle is obtuse (greater than 90 degrees).
6. A *right triangle* is one which includes a right angle (90 degrees). The longest side of a right triangle is called the *hypotenuse*. It is always the side opposite the right angle (side c). The other two sides are called *legs*.

There is a very important idea connected with right triangles. It is called the *Pythagorean Theorem*. It says that in a right triangle, the square of the hypotenuse is equal to the sum of the squares of the legs. As an equation, the Pythagorean Theorem would be expressed as follows:

$$c^2 = a^2 + b^2$$

Example: A gardener placed a 5-foot ladder against a 4-foot wall. If the top of the ladder touched the top of the wall, how far away from the base of the wall was the bottom of the ladder?

Solution: The angle formed by the base of the wall and the ground is a right angle. Therefore, we can use the Pythagorean Theorem. Since the ladder was opposite the right angle, let $c = 5$.

$$c^2 = a^2 + b^2$$
$$5^2 = 4^2 + x^2 \text{ (Clear for } x.)$$
$$5^2 - 4^2 = 4^2 - 4^2 + x^2$$
$$25 - 16 = x^2$$
$$9 = x^2 \text{ (Find the square roots.)}$$
$$3 = x$$

7. *Congruent triangles* are alike in every respect. All three sides and all three angles of one triangle are exactly the same as those of the other.
8. *Similar triangles* are triangles with exactly the same shape, but not necessarily the same size. The angles of two similar triangles are the same.

Quadrilaterals

There are several types of quadrilaterals, but all quadrilaterals contain 360 degrees.

1. A *parallelogram* is a quadrilateral with its opposite sides parallel. In a parallelogram the opposite sides and angles are also equal.
2. A *rectangle* is a parallelogram in which all angles are right angles.
3. A *square* is a rectangle all of whose sides are equal.
4. A *rhombus* is a parallelogram in which all four sides are equal.
5. A *trapezoid* is a quadrilateral with two sides parallel, and two sides not parallel.

Perimeter and Area

The *perimeter* of a polygon is the sum of all its sides.

Example: Find the perimeter of a triangle whose sides measure 3 feet, 4 feet, and 5 feet.

$$3' + 4' + 5' = 12' \text{ (perimeter)}$$

Example: Find the perimeter of a square whose side is 9 yards.

$$9 + 9 + 9 + 9 = 36 \text{ yds} \quad \text{(perimeter)}$$

Since all four sides of a square are equal, you can use the rule "perimeter (P) of a square equals four times a side (s)": $P = 4s$.

The *area* of a polygon is the space enclosed by its sides.

1. The area of a parallelogram is base times height.
$$A = bh$$
2. The area of a rectangle is length times width.
$$A = lw$$
3. The area of a square is one side, "squared."
$$A = s^2$$
4. The area of a triangle is one-half the base times the height.
$$A = \frac{bh}{2}$$

Example: Find the area of a room whose length is 20 feet and whose width is 18 feet.

$$A = lw$$
$$x = 20' \times 18'$$
$$x = 360 \text{ square feet (area)}$$

Circles

A *circle* is a closed curved line, all of whose points are equally distant from the center. A circle contains 360 degrees. There are several special "parts" to a circle.

The *circumference* of a circle is its "length"—once around the rim.
The *radius* of a circle is a line drawn from the center to any point on the circumference.
The *diameter* is a line passing through the center of a circle, and is equal to twice the radius.

Perimeter and Area

To find the circumference (perimeter) of a circle, we use a new number, *Pi* (π). Pi is actually a Greek letter. In geometry it expresses an unchanging relationship between the circumference of a circle and its diameter. In other words, the circumference is always Pi times the diameter. Since the diameter is twice the radius, we can also say that the circumference of a circle is Pi times twice the radius. Thus

$$C = (\pi)d \quad \text{OR} \quad C = (\pi)2r$$

When we do arithmetic operations with Pi, we use either 3.14 or $3\frac{1}{7}$ for Pi.

Example: Find the circumference of an ice rink whose radius is 70 yards.

$$C = (\pi)2r$$
$$C = (\pi)\,(2 \times 70)$$
$$C = 3\frac{1}{7} \times 140$$
$$C = \frac{22}{7} \times 140$$
$$C = 22 \times 20 = 440 \text{ yards}$$

The area of a circle also has a fixed relationship to Pi. The area equals Pi times the square of the radius. Thus

$$A = (\pi)r^2$$

Example: Find the area of a circular tract of land whose diameter is 20 miles.

Step 1. Find the radius (one-half of the diameter).
$20 \div 2 = 10$ miles (radius)
Step 2. Apply the formula for the area of a circle.
$$A = (\pi)r^2$$
$$A = 3.14 \times (10)^2$$
$$A = 3.14 \times 100$$
$$A = 314 \text{ square miles (area)}$$

Volumes

Volume is the space occupied by a solid figure. A *solid*, or three-dimensional object, has a flat base and height (sometimes called depth). Volume is measured in cubic units.

A *rectangular solid* has length, width, and height. The formula for finding its cubic measure is length times width times height. Thus

$$V = lwh$$

A *cube* is a solid whose length, width, and height are the same. The volume of a cube is one side, "cubed"—or one side raised to the third power. Thus

$$V = s^3$$

A circular solid is called a *cylinder*. The volume of a cylinder is the area of its base (a circle) times its height. Thus

$$V = (\pi)r^2h$$

Example: Find the difference between the capacity of a rectangular solid measuring 3' by 5' by 10' and a cylinder with a radius of 7' and a height of 3'.

Step 1. Find the volume of the rectangular solid.

$$V = lwh$$
$$V = 3' \times 5' \times 10'$$
$$V = 150 \text{ cubic feet}$$

Step 2. Find the volume of the cylinder.

$$V = (\pi)r^2h$$
$$V = 3\frac{1}{7} \times 7^2 \times 3$$
$$V = \frac{22}{\cancel{7}_1} \times \cancel{49}^{\,7} \times 3$$
$$V = 22 \times 7 \times 3$$
$$V = 462 \text{ cubic feet}$$

Step 3. Find the difference between both volumes.

$$462 - 150 = 312 \text{ cubic feet}$$

6 PARAGRAPH COMPREHENSION AND WORD KNOWLEDGE REVIEW

Basics on General Reading

General reading is the reading you do in the course of your daily life. It may be the reading you do on the job or it may be the reading you do in the evening and on weekends to find out more about the things that interest you—cooking, woodworking, travel, etc. For this, you read magazines and the family living sections of newspapers. You also consult books which deal with subjects in which you are interested.

This part of the examination tests your ability to read popular articles that deal with everyday topics. *What are the skills you will need to master?* These are not much different from the skills needed in reading materials in the social studies.

1. *You read to find the main idea of the selection.* You find it in a variety of places. It may be stated directly in the first sentence (easy to find). It may be stated in the final sentence to which the others build up (a bit harder to find). It may have to be discovered within the passage (most difficult). An example of this (note the underscored words) may be found in the following paragraph:

   > Several students were seriously injured in football games last Saturday. The week before, several more were hospitalized. Football has become a dangerous sport. The piling up of players in a scrimmage often leads to serious injury. Perhaps some rule changes would lessen the number who are hurt.

   You may also find that the main idea is not expressed at all, but can only be inferred from the selection as a whole.

   > The plane landed at 4 P.M. As the door opened, the crowd burst into a long, noisy demonstration. The waiting mob surged against the police guard lines. Women were screaming. Teenagers were yelling for autographs or souvenirs. The visitor smiled and waved at his fans.

   The main idea of the paragraph is not expressed, but it is clear that some popular hero, movie or rock star is being welcomed enthusiastically at the airport.

   > *To find the main idea of a passage,* ask yourself any or all of these questions:
   > 1. What is the *main idea* of the passage? (Why did the author write it?)
   > 2. What is the *topic sentence* of the paragraph or paragraphs (the sentence that the other sentences build on or flow from)?
   > 3. What *title* would I give this selection?

2. *You read to find the details that explain or develop the main idea.* How do you do this? You must determine how the writer develops the main idea. He will either give examples to illustrate that idea, or he may give reasons why the statement which is the main idea is true. Or he may give arguments for or against a position stated as the main idea. The

writer may define a complex term and give a number of qualities of a complicated belief (such as democracy). He may also classify a number of objects within a larger category. Finally, he may compare two ideas or objects (show how they are similar) or contrast them (show how they are different).

In the paragraph immediately above, you can see that the sentence "You must determine how the writer develops the main idea." *is* the main idea. Six ways in which the writer can develop the main idea follow. These are the details that actually develop the main idea of the paragraph.

To find the main details of a passage, the questions to ask yourself are these:
1. What examples illustrate the main point?
2. What reasons or proof support the main idea?
3. What arguments are presented for or against the main idea?
4. What specific qualities are offered about the idea or subject being defined?
5. What classifications is a larger group broken down into?
6. What are the similarities and differences between two ideas or subjects being compared or contrasted?

---

3. *You read to make inferences by putting together ideas which are expressed to arrive at other ideas which are not.* In other words, you draw conclusions from the information presented by the author. You do this by locating relevant details and determining their relationships (time sequence, place sequence, cause and effect).

How do you do this? You can put one fact together with a second to arrive at a third which is not stated. You can apply a given fact to a different situation. You can predict an outcome based on the facts given.

To make inferences from a passage, ask yourself the following questions:
1. From the facts presented, what conclusions can I draw?
2. What is being suggested, in addition to what is being stated?
3. What will be the effect of something which is described?
4. What will happen next (after what is being described)?
5. What applications does the principle or idea presented have?

Let's try to apply these skills to representative passages you will encounter in the paragraph comprehension part of the test.

Family camping has been described as the "biggest single growth industry in the booming travel/leisure market." Camping ranges from backpacking to living in rolling homes with complete creature comforts. It is both an end in itself and a magic carpet to a wide variety of other forms of outdoor recreation.

1. It can be inferred from the passage that the LEAST luxurious form of camping is
   1-A   backpacking
   1-B   travel trailers
   1-C   camping trailers
   1-D   motor homes

Answer Analysis   1-A This question requires you to make an inference from the information in the passage. The second sentence in the paragraph refers to the range of camping—from backpacking to the "creature comforts" of rolling homes. From this, it can be inferred that backpacking is the least luxurious form of camping.

Locating the Main Idea

Depending upon the type of passage—poetry, fiction, essay, drama—the technique of finding the main idea may vary. In the essay, for example, the main idea may very well appear as a straightforward statement, usually expressed in the topic sentence. In this particular case, the trick is to find the topic sentence. In works of fiction, poetry, or drama, the main idea might be found in a line of dialogue or exposition, or within a long, flowing line of verse.

In reading *prose,* the main unit is the paragraph. Since the paragraphs you will encounter on the examination have all been chosen for their "loaded" content—that is, because they contain a number of ideas offering possibilities for questions—it is important that you learn how to locate the main idea. This, in turn, will enable you to understand many of the subordinate, that is, less important elements of the paragraph—all of which may be the basis for examination questions.

The topic sentence containing the main idea is used in five standard patterns:

1. The topic sentence, expressing the main idea, may introduce the paragraph and be followed by sentences containing details that explain, exemplify, prove, or support the idea, or add interest.

   Example:

   In *Alice in Wonderland,* Lewis Carroll has created a world of fantasy out of essentially real creatures, transformed into whimsy by the odd patterns of a dream. Sitting with her sister by a stream, Alice sees a rabbit; as she dozes off, the rabbit becomes larger, dons a waistcoat and a pocket-watch, and acquires human speech.

2. The topic sentence may appear at the end of the paragraph, with a series of details leading to the main idea.

   Example:

   The small, darting rabbit on the river-bank becomes a huge White Rabbit, complete with waistcoat and pocket-watch. The cards in a discarded deck become the Queen of Hearts and her court. The real world of Alice Liddell becomes, through the odd patterns of the dream, the fantasy world of *Alice in Wonderland.*

3. The selection may begin with a broad generalization (topic sentence) followed by details that support the main idea and lead to another broad generalization which is called the "summary sentence" (conclusion).

   Example:

   The elements of the real world become, through the strange, shifting patterns of the dream, objects and creatures of curiosity and whimsy. A scurrying rabbit becomes a humanized White Rabbit, a deck of cards becomes the court of the Queen of Hearts, a kitten becomes a chess Queen. In *Alice in Wonderland* reality becomes fantasy and, for a while, fantasy becomes reality.

4. The topic sentence may appear in the body of the paragraph.

Example:

When Alice goes through the looking glass, she enters a garden where the flowers speak. In a dark forest, a fawn befriends her. The dream world reverses the events of the real world. The Lion and the Unicorn come off their shield and do battle. The Red Queen, originally a kitten of Alice's pet cat Dinah, gives Alice instructions in etiquette.

5. The selection may contain *no expressed topic sentence* but consist of a series of sentences concerning details and implying a central thought.

Example:

A deck of cards becomes a royal court. A kitten becomes a chess Queen. A scurrying wild creature becomes a sophisticated courtier, a White Rabbit in vest and pocket-watch. A proper Victorian tea-party becomes the setting for rude remarks and outrageous behavior.

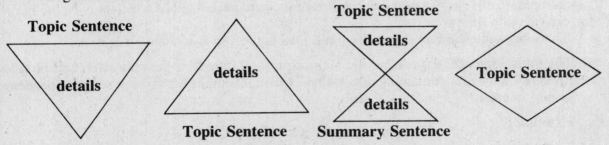

Finding Details   Very often questions on reading passages will test your ability to locate relevant details. In a descriptive passage, the author may give a general impression of a scene. Take, as an example, the famous short story by Edgar Allan Poe, ''The Fall of the House of Usher.'' The narrator conveys his reaction on seeing the house with the words: ''I know not how it was, but, with the first glimpse of the building, a sense of insufferable gloom pervaded my spirit.'' Two sentences later you get the details that made him feel that way.

Or in a passage dealing with the character of the subject of a biography, details will document the point the author is making. Sandburg's biography of Abraham Lincoln is full of passages which follow this pattern. To show the industriousness of Lincoln, Sandburg writes: ''Abe knew the sleep that comes after long hours of work outdoors. . . .'' You can almost feel certain that the ''work'' that is mentioned will be described in detail and it is. Among the jobs listed are ''clearing timberland,'' ''splitting rails,'' ''harrowing,'' ''planting,'' ''pulling fodder,'' ''helping . . . house raisings, log-rollings, corn-huskings.''

Details are also used to move the plot or story interestingly and smoothly along the way. In Hawthorne's ''The Ambitious Guest,'' we find the sentence, ''The simplest words must intimate, but not portray, the unutterable horror of the catastrophe.'' Immediately there follow the details which tell us just how horrible the catastrophe was.

Finally, details are often used to provide reasons for a conclusion that has been reached. Sherlock Holmes is talking to Dr. Watson about his solution of the case, ''The Adventure of the Speckled Band.'' ''I had come to these conclusions before ever I had entered his room,'' and Holmes proceeds to give us the details of why he reached them.

How do you locate a detail? It may be necessary for you to return to the reading passage many times to dig out the details required to answer a given question. In your search, a number of clues may help you. These involve the location of what are called *transitional words*, words which point out the purpose of the details presented.

Transitional Words

These words may indicate *illustrations* of a general idea or impression:

for example	in such cases
for instance	in the same manner
in other words	just as

Or they may signal *additional items:*

again	another	second
also	as well as	third
and	besides	

Or they may point to *opposite evidence:*

but	nevertheless	although
however	otherwise	despite

Sometimes they *identify an important detail:*

don't overlook	notice that	most important

Finally, they may announce a helpful *conclusion* which the details document:

accordingly	finally	in conclusion
as a result	hence	in short

Inferring Word Meaning   It is not necessary to memorize an extensive vocabulary to understand the meaning of an unfamiliar word. Quite often the clue to a word's meaning may be found by carefully reading the sentence in which the word appears.

Example:

It is easy to understand how the author's *misogyny* developed. His mother abandoned him at the age of five; the aunt who raised him tended to treat him as if he were one of the crosses all good "Christians" must bear; and his wife, whom he adored, ran off with his best friend.

What information are we given in this sentence? We are told that the author had a series of bad experiences in his childhood and young manhood involving people who were very important to him at those times. All of these people—mother, aunt, and wife—are women. We can assume that his treatment by these women led to the author's dislike or mistrust— even hatred—of women because of the way he was treated by some of them. Therefore, we can infer that *misogyny* means "a hatred and mistrust of women," which is, in fact, the dictionary meaning of the word.

Let's try another. Here's a double challenge.

Example:

She took *umbrage* at his critical remarks, and left in a *dudgeon*.

The key to the meaning of these unfamiliar words is the phrase "critical remarks" which obviously implies that "he" was saying certain things that were unpleasant to "her." The fact that she left, rather than staying to hear him out, tells us that she resented what he was saying, and was very likely quite angry with him. In other words, she *took umbrage* at his remarks, which is the same as saying she *took offense*.

To understand the word *dudgeon*, we must assume, first of all, that the second part of the sentence has some direct relation to the first. We cannot infer that a *dudgeon* is, for example, some sort of vehicle, since to say that she took offense at his words and left in a carriage, for example, adds an entirely new idea which has no relation to the rest of the sentence. We know, however, that her mood was affected by his remarks, and we may logically conclude that she went away angry. In fact, *dudgeon* means ill-humor or resentment, a state of mind which fits in with her having taken offense in the first place. In other words, she got angry and she left in a huff.

The fact to remember, whether you are taking an examination or merely reading for your own pleasure or information, is that unfamiliar words should not be disturbing, or appear to present obstacles that cannot be overcome. While it is true that many big words are used much more frequently in written than in spoken language, there is often a very good reason for this. Spoken language is re-enforced with gestures, facial expressions, tone of voice of the speaker. Because written language can rely on none of these, it must be much more specific; and the more words there are to express a particular idea, the more easily the author can choose those which convey his or her exact meaning. A mechanic with a large selection of good tools can accomplish much more, and do the job much better, than a man with only a wrench and a crowbar. Words are the tools of the writer, and the more he or she has and knows how to use properly, the better he or she can do the job.

Vocabulary and How to Build Yours

Why Vocabulary   In a classic study conducted over twenty-five years ago by Johnson O'Connor of the Human Engineering Institute and reported in an article called "Vocabulary and Success," the main finding was that a good vocabulary was more frequently to be found among successful persons (persons in important positions) than any other single factor. That doesn't mean that everyone with a good vocabulary is necessarily successful, but it is generally true that successful people have good vocabularies.

This discovery should really come as no surprise. A vocabulary is not merely a collection of words. It is all the ideas for which words stand. Take, for example, the following words taken from the study of government.

anarchy	fascism
autocracy	federal
autonomy	oligarchy
democracy	republic
dictatorship	totalitarian

These words all identify systems of government. Anyone who knows the meanings of those ten words has an understanding of the most widely known kinds of government and what each represents. Or, to choose a more technical (and a more dramatic) area, that of space exploration, any knowledgeable person will have as part of his vocabulary such words as

abort	injection
apogee	orbit
burnout	perigee
cislunar	phasing
docking	telemetry

among others. The point is that the person with a good vocabulary has more ideas (about government, for example) and more knowledge (about space exploration, for example) and such persons are always in demand in business and in the professions.

How to Add a Word to Your Vocabulary   The best way to find words to build your vocabulary is by reading, and not the most difficult books either. Research has shown that, to build your vocabulary, it is better to read books just a little bit more difficult than the level you find to be easy. A few new words a page are better than many. Let us take a few examples of how reading can help you add words to your vocabulary.

A fine American short story starts with the sentence:

"It was late in the afternoon, and the light was *waning*."

The sentence itself provides a clue to the meaning of the word "waning." "Late in the afternoon" the light grows dim. Reference to the dictionary confirms this guess at the meaning from the clues provided in the sentence. One definition reads: "to grow dim, as a light." It would be helpful to fix the meaning of the word if you jotted it down in a small pocket vocabulary notebook. The notation should include the following:

Word (correctly spelled)	Meaning	Example of use
wane	grow dim	The light began to *wane*.

The final clincher is your own proper use of the word in another sentence. One possibility might be: "His eyesight began to *wane*."

In the above example, you can find the four steps to take if you wish to master a word.

1. Find the word as it is used in the company of other words on the printed page. Reading is the best way to do this.
2. Make a temporary judgment as to the meaning of the word from the clues contained in the sentence where it is found.
3. Check your opinion of its meaning by referring to a dictionary at your first opportunity.
4. If possible, add the word to a continuing list you develop in a small pocket-size notebook. Include the meaning and a typical context (the sentence in which it was found).
5. Use it yourself in the same, or, preferably, in a new context (word setting).

Now try your hand at the next example.
This is taken from another fine American short story.

"It was a *desolate* country in those days; geographers still described it as The Great American Desert, and in looks it deserved the title."

How would you master the word "desolate"?

A temporary judgment as to its meaning would be based on the clue in the sentence that it was similar to a desert. But what quality or characteristic of a desert does it stand for? You find out by checking with the dictionary. The entry is found on the page with the guide words desecrate—detach. It is in its alphabetical place between Des Moines and desolation. Four meanings are given and you start with the first: "lonely; solitary." That is the original meaning and the most precise. It is best to choose the first definition in preference to the others if it fits the sentence. In this case, the others are all possible extensions of the main meaning "lonely"; uninhabited; laid waste; forlorn. Your notebook notation might read something like this:

Word	Meaning	Example of use
desolate	lonely	The abandoned child was *desolate*.

There is one more important dictionary clue in the entry for *desolate*. The origin of the word is given [<L. *de-* intens. + *solus*, alone]. The word comes to us from the Latin. "De" is an intensive, meaning "very," but the important clue is the Latin word "solus" meaning "alone." Other English words use forms of the Latin word "solus". These are some that might occur to you: sole, solitaire, solitary, solitude, solo.

Study the Parts of a Word   This means of vocabulary building requires you to work with three elements of a word: the root, prefixes, and suffixes.

The one essential part of any word is the root. It may be a word in itself (for example, *flex*) or a word element from which other words are formed (for example, *aud*). Knowing many word roots is one way of multiplying your vocabulary, for each root can lead you to several words. We shall show you how, after we define the other two elements: prefixes and suffixes.

A prefix is a word part (a syllable or group of syllables) added to the beginning of a word which changes its meaning. Let us return to the example *flex*. By itself, it means to bend or contract. The context is the human body. You can flex an arm; you can flex a muscle. If you add the syllable *re* to the beginning of the root, flex, that is, if you add the prefix *re*, you get a new word, reflex, with a new meaning. *Reflex* describes an action which you cannot control, such as a sneeze.

We can further change the meaning of the root "flex" by adding a suffix. A suffix is a word part (a syllable or group of syllables) added to the end of a word which changes its meaning. If you add the syllables "ible" to the end of the root, that is, if you add the suffix "ible," you get another new word, flexible, with a new meaning. *Flexible* means *able to bend without breaking* or, in a broader meaning, *able to adjust to change*.

It is also possible to add both a prefix *and* a suffix to a root and get still another word. If you add both the prefix *in* meaning *not* and the suffix *ible* meaning *able,* you get a new word, *inflexible*. *Inflexible* means *unbending* or, in a broader meaning, *stubborn* and *unable to adjust to change*.

To give you some idea of the flex family of words, here are a number of other words (*flect* is another form of *flex*).

flexibility   reflection
deflect   circumflex
inflection   genuflect

Here is a list of widely used prefixes in English. They are derived from Anglo-Saxon (Old English), Greek and Latin. Make up at least one word using each prefix and check your accuracy in the dictionary.

Prefix	Meaning	Source	Word
1. a	no, not	Greek	
2. ab	away, from	Latin	
3. ad	to	Latin	
4. amphi	both	Greek	
5. ante	before	Latin	
6. anti	against	Greek	
7. be	completely	Anglo-Saxon	
8. circum	around	Latin	
9. contra	against	Latin	
10. de	from, away	Latin	
11. dia	across	Greek	

Prefix	Meaning	Source	Word
12. eu	well	Greek	
13. ex	out of	Latin	
14. extra	beyond	Latin	
15. fore	before	Anglo-Saxon	
16. hyper	above	Greek	
17. hypo	below, under	Greek	
18. in	into	Latin	
19. in	not	Latin	
20. inter	between	Latin	
21. intra	within	Latin	
22. mis	wrong	Anglo-Saxon	
23. ob	against	Latin	
24. out	from, beyond	Anglo-Saxon	
25. over	above, too much	Anglo-Saxon	
26. para	beside	Greek	
27. peri	around	Greek	
28. poly	many	Greek	
29. post	after	Latin	
30. pre	before	Latin	
31. pro	forward	Latin	
32. re	back, again	Latin	
33. retro	back	Latin	
34. se	apart	Latin	
35. sub	under	Latin	
36. super	above, beyond	Latin	
37. syn	together, with	Greek	
38. trans	across	Latin	
39. ultra	beyond	Latin	
40. un	not	Anglo-Saxon	
41. under	below	Anglo-Saxon	

Here is a list of widely used Greek and Latin word roots. Make up at least one word using each root and check your word in the dictionary. Try to combine the root with one of the prefixes we have listed for you. Be careful to combine Latin prefix with Latin root, etc.

Root	Meaning	Root	Meaning
act	do	clud (e)	close
anim	spirit, life	cor	heart
anthro	man	corp	body
ann (u)	year	cred	believe
aqua	water	curr	run
aud	hear	dem	people
bene	well	dic (t)	say
cas	fall	do (n)	give
chrom	color	duc (t)	lead
chron	time	fac (t)	make
ced (e)	go	fer	carry
cid (e)	kill	fin	end

Root	Meaning	Root	Meaning
flect	bend	ortho	right
flu (x)	flow	pan	all
fract	break	pater	father
frater	brother	path	suffer, feel
graph	write	ped	foot
gress	walk	pend	hang
hetero	different	phil	love
homo	same	phon	sound
hydr (o)	water	psych	mind
ject	throw	pugn	fight
jur (e)	swear	rupt	break
litera	letter	sci	know
lith	stone	scrib	write
magn	large, great	sect	cut
mal	evil	sol	alone
man(u)	hand	soph	wise
mar	sea	spect	look
mater	mother	struct	build
ment	mind	tele	far
met (er)	measure	temp	time
micro	small	tract	draw
mit	send	vad	go
mono	one	ven (t)	come
mort	death	vert	turn
mot	move	vis	see
multi	many	vict	conquer
nom(y)	science of	voc, voke	call
norm	rule	volv	turn
nov	new		

The following is a list of prefixes both in Greek and Latin which indicate a number. Find one word for each prefix and add it to your vocabulary.

Meaning	Latin		Greek	
1. half	semi	....	hemi	....
2. one	uni	....	mono	....
3. two	bi	....	di	....
4. three	tri	....	tri	....
5. four	quadr	....	tetra	....
6. five	quint	....	penta	....
7. six	sex	....	hexa	....
8. seven	sept	....	hepta	....
9. eight	oct	....	octa	....
10. nine	nona	....	rarely used	
11. ten	dec	....	deca	....
12. hundred	cent	....	rarely used	
13. thousand	mill	....	kilo	....

Learn the Synonyms and Antonyms of a Word
A synonym is a word that has the same or nearly the same meaning as another word in the language. An antonym is a word that has the opposite or nearly the opposite meaning from another word in a language. You may ask, "How do I find these synonyms and antonyms?" The answer is again: "In the dictionary." The paperback pocket-size dictionary, because of its size, will give you little help in this particular technique. You must resort to a desk-size dictionary. Again, because of the simplicity of its definitions and its reporting of current American usage the *Webster's New World Dictionary of the American Language,* College Edition with about 150,000 entries (three times that of a paperback dictionary) is the best.

Let us take that dictionary's listing of synonyms for the word *happy*.

SYN.—happy generally suggests a feeling of great pleasure, contentment, etc. (a *happy* marriage); glad implies more strongly an exultant feeling of joy (your letter made her so *glad*), but both glad and happy are commonly used in merely polite formulas expressing gratification (I'm *glad,* or *happy,* that you could come); cheerful implies a steady display of bright spirits, optimism, etc. (he's always *cheerful* in the morning); joyful and joyous both imply great elation and rejoicing, the former generally because of a particular event, and the latter as a matter of usual temperament (the *joyful* throngs, a *joyous* family). See also *lucky.* —*ANT.* sad

In addition to giving you four synonyms for *happy*, the entry distinguishes among them. It also gives you a context (group of words in which the synonym appears) for each synonym. In addition, it refers you to *lucky* under which you find two more synonyms—fortunate and providential. Finally, it gives you one antonym, sad, which itself becomes a clue to five other antonyms—sorrowful, melancholy, dejected, depressed, and doleful. From the one word, happy, the dictionary has led us to seven synonyms and five antonyms, an additional dozen words.

Similarly, the word *large* will lead you to synonyms big and great and to antonyms small, little, diminutive, minute, tiny, miniature, and petite.

It is easier to learn related words and remember them than to learn words in isolation. Surprisingly, it is often a fact that one sign you are learning the meaning of a word is your mistake in using its antonym or opposite. You are associating the word incorrectly and incompletely, but the point is you *are* making an association.

Learn to Associate Words by Topic or Idea
One of the most helpful aids to vocabulary-building is based on this principle. It is called *Roget's Thesaurus* or the treasury (of words) of Peter Mark Roget, the man who first thought out the organization of words into 1000 related groups. The *Thesaurus* of Roget cannot be used by itself. It must be used together with a dictionary since the *Thesaurus* merely lists the words by idea. Here is an example:

Under the idea of GREATNESS, the following adjectives (descriptive words used to make the things referred to more specific) are listed, a total of no fewer than 56 (note that three are *Colloq.*)

Adjectives—1. great; greater; large, considerable, fair, above par; big, huge; ample; abundant, enough; full, intense, strong; passing, heavy, plenary, deep, high; signal, at its height, in the zenith; worldwide, widespread, extensive; wholesale; many.

2. goodly, noble; mighty; arch; profound, intense, consummate; extraordinary; important; unsurpassed; complete.

3. vast, immense, enormous, extreme; exaggerated; marvelous; unlimited, infinite. *Colloq.* whopping, fearful, terrific.

4. absolute, positive, stark; perfect, finished; remarkable, noteworthy.

It is obvious that many of these words require further investigation before you can use them. The word, *consummate*, fits into the general idea of greatness, but it refers to great mastery of a skill, both to be admired or to be disapproved, as in "with consummate artistry" or "a consummate liar." That is why the *Thesaurus must* be used together with a dictionary. Even so, you must be very careful because of the special use of many of the words.

While we are on the subject of association as a way of learning new words, there is another kind of association which you yourself can make. That is a group of words which deals with a topic or subject. A good place to start is your own interests. Let's try foods and food preparation. Words such as the following come to mind: aspic, baste, sauté, truss, buffet, entrée, ragout, simmer, braise, compote, cuisine, curried, garnish, soufflé, meringue, hors d'oeuvres. One way to build a "food" vocabulary is to study the words on a restaurant menu which you don't understand.

Now for a subject that concerns all of us—health. The following words are the stock in trade of the medical doctor: abscess, allergy, anemia, cataract, cyst, eczema, embolism, gangrene, hemorrhage, hepatitis, metabolism, neuralgia, pleurisy, sciatica, stroke, tumor.

And anyone with an interest in motors and tools should be familiar with the terms carburetor, condenser, compression, gear ratio, piston, socket wrench, dynamometer, emission, vacuum.

Many books have glossaries, lists of difficult words with definitions.

A Basic 1100 Word Vocabulary

To help you build your vocabulary, we have selected 1100 words which every high school graduate should know. They are grouped into lists of nouns, verbs, and adjectives. You should use these lists and the definitions together with a good dictionary such as *Webster's New World Dictionary of the American Language*. For each word, we have provided a definition which is most widely used but is often far removed from the first or literal meaning. You may wish to study other meanings of each word. We have also provided many words, sentences or phrases to show you how the particular word should be used.

300 Useful Nouns

ACCESS   (means of) approach or admittance (e.g. to records)

ACCORD   agreement

ADAGE   proverb (As "Better late than never")

AFFLUENCE   abundance; wealth (e.g. age of _____)

AGENDA   list of things to be done or discussed (e.g. at a meeting)

ALACRITY   brisk willingness (e.g. agreed with _____)

ALIAS   assumed name (e.g. Fred Henry, _____ John Doe)

ANIMOSITY   great hatred (e.g. towards strangers)

ANTHOLOGY   collection of writings or other creative work such as songs

APATHY   indifference (e.g. towards poverty)

APEX   the highest point (e.g. _____ of a triangle)

ATLAS   book of maps

AUDACITY   boldness

AVARICE   greed for wealth

AWE   feeling of respect and wonder (e.g. in _____ of someone's power)

BEACON   guiding light (e.g. of knowledge)

BENEDICTION   blessing

BIGOTRY   unwillingness to allow others to have different opinions and beliefs from one's own

BLEMISH   defect (e.g. on one's record)

BONDAGE   slavery

BOON   benefit (e.g. a _____ to business)

BRAWL   noisy fight

BREVITY   shortness

BROCHURE   pamphlet (e.g. a travel _____)

BULWARK   strong protection (e.g. a _____ against corruption)

CALIBER   quality (e.g. a person of high _____)

CAMOUFLAGE   disguise, usually in war, by changing the appearance of persons or materiel

CASTE   social class or distinction

CATASTROPHE   sudden disaster (e.g. an earthquake)

CHAGRIN   feeling of deep disappointment

CHRONICLE   historical record

CLAMOR   uproar

CLEMENCY   mercy (e.g. toward a prisoner)

CONDOLENCE   expression of sympathy (e.g. extended _____ to a bereaved)

CONNOISSEUR   expert judge (e.g. of paintings, food)

CONSENSUS   general agreement

CONTEXT   words or ideas just before or after a given word or idea (e.g. meaning of a word in a given _____)

CRITERION   standard of judgment (e.g. good or poor by this _____)

CRUX   the essential point (e.g. the _____ of the matter)

CYNIC   one who doubts the good intentions of others

DATA   known facts (e.g. _____ were found through research)

DEARTH   scarcity (e.g. of talent)

DEBACLE   general defeat (e.g. in a battle)

DEBUT   first appearance before an audience (e.g. actor, pianist)

DELUGE   great flood (e.g. rain or, in a special sense, mail)

DEPOT   warehouse

DESTINY   predetermined fate (e.g. it was his _____ to)

DETRIMENT   damage or loss (e.g. it was to his _____)

DIAGNOSIS   determining the nature of a disease or a situation

DICTION   manner in which words are used in writing and speech (e.g. The radio announcer's _____ was excellent.)

DILEMMA   situation requiring a choice between two unpleasant courses of action (e.g. He was in a _____.)

DIN   loud continuing noise

DIRECTIVE   a general order (e.g. from an executive or military commander)

DISCORD   disagreement

DISCREPANCY   inconsistency (e.g. in accounts, in testimony)

DISCRETION   freedom of choice (e.g. He was given _____ to spend the money as he saw fit.)

DISSENT   difference of opinion (e.g. from a decision)

DROUGHT   long spell of dry weather

EGOTIST   one who judges everything only as it affects his own interest; a self-centered person

ELITE   choice part (e.g. of society)

ENTERPRISE   an important project

ENVIRONMENT   surrounding influences or conditions

EPITOME   typical representation (e.g. She was the _____ of beauty.)

EPOCH   period of time identified by an important person or event (e.g. the _____ of space flight)

ERA   period of time marked by an important person or event (e.g. the Napoleonic _____)

ESSENCE   basic nature (e.g. of the matter)

ETIQUETTE   rules of social behavior which are generally accepted

EXCERPT   passage from a book or a document

EXODUS   departure, usually of large numbers

FACET   side or aspect (e.g. of a problem)

FACSIMILE   exact copy

FALLACY   mistaken idea; reasoning which contains an error

FANTASY   imagination (e.g. He indulged in _____.)

FEUD   continued deadly hatred (e.g. between two families)

FIASCO   complete humiliating failure

FIEND   inhumanly cruel person

FINALE   last part of a performance

FLAIR   natural talent (e.g. for sports)

FLAW   defect

FOCUS   central point (e.g. of attention)

FOE   enemy

FORMAT   physical appearance or arrangement (e.g. of a book)

FORTE   one's strong point (e.g. school grades)

FORTITUDE   steady courage (e.g. when in trouble)

FORUM   a gathering for the discussion of public issues

FOYER   entrance hall (e.g. to a building or dwelling)

FRAUD   deliberate deception

FRICTION   rubbing of the surface of one thing against the surface of another

FUNCTION   purpose served by a person, object, or organization

FUROR   outburst of excitement (e.g. over a discovery)

GAMUT   the whole range (e.g. of experiences)

GAZETTEER   geographical dictionary, usually accompanying an atlas

GENESIS   origin (e.g. of a plan)

GHETTO   section of a city where members of a particular group (formerly religious, now racial) live

GIST   essential content (e.g. of a speech or an article)

GLUTTON   one who overeats or who indulges in anything to excess

GRIEVANCE   complaint made against someone responsible for a situation believed to be unjust

HAVOC   great damage and destruction (e.g. wreak _____ on)

HAZARD   danger

HERITAGE   inheritance either of real wealth or of a tradition

HOAX   deliberate attempt to trick someone either seriously or as a joke

HORDE   crowd

HORIZON   limit (of knowledge, experience, or ambition)

HUE   shade of color

HYSTERIA   wild emotional outburst

IDIOM   expression peculiar to a language which has a different meaning from the words which make it up   (e.g. hit the road)

ILLUSION   idea or impression different from reality

IMAGE   likeness or reflected impression of a person or object

IMPETUS   moving force

INCENTIVE   spur or motive to do something (e.g. profit _____)

INCUMBENT   present holder of an office

INFIRMITY   physical defect

INFLUX   flowing in (e.g. of money into banks, tourists into a country)

INFRACTION   violation of a rule or a law

INITIATIVE   desire or ability to make the first step in carrying out some action (often a new plan or idea)

INNOVATION   introduction of a new idea or method

INTEGRITY   moral and intellectual honesty and uprightness

INTERIM   meantime (e.g. in the _____)

INTERLUDE   period of time between two events (e.g. _____ between the acts of a play)

INTRIGUE   secret plot

INTUITION   knowledge through instinct rather than thought

IOTA   very small amount

ITINERARY   route followed on a trip, actual or planned

JEOPARDY   risk of harm (e.g. put into _____)

KEYNOTE   main theme (e.g. he sounded the _____ of the convention)

LARCENY   theft (e.g. they couldn't decide whether it was grand or petty _____)

LAYMAN   one who is not a member of a particular profession (e.g. from the point of view of a _____)

LEGACY   material or spiritual inheritance (e.g. _____ from a parent)

LEGEND   story or stories passed on from generation to generation and often considered to be true

LEGION   large number

LIAISON   contact between two or more groups (e.g. _____ between headquarters and field units)

LORE   body of traditional knowledge (e.g. nature _____)

MALADY   disease (e.g. incurable _____)

MANEUVER   skillful move (e.g. a clever _____)

MANIA   abnormal absorption (e.g. She had a _____ for clothes.)

MARATHON   contest requiring endurance

MAVERICK   one who acts independently rather than according to an organizational pattern

MAXIM   saying which provides a rule of conduct (e.g. Look before you leap)

MEDIUM   means of communication (e.g. _____ of radio)

MEMENTO   object which serves as a reminder (e.g. a _____ of the war)

METROPOLIS   main city of a state or region (or any large city)

MILIEU   surroundings

MORALE   state of mind as it affects possible future action (e.g. The troops had good _____ .)

MORES   well-established customs (e.g. the _____ of a society)

MULTITUDE   a large number

MYRIAD   a large number of varied people or things

MYTH   a story which is a traditional explanation of some occurrence, usually in nature (e.g. the _____ of Atlas holding up the heavens)

NICHE   a suitable and desirable place (e.g. He found his _____ in the business organization.)

NOMAD   wanderer

NOSTALGIA   desire to return to past experiences or associations

OASIS   a place which provides relief from the usual conditions (e.g. an _____ of peace in a troubled world)

OBLIVION   place or condition in which one is completely forgotten

ODYSSEY   long journey

OMEN   something which is believed to predict a future event (e.g. an evil _____)

OPTIMUM   the best possible quantity or quality (e.g. He participated to the _____ .)

OVATION   enthusiastic reception usually accompanied by generous applause (e.g. He received a tumultuous _____ .)

OVERSIGHT   failure to include something through carelessness (e.g. His name was omitted because of an _____ .)

OVERTURE   first step which is intended to lead to others in either action or discussion (e.g. He made a peace _____ .)

PAGEANT   public spectacle in the form of a stage performance or a parade (e.g. a historical _____)

PANACEA   something considered a cure for all diseases or problems

PANORAMA   a clear view of a very broad area

PARADOX   statement of a truth which appears to contradict itself (e.g. a 20-year-old who had only five birthdays because he was born on February 29).

PASTIME   way of spending leisure time (e.g. He took up golf as a _____.)

PAUCITY   scarcity (e.g. a _____ of nuclear scientists)

PAUPER   very poor person

PEER   an equal as to age, social standing, ability or other feature

PHENOMENON   a natural occurrence such as the tides

PHOBIA   fear of something which is so great as to be unreasonable (e.g. _____ against cats)

PHYSIQUE   build (of the human body)

PILGRIMAGE   long trip to some place worthy of respect or devotion

PINNACLE   highest point (e.g. the _____ of power)

PITFALL   trap

PITTANCE   very small sum of money (e.g. He survived on a _____.)

PLATEAU   area of level land located at a height

PLIGHT   condition, usually unfavorable (e.g. the sorry _____ of the refugees)

POISE   calm and controlled manner of behavior (e.g. He showed _____ in difficult situations.)

POPULACE   the common people

POSTERITY   future generations (e.g. leave a peaceful world to our _____)

PRECEDENT   event or regulation which serves as an example or provides the basis for approval of a later action (e.g. set a _____)

PREDICAMENT   unpleasant situation from which it is difficult to free oneself (e.g. He found himself in a _____.)

PREFACE   introductory statement to a book or speech

PRELUDE   something which is preliminary to some act or work which is more important

PREMISE   statement from which a conclusion is logically drawn (e.g. Granted the _____ that . . . , we may conclude . . .)

PREMIUM   amount added to the usual payment or charge (e.g. He paid a _____ for the seats.)

PRESTIGE   respect achieved through rank, achievement, or reputation

PRETEXT   reason given as a cover up for the true purpose of an action (e.g. He gave as a _____ for stealing it his sentimental attachment to the ring.)

PRIORITY   something which comes before others in importance (e.g. He gave _____ to his studies)

PROCESS   step by step system for accomplishing some purpose (e.g. the _____ of legislation)

PROSPECT   outlook for the future (e.g. the _____ of peace)

PROVISO   requirement that something be done, usually made in writing

PROWESS   superior ability (e.g. _____ in athletics)

PROXIMITY   nearness

PSEUDONYM   assumed name, usually by an author (e.g. Mark Twain, _____ of Samuel Clemens)

PUN   play on words depending on two different meanings or sounds of the same word (e.g. Whether life is worth living depends on the *liver.*)

QUALM   uneasy doubt about some action (e.g. He had a _____ about running for office.)

QUANDARY   uncertainty over a choice between two courses of action (e.g. He was in a _____ between the careers of law or medicine.)

QUERY   question

QUEST   search (e.g. _____ for knowledge)

RAPPORT   harmonious relationship (e.g. _____ between teacher and pupil)

RARITY   something not commonly found (e.g. A talent like his is a _____.)

REFUGE   place to which one can go for protection (e.g. He found _____ in the church.)

REMNANT   remaining part (e.g. _____of the troops)

REMORSE   deep feeling of guilt for some bad act (e.g. He felt _____ at having insulted his friend.)

RENDEZVOUS   a meeting or a place for meeting

RENOWN   fame (e.g. an actor of great _____)

REPAST   meal

REPLICA   an exact copy (e.g. _____ of a painting)

REPRIMAND   severe criitcism in the form of a scolding (e.g. He received a _____ from his superior.)

REPRISAL   return of something in kind (e.g. _____ for an injury—"An eye for an eye")

RESIDUE   remainder

RESOURCES   assets, either material or spiritual, which are available for use

RESPITE   temporary break which brings relief (e.g. _____ from work)

RESUMÉ   summary

REVERENCE   feeling of great respect (e.g. _____ for life)

ROBOT   one who acts mechanically or like a mechanical man

ROSTER   list of names (e.g. _____ of guests)

SABOTAGE   deliberate damage to vital services of production and supply, usually to those of an enemy in wartime

SAGA   long tale, usually of heroic deeds

SALUTATION   greeting, written or spoken (e.g. The _____ of a letter may be "Dear Sir.")

SANCTION   approval, usually by proper authority

SARCASM   use of cutting remarks

SATIRE   attack upon evil or foolish behavior by showing it to be ridiculous

SCAPEGOAT   someone who is blamed for the bad deeds of others

SCENT   distinctive smell

SCOPE   entire area of action or thought (e.g. the _____ of the plan)

SCROLL   roll of paper or parchment containing writing

SECT   group of people having the same beliefs, usually religious

SEGMENT   part or section of a whole (e.g. _____ of a population)

SEMBLANCE   outward appearance (e.g. He gave the _____ of a scholar.)

SEQUEL   something that follows from what happened or was written before (e.g. _____ to a novel)

SHAM   false imitation (e.g. His devotion was a _____ of true love.)

SHEAF   bundle either of grain or of papers

SHEEN   luster (e.g. of furniture)

SILHOUETTE   outline drawing in black

SITE   location of an object or an action (e.g. original _____ of a building)

SLANDER   untruth spoken or spread about someone which damages his reputation

SLOGAN   motto which is associated with an action or a cause (e.g. Pike's Peak or Bust!)

SLOPE   slant (e.g. _____ of a line)

SNARE   trap

SOLACE   comfort (e.g. She found _____ in work.)

SPONSOR   one who endorses and supports a person or an activity

SPUR   something which moves one to act (e.g. a _____ to sacrifice)

STAMINA   ability to fight off physical difficulties such as fatigue

STATURE   height reached physically or morally (e.g. a man of great _____)

STATUS   standing, social or professional

STIGMA   mark of disgrace

STIMULUS   any encouragement to act

STRATEGY   skillful planning and execution (e.g. the _____ in a battle)

STRIFE   conflict (e.g. _____ between labor and management)

SUMMIT   the highest point (e.g. the _____ of his career)

SUPPLEMENT   amount added to complete something (e.g. _____ to a budget)

SURVEY   broad study of a topic (e.g. a _____ of employment)

SUSPENSE   tenseness brought about by uncertainty as to what will happen

SYMBOL   something which is used to stand for something else (e.g. Uncle Sam is a _____ of the United States)

SYMPTOM   indication of something (e.g. _____ of disease)

SYNOPSIS   brief summary

TACT   ability to say and do the right thing socially

TACTICS   skillful actions to achieve some purpose (e.g. The _____ he used to win were unfair.)

TALLY   record of a score or an account (e.g. the _____ of the receipts)

TANG   strong taste or flavor

TECHNIQUE   method or skill in doing work (e.g. the _____ of an artist)

TEMPERAMENT   natural disposition, often to act in a contrary manner (e.g. He displayed a changeable _____.)

TEMPO   pace of activity (e.g. The _____ of life is increasing.)

TENSION   mental or emotional strain (e.g. He was under great _____.)

THEME   topic of a written work or a talk

THRESHOLD   the starting point (e.g. the _____ of a career)

THRIFT   ability to save money (e.g. He became wealthy because of _____.)

TINT   a shade of color

TOKEN   sign which stands for some object or feeling (e.g. a _____ of esteem)

TONIC   something which is a source of energy or vigor

TRADITION   customs and beliefs which are received by one generation from another

TRAIT   distinguishing feature (e.g. _____ of character)

TRANSITION   movement from one situation to another (e.g. _____ from dictatorship to democracy)

TRIBUNAL   place of judgment such as a court

TRIBUTE   showing of respect or gratitude (e.g. He paid a _____ to his parents.)

TURMOIL   disturbance (e.g. great _____ at the meeting)

TUTOR   a private teacher

TYCOON   wealthy and powerful businessman

ULTIMATUM   a final ("Take it or Leave it") offer

UNREST   restless dissatisfaction

UPHEAVAL   sudden overthrow, often violent

USAGE   established practice or custom

UTENSIL   implement which is of use (e.g. a kitchen _____)

UTOPIA   ideal place or society

VALOR   courage

VENTURE   something involving risk

VICINITY   neighborhood

VICTOR   winner

VIGOR   vitality

VIM   energy

VOW   solemn pledge

WAGER   bet

WHIM   sudden notion or desire

WOE   great sorrow (e.g. He brought _____ to his friends.)

WRATH   intense anger (e.g. He poured his _____ on his enemies.)

ZEAL   eager desire

ZENITH   the highest point

ZEST   keen enthusiasm (e.g. _____ for competition)

300 Useful Verbs

ABHOR   hate

ABSOLVE   free from guilt (e.g. for a crime)

ACCEDE   agree to (e.g. a request)

ACCELERATE   speed up

ACCOST   go up and speak to

ADHERE   give support to (e.g. a cause)

ADJOURN   put off to a later time (e.g. a meeting)

ADVOCATE   act in support of (e.g. revolution)

ALLAY   calm (e.g. fears)

ALLEGE   claim

ALLOT   assign (e.g. a share)

ALLUDE   refer to (e.g. a book)

ALTER   change

ASSENT   agree

ATONE   make up for (e.g. a sin)

AUGMENT   add to

AVERT   prevent

BAFFLE   puzzle

BAN   forbid

BAR   exclude

BEFALL   happen to

BERATE   scold

BESEECH   plead

BESTOW   grant (used with on or upon)

CEDE   give up (e.g. territory)

CENSURE   blame

CHAR   scorch

CHASTISE   punish

CHIDE   scold

CITE   mention in order to prove something

COERCE   force

COLLABORATE   work with someone

COMMEND   praise

COMPLY   act in answer to (e.g. a request)

CONCEDE   admit that something is true (e.g. an argument)

CONCUR   agree

CONSTRICT   squeeze

CULL   pick out

CURTAIL   cut short or reduce

DEDUCE   make a conclusion from given facts

DEEM   consider

DEFER   postpone

DEFRAY   pay (e.g. the costs)

DELETE   remove or erase (e.g. a word)

DELVE   investigate

DEPLETE   use up

DEPLORE   be sorry about

DEPRIVE   keep someone from having or getting something

DESPISE   scorn

DETAIN   delay temporarily

DETECT   uncover something that is not obvious

DETER   keep someone from doing something

DETEST   hate

DETRACT   take away from

DEVOUR   eat up greedily

DIGRESS   depart from the subject under consideration

DILUTE   weaken by adding something less strong to the original (e.g. a mixture)

DISBURSE   pay out

DISCERN   make out clearly (e.g. a pattern)

DISDAIN   look down on with scorn

DISINTEGRATE   fall apart

DISMAY   dishearten

DISPEL   drive away

DISPERSE   scatter

DISRUPT   break up

DISTORT   present incorrectly (e.g. facts)

DIVERGE   go in different directions

DIVERT   turn from a course (e.g. a stream)

DIVULGE   reveal

DON   put on (e.g. clothing)

EFFACE   blot out

EFFECT   bring about

EJECT   throw out

ELATE   make happy

EMIT   give forth (e.g. sounds)

ENCOUNTER   meet

ENCROACH   intrude on (e.g. property)

ENDEAVOR   try

ENDOW   provide with (e.g. a desirable quality)

ENHANCE   increase the value of

ENSUE   follow as a result

ENTREAT   plead

ERR   make a mistake

ERUPT   break out

ESTEEM   value

EVADE   avoid or escape from someone or something

EVICT   expel

EXALT   raise to greater heights

EXCEED   surpass

EXPEDITE   speed up the handling of

EXPLOIT   take advantage of a situation or a person

EXTOL   praise highly

FALTER   stumble

FAMISH   starve

FEIGN   pretend

FLAUNT   show off

FLOURISH   thrive

FLOUT   defy mockingly

FOIL   prevent

FORGO   do without

FORSAKE   abandon

FRUSTRATE   prevent someone from achieving something

GAUGE   estimate

HARASS   disturb constantly

HEAVE   lift and throw

HEED   pay attention to (e.g. advice)

HINDER   keep back

HOVER   hang in the air above a certain spot

HURL   throw with force

IGNITE   set fire to

IMMERSE   plunge into a liquid

IMPAIR   damage

IMPEDE   stand in the way of

IMPLY   suggest

INCITE   arouse

INCUR   bring upon oneself (e.g. criticism)

INDUCE   persuade

INDULGE   satisfy (e.g. a desire)

INFER   come to a conclusion based on something known

INHIBIT   restrain

INSTIGATE   spur to action

INSTILL   put a feeling into someone gradually (e.g. fear)

INTERCEPT   interrupt something (or someone) which is on its way

INTERROGATE   question

INTIMIDATE   frighten by making threats

INVOKE   call upon

IRK   annoy

JAR   shake up (e.g. as in a collision)

JEER   poke fun at (e.g. as by sarcastic remarks)

LAMENT   feel sorrow for

LAUNCH   set in motion

LOOM   appear in a threatening manner

LOP   cut off

LURE   tempt

LURK   remain hidden

MAGNIFY   make larger

MAIM   cripple

MIMIC   imitate

MOCK   ridicule

MOLEST   bother

NARRATE   tell (e.g. a story)

NAVIGATE   steer (e.g. a ship)

NEGATE   deny

ORIENT   adjust oneself or someone to a situation

OUST   expel

PARCH   make dry

PEER   look closely

PEND   remain undecided

PERFECT   complete

PERPLEX   puzzle

PERSEVERE   continue on a course of action despite difficulties

PERTAIN   have reference to

PERTURB   upset to a great extent

PERUSE   read carefully

PINE   long for

PLACATE   make calm

PONDER   think through thoroughly

PRECLUDE   prevent something from happening

PRESCRIBE   order (e.g. for use or as a course of action)

PRESUME   take for granted

PREVAIL   win out over

PROBE   investigate thoroughly

PROCURE   obtain

PROFESS   claim with doubtful sincerity

PROSPER   be successful

PROTRUDE   project

PROVOKE   arouse to action out of irritation

PRY   look closely into

QUELL   subdue

RAVAGE   ruin

REBATE   give back, usually part of an amount paid

REBUFF   repulse

REBUKE   disapprove sharply

RECEDE   move backward

RECOMPENSE   repay

RECONCILE   bring together by settling differences

RECOUP   make up for (e.g. something lost)

RECTIFY   correct

RECUR   happen again

REDEEM   buy back; make good a promise

REFRAIN   keep from

REFUTE   prove false

REIMBURSE   pay back

REITERATE   repeat

REJECT   refuse to take

RELINQUISH   give up

REMINISCE   recall past happenings

REMIT   send (e.g. money)

REMUNERATE   pay for work done

RENOUNCE   give up (e.g. a claim)

RENOVATE   restore (e.g. a house)

REPENT   feel regret for (e.g. a sin)

REPLENISH   make full again

REPOSE   rest

REPRESS   hold back (e.g. a feeling)

REPROACH   blame

REPUDIATE   refuse to recognize

REPULSE   drive back (e.g. an attack)

RESCIND   cancel (e.g. a rule or regulation)

RESPIRE   breathe

RESTRAIN   hold back

RETAIN   keep

RETALIATE   return in kind (e.g. a blow for a blow)

RETARD   delay

RETORT   answer sharply

RETRACT   take back (e.g. something said)

RETRIEVE   get back

REVERE   have deep respect for

REVERT   go back to a former condition

REVOKE   withdraw (e.g. a law)

RUPTURE   break

SALVAGE   save something out of a disaster such as fire

SCALD   burn painfully with steam or hot liquid

SCAN   look at closely

SCOFF   mock

SCORN   treat with contempt

SCOUR   clean thoroughly; move about widely in a search

SCOWL   make an angry look

SECLUDE   keep away from other people

SEEP   ooze

SEETHE   boil

SEVER   divide

SHEAR   cut with a sharp instrument

SHED   throw off (e.g. clothing)

SHIRK   seek to avoid (e.g. duty or work)

SHRIVEL   contract and wrinkle

SHUN   avoid

SHUNT   turn aside

SIFT   sort out through careful examination (e.g. evidence)

SIGNIFY   mean

SINGE   burn slightly

SKIM   read over quickly

SMITE   hit hard

SMOLDER   burn or give off smoke after the fire is out

SNARL   tangle

SOAR   fly high in the air

SOJOURN   live temporarily in a place

SOLICIT   plead for (e.g. help)

SPURN   reject scornfully

STARTLE   surprise

STIFLE   suppress (e.g. feelings)

STREW   scatter

STRIVE   try hard

STUN   daze

SUBSIDE   lessen in activity

SUBSIST   continue to live with difficulty

SUCCUMB   yield to

SUFFICE   be enough

SUPPRESS   put down (e.g. a revolt)

SURGE   increase suddenly

SURMOUNT   overcome (e.g. an obstacle)

SUSTAIN   support

SWARM   move in great numbers

SWAY   move back and forth

TAMPER   meddle with

TARNISH   discolor

TAUNT   reproach mockingly

THAW   melt

THRASH   defeat thoroughly

THRIVE   prosper

THROB   beat insistently

THROTTLE   choke

THRUST   push forcefully and suddenly

THWART   prevent someone from achieving something

TINGE   color slightly

TORMENT   afflict with pain

TRANSFORM   change the appearance of

TRANSMIT   send along

TRANSPIRE   come to light

TRAVERSE   cross over

TRUDGE   walk with difficulty

UNDERGO   experience

UNDO   return to condition before something was done

USURP   seize power illegally

UTILIZE   make use of

UTTER   speak

VACATE   make empty

VANQUISH   conquer

VARY   change

VEND   sell

VERGE   be on the point of

VERIFY   prove the truth of

VEX   annoy

VIBRATE   move back and forth

VIOLATE   break (e.g. a law)

VOUCH   guarantee

WAIVE   give up (e.g. a right or privilege)

WANE   decrease in strength

WARP   twist out of shape

WAVER   sway back and forth

WHET   sharpen

WIELD   put to use (e.g. power or a tool such as a club)

WILT   become limp

WITHER   dry up (e.g. a flower)

WITHSTAND   hold out against (e.g. pressure)

WREST   pull violently

WRING   force out by squeezing

WRITHE   twist and turn about

YEARN   long for

YIELD   give up

500 Useful Adjectives

ACRID   sharp to taste or smell (e.g. odor)

ADAMANT   unyielding

ADEPT   skilled

ADROIT   skillful

AESTHETIC   having to do with beauty

AGILE   nimble

AMBIDEXTROUS   equally skilled at using both hands

AMENABLE   disposed to follow (e.g. advice)

AMIABLE   friendly

APT   suitable

AQUATIC   living in or practiced on water

ARDENT   passionate

ARROGANT   overly proud

ARTICULATE   able to express oneself clearly (e.g. a person)

ASTUTE   shrewd

AUSPICIOUS   favorable (e.g. circumstances)

AUSTERE   harsh

AUTHENTIC   genuine

AUXILIARY   helping

BARREN   unfruitful

BIZARRE   strange

BLAND   gentle

BLATANT   overly loud

BOISTEROUS   rambunctious

BRUSQUE   rudely brief

CALLOUS   unfeeling

CANDID   honest

CASUAL   offhand

CHIC   stylish

CHRONIC   continuing over a long period of time

CIVIC   municipal

CIVIL   courteous

COGENT   convincing (e.g. argument)

COHERENT   clearly holding together

COLLOQUIAL   conversational

COLOSSAL   huge

COMPATIBLE   capable of getting along together

COMPLACENT   satisfied with oneself

CONCISE   brief but complete

COPIOUS   plentiful

CRAFTY   sly

CREDIBLE   believable.

CREDULOUS   given to believing anything too easily

CUMBERSOME   bulky

CURSORY   done quickly but only on the surface (e.g. an examination)

CURT   rudely brief

DEFT   skillful

DEFUNCT   dead

DEMURE   overly modest

DEROGATORY   belittling

DESOLATE   lonely

DESPONDENT   depressed

DESTITUTE   poverty-stricken

DETERGENT   cleansing

DEVIOUS   indirect

DEVOID   completely free of (e.g. feeling)

DEVOUT   very religious

DIFFIDENT   shy

DIMINUTIVE   tiny

DIRE   dreadful

DISCREET   careful

DISCRETE   distinctly separate

DISINTERESTED   impartial

DISMAL   gloomy

DISTRAUGHT   driven to distraction

DIVERSE   varied

DOCILE   easily led

DOGMATIC   stubbornly positive (e.g. opinion)

DOMESTIC   having to do with the home

DOMINANT   ruling

DORMANT   sleeping

DRASTIC   extreme (e.g. changes)

DREARY   gloomy

DUBIOUS   doubtful

DURABLE   lasting

DYNAMIC   energetic

EARNEST   intensely serious

EBONY   black

ECCENTRIC   peculiar (e.g. behavior)

EDIBLE   fit to be eaten

EERIE   weird

ELEGANT   tastefully fine

ELOQUENT   powerfully fluent in writing or speech

ELUSIVE   hard to get hold of

EMINENT   distinguished (e.g. author)

EPIC   heroic in size

ERRATIC   not regular

ETERNAL   everlasting

ETHNIC   having to do with race

EXORBITANT   unreasonable (e.g. price)

EXOTIC   foreign

EXPEDIENT   suitable in a given situation but not necessarily correct

EXPLICIT   clearly indicated

EXQUISITE   extremely beautiful

EXTEMPORANEOUS   spoken or accomplished with little preparation

EXTENSIVE   broad

EXTINCT   no longer existing

EXTRANEOUS   having nothing to do with the subject at hand

FANATIC   extremely emotionally enthusiastic

FEASIBLE   possible to carry out (e.g. a plan)

FEEBLE   weak

FERTILE   productive

FERVENT   warmly felt

FESTIVE   in the spirit of a holiday (e.g. celebration)

FICKLE   changeable

FLAGRANT   noticeably bad (e.g. violation)

FLEET   swift

FLIMSY   not strong (e.g. platform)

FLUENT   smooth (e.g. speech)

FORLORN   hopeless

FORMIDABLE   fear-inspiring because of size or strength (e.g. enemy)

FRAGILE   easily broken

FRAIL   delicate

FRANK   outspoken

FRATERNAL   brotherly

FRIGID   extremely cold

FRUGAL   thrifty

FUTILE   useless

GALA   festive

GALLANT   courteously brave (e.g. conduct)

GAUDY   tastelessly showy

GAUNT   overly thin and weary-looking

GENIAL   kindly

GERMANE   pertinent

GHASTLY   frightful (e.g. appearance)

GIGANTIC   huge

GLIB   fluent but insincere

GLUM   gloomy

GORY   bloody

GRAPHIC   vividly realistic

GRATIS   free

GRIEVOUS   causing sorrow

GRIM   sternly forbidding (e.g. future)

GROSS   glaringly bad (e.g. injustice)

GROTESQUE   distorted in appearance

GRUESOME   horrifying

GULLIBLE   easily fooled

GUTTURAL   throaty (e.g. sound)

HAGGARD   worn-looking

HALE   healthy

HAPHAZARD   chance

HARDY   having endurance

HARSH   disagreeably rough

HAUGHTY   overly proud

HEARTY   friendly (e.g. welcome)

HECTIC   feverish

HEINOUS   outrageous (e.g. crime)

HIDEOUS   extremely ugly

HILARIOUS   very gay

HOMOGENEOUS   of like kind (e.g. group)

HORRENDOUS   horrible

HOSTILE   unfriendly (e.g. unwelcome)

HUMANE   merciful

HUMBLE   modest

HUMID   damp

ILLICIT   illegal

IMMACULATE   spotlessly clean

IMMENSE   very large

IMMINENT   about to happen (e.g. storm)

IMPARTIAL   unbiased

IMPERATIVE   necessary

IMPERTINENT   rude

IMPETUOUS   acting on impulse

IMPLICIT   implied

IMPROMPTU   without any preparation (e.g. remarks)

IMPUDENT   rudely bold

INANE   silly

INCENDIARY   causing fire (e.g. bomb)

INCESSANT   uninterrupted

INCLEMENT   rough (e.g. weather)

INCOGNITO   with real identity hidden

INCOHERENT   not clearly connected

INDELIBLE   unable to be erased

INDIFFERENT   showing no interest

INDIGENT   poor

INDIGNANT   very angry

INDISPENSABLE   absolutely necessary

INDUSTRIOUS   hard-working

INEPT   ineffective

INFALLIBLE   unable to make a mistake

INFAMOUS   having a bad reputation

INFINITE   endless

INFINITESIMAL   very very small

INFLEXIBLE   unbending

INGENIOUS   clever

INGENUOUS   naturally simple

INHERENT   existing in someone or something

INNATE   inborn

INNOCUOUS   harmless

INSIPID   uninteresting (e.g. conversation)

INSOLENT   boldly rude

INTEGRAL   essential to the whole

INTENSIVE   thorough (e.g. study)

INTERMITTENT   starting and stopping (e.g. rain)

INTOLERANT   unwilling or unable to respect others or their beliefs

INTRICATE   complicated

INVINCIBLE   unable to be conquered

IRATE   angry

IRRATIONAL   unreasonable

JOVIAL   good-humored

JUBILANT   joyous

JUDICIOUS   showing good judgment (e.g. decision)

LABORIOUS   demanding a lot of work

LANK   tall and thin

LATENT   hidden (e.g. talent)

LAUDABLE   worthy of praise

LAVISH   extremely generous (e.g. praise)

LAX   loose (e.g. discipline)

LEGIBLE   easily read (e.g. print)

LEGITIMATE   lawful (e.g. claim)

LETHAL   fatal

LISTLESS   lacking in spirit

LITERAL   following the exact words or intended meaning of the original (e.g. translation)

LITERATE   educated to the point of being able to read and write (e.g. person)

LIVID   discolored by a bruise (e.g. flesh)

LOATH   reluctant

LOFTY   very high

LOQUACIOUS   talkative

LUCID   clear

LUCRATIVE   profitable (e.g. business)

LUDICROUS   ridiculous

LURID   shockingly sensational (e.g. story)

LUSTY   vigorous

MAJESTIC   grand (e.g. building)

MALICIOUS   spiteful

MALIGNANT   harmful

MAMMOTH   gigantic

MANDATORY   required

MANIFEST   evident

MANUAL   done by the hands (e.g. labor)

MARINE   of the sea (e.g. life)

MARTIAL   warlike

MASSIVE   bulky and heavy

MEAGER   scanty

MENIAL   lowly (e.g. task)

MERCENARY   working only for financial gain (e.g. soldier)

METICULOUS   extremely careful

MILITANT   aggressive

MOBILE   movable (e.g. home)

MOOT   debatable (e.g. question)

MORBID   unhealthily gloomy

MUTUAL   reciprocal (e.g. admiration)

NAIVE   innocently simple

NAUSEOUS   disgusting

NAUTICAL   having to do with ships and sailing

NEGLIGENT   neglectful

NEUROTIC   describing the behavior of a person suffering from an emotional disorder

NIMBLE   moving quickly and easily

NOCTURNAL   of the night (e.g. animal)

NOMINAL   small in comparison with service or value received (e.g. fee)

NONCHALANT   casual and unexcited

NOTABLE   important (e.g. person)

NOTORIOUS   well-known in an unfavorable way (e.g. criminal)

NULL   having no effect

OBESE   overly fat

OBJECTIVE   free from prejudice (e.g. analysis)

OBLIQUE   indirectly indicated (e.g. suggestion)

OBNOXIOUS   extremely unpleasant (e.g. behavior)

OBSOLETE   out-of-date (e.g. machine)

OBSTINATE   stubborn

OMINOUS   threatening (e.g. clouds)

ONEROUS   burdensome (e.g. task)

OPPORTUNE   timely

OPULENT   wealthy

ORNATE   elaborately decorated

ORTHODOX   usually approved (e.g. religious beliefs)

OSTENSIBLE   apparent

OUTRIGHT   complete

OVERT   open

PALTRY   insignificant (e.g. sum of money)

PARAMOUNT   chief (e.g. importance)

PASSIVE   not active (e.g. participation)

PATENT   obvious

PATHETIC   pitiful

PEDESTRIAN   unimaginative (e.g. ideas)

PEEVISH   irritable

PENITENT   repentant

PENSIVE   thoughtful

PERENNIAL   lasting for a long time (e.g. problem)

PERILOUS   dangerous

PERTINENT   relevant

PETTY   relatively unimportant

PICAYUNE   petty

PIOUS   devoutly religious

PLACID   calm (e.g. waters)

PLAUSIBLE   apparently true (e.g. argument)

PLIABLE   flexible

POIGNANT   keenly painful to the emotions

POMPOUS   self-important (e.g. person)

PORTABLE   capable of being carried (e.g. radio)

POSTHUMOUS   taking place after a person's death (e.g. award)

POTENT   powerful (e.g. drug)

POTENTIAL   possible (e.g. greatness)

PRACTICABLE   capable of being done (e.g. plan)

PRAGMATIC   practical

PRECARIOUS   risky

PRECISE   exact

PRECOCIOUS   advanced to a level earlier than is to be expected (e.g. child)

PREDOMINANT   prevailing

PREPOSTEROUS   ridiculous

PREVALENT   widespread

PRIMARY   fundamental (e.g. reason)

PRIME   first in importance or quality

PRIMITIVE   crude (e.g. tools)

PRIOR   previous (e.g. appointment)

PRODIGIOUS   extraordinary in size or amount (e.g. effort)

PROFICIENT   skilled

PROFUSE   abundantly given (e.g. praise)

PROLIFIC   producing large amounts (e.g. author)

PRONE   disposed to (e.g. accident)

PROSAIC   ordinary

PROSTRATE   laid low (e.g. by grief)

PROVINCIAL   narrow (e.g. view of a matter)

PRUDENT   discreet (e.g. advice)

PUGNACIOUS   quarrelsome (e.g. person)

PUNGENT   sharp to taste or smell (e.g. odor)

PUNITIVE   inflicting punishment (e.g. action)

PUNY   small in size or strength (e.g. effort)

PUTRID   rotten

QUAINT   pleasantly odd (e.g. custom)

RADIANT   brightly shining

RAMPANT   spreading unchecked (e.g. violence)

RANCID   having the bad taste or smell of stale food (e.g. butter)

RANDOM   decided by chance (e.g. choice)

RANK   complete (e.g. incompetency)

RASH   reckless

RAUCOUS   harsh (e.g. sound)

RAVENOUS   extremely hungry

REFLEX   of an involuntary response (e.g. action)

REGAL   royal

RELENTLESS   persistent (e.g. chase)

RELEVANT   pertinent

REMISS   careless (e.g. in one's duty)

REMOTE   far distant (e.g. time or place)

REPLETE   filled (e.g. with thrills)

REPUGNANT   extremely distasteful

REPULSIVE   disgusting

REPUTABLE   respectable (e.g. doctor)

RESIGNED   submitting passively to (e.g. one's fate)

RESOLUTE   firmly determined

RESONANT   resounding (e.g. sound)

RESTIVE   restless (e.g. pupils)

RETICENT   speaking little (e.g. child)

RIGID   stiff

ROBUST   strong and healthy

ROWDY   rough and disorderly (e.g. mob)

RUGGED   rough

RUSTIC   of the country (e.g. life)

RUTHLESS   pitiless (e.g. dictator)

SAGE   wise (e.g. advice)

SALIENT   prominent (e.g. points)

SALUTARY   healthful (e.g. climate)

SANE   mentally sound

SANGUINARY   bloody

SANGUINE   cheerfully hopeful

SCANTY   meager

SCHOLASTIC   having to do with school and education (e.g. record)

SCRAWNY   thin

SCRUPULOUS   careful and honest (e.g. accounting)

SECRETIVE   given to secrecy

SECULAR   not religious (e.g. education)

SEDATE   dignified

SERENE   calm

SHEER   very thin (e.g. stockings); utter (e.g. nonsense)

SHIFTLESS   lazy

SHIFTY   tricky

SHODDY   inferior in quality (e.g. material)

SHREWD   clever in one's dealings (e.g. businessman)

SIMULTANEOUS   happening at the same time (e.g. events)

SINGULAR   remarkable; strange (e.g. behavior)

SINISTER   threatening evil

SKEPTICAL   showing doubt (e.g. attitude)

SLACK   not busy (e.g. business season); loose (e.g. rope)

SLEEK   smooth and glossy (e.g. appearance)

SLENDER   small in size or amount (e.g. contribution)

SLOVENLY   untidy

SLUGGISH   slow-moving

SMUG   self-satisfied

SNUG   comfortable

SOBER   serious

SOLEMN   grave (e.g. occasion)

SOLITARY   lone

SOMBER   dark and gloomy (e.g. outlook)

SOPHISTICATED   wise in the ways of the world

SORDID   wretched (e.g. condition)

SPARSE   thinly scattered

SPIRITED   lively

SPIRITUAL   of the spirit or soul

SPONTANEOUS   happening as a result of natural impulse (e.g. reaction)

SPORADIC   happening at irregular times (e.g. shooting)

SPRY   nimble

STACCATO   with breaks between successive sounds

STAGNANT   dirty from lack of movement (e.g. water)

STALWART   robust

STAUNCH   firm (e.g. friend)

STARK   bleak (e.g. outlook)

STATELY   dignified

STATIC   stationary

STATIONARY   not moving

STEADFAST   firm

STERN   severe (e.g. look)

STOCKY   short and heavily built

STODGY   uninteresting

STOICAL   unmoved emotionally

STOUT   fat; firm (e.g. resistance)

STRAIGHTFORWARD   honest (e.g. answer)

STRENUOUS   demanding great energy (e.g. exercise)

STUPENDOUS   amazing (e.g. effort)

STURDY   strongly built

SUAVE   smoothly polite (e.g. manner)

SUBLIME   inspiring admiration because of noble quality (e.g. music)

SUBSIDIARY   of less importance (e.g. rank)

SUBSTANTIAL   of considerable numbers or size

SUBTLE   suggested delicately (e.g. hint)

SULLEN   resentful

SULTRY   extremely hot and humid (e.g. weather)

SUMPTUOUS   costly (e.g. meal)

SUNDRY   various

SUPERB   of a high degree of excellence

SUPERFICIAL   not going beyond the obvious (e.g. examination)

SUPERFLUOUS   beyond what is needed

SUPERLATIVE   superior to all others (e.g. performance)

SUPPLE   limber (e.g. body)

SURLY   offensively rude

SUSCEPTIBLE   easily affected by (e.g. colds)

SWARTHY   dark-skinned

TACIT   not openly said but implied (e.g. approval)

TANGIBLE   capable of being touched; actual (e.g. results)

TARDY   late (e.g. student)

TART   having a sharp taste (e.g. food)

TAUT   tightly stretched (e.g. rope)

TEDIOUS   long and tiresome (e.g. study)

TEMPERATE   moderate (e.g. climate)

TENACIOUS   holding fast (e.g. grip)

TENTATIVE   for a temporary period of trial (e.g. agreement)

TEPID   lukewarm (e.g. water)

TERMINAL   concluding

TERSE   brief but expressing a good deal (e.g. comment)

THANKLESS   unappreciated (e.g. task)

TIDY   neat (e.g. appearance)

TIMELESS   eternal (e.g. beauty)

TIMELY   happening at a desirable time (e.g. arrival)

TIMID   shy

TIRESOME   tiring

TITANIC   of enormous size or strength

TORRID   intensely hot

TRANQUIL   calm (e.g. waters)

TRANSIENT   passing away after a brief time

TRIFLING   of little importance

TRITE   ordinary (e.g. remark)

TRIVIAL   insignificant

TURBULENT   agitated

ULTIMATE   final (e.g. conclusion)

UNANIMOUS   in complete agreement (e.g. decision)

UNASSUMING   modest

UNCANNY   unnatural (e.g. accuracy)

UNCONDITIONAL   absolute (e.g. surrender)

UNCOUTH   crude and clumsy (e.g. adolescent)

UNDAUNTED   not discouraged

UNDERHAND   sly

UNDULY   overly (e.g. concerned)

UNEASY   disturbed

UNGAINLY   awkward (e.g. youth)

UNIQUE   only one of its kind (e.g. specimen)

UNKEMPT   not combed

UNRULY   disorderly (e.g. crowd)

UNSCATHED   uninjured

UNWIELDY   clumsy to use, usually because of size (e.g. implement)

UPRIGHT   honest (e.g. citizen)

UTMOST   most extreme (e.g. in distance, height or size)

UTTER   complete (e.g. failure)

VAIN   futile (e.g. attempt); conceited (e.g. person)

VALIANT   brave

VALID   (legally) sound (e.g. argument)

VAST   very large in extent or size (e.g. distances)

VEHEMENT   violent in feeling (e.g. protest)

VERBATIM   word for word (e.g. report)

VERSATILE   able to perform many tasks well (e.g. athlete)

VIGILANT   watchful (e.g. sentry)

VILE   highly disgusting (e.g. conduct)

VISIBLE   able to be seen (e.g. object)

VITAL   essential (e.g. contribution)

VIVACIOUS   lively

VIVID   bright (e.g. color)

VOID   not binding legally (e.g. contract)

VOLUMINOUS   very great in size (e.g. writings)

VORACIOUS   greedy for food (e.g. appetite)

VULNERABLE   open to attack (e.g. position)

WARY   cautious

WEARY   tired

WEE   very small

WEIGHTY   important (e.g. decision)

WHOLESOME   causing a feeling of well-being (e.g. entertainment)

WILY   cunning (e.g. magician)

WISHFUL   showing desire that something be so (e.g. thinking)

WITTY   amusingly clever (e.g. remark)

WORDY   using too many words (e.g. reply)

WORLDLY   enjoying the pleasures and experiences of this world (e.g. person)

WORTHY   deserving (e.g. choice)

WRETCHED   miserable

7 CODING SPEED SKILLS

Improving Your Memory

Science has yet to discover exactly how the human brain works. It knows enough to tell us that the brain is an awesomely complex structure that makes the most advanced computer look crude. We also know that it has enormous untapped potential. One commonly cited bit of knowledge has it that the average people use only about ten percent of their ten billion brain cells. If we were able to tap the unused powers of our mind, we might be able to accomplish wondrous things. Studies that have been made of individuals with just such extraordinary mental abilities bear out the supposition.

One famous case that was extensively documented is that of Mr. S. He was an obscure Russian who had a fantastic memory. He was able to memorize a list of 18 six-digit numbers in 3 minutes. He retained it so well that he could repeat the list in any order, even reciting each number in reverse! Amazingly, he was able to repeat these feats years later, even though he had not seen the list in the interim! Extraordinary displays of memory also are given by professional entertainers, the so-called memory experts who can learn the names and addresses of dozens of members of an audience they have never met before. In addition, we all have heard stories about famous generals, hostesses, and politicians who never forget a name or a place.

Intensive studies of people with "super-memories" have helped psychologists understand how those of us with ordinary memories, may improve them. The methods outlined below are based on such studies

Techniques for Remembering Words

Association and Imagery

If you are like most people, you find it easier to remember names than numbers. This is because names bring forth a meaningful association with something familiar. They may remind us of a place, a thing, or a word we know about. Even better, the name may bring a vivid picture to mind. For example, take the word *ice*. As soon as we see or hear this word, we may form an association with the words *cream* or *snow*. We may also associate *ice* with ideas or feelings such as *cold* and *chilly*. In our mind's eye, the image of an *iceberg* or an *ice cube* may form without conscious effort.

When we see a name that carries a meaningful association and presents an image, the name will probably stick in our memory. Two key memorization techniques to use, therefore, are *association* and *imagery*.

Look at the sample below. This represents the type of coding question that you will find on the test. Remember, this is a speed test. You must remember the words and numbers in the Key. Then, from the list of possible answers, you must find the number that is the correct code for that word. *Note: The test is organized in a way to help you as you learn your memory techniques:*

1. The words in the Key are always listed in *alphabetical order.*

2. The numbers in the Answer Choices are always in *ascending order.*

Key		
bargain . .8385	house . . .2859	owner . . .6227
chin 8930	knife 7150	point 4703
game 6456	music . . .1117	sofa 9645
	sunshine .7489	

	Answers				
	A	B	C	D	E
1. music	1117	2859	7489	8385	9645
2. knife	6227	6456	7150	7489	8485
3. sunshine	4703	6227	6456	7489	8930
4. chin	1117	2859	4703	7150	8930
5. sofa	4703	6227	7150	8485	9645
6. bargain	2859	6456	8385	8930	9645
7. point	1117	4703	6227	6456	7150

Now let's label the elements in the Key so that you can easily grasp the important items.

X	Y	Z
bargain 8385	house 2859	owner 6227
chin 8930	knife 7150	point 4703
game 6456	music 1117	sofa 9645
	sunshine 7489	

Try to associate with either 3 words horizontally, or 3 to 4 words vertically. For example, take the 3 horizontal words:

> bargain house owner

Imagine an owner who wants to sell a house and puts a sign with the word BARGAIN on the front lawn. This image is vivid,, and it forms a good association among the 3 words. 3 words.

Now let's try this technique with the 3 vertical words: *owner, point,* and *sofa.*

> owner
> point
> sofa

What images do you see? What about an *owner* pointing to his *sofa* and saying that he bought it for a mere $9645? This also conjures up a vivid picture. And besides helping you remember the words and their placement, you'll probably remember the number as well!

Note that putting the words in an imaginary box and labeling the box can help your memory.

X	Y	Z
bargain	house	owner
chin	knife	point
game	music	sofa
	sunshine	

The "LOCI" Technique

Mr. S., the Russian with the fabulous memory, partially explained it by telling about a system of "places" he used. (*Loci* is a Greek word meaning "places.") He said that he remembered long lists of objects by mentally putting each object in a particular place that was familiar to him. By remembering the place, he could "see" the object. For example, assume that Mr. S. were given a list of objects to remember such as a hat, cane, dog, violin. He would assign each of them to a particular place in a certain scene. A scene that he sometimes used was a street near his home. He knew every inch of it because he walked it daily. To remember the list of objects, he merely imagined himself walking down the street. On his imaginary walk, he put the *hat* on a lamp post, leaned the *cane* against the side of a shop, saw the *dog* near a tree across the road, put the *violin* in a pawnshop window, etc. He could recall each object by mentally retracing his path down the street. So, when he saw the tree, he saw the dog, too! Each of the other objects on his list was recalled in the same way.

Performers, politicians, students, and others from all walks of life have been using the loci system, or a variation on it, through the ages. It will work for you, too, provided you do two things:

1. Decide on your personal system of places, or loci.
2. Become so familiar with your loci that you can immediately "see" every one of the places.

You might choose a street on the way to work, your shop or office, a room in your house. The objects can range from your kitchen shelf to your desk drawer. Make the scene as detailed as you wish. The more "places" it has in it, the more items you will be able to remember.

Reduction Coding

This is the third of our memory tools. It means that we cut down, or *reduce,* the amount we have to remember and then put what remains into a special, easy-to-remember form. Here are some simple examples:

SAMPLE

We can remember the order in which the colors of the rainbow appear (*r*ed, *o*range, *y*ellow, *g*reen, *b*lue, *i*ndigo, *v*iolet) by using their initials, ROYGBIV.

SAMPLE

If you want to remember the names of the Great Lakes, just remember the word HOMES:
- *H*uron
- *O*ntario
- *M*ichigan
- *E*rie
- *S*uperior

In each case, *one* word replaces many words.

One more example. This time it is a word frequently used by those preparing for a test to select managers.

SAMPLE

The word is POSDCORB, and it stands for the seven basic duties of every manager:
- *P*lanning
- *O*rganizing
- *S*taffing
- *D*irecting
- *C* }
- *O* } ordinating
- *R*eporting
- *B*udgeting

Seven different words made into one! Although POSDCORB, as a word, doesn't mean anything, it can be *sounded out* and seen in the mind's eye very easily. In his way, it will be remembered far longer and better than by drilling on the original seven.

Try this technique using the example on page 294.

Techniques for Remembering Numbers

Chunk the Number

SAMPLE

Try this experiment. Get a pencil and a blank sheet of paper. Next, study line 1 below for 5 seconds. Then look away and write, in order, the numbers you saw.

Line 1: 7 4 3 0 1 9 4 1 1 8 6 5

That was not easy. Try it once more using line 2 below. Study it for 5 seconds, look away, and write the numbers from memory.

Line 2:   7430   1941   1865

It was much easier to do the second time, wasn't it? Although the numbers were identical, the fact that they were organized into "chunks" made all the difference. Here is why.

The way our mind works, most of us cannot retain more than seven or eight pieces of information presented to us separately. The way the numbers were displayed on line 1, you were required to remember *twelve* separate items. On line 2, the same numbers were gathered into chunks of four numbers each. Each of these chunks, believe it or not, is as difficult (or easy) to remember as just *one* of the original digits. In effect, a chunk counts as a single piece of information. This is particularly true when the chunks have a meaningful association. In the example above, most of us will associate 1941 with Pearl Harbor, and 1865 with the end of the Civil War or President Lincoln's assassination. The chunking technique will make it far easier to remember the numbers.

Let's look again at the numbers in the exercise on page 294.

X	Y	Z
8385	2859	6227
8930	7150	4703
6456	1117	9645
	7489	

Use your powers of visualization. Help your memory by placing each set of numbers in an imaginary box and labeling the boxes. In that way, you will be able to identify in which box each part belongs. You will get the correct answer if you visualize "chunks" 8385, 2859, and 6227 "floating" on the top line, *where the sign* **BARGAIN** *shows a* **house** *being sold by its* **owner for $8385 2859 6227.** What a bargain! (Remember that you can combine the techniques " chunking" numbers with associating" names.)

Try the same thing with the vertical numbers 6227, 4703, and 9645. Remember, you already know that the *sofa* is being sold for a mere $9645!

Use Associations

Using associations to remember the names was discussed previously. It can work quickly and easily, with many names, i.e. *Pearl*—Bailey, necklace; *Magnet*—pull, iron; *Cedar*—tree, chest, red.

Numbers may be remembered in the same way.

Now See Why

1. *There are numbers which hold immediate associations for almost everyone.*

   1492—Columbus, Discovery of America
   1776—Declaration of Independence, Revolutionary War
   1914—Outbreak of World War I
   1929—Stock Market Crash

2. *Some numbers hold personal associations.* The chances are that most of us make an immediate connection with all or part of some of the following items.

address—	home, business friend
age—	yours, wife, child
telephone number-	home, job, friend
Social Security number—	_____
license plate number-	_____
anniversary—	wedding, job, retirement
birthdate—	yours, loved one's
credit card number—	_____

Associate Numbers with Your "Loci"

If you have a system of "loci" (see page 295), it may be used to "place" some numbers. For example, you might see your hi-fi set in the living room playing a *45* r.p.m. record. Nearby, in the dining room a stack of *33* r.p.m. L.P.'s sits on the table to be played next.

Look for One-of-a-Kind Numbers and Number Positions

After you have reduced the numbers, chunked them, and tried to associate them with their boxes, examine them quickly to see if any of them are "one-of-a-kind"! Also, look to see if any of the numbers fall into easy-to-remember positions.

Let's turn again to the sample on page 294.

1. Out of all of the numbers, only two are below 4500. See 2859 and 1117 in your imaginary box Y:

X	Y	Z
8385	2859	6227
8930	7150	4703
6456	1117	9645
	7489	

Whenever the boxes contain only one number in a category (the 10's, 20's 30's etc.) or even two, those number(s) take on a special association with the box in which they are located.

2. *Notice the numerical relationships:*
   a. *The only two chunks starting with the same digit—8385 and 8930— lie one above the other.*
   b. The numbers on the bottom line gradually increase from Box X to Z —6456, 7489, 9645.

When you train your eye to quickly pick up relationships like these, you are embedding those numbers more firmly in your mind. It is far easier to remember a pattern than a group of numbers at random.

Use a Rhyming Code

This memory system is designed especially for remembering numbers. In it, each of the numbers from 1 to 20 is associated with one or more designated words with which it rhymes. (See table below.) You memorize a number by translating it into a word picture or story, using the rhyming code words. Make the story picture as unusual, funny, and active as you can. Later, when you wish to recall the numbers, just bring that story picture back to mind. The words in it should automatically bring back the numbers too.

For example, if this method were used to remember the 4-digit number 2148, the story would go like this:

I found a *shoe* that had a *bun* in it and took it to the *door* and *ate* it.

RHYMING TABLE FOR NUMBERS

Number	Word(s)
1	Bun, Won
2	Shoe, Flew
3	Tree, See
4	Door, Score

5	Hive, Strive
6	Sticks, Picks
7	Heaven, Leaven
8	Gate, Ate
9	Spine, Dine
10	Hen, Pen
11	Eleven (as in football), Enliven
12	Delve, Shelve
13	Flirting, Thirsting
14	Courting, Sorting
15	Lifting, Drifting
16	Fixing, Sicking (as in dog)
17	Leavening, Leveling
18	Mating, Grating
19	Pining
*20	Plenty

---

*Although this table is sufficient for you to encode all possible number combinations, it will help if you add some key words:

0	. . . hero, zero
30	. . . dirty, thirsty
40	. . . naughty, haughty
50	. . . nifty, swiftly
60	. . . sickly, sexy
70	. . . TNT, sentry
80	. . . lately, Haiti
90	. . . Numbly, pine tree

If you had a command of the extra code words and numbers shown at the bottom of the table, you also could have used this story for the same number.

I saw *plenty* of *buns* (21) on the wedding table. I jumped on the table and *haughtly ate* (48) them.

The story is ridiculous, but it is vivid. It can be made up quickly and recollected just as easily. With practice, stories like these can be made up in 15 to 20 seconds. See if you have the knack for doing it. First, memorize the above table. Then, try to make up stories for the key on page 294.

You will increase the flexibility and power of this system if you incorporate some of your favorite personal associations with it. The fact that they may not rhyme is not important, so long as they give you a key for additional numbers. For example, to remember the number 72 in a box, you may prefer to use an image of your father (if he is 72) instead of an image of a *sentry* without *shoes* (72).

Final Guidelines

What method to use for memorization? Use any of the memorization methods, or combination of methods, that work best for you. As you do the practice tests, you will be in a good position to make a final decision on how to proceed on the real test. Make this decision by the time you complete all of the practice tests in this book and, definitely, *before* you take the actual exam. For example, if you have been getting good scores on the practice tests

by the use of Reduction Coding, stick to it. For memorizing numbers, you may be doing very well remembering Number Associations. Others will have found they are good at Chunking and should immediately use that technique of the test.

Tips for Names

1. *Association and Imagery.* Attach a vivid, colorful, or active image to the address; and it comes alive and is easier to remember. For example, Grand with Canyon, Crescent with Moon, Carpenter with Swinging a Hammer.
2. *Loci.* Decide on a familiar setting and visualize the objects in your imaginary boxes to be part of that scene. For example, assume that on your test you can see the words:

```
            X
    ┌ ─ ─ ─ ─ ┐
    | cheese  |
    | bread   |
    | desk    |
    └ ─ ─ ─ ─ ┘
```

The picture you can come up with would show a big, smelly piece of cheese between two slices of bread lying on top of your desk — Box X.
3. *Reduction Coding.* NATO is easier to remember than North Atlantic Treaty Organization. U.I.B., FBI, UNICEF are other examples of how lengthy words and phrases may be easily remembered by using their initials to form a new word. On the test you can use this principle to remember each imaginary box individually.
   A. *Check the Sound.* The three- or five-initial words may have a distinctive sound, like "BUZ" or "CRUMP."
   B. *Check For Meaning.* The new word may mean something like the one formed by the initials of the names.
   Game   Roof   Owner   Water   Sofa
   C. *Make Up a Story/Slogan.* Use initials to make up a story or slogan. For example, if five letters are TRMAB you could think of The Red Monkey Ate Bananas.

Tips for Numbers

1. *Chunk the Number.* Place the numbers in imaginary boxes and label the boxes so that you can easily identify where each part belongs.
2. *Association.* Numbers can evoke associations, just as names can. Look for numbered addresses that mean something to you, like your birthday, your address, your height, your weight.
3. *Look for One-of-a-Kind Numbers and Number Positions.* Do numbers increase or decrease vertically or horizontally? Are all high or low, except for one number? Practice noting relationships.
4. *Rhymes and Codes.* Numbers can be associated with a word with which they rhyme. For example, 1 with "won," 2 with "shoe," 10 with "hen." With practice, you can make up a story or picture using two-, four- or six-digit chunks.
5. *Loci.* The technique explained for letters can also be applied to numbers.
6. Practice-Practice-Practice.

8 AUTOMOTIVE INFORMATION REVIEW

Automobiles are the basis of our transportation system and a necessary part of our whole way of life. The bright and colorful finish of the new car, the closed body, solid top and glass windows—all this bears little resemblance to the early cars. Electronic ignition, automatic transmission, soft springs and comfortable seats, fuel-efficient engines—these and many other items of safety and convenience have increased the numbers of people able and eager to drive.

We do not have the space in this section to cover all the changes and new devices on automobiles today. This section attempts to explain simply the basic parts of an automobile and how they operate, to discuss in some detail basic mechanical principles as they apply to the internal combustion engine, and finally to provide a guide to recognizing common problems that may occur with a car.

Parts of an Automobile

Fundamentally the automobile is a compartment mounted on wheels with some self-contained means for propelling it over ground. Of course, today's automobiles consist of a great deal more than that—easy riding suspension systems, soft comfortable seats, headlights for night-driving, windshield wipers, rear-view mirrors and many other driver conveniences and safety features. If these were lacking we would feel that the car was quite incomplete. Yet the fundamentals are still there, and there was a time when many of these "extras" were unknown to builders of automobiles.

One of the fundamentals is without doubt the wheel. For thousands of years the wheel has made transportation easier. But for most of that time the wheel served only as a support for the vehicle, to make it easier for something to pull it or push it. A separate motive power propelled the vehicle—slaves, animals, or even the wind. Then the internal combustion engine, with its light weight and comparatively high efficiency, made the automobile a practical mechanism for transporting people from where they were to where they wanted to be. This was the beginning of the automobile we know today.

It is easy to see that the very least we need to make an automobile go is an engine and some means of connecting the engine to the wheels. The engine turns the shaft, which runs back toward the rear wheels. It has a gear on the end which meshes with a gear on the axle connecting the rear wheels together. As the first shaft turns, it rotates the axle and the wheels propel the car. If there were no hills around, and we didn't want to go very fast and didn't want to turn any corners, this arrangement might work. But in an actual automobile, we have some more parts between the engine and the wheels. From here on in this section, we're going to take them up one by one and try to explain what they are and what they do and how the wheels revolve.

The Engine

The power of an automobile engine comes from the burning of a mixture of gasoline and air in a small, enclosed space. When this mixture burns it expands greatly, and pushes out in all directions. It happens so quickly that we sometimes call it an explosion. This push or pressure can be used to move a part of the engine, and the movement of this part is eventually transmitted back to the wheels to drive the car.

Looking at an engine under the hood of an automobile, it seems to be a complicated sort of thing with hundreds of pieces and attachments. But we can forget about most of these for the present, and consider only the basic parts.

First, we must have a cylinder. This is something like a tall metal can, or a pipe closed at one end. In fact some of the early automobiles used cast iron pipe for cylinders.

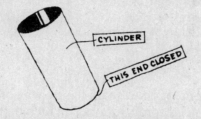

Inside the cylinder we have a piston. This is a plug which is close-fitting but which can slide up and down easily. It is the part of the engine mentioned above which is moved by the expanding gases, being driven down on each power impulse or explosion.

Now we must find some way to change that up-and-down motion to rotary motion to propel the car. For this we have a connecting rod and crankshaft. The crankshaft is a shaft with an offset portion, the crank, which describes a circle as the shaft rotates. The top end of the connecting rod is fastened to the piston, so it goes up and down in a straight line. The bottom end is fastened to the crank, so that end has to go around in a circle as the piston moves up and down.

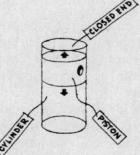

This is the most common way of changing straight line motion to rotary motion. Familiar examples of it are a kitchen meat grinder or a bicycle. In the latter the foot pedal is the crank and our leg the connecting rod. Our knee moves up and down in a straight line while our foot goes round in a circle.

On one end of the crankshaft is a heavy wheel called the flywheel. If we turn a grindstone or emery wheel rapidly by hand, and then let go, the wheel will keep on rotating. This is the same action as the flywheel. It keeps the engine turning between power impulses.

These are the basic parts of an engine. However, these parts would make only a single-cylinder engine. All automobile engines today have four or more cylinders. They can be arranged in one straight row, which we call an in-line engine, or in two rows set at an angle, descriptively called a V-type engine. In either case we have only one crankshaft, but it has a number of cranks instead of only one. With a number of cylinders the flywheel does not have such a big job to do because the power impulses occur more often and thus keep the crankshaft turning.

This basic engine we have put together so far has no way of getting the fuel-air mixture into it or burned gases out of it. We need some "doors," which in this case we call valves. Two holes are cut in the top of the cylinder, one for intake and one for exhaust. Metal discs are arranged to fit tightly over the holes to close them, but when pushed down they open the holes to allow passage of the gases through them. They work very much like the familiar stopper in a wash-bowl, but turned upside down.

The valves are controlled by rocker arms and rods which are moved by a camshaft. This is a shaft with cams or bumps on it—one bump for each valve—which push up on the rods to open the valves. The camshaft is driven by the crankshaft, at one-half speed. The cams are accurately shaped and located, and the shaft rotates at just the proper speed, as the valves must open and close at exactly the right moment.

Carburetors and Fuel Pumps

In order to produce power, the engine needs a supply of gasoline and air mixed in the proper proportions. The carburetor does the mixing job. Gasoline is pumped from the tank to the carburetor by the fuel pump. This operates in much the same manner as the old-fashioned water pump, each stroke pushing a little fuel on to the carburetor where it goes first to the float chamber.

Air enters the carburetor through the air cleaner, being pulled in by the pumping action of the engine pistons working in the cylinders. The air flows through a venturi (a reduced passage in the carburetor) at high speed, then past the end of a tube leading from the float chamber. This sucks out the fuel into the air stream, breaking the liquid up into a fine mist and mixing it thoroughly with the air. An atomizer or garden sprayer works in a similar manner. Then the fuel and air mixture goes on into the engine. The amount of the mixture going into the engine is controlled by a throttle valve at the base of the carburetor, which is opened or closed by movement of the accelerator pedal.

A good mixture for burning in an engine is about 15 pounds of air to 1 pound of gasoline. Air being so much lighter than gasoline, this means that for every gallon of gasoline we burn, we use enough air to fill a room 10 feet square and more than 10 feet high. We call them gasoline engines, but it is easy to see that in some ways air plays the more important part.

Electronic Carburetors and Fuel Injection Systems

Many modern automobiles are equipped with electronically controlled carburetors. This type of carburetor results from integrating the sophisticated electronics used in electronic fuel injection with the basic carburetor. The primary difference between a basic carburetor and an electronic carburetor is the addition of an electrically operated device called a fuel solenoid. The fuel solenoid is an electronically controlled valve used to regulate the amount of fuel delivered to the engine through the main metering circuit.

There are three basic types of fuel injection in use today: (1) multi-injector electronic, (2) mono-injector electronic, and (3) manual continuous flow. The two electronic types are very similar and use most of the same components. They differ mainly in the number of injectors used. The multi-injector, the first electronic fuel injection system used and one that is still popular, uses one injector for each cylinder, all connected to a common fuel rail. Each individual injector has a separate internal solenoid and fuel valve, yet all are connected to one control system.

A typical fuel injection system control usually contains most of the following units, which are interconnected by an electrical harness:

1. A *manifold absolute pressure sensor,* or vacuum transducer, that controls the *basic* quantity of fuel at each engine speed.
2. An engine *speed,* or *timing, sensor* that determines exactly when each injector valve is to be opened (or, as is generally the case, two or four valves may be opened simultaneously).
3. A *throttle-position switch* that controls the amount of fuel needed for the engine speed called for by the throttle position.
4. *Temperature sensors* for engine coolant and intake air that vary the basic fuel quantity in accordance with immediate engine operating temperatures.
5. *An airflow sensor* for determining the volume of air entering the cylinders and controlling the basic quantity of fuel delivered.
6. A *fast-idle* valve that increases the normal (warm-engine) idle speed during periods of cold starting and warm-up. In some systems, an *air solenoid valve* is also used to supplement the fast-idle valve.
7. An *oil-pressure sensor* that closes down the system if oil pressure becomes dangerously low.
8. Finally, a *control unit* (ECU) that converts all the foregoing signals into the pulses that operate the injector valves.

In manual fuel injection systems the function of a manifold absolute pressure may be accomplished by a *pressure sensor* and a *pressure switch* . There may also be more than two *temperature sensors.* And a fuel-injection pump to which the various system signals are transmitted, may replace the control unit and injector valves and meter fuel directly to injection nozzles.

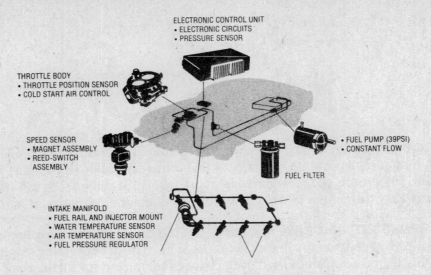

Fuel injector valves are used with electronic fuel injection systems. They are solenoid-operated pintle valves with integral fine-mist nozzles that project into the intake manifold above the respective intake ports. Each valve is operated by a pulsed signal from the control unit, which opens the valve for the proper time interval (pulse width) to deliver the amount of fuel determined by the control unit.

Fuel for the valves of an engine (one valve for each cylinder) is delivered by the *fuel rail,* which is attached to the tops of the valve bodies and in which fuel is kept at a constant, predetermined pressure. Generally with V-type engines, the fuel rail is divided into two parts, each of which serves half the total number of valves. The two parts are so assembled that one pressure regulator, installed in the complete assembly, serves both halves.

Fuel Pumps. Two electric fuel pumps are usually used. The first, located in the fuel tank, is generally a diaphragm-type booster pump that is integral with the fuel gauge and a simple, replaceable-element filter. The second, located somewhere in the fuel line ahead of the pressure regulator, is usually a roller-vane pump driven by a motor and designed to produce a constant displacement. This (second) pump has a check (one-way pressure-opened) valve at the output side that prevents backflow to maintain pressure in the line when the pump is not operating. In general, pumps have built-in design factors that cannot be altered by service procedures. It is generally contained within a compact housing designed for mounting as desired and for connection, by a designed electrical harness, to the other components of a system. This is a nonserviceable unit which must be replaced if faulty.

Fuel Pressure Regulator. Because the second fuel pump operates continuously at maximum output, regardless of engine speed or load, the engine seldom requires all the fuel the pump makes available. It is the function of the pressure regulator to return excess fuel through a bypass line back to the tank, and thus to maintain a constant pressure in the fuel rail.

Electronic Control Unit. This may be an analog or digital computer (with electronic circuits) that is preprogrammed by the manufacturer to "accept" certain signals from the various sensors of the system and to "translate" these into a pulsed signal for operation of the fuel injection valves. It is generally contained within a compact housing designed for mounting as desired and for connection, by a designed electrical harness, to the other components of the system. This is a nonserviceable unit that must be replaced if faulty.

Engine Ignition   Now we have everything we need to make an engine run except something to start the mixture burning in the cylinder. Any kind of a spark will do it. In a cigarette lighter we make a spark by friction against a special metal. In an engine we do it electrically. A spark

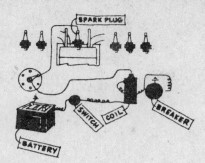

plug is inserted in the top of each cylinder, and a spark is created by electricity jumping across the gap between the two electrodes of the plug.

A battery furnishes the electricity, but several additional pieces of equipment are necessary for a complete ignition system. The coil and the breaker cooperate to develop a very high voltage, and the distributor is responsible for getting the high voltage electricity to the right spark plug at the right time.

All of this must take place very rapidly. In an eight-cylinder engine driving a car 55 miles per hour, the ignition system would have to furnish about 7,350 sparks per minute, or 123 each second. And it must do this at exactly the right time and without a miss.

The reason the valve mechanism and ignition system must perform their duties at just the right time is that an engine operates with a certain definite cycle of events—over and over again, at a high rate of speed. Now that we have all the necessary parts of an engine, we can see how it actually works.

How an Engine Works

Most automobile engines are four-cycle engines. This means they operate on a four-stroke cycle, taking four strokes of the piston—down, up, down, up—for one complete cycle of events.

On the first stroke the intake valve is open and the piston moves down, pulling in the fuel-air mixture until the cylinder is full. This is the *intake stroke.*

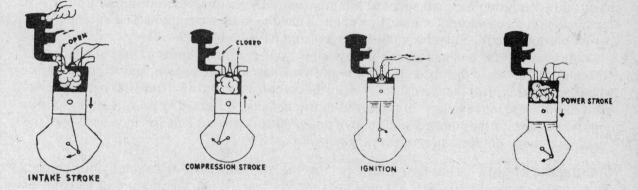

INTAKE STROKE   COMPRESSION STROKE   IGNITION   POWER STROKE

Then the intake valve closes and the piston starts up on the *compression stroke.* It squeezes the mixture into a small space at the top of the cylinder which increases the pressure in the cylinder to almost 200 pounds per square inch.

Between the second and third strokes, ignition or firing takes place. The spark, jumping the gap of the spark plug, ignites the mixture of fuel and air squeezed at the top of the cylinder. In burning, the mixture of course gets very hot and tries to expand in all directions. The pressure rises to about 600 or 700 pounds per square inch. The piston is the only thing that can move, so the expanding gases push it down to the bottom of the cylinder. This is the *power stroke.*

The fuel is burned and the energy in the gases has been used up in pushing the piston downward. Now it is necessary to clear these burned gases out of the cylinder to make room for a

new charge. On the *exhaust stroke*, the exhaust valve opens and the piston pushes the gases out through the opening.

So the cycle is completed and we are ready to start over again with the intake stroke of the next cycle. Intake—Compression—Power—Exhaust. Over and over again through the same series of actions. The crankshaft is going around continuously while the piston is going up and down, but we should note that it is only on the power stroke that the piston is driving it around. On the other three strokes, the crankshaft is driving the piston. There is one power stroke to every two revolutions of the crankshaft. This is for each cylinder, of course; with an eight-cylinder engine there are 4 power strokes for each revolution.

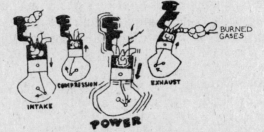

We described what happens on the compression stroke, but we did not go into detail as to its importance. We hear talk of "compression ratio" and "high compression ratio," all of which has to do with how much we squeeze the mixture in the cylinder before igniting it. It is a fundamental fact of internal combustion engines that the more we compress the mixture—the harder we squeeze it—the more power we get from it.

Compression ratio is a measure of how much we squeeze the mixture. If the cylinder holds 100 cubic inches when the piston is all the way down in its lowest position, and 10 cubic inches when the piston is up as far as it can go, we say the compression ratio is 10 to 1. The mixture has been compressed into a space $1/10$ as large as it originally occupied. Fifty years ago 4 to 1 was a common figure for the compression ratio of automobile engines. This has increased over the years, and today compression ratios range upward of 8 to 1.

Cooling the Engine Thus far we have put together the main parts of an automobile engine. Such an engine would run—but it would not run very long. When the mixture of fuel and air burns in the cylinder, it creates a temperature of 4000 to 4500 degrees Fahrenheit. This is almost twice the temperature at which iron melts. So it is easy to see that if we did not have a cooling system our engine would not last very long.

The usual way of cooling the engine is to put water jackets around the hottest parts. Water is constantly circulated through these by a small pump. The heat of the cylinder makes the water hot, and it then goes to the radiator where it is cooled by the outside air passing through. Then it starts back to the engine again to do more cooling. It is actually very much like a steam or hot water heating system in a home. The engine is our boiler which heats up the water which then goes to a radiator where it gives up its heat to the air.

Lubricating the Engine

We also need a lubrication system for our engine. If all the rotating and reciprocating parts were running metal against metal, with no film of oil between them, they would soon heat up and stick. The friction would also make it harder for the parts to turn. So we have a reservoir of oil in the crankcase, where a pump forces it to the bearings and more critical points in the engine. Some of it flows through tubes and some through passages drilled in the crankshaft and connecting rods. The lubrication system might be compared to the water system in a house. The liquid is forced from one central place through pipes to many different locations where it is needed.

Starting the Engine

We must have some way of starting the engine. It has to be turning over before it can run under its own power, and we give it this initial start by means of an electric motor. This is somewhat similar to the motor in our vacuum cleaner or washing machine. It runs on electricity from the battery, and the starter switch is similar to the electric wall switch which turns on the lights in our home.

There is one more important piece of electrical equipment. This is the alternator. It looks something like the starter motor, but its job is just the opposite. Instead of taking electricity from the battery to start the engine, the alternator is driven by the engine and generates electric current which feeds back into the battery to keep it charged for starting. The alternator also supplies power for the ignition system, lights, radio, and other electrical units.

Controlling Engine Emissions

We have put together a complete automobile engine—at least enough parts of one so that it will start and keep on running. But before we talk about how power from the engine is sent back to the rear wheels to drive the car, let's look briefly at something that is found on all cars produced today—the systems that are used to control the emission of pollutants to the atmosphere.

There are three major pollutants that are emitted from automobiles into the atmosphere—hydrocarbons, carbon monoxide, and oxides of nitrogen. Hydrocarbons, which we can think of as essentially unburned gasoline, come from the exhaust pipe and the engine's crankcase as a result of the combustion process. They also enter the atmosphere from the carburetor and the fuel tank through an evaporation process. Carbon monoxide (CO) results from partially burned fuel when rich fuel/air mixtures do not allow complete combustion all the way to

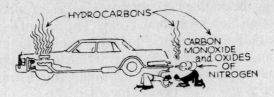

carbon dioxide (CO_2). Oxides of nitrogen, on the other hand, are gases formed during combustion due to the high temperatures.

Today's cars have built-in systems designed to reduce the three major pollutants emitted from these sources. The systems may vary somewhat between different makes of cars, but they all work to perform the same job—reducing emissions of hydrocarbons, carbon monoxide, and oxides of nitrogen. Let's see what the systems are and what they do.

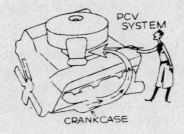

The first emission control applied to automobile engines was called the positive crankcase ventilation (PCV) system. This system, introduced in the early 1960's, is still in use today. During the "compression strokes" of the pistons, small amounts of gasoline vapors are forced past the piston rings from the combustion chamber and into the engine crankcase. These infinitesimal amounts of vapors expelled each engine cycle would add up to significant quantities of hydrocarbon (HC) emissions if they were allowed to enter the atmosphere. They don't, however, because the PCV system directs these vapors back to the intake system so that they are burned in the combustion chambers. The system also increases gas mileage since the fuel vapors are not lost but are burned in the engine.

Another system—Air Injection—helps control hydrocarbon and carbon monoxide (CO) emissions in the exhaust. Air is injected by a pump into the engine's exhaust ports to cause further burning of the hot gasoline vapors before they pass out the exhaust pipe.

As government emission standards became more strict, engineers and scientists had to find new ways to achieve the required control. At the same time, they had to come up with a system that would provide good fuel economy and not affect the smooth operation of an automobile.

The result was the development of a device called a *catalytic converter,* which was first introduced on most 1975-model cars made in the United States. This emission control system oxidizes hydrocarbons and carbon monoxide into harmless water vapor and carbon dioxide as the exhaust gases pass through a canister containing pellets which are coated with a catalyst material. A catalyst promotes chemical reactions, allowing them to take place at much lower than normal temperatures and more rapidly than a chemical reaction ordinarily would proceed. In the case of the catalytic converter emission control system, this means that catalysts allow more nearly complete oxidation of hydrocarbons and carbon monoxide at a much lower temperature than ordinary "burning."

The catalytic converter has played a major role in reducing the emission of hydrocarbons and carbon monoxide from exhaust pipes into the atmosphere. It has also promoted improved fuel economy and has helped engineers "tune" the engine for a more pleasant car to drive.

Although the present catalytic converter, an oxidizing converter, does an excellent job in controlling hydrocarbon and carbon monoxide emissions, it isn't effective in controlling oxides of nitrogen (NOx), the third type of pollutant in exhaust gases. Oxides of nitrogen are

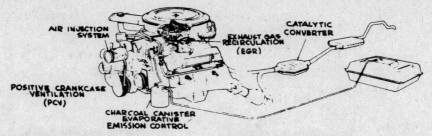

different from hydrocarbons and carbon monoxide because they will not burn to harmless combustion products. Instead, control of oxides of nitrogen in the engine exhaust usually requires measures to prevent their formation.

Oxides of nitrogen are formed anytime you have very high temperatures in the oxidation process (usually above 3000°F or 1090°C) when air is used to provide the oxygen. Air contains 79% nitrogen and 21% oxygen, so you could say the air burns.

The formation of oxides of nitrogen in an engine is minimized by diluting the fuel/air mixture entering the combustion chamber. This helps reduce the peak combustion temperature. One system being used is call Exhaust Gas Recirculation (EGR). With this system, small quantities of exhaust gases are recirculated back into the intake system of the engine to dilute the fuel/air mixture. Engineers are also looking at a "Three-Way Catalyst Closed Loop System" in which all three pollutants can be removed from the exhaust gases by a single catalytic converter. Such a system has been used already in a limited number of cars.

To reduce hydrocarbons that evaporate from the carburetor and the fuel tank when the engine is not running, there's a system that vents gasoline vapors into a canister filled with carbon granules. These granules act like a sponge and soak up the fumes and store them while the car is parked. When the engine starts up, the fumes are fed back to the engine and burned.

Further control of exhaust emissions has been brought about within the engine by changing the shape of the combustion chambers, using a leaner air-fuel ratio (more air in the mixture that goes to the cylinders for combustion), regulating the temperature of the air entering the carburetor, increasing the speed at which the engine idles, and modifying spark timing for stop and go driving. These changes to the engine all combine to help achieve more complete combustion and decrease exhaust emissions.

The Drive System

The first thing needed in the drive system is a device that will completely disconnect the engine from the rear wheels and the rest of the power transmission system. This will allow the engine to run when the car is standing still.

Suppose we mount two ordinary pie tins, each on a shaft, as shown. As long as they are not touching each other, we can spin one as fast as we want to without affecting the other at all. But if we move them together when one of them is spinning, the other will begin to turn and almost immediately both shafts will be turning together as one unit. This is the general principle of operation of the disc, or friction, clutch used in automobiles having manual shift transmissions. The discs are forced together by strong springs, and are separated by pushing down on the clutch pedal in the driver's compartment.

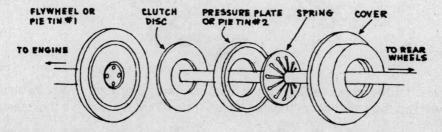

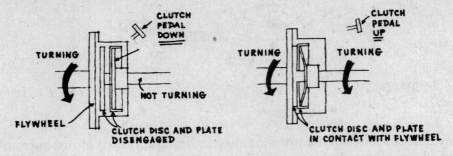

Cars equipped with automatic transmissions do not have a friction clutch or clutch pedal. We will discuss those shortly but, first we will cover the manual shift type transmission and drive system.

Manual Shift Transmission A transmission is used in automobiles to enable us to change the speed of the engine in relation to the speed of the rear wheels. When a car is starting up or in heavy going at low speed, we need more twisting force on the rear wheels to make it go than we need cruising along a good highway at constant speed. The transmission gives us this increased twisting force, and also allows the engine to run faster. The latter is important because an internal combustion engine does not develop very much power at low speed. When the car has picked up speed, the transmission is shifted to change the speed ratio between the engine and the wheels, and eventually is shifted into its highest gear.

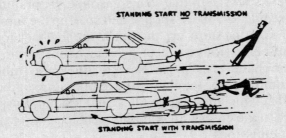

The transmission is a system of gears. Suppose we have a small gear with 12 teeth driving a larger gear with 24 teeth. When the first gear has made one complete revolution, we might say that it has gone around a distance equivalent to 12 teeth. The second one has gone around the same distance—12 teeth—but this means only one-half a revolution for the larger gear. So this second gear, and the shaft it is fastened to, always turn at one-half the speed of the first gear and its shaft.

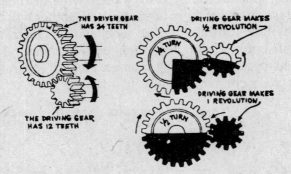

A familiar household example of gears is the hand-operated egg beater. We can turn the large gear fairly slowly and the small gears meshing with it turn rapidly to drive the beaters at high speed.

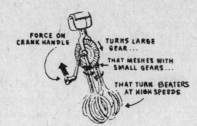

In a manual shift automobile transmission we have several combinations of gears arranged so that we can select the one we want to use at any moment. For low gear, or first, a small gear on the engine shaft drives a large gear on another shaft. This reduces the speed and increases the twisting force. Then a small gear on the second shaft drives a large gear on the drive shaft which goes to the rear axle. This reduces the speed and increases the twist still more, giving a ratio of about 3 to 1 for starting up or heavy pulling.

When the car has started we need less twisting force to turn the rear wheels and we would like more speed. For intermediate or second gear, we use the same first pair of gears as in low. We disconnect the second pair, however, and drive through two other gears. These are arranged with the larger one driving the smaller, so there is less overall speed reduction than in first gear, about 1⅔ to 1.

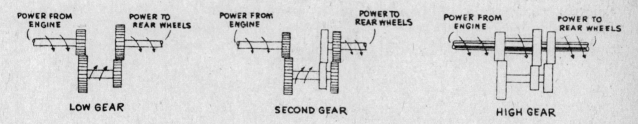

LOW GEAR   SECOND GEAR   HIGH GEAR

Most of the time while we are driving we need no reduction at all in the transmission. This is third, or high gear, and the engine shaft is connected directly to the drive shaft. They both revolve at the same speed, that is a 1 to 1 ratio.

One very important requirement of a transmission is to provide means to make a car back up. Reverse gear is very much like first, giving about the same ratio and using the same four gears. It also uses a fifth gear, however, which causes the drive-shaft to turn in the opposite direction.

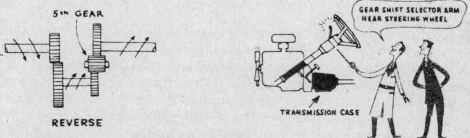

5th GEAR

REVERSE

This makes a complete manual shift transmission of the conventional type, with three speeds forward and one reverse. The gears are mounted in a metal case filled with oil to lubricate the gears and bearings. The various speeds are selected by moving a gearshift in the driver's compartment.

Many manual transmissions today have four or five speeds, sometimes called overdrive. In these higher gear ratios, the engine is actually turning slower than the drive shaft and rear axle. With the higher gear ratios and lower engine speeds, fuel economy can be significantly improved.

Automatic Transmission   Most cars built today have some form of automatic transmission, which eliminates the clutch and the need to shift gears manually to obtain the right gear ratios. There are various types, but most of them are similar in the way they affect the driving of the car.

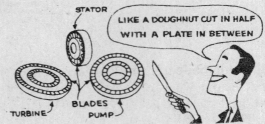

They usually have a hydraulic drive of some sort. The type that is in wide use today is the three-element torque converter. Imagine taking a doughnut, slicing it in two, and putting blades on the inside of each half. Both halves represent two elements of the torque converter—the pump, or driving element, and the turbine, or driven element. Now, between these two halves place a plate that also has blades. This is the third element of the converter called the stator. All three elements are in a casing filled with oil, which is circulated by means of the blades.

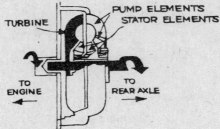

Let's see what happens when we place the automatic transmission selector in the Drive position.

The pump is mechananically connected to the engine's crankshaft, so it always rotates when the engine runs. When the engine is started, the pump begins rotating and sends oil, spinning in a clockwise direction, against the blades of the turbine to start it turning. The spinning oil has energy which the turbine absorbs and converts into torque, or twisting force, which then is sent to the rear wheels. When the oil leaves the turbine it spins in a counterclockwise direction, and if it went back to the pump spinning in this direction it would slow it down. We would lose any torque that had been gained. To make sure this doesn't happen, we use the blades of the stator which does not rotate (not just yet, anyway) to change the direction of the oil flow so it spins again in a clockwise direction. When the oil now enters the pump it adds to the torque the pump receives from the engine, the pump starts to turn faster, and we start to obtain torque multiplication. The cycle of oil going from the pump to the turbine, then through the stator, and back to the pump is repeated over and over until the car reaches a speed where torque multiplication is no longer needed. When this happens, the stator starts to turn freely (it's fixed to rotate only clockwise). The pump and turbine then rotate at nearly the same speed and act like a fluid coupling, or clutch. We now have a situation similar to high gear in a manual shift transmission

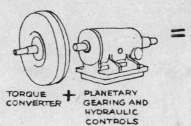

TORQUE CONVERTER + PLANETARY GEARING AND HYDRAULIC CONTROLS = Automatic Drive

where the crankshaft is connected directly to the driveshaft and both revolve at nearly the same speed. The stator stops rotating when torque multiplication is needed again.

The turbine is connected by a shaft to a gear transmission located behind the converter. The transmission usually used contains planetary gear sets and provides the desired number of forward speed gear ratios automatically. These gear ratios may also be selected manually for greater engine braking or exceptionally hard pulling. A reverse gear and neutral are also provided. The planetary type of gear transmission has its gears in mesh at all times. Gear ratios for different driving conditions are obtained using hydraulic controls that cause friction bands and clutches to grab and hold certain gears of the set stationary while the others rotate.

Hydraulic torque converters can have variations in the design of their basic components. Some elements may have their blades set at a fixed angle to the flow of oil. Others may have blades that are hydraulically operated to provide varying blade angles automatically. For example, a stator could have a low angle for maximum efficiency during the average operating range of the transmission and a high angle for increased acceleration and performance (when more torque is needed at the rear wheels). There also are variations in the way the components are arranged in hydraulic torque converters. Some have two stators, others have multiple sets of pump and turbine blades. Differences can exist, too, in the way the planetary gears are combined with the pump, turbine, and stator elements.

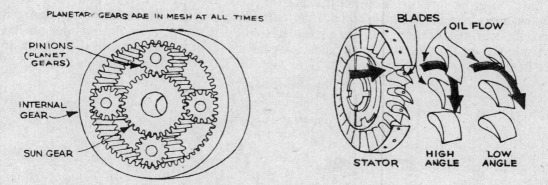

PLANETARY GEARS ARE IN MESH AT ALL TIMES

PINIONS (PLANET GEARS)

INTERNAL GEAR

SUN GEAR

BLADES   OIL FLOW

STATOR   HIGH ANGLE   LOW ANGLE

Under ordinary circumstances, however, these variations will not make a great deal of difference to the driver of the car. He still will find no clutch pedal and will have no shifting to do, except when he wants to back up. And for forward driving, all he has to do is step on the accelerator to go and the brake pedal to stop.

UNIVERSAL JOINTS

TRANSMISSION

PROPELLER SHAFT

REAR AXLE

UNIVERSAL JOINT

THERE ARE TWO COMMON METHODS FOR CONNECTING THE ENGINE AND TRANSMISSION TO THE REAR AXLE

Shaft and Universal Joint From the transmission the propeller shaft, or drive shaft, goes back to the rear axle. This is simply a solid or tubular steel shaft. The universal joint allows the rear axle to move up or down in relation to the transmission without bending or breaking the shaft. It is something like the gimbals of a compass on a boat, which allows the compass to remain level at all times no matter how the boat rolls or pitches.

Rear Axle In the rear axle we have two sets of gears. The first—ring gear and pinion—is simply to transmit the power around a corner. It enables the propeller shaft to drive the axle shafts which are at right angles to it. The old-fashioned ice cream freezer has a set of gears to do the same thing.

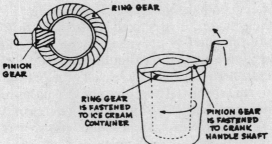

If we didn't ever have to turn a corner that is all the gearing we would need at the rear axle. But when we turn a corner the outside wheel has to travel farther than the inside wheel, and so it has to go faster during that time. It is like a squad of soldiers making a turn; the outside man has to march much faster than the one on the inside. We have a set of gears called the differential to take care of this.

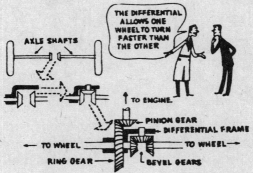

The *differential* consists of two small bevel gears on the ends of the axle shafts meshed with two bevel gears (for simplicity we show only one) mounted in the differential frame. This frame is fastened solidly to the ring gear. When the car is going straight ahead, the frame and the gears all rotate as a unit, with no motion between one another. But when the car is turning, one wheel wants to go faster than the other, so the gears on the axle shafts rotate relative to the other small gear. If the ring gear were stationary, one axle would turn frontward and the other one backward. But inasmuch as the ring gear is turning the whole unit, it means that one axle is turning faster than the ring gear and the other is turning slower by the same amount. This can be carried to the point where one wheel is stationary and the other one is turning at twice ring gear speed, which is the situation we sometimes get when one wheel is on a slippery spot and the

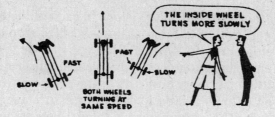

other isn't. Some cars, however, can be equipped with a limited slip differential, a type of differential that allows the major driving force to go to the wheel having greater traction.

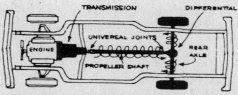

COMPLETE POWER PATH - ENGINE TO REAR WHEELS

The axle shafts, of course, drive the wheels and make the car move, which is the point we have been getting to all this time. We now have a complete rear wheel drive system, just as outlined at the beginning. Power starts at the engine and eventually gets to the rear wheels, after passing through various mechanisms so that it will arrive there in proper form.

Front Wheel Drive Cars
There also are cars that have front wheel drive. The same basic components are used as for the rear wheel drive system, but all the components are arranged up front of the driver. The power flow from the engine is to the front wheel axle shafts. Instead of the rear wheels pushing the car forward, the front wheels pull the car along.

Braking System

There is one more part of the car we should mention before we are through. We have shown how we get the car to move, but another very important point is to be able to stop it.

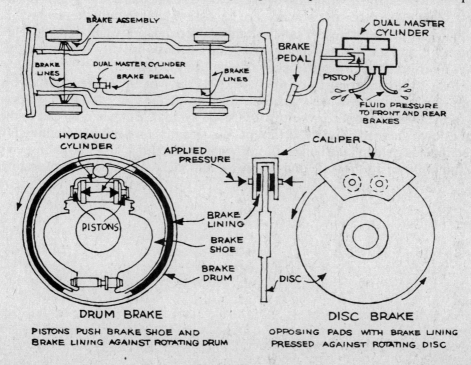

DRUM BRAKE
PISTONS PUSH BRAKE SHOE AND
BRAKE LINING AGAINST ROTATING DRUM

DISC BRAKE
OPPOSING PADS WITH BRAKE LINING
PRESSED AGAINST ROTATING DISC

Brakes are provided for this purpose. There is one in each of the four wheels, and they are simply a method of applying friction to the rotating wheels to stop them. It is like rubbing a stick against the rim of a child's wagon wheels.

Two types of brake systems can be found on today's cars—the drum brake or the disc brake. In the drum brake system, two stationary brake shoes covered with a special friction material, called brake lining, are forced outward by hydraulic pressure against the inside of a metal drum that rotates with the wheel. A system of steel tubes filled with a special hydraulic brake fluid runs from a master cylinder to each brake. When the driver steps on the brake pedal, pressure is built up in the master cylinder and this pressure is transmitted through the tubes, called brake lines, to pistons located inside a hydraulic cylinder in each wheel. The pistons move outward and push the shoes against the brake drum. As a safety feature, today's cars have a dual master cylinder which provides two independent hydraulic systems, one for the front wheels and one for the rear.

In the disc brake system, the brake lining is bonded to brake shoes positioned on each side of a rotating disc located in the wheel. When the brake pedal is applied, hydraulic pressure transmitted from the dual master cylinder causes a caliper to clamp the opposing shoes against the disc (it's like taking your thumb and forefinger and squeezing them together against a rotating plate).

The brake is a friction device that converts work into heat, and the amount of heat created by the brakes during a fast stop from high speed is amazing. Because of this, proper cooling of the brakes is an important consideration during their design.

Stoplights   Stoplights are controlled by stoplight switches, which are spring-loaded electrical switches. Most cars have mechanically operated switches, operated by contact with the brake pedal or with a bracket attached to the pedal. When the brakes are released, the electrical circuit through the stoplight is open—broken. When the brake is applied, the circuit through the switch closes and the stoplight lights.

The hydraulic type of spotlight switch operates on the same principle, it's operation depends on hydraulic pressure in the master cylinder of the brake.

So now we have everything we need to make a car go and to make it stop. It is not a complete car of course. There are other parts which are necessary, and many others which have been added over the years in the interest of safety, comfort, dependability and so forth. The research people—engineers and scientists of many sorts—have been constantly improving the automobile until it is a far cry from the horseless carriage of its early days.

When we look at the cars going by on the street, we don't see any of these parts we have been talking about—except the tires. And when we look inside the car, even then we don't see all those parts of the engine and the power transmission system. But when we get in the driver's seat and drive down the road, then it is different. We certainly know that something is there. We hope this section has given you a better idea of what "something" is—those unseen parts that make an automobile an automobile and not just a stationary room with comfortable seats.

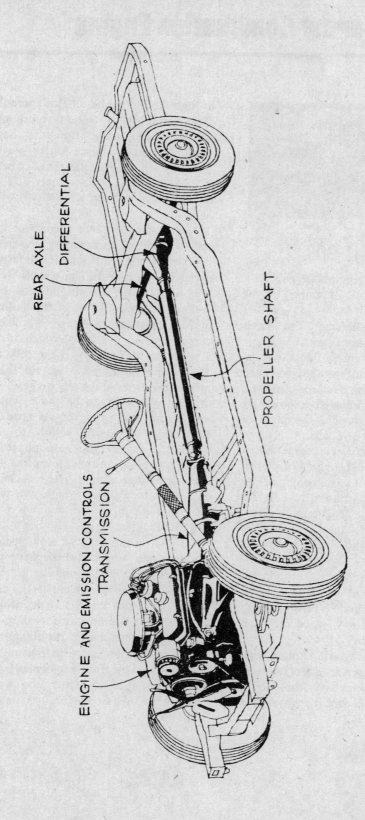

REAR AXLE

DIFFERENTIAL

PROPELLER SHAFT

ENGINE AND EMISSION CONTROLS

TRANSMISSION

Internal Combustion Engine

WHAT MAKES IT GO?

"What makes an automobile go?"

"Why, the engine, of course," is the reply.

"No," someone objects. "The wheels turning around make it go."

Such an argument is ridiculous because it is easy to see that we need both. We must have a source of power, an engine, and we must have something which actually furnishes the push or pull that moves the vehicle.

Many people, however, forget about the second part of this chain of power. Everybody talks of gasoline engines or Diesel engines, and they take it for granted that if the engine runs there is nothing else to think about. The curious person who does try to find out what happens beyond the engine immediately runs into complicated equations, talk of involute curves, compound gears, and so forth. And he decides that here is a place for engineers, not for him.

In this booklet we will explain what happens to the power after it leaves the engine — particularly the power from *internal combustion* engines used in automobiles. The engine's crankshaft rotates at a certain speed and with a certain force. But what happens between the place where power is developed (the engine) and where it finally is used (the wheels)? This is what we will be concerned with here.

Not too many years ago about the only method of transmitting power to a vehicle was a shaft or straps to fasten it behind an animal. The wheels were only to make it easier to pull—they did not make it move. One of the earliest and simplest examples of a vehicle carrying its own engine, which turns a wheel to make it go, is the bicycle. The engine, of course, is the rider. He makes the front sprocket, or gear, go around, which drives the chain, which makes the rear sprocket go around. Since this is fastened solidly to the wheel, the wheel goes around, rolls along the ground, and moves the bicycle and rider with it. Here we have a familiar mechanism which is a definite example of generating power in one place and using it in another place.

But when the internal combustion engine came along, it brought some new problems in transmitting power. The internal combustion engine has certain fundamental characteristics which require rather complicated gearing to make an automobile do the things we want it to do. Power can be transmitted in various ways. But as it comes from the crankshaft of an engine, it is in the form of twist. The engine acts like a

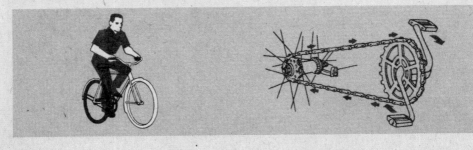

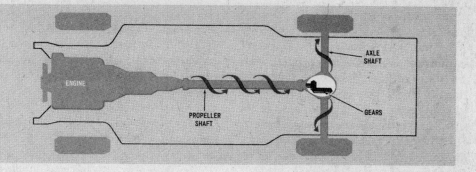

AXLE
SHAFT

ENGINE

PROPELLER
SHAFT

GEARS

powerful giant turning a crank handle which exerts this twisting force on the shafts and gears which connect the engine to the driving wheels.

Let us see how this would work in a very simplified form of an automobile power transmission system. This system would not be very satisfactory for starting the car, turning corners, or climbing hills, but for just driving along on a straight, level road it would be all right. There is a long shaft, called the propeller shaft, with one end fastened to the rear of the engine crankshaft, and on its other end, between the rear wheels, is a gear. Running from the center of one rear wheel to the other—fastened solidly to each—is the axle shaft. And at the center of this axle is fastened a circular gear with gear teeth on one side. The two gears fit together, so that as the propeller shaft turns, or twists, the axle also turns and causes the wheels to go around. Since the wheels rest solidly on the ground, we might say that they try to push the ground backward when they begin to turn. But the ground does not move—so in order to turn, the wheels must roll forward. They necessarily move the car forward with them, which is what we have been trying to do all the time.

As we said, this is a very simplified arrangement. In fact about all we are doing is to make our path of power turn a corner. Or to be more accurate, perhaps we should say that our path splits and each half goes off at a right angle. Our only object is to get that twisting force of the crankshaft back to the rear of the vehicle and facing in a direction where it can twist the wheels. All we have been trying to do is get power from one place to another.

But that is only a part of most power transmission systems. And in many cases the least important part. We often use gears—or wheels, pulleys, etc.—for other purposes.

First, there is the question of speed. Suppose there is an engine running at one speed, but we have a machine we want to drive at half that speed. We can do this with gears. If we want the machine to run twice as fast as the engine, we can do that also—with dif-

Torque
is twist

ferent gears. We will see how a little later.

Second, there is torque. Webster says torque is "that which produces or tends to produce rotation or torsion." In everyday words, it is a force which tries to make something rotate. It is a twist. We usually can put the word "twist" in the place of "torque" and the meaning will be exactly the same but engineers prefer "torque."

We use gears to increase or reduce torque. We might have an engine connected directly to a machine by a solid shaft, and the engine could not produce enough torque, or twist, to turn that shaft and run the machine. By putting the right size and kind of gears between the engine and machine, we could increase the twisting force enough to run the machine.

Speed changes and torque changes are related. Gear systems which change one will almost always change the other. But before we get into the why's and wherefore's of that, we are going to discuss briefly some fundamentals of mechanics. These may be old and familiar, but they will help explain a lot that follows.

Machines

There are a number of ways a man can increase the force he can apply with his own muscles. Some get to be rather complicated, but they are all made up of one or more simple machines. There are six of these machines —the lever, pulley, wheel and axle, inclined plane, wedge, and screw. Let us look at them briefly, with particular attention to one or two which we are going to hear more about later.

We are all familiar with the *lever,* an example of which is the teeter totter. If a child is on one end and his father on the other, the child will go up and the heavier person down. But if his father moves closer to the center of the board, nearer and nearer the pivot point, there will come a time when the small weight of the child will raise the heavier person on the other side. If the father weighs twice as much as the child, they will just balance when the father is half as far from the pivot as the child is. That is leverage, or mechanical advantage—a weight in one place lifts a heavier weight in another place, or a force applied at one point of the lever produces a greater force at another point.

The point of support, or the pivot point, is called the *fulcrum.* This may be between the two forces, as shown, or at one end. And the forces or weights may be arranged in different ways.

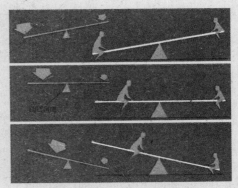

We have examples of levers all around us. A pair of pliers pinches something with much more force than we apply with our fingers. With a crowbar we can lift more than we can lift directly. A nut cracker and a

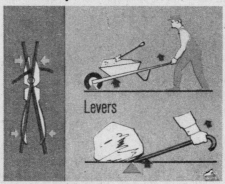

Levers

wheelbarrow are other levers in common use.

There are also examples of levers in which the force is decreased. We simply turn things the other way around. Fire tongs do not hold the chunk of coal as tightly as we are squeezing the handles. The fish end of a fishing pole does not have the same force that we are supplying near the other end. Our own forearm is a good example of this type of lever. The muscle pulls at a point very close to the fulcrum, and the weight we are lifting is way out at the end.

One thing should be noticed in all of these cases. When the force is increased, it does not move as far. We may move the handles of a pair of pliers an inch to get a movement of an eighth of an inch at the jaws. The long end of the crowbar moves several feet to move the weight a few inches. Looking at the other side of it, we can jerk a fish out of ten feet of water by moving our hands less than a foot. Whatever we gain in force, we sacrifice in distance, and vice versa.

There are many arrangements of *pulleys*. With the simple one shown

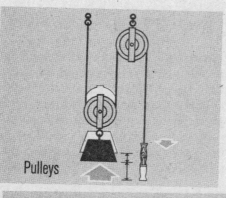

Pulleys

here we can hold 100 pounds with a force of 50 pounds. Each rope supports 50 pounds. By arrangements of more pulleys and thus more supporting ropes, we can get a greater mechanical advantage than the 2 to 1 shown. However, we have the same condition we mentioned with the lever. If our 50 pound force moves 1 foot, it will raise the 100 pound weight only ½ foot.

The *wheel and axle* is usually just a wheel fastened to a rod, like the steering wheel of an automobile. A force applied to the outside of the big wheel produces a greater twisting force on the small rod than if we twisted the rod itself. Sometimes we use a handle instead of a wheel, a crank, but this does not change the principle. Take a crank and a rod with a rope around it and we have a windlass. The hand will move several feet in turning the crank around once. This will turn the rod around once which will wind the rope up only a few inches. But it will lift a much greater weight than we could lift by pulling directly on the rope.

If a truck driver wants to get a barrel onto his truck, he lays a plank from the ground to the edge of the truck platform and rolls the barrel up. This plank is an *inclined plane*. He has to move the barrel a greater distance than he would by lifting it straight up, but it is a lot easier. He can get a barrel on the truck this way that he could not possibly lift.

The *wedge* is just a form of inclined plane. We push it under or between the objects to be moved instead of moving the object up the incline.

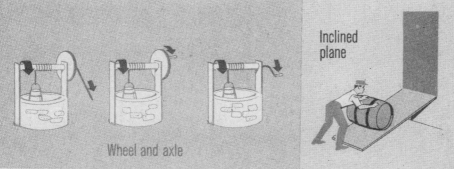

Wheel and axle

Inclined plane

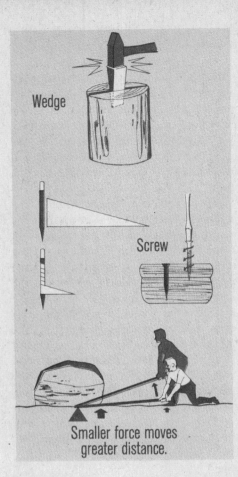

Wedge

Screw

Smaller force moves
greater distance.

the inside which will fit exactly the threads on the outside of the screw, but the wood screw cuts its own threads in the wood as it moves inward.

These few devices we have named often are combined in more complicated mechanisms, and sometimes it is difficult to recognize them as these same simple things. But if we take them apart and look them over carefully, we will find the familiar characteristics of the lever, the screw, or one of the others.

We shall find also that all these devices work on the same principle. That principle is that if we increase a force by means of one of these machines, that force cannot move as far as the original smaller force moves. As we have pointed out in each case, when we increase the force, we sacrifice distance. In textbooks, the formula says that *work equals force times distance*. And we cannot increase work by means of a lever. If we could, we would have perpetual motion. So the work remains the same, and if force increases, distance decreases, and vice versa.

The action of gears—the principle on which they work—is exactly the same as this. But before we get into that, let us see what a gear is, and what different kinds there are.

What is a Gear?

A gear is a wheel with projections on it called *teeth*. These teeth may be on the edge, on the side, or halfway between. A gear usually is fastened to a shaft. Sometimes it turns and applies a twisting force to the shaft, and sometimes the shaft is turning and turns the gear with it.

The *screw* is also a member of the the same family. It is an inclined plane wrapped around a rod. As we follow the thread around the outside of the rod, we are continually going up hill. One complete turn of the screw moves the nut only the short distance between two threads. This distance is called the *pitch* of the screw. With a wood screw the action is just the same. Each turn of the screw moves it into the wood a distance equal to the pitch. The metal nut must have threads on

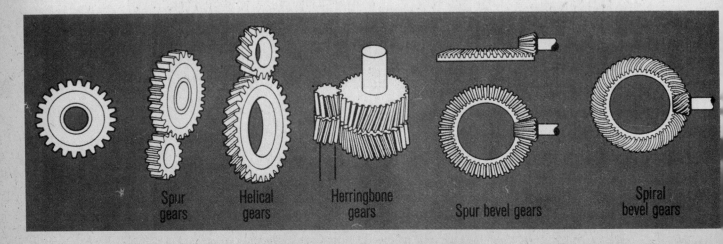

Spur
gears

Helical
gears

Herringbone
gears

Spur bevel gears

Spiral
bevel gears

The simplest type of gear is the *spur* gear. This has its teeth cut straight across the edge. For years it was almost universal, but other types have become more common in the transportation field. We will use it a lot in this book, however, even in places where it is not ordinarily used. It is easier to see and understand its motions, and the principle is exactly the same.

Another type is the *helical gear*. This is the same as the spur gear, but its teeth are cut at an angle. The teeth of the gear it meshes with must be cut at the same angle. It is usually quieter than the ordinary spur gear, and for that reason is preferred for many uses. For the same reason we sometimes use *herringbone* gears. This is like two helical gears fastened together tightly side by side.

When our power must turn a corner, we ordinarily use a *bevel* gear. The teeth of this gear are not cut on the edge. They are cut, we might say, across the corner. Sometimes it is a spur bevel gear, with straight teeth, but it is more likely to be a *spiral bevel* gear. This is somewhat like a helical gear, except that the teeth, in addition to being cut at an angle, also are curved.

We are going to leave out all the technical terms we can, but there is one we should explain. *Pitch diameter* is the diameter of the *pitch circle*. The pitch circle is a purely imaginary line running through the gear teeth at a point usually a little outside the half way point of the tooth. The easiest way to define it is to suppose we have two smooth rollers running together instead of toothed gears. They are of such a size that they run at exactly the same speeds as the gears. In such a case the pitch diameter of a gear would be the same as the diameter of the corresponding roller. From now on in this book, when we speak of the size of a gear we will mean the pitch diameter, as that is what really determines its speed and other characteristics.

There is still another way of classifying gears. They can be external or

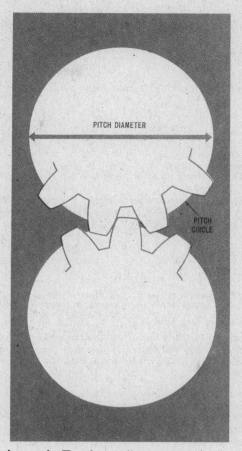

internal. To the ordinary person the word "gear" will always bring to mind a picture of an external gear, and he usually will be right. But internal gears do play an important part in some mechanisms, as we will see later. An internal gear is simply a ring with teeth cut on the inside instead of the outside. To mesh with it we must have an external gear of smaller size.

What Does a Gear Do?

A gear is a spinning lever. It can increase or decrease torque in exactly the

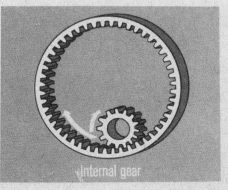

Internal gear

A GEAR IS A SPINNING LEVER

Take an ordinary lever, 20 inches long, pivoted on a fulcrum.

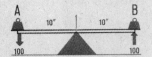

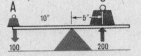

A 100 pound force down at A exerts a 100 pound force up at B.

100 x 10 = 100 x 10

A 100 pound force down at A exerts a 200 pound force up at C.

100 x 10 = 200 x 5

Now change the fulcrum into a shaft, fastened solidly to the lever. If a force pushes down on one end of the lever, this applies a twist, or torque, to the shaft.

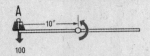

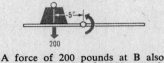

A force of 100 pounds at A causes a torque of 1000 pound-inches on the shaft.

100 x 10 = 1000

A force of 200 pounds at B also causes a torque of 1000 pound-inches on the shaft.

200 x 5 = 1000

What happens if we turn things around the other way, and have the shaft try to turn the lever? If the shaft exerts a torque of 1000 pound-inches, it will create a force of 100 pounds at A, or 200 pounds at B.

* * *

Now let us take two of these levers, one 10 inches long and the other 20 inches long. Arrange them so one end of the short one is resting on one end of the long one. A torque of 500 pound-inches is applied to the shaft of the shorter one. The shafts are at the mid-point of each lever.

There will be a force of 100 pounds down at A, the end of the short lever. (100 x 5 = 500)

This will exert the same force, 100 pounds, down at the end of the long lever. This force will create a torque on the second shaft of 1000 pound-inches. (100 x 10 = 1000)

Our input torque was 500 pound-inches, and our output torque is now 1000 pound-inches, because the lever is longer.

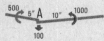

But these two levers would not move the shaft very far. So we add another pair of levers, and then another.

When we have added enough of these to fill the circle, we have a set of gears.

The driving gear is 10 inches in diameter; the driven gear 20 inches. The input torque is 500 pound-inches; the output torque 1000 pound-inches. Thus the torque is multiplied in the same ratio as the size of the gears.

same way that a lever increases or decreases force. If you are interested in the explanation of this, details are given to the left. But these details are not necessary to understand what gears do and why we use them. The main thing to remember is that if we have a small gear fastened on one shaft driving a bigger gear on another shaft, the torque of the second shaft will be increased. The second shaft will have more twisting force than the first shaft. If we have an engine driving the small gear, our system now will be able to turn something—say a machine of some sort—that the engine could not turn when they were connected directly together.

The amount of torque increase depends on the relative size of the gears. If the pitch diameter of the second gear is twice the diameter of the first gear, the torque will be doubled. If the second gear is three times as big the torque will be three times as much. But, if the *driving* gear is twice as big as the *driven* gear, the output torque will be cut down to ½ the input torque.

We can also think of a gear as another class of simple machine — the wheel and axle. A force applied at the outside edge of a gear, that is, where the teeth are, will exert a twist on the shaft. And the bigger the gear is, the greater will be this twist. With equal forces on the teeth of two gears, the shaft of the larger gear will have the greater torque. This is what we have when two gears are in mesh and one is driving the other.

In all this we have to remember one thing. We do not obtain this increased torque for nothing. We are not discoverers of perpetual motion and claim that we obtain more power out of the engine because we have added some gears to the system. We are still dealing with levers and they still follow the same rules. With levers we said that *whatever we gain in force we lose in distance.* When talking about gears and shafts we say *whatever we gain in torque we lose in speed.* The two statements are not exactly the same, but we

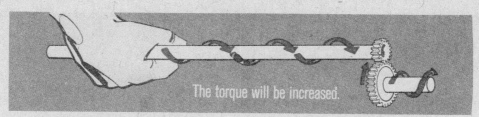

The torque will be increased.

have twice as many teeth as the small one. Let us say 24 and 12 teeth respectively. As the small one, the driving gear, goes all the way around once, its 12 teeth have meshed with 12 teeth of the larger gear. That means the large one has turned around only halfway. The small one has to go around again before the large one completes one revolution. So, for every two revolutions of the small driving gear the large driven gear revolves once. And for every 1,000 revolutions of the small one the large one has made 500 revolutions. So, if an engine driving the small gear is running at a speed of 1,000 revolutions per minute (rpm) the machine driven by the large gear is turning over only 500 rpm. We have doubled the torque furnished by the engine. We have increased the twist on the second shaft so now it can turn the machine when perhaps it could not before. But the machine turns only half as fast as it would if it were connected directly to the engine.

Counting the number of teeth on gears is usually easier than measuring the pitch diameter. And as we have just shown it will give us the same information concerning the gear ratio—that is, the amount of change in torque and speed. If the driving gear has 10 teeth and the driven gear 30 teeth, it will take 3 revolutions of the first to get the second all the way around through one

can think of them that way for the moment.

The best way to show this is to count the number of teeth on two gears. The teeth must all be the same size to fit together properly. Therefore, if the diameter of one gear is twice the diameter of the other, the big one must

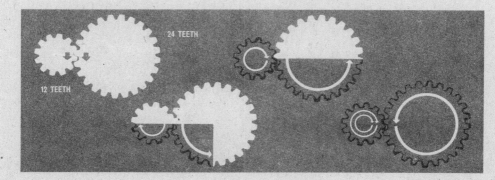

24 TEETH

12 TEETH

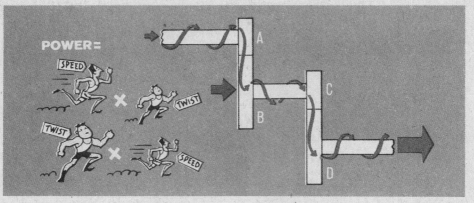

revolution. Thus the speed of the driven gear will be ⅓ the speed of the driving gear, and we know from this that the torque will be multiplied by 3. We would say that the gear ratio was 30/10 or 3 to 1. This applies equally as well if we have an odd combination of numbers, such as 39 and 19, only it is not so easy to do the mathematics in our head. The gear ratio would be 39/19, or a little over 2 to 1.

The gear with the greater number of teeth will always turn slower and will produce the greater torque.

Sometimes we are glad to have this reduction in speed along with the torque increase. In fact the main purpose of gears in some mechanisms is to act as speed reducers. In other cases we need both more torque and less speed, so we gain both ways. On the other hand, sometimes we may wish to increase the speed. Maybe we have a machine that has to run at 2,000 rpm and an engine running at 1,000 rpm. In that case we use a gear ratio of 2 to 1 again, but we have to put the large gear on the engine shaft and the small one on the machine shaft. The torque will be cut in half, but if the engine has enough power to drive the machine under those conditions, the machine will run at the required speed of 2,000 rpm. But we cannot eat our cake and have it too. If we need both more torque and more speed, there is nothing we can do about it—except get more power from the engine.

What we have been saying is really the same thing as is expressed by the formula found in text books — that *power equals torque times speed*. The gears cannot change the power; that stays the same. Therefore, if the torque increases, the speed must decrease; if the speed goes up, the torque must go down.

WARNING

Everything said thus far has to do with gear mechanisms all by themselves, or we might say, with gear mechanisms driven by an engine which is running at *constant speed and constant power*. The statements are not necessarily true when applied to the over-all mechanism as in an automobile where the speed and torque of the engine can change at any time. But even there, if we consider it at any one moment, the same rules apply.

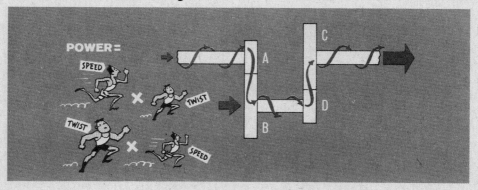

In some mechanisms we have more than two gears between the input and output. A clock or watch—one of the very early users of gears—is a good example of multiple gears in series.

But suppose we look at something simpler to begin with. We will use our same two gears with 12 and 24 teeth and call them *A* and *B*. To these we add another pair of gears *C* and *D* which also have 12 and 24 teeth respectively. The small gear *C* is fastened on the same shaft as large gear *B*. Now let us follow the path of the power flowing through this gear train. The engine is connected to the top shaft and is still running at 1,000 rpm. We already know what happens with the first two gears. The speed is cut in half and the torque doubled. So our second shaft is turning only 500 rpm which means that gear *C* is turning at that same speed. Now we can forget about the first two gears and consider only *C* and *D*. We know what happens there, too, because they are just the same gears with a ratio of 2 to 1. Our speed will be halved again and the torque doubled once more. So our last shaft, which is driving the machine, is turning at only 250 rpm, but it is applying to the machine a torque or twist 4 times as much as that delivered by the engine. The over-all ratio of the whole system is 4 to 1.

In any simple case such as this we can get the same effect by using only two gears of the proper ratio. Sometimes, however, there is too great a difference to be efficient, and sometimes it is a matter of convenience or space saving. In actual practice we ordinarily would not arrange the gears as we have here. We would save room by moving the third shaft up above the second. The result would be exactly the same, and we would have the added advantage that the first and third shafts would be directly in line. What we really have here now is a simplified arrangement of a manual shift automobile transmission. The third shaft would extend back to the rear axle to drive the wheels. But we will get into that a little later.

There is another feature in using four gears here instead of two which is sometimes an advantage. And this brings up a characteristic of gears which has probably been self-evident but which we have not mentioned. It has to do with direction of rotation. Looking at a pair of gears it is easy to see that if one shaft rotates clockwise, the

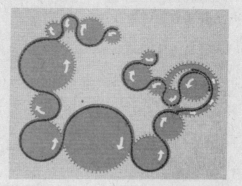

other must go counterclockwise. This may be a nuisance in some installations, and in some others it may be just what we want. Sometimes gears are used to reverse the direction of rotation and for no other reason. But if we want the output shaft to run the same way as the input shaft, we must use at least three gears. Or, we can use a combination of more gears such as we have just been discussing. To find out which way the final shaft runs in any complicated system of gearing, the best procedure is to go through the whole system and figure out which way each gear turns. And do not forget the exception to the above—when an ordinary external gear is driving an internal gear, both shafts will rotate in the same direction.

We should point out one more thing before we leave this subject. If we consider the gear system of any wheeled vehicle, we must consider the wheels themselves. The size of the wheels has just as much to do with the overall drive ratio as do the gears. It is the backward force the wheel exerts on the ground which makes the vehicle go, and if we have a certain torque or twist on the wheel shaft, this force at the ground depends on the size of the wheel. The larger the wheel, the less the force.

Pedals go around once, wheel goes around once.

Pedals go around once, wheel goes around twice.

As an example, let us look at the bicycle as it was back in the early 1890's—that great high front wheel with the rider perched on top. The size of the front wheel was a matter of much pride and argument in those days. A 56-inch wheel was fairly good. But a long-legged person who could straddle a 60-inch wheel really had something to brag about.

Why was the wheel made so big? It is very simple. They used a big wheel instead of using gears. The pedals were connected directly to the hub of the wheel, so every time the rider's feet went around once the wheel went around once. With a wheel of the size used today that would mean that the bicycle would move forward about 7 feet. But one revolution of that big wheel would roll it forward about 15 feet. This meant that pedalling at the same speed would make the high-wheeler go twice as fast. It might be harder to get started and tough-going on hills, but speed was what counted.

Eventually, the driving wheel was reduced to about half its former size and gears were used to give the rider the same effect he had before. Let us say we have 20 teeth on the front sprocket (gear) and 10 teeth on the rear sprocket. Disregard the chain because all it does is allow us to separate the gears. As far as the ratio is concerned we can think of the gears as meshing together directly. So we have a ratio of 1 to 2. The back gear will revolve twice as fast as the front gear, and thus the wheel will go around twice each time the pedals go around once. This gives us exactly the same result as if the wheel were twice as big and

the pedals connected directly to it. The gears have cut the torque in half, but the driving wheel is only half the size of the big wheel, so the force between the wheel and the ground is the same in both cases.

Friction

Thus far we have neglected to mention friction, which always enters into the transmission of power. Friction has its good points and its bad points. We would have difficulty doing a great many things if there were no friction.

Try walking without it, for example. The only reason an automobile moves is because of the friction between the tires and the road. Also, an automobile clutch depends entirely on friction.

But in transmitting power, most of the effects of friction that we think about and talk about are the troublesome ones. That is probably because they are the ones we have to do something about. Whenever two gears run together, there is friction. This means that some of the power is used up—wasted—in overcoming that friction. A shaft running in a bearing creates friction, which means more wasted power. If there is too much of this friction in any one place, it means that the part will get very hot. This may result in swelling and sticking and all sorts of damage.

So we have to do the same things that are done in almost every moving mechanism. We have to use bearings to cut down the friction of all rotating shafts, and we have to furnish lubrication to these bearings and to the gears.

A little oil makes all the difference in the world in the amount of friction.

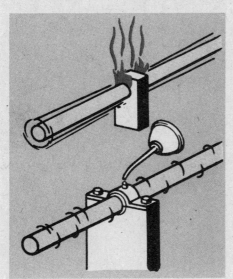

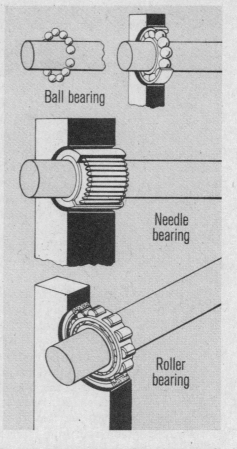

Ball bearing

Needle bearing

Roller bearing

A thin film of oil—no matter how thin —permits two metal surfaces of the right kind to rub against each other for very long periods with little wear and no damage. There are various ways to get this lubricant to the right place. Sometimes a pump forces oil under pressure to the points needing it; it circulates all the time the mechanism is running. Many parts are oiled by the mist and spray splashed up by gears churning the oil in the bottom of the case. Other points are packed permanently with grease, or have means to force grease into them every so often.

Plain bearings are used in many places—that is, bearings in which a metal shaft runs inside a metal ring of special bearing material. But in power transmission systems we use a number of anti-friction bearings. These are ball bearings, roller bearings, or needle bearings. They let us do things which without them would be difficult and complicated, if not impossible. They

have a lot to do with the high speeds at which shafts and gears now run.

In all our discussion and figures so far we have not taken friction into account. All our mechanisms were perfect machines, with no losses due to friction. We are going to continue to do that to a large extent in the rest of this booklet. Friction is a variable factor and hard to pin down. Bearings and lubrication are a very important subject, but too large a subject to cover here. So in most of the examples we will show, we will just assume that the mechanism has proper bearings and is well lubricated in some way or other.

Why a Transmission?

The question might be asked, "Why use a transmission anyway? If any gain in torque is at the expense of speed, and vice versa, why not just put in an engine of the proper size and use only the gears necessary to get the power to where we need it?"

This argument might hold good for certain conditions. But in the cases we are going to consider in this book, where we have an internal combustion engine driving a vehicle, there are two things against it. First, the car needs different amounts of power to make it go properly under different conditions. Second, the power provided by the engine also can change greatly, depending on the operating conditions.

When we are considering an automobile, quite a lot of force is needed to start it moving. Less force is needed to keep it moving at a moderate speed. A lot of force is needed again to move it at very high speeds, and of course we have hills to contend with. So it is easy to see that we never know from one moment to the next just what force is going to be required at the wheels.

If we consider the characteristics of the engine, it is easy to see that we do not always get the power from it when we want it. We just said we needed a lot of force to get started, when the vehicle is standing still or moving very slowly. And that is just the time that the engine does not furnish very much power. One of the characteristics of an internal combustion engine is that it must run fairly fast before it can produce much power. Its shaft does not twist very hard when it turns over slowly.

But if we use the right size and kind of gears we can let the engine run at high speed while the wheels are turning slowly, and at the same time they themselves increase the torque being delivered by the engine. Thus the trans-

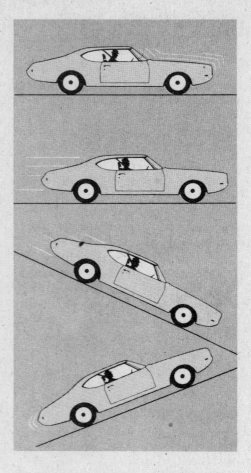

mission is responsible for more twist on the propeller shaft because it lets the engine run faster and deliver more power. It increases that twist still more by its multiplication of torque. So for starting, this arrangement is fine. But it is not so good for higher speeds, and that is why automobiles have some means for changing the gear ratio, depending on the load and speed of the car and the judgment of the driver.

It is possible to drive a car without ever shifting gears if we are careful to stay on hard level roads and if we do not object to other cars going by us and leaving us behind at traffic signals.

We gain in two ways.

POWER TRANSMISSION SYSTEM IN AN AUTOMOBILE

In an automobile there are a lot of things between the engine and the drive wheels. Some kinds of cars have more, others have less. Some have one thing, others have something else. They all have more than the simplified system shown in the early part of this booklet. As we said, that might be all right for driving straight ahead on a level road, but there would be a lot of places where it would not be all right. So we will start out here with a complete power transmission system of a typical automobile. We will explain briefly what each part does, without much attention to how it does it, and we may take liberties with what it looks like. Later on we will take up the more important parts individually and go into greater detail.

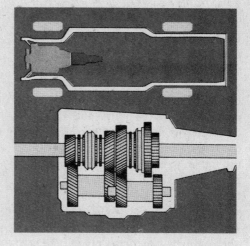

Clutch

Starting from the engine, the first thing we come to is the clutch. Its job is to disconnect the engine from the power transmission system when the driver so desires. When it is disengaged, the driving and driven plates are separated. What the engine does has no effect on the rest of the drive system and what the wheels are doing has no effect on the engine. There are several reasons why we want to be able to do that at certain times and under certain conditions.

Transmission

After the clutch comes the transmission. The reason for calling it this is not too clear. "Torque converter" or the English expression "gear set" gives us a better idea of what it is and what it does. But everyone still calls it "transmission." Its purpose is to let us change the ratio of speed between the engine and the rear wheels. When the car is starting we can run the engine fast and drive the wheels slowly, increasing the torque or driving force at the same time. When we are going faster we can change the ratio, so that the wheels are turning at more nearly the same speed as the engine. Finally, in direct drive, the shaft behind the transmission is connected directly to the shaft from the clutch, and it is just as if the transmission were not there at all. There is also a reverse gear in the transmission, so that we can make the car go backward, and a neutral position, in which no movement or power is transmitted.

A large part of the rest of this booklet will be about the transmission and the various forms it takes. So we will save the rest for later.

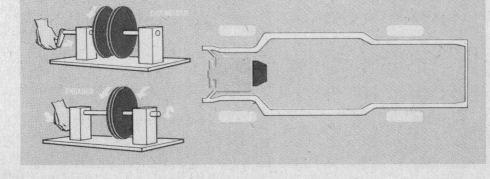

Propeller Shaft, Universal Joints

Back of the transmission is the propeller shaft which runs to the rear of the car. This is a hollow or solid steel shaft, sometimes enclosed in an outer tube, sometimes left open. At the front end is a universal joint, and in many cars there is another universal joint at the rear end of the shaft. These usually are made up of two U-shaped pieces at right angles to each other and fastened together by a cross having arms of equal length. The U-shaped yokes pivot on the arms of the cross. Since there are two of these pivots, the two shafts can be at an angle to one another and can still turn around and transmit

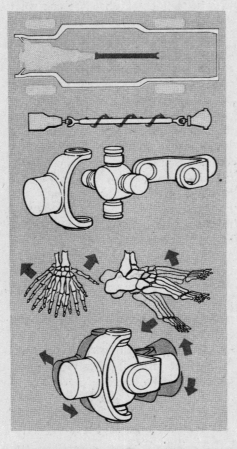

power. They do not have to be in a straight line. This is very important, because even if we could design the car to have them in a straight line to begin with, every time we went over a bump they would get out of line. The rear axle moves with the wheels, up and down with every bump, while the transmission does not move so much, being fastened to the frame. So the universal joint lets the propeller shaft keep on turning even though its two ends are moving around relative to each other.

Final Drive

At the rear end of the propeller shaft is fastened a short shaft carrying a gear on the end. This is a bevel gear and is called the *pinion*. It meshes with the *ring gear* which is mounted on the rear axle. The job of the pinion and ring gear combination, or *final drive* as it often is called, is to take the torque provided by the propeller shaft, increase it, and turn it at right angles so it can twist the wheels and drive the car.

For many years these rear axle gears were of the spiral bevel type. But now most cars use what are called *hypoid* gears. They are about the same as spiral bevel gears, except that the pinion does not meet the ring gear at its centerline. It meets it at a lower point, which means that the shape of the teeth must be different. This allows the propeller shaft to be lowered and, in turn, the overall car height.

Since the pinion is much smaller than the ring gear, we know immediately that there is a speed reduction here, and an increase in torque. In today's passenger cars the rear axle ratios generally average about 3 to 1.

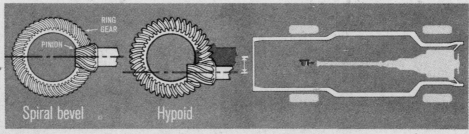

RING GEAR · PINION · Spiral bevel · Hypoid

The axles and wheels are turning only about one third as fast as the propeller shaft. It should be noted that this speed reduction and torque increase are always there and always stay the same. Even when we say that we are in direct drive we are referring only to the transmission, and this rear axle ratio is still effective. And if the transmission is in low gear, say a ratio of 3 to 1 (it is actually less than this in most of today's cars), the overall ratio between the engine and rear wheels will be 3×3, or 9 to 1.

Differential

In the simplified automobile drive system which we showed in the first part of this booklet, the ring gear was fastened directly to a solid axle which ran from one wheel to the other. This would be all right for going straight. But when the car turns a corner, the wheel on the outside of the turn must travel farther than the inside wheel. It is like a horse race. The jockeys all try to get the inside position on the curves because the inside horse does

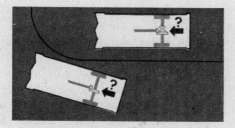

not have to run as far as those on the outside. In an automobile we use a differential to take care of this. The differential is meant for just one thing—to let the wheels turn at different speeds while still driving the car. It transmits equal torque to both wheels even when one is going faster than the other. If it was not necessary to have this difference in speed, we could do without the differential and have a much simpler rear axle and drive system.

A differential is one of those mechanisms whose action is easy to see when it is working right in front of you, but it is not so easy to describe. We will build it up piece by piece, however, and try to show how simple it really is.

First we have the two axles, each with a wheel on one end and a gear on the other end. These are small spur bevel gears, and are called *differential gears* or *side gears*. Then we add what is called the differential case, which we show as just a crooked bar fastened around one of the axles. It is loose on the axle, however, so it can turn around on it. In this case we mount another gear, the *differential pinion*. This is a small bevel gear which fits in between the two side gears and meshes with both of them. There we have all the necessary parts for a differential—just three gears and a case.

We will add one more part, however, to make it easier to tell the story. That

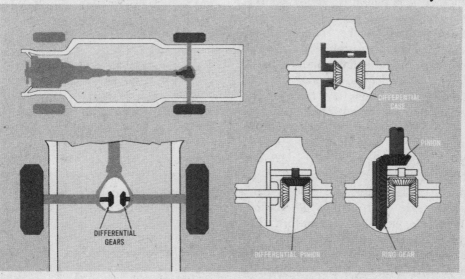

DIFFERENTIAL GEARS

DIFFERENTIAL CASE

PINION

DIFFERENTIAL PINION

RING GEAR

is the ring gear mentioned before. It is fastened solidly to the differential case. Thus the case rotates all the time, at the same speed as the ring gear. This should be noted carefully, as we are likely to think of a "case" as something stationary, just an enclosure for the working parts. But here it is the driving member of the differential. As long as the ring gear rotates the case goes around, too, at the same speed. It carries the differential pinion around with it, but otherwise it knows nothing about what is going on in the differential. It just keeps rotating.

When we go straight ahead on a smooth road, the wheels turn at the same speed. Engine power drives the ring gear, so the differential case goes around, carrying the pinion with it.

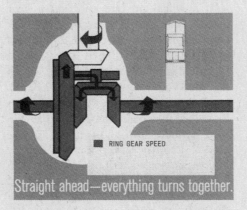

RING GEAR SPEED

Straight ahead—everything turns together.

This turns the two side gears, and the whole mechanism revolves as one solid unit. The gears are not turning on one another. The pinion is simply connecting the two side gears together; they could just as well be bolted together solidly. They are turning at the same speed as the differential case. It is the same as if we had no differential at all, because our wheels are traveling together and we do not need one.

Now let us take the other extreme and hold one wheel so it cannot turn. What happens in the differential? The case turns as before, carrying the pinion with it. But one axle is held, so its side gear cannot go around. Therefore, the pinion must turn. The pinion is being carried around by the case, but at the same time is revolving around its own short shaft. It must in

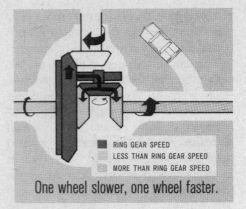

RING GEAR SPEED
LESS THAN RING GEAR SPEED
MORE THAN RING GEAR SPEED

One wheel slower, one wheel faster.

order to stay meshed with the stationary side gear. It is running around the stationary gear.

But what is happening to the other side gear while this is going on? It is meshed with the pinion too, but it is free to turn. It is being turned just the same as it was in the first case, but *in addition* it is being turned more by the revolving of the pinion on its own shaft. The pinion is revolving in the right direction so that its motion is added to the movement of the differential case. So the second side gear is turning faster than before. In fact this axle and wheel are turning exactly twice as fast as when the two wheels were running at the same speed.

Now let us take a situation in between these two extremes. Both wheels are turning, but one is going faster than the other. This is the case we ordinarily have in an automobile turning a corner. The inside wheel travels a shorter distance than the outside wheel; therefore it must turn around more slowly.

The inside wheel—and thus the differential gear on its axle shaft—is re-

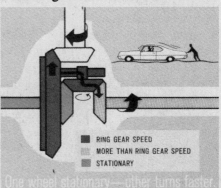

RING GEAR SPEED
MORE THAN RING GEAR SPEED
STATIONARY

One wheel stationary—other turns faster.

volving more slowly than the differential case. The differential gear is turning more slowly than the pinion is being carried around. So we have the same general effect as when it was held tight—the pinion must turn on its own shaft. It will not turn as fast as before but it will turn. And it again turns in a direction to add to the speed of the opposite differential gear. It adds to it exactly the amount taken away from the slower gear and wheel. That is the way a differential must work—what is subtracted from one side must be added to the other. The ring gear speed always splits the difference between the two.

To make our mechanism look more like the real thing, we will add a little to it. This does not change its operation in any way however. We will complete the case, and add another pinion to the bottom. This pinion simply does

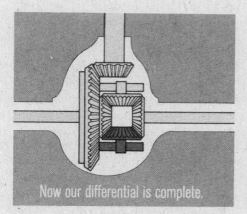

Now our differential is complete.

exactly the same thing as the first one, and helps it do the job we have just described.

Limited Slip Differential

The differential is a very necessary thing. It acts as a sort of balance between the rear wheels. But it can be a nuisance at times. This is usually when we have a situation giving us the result we mentioned earlier—one wheel standing still, the other going twice as fast as usual. It is easy to do this. All we have to do is stop the car so one rear wheel is on dry pavement or road, and the other is on a slick patch of ice. The differential will drive the wheel which is the easier to turn. So the wheel on the ice will just spin, the other one will stand still, and—which is usually more important—the car will stand still. We get the same effect when one wheel is stuck in deep sand or mud, and the other one is comparatively free to turn. To avoid this trouble, limited slip differentials have been developed which permit the major part of the driving force to go to the wheel having the most traction.

Axles, Wheels

The axles are comparatively slender steel shafts. They have a flange at the outer end to which the wheel and brake drum are bolted. Around the axle is the axle housing. This holds the parts of the brake which do not turn with the wheel, and supports the bearing in which the outer end of the axle shaft runs.

The wheel itself is essentially a metal disc with a rim around the outside into which the tire fits. It is the outside surface of the tire which pushes on the

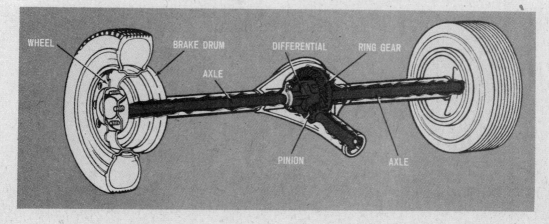

WHEEL   BRAKE DRUM   DIFFERENTIAL   RING GEAR   AXLE

PINION   AXLE

ground and really makes the car move. But the engine furnishes the force, and all the other things we have just mentioned have a certain part of the job to do in getting that force from one place to the other.

This completes a general discussion of the main components of an automotive power transmission system. We will now go into more detail about the kinds of power transmission systems found in today's cars, show how they operate, and discuss some of their more important parts. We will begin with the manual shift transmission, then talk about automatic transmissions. Finally, we will mention some of the different arrangements found in power transmission systems today, such as front wheel drive.

MANUAL SHIFT TRANSMISSION

A manual shift transmission allows the driver control over the speed at which the gear ratios are to be changed to provide power at the driving wheels. Most of the manual shift transmissions used in today's cars have three forward gear ratios, or "speeds", although four-speed transmissions also are available. In any case, before the gears can be shifted, the clutch must be disconnected from the engine. This was touched on briefly before but now we'll explain in more detail just how this is accomplished.

Clutch

It is sometimes said that a good clutch *must slip* while being engaged and *must not slip* when it is engaged. This

is almost a definition of a clutch. It is easy to see why when we consider what a clutch is for and what we want it to do.

First, we need something to disconnect the engine from the wheels, so that the engine can run while the car is standing still. Otherwise we would have to stop the engine every time we came to a traffic light. And it would be a problem to start the engine while it was connected to the drive system. Also, with manual shift transmissions, we have to disconnect it from the engine to shift gears easily.

There are various ways in which we could take care of these things, but we need something else. We need something which will take hold *gradually,* which will not jump abruptly from no connection at all to a direct, solid connection. When we want to start a car, we have to speed the engine up to get enough power to move it. At the same time the wheels are standing still. We cannot, in one moment, bring the speed of the wheels up to the speed of the engine; there would be a terrible jerk. And when we shift gears after the car is moving, we have almost the same situation—the wheels and propeller shaft are not turning at the same speed as the engine. So we want something which will slip a little, which will take hold gently at first and gradually grab harder and harder. Thus the rear wheels can start to move slowly and gradually pick up speed, until finally everything is turning at the same rate and the clutch is solidly engaged. From then on, of course, we do not want any slipping, because that

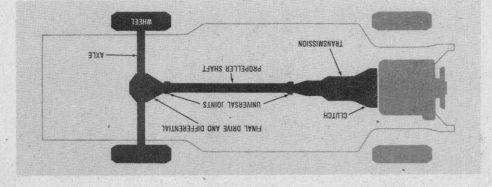

is just wasting power and heating things up.

The kind of clutch we are talking about depends on friction for transmitting power. In fact, its full name is "friction clutch," as there are other types of devices commonly called clutches. In most automobiles the clutch consists of one plate squeezed tightly between two other plates. The one in the middle is the *driven member;* it is connected to the shaft leading back into the transmission. The other two are the *driving members;* they are connected directly to the engine. A strong spring, or springs, forces the two driving members together. This tightens their grip on the middle plate until they are all turning together as one unit.

The engine flywheel is used for the first driving member. Its surface is made very smooth where the driven plate pushes up against it.

The other driving member is called the *pressure plate*. It is a fairly heavy ring of cast iron, smooth on one side. It is fastened to the cover, which is bolted to the flywheel, so they all turn together. It is fastened in such a way that it can slide back and forth.

The *driven plate* is a flat disc of steel with friction facing fastened on each side. The plate is fastened by *splines* to a shaft going to the transmission. This means it fits into grooves on the shaft so that they must turn together but the plate can slide forward and backward on the shaft.

A series of coil springs, or sometimes one large flat spring, act between the clutch cover and the pressure plate. They push the pressure plate toward the flywheel, squeezing the driven plate between the two. The springs are always trying to engage the clutch, and they are strong enough to keep it from slipping under any ordinary conditions. To disengage the clutch, the driver pushes on the pedal. This works through levers to pull back the pressure plate against the force of the

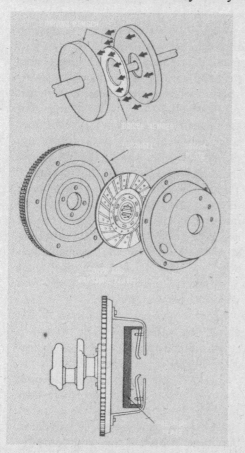

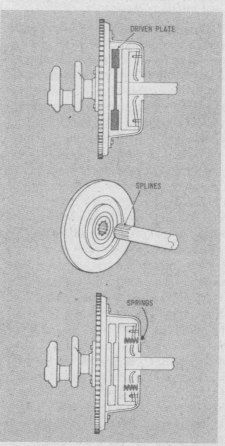

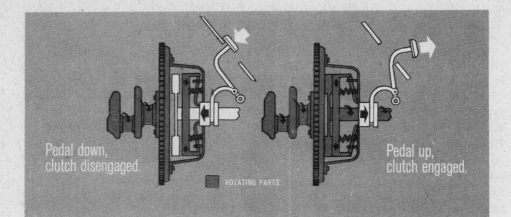

Pedal down,
clutch disengaged.

Pedal up,
clutch engaged.

ROTATING PARTS

springs. This loosens the driven plate and disconnects the transmission shaft from the engine crankshaft.

There have been many different designs of clutches in the past and the present ones do not all look just like what we have shown. Sometimes more than one driven plate is used, with a corresponding increase in the number of driving plates. And there are other differences. But they all work on the same principle.

Transmission Gearing

The transmission is a case full of gears located behind the clutch. The case is usually fastened to the clutch housing, so the whole thing looks like an extension of the engine. The purpose of the transmission, as mentioned, is to vary the speed and torque of the rear axle in relation to the speed and torque of the engine.

Most passenger cars in this country have three ratios or "speeds" in the transmission for forward driving, and what we say here will apply to the simple, three-speed manual shift.

First speed, or *low gear,* is used for starting and for steep hills or heavy going in sand or mud. It lets the engine run fast while the car runs slowly. The engine runs 2½ to 3 times as fast as the propeller shaft. The exact figure varies in different cars. This means, of course, that the torque of the propeller shaft is increased just as much as its speed is cut down. Thus we have a lot of twist on the rear wheels to get the car started from a stand-still, or for use any other time we need it.

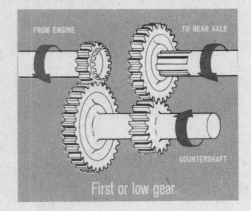

FROM ENGINE   TO REAR AXLE

COUNTERSHAFT

First or low gear.

This is done with four gears and three shafts. A small gear on the shaft from the clutch drives a larger gear fastened to the transmission *countershaft.* Another smaller gear fastened on the countershaft drives a large gear on the third shaft. This last shaft goes to a universal joint on the front end of the propeller shaft. Thus we have the same arrangement shown earlier. There is a certain speed reduction in the first two gears, and then some more reduction in the second set of two gears. The countershaft is running at a speed between the speeds of the other two shafts. And the third shaft of course is running most slowly and with the greatest torque.

Second, or *intermediate gear,* works about the same way. The first two gears are the same as we used in low gear. The next pair are different, however. They are almost the same size, and sometimes the countershaft gear may be the larger. Thus the countershaft runs at the same speed as before, but there is little if any additional re-

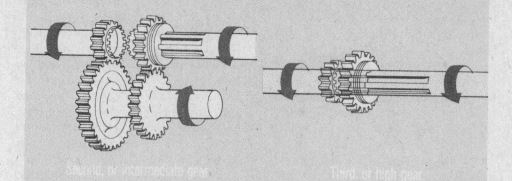

Second, or intermediate gear   Third, or high gear

duction from that to the third shaft. So the wheels will run faster for the same engine speed than they did in low gear. The usual ratio in second speed is around 1⅔ to 1. This means that the propeller shaft will run at 1,000 rpm when the engine is running 1,670.

Third, or *high speed,* is direct drive. The transmission does not do anything. We simply connect the first and third shafts together, and they turn as one. The propeller shaft turns at the same speed as the engine, and delivers engine torque. Sticking to figures, we would say the ratio is 1 to 1.

Besides the three forward speeds, there are two other combinations we can get in a transmission. There is *neutral,* in which the transmission shaft is entirely disconnected from the clutch shaft, and the engine cannot drive the propeller shaft or anything beyond the transmission. It has about the same effect as disengaging the clutch. And there is *reverse.* It is a complicated matter to make an internal combustion engine run backwards, so we run it in one direction all the time and use gears to reverse the direction of rotation. We put an extra gear between the countershaft and the final drive shaft. It is called the *reverse idler.* We drive the countershaft in the same way as before, it drives this reverse idler which in turn drives the low speed gear on the final drive shaft. The system is just like low gear except for this extra gear. This changes the direction of rotation, and we can see that the final shaft is turning opposite to what it was

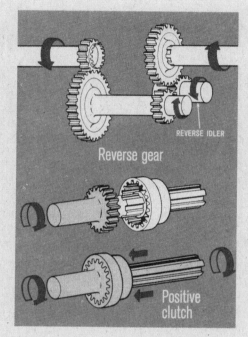

REVERSE IDLER

Reverse gear

Positive clutch

in all the previous cases. The ratio of reverse is about the same as low gear, or even lower. This is logical, because we may want to pull hard in reverse but we never want to back up very fast.

We have shown all the combinations found in a typical three-speed transmission. These can be put together in various ways to make a complete transmission, but we cannot show them all here. They first used to slide the gears back and forth on the shafts to get them into mesh and out of mesh. This can be done by using a square shaft or a splined, or grooved, shaft. In this way a gear is fastened solidly to its shaft as far as revolving is concerned, but it can slide along it.

Now we commonly use the so-called

constant mesh transmission. **Some of** the gears still slide, but some are constantly in mesh with each other and rotate all the time. But these gears do not necessarily drive the shaft. They are free to rotate on it until they are connected to it by a clutch. We should explain that this is not a friction clutch. It is a *positive clutch*—more like a gear —having teeth that fit into similar teeth on the gear. It is called a clutch because its only job is to connect or disconnect the gear and the shaft.

Let us look at a complete constant mesh transmission, and note briefly what gears and shafts there are. There is the clutch shaft with gear *A* fastened solidly to it. There is the countershaft with all three gears, *B, C,* and *D,* fastened solidly to it. *A* and *B* are constant mesh gears, so whenever the engine is running and the clutch engaged, the countershaft and its three gears are turning. Then there is the transmission main shaft, with the two gears *E* and *F.* Gear *E* is in constant mesh with *C,* but is free to rotate on its own shaft except when connected to it by a clutch arrangement. Gear *F* is splined to the main shaft, so it turns with it but can slide back and forth. Finally we have the reverse idler, which is now a short shaft with the two gears *G* and *H* solidly fastened to it. *G* is always in mesh with *D.*

This may look rather complicated, but there is not really a great deal to it. And with this arrangement it is very simple to get any speed or gear we want. We can see that even in neutral the countershaft gears, gear *E,* and the reverse idler gears all revolve. But the main shaft stands still. Now suppose we slide gear *F* along the shaft. If we slide it in one direction it meshes with *D* and we have low gear. If we slide it the other way it meshes with *H* and we have reverse. We are using two gears on the reverse idler now, but as they are both fastened solidly on the same shaft and rotate in the same direction, the principle has not changed from that in our first example.

The path the power takes through the transmission in the various speeds is shown more clearly on page 207.

The other speeds we need are second and high. We get these by means of a positive clutch arrangement which slides between gears *A* and *E.* When it slides to the right it connects *E* to its shaft and we have second speed. When it slides to the left it connects the main shaft to the clutch shaft and we have direct drive.

We should mention one thing here. For the sake of convenience, we have shown spur gears being used in the transmission. In passenger cars, the usual practice is to use helical gears because of their quieter operation. Spur gears are used sometimes in truck transmissions.

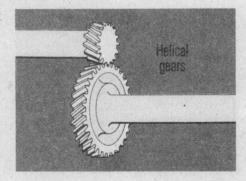

Helical gears

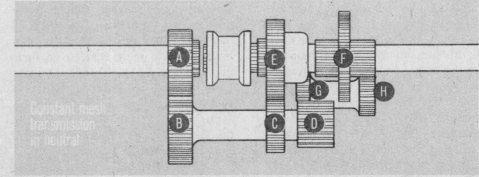

Constant mesh transmission in neutral

How do we shift these gears and clutches to get the different speeds? We have seen that we only have to move two things—the low speed gear and the double clutch. These both have grooves in them into which *shifting forks* fit loosely. The forks do not interfere with these parts turning around, but they can be used to slide them endwise.

Then we connect the forks to the gearshift lever in the driver's compartment in such a way that he can select either one and move it in either direction. Thus with the one lever he can take his choice of any one of the four positions of the gears—five, counting neutral.

We have to disengage the main friction clutch when we shift gears. Otherwise there would be jerks and much loud clashing of gears. Some gears are running and some are standing still, or they are running at different speeds. Also there is considerable pressure on the gear teeth when they are driving, so the gears do not slide apart easily.

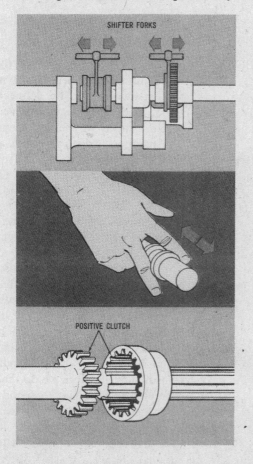

SHIFTER FORKS

POSITIVE CLUTCH

And of course it gives the clutch a chance to cushion the shock or jerk of suddenly changing the ratio between the engine and the rear wheels.

There has been a lot of work done to make it easier to shift gears. The most successful result has been the development of gear synchronizers, or *synchronous transmissions*. This is a refinement of the constant mesh type we have described. Synchronizers are used for all forward speeds in the majority of today's manual shift transmissions, although some transmissions use synchronizers only for second and third speeds. There are several types, but they all have the same object.

Most of the trouble in shifting gears comes from the gears or clutches running at different speeds. If we could synchronize them, get them running at approximately the same speed before we tried to mesh the teeth, there would be little clash or clatter. This is just what we do. When the second and high speed clutch slides on the shaft—in either direction—it does not mesh with the teeth on the other half of the clutch right away. Instead a small friction clutch takes hold first. (The illustrations show only the general principle of it; the parts do not look anything like those shown.) This is a cone-shaped clutch, with metal faces, but it acts like the friction clutches we have described. It can slip enough to prevent a shock, but almost immediately it is solidly engaged. In doing this it has brought the speed of the gear up to the speed of the shaft. As soon as they are turning at the same speed, it is easy to push in the toothed part of the clutch which gives a positive connection. The first part of the motion engages the friction clutch, and the second part engages the positive toothed clutch. This arrangement enables even a new driver to shift gears without trouble.

All manual shift transmissions do not look like those we have shown. Some have a greater number of forward speeds, particularly trucks, and the gears may be arranged in a different order on the shafts. Most manual trans-

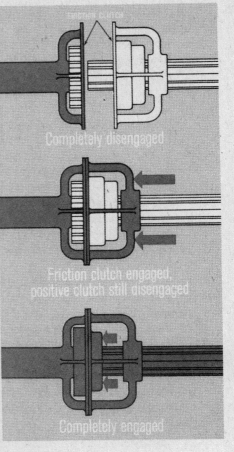

Completely disengaged

Friction clutch engaged, positive clutch still disengaged

Completely engaged

missions, however, operate on the principles discussed. There are a number of gears which can be connected together in different ways to give us the different ratios we want. Except when it is in direct drive, a certain amount of torque comes in at the front end from the clutch shaft, and a different amount goes out the back end to the propeller shaft.

We have described to some extent the main parts of the power path in a car with a manual shift transmission. These are the clutch and transmission gearing. We covered the propeller shaft, universal joints, axles, differential, and wheels and tires earlier. We will soon discuss automatic transmissions and how they make the power path different from those in cars with manual shift transmissions. Before we do that, however, it would be best to spend a little time talking about planetary gears since they play such an important role in the operation of an automatic transmission.

PLANETARY GEARS

Planetary gears are used in a variety of arrangements in the automobile. Probably the main reason for this is that we can make them do a number of different things, depending on how we connect them into the power system. This is

what makes a planetary gear set so interesting. But, first, let us look at one and see what it is.

In its simplest form, a planetary gear set is comprised of three gears. There is a *sun gear,* or pinion, in the center. Then there is a small *planet gear* meshing with it. (We show two of them here but usually there are three or four.) On the outside is the *ring gear,* an internal gear meshing with the planets. The planet gears are fastened together by the *planet carrier.* This holds them in place but lets them rotate. Just how these gears and carriers are fastened to the shafts depends on what we want the mechanism to do. We will explain one of the forms here, and others are shown on page 209.

Suppose we connect the sun gear to the input, or driving shaft, and the planet carrier to the output, or driven shaft. We put a brake band around the

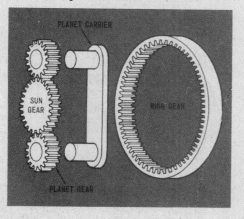

PLANET CARRIER

SUN GEAR

RING GEAR

PLANET GEAR

outside of the ring gear and hold it tight so it cannot move.

If the engine drives the sun gear, the planet gears must turn around. But they cannot stand still and rotate on their shafts because that would mean the ring gear must move, and we are holding that with the brake. So they have to move around the ring gear and the planet carrier moves with them. It is something like the differential we described. There are two motions in the planet gears. Each one is rotating about its own shaft, and at the same time they are all moving around in a circle on the teeth of the ring gear. This is where this type of gearing gets its name. The motion is much the same as the Earth and other planets about the sun. Each one rotates on its own axis, but they also continually circle around the sun.

The planet carrier, and thus the driven shaft, is turning much more slowly than the sun gear and drive shaft and in the same direction. Just what the ratio is depends on the size of the gears, and we will not go into the details of how it is figured. As an example, however, with the smallest practical planets the ratio cannot be less than 2½ to 1. When the planets and the sun gear are the same size, the ratio is 4 to 1. This of course means that the speed is reduced to ¼, and the torque increased 4 times.

To shift into direct drive, we release the brake on the ring gear and engage a clutch connecting the drive shaft directly to the driven shaft. If we wish, this can be done by clutching the planet carrier to either the sun gear or ring gear. In either case none of the gears can turn on each other, so the whole mechanism is locked and rotates all together without affecting the drive.

We mentioned that we can get various results with a planetary transmission by connecting it up in different ways. If we drive the ring gear and hold the sun gear still, we will still increase torque as we did in the case just described, but it will not be increased so much. By other arrangements we can increase the speed and reduce the torque, and by still other means we can get reverse. We have three units, any one of which we can hold stationary, and either of the other two can be the driving or driven member. So there are six possible combinations, shown below. Practically all of them are used in transmissions in one way or another.

There are various modifications of this simple planetary gear. There are some with double planets of different sizes, and there are compound planetary gears, which consist of two planetary

gear-sets with certain gears of one connected to certain gears of the other. These act in fundamentally the same way as the simple planetary, but follow-

PLANETARY GEAR COMBINATIONS

There are three units in a planetary gear—sun gear, planet gears and carrier, and ring gear. To get various results we can hold any one of these units stationary, and either of the other two can be the driving or driven member. So there are six possible combinations. We show them here, with colors indicating the driving, driven, and locked members, and the labels telling what kind of gear results from each arrangement.

They are all planetary gears, but a number of different results are obtained by hooking them up differently.

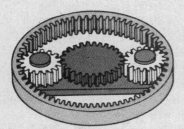

Reduction gear—less speed, more torque.

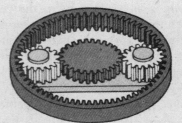

Reversing overdrive — more speed, less torque, turns backward.

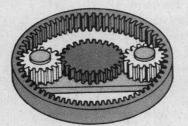

Reversing reduction gear — less speed, more torque, turns backward.

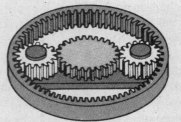

Overdrive—more speed, less torque.

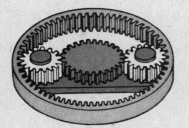

Reduction gear—less speed, more torque.

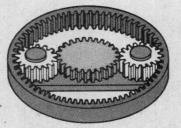

Overdrive—more speed, less torque.

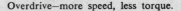

■ DRIVING   ▨ DRIVEN   ▨ LOCKED

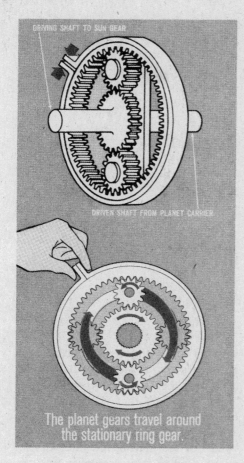

DRIVING SHAFT TO SUN GEAR

DRIVEN SHAFT FROM PLANET CARRIER

The planet gears travel around the stationary ring gear.

ing the power flow through them is rather complicated and figuring the gear ratio is not worth the trouble unless we are in the business of designing transmissions.

Planetary gears are used in automobiles mostly in automatic or semi-automatic transmissions. In the next section we will show how they work in the hydraulic torque converter type of automatic transmissions used in many cars built today.

AUTOMATIC TRANSMISSION

The name *automatic transmission* has been used to cover a lot of different things. Ordinarily it means any arrangement which will change the ratio between the engine and the wheels *by itself*—without the driver having to do anything.

In discussing the manual shift transmission, the first part after the engine in the power path was the clutch. In automatic power transmission systems, the clutch—or its replacement—also must be automatic. We must have a device that does the work of the friction clutch without requiring the driver to operate it.

Various ways have been tried to make the clutch work automatically, that is, to engage and disengage without effort on the part of the driver. Some early designs used vacuum power to operate the linkage of a standard clutch. In others, the clutch itself was changed to operate centrifugally. We won't go into the details of it. The principle remains the same, but centrifugal weights were arranged to engage the clutch when the engine reached a certain speed, then disengaged it when it dropped below a certain speed.

Hydraulic Coupling

Another device to replace the friction clutch is the *hydraulic coupling,* sometimes called the *fluid flywheel*. Some early automatic power transmission systems used the hydraulic coupling to replace the clutch entirely. In other arrangements, the coupling was placed just behind the engine, followed by a friction clutch, and finally the transmission. The hydraulic coupling does not do everything the friction clutch can do, but does some things the clutch cannot. The coupling can be called a centrifugal clutch because of the way it operates. If we run the engine slowly, it will not start the drive wheels turning. When we speed up the engine, it gradually takes hold until finally the engine is driving the wheels with practically no slip.

How does it work? Suppose we start with a simple example. If we shoot steel balls at the blades of a paddle wheel, each ball will give the wheel a little push, will try to turn it around. If we can shoot them fast enough and hard enough, the wheel will keep spinning. Now if we think of water or oil as being made up of a lot of small liquid balls, we can shoot these at the wheel and get the same results. You probably have seen water wheels which worked much like this, driven by the water falling over a dam or by the flow of a swift stream.

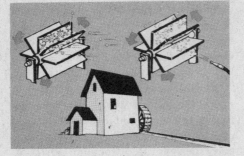

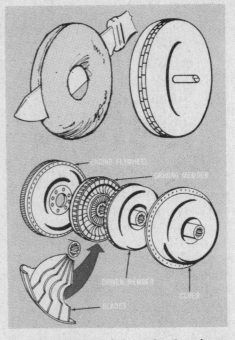

This is about what we do in a fluid flywheel. But in an automobile we have to make an artificial stream. What it amounts to is a pump forcing oil against a turbine, or hydraulic motor. Many years ago it was found that the most efficient way to do this was to get the pump and motor close together, to more or less combine them. The result was a hydraulic coupling essentially the same as the fluid flywheel.

The working parts of a hydraulic coupling look very much like a doughnut. But the doughnut is sliced down the middle, so there is no connection between the two halves. One half is fastened to the engine crankshaft; the other to the clutch, or transmission, or some part eventually leading to the rear wheels. The doughnut is hollow, but each half has a number of straight radial blades leading from the hub to the outside edge. Very often a section of each blade is cut away, and in that space is put a metal plate or guide ring shaped like half of another, smaller doughnut. The two halves of the hydraulic coupling are just alike. When we put them together we have what looks like a skinny doughnut inside a fat one, with thin blades connecting the two.

To make this complete we put a cover around it all, the cover often being fastened solidly to one of the rotating members. Then we fill it almost full of oil. Now if the engine is running, the first half of the hydraulic coupling, the *driving member,* is turning with it. If it is turning fairly fast, the oil is being thrown toward the outside of the doughnut by centrifugal force, just like marbles on a phonograph turntable. When it gets to the outside it wants to

keep on going, and the only place it can go is across into the other half of the doughnut, the *driven member.*

All this time that the oil is being forced outward, it is also being whirled around in the other direction by the blades of the driving member. Consequently, when it crosses over into the driven member, it hits against those blades just as in the water wheel we mentioned and pushes them around. This tends to slow up the drops of oil, and they travel toward the hub, or center, of the driven member, then across the driving member and repeat the whole process. Thus we have the oil continually circulating, outward in the driving member, inward in the driven member. And at the same time it is traveling in a direction at right angles to this, being pushed by the blades of the driving member and pushing on the blades of the driven member.

The driven member can never go quite as fast as the driving member. There is always a certain amount of slip no matter how fast they are turning. But at ordinary driving speeds this may amount to less than one per cent so it is not serious. When we get below a certain speed however, this slip begins to get greater. Finally it gets down to the point where the driven member does

Oil flows outward in driving member, inward in driven member, and is also forced in other direction by blades of driving member.

not turn at all. There is still some torque being applied to it, but it is not enough to make the rear wheels turn and move the car. This means that we can stand at a traffic signal with the transmission in gear and the car will stand still just as if a friction clutch were disengaged. Then as we speed up the engine, the driven member begins to turn, gradually picks up speed, and finally is running at approximately the same speed as the engine.

We mentioned that the driving member and driven member were just alike.

There may be slight differences in them, but they are enough alike that a hydraulic coupling can drive in one direction as well as the other. The oil just circulates in the opposite direction, from what was the driven member to the driving member. Thus if the car is coasting or being pushed, the wheels drive the engine just about the same as if there were a solid connection there.

The use of a hydraulic coupling gives smoother pickup and makes it impossible to stall the engine when starting or climbing a hill. It also smooths out

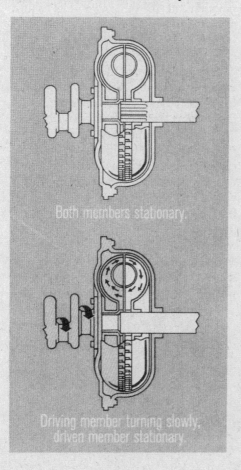

Both members stationary.

Driving member turning slowly, driven member stationary.

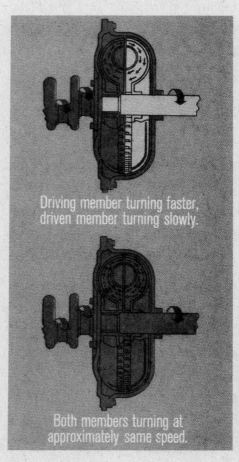

Driving member turning faster, driven member turning slowly.

Both members turning at approximately same speed.

jerks, especially at low speeds, and in some ways acts as a centrifugal clutch. As we will see later, those characteristics let us use certain types of transmissions and shift gears in certain ways which would not be satisfactory without a fluid flywheel. But we must remember that this is just a clutch. It is not a transmission. It cannot replace the transmission because it does not increase the torque—it only transmits the torque which the engine delivers to it.

A fluid flywheel does not increase the torque

We will see later on in this book a mechanism that looks very much like it and which does multiply torque. But it is different. We will point out just how it is different when we get there.

Coupling-Planetary Combination

When automatic transmissions first came into wide use, the majority used a hydraulic coupling in combination with planetary gear sets. Although this design is no longer used today, it is worthwhile to discuss briefly how it operated since it was used so widely.

The hydraulic coupling-planetary gear combination was a four-speed automatic transmission, the top gear being direct drive, and a low rear axle ratio was used. A low axle ratio usually means slower pickup or acceleration in

high gear, so third speed was arranged so that it could be brought into use at almost any speed when more acceleration was desired.

The transmission consisted of two planetary gear sets, one behind the other. Each planetary had two speeds, a reduction ratio and direct drive, but the reduction ratios were not the same. We could get the four speeds we wanted by choosing the proper ratios. In low gear, both planetaries were in action, giving us a double reduction. In second speed the front unit was in direct drive, and the rear unit alone gave a reduction of about 2½ to 1. In third speed we did just the opposite; the rear unit was in direct drive and the front unit was working. This had a ratio of approximately 1½ to 1. In fourth speed, both units were in direct drive, so engine torque flowed straight through to the rear axle. There also was a reverse gear which was a third planetary unit behind the other two. It acted in combination with the other two units to furnish a low ratio in the reverse direction.

The hydraulic coupling was a very important part of this combination. It was located between the engine and the transmission, but the flow of power from the engine actually went first to the front planetary unit, then to the fluid coupling, and then to the second planetary unit. The effect was just the same, however, except that the coupling was at a reduced speed at certain times, which had advantages. There was no friction clutch. The transmission shifted from one speed to another under load, without being disconnected from the engine. This was possible because the fluid flywheel cushioned the shock, and was one of the big differences between

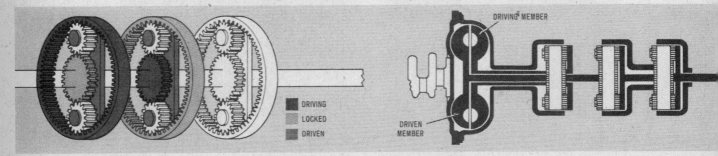

DRIVING
LOCKED
DRIVEN

DRIVING MEMBER

DRIVEN MEMBER

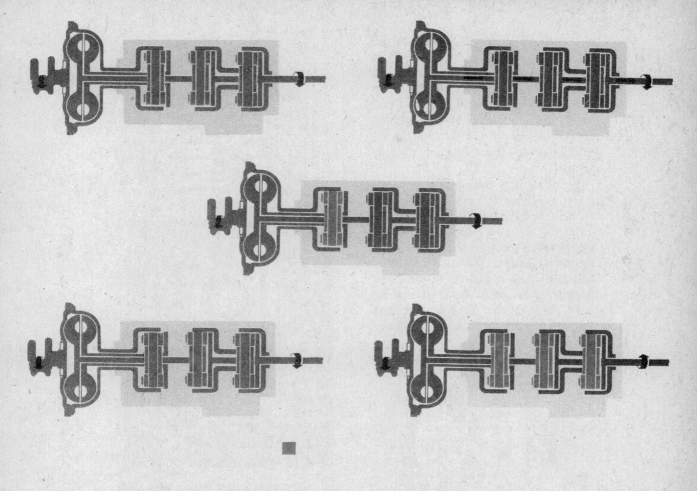

this and most other transmissions, even some which used a fluid flywheel.

The planetary gears were controlled by brake bands and friction clutches. A brake band held the proper member stationary in each unit when it was in low ratio, and a clutch locked each unit together when direct drive was needed in that unit. Oil pressure made these brakes and clutches work at the right time, depending on how fast the car was going and how far the accelerator pedal was pushed down. All the driver had to do was control the speed of the engine, and the gear shifting took care of itself.

Hydraulic Torque Converter

In our discussion of the hydraulic coupling, we pointed out that it is simply a hydraulic clutch which cannot deliver any more torque than is put into it. It is a very useful addition to a transmission, but it cannot replace the transmission because it is not a torque multiplier.

But we can make a torque multiplier out of it, and most automatic transmissions built today are of the multiplying type, commonly designated as *three-element hydraulic torque converters.*

In principle, all we have to do to a hydraulic coupling to make a torque converter is add another set of blades—*stationary* blades. There is the old rule that for every force there must be an equal and opposite reacting force. In transmissions this means that we cannot multiply torque unless we have some solid point to push on. We usually say we must have a reaction member, some stationary part connected to the frame of the vehicle. In a manual shift transmission the whole casing is fastened solidly and this holds the shafts in place. In the planetary gear set we have to grab hold of one of the three members before we can multiply torque—we have to hold it stationary in relation to the frame. And we have the same situation here. In a hydraulic coupling the whole thing turns around together. But if we put in a new part, a set of blades tied solidly to the frame, we have something to take the reaction, to furnish the reacting force. Then it can multiply torque.

We show here the simplest arrangement. We have the pump, or driving element, and the turbine, or driven element, just as in the hydraulic coupling. But between them we add a *stator,* the reaction element. The casing is filled with oil which circulates in the usual manner, outward from the pump, inward .through the turbine, and then through the stator back to the pump.

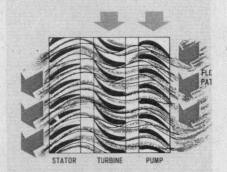

STATOR   TURBINE   PUMP

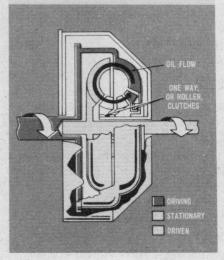

OIL FLOW

ONE WAY, OR ROLLER, CLUTCHES

DRIVING
STATIONARY
DRIVEN

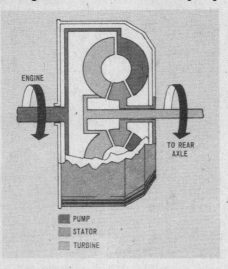

ENGINE

TO REAR AXLE

PUMP
STATOR
TURBINE

The blades are not straight and flat however. If we could spread the three members out flat and look down on them, we would get an idea of their shape and how the liquid flows through them. The pump pushes the oil in the direction it is turning, and this oil hits the turbine and forces it to turn in the same direction. In doing this the oil bounces off the turbine blades in the opposite direction, and is flowing somewhat backward when it reaches the stator. If this reaction member were free to turn it would turn backward, but it is held tight. So it straightens out the oil and gets it moving in a forward direction again before it returns to the pump. In this way the motion of the oil

assists the pump, and that is why such an arrangement can multiply torque.

A hydraulic torque converter is completely automatic in itself. It furnishes the greatest multiplication of torque when the car is starting from standstill, and this becomes less as the car picks up speed. The torque converter does not shift. It just smoothly changes from one ratio to another and to another in a continuous fashion, without definite steps. It is what we know as a continuously variable transmission.

This seems like the perfect way to drive a car, but there are some problems. If we tried to use the simple design we have shown, the results would be disappointing. Such an arrangement gives maximum efficiency at only one speed, and a large part of the time we would be wasting fuel. The stationary blades are necessary for multiplying torque, but when we are cruising along they just get in the way and churn up the oil. The curvature of the blades in all three elements is important, and if we design them for one condition they may not be so good for others. It is difficult to get as much torque multiplication as we desire to give good performance in starting up, and if the designer concentrates on this problem, he must sacrifice something else.

The approach used to improve the efficiency is to mount the stator on a one-way, or roller, clutch. This prevents the stator from turning backward, and thus it can act as the reaction element for multiplying torque. When the car speed reaches the point at which no further torque multiplication is needed, however, there is no backward force on the blades and the stator turns forward, or free-wheels, with the oil flow. What this actually means is that the torque converter now operates as a hydraulic coupling which wastes very little power under these conditions.

In some converter designs, the blades of the stator are mounted on pivots. This arrangement, known as variable pitch control, allows the angle at which the oil impinges on the stator blades to be changed to a low angle position for maximum efficiency of the converter and economical cruising or to a high angle position when more torque multiplication is needed for increased acceleration or pull. The blade angles can be changed automatically by means of a hydraulically controlled mechanism that is activated by the engine's throttle linkage.

If we wanted a simple form of automatic transmission, we could use the three-element torque converter by itself and connect the turbine shaft directly to the propeller shaft. Such an arrangement might satisfy a car's normal speed and torque requirements. But, unfortunately, the needs of an automatic transmission are more demanding than this. We need some way to provide additional torque multiplication, a reverse gear to back the car, and a neutral gear. We can do all these things with planetary gears.

Today's three-element torque converter transmissions use compound planetary gear sets, which means that

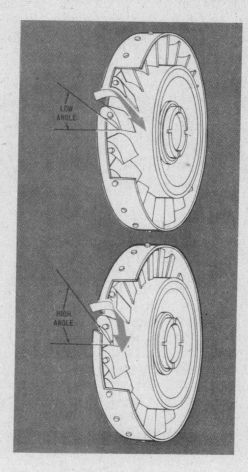

gears of both sets are interconnected. The planetary gears, along with the necessary clutches and bands, give the added torque multiplication needed as the car accelerates through the forward speed gear ratios. They also provide a low gear for slowing down the car or for hard pulling, such as when going either down or up a steep hill, and the necessary reverse gear and neutral.

The forward speed gear ratios provided by the planetary gears are changed automatically, and at exactly the right time. This is done by means of a hydraulic system that is an integral part of the torque converter-planetary gear transmission assembly. The hydraulic system applies the clutches and bands that grab or release the gears of the planetary set, as we explained earlier, to provide the proper gear ratio and control the automatic shifting. The hydraulic pressure that activates the specific bands and clutches used in the transmission varies with car speed and

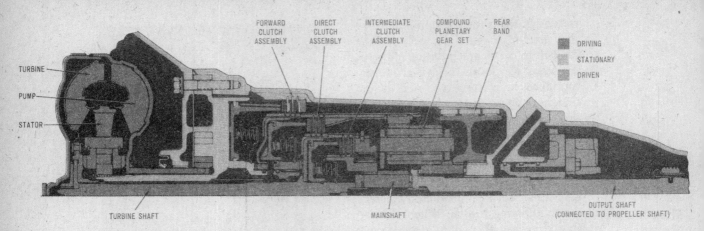

TURBINE

PUMP

STATOR

FORWARD CLUTCH ASSEMBLY

DIRECT CLUTCH ASSEMBLY

INTERMEDIATE CLUTCH ASSEMBLY

COMPOUND PLANETARY GEAR SET

REAR BAND

DRIVING
STATIONARY
DRIVEN

TURBINE SHAFT

MAINSHAFT

OUTPUT SHAFT
(CONNECTED TO PROPELLER SHAFT)

torque input to the transmission. An explanation of exactly how this is done is too complex for the scope of this booklet. We would have to get into a discussion on governor valves, servos, accumulator pistons, modulator valves and other components that make up the hydraulic system. For our purposes, it is sufficient to say that the system is designed to make sure that the gears are shifted (clutches and bands are held or released) at the proper time for all conditions of car speed and torque requirements.

The accompanying cut-away diagram shows how the components are arranged in a typical three-element torque converter transmission that provides three forward gear ratios and one reverse. Because of the difficulty in showing exactly how each part looks, simple shapes have been used for illustration. The diagram, however, indicates where the various components are located. Also, only the upper half of the overall transmission is shown, since the bottom half, of course, would look the same.

The flow of power from the engine to the rear wheels is through the torque converter assembly (pump, turbine, stator), the turbine shaft, mainshaft, the various clutches indicated, the compound planetary gear set, and finally the output shaft connected to the propeller shaft. Let's see what happens when the engine is running and the driver places the transmission selector lever in the Drive position.

As soon as the lever is placed in the Drive position, the forward clutch as-

sembly is applied and the transmission is in first gear. This clutch is connected to both the turbine shaft and the mainshaft. The mainshaft, in turn, is connected to the planetary gear sets. As the accelerator pedal is depressed and car speed increases, power flows through the turbine shaft and into the mainshaft which causes the gears in the planetary set to rotate and provide the proper gear reduction (about 2.5 to 1) and the proper torque to the output shaft. As car speed increases, less torque multiplication is needed and the hydraulic system receives a signal to apply the intermediate clutch. The transmission is now in second gear. This action results in the planetary gearing providing a lower gear ratio of about 1.5 to 1.

As the car continues to accelerate, we eventually get to a speed where no more torque multiplication is needed. When this point is reached, the hydraulic system applies the direct clutch and the car is in direct drive or third gear. The planetary gear set rotates as a unit and there is a ratio of 1 to 1, since the output shaft now rotates at the same speed as the turbine shaft.

The forward clutch not only provides the means for obtaining the proper gear reduction ratio for the first gear, but also lets the transmission be placed in Neutral. When the transmission selector lever is placed in Neutral, the forward clutch is released. This interrupts the flow of power from the turbine shaft to the mainshaft and, in turn, the output shaft.

The rear band assembly is used for reverse gear. When the transmission selector is placed in Reverse, the front and intermediate clutches are released and the direct clutch and rear band are applied. The direct clutch lets torque from the turbine be transmitted through the turbine shaft and into the planetary gear set (the mainshaft is by-passed). The rear band makes the planetary gears rotate opposite to the way they rotated for the forward speed gear ratios. This causes a similar change in output shaft and propeller shaft rotation.

Most torque converter transmissions also provide an intermediate and low gear range which can aid to brake the car when coming down steep hills or for hard pulling. When the transmission selector is placed in the intermediate range (this might be indicated as D_1, S, or L_2 on the quadrant), the transmission immediately shifts to second gear. The front band is applied to the direct clutch assembly to keep the transmission in second gear. When the driver's foot is taken off the accelerator pedal, the car will decelerate by using engine compression as the braking force.

The low gear provides even greater engine braking. Actually, low gear is the same as first gear—that is, moving the transmission to Lo, or L, on the quadrant places the transmission in first gear. (Shifting the transmission into the Lo range can only be done below a certain speed). When the transmission shifts into the low gear, the rear band and forward clutch assemblies are applied and the direct and intermediate clutch assemblies are released. The transmission will stay in the low gear range regardless of car speed until the driver shifts the transmission.

The automatic transmission also provides a Park position. This locks the output shaft and prevents the car from moving. Because the output shaft is mechanically locked to prevent its rota-tion, the Park position is never selected until the car is completely stopped.

We have now discussed all of the common ways of transmitting power in automotive vehicles. We have seen that there are many different ways of doing it. There are various types of mechanical drives and hydraulic devices. But if we look at them more closely, we find that they are simply entirely different ways of doing exactly the same thing. In all of them we are just transmitting power from one place to another, and providing something which will change the speed and torque when necessary.

We get a certain twist from the engine crankshaft and we carry that back to where it can apply a certain different twist to the wheels. To go a step further, we carry it back until it can apply a certain backward force to the ground, which makes the vehicle move forward. Just as there are different ways to transmit the engine's power to the rear wheels, so are there different ways in which the various components used to transmit this power are arranged in an automobile. We'll examine these arrangements in the next section.

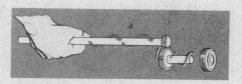

POWER TRAIN CONFIGURATIONS

Most of the automobiles we see on the road today—whether they have manual shift or automatic transmissions—have the engine located in the front with the power transferred to the rear drive wheels. This is the kind of power train configuration we have been talking about in this book.

Other automobiles are manufactured with different power train configurations. This means that while the engine and power transmission system are doing the same job, the arrangement of the system's components in the car, as well as the shape or form of each component, may be different.

In this section we'll discuss three other common power train configurations—front wheel drive, rear engine cars, and four and six-wheel drive.

Front Wheel Drive

Pulling a car by providing power at the front wheels instead of pushing it with the rear wheels is not a new idea. During the early days of automobiles, several models were produced with front wheel drive. But as cars became larger and more powerful, this power transmission system configuration became impractical.

It was not until recently that the knowledge of design, materials, and manufacturing had advanced enough to make front wheel drive practical on a modern, large-sized car with automatic transmission. In this section we will discuss only the power transmission system used on one of the present day front wheel drive cars and show how power from the engine can be transferred to the front wheels.

In this car, we are taking power from one place and putting it to work in another, just as we did before. Most of the components of the power train are the same as those in rear wheel drive cars. But now we are driving the front wheels. So, instead of being stretched out in a line from the engine back to the rear wheels, the power train is arranged to bend from the back of the engine forward to the front wheels.

The engine is located in the usual position, but there are major changes in the transmission. As we saw earlier, the usual automatic transmission has the torque converter attached to the engine with the rest of the transmission extending behind it. In the front wheel drive car, the transmission is split between the converter and the other section, which contains the planetary gearing. The converter is attached to the back of the engine, but the other section is swung around alongside the engine—like the hinged lid of a cigarette

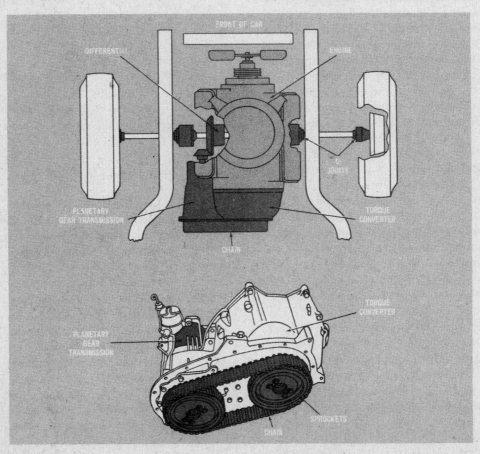

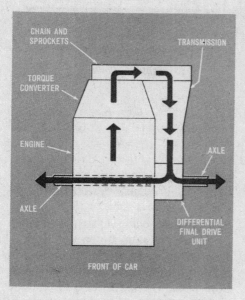

CHAIN AND SPROCKETS

TRANSMISSION

TORQUE CONVERTER

ENGINE

AXLE

AXLE

DIFFERENTIAL FINAL DRIVE UNIT

FRONT OF CAR

lighter that has been opened all the way.

Now what used to be the back of the transmission is facing the front of the car. But something else is needed. We must connect the converter and the rest of the transmission where we split them. One way to do this is with a chain and sprockets, which work something like those on a bicycle would if its sprockets were the same size. By attaching one sprocket to the torque converter and the other to the rest of the transmission where we split it, we have two sprockets of equal size side by side. When we put a chain around these sprockets, we can keep the power flowing through both parts of the split transmission.

Now the power comes from the engine through the torque converter, and is transferred into the transmission gearing. From there it flows directly into the final drive. Thus, we see another advantage of front wheel drive—the long propeller shaft has been replaced by a direct connection between the transmission and the differential.

The differential is located directly in front of the transmission gearing. A separate axle runs from the differential to each front wheel. Since the front wheels must pivot to steer the car as well as provide the drive, they undergo a wide range of movement while under power. To handle this, two universal

joints are placed on each axle—one at each end.

This power transmission system is typical of those used in the large, front wheel drive cars being made today. Some smaller cars also are made with front wheel drive, and use a manual shift transmission in the power train. But we won't go into the details. The arrangement of their components is similar to what we have described.

Rear Engine Cars

Another power train configuration found in many cars—especially small cars—is one with the engine and power transmission system in the rear of the vehicle. This arrangement gives a compact power train that can be thought of as a single unit, much like the front wheel drive arrangement already described.

Although there are several ways to arrange the power transmission components in a rear engine car, we'll discuss only one. It gives us a good idea of how power can be transferred from an engine in the rear of the car to the rear drive wheels.

As with front wheel drive, putting the entire power train in the rear of the car makes finding room a problem. The car we're going to look at solves this problem by placing the engine and transmission on opposite sides of the rear axle.

The engine is the rearmost power train component. In this car, its output shaft faces the front of the vehicle. Attached to the engine is the clutch. Then directly in front of the clutch is the final drive, and beyond it the transmission.

Now we know that in the power path the transmission must come between the clutch and the final drive. Although in this car the physical units themselves are not arranged in this order, a mechanical arrangement makes sure that the actual flow of power is.

This is done by using concentric shafts—a smaller shaft that is free to turn inside a larger, hollow shaft, which also is free to turn. In this way,

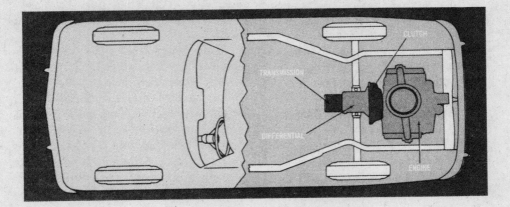

each shaft can be used to transmit power without having any effect on or being affected by the other. Different ratios of power can be transferred in opposite directions at the same time.

In this car, the hollow shaft is the pinion shaft that carries power from the transmission to the differential. Running inside this shaft and passing completely through the differential is the shaft connecting the clutch with the transmission.

Thus, power flows from the engine through the clutch and into the transmission by way of the "inside" shaft. Then, after the power ratio is changed in the transmission, it flows by way of the "outside" shaft back into the differential. Finally, it goes through the axles to the rear wheels.

On rear engine cars with automatic transmissions, the torque converter takes the place of the clutch, while the transmission planetary gearing and controls occupy the position of the standard transmission.

Again, the car we have described is only one of several rear engine cars. And its power train configuration is only one of several. But it shows us how power in a rear engine can be transferred to the rear wheels successfully.

Four-Wheel and Six-Wheel Drive

Trucks and other utility vehicles often are driven in places where the going is rough. Sometimes better traction than usual is needed. For example, two wheels might get stuck in a mud hole and not be able to pull out of it. So instead of having the engine drive just two wheels, it drives four wheels or six wheels. A four-wheel vehicle driving on all four wheels is known as a 4 × 4, and one with six wheels, all driving, is a 6 × 6. A 4 × 6 is a six-wheel truck with four driving wheels.

To get such a drive we use a *transfer case*. In back of the regular transmission is another set of gears. Essentially this consists of three gears meshing to-

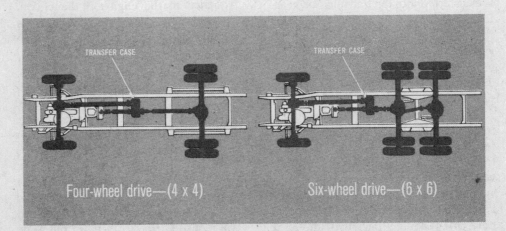

Four-wheel drive—(4 x 4)   Six-wheel drive—(6 x 6)

gether in series, extending out to one side of the transmission. The first and third gears are the same size. From each side of the third gear a propeller shaft extends, one forward to the front axle, one back to the rear axle. Each axle is driven just as we have shown in the two-wheel drive, except that in the front axle we must have some universal joints in order to steer.

For a six-wheel drive a third propeller shaft extends straight back from the first gear in the transfer case; that is, in line with the regular transmission. Thus, we have one input shaft into the transfer case and three output shafts.

With the first and third gears the same size we have no change of speed or torque in the transfer case. Usually, however, there is another pair of gears in it which can be shifted to give us a different ratio. A two-speed transfer case doubles the number of gear ratios available in the regular transmission.

TRANSMISSION AND ENGINE— A SUMMARY

This completes our look at the automobile and what makes it go.

We have found that the wheels do the driving, and that we must use the power of the engine to turn those wheels and push the car forward. An automobile must do this over a wide range of operating conditions. It must be able to go fast and slow with equal ease. It must start from rest and accelerate quickly. It must go up hills and down hills, on mud roads and smooth pavement. All this means that we need a lot of flexibility in both engine and transmission.

The engine furnishes power in the form of a twisting force, and this twist must be transmitted to a point where it can turn the wheels. That is the first requirement—simply to get power from one place to another.

But that power must be changed while it is being transmitted. We *increase the torque and decrease the speed*. We run the wheels at slower speed than the engine, but with a greater twisting force.

The reason why this is done is based on a fundamental characteristic of the internal combustion engine. It is a *high speed* engine. That is, to get the most power out of a given size engine, it has to run fairly fast—at least faster than we want the wheels to turn. We cannot run an engine at a slow speed and get the torque or twist we need to move a vehicle efficiently. So the easiest thing to do is what we have described—run the engine faster and use some sort of a transmission system to reduce the speed and increase the torque.

Thus, our power transmission system depends largely on the type of engine we use it with. It is the over-all effect of the engine-transmission combination in which we are interested. If new types of engines are developed in the future, our transmission system will change accordingly. What way it will change depends on how the engine changes. On the other hand, transmission systems will undoubtedly change whether or not engines change. And they will change for the better. They will be more efficient, quieter, smaller, more automatic, or more convenient for the operator.

Progress due to research and invention will be apparent in the power transmission field just as in every other. But, no matter what changes take place, the fundamental purpose will be the same—to take power from the engine, deliver it to the proper place and in the proper form, and use it in the best way to make the vehicle go. That is power transmission. That is how POWER GOES TO WORK in the automobile.

Common Problems

Basically all internal combustion engines depend for their proper performance on a supply of correct fuel mixture, good compression, and an adequate spark to ignite the mixture at the proper time. This section lists problems that may occur, their possible causes and remedies. (The remedies tell what to do, not how to do it)

1. **Engine will not start**
    Possible Common Causes:
    a. Weak battery.
    b. Corroded or loose battery terminal connections.
    c. Dirty or corroded distributor cap or rotor.
    d. Weak coil.
    e. Broken or loose ignition wires.
    f. Moisture on ignition wires, cap or plugs.
    g. Fouled spark plugs.
    h. Malfunctioning electronic ignition.
    i. Improper timing (ignition).
    j. Dirt or water in gas line or carburetor.
    k. Carburetor flooded.
    l. Fuel level in carburetor bowl not correct.
    m. Supply of fuel insufficient.
    n. Defective fuel pump.
    o. Vapor lock.
    p. Defective starting motor.
    q. Open ignition switch circuit.
    r. Inoperative breaker points.

    Remedies:
    a. Recharge and test battery. If necessary, replace battery.
    b. Clean, inspect and tighten battery terminals and clamps. Replace battery cables and clamps if badly eroded.
    c. Clean and inspect; if badly burned or pitted, replace cap or rotor. Check for carbon tracking between terminals.
    d. Replace weak coil with a new one.
    e. Replace broken ignition wires or those with cracked insulation. Tighten all connections at distributor, coil, ammeter and ignition switch. Be sure the spark plug wires are secure in distributor cap and coil tower.
    f. Dry the wet ignition system with compressed air or a clean, dry cloth. Remove the individual spark plug wire from cap; dry cavity and wire ends thoroughly. Inspect inside of cap and remove all traces of moisture and dirt.
    g. Clean and tighten spark plugs. Adjust gaps to manufacturer's specifications.
    h. Check electronic ignition system by manufacturer's procedure and replace bad components.
    i. Check ignition timing. Adjust to manufacturer's specifications.
    j. Disconnect fuel lines and clear with compressed air. Remove and clean carburetor. Drain tank and refill.
    k. Check carburetor float level and needle seat assembly. Check float for leaks and replace parts as necessary to correct this condition.
    l. Check carburetor for dirt, varnish or gumming; disassemble and clean.
    m. Set float level to manufacturer's specifications.
    n. Replace defective fuel pump with a new one to correct this condition.

   o. Check for air and fuel restrictions around fuel pump and check for misplacement of heat shield. Repair as necessary to correct this condition.

   p. Repair or replace defective starting motor. Replace worn or damaged parts as required.

   q. Turn ignition switch on; if ammeter shows a slight discharge, it indicates that current is flowing. A glance at the fuel gauge will indicate whether or not there is fuel in the tank. If no indication is obtained when turning the ignition switch on, the circuit is faulty and should be repaired.

   r. Inspect operation and condition; clean or replace as necessary. Set to manufacturer's specifications.

2. Engine stalls

Possible Causes:

   a. Idling speed too low.
   b. Idle mixture too lean or too rich.
   c. Dirt or water in gas line or carburetor.
   d. Incorrect carburetor float level.
   e. Leak in intake manifold vacuum.
   f. Defective accelerator pump (stall occurs on acceleration).
   g. Improper choke adjustment (stalls before warm-up).
   h. Carburetor icing (cold wet weather).
   i. Weak fuel pump.
   j. Fuel system emission controls malfunction.
   k. Weak battery and charging system.
   l. Spark plugs dirty, or gaps incorrectly set or worn.
   m. Coil defective, with low output.
   n. Distributor cap and rotor burned, worn or tracked.
   o. Improper ignition timing.
   p. Leaks in ignition wiring.
   q. Burned or pitted valves.
   r. Engine overheating.

Remedies:

   a. Reset throttle adjustment screw until engine idles at manufacturer's specifications.
   b. Reset idle adjustment screw for correct idle mixture. For richer mixture, turn screw out.
   c. Disconnect lines and clear with compressed air. Remove and clean carburetor.
   d. Fuel level should be adjusted to manufacturer's specifications.
   e. Check intake manifold, gasket and vacuum hoses. Replace parts as required to correct this condition.
   f. Replace or repair defective accelerator pump. Replace parts as required.
   g. Readjust automatic choke.
   h. Open throttle as engine starts to stall. Keep engine at fast idle until condition clears. Check heat riser valve and passages.
   i. Check fuel pump pressure at carburetor and replace if necessary.
   j. Check vapor emission systems as to manufacturer's specifications.
   k. Recharge and test battery and charging system. If necessary, replace any defective part with a new one of the same type and capacity.
   l. Clean or replace spark plugs. Adjust plug gaps to manufacturer's specifications.
   m. Replace defective coil.
   n. Replace distributor cap and rotor.

    o. Set ignition timing to manufacturer's specification.

    p. Replace broken ignition wires or those with cracked insulation. Tighten all connections at coil and distributor. Be sure the spark plug wires are secure in distributor cap and coil tower.

    q. Replace or reface and grind valves.

3. Engine has no power

  Possible Causes:

    a. Incorrect ignition timing.

    b. Coil has low output.

    c. Electronic ignition malfunctioning.

    d. Defective mechanical or vacuum advance (distributor).

    e. Emission controls malfunctioning.

    f. Worn or misadjusted points.

    g. Spark plugs dirty or worn.

    h. Poor fuel used.

    i. Carburetor in poor condition.

    j. Dirt or water in gas line or carburetor.

    k. Partially plugged fuel filter.

    l. Defective fuel pump.

    m. Valve timing incorrect.

    n. Malfunctioning fuel injection.

    o. Low compression.

    p. Plugged or restricted exhaust system.

    q. Clutch slipping.

    r. Engine overheating.

  Remedies:

    a. Check and reset ignition timing. Replace parts as necessary to correct this condition.

    b. Replace defective coil.

    c. Check electronic ignition system by manufacturer's procedure and replace bad components.

    d. Check vacuum-advance mechanism. Make adjustments or replace parts as necessary to correct this condition.

    e. Check EGR system and gas tank venting components and set to manufacturer's specifications.

    f. Install and adjust new points.

    g. Clean or replace spark plugs. Adjust plug gaps.

    h. Drain fuel tank and refill with a clean fresh fuel.

    i. Remove and recondition carburetor. Replace parts as required to correct this condition.

    j. Disconnect lines and clear with compressed air. Remove and clean carburetor. Drain tank and refill.

    k. Replace fuel filter.

    l. Replace defective fuel pump with a new one to correct this condition.

    m. Replace timing chain or belt, reset valve timing to manufacturer's specifications.

    n. Check fuel injection by manufacturer's procedure and replace bad components.

    o. Replace or reface and grind valves. Replace piston rings.

    p. Remove plugged or restricted muffler, catalytic converter or pipe and replace with a new one. Check for excessive carbon in combustion chamber.

4. Engine "skips" or misses at idle or low speeds

Possible Causes:

a. Spark plugs dirty, damp, or worn.
b. Moisture on ignition wires, caps or plugs.
c. Leaks in ignition wiring.
d. Incorrect carburetor idle adjustment.
e. Dirt or water in gas line or carburetor.
f. Incorrect ignition timing.
g. Dirty jets or plugged passages in carburetor idle or main circuit.
h. Excessive wear in distributor cap or rotor.
i. Defective electronic ignition pickup.
j. Defective electronic ignition control unit.
k. Burned, warped or pitted valves.
l. Malfunctioning fuel injection system.

Remedies:

a. Clean or replace spark plugs. Adjust plug gaps to manufacturer's specifications.
b. Dry the wet ignition system with compressed air or a clean, dry cloth. Remove the individual spark plug wires from cap; dry cavity and wire ends thoroughly. Inspect inside of cap and remove all traces of moisture and dirt.
c. Replace broken ignition wires or those with cracked insulation. Tighten all connections at distributor and ignition coil. Be sure the spark plug wires are secure in distributor cap and coil tower.
d. Reset idle adjustment screw for correct idle mixture.
e. Disconnect lines and clear with compressed air. Remove and clean carburetor. Drain tank and refill.
f. Check and reset ignition timing.
g. Remove carburetor and recondition. Replace parts as necessary to correct this condition.
h. Check distributor shaft play. Replace parts as required to correct this condition.
i. Test pickup according to manufacturer's specifications and replace as necessary.
j. Test control unit according to manufacturer's procedure and replace if necessary.
k. Replace, or reface and grind valves.
l. Check fuel injection system according to manufacturer's procedure and replace defective parts.

5. Engine misses on acceleration

Possible Causes:

a. Distributor points worn or incorrectly spaced.
b. Coil defective.
c. Incorrect ignition timing.
d. Spark plugs dirty, damp, or worn.
e. Poor ignition wires.
f. Dirty jets in carburetor, especially enrichment circuit; or accelerator pump operating improperly.
g. Fuel injection malfunctioning.
h. Defective electronic ignition component.

Remedies:

a. Clean and inspect contact points; if badly burned or pitted, replace points and condenser. Adjust point gap to manufacturer's specifications and then check timing.
b. Replace defective coil.

   c. Check and reset ignition timing.
   d. Clean or replace spark plugs. Adjust plug gaps to manufacturer's specifications.
   e. Replace faulty ignition wires.
   f. Remove carburetor and recondition. Replace parts as required to correct this condition.
   g. Test fuel injection according to manufacturer's procedure and replace necessary components.
   h. Test electronic injection according to manufacturer's procedure and replace necessary components.

6. Engine misses at high speed
  Possible Causes:
   a. Dirt or water in gas line or carburetor.
   b. Dirty jets or enrichment circuit in carburetor.
   c. Coil defective.
   d. Incorrect ignition timing.
   e. Distributor points worn or incorrectly set.
   f. Rotor or cap severely worn.
   g. Loose or bad ignition wires.
   h. Defective electronic ignition pickup.
   i. Spark plugs dirty, damp or worn.
   j. Defective electronic ignition control unit.
   k. Defective fuel injection.

  Remedies:
   a. Disconnect lines and clear with compressed air. Remove and clean carburetor. Drain tank and refill.
   b. Remove carburetor and recondition. Replace parts as necessary to correct this position.
   c. Replace defective coil.
   d. Check and reset ignition timing.
   e. Clean and inspect contact points; if badly burned or pitted, replace points and condenser. Adjust point gap to manufacturer's specifications and then check timing.
   f. Replace worn rotor with a new one. Check contacts in cap for burning or pitting. If necessary, replace distributor cap.
   g. Replace broken ignition wires or those with cracked insulation. Tighten all connections and be sure the spark plug wires are secure in distributor cap.
   h. Test pickup according to manufacturer's specifications and replace as necessary.
   i. Clean or replace spark plugs. Adjust plug gaps to manufacturer's specifications.
   j. Test according to manufacturer's specifications and replace if necessary.
   k. Test according to manufacturer's specifications and replace defective components.

7. External oil leakage
  Possible Causes:
   a. Tappet or valve cover gaskets.
   b. Oil filter gasket.
   c. Oil pan drain plug.
   d. Fuel pump or gasket.
   e. Oil pressure sending unit.
   f. Oil pan gaskets.
   g. Rear main bearing oil seal.

    h. Timing gear case cover oil seal.
    i. Intake manifold (V type).
    j. Timing chain cover gasket.
    k. Outside oil lines.

Remedies:

    a. Remove gaskets from tappet or valve covers and replace with new ones. Before installing, be sure all traces of old gasket have been removed from the machined faces of block. Wipe surfaces dry and install covers. Always open drain holes.
    b. Clean filter and cover, removing all traces of old gasket. Install new gasket, using care to be sure gasket is centered. Make hand tight only, then run engine for five minutes; inspect for leakage.
    c. Replace worn oil pan plug, using a new gasket.
    d. Replace fuel pump or gasket. Check fuel pump for oil leaks after installing.
    e. Clean off sending unit and run for 10 minutes; inspect for leaks; replace if necessary.
    f. Replace faulty oil pan gaskets to correct this condition.
    g. Replace rear main bearing oil seal. Be sure seal and gaskets are in correct location in the cap before installation.
    h. Replace chain case cover oil seal. Be sure to use a new cover gasket. Check seal surface of balancer or shaft for wear.
    i. Remove intake manifold and check drain hole. Check and clean gasket surface; install with new gaskets.
    j. Replace timing chain cover gasket. Inspect oil seal and if necessary, replace.
    k. Check for oil leaks at filter tubes and oil gauge lines. Replace tubing or fittings to correct this condition. Be sure filter mounting bracket is fastened tightly.

8. Oil pumping at rings

Possible Causes:

    a. Worn or broken rings.
    b. Incorrect size rings.
    c. Out-of-round cylinders.
    d. Rings stuck in grooves.
    e. Carbon in oil drain holes or slots.
    f. Insufficient tension in rings.
    g. Excessive rod bearing clearance causing excessive oil to be splashed on cylinder walls.

Remedies:

    a. Replace worn rings after a careful inspection of cylinder walls. Worn, wavy or scored walls are a contributing factor to high oil consumption. Recondition cylinder walls.
    b. Replace incorrect size rings with new piston rings of the proper type.
    c. Rebore out-of-round cylinders after checking cylinder bore.
    d. Replace frozen or stuck rings with new piston rings. Check oil ring clearance in groove.
    e. Remove rings and clean piston ring slots with a suitable cleaning tool. Check cylinder bore and rings.
    f. Replace weak rings with new rings after checking condition of cylinder walls.
    g. Measure rod bearing clearances and replace if necessary.

9. **Oil pumping at valves**

   Possible Causes:

   a. Worn or heat damaged valve seals.
   b. Plugged oil return drain holes.
   c. Worn valve stems or guides.

   Remedies:

   a. Replace worn or damaged seals whenever this condition is apparent.
   b. Remove valve or tappet covers; open drain holes.
   c. Replace worn valves and guides as necessary to correct this condition.

10. **High oil consumption due to lubricating oil**

   Possible Causes:

   a. Oil level too high.
   b. Water-contaminated oil.
   c. Poor grade of oil.
   d. Thin, diluted oil.
   e. Oil pressure too high.
   f. Sludge in engine blocking return drain holes.

   Remedies:

   a. Add oil only when level reaches add oil mark. If oil level is over "full," drain sufficient oil to obtain correct level.
   b. Drain and refill crankcase with a good-quality oil of the proper type and grade. Replace filter cartridge or filter.
   c. Drain and refill crankcase with a good-quality oil of manufacturer's specified weight. Replace filter cartridge or filter.
   d. Drain and refill crankcase with a good-quality oil. Replace filter cartridge or filter. Check operation of automatic choke and carburetor for source of fuel.
   e. Free up sticking relief valve or replace oil pressure relief valve spring.
   f. Drain and refill crankcase with a good-quality oil. Replace filter cartridge or filter after thoroughly cleaning all return drain holes under valve or tappet covers and intake manifold. Check thermostat. A thermostat that remains in the open position allows the engine to operate below normal temperatures, thus allowing sludge formation. Also check PCV valve and breather system.

11. **High oil consumption—miscellaneous**

   Possible Causes:

   a. Overheating engine.
   b. Sustained high speeds.
   c. Plugged breather cap causing excessive crankcase ventilation vacuum.
   d. Plugged PCV system causing crankcase pressure.

   Remedies:

   a-b Avoid sustained high speeds at wide-open throttle whenever possible or change to heavier-weight oil.
   c. Check breather. Inspect crankcase ventilator outlet tube and oil drain passage in block for restrictions. Clean or repair as required to correct this condition.
   d. Replace PCV valve and open all passages and hoses.

12. **Piston noise**

   Possible Causes:
   - *a.* Piston pin fit too tight or too loose.
   - *b.* Excessive piston-to-bore clearance.
   - *c.* Collapsed piston skirt.
   - *d.* Insufficient clearance to cylinder head due to carbon buildup.
   - *e.* Broken piston or skirt.

   Remedies:
   - *a.* Refit piston pins as required.
   - *b.* Replace pistons as required. Check cylinder walls for excessive wear; if necessary, recondition cylinder walls and install new pistons to fit manufacturer's specifications.
   - *c.* Replace pistons as required. Check cylinder walls for possible scoring; recondition as necessary to correct.
   - *d.* Remove cylinder head and clean carbon from chamber, pistons, and valves.
   - *e.* Replace pistons as required. Check cylinder walls for possible scoring or damage. Recondition walls if necessary and install new pistons.

13. **Valve noise**

   Possible Causes:
   - *a.* Excessive valve clearance.
   - *b.* Worn or stuck hydraulic valve lifters.
   - *c.* Gum formation on stem causing valves to stick.
   - *d.* Weak valve springs.
   - *e.* Worn camshaft.

   Remedies:
   - *a.* Check and adjust valves with engine at normal operating temperature.
   - *b.* Replace hydraulic lifters. Check camshaft for pitting and wear.
   - *c.* Remove gum from valve stems, grind, reinstall and adjust. Replace valves, if necessary.
   - *d.* Valve springs can be checked with testing gauge.
   - *e.* Replace worn camshaft and always install new lifters.

14. **Connecting rod noise**

   Possible Causes:
   - *a.* Low oil pressure.
   - *b.* Insufficient oil supply (splash lubrication system).
   - *c.* Thin or diluted oil.
   - *d.* Misaligned rods.
   - *e.* Excessive bearing clearance.
   - *f.* Eccentric or out-of-round crank pin journal.

   Remedies:
   - *a.* Check oil pump thoroughly.
   - *b.* Check oil level in crankcase; if necessary, add oil to obtain correct level, or drain and refill. Test for possible loose or damaged rod bearings.
   - *c.* Drain and refill crankcase and then test for possible loose or damaged rod bearings.
   - *d.* Check rods for alignment; if necessary, straighten rod or install new one to correct

this condition. Check bearing and journal for excessive wear. Replace parts as required.

e. Replace worn bearings as required. Fit connecting rod bearings to manufacturer's clearance.

f. Replace or regrind crankshaft as necessary. Replace with new fitted undersize bearings after grinding operation is completed.

15. Main bearing noise

Possible Causes:

a. Low oil pressure.
b. Insufficient oil supply (splash lubrication system).
c. Thin or diluted oil.
d. Excessive bearing clearance.
e. Excessive end play or thrust bearing.
f. Eccentric or out-of-round journals.

Remedies:

a. Check pump thoroughly.
b. Check oil level in crankcase; if necessary, add oil to obtain correct level, or drain and refill. Test for possible loose or damaged main bearings.
c. Drain and refill crankcase; then test for possible loose or damaged main bearings.
d. Replace worn bearings as required. Fit main bearings to manufacturer's clearance.
e. Replace thrust bearing; measure and replace crankshaft if necessary.
f. Replace crankshaft or regrind journals as necessary. Replace with new fitted undersize bearings when grinding operation is completed.

16. Broken piston rings

Possible Causes:

a. Wrong type or size.
b. Worn pistons (excessive clearance).
c. Ring striking top ridge.
d. Worn ring grooves.
e. Broken ring lands.
f. Insufficient end gap clearance.
g. Excessive side clearance in groove.
h. Uneven cylinder walls (particularly due to a previous ring wear in same cylinder).

Remedies:

a. Replace rings as required, after checking cylinder walls for possible scoring or grooving. When replacing rings, use only those that are factory engineered and inspected and the correct type and size for the engine being worked on.
b. Fit new pistons and rings. Rebore or sleeve cylinders.
c. Replace rings as required, after checking cylinder walls for possible scoring or grooving. Remove ridge and recondition walls, if necessary.
d. Replace pistons and rings, after checking cylinder walls for possible scoring or grooving. Recondition cylinder walls as required.
e. Replace pistons and rings as required, after checking cylinder walls for possible scoring or grooving. Recondition cylinder walls if necessary.
f. Replace rings as required. Check walls for damage and recondition if necessary. Correct ring gap to manufacturer's specifications.

g. Replace pistons as required. Inspect cylinder walls for damage and recondition if necessary.

h. Fit new pistons and rings, after reboring or sleeving cylinder walls.

17. Broken pistons
Possible Causes:
a. Undersize pistons (excessive clearance).
b. Eccentric or tapered cylinders.
c. Misaligned connecting rods.
d. Engine overheating.
e. Excessive engine speed or loading at low rpm.
f. Water or fuel leakage into combustion chamber.
g. Detonation or preignition.

Remedies:
a. Recondition cylinder walls and fit oversize pistons.
b. Recondition cylinder walls and fit new pistons and rings.
c. Recondition cylinder walls if necessary; then fit new pistons and rings. Realign connecting rods.
d. Recondition cylinder walls if necessary; then fit new pistons and rings.
e. Recondition cylinder walls if necessary; then fit new pistons and rings. Avoid the practice of "racing" or "lugging" the engine.
f. Recondition cylinder walls if necessary; then fit new pistons and rings. Check cylinder head, gasket and cylinder block for leaks. Repair as necessary to correct this condition.
g. Recondition cylinder walls if necessary; then fit new pistons and rings. Check for excessive spark advance and insufficient octane fuel.

18. Low oil pressure
Possible Causes:
a. Thin or diluted oil.
b. Oil relief valve spring broken or weak; oil pressure relief valve sticking.
c. Restricted oil pump screen.
d. Excessive clearance in main or connecting rod bearings.
e. Excessive clearance in camshaft bearings.
f. Low oil level.
g. Loose connections or restricted oil lines.
h. Worn oil pump.
Remedies:
a. Drain, flush and refill crankcase.
b. Replace broken or weak relief spring, clean relief valve and bore.
c. Remove strainer, disassemble and wash in solvent or replace; Clear with an air hose and install.
d. and e. Check clearance in main, connecting rod and camshaft bearings. Correct as necessary.
f. Add oil to bring capacity up to the proper level. Check for bearing damage.
g. Check for restricted lines and clean out or replace where necessary. Check for leaking connecting lines.
h. Check pump according to manufacturer's procedure and specifications. Rebuild or replace as necessary.

Problems may also occur with the exhaust system. Vibrating or rattling exhaust system parts may be caused by a broken exhaust manifold valve or valve spring or by loose or broken clamps or pipes. Leaking or noisy exhaust systems may be caused by cracked or corroded pipes, defective mufflers, loose parts or improperly aligned parts. These types of problems can be corrected by repairing or replacing all worn and broken parts, by tightening all connections and by checking that all parts are properly aligned. Restricted exhaust can also sometimes occur from excessive backpressure resulting from a bent or obstructed pipe, an exhaust manifold valve stuck in the closed position, or other problems. Replacement of worn parts and attention to the removal of all obstructions or kinks in the pipes will solve the problem.

9 SHOP INFORMATION REVIEW

A person interested in making or repairing things is lost without tools. Tools make the difference between a person who works efficiently and one who struggles laboriously. There are some tools that are basic to any home shop and are generally used for simple carpentry work. Others are used for more specialized purposes, including working with concrete, wood, or sheet metal.

Common Tools for a Carpenter and Home Mechanic

Measuring devices. One of the first tools you need is a measuring device. This may take the form of a folding rule, a tape measure, a ruler, or a yard stick (Fig. 9.1).

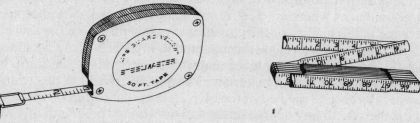

Fig. 9.1. Tape measure and folding rule

When using a folding rule, place it flat on the work. The "0" end of the rule should be exactly even with the end of the space or board to be measured. The correct distance is indicated by the reading on the rule.

A very accurate reading may be obtained by turning the edge of the rule toward the work. In this position, the marked graduations of the face of the rule touch the surface of the board. With a sharp pencil, mark the exact distance desired. Start the mark with the point of the pencil in contact with the mark on the rule. Move the pencil directly away from the rule while making the mark.

A problem may be noticed with a folding rule: if it is twisted, it breaks. This happens commonly when folding or unfolding the rule and may not be noticed at the time. You should keep the joints oiled lightly so that the rule operates more easily.

Beginners may find a pocket tape (Fig. 9.2) the most useful measuring tool for all types of work. It extends smoothly to full length. It returns quickly to its compact case when the return button is pressed. Steel tapes are available in a variety of lengths. For most carpentry work a rule 6, 8, 10, or 12 feet long is suggested.

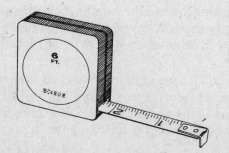

Fig. 9.2. Tape measure

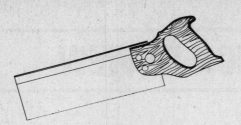

Fig. 9.3. Back saw

Fig. 9.4. Standard skew-back saw

Saws. Many home mechanics and carpenters use saws to cut wood or metal. There are different types made for wood or metal and different types designed for specific types of work. The blade determines the use of the saw.

The *back saw* (Fig. 9.3) gets its name from the piece of heavy metal that makes up the top edge of the cutting part of the saw. It has a fine tooth configuration. This means it can be used to cut cross-grain—cut wood across the grain—and it leaves a smooth finished piece of work. This type of saw is used by finishing carpenters who want to cut trim or molding. The standard *skew-back saw* (Fig. 9.4) has a wooden handle. It has a 22-inch length. A 10-point saw (with 10 teeth per inch) is suggested for crosscutting.

The 26-inch length, 5½ point saw is suggested for ripping—cutting with the wood grain. This saw is used in places where an electric saw cannot be used. The sharpness of the blade makes a difference in the quality of the cut and the ease with which the saw can be used.

The *mitre box* (Fig. 9.5) has a backsaw mounted in it. This box can be adjusted for the cut you wish from 90° to 45° using the lever under the saw handle. The mitre box is used for finishing cuts on moldings and trim materials. The angle of the cut is determined by the location of the saw in reference to the bed of the box. Release the clamp on the bottom of the saw support to adjust the saw to any degree desired. The wood is held with one hand against the fence of the box and the bed. Then the saw is used by the other hand. As you can see from the setup, the cutting should take place when the saw is pushed forward. The backward movement of the saw should be made with the pressure on the saw released slightly. If you try to cut on the backward movement, you will just pull the wood away from the fence and decrease the quality of the cut.

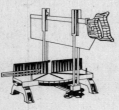

Fig. 9.5. Mitre box

Fig. 9.6. Coping saw

The *coping saw* (Fig. 9.6) comes in handy to make cuts that are not straight. The coping saw can cut small thicknesses of wood at any curve or angle desired. It can be used to make a piece of paneling fit properly or a piece of molding fit another piece in the corner. The blade is placed in the frame with the teeth pointing toward the handle. This means it cuts only on the downward stroke. Make sure you properly support the piece of wood being cut. A number of blades can be obtained for this type of saw. The number of teeth in the blade determines the smoothness of the cut.

Hammers. Hammers (Fig. 9.7) come in many sizes and shapes, made for different types of jobs. The *claw hammer* is used by carpenters. It has the ability to extract nails from wood if they are bent or have been put in the wrong way. Claw hammers can be bought in 20-ounce, 24-ounce, 28-ounce, and 32-ounce weights for carpentry work; the usual carpenter choice is

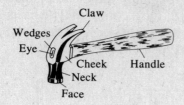

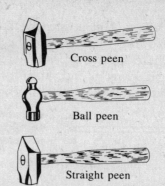

Cross peen

Ball peen

Straight peen

Fig. 9.7. (A) A claw hammer is used for building with wood and for driving nails.

(B) Three types of metal working hammers.

the 20-ounce. You have to experiment to find out which is best for you. The hammer should be made of tempered steel.

Nails. Nails (Fig. 9.8) are driven by hammers. Note the relationship between gage, penny *(d)*, and inches. The *d* after the number means penny. This is a measuring unit inherited from the English in the colonial days. There is little or no relationship between penny and inches. If you want to be able to talk about it intelligently, you'll have to learn both inches and penny. The gage is nothing more than the American Wire Gage number for the wire that the nails are made from originally. Finish nails have the same measuring unit (the penny) but do not have the large flat heads.

Nail Sets. Nail sets are used to drive finish nails below the surface of the wood. The nail set is placed on the head of the nail. The large end of the nail set is struck by the hammer. This causes the nail to go below the surface of the wood. Then the hole left by the countersunk nail is filled with wood filler and finished off with a smooth coat of varnish or paint.

Scratch Awl. A scratch awl is a handy tool for a carpenter. It can be used to mark wood with a scratch mark. It can also be used to produce pilot holes for screws. Once it is in your tool box, you can think of a hundred uses for it. Since it has a very sharp point, it is best treated with respect. Fig. 9.9 shows the point.

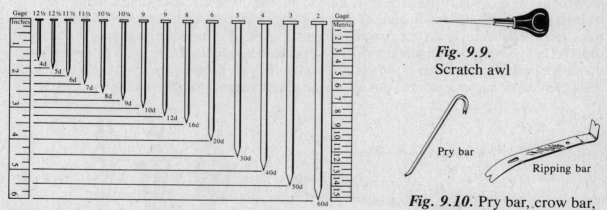

Fig. 9.9. Scratch awl

Pry bar

Ripping bar

Fig. 9.10. Pry bar, crow bar, or wrecking bar

Fig. 9.8. Nails

Wrecking Bar. The wrecking bar (Fig. 9.10) has many names. It is called a crow bar, a pry bar or a wrecking bar depending on what part of the country you are in. It is a tool with a chisel-sharp flat surface to get under boards and pry them loose. The other end is so hooked that the slot in the end can pull nails with the leverage of the long handle. This specially treated steel bar can be very helpful in prying away old and unwanted boards. It can be used to help give leverage when you are putting a wall in place and making it plumb. This tool is also used for many other purposes.

Screwdrivers. This is one tool that cannot be left out of a tool box for a mechanic, carpenter or anyone doing work around the house. It can be used for many things other than turning screws. There are two types of screwdrivers. The standard, most common type has a straight slot-fitting blade at its end. The Phillips-head screwdriver has a cross or X on the end; this fits a screw head of the same design. Fig. 9.11 shows the two types of screwdrivers.

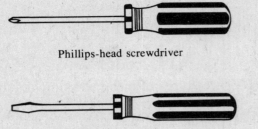

Phillips-head screwdriver

Standard screwdriver

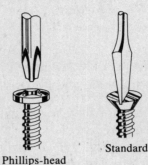

Phillips-head

Standard

Fig. 9.11. Screwdrivers, standard and phillips-head

Chisels. Chisels are used to cut wood. They are sharpened on one end. When the other end is struck with a hammer, the cutting end will do its job. That is, of course, if you have kept it sharpened. Fig. 9.12 shows a wood chisel.

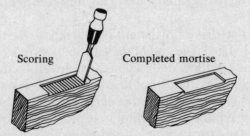

Scoring

Completed mortise

Fig. 9.12. Wood Chisel

Level and Plumb bob. Levels are used for a number of purposes. The most important is to make sure that things are properly oriented so that mechanisms will work properly. A refrigerator, for example, usually has to be level for it to operate correctly; doors and windows have to be level to move up and down, and, of course, things look better when they are level. A level has a vertical indicator and a horizontal indicator (Fig. 9.13). The bubbles in the glass tubes in the level tell you if the level is obtained. The carpenter's level is used to make sure windows and doors are properly installed. If the vertical and horizontal bubbles are lined up between the lines then the window or door is plumb. Being plumb means that the window is vertical.

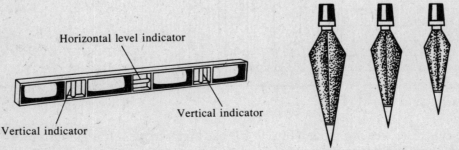

Horizontal level indicator

Vertical indicator

Vertical indicator

Plumb bobs

Fig. 9.13. Level and plumb bob

A *plumb bob* is a small, pointed weight. It is attached to a string and dropped from a height. If the bob is just above the ground, it will indicate the vertical direction by its string. Keeping windows and doors and frames square and level makes a difference in fitting. It is much easier to fit prehung doors into a frame that is square.

Files. A number of types of files are available. A carpenter, for instance, finds use for different surfaces to do different jobs. Tapping out a hole to get something to fit may be just the job for a file. Some files are used for sharpening saws and touching up tool cutting edges. Fig. 9.14 shows different types of files. Other files may also be useful for working with metals.

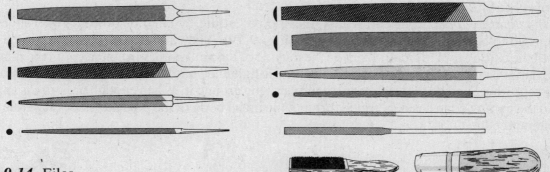

Fig. 9.14. Files

Hole Cutter or Saws. Hole saws (Fig. 9.15) are used in the metal cutting, electrical, plumbing, and automotive trades. The high speed steel cutting edge, welded to a tough alloy back, will cut clean, round holes in any machinable material up to 1 inch depth and from 9/16 to 6 inches in diameter. Similar designs can be used for cutting holes in wood.

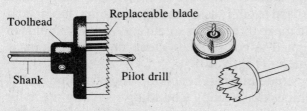

Fig. 9.15. Hole saw

Fig. 9.16. Cold Chisel

Cold Chisel. The cold chisel (Fig. 9.16) is made with a very sharp edge that can cut metal. This means it can be used to remove a nail. The nail head may have broken off and the nail must be removed. The chisel can cut the nail and permit separation of the wood pieces. Cold chisels are used for many operations involving the removal of small amounts of metal.

If a chisel of this type starts to "mushroom" at the head, you should remove the splintered ends with a grinder. Hammering on the end can produce a mushrooming effect. These pieces should be taken off since they can easily fly off when hit with a hammer. This is but one reason for wearing eye protection when using tools.

Other Types of Tools

Welding can be done by arc welders using electricity to cause metals to heat sufficiently to run together and hold permanently. Oxygen and acetylene are used in welding and also in cutting metal. The *welding torch* has adjustments for making the flame hot enough to melt the metal sufficiently to bond (Fig. 9.17). The oxyacetylene cutting torch (Fig. 9.18) can be

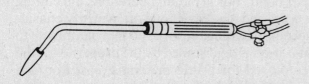

Fig. 9.17. Welding torch

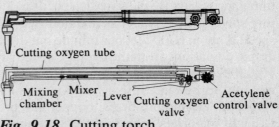

Fig. 9.18. Cutting torch

manipulated manually to cut thick metal or to remove bolts from rusty mufflers on a car. The tip of the torch contains a circular array of small holes through which the oxygen-acetylene mixture is supplied for the heating flame. A larger hole in the center supplies a stream of oxygen, controlled by a lever valve. The rapid flow of the cutting oxygen not only produces rapid oxidation but also blows the oxides from the cut. If the cut is adjusted and manipulated properly a smooth cut results.

Pipe cutting tools are used for fast, clean pipe cutting by hand or power. Two rollers are adjusted to come in contact with the pipe (Fig. 9.19). They are then pushed against the pipe until the cutting tool (a small wheel on the outside of the tool) comes in contact with the pipe. As the cutter is turned around the pipe the handle is tightened until the cutting edge has penetrated the pipe lining and caused it to have a complete ring around it. When enough pressure is applied and the cutting edge has penetrated through the metal body of the pipe the pieces separate with a smooth edge.

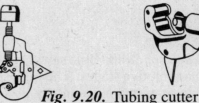

Fig. 9.19. Pipe cutter   *Fig. 9.20.* Tubing cutter

Tubing cutters are smaller versions of the pipe cutters. They are about 5 inches long with a lightweight frame of aluminum alloy. They are used to cut brass, copper, aluminum tubing and thinwall conduit. Rollers smooth the tubing and make it ready for soldering. A reamer folds in when the cutter is in use. They are also designed to cut stainless steel tubing. Capacity is usually limited to tubing up to 2½ inches diameter (Fig. 9.20).

Grinders are made for many purposes. They come in small bench top units for home work and small shop use all the way up to huge machines that occupy a building specially made for them. In the small shop you will find a grinder used for many purposes, most often for removing metal.

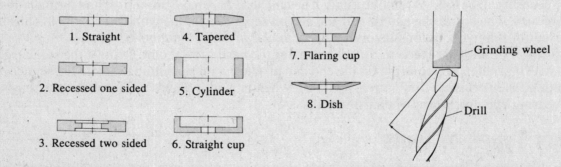

1. Straight   4. Tapered

2. Recessed one sided   5. Cylinder   7. Flaring cup   Grinding wheel

8. Dish

3. Recessed two sided   6. Straight cup   Drill

Fig. 9.21. (A) Grinding wheels   (B) Sharpening a drill bit

The shape of the grinding wheel runs from straight to dish (Fig. 9.21). There are a dozen standard face contours for straight grinding wheels (Fig. 9.22). The size of the wheel is determined primarily by the spindle speeds available for the grinding machine and the proper cutting speed for the wheel as dictated by the type of bond. For grinding operations the cutting speed is about 6500 feet per minute but different types and grades of bond often justify considerable deviations from the average speed. The speeds may range from 4500 feet per minute to 10,000 feet per minute. The kind of abrasive that is used is determined by the properties of the material to be cut. Silicon carbide usually is employed for brittle materials, cast iron and ceramics, aluminum, brass, copper and bronze. Aluminum oxide is used for tougher, higher strength materials such as steel, wrought iron or hardened steel. Selection of grain size is

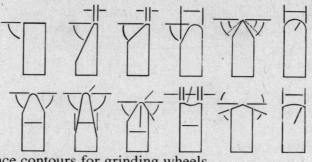

Fig. 9.22. Standard face contours for grinding wheels

determined by whether coarse or fine cutting and finish are desired. As you can see it takes some time to study the situation to become well informed on grinding wheel selection.

Working with Concrete

Working with concrete calls for proper concrete mix. The concrete mix can be selected in bags or ordered ready-mixed and delivered by a truck that keeps the material properly mixed until needed. Or, you can mix the cement, sand, and gravel as needed to make concrete. However, you must use the proper proportions and add water and turn the mix until it reaches the proper consistency.

In most instances you will want to place the concrete in a *form* that has previously been prepared for it. You first have to excavate the site. This calls for outlining with stakes the area to be covered with concrete. The area should extend at least 1 foot beyond the edge of a planned site—a patio, for instance. This helps prevent undercutting, which can occur when a base has eroded or fallen away leaving the slab without sufficient base. Tie a string tautly between all stakes. To make the pattern for digging simply sprinkle sand or lime over the string onto the ground, thus outlining the pattern for digging.

Then you must prepare the base. This means you should remove all grass, roots and other organic matter from the surface. Dig to a depth of 6 to 8 inches, sloping gently away from the nearest building. Use sand, gravel or other fill with a minimum of four inches to bring the site to a uniform grade. Compact the fill with a tamper or similar device such as a concrete block or 4″ x 4″ piece of wood. Dampen the fill to aid in packing. The base should be uniform, hard, and free from foreign matter.

Make the form to fit the pattern needed. Dampen the forms and base thoroughly, but leave no puddles. Shovel or place the mix into the form. Fill to the full depth of the forms. Start at a corner and do not drag or flow the concrete unnecessarily. After the concrete has been spread, completely filling the forms, strike off and float immediately (Fig. 9.23).

To "strike off" means to use a straight 2″ x 4″ x 6′ board, moving the edge back and forth with a sawlike motion, smoothing the surface. Then use a "darby" (made from a smooth, flat board approximately 3.5 inches wide and 3.5 feet long with a handle on top) to float the surface. This helps level any ridges and fills voids left by the straight edge. These two procedures help embed all particles of coarse stone or gravel slightly below the surface. Do not "overwork" the concrete. This can cause separation and create a less durable surface.

Fig. 9.23. Striking off concrete

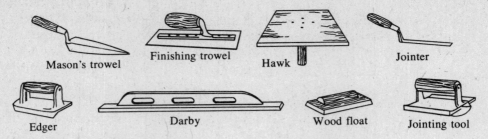

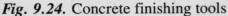

Fig. 9.24. Concrete finishing tools

Before finishing the concrete allow it to stiffen slightly. This allows all water to evaporate from the surface before troweling. When the surface has turned dull, smooth and compact the concrete with a trowel. For best results keep the trowel pressed firmly and flat. Sweep it back and forth, each pass overlapping half of the previous pass. Good results can be attained by using a trowel measuring 4″ x 14″ (Fig. 9.24). Use an edging tool to round the edges along all forms. An edger with a half-inch radius is recommended. To produce a textured, non-skid surface, use a wood float for final troweling. Then use a wet broom to place the marks in the surface that are needed for your purposes.

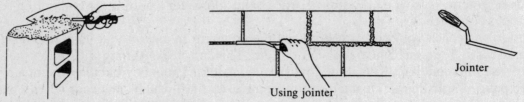

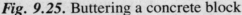

Fig. 9.25. Buttering a concrete block

Other tools used by persons working with concrete and masonry are the *mason's trowel* which is used to "butter" a block or brick (Fig. 9.25). The *jointer* is used to finish up the joints between the blocks (Fig. 9.26). When a wall needs to be covered with mortar, the *hawk* can be used to keep enough near at hand so it can be spread on the surface of the blocks (Fig. 9.27).

Fig. 9.26. Using a jointer   *Fig. 9.27.* Hawk being used to hold mortar

In order to cure concrete properly you should keep it damp for a period of five to seven days after it has been poured. This helps the hardening (hydrating) process, thus producing a more durable surface. Proper curing of all cement mixes is necessary for maximum strength. Concrete which has been moisture cured will be approximately 50% stronger than that exposed to dry air. Concrete reaches 98% of its strength in 28 days.

Working with Wood

Wood is the basic substance of trees, and there are many types of wood used for different purposes—furniture making, home building, and many other uses. Wood is easy to work with. It is made up of long cells which grow closely together, forming a compact, yet porous, material. It is elastic, plastic, and honeycomb. The relatively light weight of wood is explained by the fact that approximately half of its volume is made up of hollow cells. If wood is dried and crushed into solid material, it weighs approximately 1.5 times as much as an equal volume of water and consequently sinks in water. It is because of its hollow cell structure that most woods are buoyant, can take finishing materials, and can hold nails, screws, glue, and other fasteners.

Wood is named and classified as hard or soft according to the species of tree from which it is cut. Hardwood comes from the deciduous or broad-leaved trees and softwoods come from the coniferous or needle-bearing trees. This classification does not however indicate the degree of hardness of the wood. Some woods classified as hardwoods are actually soft. The pines, firs, and other evergreens are softwoods, and the maples, oaks, elms, poplars, and other shade and fruit trees are the hardwoods.

Trees are cut into logs, usually eight or more feet long. The individual logs are squared by slabbing, or the log is first split through the center and squared into a *cant*. In most cases, the cant is then sawed into timbers, planks, and boards. Sometimes logs are selected for special purposes and cut accordingly.

New lumber contains an excess of moisture. This may run as high as 200% when a freshly cut log is sawed. The evaporation of this moisture must be controlled if good lumber is to be obtained for building or furniture making. Rapid drying causes checking and cracks (Fig. 9.28). To help prevent rapid drying, freshly cut logs are often submerged in water until they are to be cut into lumber.

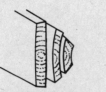 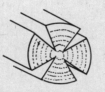 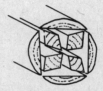

Warp due to shrinkage   Shrinkage in circumference   Shrinkage in quartered logs

Fig. 9.28. Warpage and shrinkage of wood

Controlled drying conditions reduce the intensity of the forces acting on the logs. Drying must be done by air seasoning or by the modern, faster method of kiln drying. Air dried lumber is better for use outside and kiln dried lumber is better for use inside. Kiln drying is done by using forced air or fans. It reduces the moisture content to 5 to 8 percent within two to three weeks for one-inch lumber.

Recent developments have produced lumber that will not rot quickly when left outside. Dipping the wood in polyethylene glycol or other chemicals has been found to stabilize the wood over a wide range of relative humidity conditions. The solution replaces most of the water in the wood and causes a reduction of shrinkage.

The study of woodworking can take years. There is much to be learned about woods and what can be done with them. Newer finishes and treatments extend the life of furniture and buildings made of wood. More exciting uses for wood fibers for alcohol, medicines, and paper are found every year. Wood is a valuable resource for the United States and represents a good source of energy and construction material for years to come.

Working with Sheet Metal

Metal is available in all shapes and forms, but the sheet form is the most commonly used. One type of very thin sheet metal, referred to as foil, is used for wrapping chewing gum, cereal, candy bars, and cigarettes. Gold can be made so thin it is thinner than a coating of paint.

Other types of sheet metal—for example, the sheet metal that makes up the body of an automobile, are not so thin. Shaping and forming automobile sheet metal takes some special tools. People spend their lives learning the trade and developing the skill to make an old car look new.

Many tools used in sheet metal work are also used in other trades to work with metal of different thicknesses and forms. Hammers have been designed for setting rivets that hold sheet metal together. Wooden mallets and soft-faced hammers are used in forming sheet metal because they do not stretch it as much as metal hammers do. A *bumping hammer* is used by auto body repairmen to smooth out dents.

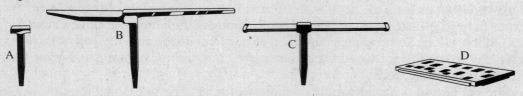

Fig. 9.29. Stakes (A) Square stake (B) Beakhorn stake (C) Double-seaming stake (D) Stake holder

Stakes are used so that sheet metal can be formed by hammering it over T-shaped anvils of steel (Fig. 9.29). *Punches* are used to make holes in sheet metal. It is safer to punch a hole in sheet metal than to drill it. A *groover* is used to lock seams together. You use one that fits the seam and tap it with a mallet as you slide it along the seam. Lay the seam over an anvil while tapping (Fig. 9.30).

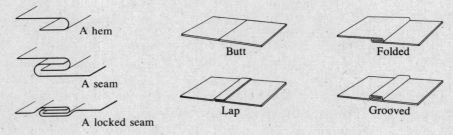

Fig. 9.30. Sheet metal seams

Tin snips, another sheet metal tool, are similar to scissors. They shear sheet metal just as scissors cut paper or cloth. To cut sheet metal lay the sheet on a bench and slide snip jaws over the sheet at the side of the cutting mark. Press down on the top handle and let the bench push against the bottom (Fig. 9.31).

Sheet metals are processed by both hand-driven and automatic machines. A *squaring shear* cuts off sheet metal to a straight line. Edges are turned and hems formed on *bar folders* and brakes. Sheet is formed into round cylinders on a *slip roll.* Turned and wired edges are made on *rotary machines.* Sheet is pressed into form on presses. It is cut to shape or punched on *punch presses.*

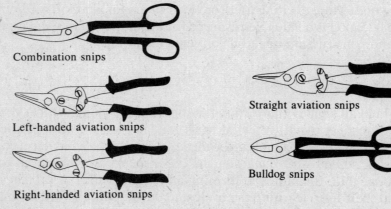

Fig. 9.31. Tin snips

Joining sheet metals by welding is a common practice today. There are a number of welding methods applicable to sheet metal. One of the most often used is the spot welder, but the joint may also be welded continuously along its length. Soft and hard soldering are used in place of welding in some products when little heat can be applied. Riveting is less common now than before the perfection of welding. Hems and seams are the joints in such products as tin cans, pails, boxes, and air conditioning and heating ducts.

Sheet metal work means working with patterns in much the same way as dressmaking or box folding work involves patterns. A seam is a fold, whether it is in cloth or in metal. You may not have thought of the medieval armorer as a tailor, but he was, and a metal worker too. A hem in cloth is sewed in place. In metal, the ends are folded, or hemmed, and then hooked together and locked, making a seam. To stiffen the joint even more and to make sure it holds water, solder is flowed into the folds.

Galvanized and tin-plated steel can be soldered with a *soldering iron* (in this case the *soldering copper*). These metals do not conduct heat away as rapidly as do copper and brass. Brass usually requires a flame to solder rather than a copper tipped iron (Fig. 9.32).

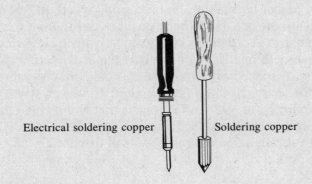

Electrical soldering copper   Soldering copper

Fig. 9.32. Soldering copper

When using the soldering copper to solder sheet metal, first, heat the copper until it will melt solder. This is at about 450°F. Then wipe the tip clean with a damp cloth, and dip the hot tip into flux and rub on a small amount of solder. If the tip does not take the solder all over, rub it on a block of wood until it does. This is called *tinning*. A well-tinned copper holds solder better and transfers more heat to the metal than does a dirty one. You are now ready to solder with the tinned end of the soldering copper.

Clean the surfaces of the metal to be soldered. Do not use steel wool on galvanized metal or tin plate. Apply flux to the joint. Hold the tip of the copper against the joint until the metal is hot enough to melt the solder. Then add as much solder as needed to cover the area to be joined.

Sheet metal has wide application and the need for people to work in this trade is increasing. The number of older workers is increasing and younger replacements are not coming along as fast as needed. The future looks bright for those who want to enter this trade. All new buildings need air conditioning and heating ducts made and installed. This field alone requires many sheet metal specialists.

10 BASIC MECHANICS REVIEW

The ASVAB subtest on Mechanical Comprehension tests knowledge of basic mechanical and physical principles and the ability to visualize how illustrated objects and simple machines work. This chapter reviews some basic principles of physics and how some simple machines make work easier.

Force

One of the basic concepts of physics is the concept of force. Force is something that can change the velocity of an object by making it start, stop, speed up, slow down, or change direction. Let's think for a minute of a car. When you take your foot off the gas pedal, your car does not suddenly come to a stop. It coasts on, only gradually losing its velocity. If you want the car to stop, you have to do something to it. That is what your brakes are for: to exert a force that decreases the car's velocity. A spacecraft also illustrates the point. Voyager has been coasting through the solar system for years. Nothing is pushing it. However, when we want it to speed up, slow down, or change direction, we send it signals that fire control rockets—or, in other words, we exert a force on it to change its velocity.

There are many types of force, some of which we will discuss.

Kinds of Force

Friction. Your car has three controls whose function is to change its velocity: the gas pedal, the brake pedal, and the steering wheel. The brakes make use of the same force that stops your car if you just let it coast: friction.

Sliding friction is a force that is generated whenever two objects are in contact and there is relative motion between them. When something is moving, friction *always* acts in such a direction as to retard the relative motion. Thus the direction of the force of friction on a moving object will always be directly opposite to the direction of the velocity. The brake shoes slow down the rotation of the wheels, and the tires slow the car until it comes to rest.

In the simplest case, the force of friction can be measured quite easily by means of a spring scale. (The spring scale can be used to measure all kinds of forces. Basically, it measures the force pulling on its shackle.) A spring scale is calibrated in force units—pounds, or (in the SI) *newtons.* A newton (abbreviated N) is a rather small unit of force; it takes 4.45 newtons to equal 1 pound.

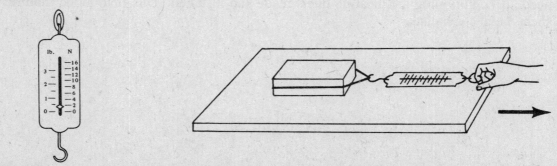

Fig. 10.1.   Fig. 10.2

Fig. 10.2 shows a spring scale being used to measure the force of sliding friction between a brick and the horizontal surface on which it is resting. The scale is pulling the brick along at constant speed. In this condition, the brick is said to be in *equilibrium*. Since its velocity is not changing, it follows that the net force acting on it is zero.

However, the spring scale is surely exerting a force, which is indicated on its face. This force is pulling the brick to the right. The brick can remain in equilibrium only if there is an equal force pulling it to the left, so that the net force acting is zero. In the situation shown, the only force pulling the brick to the left is the frictional force between the brick and the surface. Therefore the reading on the spring scale is equal to the force of friction.

Anyone who has ever moved furniture around, or slid a box across the floor, knows that the frictional force is greater when the furniture or the box is heavier. The force of friction does not change much as the object speeds up, but it depends very strongly on how hard the two surfaces are pressed together.

When a solid moves through a liquid, such as a boat moving through the water, there is a frictionlike force retarding the motion of the solid. It is call *viscous drag*. Like friction, it always acts opposite to velocity. Unlike friction, however, it increases greatly with speed, and it depends more on the shape of the object and on the nature of the liquid than on the object's weight. Gases also produce viscous drag, and you are probably most familiar with this as the air resistance that acts on a car at high speed.

To summarize, friction and viscous drag are forces that act to retard motion.

Gravity. Probably the first law of physics that everyone learns is this: If you drop something, it falls. Since its velocity keeps on changing as it falls, there must be a force acting on it all the while. That is the force we call *gravity*.

You can measure gravity by balancing it off with a spring scale. When you hang something on a spring scale and read the scale in pounds or newtons, you usually call the force of gravity acting on the object by a special name. You call it the *weight* of the object.

Weight is not a fixed property of an object; it varies with location. A person who weighs 160 pounds at the North Pole will check in at 159.2 pounds at the equator. If he should step on a scale on the moon, it would read only 27 pounds. Everything weighs less where the acceleration due to gravity is smaller. Weight, in fact, is directly proportional to the acceleration due to gravity.

Obviously, weight also depends on something else, since things have different weights even if all are at the same place. Weight depends on how much stuff there is in the object. If you buy 10 pounds of sugar, you expect to get twice as much as if you buy 5 pounds. And if you take both sacks to the moon, one will still weigh twice as much as the other. The amount of sugar, the *mass* of the sugar, did not change when it was brought somewhere else. And the more sugar you have, the more it weighs.

Weight, then, is proportional both to mass and to the acceleration due to gravity.

This equation works nicely, without introducing any constants, if the units are carefully defined. Mass is measured in kilograms; the kilogram is one of the basic units of the SI. By definition, when you multiply the mass in kilograms by the acceleration in meters per second squared, the weight comes out in newtons.

To summarize, weight, the force of gravity, is the product of mass and the acceleration due to gravity.

Elastic Recoil. The basic feature of a solid, as opposed to a liquid or a gas, is that it has a definite shape. It resists changes in its shape and, in so doing, exerts a force against whatever force is applied to it.

Look, for example, at the meter bar supported at its ends, shown in Fig. 10.3. If you push down on it, you bend it, and you can feel it pushing back on you. The harder you push, the more the bar bends and the harder it pushes back. It bends just enough to push on you with the same force that you exert on it. The force it exerts is called *elastic recoil*.

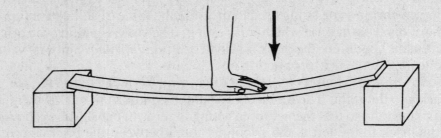

Fig. 10.3

The same thing happens when you stand on the floor, or on the ground. You can't see the floor bend, but it bends just the same, although not very much. Even a feather resting on the floor bends it a little. The elastic recoil force needed to support the feather is very small, so the amount of bending is too small to detect.

A rope does not resist bending, but it certainly does resist stretching. When a rope is stretched, it is said to be in a state of *tension*. The tension can be measured by cutting the rope and inserting a spring scale into it, as shown in Fig. 10.4. The spring scale will read the tension in the rope, in pounds or newtons. If you pull with a force of 30 N, for example, the tension in the rope is 30 N, and that is what the scale will indicate. Something, such as the elastic recoil of the wall to which the scale is attached, must be pulling on the other end with a force of 30 N. The tension in the rope is the same throughout, and is equal to the elastic recoil force that the rope exerts at its ends.

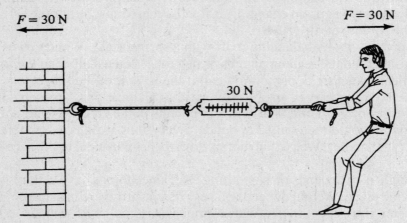

Fig. 10.4

To summarize: A force applied to a solid distorts the shape of the solid, causing it to exert a force back on the force that distorted it.

Buoyancy. If you take a deep breath and dive into a pool, you will have a lot of trouble keeping yourself submerged. Something keeps pushing you up. That force is called *buoyancy*.

The force of buoyancy acts in an upward direction on anything submerged in a liquid or a gas. Buoyancy is the force that makes ships float and helium-filled balloons rise. A rock sinks because its weight is larger than the buoyancy of the water. A submerged cork rises because the buoyancy is more than its weight. When it reaches the surface, some of it emerges, but the rest is still under water. The amount under water is just enough to produce a buoyant force equal to its weight, so it stays put.

Other forces. There are some other familiar forces, and others not so familiar. You know about magnetism, which attracts iron nails to a red horseshoe. You have met electric force, which makes a nylon shirt cling to you when you try to take it off, or which refuses to release the dust particles from your favorite record. Airplanes stay up because of the lift force generated by the flow of air across their wings. A rocket takes off because of the force generated by the gases expanding in it. We will meet other forces from time to time, but we have enough to get along with for now.

Action and Reaction

The batter steps up to the plate and takes a healthy swing, sending the ball into left field. The bat has exerted a large force on the ball, changing both the magnitude and the direction of its velocity. But the ball has also exerted a force on the bat, slowing it down. The batter feels this when the bat hits the ball.

Next time up, he strikes out. He has taken exactly the same swing, but exerts no force on anything. (Air doesn't count.) The batter has discovered that it is impossible to exert a force unless there is something there to push back. Forces exist *only* in pairs. When object A exerts a force on object B, then B must exert a force on A. The two forces are sometimes called *action* and *reaction,* although which is which is often rather arbitrary. The two parts of the interaction are equal in magnitude, are opposite in direction, and act on different objects.

The law of action and reaction leads to an apparent paradox, if you are not careful how it is applied. The horse pulls on the wagon. If the force of the wagon pulling the horse the other way is the same, as the law insists, how can the horse and wagon get started?

The error in the reasoning is this: If you want to know whether the horse gets moving, you have to consider the forces acting *on the horse.* The force acting on the wagon has nothing to do with the question. The horse starts up because the force he exerts with his hooves is larger than the force of the wagon pulling him back. And the wagon starts up because the force of the horse pulling it forward is larger than the frictional forces holding it back. To know something moves, consider the forces acting *on it.* The action and reaction forces *never* act on the same object.

Again, to summarize, forces exist only in pairs, equal in magnitude and opposite in direction, acting on different objects.

Balanced Forces

If a single force acts on an object, the velocity of the thing must change. If two or more forces act, however, their effects may eliminate each other. This is the condition of equilibrium, in which there is no net force and the velocity does not change. We saw such a condition in the case in which gravity is pulling an object down and the spring scale, used for weighing it, is pulling it upward.

An object in equilibrium may or may not be at rest. A parachutist, descending at constant speed, is in equilibrium. His weight is just balanced by the viscous drag on the parachute, which is why he put it on in the first place. A heavier parachutist falls a little faster; his speed increases until the viscous drag just balances his weight.

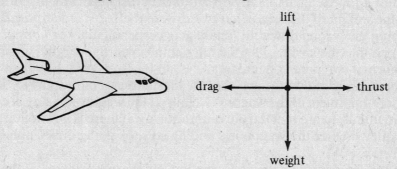

Fig. 10.5

Balancing the vertical forces is not enough to produce equilibrium. An airplane traveling at constant speed is in equilibrium under the influence of four forces, two vertical and two horizontal. Vertical: gravity (down) is just balanced by the lift produced by the flow of air across the wing. Horizontal: viscous drag is just balanced by the thrust of the engines. Both the vertical and the horizontal velocities are constant.

The brick of Fig. 10.2, resting on a tabletop and being pulled along at constant speed, is another example. Vertical: the downward force of gravity is balanced by the upward force of the elastic recoil of the tabletop. Horizontal: the tension in the spring scale, pulling to the right, is balanced by the friction pulling it to the left, opposite to the direction of motion.

If an object is in equilibrium—at rest or moving at constant speed in a straight line—the total force acting on it in any direction is exactly equal in magnitude to the force in the opposite direction.

Components of a Force

The crate of Fig. 10.6 is being dragged along the floor by means of a rope, which is not horizontal. The rope makes an angle θ to the floor.

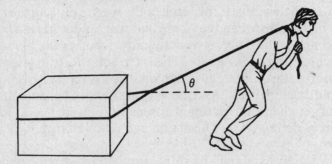

Fig. 10.6

The tension in the rope, acting on the crate, does two things to it. First, it drags the crate across the floor. Second, it tends to lift the crate off the floor. The smaller the angle θ, the larger the effective force that is dragging the crate, and the smaller the effective force that is lifting it. When $\theta = 0$, the entire force is dragging and there is no lifting at all. Conversely, when $\theta = 90°$, the entire force is lifting the crate.

The Inclined Plane

A wagon rolls downhill, propelled only by its own weight. But gravity pulls straight down, not at an angle downhill. What makes the wagon go is a *component* of its weight, a part of its weight acting downhill, parallel to the surface the wagon rests on.

A component of a force can act in any direction, not just vertically or horizontally. On the inclined plane, the weight of the wagon has two different effects: it acts *parallel* to the surface of the hill, pushing the wagon downhill; and it acts perpendicular (or *normal*) to the surface, pushing the wagon into the surface. As the hill gets steeper, the parallel component becomes larger and the normal component decreases.

When the wagon is resting on the surface, the elastic recoil of the surface is just enough to cancel the normal component of the wagon's weight. If the wagon is to stay in equilibrium, you have to pull on it, uphill, to prevent it from running away. If there is no friction, the uphill force needed is the same whether the wagon is standing still, or going either uphill or downhill at constant speed.

The situation is different if the wagon is moving and there is friction. If the wagon is going uphill, you have to pull harder, because the friction is working against you, holding it back. The total force you need to keep the wagon going is then equal to the parallel component of the weight plus the friction. On the other hand, if you are lowering the wagon down the hill, holding the rope to keep it from running away from you, friction is acting uphill, helping you to hold the wagon back. Then the force you must exert is the parallel component of the weight *minus* the friction.

Simple Machines

There are devices that make work easier. These devices are known as simple machines. Without thinking about it, everybody uses a hundred simple machines every day—a light switch, doorknob, pencil sharpener, to name just a few.

A pulley illustrates how machines make work easier. After discussing the pulley principle and learning some basic work terms, we will go on to discuss briefly some other simple machines—levers, hydraulic jacks, loading ramps, vises, and machines that spin (for example, winches and gears).

The Pulley Principle

A piano mover, unable to fit the instrument into the staircase, decides to raise it outside the building to a window. He attaches it to a set of ropes and wheels which, somehow, make it possible for him to lift it with a force considerably smaller than the weight of the piano. How does it work?

Consider first the heavy block in Fig. 10.7 suspended from two ropes. The upward force on the block is the tension (T) in the ropes, and the sum of the two tensions must equal the weight of the block. If the whole system is symmetrical, each rope is under tension equal to half the weight of the block.

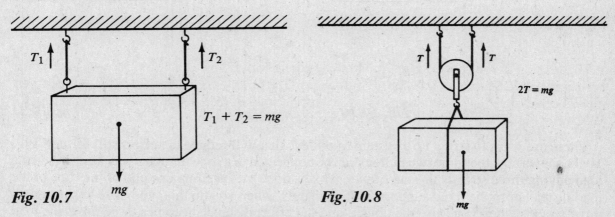

Fig. 10.7

$T_1 + T_2 = mg$

Fig. 10.8

$2T = mg$

Now look at Fig. 10.8, where the block has been attached to a wheel. There is now only one rope, which passes over the wheel. The tension in the rope is the same throughout; if it were different on one side than on the other, the wheel would turn until the tension on the two sides equalized. The tension in the rope is still only half the weight of the block, since it exerts *two* upward forces on the block. Now we have a system that helps in lifting things. Just fasten one end of the rope to a fixed support and pull on the other end (Fig. 10.9). Now you can raise the block with a force equal to only half its weight.

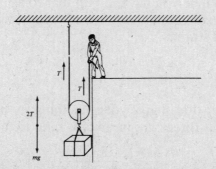

Fig. 10.9

Are you getting something for nothing? Well, yes and no. True, you can now lift the weight with less force, but you have to pull the rope farther than you would if you lifted the block directly. Every time you pull 10 feet of rope through your hands, the block rises 5 feet. You might look at it this way: If the block rises 5 feet, *both* sides of the supporting rope have to shorten 5 feet, and the only way to accomplish this is to pull 10 feet of rope through. You raise the block with only half the force, but you have to exert the force through twice the distance.

You might prefer to pull in a downward direction rather than upward, and you can manage this by attaching a fixed wheel to the support and passing the rope around it as in Fig. 10.10. The tension in the rope is still only half the weight of the block; the fixed pulley does nothing but change the direction of the force you exert.

Let's adopt some vocabulary. The weight of the object being lifted we will call the *load*, and the distance it rises is the *load distance*. The force you exert on the rope is the *effort*, and the distance through which you exert that effort is the *effort distance*. With a single movable pulley in use, the effort is half the load and the effort distance is twice the load distance.

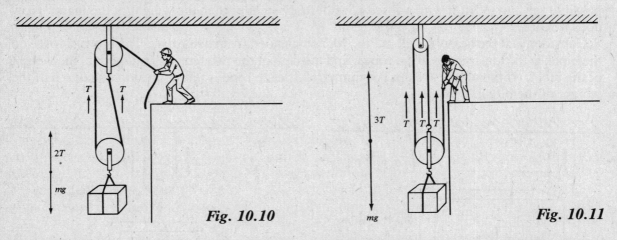

Fig. 10.10   **Fig. 10.11**

There are ways to string up a system of pulleys that will reduce the effort still further. Fig. 10.11 shows how the same two pulleys can be connected to a rope in such a way as to divide the load among three strands instead of two. This is done by fastening one end of the rope to the load instead of to the fixed support. Unfortunately, when you do this, you have to shorten all three strands when you raise the object, and the effort distance becomes three times the load distance. By using more pulleys you can reduce the effort still further. Unfortunately, there is a limit to how much you can reduce the effort. The analysis we did so far neglects a few things, such as friction and the weight of the movable pulleys themselves. Every time you add a pulley, you increase the friction in the system; if it is a movable pulley—the only kind that produces a reduction in force—you have to lift it along with the load. The effort in any real system is always larger than the ideal effort we calculated by dividing up the load. If there are a lot of pulleys, it may be considerably larger. And friction, while it increases the force you must exert, has no effect on the distance you have to pull that rope.

Effort distance is load distance times the number of supporting strands; effort is larger than load divided by the number of strands.

The Work Principle

While pulleys are useful, they do not give you something for nothing. Ignoring the problem of friction, the input and output forces are in inverse ratio to the respective distances:

$$\frac{\text{effort}}{\text{load}} = \frac{\text{load distance}}{\text{effort distance}}$$

or, to put it another way,

(effort)(effort distance) = (load)(load distance)

The frictionless pulley, then, does not alter the product of force and distance; it is the same for the mover who pulls on the rope as it is for the piano. This product occurs repeatedly in physical situations, so it is given a special name. Force times distance is called *work*.

Work is done whenever a force moves something through a distance. If you stand still holding a boulder over your head, you might get tired, but—in the physical sense—you are doing no work.

There is another limitation on the definition of work. Only the force in the direction of motion counts. For example, look at Fig. 10-12—the child on the sled. The tension in the rope is pulling the sled, but it is also lifting the sled. Only the component of the force that is acting in the direction the sled is going is doing work on the sled. Since the sled is moving horizontally, the horizontal component of the tension is the only part that is doing the work of moving the sled.

Fig. 10.12

The effort times the effort distance is called the *work input,* and the load times the load distance is the *work output*. While there are no real frictionless pulleys, we can use the ideal of a frictionless, weightless pulley in doing useful calculations. With such an ideal pulley, the work output is exactly the same as the work input. If you use this idea to calculate how hard you will have to pull on the rope, the best you can do, when you have finished the calculation, is to say that the effort will be *at least* the amount you figure. How much more it will be depends on the friction and on the weight of the wheels.

With a real pulley, you always have to pull a little harder than that calculated value. The work input is therefore always more than the work output. The ratio between the work output and the work input is called the *efficiency* of the machine:

$$\text{efficiency} = \frac{W_{\text{out}}}{W_{\text{in}}}$$

Efficiency is usually expressed as a percent. It tells you what fraction of the work you put into a machine comes out as useful work at the other end. Or, in other words, *efficiency* is the fraction of the work input that emerges as useful work output.

Levers

Another type of simple machine is a *lever*. A lever consists of a rigid bar, pivoted at some point. An effort force applied to the bar at some point produces a different force on a load at some other position on the bar. The crowbar of Fig. 10.13 is typical. The load is the weight of the rock being lifted. The effort is the force exerted by the person who is trying to move the rock.

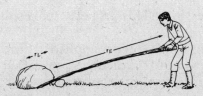

Fig 10.13

Usually, the purpose of a machine is to make it possible to exert a large load force with a smaller effort. The machine magnifies force. The amount of this magnification, the ratio of load to effort, is called the *mechanical advantage* of the machine. It can be defined algebraically as the ratio of the two forces:

$$MA = \frac{F_L}{F_E}$$

In a pulley, the mechanical advantage is equal to the number of strands of rope supporting the load. For a lever, it can be found by considering the torques acting on the bar.

The torque around the pivot that is exerted by the worker is $F_E r_E$, where r_E (the *effort arm*) is the distance from the point where the effort is applied to the pivot. Similarly, the torque produced by the weight of the rock is $F_L r_L$, where r_L is the *load arm*. If the system is rotating in equilibrium, these two torques must have the same magnitude, so

$$F_E r_E = F_L r_L$$

From which we find that the mechanical advantage, F_L/F_E, is given by

$$MA_{lever} = \frac{r_E}{r_L}$$

Or, in other words, in a lever the mechanical advantage is equal to the ratio of effort arm to load arm.

For many kinds of levers, friction at the pivot is quite small, so efficiencies approach 100 percent, and the arm ratio is very near the force ratio. Usually, no correction is needed.

Levers are classified according to the relative positions of the pivot, load, and effort. The three classes are represented by the tools shown in Fig. 10.14. In the pliers (first class) the pivot is between the effort and the load. In the nutcracker (second class) it is the load that is between the other two. And in the sugar tongs (third class), the effort is in the middle.

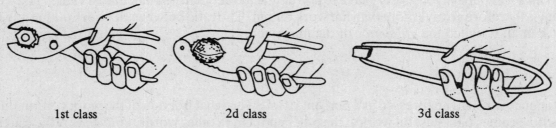

1st class   2d class   3d class

Fig. 10.14

Note that in the third-class lever (the sugar tongs), the load arm is longer than the effort arm, so the mechanical advantage is less than. 1. This lever magnifies distance at the expense of force.

Mechanical advantage is the ratio of load to effort; in a lever, it is equal to the ratio of effort arm to load arm.

Hydraulic Jack

Liquids are nearly incompressible. This property makes them suitable as means of transforming work.

A hydraulic jack is a device in which force is applied to the oil in a small cylinder. As shown in Fig. 10.15, this force causes some of the oil to be transferred to a larger cylinder. This forces the piston in the larger cylinder to rise, lifting a load.

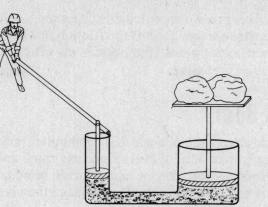

Fig. 10.15

This device takes advantage of the fact that oil, being nearly incompressible, transmits whatever pressure is applied to it. The pressure applied in the small cylinder appears unchanged in the big one, pushing up its piston.

Ideal mechanical advantage is the ratio between effort distance and load distance; for a hydraulic jack, it is equal to the ratio of the area of the load piston to that of the effort piston:

A Loading Ramp

A ramp is a device commonly used to aid in lifting. To raise a heavy load a couple of feet onto a platform, it is common practice to place it on a dolly and wheel it up an inclined plane.

The work output of an inclined plane is the work that would have to be done to lift the load directly: the weight of the load times the vertical distance it goes. The work input is the actual force exerted in pushing the dolly up the ramp times the length of the ramp.

The ideal mechanical advantage of an inclined plane is equal to its length divided by its height.

A Vise

The vise of Fig. 10.16 is a complex machine in which the handle acts as a lever operating a new kind of machine: a screw. How can we calculate the constants of this gadget?

It would be very difficult to calculate the ratio of the force the jaws apply to the force on the handle. The best we can do is work with the distances.

A screw consists of a single continuous spiral wrapped around a cylinder. The distance between ridges is known as the *pitch* of the thread, as shown in Fig. 10.17. Every time the screw makes one complete turn, the screw advances a distance equal to the pitch. In the vise, one complete turn is made when the end of the handle travels in a circle whose radius is the length of the handle *(l)*. Therefore, when the effort moves a distance $2\pi l$ the load moves a distance equal to the pitch of the thread. Therefore, for a screw,

$$\text{ideal MA} = \frac{2\pi \text{ (length of handle)}}{\text{pitch of thread}}$$

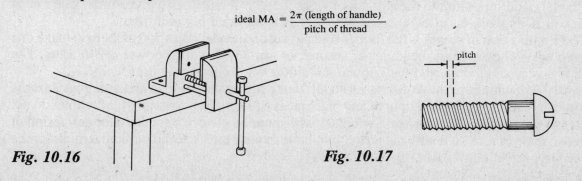

Fig. 10.16   *Fig. 10.17*

However, if you use this expression to calculate the forces, you will get it all wrong. The vise is a high-friction device. It has to be, for it is the friction that keeps it from opening when you tighten it. A vise is a self-locking machine because its efficiency is considerably under 50 percent.

Machines That Spin

What is the mechanical advantage of a winch, such as that shown in Fig. 10.18? The principle is not much different from that of a lever. Since the crank and the shaft turn together, the torque exerted by the effort (the force on the handle) must be equal to the torque exerted by the load (the tension in the rope). The mechanical advantage then is the ratio of the radius of the crank to the radius of the shaft.

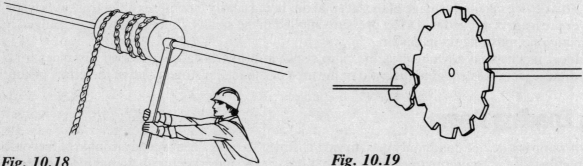

Fig. 10.18   *Fig. 10.19*

In mechanical devices, gears are commonly used to change torque. Consider the gears of Fig.10.19, for example. We assume that both gears are mounted on shafts of equal diameter, and that the small gear is driving the large one. What is the mechanical advantage of this combination?

First of all, the teeth must have the same size and spacing on both gears in order for them to mesh properly. With 12 teeth in the large gear and only 4 in the small one, the small gear has to make three complete revolutions to make the big one turn once. The large, load gear moves only one-third as far as the smaller, effort gear. And the ratio of the two distances is the same as the ratio of the number of teeth in the two gears. Then we can say that the ideal mechanical advantage of a gear is the ratio of the number of teeth in the load gear to the number of teeth in the effort gear.

Power

When the piano mover rigs his tackle, he has to consider many factors. For one, the more pulleys he puts in, the longer it will take him to get the job done. If he has to pull more rope—using less force, to be sure—he will have to keep pulling for a longer time.

There is a definite limit to the amount of work the mover can do in a given time. The rate at which he does work is called his *power*. Power is work done per unit time.

The English unit of power is the foot-pound per second, and it takes 550 of them to make one horsepower. The SI unit is the joule per second, or *watt* (W). A horsepower is 746 watts. The watt is a very small unit, and the kilowatt (=1,000 W) is commonly used.

In all the machines we have discussed so far, work comes out the load end as it goes in at the effort end. Thus, the power output of any machine is equal to the power input. Machines do not increase your power. A pulley or a windlass will spread the work out over a longer period of time, so that you can do it with the power available in your muscles and without straining for a force larger than convenient.

11 ELECTRONICS INFORMATION REVIEW

The Greeks are believed to have discovered electricity in the process of conducting some of their experiments. While working with a piece of amber (the fossilized resin from an ancient species of tree), which is translucent and golden in color, they found that if the amber was rubbed briskly, it would exhibit an attraction for tiny bits of lightweight material. You have probably seen this happen when you run a comb through your hair on a dry day and pick up bits of paper with it. The Greeks believed that the forces of amber were at work in this phenomenon. Similarly, the Romans found that lignite (a form of coal) could be rubbed and could produce, by friction, the same reaction. However, it is the Greeks who have been given credit for the first experiments that later led in 1600 to the work of William Gilbert (an Englishman) with friction and static electricity. Gilbert wrote a book on the substances with which he had experimented. He showed that amber was not the *only* such material that produced an attraction for the bits of paper.

Gilbert is given credit for coining the word *electrics*. The Latin word *electrum* is derived from the Greek *elektron* which in turn means "amber." Gilbert was influenced by the Latin being studied at the time. In all probability this is how the name worked its way into print and history.

Gilbert has been called the father of electricity since he was the first to classify objects that would produce an electrostatic field when rubbed. He called these substances *electrics*.

Electronics is the application of electrical principles. Electrical principles are derived from the uses and generation of electric energy. Therefore, electricity is necessary for the proper operation of electronic devices and electronic circuits. In order to understand electronics it is first necessary to know how electricity is generated, distributed, and put to work in circuits.

Basic Atomic Structure

Electricity is defined as the flow of electrons along a conductor. A conductor is an object that allows electrons to pass easily. That means electrons must be organized and pushed toward a goal. This is done in a number of ways. But first, we must know what an electron is before we can start working with it.

Elements are the most basic materials in the universe. There are 106 elements including some that have been made in the laboratory. Elements such as iron, copper, gold, lead, and silver have been found in nature. Eleven others have been made in the laboratory. Every known substance—solid, liquid, or gas—is composed of elements.

An electron is the smallest part of an atom. An atom is the smallest particle of an element that retains all the properties of that element. Each element has its own kind of atom. That is, hydrogen atoms are alike, and they are different from the atoms of all other elements. However, all atoms have certain things in common. They all have an inner part, the nucleus. The nucleus is composed of very small particles called *protrons* and *neutrons*. An atom also has an outer part, consisting of other small particles. These very small particles are called *electrons*. the electrons orbit around the nucleus.

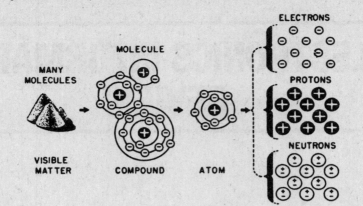

Fig. 11.1.   Molecular structure. the negative (−) particles are electrons.

Neutrons have no electric charge, but protons are positively charged. Because of these charges, protons and electrons are particles of energy. That is, these charges form an electric field of force within the atom. These charges are always pulling and pushing one another; this action produces energy in the form of movement.

The atoms of each element have a definite number of electrons, and they have the same number of protons. A hydrogen atom has one electron and one proton (Fig 11-2). The aluminum atom has thirteen of each (Fig. 11-3). The opposite charges—negative electrons and positive protons—attract each other and tend to hole electrons in orbit. As long as this arrangement is not changed, an atom is electrically balanced.

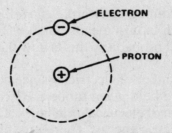

Fig. 11-2.   The hydrogen atom has one electron and one proton.

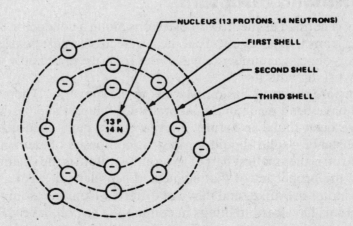

Fig. 11-3.   The aluminum atom has 13 electrons.

When electrons leave their orbits, they move from atom to atom at random, drifting in no particular direction. Electrons that move in such a way are referred to as *free electrons*. Electrons in copper drift along in a random fashion when at room temperature.

Heat is only one of the types of energy that can cause electrons to be forced from their orbits. A magnetic field can also be used to cause electons to move in a given direction. Light energy and pressure on a cystral are also used to generate electricity by forcing electrons to flow along a given path. A force can be used to cause electrons to move in a given direction. That is how electricity (the flow of electrons along a conductor) is generated. A *conductor* is any material that has many free electrons by virtue of its physical makeup.

Electric Energy

So far you have read about electrons being very small. Just how small are they? Well, electrons are incredibly small. The diameter of an electron is about 0.00000000000022 inch (in.). You may wonder how anything so small can be a source of energy. Much of the answer lies in the fact that electrons move at nearly the speed of light, or 186,000 miles per second (mi/s). In metric terms that is 300 million meters per second (m/s). As you can see from their size, billions of them can move at once through a wire. The combination of speed and concentration together produces great energy.

When a flow of electrons along a conductor occurs, this is commonly referred to as *current flow*. Thus, you can see that the movement of electrons is related to current electricity.

Electric Current

In the early years of electrical study, electric current was erroneously assumed to be a movement of positive charges from positive to negative. This assumption, termed *conventional current flow,* is a concept that became entrenched in the minds of many scientists. Consequently, conventional current flow is found in many textbooks and its existence should be realized.

Since it has been proven that electrons (negative charges) move through a wire, *electron current* will be used throughout the explanation of electric current in this chapter and throughout the remainder of the text. Electron current is defined as the directed flow of electrons. The direction of electron movement is from a region of negative potential to a region of less negative potential or more positive potential. Therefore, electric current can be said to flow from a negative potential to a positive potential. The direction is determined by the polarity of the voltage source.

Electric current is generally classified into two general types—direct current and alternating current. A direct current flows continuously in the same direction whereas an alternating current periodically reverses direction.

A circuit is a pathway for the movement of electrons. An external force exerted on electrons to make them flow through a conductor is know as *electromotive force*, or emf. It is measured in volts. Electric pressure, potential difference, and emf mean the same thing. The words *voltage drop* and *potential drop* can be interchanged.

For electrons to move in a particular direction, it is necessary for a potential difference to exist between two points of the emf source. If 6,250,000,000,000,000,000 electrons pass a given point in one second, there is said to be one *ampere* (A) of current flowing. The same number of electrons stored on an object (a static charge) and not moving is called a *coulomb* (C).

Measurement of Current   The magnitude of current is measured in *amperes*. A current of one ampere is said to flow when one coulomb of charge passes a point in one second. Expressed as an equation:

$$I = \frac{Q}{T}$$

where:

I = current in amperes
Q = charge in coulombs
T = time in seconds

Frequently, the ampere is much too large a unit. Therefore the *milliampere* (*m*A), one thousandth of an ampere, or the *microampere* (µA)—one millionth (0.000001) of an ampere are used. (You may want to become familiar with the Greek alphabet. The table on page 263 defines the terms used in electricity and electronics and their corresponding Greek letters)

Current flow is assumed to be from negative (−) to positive (+) in our explanations here. Electron flow is negative (−) to positive (+), and we assume that current flow and electron flow are one and the same. It makes explanations simpler as we progress into electronics. The *conventional* current flow is the opposite, or positive (+) to negative (−).

An *ammeter* is used to measure current flow in a circuit. A *milliammeter* is used to measure smaller amounts, while the *microammeter* is used to measure very small amounts of current.

A *voltmeter* is used to measure voltage. In some instances it is possible to obtain a meter which will measure both voltage and current plus resistance. This is called a *multimeter,* or *volt-ohm-milliammeter* (VM).

Example. Two coulombs of charge flow past a point in a conductor in 10 minutes. What is the current flow?

I = ?
Q = 2 coulombs
T = 10 minutes

Solution:

$$I = \frac{Q}{T}$$

10 minutes = 600 seconds

$$I = \frac{2 \text{ coulombs}}{600 \text{ seconds}}$$

$$I = 0.00333 \text{ amperes, or } 3.33 \text{ } m\text{A}$$

Conductors

A material through which electricity passes easily is called a *conductor* because it has free electrons. In other words, a conductor offers very little resistance or opposition to the flow of electrons.

All metals are conductors of electricity to some extent. Some are much better than others. Silver, copper, and aluminum let electricity pass easily. Silver is a better conductor than copper. However, copper is used more frequently because it is cheaper. Aluminum is used as a conductor where light weight is important.

Why are some materials good conductors? One of the most important reasons is the presence of *free electrons*. If a material has many electrons which are free to move away from their atoms, that material will be a good conductor of electricity.

Although free electrons usually move in a haphazard way, their movement can be controlled. The electrons can be made to move in the same direction, and this flow is called *electric current*.

Conductors may be in the form of bars, tubes, or sheets. The most familiar conductors are wire. Many sizes of wire are available. Some are only the thickness of a hair. Other wire may be as thick as your arm. To prevent conductors from touching at the wrong place they are usually coated with plastic or cloth material. This covering on the conductor is called an *insulator.*

Wire Gage
Various electrical applications demand different *conductor* sizes. Some wires are extremely large, and others are almost as fine as human hair. All wire is designed by definite gage sizes. Each number designates a wire of specific diameter. As the diameter of the wire decreases, the gage number increases. The following table which refers to standard annealed solid copper wire, illustrates some various wire sizes, their comparative areas and resistance per 1000 ft. The resistance values apply only to copper conductors.

Gage Number	Diameter (mils)	Cross Section Circular (mils)	Ohms per 1000 ft 25°C (=77°F)
0000	460.0	212,000.0	.0500
2	258.0	66,400.0	.159
6	162.0	26,300.0	.403
10	102.0	10,400.0	1.02
14	64.0	4,110.0	2.58
18	40.0	1,620.0	6.51
22	25.3	642.0	16.51
26	15.9	254.0	41.6
30	10.0	101.0	105.0
36	5.0	25.0	423.0
38	4.0	15.7	673.0
40	3.1	9.9	1,070.0

Much wire in common use today, however, is not solid. It is stranded.

Stranded Wire
Copper wire is stranded for one reason: stranded wire is easily bent. In order to bend or flex wire constantly it is necessary to make many smaller strands into a cable or bundle. This allows for flexing of the cable or wire. The lamp cord in your home is made of many fine strands of copper wire. This allows it to be flexible and bend where you want it on the way from the plug to the lamp.

Larger wires used for wiring commercial or industrial buildings are also stranded. Any number of smaller wires are grouped in a cable to carry the same amount of current as a solid conductor wire in a solid mass. The larger cables have to be stranded or it would be next to impossible to bend them or work with them.

The physical size of the flexible wire is greater than the same size, electrically, of solid wire. A solid No. 18 wire is easily bent, but is not as flexible as a multiple strand cable made up of smaller gage wire to equal the No. 18 wire used in a lamp cord.

Insulators

An insulator is a material with very few, it any, free electrons. No known material is a perfect insulator. However, there are materials that are such poor conductors that they are classified as insulators. Glass, dry wood, rubber, mica, and certain plastics are insulating materials.

Semiconductors

So far you have looked at insulators and conductors. In between the two extremes are semiconductors. Semiconductors in the form of transistors, diodes, and integrated circuits or chips are used every day in electronic devices. Now is the time to place them in their proper category.

Materials used in the manufacture of transistors and diodes have a conductivity halfway between that of a good conductor and a good insulator. Therefore, the name *semi*conductor is given them. Germanium and silicon are the two most commonly known semiconductor materials. Through the introduction of small amounts of other elements (called impurities) these nearly pure (99.999999%) elements become *limited* conductors. The opposite of conductors is resistors. *Resistors* are devices used to give a measured amount of opposition or resistance to the flow of electrons. This opposition to current flow is measured in ohms (Ω) and indicates the amount of resistance a piece of material offers to the flow of electrons. Take a look at Fig. 11.4 to see how these semiconductor materials are placed between good conductors and poor conductors.

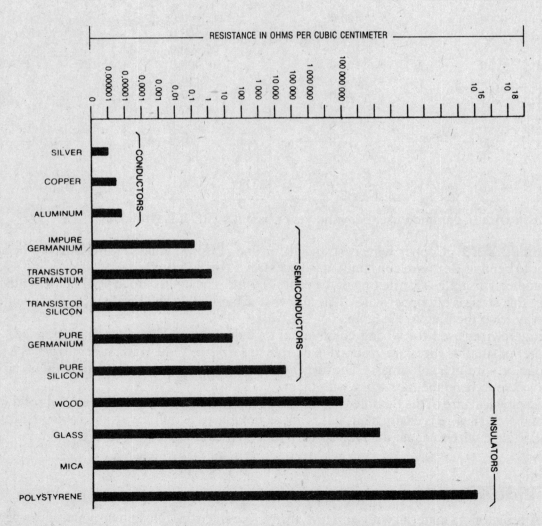

Fig. 11.4. Location of insulators, semiconductors, and conductors in relation to one another in terms of inherent resistance.

THE GREEK ALPHABET USED IN ELECTRICITY AND ELECTRONICS

Name	Capital	Small	Used to Designate
Alpha	A	α	Angles, area, coefficients, and attenuation constant.
Beta	B	β	Angles and coefficients.
Gamma	Γ	γ	Electrical conductivity and propagation constant.
Delta	Δ	δ	Angles, increment, decrement, and determinants.
Epsilon	E	ϵ	Dielectric constant, permittivity, and base of natural logarithms.
Zeta	Z	ζ	Coordinates
Eta	H	η	Efficiency, hysteresis, and coordinates.
Theta	Θ	ϑ θ	Angles and angular phase displacement.
Iota	I	ι	Coupling coefficicent.
Kappa	K	κ	
Lambda	Λ	λ	Wavelength
Mu	M	μ	Permeability, amplification factor, and prefix *micro*.
Nu	N	ν	
Xi	Ξ	ξ	
Omicron	O	o	
Pi	Π	π	Pi=3.1416.
Rho	P	ρ	Resistivity and volume charge density.
Sigma	$\Sigma \sigma \varsigma$	Summation.	
Tau	T	τ	Time constant and time-phase displacement.
Upsilon	Υ	υ	
Phi	Φ	$\phi \varphi$	Magnetic flux and angles.
Chi	X	χ	Angles.
Psi	Ψ	ψ	Dielectric flux.
Omega	Ω	ω	Resistance in ohms and angular velocity.

Power

Power is defined as the *rate* at which work is done. It is expressed in metric measurement terms of watts (W) for power and joules (J) for energy work. A *watt* is the power which gives rise to the production of energy at the rate of one joule per second (W = J/s). A *joule* is the work done when the point of application of force of one newton is displaced a distance of one meter in the direction of the force (J = N · m).

It has long been the practice in this country to measure work in terms of horsepower (hp). Electric motors are still rated in horsepower and probably will be for some time inasmuch as the United States did not adopt the metric standards for everything.

Power can be electric or mechanical. When a mechanical force is used to lift a weight, *work* is done. The rate at which the weight is moved is called *power. Horsepower* is defined in terms of moving a certain weight over a certain distance in one minute (e.g., 33,000 lb lifted 1 ft in 1 min equals 1 hp). Energy is consumed in moving a weight or when work is done. The findings in this field have been equated with the same amount of work done by electric energy. It takes 746 W of electric power to equal 1 hp.

The horsepower rating of electric motors is arrived at by taking the voltage and multiplying it by the current drawn under full load. This power is measured in watts. In other words, one volt times one ampere equals one watt. When put into a formula it reads:

$$\text{Power} = \text{volts} \times \text{amperes} \quad \text{or} \quad P = E \times I$$

where E = voltage, or emf

I = current, or intensity of electron flow

Kilowatt. The kilowatt is commonly used to express the amount of electric energy used or available. The term *kilo* (k) means one thousand (1000). A kilowatt (kW) is one thousand watts.

When the kilowatt is used in terms of power dissipated or consumed by a home for a month it is expressed in kilowatthours. The unit kilowatthour is abbreviated as kWh. It is the equivalent of one thousand watts used for a period of one hour. Electric bills are figured or computed on an hourly basis and then read in the kWh unit. The entire month's time is equated to one hour's time.

Milliwatt is a term you will encounter when working with electronics. The *milliwatt* (mW) means one-thousandth (0.001) of a watt. The milliwatt is used in terms of some very small amplifiers and other electronic devices. For instance, a speaker used on a portable transistor radio will be rated as 100 milliwatts, or 0.1 W. Transistor circuits are designed in milliwatts, but power line electric power is measured in kilowatts. Keep in mind that *kilo* means 1000 and *milli* means 0.001.

Resistance

Any time there is movement there is resistance. This resistance is useful in electric and electronic circuits. Resistance makes it possible to generate heat, control electron flow, and supply the correct voltage to a device.

Resistance in a conductor depends on four factors: material, length, cross-sectional area, and temperature.

Material. Some materials offer more resistance than others. It depends upon the number of free electrons present in the material.

Length. The longer the wire or conductor, the more resistance it has. Resistance is said to vary *directly* with the length of the wire.

Cross-Sectional Area. Resistance varies *inversely* with the size of the conductor in cross section. In other words, the larger the wire, the smaller the resistance per foot of length.

Temperature. For most materials, the higher the temperature, the higher the resistance. However, there are some exceptions to this in devices known as *thermistors*. Thermistors change resistance with temperature. They *decrease* in resistance with an increase in temperature. Thermistors are used in certain types of meters to measure temperature.

Resistance is measured by a unit called the *ohm*. The Greek letter omega Ω is used as the symbol for electrical resistance.

Resistors   *Resistors* are devices which provide measured amounts of resistance. They are valuable when it comes to making sure the proper amount of voltage is present in a circuit. They are useful when generating heat.

Resistors are classified as either *wirewound* or *carbon-composition*. The symbol for a resistor of either type is ⎓⎓⎓⎓

Wirewound resistors are used to provide sufficient opposition to current flow to dissipate power of 5 W or more. A watt is a unit of electric power. A watt is equal to one volt times one ampere.

Wirewound resistors are made of wire that has controlled resistance per unit length.

Resistance causes a voltage drop across a resistor when current flows through it. The voltage is dropped or dissipated as heat and must be eliminated into the air.

Some variable resistors can be varied but can also be adjusted for a particular setting. Resistors are available in various sizes, shapes, and wattage ratings.

Carbon-composition resistors are usually found in electronics devices. They are of low wattage. They are made in ¹/8-W, ¹/4-W, ¹/2-W, 1-W, and 2-W sizes. The physical size determines the wattage rating or their ability to dissipate heat.

Carbon-composition resistors are usually marked according to their ohmic value with a *color code*. The colors are placed on the resistors in rings (see Fig. 11.5).

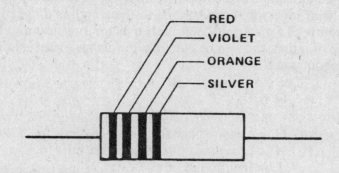

RED
VIOLET
ORANGE
SILVER

Fig. 11.5. A 27,000-ohm (Ω)resistor.

The table below shows the values for reading the color code of carbon-composition resistors.

RESISTOR COLOR CODE

0 Black	5 Green
1 Brown	6 Blue
2 Red	7 Violet
3 Orange	8 Gray
4 Yellow	9 White

Take a close look at a carbon-composition resistor. The bands should be to your left. Read from left to right. The band closest to one end is placed to the left so you can read it from left to right. The first band gives the first number according to the color code. In this case it is red, or 2. The second band gives the next number, which is violet, or 7. The third band represents the multiplier or divisor.

If the third band is a color in the 0 to 9 range in the color code, it states the number of zeros to be added to the first two numbers. Orange is 3; so the resistor in Fig. 11.5 has a value of 27,000 Ω of resistance.

The 27,000 Ω is usually written as 27 kΩ. The k stands for thousand; it takes the place of three zeros. In some cases, resistors are referred to as 27 MΩ (which means 27,000,000, or 27 million Ω), because the M stands for *mega,* and that is the unit for million.

If there is no fourth band, the resistor has a tolerance rating of ± 20 percent (± means plus or minus). If the fourth band is silver, the resistor has a tolerance of ± 10 percent. If the fourth band is gold, the resistor has a tolerance of ± 5 percent.

Silver and gold may also be used for the *third* band. In this case, according to the color code, the first two numbers (obtained from the first two color bands) must be divided by 10 or 100. Silver means divide the first two numbers by 100. Gold means divide the first two numbers by 10. For example, if the bands of the resistor are red, yellow and gold, then the value is 24 divided by 10, or 2.4Ω. If the third band is silver and the two colors are yellow and orange, then the 43 is divided by 100 to produce the answer of 0.43Ω. Keep in mind, though, that the fourth band will still be either gold or silver to indicate the tolerance.

Resistors marked with the color code are available in hundreds of size and wattage rating combinations. Wattage rating refers to the wattage or power consumed by the resistor.

Conductance

Electronics is a study that is frequently explained in terms of opposites. The term that is just the opposite of resistance is conductance. Conductance is the ability of a material to pass electrons. The factors that effect the magnitude of resistance are exactly the same for conductance, but they affect conductance in the opposite manner. Therefore, conductance is directly proportional to area, and inversely proportional to the length and specific resistance of the material. The temperature of a material is definitely a factor, but assuming a constant temperature, the conductance of a material can be calculated if its specific resistance is known.

The formula for conductance is:

$$G = \frac{A}{pL}$$

where:

G = conductance measured in siemens (S)
A = cross-sectional area in cir mils
L = length measured in feet
p = specific resistance

The unit of conductance is the *siemen* (formerly the MHO, which is ohm spelled backwards). Whereas the symbol used to represent the magnitude of resistance is the Greek letter omega (Ω), the symbol used to represent conductance is S (formerly   ). The relationship that exists between resistance and conductance is a reciprocal one. A reciprocal of a number is one divided by that number. In terms of resistance and conductance:

$$R = \frac{1}{G}$$

$$G = \frac{1}{R}$$

If the resistance of a material is known, dividing its value into one will give its conductance. Also, if the conductance is known, dividing its value into one will give its resistance.

Ohm's Law

A German physicist by the name of Georg Ohm discovered the relationship between voltage, current, and resistance in 1827. He found that in any circuit where the only opposition to the flow of electrons is resistance, there is a relationship between the values of voltage, current, and resistance. The strength or intensity of the current is directly proportional to the voltage and inversely proportional to the resistance.

It is easier to work with Ohm's law when it is expressed in a formula. In the formula, E represents emf, or voltage; I is the current, or the intensity of electron flow; R stands for resistance. The formula is $E = I \times R$. It is used to find the emf (voltage) when the current and the resistance are known.

To find the current, when the voltage and resistance are known, use

$$I = \frac{E}{R}$$

To find the resistance, when the voltage and current are known, use

$$R = \frac{E}{I}$$

Ohm's law is very useful in electrical and electronics work. You will need it often to determine the missing value. In order to make it easy to remember the formula take a look at Fig. 11.6. Here the formulas are arrived at by placing your finger on the unknown and the other two will have their relationship displayed.

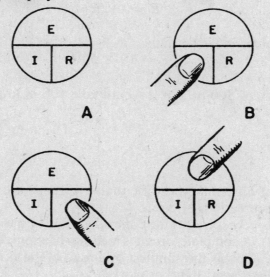

Fig. 11.6. Ohm's law. Place your finger on the unknown value and the remaining two letters will give the formula to use for finding the unknown value.

The best way to become accustomed to solving problems is to start with something simple, such as:

1. If the voltage is given as 100 V and the resistance is 25 Ω, it is a simple problem and a practical application of Ohm's law to find the current in the circuit. Use

$$I = \frac{E}{R}$$

Substituting the values in the formula,

$$I = \frac{100}{25}$$

means 100 is divided by 25 to produce 4 A for the current.

2. If the current is given as 2 A (you may read it on an ammeter in the circuit), and the voltage (read from the voltmeter) is 100 V, it is easy to find the resistance. Use

$$R = \frac{E}{I}$$

Substituting the values in the formula,

$$I = \frac{100}{25}$$

means 100 divided by 2 equals 50 Ω for the circuit.

3. If the current is known to be 10 A, and the resistance is found to be 50 Ω (measured before the circuit is energized), it is then possible to determine how much voltage is needed to cause the circuit to function properly. Use

$$E = I \times R$$

Substituting the values in the formula,
$$E = 10 \times 50$$

means 10 times 50 produces 500 or that it would take 500 V to push 10 A through 50 Ω of resistance.

Circuits

There are a number of different types of circuits. Circuits are the pathways along which electrons move to produce various effects.

The *complete* circuit is necessary for the controlled flow or movement of electrons along a conductor (see Fig. 11.7). A complete circuit is made up of a source of electricity, a conductor, and a consuming device. This is the simplest of circuits. The flow of electrons through the consuming device produces heat, light, or work.

In order to form a complete circuit, these rules must be followed:

1. Connect one side of the power source to one side of the consuming device: *A* to *B*. (See Fig. 11.7)
2. Connect the other side of the power source to one side of the control device, usually a switch: *C* to *D*. (See Fig. 11.7)
3. Connect the other side of the switch to the consuming device it is supposed to control: *E* to *F*. (See Fig. 11.7). When the switch is closed the circuit is complete.

However, when the switch is open, or not closed, there is no path for electrons to flow, and there is an *open circuit* condition where no current flows.

This method is used to make a complete path for electrons to flow from that side of the battery with an excess of electrons to the other side which has a deficiency of electrons. The battery has a negative (−) charge where there is an excess of electrons and a positive (+) charge where there is a deficiency of electrons. Yes, you read it right: the − means excess and + means deficiency. This is due to the fact that we are using the current flow and electron flow as both the same and from − to + in the circuit.

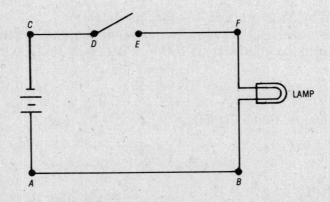

Fig. 11.7. A simple circuit with a switch.

A single path for electrons to flow is called a *closed*, or *complete*, circuit. However, in some instances the circuit may have more than one consuming device. In this situation we have what is called a *series circuit* if the two or more resistors or consuming devices are placed one after the other as shown in Figure 11.8.

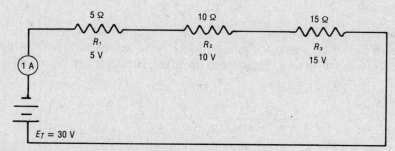

Fig. 11.8.   A series circuit with three resistors.

Series Circuit

Fig. 11.8 shows a series circuit. The three resistors are connected in series, or one after the other, to complete the path from one terminal of the battery to the other. The current flows through each of them before returning to the positive terminal of the battery.

There is a law concerning the voltages in a series circuit. *Kirchhoff's voltage law* states that the sum of all voltages across resistors or loads is equal to the applied voltage. Voltage drop is considered across the resistor. Fig. 11.8 shows the current flow through three resistors. The voltage drop across R_1 is 5 V. Across R_2 the voltage drop is 10 V. And, across R_3 the voltage drop is 15 V. The sum of the individual voltage drops is equal to the total or applied voltage of 30 V. E_T means total voltage. It may also be written as E_A for applied voltage or E_S for source voltage.

To find the total resistance in a series circuit, just add the individual resistances or $R_T = R_1 + R_2 + R_3$. In this instance (Fig. 11.8) the total resistance is $5 + 10 + 15$, or 30 Ω.

Parallel Circuits

In a parallel circuit each resistance is connected directly across the voltage source or line. There are as many separate paths for current flow as there are branches (see Fig. 11.9).

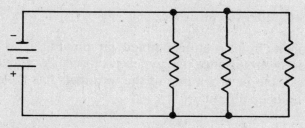

Fig. 11.9.   A parallel circuit.

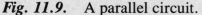

The voltage across all branches of a parallel circuit is the same. This is because all branches are connected across the voltage source. Current in a parallel circuit depends on the resistance of the branch. Ohm's law can be used to determine the current in each branch. You can find the total current for a parallel circuit by simply adding the individual currents. When written as a formula it reads

$$I_T = I_1 + I_2 + I_3 + \ldots$$

The total resistance of a parallel circuit cannot be found by adding the resistor values. Two formulas are used for finding the total resistance (R_T). If there are *only* two resistors in parallel, a simple formula can be used:

$$R_T = \frac{R_1 \times R_2}{R_1 \times R_2}$$

If there are more than two resistors in a parallel, you can use the following formula. This formula may also be used with two resistors in parallel. In fact it can be used for *any* number of resistors.

$$\frac{1}{R_T} = \frac{1}{R_1} + \frac{1}{R_2} + \frac{1}{R_3} + \frac{1}{R_4} + \cdots$$

One thing should be kept in mind in parallel resistances: The total resistance is *always* less than the smallest resistance.

Series-Parallel Circuits   The series-parallel circuit is a combination of the series and the parallel arrangement. Fig. 11.10 shows an example of the series-parallel circuit. It takes a minimum of three resistances to make a series-parallel circuit. This type has to be reduced to a series equivalent before it can be solved in terms of resistance. The parallel portions are reduced to the total for that part of the circuit, and then the equivalent resistance is added to the series part to obtain the total resistance.

Total current flows through the first series resistor but divides according to the branch resistances after that. There are definite relationships which must be explored here before that type of circuit can be fully understood. This will be done in a later part of this book.

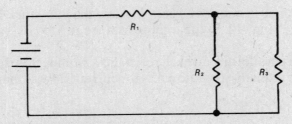

Fig. 11.10.   A series-parallel circuit.

Open Circuits   An open circuit is an incomplete circuit. Fig. 11.11 shows an open circuit that will become a closed circuit once the switch is closed. A circuit can also become open when one of the leads is cut or when one of the terminals has the wire removed. A loose connection can cause an open circuit.

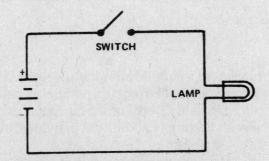

Fig. 11.11.   An open circuit produced by an open switch.

Short Circuits   The short circuit is something to be avoided because it can cause a fire or over-heating.

A short circuit has a path of low resistance to electron flow. This is usually created when a low-resistance wire is placed across the consuming device (see Fig. 11.12). The greater number of electrons will flow through the path of least resistance rather through the consuming device. A short usually generates an excess current flow which can result in damage to a number of parts of the circuit. If you wish to prevent the damage caused by short circuits, you use a fuse.

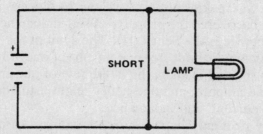

Fig. 11.12.   A short circuit. The wire has less resistance than the lamp.

Fuses   Fuses are available in a number of sizes and shapes. They are used to prevent the damage done by excess current flowing in a circuit. They are places in series with the consuming devices. Once too much current flows, it causes the fuse wire inside the fuse case to melt. This opens the circuit and stops the flow of current and prevents the overheating that occurs when too much current is present in a circuit.

The symbol for a fuse is ⌇ . It fits into a circuit as shown in Fig. 11.13.

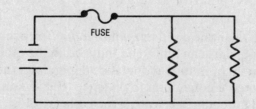

Fig. 11.13.   The location of the fuse in a circuit.

Resistors and resistance are very important in the study of electricity and electronics. However, when two other devices are introduced into the circuits, there is the possibility of various combinations that can produce rather interesting final results. One of these devices is the inductor, which produces inductance.

Inductance

Inductance is the ability of a coil, or choke, or inductor (all three mean the same thing and are interchangeable) to oppose any change in circuit current. This is not so important in a direct current (dc) circuit because the current flows in only one direction, from negative to positive, when it is first turned on, and then it stops when it is turned off. The collapsing magnetic field that was produced by the coil of wire with a current through it produces an emf in the coil when it decays or collapses. This emf is in the opposite polarity to that which caused it to be produced. The emf is called a *counter emf,* abbreviated as *cemf.*

Michael Faraday was an Englishman who performed early experiments with coils of wire and electric current. Faraday started to experiment with electricity about 1805. It was not until 1831 that he performed experiments on magnetically coupled coils. A voltage was induced in one of the coils by means of a magnetic field created by current flow in the other coil. From this experiment came the induction coil. Faraday's experiment and discovery made possible many of our modern conveniences. The automobile, doorbell, automobile radio, and television are all possible because of inductance.

Faraday also invented the first transformer. A *transformer* changes electricity into a higher or lower voltage. At that time it had very few practical uses. At the time Faraday was working in England, Joseph Henry was making almost the same discoveries in the United States. Henry worked in New York and discovered the property of self-inductance before Faraday. The unit of measurement for inductance is the henry (H). The symbol for inductance is *L*.

An inductor has an inductance of one *henry* if an emf of one volt is induced in the inductor when the current through the coil is changing at the rate of one ampere per second. Keep in mind that the one-volt, one-ampere, and one-henry relationship deals with the basic units of measurement of voltage, current, and inductance.

Inductors come in many sizes and shapes. Air-core inductors are coils that are wound without a core. They are used in circuits where the frequencies cannot be heard, such as radio frequencies. Radio frequencies are above the human hearing range. The symbol for a radio frequency coil is ⌒⌒⌒ .

Inductors are also called *chokes* because of the way they hold back current or choke it. They are also called *coils* for the simple construction technique used to make them. They are nothing more than a coil of wire.

Inductors with iron cores are used in circuits where the frequencies can be heard. These are called *audio frequencies* and they are referred to as audio chokes or audio inductors. The iron core is usually laminated sheets of iron. The iron is specially made silicon steel. Silicon steel is used because it can change its magnetic orientation rapidly without causing too much opposition to the changing field or polarity reversals. The symbol for an iron core choke is ⌒⌒⌒ .

When two coils are placed near one another *mutual induction* occurs. A change in the flux or magnetic field in one coil will cause an emf to be induced in the other coil. The two coils have mutual inductance. The amount of mutual inductance depends on the distance between the two coils. If the coils are separated a considerable distance, the amount of flux common to both coils is small and the mutual inductance is low. If the coils are close together nearly all the flux on one coil will link the turns of the other. The mutual iductance can be increased greatly by mounting both coils on the same iron core.

Mutual inductance of two adjacent coils depends upon the physical size of the two coils, the number of turns in each coil, the distance between the two coils, the distance between the axes of the two coils, and the permeability of the cores. *Permeability* is the ease with which magnetic lines of force distribute themselves throughout a material.

Alternating Current

Most of us have grown up with alternating current (ac). We are used to the 60-hertz (Hz) line current that is furnished to every house in the United States. It is much better than direct current (dc) when it comes to transporting power over long distances without huge losses. It is also important since electronics relies so heavily on alternating current. The radio frequencies which bring us radio and television are also ac. In order to get a better understanding of ac, we should look at how it is generated and distributed.

Alternating current was developed by Nicholas Tesla. Its use was introduced around 1900.

Niagara Falls, New York had one of the first commercial ac generators, which was in operation until 1948 when a rock slide ruined it.

Alternating current has a distinct advantage over direct current. Alternating current can be stepped up to obtain higher voltages and lower currents and still produce the same amount of power at the other end of the line. It can be transported over long distances through small wires because of the higher voltages and lower currents. Current determines the size of the wire. Then it is stepped down for local distribution. Since transformers are very efficient machines, very low losses are experienced with ac.

Usually, alternating current is generated at 13,800 volts (V). This is then stepped up to at least 138,000 V for distribution. The most commonly used high voltages for long-distance transmission are 138,000, 250,000 and 750,000 V. Once the power reaches its destination, it is reduced to as low as 240 V for home use. This is further split for home circuits of 120 V.

Nature of Alternating Current
Alternating current changes its direction of flow as it moves along a wire. If flows in one direction and then the other. Fig. 11.14 shows a simple ac generator; Fig. 11.15 shows the output of the generator.

Alternating current is constantly changing. It changes in magnitude and direction. The ac pattern, or *waveform,* is shown in Fig. 11.15. The time base of one second (s) is standard in the electrical field. Whenever you see 60 Hz, you know it means 60 complete sine waves are generated in l s.

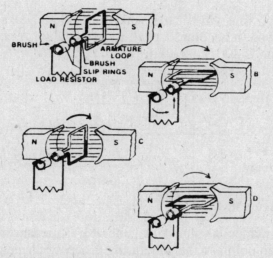

Fig. 11.14.   Simple ac generator called an alternator.

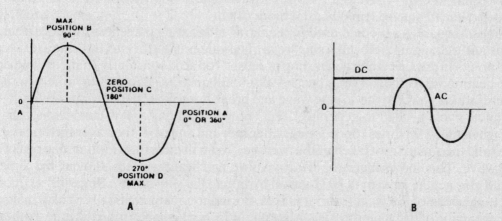

Fig. 11.15.   A. The sine wave. B. Comparison of ac to dc.

The term *frequency* is used to indicate how many times the alternating current changes direction. The ac you use at home changes direction 60 times per second. This means it moves back and forth 60 times per second. This current is described as having a frequency of 60 Hz. It is said to be 60-Hz ac. Frequency can be expressed in megahertz, or MHz. This is 1 million Hz/s. It can also be expressed in kilohertz, which means 1000 times or hertz per second. Kilohertz is abbreviated as kHz. Note that k is a small letter. However, MHz uses M since it stands for *mega,* or one million.

Fig. 11.16 shows the difference between 4 Hz and 1 Hz. Note that both of them occur in 1 s. Note how the waveform becomes closer together as it becomes part of a higher frequency.

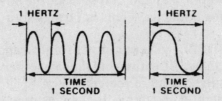

Fig. 11.16.   4 Hz and 1 Hz compared.

Three values are used to describe alternating current: peak, average, and root-mean-square (rms).

The maximum point on a sine wave is the peak value. Both peaks of a single hertz may be included in a reference. If so, it becomes a peak-to-peak value. A peak value of 100 V means that the peak-to-peak value is 200 V (see Fig. 11.17).

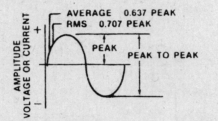

Fig. 11.17.   Ac sine wave values.

The average of all instantaneous values of a generator is measured at regular intervals. The values are taken at selected points in the generating process. The average of these is the average value of ac current. The average value is 0.637 times the peak. This means that a peak of 100 V is equal to 63.7 V average. However, average is not often used in reference to ac. Instead, root-mean-square (rms) is used more often.

Root-mean-square is a method used for equating alternating current to direct current. Since ac is constantly changing, it forms a sine wave. The values used for rms figuring are taken from selected points in the sine wave generating process. The ac is constantly changing and does not have the heating value of dc. That is because dc comes up to its peak and stays there until turned off. Therefore, if you take the ac sine wave and break it into four parts, each containing 90° of the complete cycle needed to generate 1 Hz, you will find that the instantaneous voltage and current when taken 90 times (once for each degree) and squared, then averaged (*mean* means average) and the square root taken of the average, you will have 0.7071 times the peak value of the sine wave. This shows that rms, effective heat, and heating effect all mean the same thing. You could also get the rms, or 0.7071 value, by taking the *sine* of 45°. Since 45° is one-half of the 90° to the peak of the waveform, it makes more sense mathematically. It also makes sense because the shape of the waveform is not a semicircle, but is shaped more like the mathematical equivalent to a sine value.

Transformers

A practical application of alternating current is its use with the transformer. It has the ability to step up and step down voltages. But, only ac; direct current does not work with a transformer.

A *transformer* is a device consisting of two coils that can change voltages. The voltage put into a transformer is either stepped up or stepped down. (In some instances, however, isolation transformers are used so that they have the same output as input voltage. They are used to eliminate the ground connection in convention line current. That way you must come across both terminals to receive a shock instead of any ground and the hot side of the line.)

Fig. 11.18 shows how transformers are used to distribute electric power from the generator to the consumer. Note that the symbols used for the transformer are two coils of wire with straight lines in between to designate the iron core.

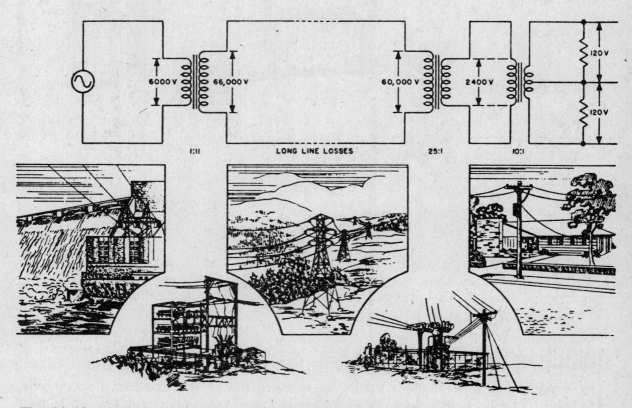

Fig. 11.18.   Using transformers to distribute ac over long distances.

A transformer has a primary winding and a secondary winding. A transformer is simply a coil when it has no load on the secondary. When a load is placed on the output side (the secondary winding), the device actually becomes a transformer.

Transformers come in many sizes and shapes (see Fig. 11.19). They may be used on alternating currents at power line frequencies of 25, 50, or 60 and also on frequencies of more than 1 million Hz. The transformers used on radio frequencies do not have cores. They have air for a core, and their physical size is much smaller than power frequency transformers.

Since there are no moving parts in a transformer, it can be up to 99 percent efficient. The only moving part is the current. Losses are eliminated by using silicon steel for the core laminations. The silicon steel reduces the losses due to hysteresis that are caused by changing the polarity many times per second. Eddy currents are small currents induced in the metal by the changing magnetic field. Laminations eliminate the losses caused by eddy currents. Copper losses are reduced to a minimum by using the proper size wire for the amount of current being handled.

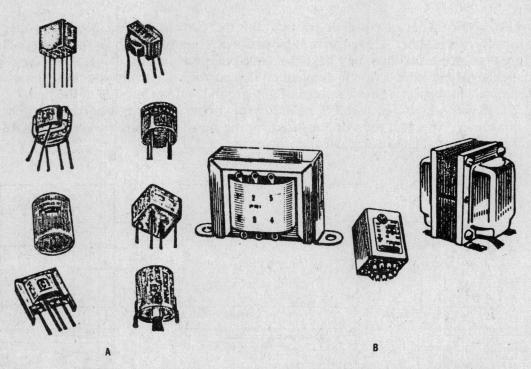

Fig. 11.19. A.   Various sizes and types of transformers. B. Power transformers.

Power Transformers   A power transformer can be both a step-up and a step-down unit (see Fig. 11.20). The secondary windings can furnish a number of different voltages. These voltages may be either higher or lower than the primary voltage. This type of transformer is used in electronics equipment where a number of different voltages are needed.

Inductive Reactance

Inductive reactance is the opposition put up to alternating current by a coil. The coil has a definite time or delay built in due to the ratio of inductance to resistance. This built-in delay of current comes in conflict with the ac since the current is constantly changing and not necessarily at the same rate as the natural tendency of the coil. Therefore, the reaction or reactance is in the form of an opposition. Since it is an opposition, it is measured in ohms. Reactance is represented by the symbol X. Inductance is represented by its symbol L. When the inductive reactance is represented it is written as X_L. It is measured in ohms.

A number of factors determine X_L. One is the frequency of ac, which affects reactance. Another is the size of the inductor. The formula used to calculate X_L is

$$X_L = 2\pi f L$$

In this equation, f is the frequency, measured in Hz. L is inductance, measured in henrys (H). Pi (π) is a standard mathematical term with a value of 3.141592654. Thus, 2π equals 6.28 when rounded off for quick answers.

By increasing the f, the X_L increases. If the f is decreased, the X_L decreases. The same is true for L, or inductance. Since the 2π is a constant, it does not change. Therefore, the only two variables for X_L are frequency and inductance.

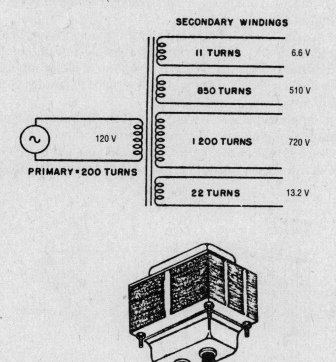

SECONDARY WINDINGS

II TURNS	6.6 V	
850 TURNS	510 V	
I 200 TURNS	720 V	
22 TURNS	13.2 V	

120 V

PRIMARY = 200 TURNS

Fig. 11.20.   Power transformer schematic.

Resistors and inductive reactances both produce opposition, and both are measured in ohms. This means that inductive reactances which are in series are simply added to obtain the total inductive reactance in a circuit:

$$X_{LT} = X_{L1} + X_{L2} + X_{L3} + \ldots$$

Inductive reactances which are in parallel are treated the same as resistors in parallel. You can use the product divided by the sum formula or the reciprocal formula:

$$X_{LT} = \frac{X_{L1} \times X_{L2}}{X_{L1} + X_{L2}}$$

$$\frac{1}{X_{LT}} = \frac{1}{X_{L1}} + \frac{1}{X_{L2}} + \frac{1}{X_{L3}} + \cdots$$

The major use of inductance is to provide a minimum reactance for low frequencies. Inductors produce high opposition to higher frequencies.

One specific use of inductance is in filters. Filters are used when certain frequencies are desired and others are to be avoided. An inductor is used that has an X_L that passes certain frequencies and opposes others.

The main use for inductive reactance is in electronic circuits. Such circuits, along with capacitors, tune in certain frequencies and reject others. An example is the tuner of your radio or television.

Capacitors

Capacitors play an important role in the building of circuits. A *capacitor* is a device that opposes any change in circuit voltage. That property of a capacitor which opposes voltage change is called *capacitance.*

Capacitors make it possible to store electric energy. Electrons are held within a capacitor. This, in effect, is stored electricity. It is also known as an *electric potential,* or an *electrostatic field.* Electrostatic fields hold electrons. When the buildup of electrons becomes great enough, the electric potential is discharged. This process takes place in nature: clouds build up electrostatic fields. Their discharge is seen as lightning.

Fig. 11.21 shows a simple capacitor. Two plates of a conductor material are isolated from one another. Between the two plates is a dielectric material. The dielectric does conduct electrons easily. Electrons are stored on the plate surfaces. The larger the surface, the more area is available for stored electrons. Increasing the size of the plates therefore increases the capacitance.

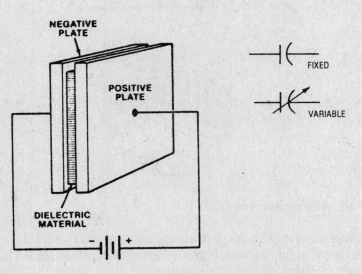

Fig. 11.21. Design of a capacitor. Symbols for a capacitor.

Operation of the Capacitor   If a capacitor has no charge of electrons, it is uncharged. This happens when there is no voltage applied to the plates. An uncharged capacitor is shown in Fig. 11.22 A. Note the symbol for a capacitor in this drawing. This is the preferred way to show a capacitor: a straight line and a curved line facing each other. Note that the circuit has a dc source and a three-position switch that is in the open position.

In Fig. 11.22B, the switch has been closed to position 1. This causes current to flow. A difference in potential is created by the voltage source. This causes electrons to be transferred from the positive to the negative plate. This transfer continues as long as the voltage source is connected to the two plates and until the accumulated charge becomes equal to the potential difference of the applied voltage. That is, charging takes place until the capacitor is charged.

In Fig. 11.22C, the voltage has been removed. The switch is open. At this point, the potential difference, or charge, across the capacitor remains. That is, there is still a surplus of electrons on the negative plate of the capacitor. This charge remains in place until a path is provided for discharging the excess electrons.

In Fig. 11.22D, the switch is moved to position 3. This opens the path for discharging the surplus electrons. Notice that the discharge path is in the opposite direction from the charge path. This shows how a change in circuit voltage results in a change in the capacitor charge.

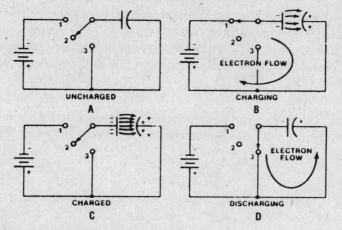

Fig. 11.22.   Charge and discharge of a capacitor.

Some electrons leave the excess (negative) plate. They do this in an attempt to keep the voltage in the circuit constant.

As you can see from the foregoing, the ability of a capacitor to charge and discharge can be useful in many types of circuits. Its ability to oppose any change in the circuit voltage can also be helpful. All this will be put to work later in electronic circuits.

Capacity of a Capacitor   The two plates of the capacitor may be made of almost any material. The only criterion is that the material will allow electrons to collect on it. The dielectric may be air, vacuum, plastics, wood , or mica.

Three factors determine the capacity of a capacitor: the area of the plates, the distance between the plates, and the material used as a dielectric. The larger the plate area, the greater the capacity, or capacitance. The distance between the plates of a capacitor determines the effect that electrons have upon one another. That is because electrons possess a charge, or field, around them that can react with those close by. Capacitance increases when the plates are brought close together. One of the effects of the dielectric materials is determined by its thickness. The thinner the dielectric, the closer the plates will be. A thin dielectric can thus increase capacitance. Some dielectrics have better insulating qualities than others and will allow greater voltages to be applied between the plates before breaking down. Take a look at the dielectric materials listed in the table below to see how various materials affect the capacitance of a capacitor.

Material	Dielectric Constant (K)
Air or Vacuum	1
Rubber	2-4
Oil	2-5
Paper	2-6
Mica	3-8
Glass	8
Ceramics	80-1,200

Working Voltage DC   The maximum safe working voltage of a capacitor in a direct current circuit is identified as the working voltage dc, or WVDC. Above this voltage, a capacitor is expected to puncture or develop a short circuit. If the temperature in which a circuit operates reaches 60°C or higher, the voltage rating is lowered.

Voltage ratings for mica, paper, and ceramic capacitors are usually 200, 400, and 600 V dc. Oil-filled capacitors have voltage ratings ranging up to 7500 V. As the voltage ratings become higher, the physical size of the capacitors becomes greater. Never operate a capacitor above its rated WVDC. It is customary to use a capacitor in a circuit with about 50 to 75 percent of its rated voltage.

Capacitors in Series. Capacitors can be connected in series, but the series reduces the capacitance. The formula used for finding capacitance for two capacitors in series is

$$C_r = \frac{C_1 \times C_2}{C_1 + C_2}$$

$$\frac{1}{C_r} = \frac{1}{C_1} + \frac{1}{C_2} + \frac{1}{C_3} + \cdots$$

As you increase the distance between the plates, effectively, when placing them in series, you also increase the WVDC rating. Just add the WVDC ratings of the capacitors to obtain the higher value created with the placement in series.

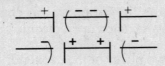

Capacitors in Parallel. Capacitors can be connected in parallel in their polarity is observed in the case of electrolytics. For standard, nonpolarized types, it is not necessary to observe any particular connection procedure except to place the leads together in order to produce a parallel connection. Placing capacitors in parallel *increases* the capacitance. Just add the individual capacitances to obtain the total capacitance. However, keep in mind that the WVDC will be the rating of the *smallest* value of voltage in the WVDC ratings.

Measuring Capacitance

Capacitance is measured in farads (F). The *farad* is defined as having the ability to store enough electrons to produce a voltage difference of one volt across the terminals while producing one ampere of current for one second.

The farad is a very large unit of capacitance. The capacitors we use in electricity and in electronics are much, much smaller. They are measured in *microfarads* (0.000001 F) and in micromicrofarads, now called *picofarads* (0.000000000001 F).

It is often necessary to interpret or change values. This occurs as you read circuit drawings or markings on capacitors. You may, for example, find yourself working with capacitors marked in terms of pF and drawings indicated in μF. Keep in mind the following to make sure you get the conversion correct and that you are tuned in to the correct formulas.

- pF to μF, move the decimal six places to the left.
- μF to F, move the decimal six places to the left.
- F to μF, move the decimal six places to the right.
- μF to pF, move the decimal six places to the right.
- pF to F, move the decimal 12 places to the left.
- F to pF, move the decimal 12 places to the right.

Capacitive Reactance

Capacitive reactance is that opposition that a capacitor presents to alternating current (ac). A capacitor has a definite time period for charging: $T = R \times C$. The time T in seconds (s) is equal to the resistance (Ω) times the capacitance (F). This produces a time constant which is 63.2 percent of the maximum voltage presented to the capacitor. It takes five time constants for a capacitor to charge to its full, or 99.3 percent level. It also takes the same amount of time to discharge when presented with a resistance across its terminals.

When ac is present across the terminals of a capacitor, it changes faster than the capacitor can charge and discharge. This reaction or reactance is determined by the frequency of the ac and the capacity of the capacitor. A formula used to express capacitive reactance is

$$X_c = \frac{1}{2\pi fC}$$

where f = frequency, expressed in hertz
C = capacitance, expressed in farads
X_c = capacitive reactance, expressed in ohms since it is opposition to current flow

The following are conditions which occur when a capacitor is introduced into an ac circuit.

1. If the capacitance decreases, the capacitive reactance will increase for the same frequency.
2. If the capacitance increases, the capacitive reactance will decrease as long as the same frequency is presented to the capacitor.
3. If the frequency is decreased and the capacitor is the same, then the capacitive reactance will increase.
4. If the frequency is increased, then the capacitive reactance will decrease provided the capacitance stays the same.

As you can see from these statements and observations, the increase of decrease of the frequency or capacitance will cause the reverse reaction with the X_c.

Resonance

Resonance is a very important part of electronics. It is necessary for the operation of the many types of television receivers and FM and AM radios. Resonance is created through the proper arrangement of a coil and capacitor.

Circuits with resistance, capacitance, and inductance behave differently from those with only one or two of these factors. For instance, a circuit with resistance reacts to alternating current (ac) and direct current (dc) the same way. However, when both a resistor and inductor are in a circuit, another factor is introduced because ac is applied to the combination. It behaves completely different from the dc circuit consisting of only a resistor and coil. The same is true with a resistor and capacitor combination. The ac introduces the capacitive reactance, but dc causes only the charging of the capacitor at a time determined by the values of the resistor and the capacitor.

It becomes important, then, for us to look closely at the combination of devices connected to a circuit. It is very evident that ac and dc cause different things to happen in an electric circuit.

The use of vectors will aid in the understanding of phase angle introduced by various combinations of these three devices (inductors, capacitors, and resistors).

Resistance, Capacitance, and Inductance   Resistance produces an opposition to current flow in a circuit. The resistor is the device that produces the opposition. It behaves the same with either ac or dc.

Capacitive reactance produces an opposition to current flow in a circuit. The capacitor is the device that produces the opposition. The capacitor behaves differently with ac than with dc.

Remember (just as in resistance) the opposition, or capacitive reactance, is measured in ohms.

Inductive reactance produces an opposition to current flow in a circuit. The inductor is the device that produces the opposition. The inductor behaves differently with ac than with dc. Inductive reactance is also measured in ohms.

Bear in mind, also, that the capacitor opposes any *change* in circuit *voltage*. The inductor opposes any *change* in circuit *current*. These two simple statements make a great deal of difference between understanding resonance and not being able to visualize it. So reread them to make sure you have them clearly in mind.

The relationship between current and voltage is vital to an understanding of electronics and electric circuits.

Impedance

The *total* opposition to current flow within a circuit is impedance. The symbol for impedance is Z. Impedance impedes or opposes current flow. It is a term used when either resistance, capacitive reactance, inductive reactance, or any combination of the three is used. In dc circuits, opposition to voltage and current is resistance only, since capacitors and inductors do not have reactance with dc—only ac. Z is measured in ohms.

Impedance can be R and X_L. It can be R and X_c, or it can be R and X_c and X_L. Impedance (Z) can also be used when there is X_L and X_C. Any combination of these oppositions can be referred to as an impedance.

Voltage lags the current in a capacitive circuit. Current lags the voltage in an inductive circuit. Voltage lagged the current in a capacitor by 90° in a purely capacitive circuit. Voltage led the current in a purely inductive circuit. That is another way of saying that the current lagged the voltage by 90°. This leading and lagging is very important in any understanding of impedance for it takes into account the *phase angle*.

The phase angle is the difference between the voltage and the current in a circuit caused by either capacitance or inductance in an ac circuit. If we want to combine these phase angles such as when a capacitor and inductor are in a circuit, we have to do it vectorially (see Fig. 11.23). Fig. 11.23 is a diagram of how impedance is represented by Z, resistance by R, and reactance by X_L. Note the angle formed by lines *BA* and *AD*. Z is shown halfway between the two lines and as a result shows a phase angle of 45°. This happens when the resistance *(R)* and inductive reactance X_L) are equal. As you can see, impedance is the *vector sum* of resistance and reactance. A *vector* is a line segment used to represent a quantity that has both direction and magnitude. Vectors are used to represent current, voltage, or any combination of the electrical quantities encountered.

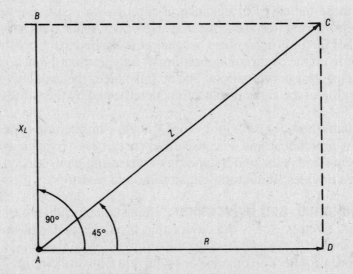

Fig. 11.23. Impedance shown in vector form.

A vector can show direction of current flow. It can also show the magnitude, or amount, of current flowing. A vector sum is a line representing the total of two or more vectors. Impedance is stated in terms of a vector sum.

Inductive reactance causes the current in an inductor to lag 90° behind the voltage. Therefore, a graphic way of presenting the impedance of current can be drawn as shown in Fig. 11.23. In this illustration, resistance is plotted on the horizontal line AD. The length of the line AD is proportional to the amount of resistance in the circuit. Proportional means that the quantity of resistance within the circuit is represented by line AD. Zero resistance is indicated by point A. The value of resistance in the circuit is indicated at point D. Using the same scale, the amount of inductive reactance is plotted on a line 90° from the resistance line. This is because the voltage and current in the resistor are in phase with one another. This means that the resistance line AD can be used as the horizontal reference and everything else will be plotted up or down in reference to this horizontal reference.

The vertical line AB represents the inductive reactance. This is also proportional. Zero inductive reactance is shown at point A. The value of inductive reactance is indicated at point B.

The impedance Z is the vector sum of the two lines. It is represented by line AC. To find the value of C, begin by constructing a parallelogram. This is shown in Fig. 11-23 by the dotted lines finishing up the Figure. A *parallelogram* is a four-sided figure whose opposite sides are parallel and equal. In Fig. 11-23, the dotted line CD is parallel to AB, and BC is parallel to AD.

C is the point where the parallelogram is completed. The value of Z is found by drawing a straight line between C and A. This line can be measured and the value of Z found by equating it to the units used in X_L and R.

The value of this graphic method is that it helps you to visualize the procedure. In practice there are faster methods for calculating impedance. This is a simple operation on most calculators. Using a calculator becomes even easier once you can visualize and understand the values involved.

Changing Alternating Current to Direct Current

Since alternating current (ac) is inexpensive, it is used in thousands of devices. It can be stepped up or stepped down by using a transformer. It is a versatile type of power that can easily be changed to fit the voltage or current needs of particular circuits. However, direct current (dc) is also useful for many devices. Electronics depends upon dc for many of its circuit components. This dependence upon dc requires a source of inexpensive direct current for a variety of voltages and currents.

Historically the changing of ac to dc began around the turn of the century when ac became available at Niagara Falls, New York, but was not easily transported to Buffalo (26 miles away) where it was needed by the milling industry. The demand for soap products became rather important in our country around 1900 when the newly "arrived" middle class was demanding the cleanliness of everything, and it became apparent that dc current could be used to produce any number of soap products from various cheap chemicals. Niagara Falls with its inexpensive source of falling water-generated ac would easily become one of the chemical centers of the country if only the ac could be converted to dc. The change was vital because dc was much more easily used in the chemical processes of the time.

Metallic Rectifiers   Large copper oxide rectifiers were designed to change the ac to dc. One side of the rectifier disk was copper, and the other was copper oxide. The copper allowed the current to flow easily, but the copper oxide side put up a great opposition to the flow of current in the other direction. This meant the ac could be rectified since the copper oxide rectifier allowed the current to flow in only one direction. This produced pulsating dc which was useful for a number of chemical processes and for driving motors which were being developed at the time.

In the copper oxide rectifier (see Fig. 11.24) the oxide is formed on the copper by partial oxidation of the copper by a high temperature. In this type of rectifier the electrons flow more readily from the copper side to the oxide than from the oxide to the copper. External electrical connection may be made by connecting terminal lugs between the left pressure plate and the copper and between the right pressure plate and the lead washer.

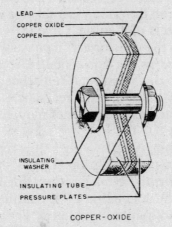

Fig. 11.24.   Construction of the metallic rectifier.

For the rectifier to function properly, the oxide coating must be very thin. Thus, each individual unit can stand only a low inverse voltage. Rectifiers designed for moderate-and high-power applications consist of many of these individual units mounted in series on a single support. The lead washer enables uniform pressure to be applied to the units so that the internal resistance may be reduced. When the units are connected in series, they normally present a relatively high resistance to the current flow. The resulting heat developed in the resistance must be removed if the rectifier is to operate satisfactorily. Many commercial rectifiers have copper fins between each unit to dissipate the excess heat. The useful life of the unit is extended by keeping the temperature low, below 140°F (60°C). The efficiency of this type of rectifier is generally between 60 and 70 percent. They are found in older types of equipment. Today, however, no one uses this type of rectifier in newly designed equipment because inexpensive semiconductor devices with over 90 percent efficiency are now readily available.

Selenium rectifiers are similar to and function much the same as copper oxide rectifiers. The selenium rectifier is made up of an iron disk coated with a thin layer of selenium. In this type of rectifier, the electrons flow from the selenium to the iron.

Commercial types of selenium rectifiers were used in early models of television sets. This type of rectifier may be operated at a somewhat higher temperature than the copper oxide type. The efficiency is between 65 and 85 percent. Many units may be bolted together to increase the voltage rating when connected in series. Larger element disks and larger cooling fins must be used if higher currents are drawn. Forced-air cooling is required in some instances to keep them cool.

Metallic rectifiers may be used in battery charges, instrument rectifiers, and many other applications including welding and electroplating. Commercial radios and television sets have been designed to utilize the selenium type of metallic retifier.

One caution: If you are going to reuse one of these unites, and you overheat the selenium type, a pungent odor will be quickly detected. It smells something like rotten eggs, or hydrogen sulfate, or like molten sulfur. Thus, one easy way to tell if the selenium rectifier is "gone" is by the odor. It can be replaced in most instances with a newer type of semiconductor diode.

Solid State Rectifiers   Semiconductor materials are used to make a diode. A *diode* is a device which allows current to flow in one direction and not the other. Germanium and silicon are used as the materials for semiconductor diodes.

Crystals of germanium or silicon are grown from a *melt* which includes small quantities of impure substances such as phosphorus, indium, boron, and other *impurity* atoms. The crystal structure of the resulting metallic chips or wafers permits current flow in one direction only.

Historically, the crystal diode dates to the crystal set used by the first amateurs who worked on making their own receivers of radio signals. Fig 11.25 shows how a crystal set may have looked in the early days of radio. Note particularly the crystal and cat whisker. This was the forerunner of today's cyrstal diodes.

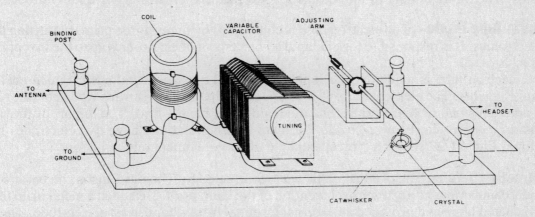

Fig. 11.25   Early receiver consisting of a crystal, cat whisker, coil, and capacitor, known as the *crystal set* to early radio buffs.

The first use of the crystal semiconductor as a rectifier (detector) was in the early days of radio. A crystal was clamped in a small cup or receptacle and a flexible wire (cat whisker) made light contact with the crystal. Tuning the receiver was accomplished by operating the adjusting arm until the cat whisker was positioned on a spot of the crystal that resulted in a sound in the headset. Tuning the variable capacitor provided maximum signal in the headset. Trying to find the correct or loudest point on the crystal was quite time-consuming. Today's point contact diode is identical to the crystal diode of yesteryear (see Fig. 11.26).

The development of the point contact transistor was announced in 1948. The physical construction of the point contact transistor is similar to that of the point contact diode except that a third lead with a metallic point contact is placed near the other metallic point contact on the semiconductor.

The junction diode was first announced in 1949. The junction diode consists of a junction

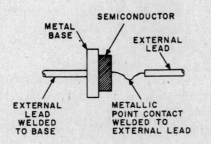

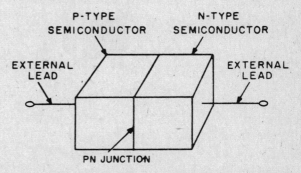

Fig. 11.26.   Physical construction of the point contact diode.

Physical construction of the junction diode.

between two dissimilar sections of semiconductor material. One section, because of its characteristics, is called a P semiconductor. The connections to the junction diode consist of a lead to the P semiconductor material and a lead to the N semiconductor. The P material has a deficiency of one electron for every covalent bond of the material. The N material has an extra electron [therefore the (−) or N designation] for every covalent bond of the material. *Covalent* means that the atoms share electron orbits with adjacent atoms.

The junction diode handles larger power than the point contact diode, but the junction diode has a larger shunt capacitance.

Many types of semiconductor diodes are available. They vary in size from so small that they are hard to see to as large a 2 in. in diameter. They can withstand high voltages and carry large currents. The improvement of the semiconductor material creates better-quality diodes.

Vacuum Tube Diode

The electron tube is considered by many as the primary starting point for electronics. It is responsible for the rapid advancement of electronics up to the invention of the transistor.

The electron tube is made up of a highly evacuated glass or metal shell, which encloses several elements. The elements consist of the cathode that emits electrons when hot, the plate, and sometimes one or more grids. The diode does not have a grid. The *di* part of the name means *two; ode* is short for *electrode.* Put them together and you have two electrodes in an envelope. Fig. 11.27 shows a typical example of a two-element tube.

Construction Details. The original diode was constructed by Thomas Edison, inventor of the incandescent lamp, shortly after his invention of the lamp itself. He added a metal plate inside his evacuated lamp and provided an external terminal from it for use as an electrode. Then he used his heated filament as another electrode and arranged that diode as shown in Fig. 11.28.

Operation of the Vacuum Tube Diode. The operation of the tube can be observed when it is connected in a circuit. Fig. 11.28 is composed of a diode vacuum tube, a battery, a milliammeter, and a resistor. Note what happens to the meter in A as compared with B in Fig. 11.28. As

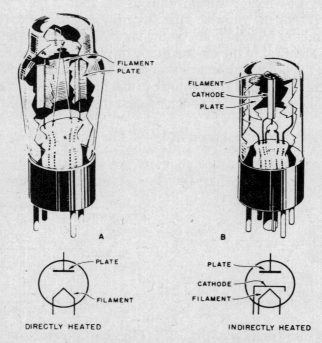

Fig. 11.27.   Cutaway view of a diode or vacuum tube rectifier.

the battery polarity is changed, the action of the vacuum tube changes. When the cathode is negative, the electrons flow through he vacuum from the cathode (K) to the plate (P). The plate has a positive potential applied.

When the plate is connected to the negative potential and the cathode to the positive terminal of the battery, the electrons—being of a negative charge—are repelled by the like potential on the plate. Therefore, there is no current flow (or electron flow) through the tube when it is *reverse-biased*.

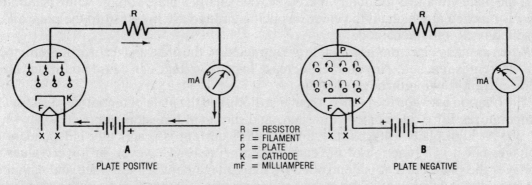

R = RESISTOR
F = FILAMENT
P = PLATE
K = CATHODE
mF = MILLIAMPERE

A — PLATE POSITIVE
B — PLATE NEGATIVE

Fig. 11.28. Operation of the vacuum tube diode circuit.

Now try to visualize how an alternating current (ac) is applied between the cathode and plate. As the polarity reverses itself in ac, the tube will conduct and not conduct according to the polarity of the two elements. Thus, the current will flow during one-half of the hertz applied to the tube and not conduct when the other half is applied. That action produces a half-wave rectified output from the circuit. (see Fig. 11.29).

How does the vacuum tube operate? Well, now that we have seen some of its action, let us take a closer look at the inside workings of the device. First, we will need a source of electrons. The electrons are obtained by heating a cathode made up of a nickel sleeve or cylinder coated with thoriated tungsten. The thoriated tungsten gives off electrons when heated to about 2000°C (3657.6°F). The cathode (emitter) is brought up to temperature by applying the rated voltage across the heater terminals marked with an X in Fig. 11.28.

If the battery is connected so that the plate is positive and the cathode is negative, the meter will indicate a current flow in the external circuit. This phenomenon, the emission of electrons from a hot body, was first observed by Edison in 1883 an is called the *Edison effect*. However, if the battery is reversed in its connection to the electrodes of the tube, there is no current flow.

The total number of electrons emitted by the hot electrode at a given operating temperature is always the same, regardless of the plate voltage. This same condition exists regardless of the plate polarity because the electrons fly into the space surrounding the emitter to produce a cluster or cloud, which is in turbulence or great agitation. This cloud constitutes a negative space charge that constantly tends to repel the electrons toward, and into, the emitter as fast as they are being emitted. the negative charge on the plate only repels the nearby electrons within

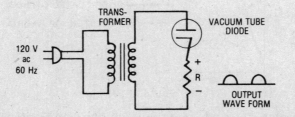

TRANS-FORMER

120 V ac 60 Hz

VACUUM TUBE DIODE

R

OUTPUT WAVE FORM

Fig. 11.29. Output of the rectifier when connected to an ac source.

the cloud, but the action is so effective that none of the electrons reaches the plate regardless of the plate voltage, as long as the plate remains negative.

Examine Fig. 11.28A again. With low values of positive plate voltage, only those electrons of the space-charge cloud that are nearest to the plate are attracted to it, and the plate current is low. As the plate voltage is increased (the cathode temperature remaining constant), greater numbers of electrons are attracted to the plate and, correspondingly, fewer of those being emitted are repelled back into the cathode.

If the plate voltage is gradually increased, eventually a plate voltage value (saturation voltage) is reached at which all the electrons being emitted are in transit to the plate and none is repelled back into the cathode.

When as many electrons as possible are attracted by the plate and it absorbs them, the saturation current is reached. Any further increase in plate voltage can cause no further increase in plate current flowing through the tube.

The relation between the plate current in a diode and the plate potential for different cathode temperatures for oxide-coated, tungsten, and thoriated-tungsten cathodes is shown in Fig. 11.30. At high plate voltages, the flow of plate current is practically independent of plate voltage, but it is a function of the cathode temperature. However, at lower values of plate voltage, the plate current is controlled by the voltage between the plate and cathode and is substantially independent of the cathode temperature. In other words, with a fixed plate voltage, electron emission and plate current will increase with cathode temperature until at some value of temperature the plate current is limited by the space charege. Thus, more electrons are being emitted by the cathode than are being attracted by the plate. Continued increase to cathode temperature fails to produce any further increase in plate current. The temperature at which the plate current stops increasing is called the *saturation temperature*.

In Fig. 11.30 the dotted portion of the characteristic curves is representative of tungsten and thoriated-tungsten emitters, and the solid curves are typical of oxide-coated emitters. It is unlikely that the plate current in a tube using an oxide-coated emitter will ever be entirely independent of the plate voltage. Before the plate voltage could be increased sufficiently to produce emission saturation, it is probable that the cathode would be damaged seriously.

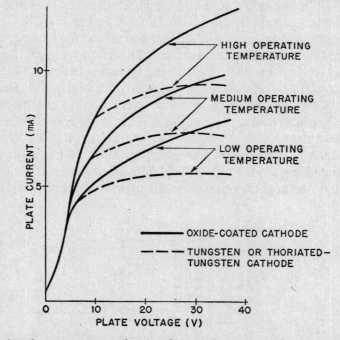

Fig. 11.30.   Diode plate-current, plate-voltage characteristic curves for various operating temperatures.

Types of Diodes   The diodes discussed so far are of the high-vacuum type. Other types of diodes contain gas at a relatively low pressure. For example, hot-cathode mercury-vapor rectifier tubes are used to provide plate power for transmitters. In other applications cold-cathode diodes containing a gas at low pressure are used in voltage regulators, relaxation oscillators, and transmit-receive switching devices for radar units. Most of these devices have been replaced today by semiconductor devices. They are mentioned here in case you run across some older equipment that is still operational.

The original use of the word diode was restricted to vacuum tubes. Scientific research has extended our knowledge about other products that have identical properties of those earlier diodes, although they are not vacuum tubes. Later you will learn about semiconductor diodes, which are identified by their predominating constituent such as silicon diode, germanium diode, and selenium diode. Therefore, the present definition of diode has been extended to refer to many types of devices which can do the same jobs as a vacuum tube and, in some cases, even more.

Power Supply Rectifiers

Older electronics equipment needed a power supply that would furnish more than one voltage. Most of the vacuum tubes needed filament voltages of 5.0, 6.3, or 12.6 volts (V). A winding on the power transformer had to provide these voltages and the current necessary to heat the filaments to boil off the electrons to cause the tubes to operate. Also on the power transformer was a high-voltage winding that would take the 120 V ac put into the primary of the transformer and step it up to over 300 V. This 300 V ac coming out of the transformer had to be changed to dc before the tubes could utilize it on their plates and screen grids. This changing of ac to dc was the job of the diode or rectifier tube.

The majority of rectifier systems that use electron tubes utilize either high-vacuum tubes of the diode design or gas-filled tubes. The high-vacuum tubes are used mostly for low-current applications. The hot-cathode mercury-vapor tubes are used in high-current circuits. The presence of mercury vapor in the tube envelope reduces the vacuum and results in low internal resistance, thus allowing a large amount of current to flow through the tube.

On the other hand, dry-disk rectifiers, such as selenium and copper oxide rectifiers, do not use electron tubes. Selenium rectifiers are sometimes used as plate supply rectifiers in small radio receivers (see Fig. 11.31). Copper oxide rectifiers have miscellaneous applications, for example, they may be used as instrument rectifiers or bias-supply rectifiers. Both these rectifiers have the advantage of not requiring heater current or warmup time.

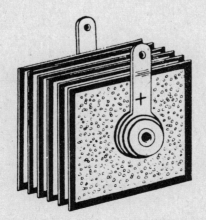

Fig. 11.31.   Selenium dry-disk rectifier stack. Used in older television sets and radios.

High-Vacuum Tubes as Rectifiers

A diode acts as a rectifier because it passes current in only one direction from the cathode to the plate. Conduction takes place only when the plate is positive with respect to the cathode.

The important characteristics of the high-vacuum rectifier tube are its maximum peak plate current and its maximum inverse peak plate voltage ratings.

The peak plate current is limited by the number of electrons emitted by the cathode and therefore is dependent upon cathode construction. Generally speaking, the directly heated type is used with dc filament voltage and the indirectly heated cathode is used with ac filament voltage. This reduces the hum picked up by the tube when it is used in an amplifier application.

It is evident that the current in a single-diode rectifier never flows for more than one-half of each ac hertz. At the power frequency, 60 Hz, the dc output current as indicated by a meter is less than one-half of the peak plate current.

The peak inverse plate voltage is the peak negative voltage that is applied to the plate during the portion of the hertz when the tube is not conducting. The dc output voltage and peak inverse voltage vary with the type of circuit. In general, the peak inverse voltage is equal to or twice the peak value of the dc output voltage.

In addition to low-power applications, high-vacuum rectifiers for high-voltage use have been designed to withstand a peak inverse voltage of 100,000 V. This is still well beyond the capabilities of semiconductor diodes. This is why some high-quality, high-powered amplifiers used by rock musicians still have vacuum tubes instead of semiconductors.

Commercial units have been built to provide peak plate currents as high as 7.5 amperes (A). High-vacuum rectifiers are seldom used for high-voltage, high-current applications except where inherent ruggedness outweighs the other disadvantages. The mercury-vapor rectifier is used in the majority of medium- and high-power equipment.

Rectifier Circuits

Three types of rectifier circuits will be mentioned briefly: the half-wave, the full-wave, and the bridge rectifier. A half-wave rectifier is a device by means of which ac is changed to pulsating direct current (pdc) by permitting current to flow through the device during one-half of the power supply hertz.

Fig. 11.32 shows a simple half-wave rectifier circuit. Note that inside the diode there is a vacuum or a gas, according to which type is needed. The electrons are attracted to the plate of the diode when it is more positive than the cathode. When the plate becomes negative with respect to the cathode, electrons are repelled by it, and no electron stream can flow in the tube. Therefore, a single diode may be used as a half-wave rectifier because the electrons can flow in the tube during only the half of the hertz when the plate is positive relative to the cathode.

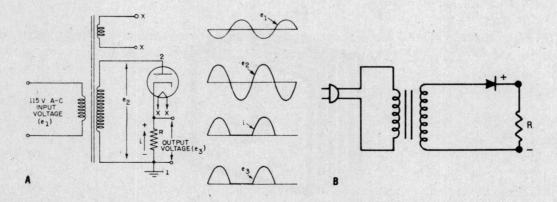

Fig. 11.32.   Half-wave vacuum tube rectifier circuit with waveforms.

A full-wave rectifier is a device that has two or more elements so arranged that the current output flows in the same direction during each half-hertz of the ac power supply. Full-wave rectification may be accomplished by using two diodes in the same envelope (a duo-diode) with a common cathode connected to one end of the load resistor, such as shown in Fig. 11.33. The other end of the load resistor is connected to the center tap of the transformer.

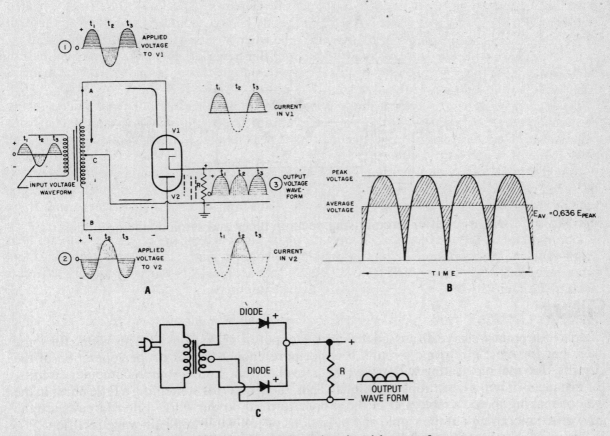

Fig. 11.33.   Full-wave vacuum tube rectifier circuit with waveforms.

Take a look at Fig. 11.34 for a four-vacuum-tube-diode arrangement referred to as a *bridge rectifier circuit*. This is a full-wave rectifier; the output is full-wave as shown in the previous two-diode circuit. There are a couple of advantages to the bridge rectifier over the regular two-tube, or semiconductor, diode, full-wave rectifier. First, the bridge arrangement allows for twice the voltage output from the same power transformer. Secondly, a bridge rectifier circuit is so designed that it has only half the peak inverse voltage impressed on a tube as the full-wave rectifier with only two diodes. *Peak inverse voltage* (piv) is a negative voltage applied across the tube when there is no current flowing through the tube, or diode in the case of semiconductor diodes.

The bridge rectifier that uses vacuum tubes has a disadvantage since it needs three filament transformer windings. This disadvantage, of course, does not apply to the bridge circuit composed of dry-disk or semiconductor diodes since they do not have filaments to contend with.

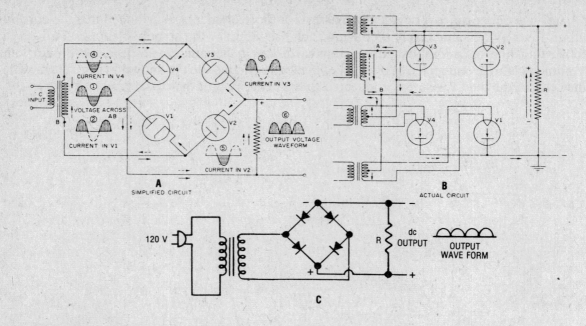

Fig. 11.34. Bridge-rectifier circuit using vacuum tubes and semiconductor diodes.

Filters

Up to this point we have discussed the making of pulsating dc from ac. This is fine for some uses, but for most electronic circuits it is not pure enough dc for proper operation of the circuits. Too much pulsating will make a high level of hum, and in some—computer circuits, for instance—it will give unreliable results. That, then, calls for something a little purer in the way of making the dc usable and of the proper form to do the work. Filter circuits are the answer to smoothing out the ripple and pulsations of full-wave and half-wave rectifiers.

The unfiltered output of a full-wave rectifier is shown in Fig. 11.35. The polarity of the output voltage does not reverse, but its magnitude fluctuates about an average value as the successive pulses of energy are delivered to the load. In Fig. 11.35 the average voltage is shown as the line that divides the waveform so that area A equals area B. The fluctuations of voltage above and below this average value is called the *ripple*. The output of any rectifier is composed of a direct voltage and an alternating or ripple voltage. For most uses, the ripple voltage must be reduced to a very low amplitude. The amount of ripple that can be tolerated varies with different uses of electron tubes and semiconductors. A circuit that eliminates the ripple voltage from the rectifier output is called a *filter*. Filter systems in general are composed of a combination of capacitors, inductors, and in some cases, resistors.

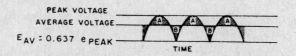

Fig. 11.35. Unfiltered output voltage of a full-wave rectifier.

Vacuum Tubes

When someone who knows something about electronics sees vacuum tubes in a book or article today, he or she thinks the book is dated. However, the day of the vacuum tube is not over. There are a number of good circuits which a vacuum tube can use to great advantage over the transistor. For example, certain types of amplifiers in the musical field contain vacuum tubes for a particular reason: Design engineers want the best-quality sound by the most reliable route. The vacuum tube is rugged in operation and will take many abuses that the semiconductor amplifier will not forgive. The vacuum tube can be overloaded and overdriven and produces some interesting output sounds that are not consistently available with other types of amplification.

Another important application of vacuum tubes is in the field of television. The vacuum tube is used for the *picture tube* in every television set made of any size. The cathode ray tube (CRT) is very much in evidence in computers and terminals located in all types of equipment. The basic knowledge that comes with understanding the vacuum tube should not be amiss if you wish to become a well-rounded, capable electronics technician or engineer.

Vacuum tubes and gas-filled tubes are not a thing of the past. They are used in many sophisticated pieces of equipment even today. The picture *tube of* the television set and the CRT monitor of the computer are *tubes*. They will be around until the liquid crystal display (LCD) can replace them.

The diode (Fig. 11.36) is a tube with two elements. It is used primarily as a rectifier. It comes in both signal type for low voltages and currents and also on the larger variety which can handle power line frequencies and rectify them to provide high voltage and higher currents that signal diodes. Electrons are boiled off the cathode, and the emitted electrons are attracted to the plate of the tube by high positive voltage.

The triode (Fig. 11.37) is made up of three electrodes. It contains a control grid which can cause the tube to amplify signals presented between the grid and cathode. The output of the

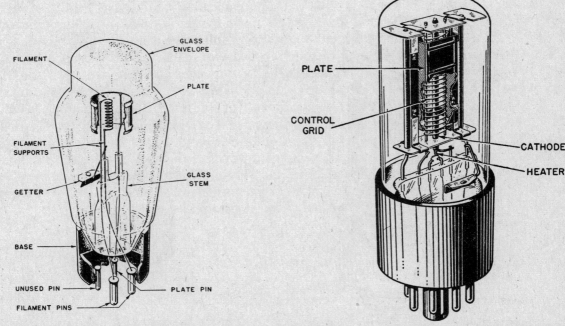

Fig. 11.36. Early model of the diode with a single plate and cathode. The filament was also the cathode in this directly heated tube.

Fig. 11.37. The triode. Note the location of the parts of the tube.

triode has a load resistance usually that has a high voltage drop which varies with the signal applied between the grid and cathode. This increase in voltage from the input to the output makes for amplification. The primary purpose of the triode is amplification, but it does have some frequency limitations that have to be corrected. This is where the tetrode and pentode enter the picture. They were designed to eliminate the interelectrode capacitance between the grid and plate that could cause feedback and unwanted oscillations, producing squeals and howls.

The tetrode (Fig. 11.38) has four elements. It has a screen grid added with a positive potential to get rid of some of the interelectrode capacitance of the triode. This additional grid did produce some rather unwanted results like a dip in the plate current at the beginning part of the characteristic curve. It was overcome by the addition of another grid called the suppressor grid. By the addition of another grid it became the pentode, of five-element, tube. The pentode (Fig.11.39) has a suppressor that is placed near the plate and has a negative potential on it so that the electrons which are emitted from the plate are kept near the plate and will not get in the way of the stream of electrons from the cathode. The measurement for transconductance, or the ability of a tube to conduct current, is the siemen (S) (formerly the mho, or reverse of ohm).

The beam power tube is a pentode with beam-forming plates instead of the suppressor grid. The tube is capable of handling relatively high levels of electric power for use in output stages of receivers and amplifiers. It is used in parts of a transmitter and for power-handling requirements in amplifiers. The ability of the beam power tube to handle power or larger currents makes it ideal as a power amplifier tube.

A number of tubes have more than one tube in an envelope. They have a number of purposes and can be found in many pieces of electronic equipment. A multiunit, or dual-purpose, tube is one in which two or more individual tubes are combined within a single envelope. As a result, economy, compactness, and more satisfactory operation for certain purposes are achieved.

The filament voltage of a vacuum tube is given in the numbers preceding the first letter in its designation, that is, a 5U4 has a 5.0-V filament.

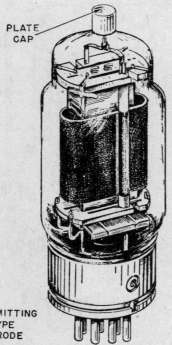

Fig. 11.38.   Various shapes of tetrodes available.

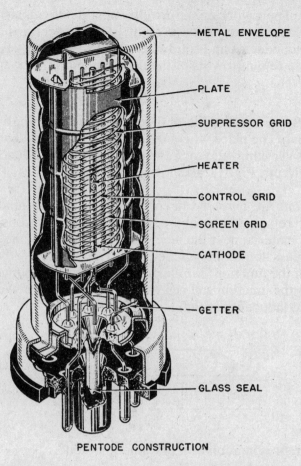

METAL ENVELOPE

PLATE

SUPPRESSOR GRID

HEATER

CONTROL GRID

SCREEN GRID

CATHODE

GETTER

GLASS SEAL

PENTODE CONSTRUCTION

Fig. 11.39.   Construction details of a metal-enveloped pentode.

Semiconductors

The term *semiconductor* is applied to both diodes and transistors as well as to certain special types of electronic devices. The word comes from the fact that germanium and silicon perform somewhere between a conductor and an insulator in terms of opposition to current flow. The amount of opposition is programmed into or manufactured into the device by means of controlling the impurities introduced into a pure germanium or pure silicon atom. Germanium and silicon can be purified to better than 99.999999 percent. Therefore, any introduction of another element is called an *impurity,* or *doping agent.* By controlling the amount of doping agent introduced into each crystalline structure, you can control the amount of opposition to current flow.

A Bit of History   In 1833 Michael Faraday, an English scientist, made a contribution to the crystalline amplifier by working with silver sulfide. He learned that the resistance of silver sulfide varies *inversely* with the temperature. As the temperature increases, the resistance decreases. This was noted as being different since most conductors will have an increase in resistance along with an increase in temperature.

It took over a hundred years before the Faraday discovery was utilized in any meaningful way. The development of the *crystal amplifier* (the transistor's original name) by three Bell Laboratory scientists utilized the work of Faraday and expanded on it. In June of 1948 John Bardeen, William Shockley, and W. H. Brattain shared an office and rode to work together at

Bell Labs in New Jersey. Their work on the development of the transistor led to Nobel Prizes for each. From the announcement day to the present, there has been no letup in the research and development of the semiconductor and solid state physics. Present-day computers and space communications devices are outgrowths of the development of a crystal that would amplify and switch.

Semiconductor Diodes   A semiconductor diode is made by joining a piece of the P material with a piece of N material. The place where the two materials are joined is referred to as the *junction*. This junction is very thin, and each end has a piece of wire attached for connecting the diode thus made into a circuit. Fig. 11.40 shows how the two pieces of material form a diode junction.

Both holes and electrons are involved in conduction in the PN junction diode. There are minority carriers in both regions: holes in the N material and electrons in the P material. The holes produced in the N material near the junction are attracted by the negative ions on the P side of the junction and pass across the junction. These holes will tend to neutralize the negative ions on the P side of the junction. Similarly, free electrons produced on the P side of the junction will pass across the junction and neutralize positive ions on the N side. This action is an example of intrinsic conduction, which is undesirable.

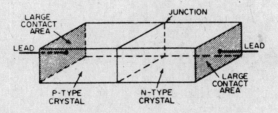

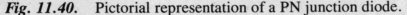

Fig. 11.40.   Pictorial representation of a PN junction diode.

This flow of minority carriers weakens the potential barrier around the atoms that they neutralize. When this happens, majority carriers are able to cross the junction at the location of the neutral atom. This means that holes from the P material will cross over to the N material, and electrons from the N material will cross over to the P material.

This action results in both holes and electrons crossing the junction in both directions. These motions cancel each other and the net movement contributes nothing toward the net charge or current flow through the junction. Because of intrinsic conduction, the junction is no longer a rectifier when an external voltage is applied across it. It is analogous to an electron tube diode in which not only the cathode emits electrons, but the plate is heated to the point where it also will emit enough electrons to break down the rectifying properties of the diode.

Operation of the Junction Diode   When an electron leaves the donor atom in the N region and moves over to the P region (see Fig. 11.41), the atom has fewer electrons than it needs to neutralize the positive charge on the nucleus, and it becomes charged (ionized). It has one extra positive charge equal to the negative charge of the electron which it lost.

Similarly, when a hole leaves an acceptor atom in the P region, the atom takes on a negative charge, because the hole has been filled by an electron, and the atom has one more electron than it needs to neutralize the charge on its nucleus.

These charged atoms, or ions as they are called, are fixed in place in the crystal lattice structure, and cannot move. Thus, they make up a layer of fixed charges on both sides of the junction. On the N side of the junction there is a layer of positively charged ions; on the P side there is a layer of negatively charged atoms or ions.

In Fig. 11.41 there is a barrier of negative ions on the P side of the junction. This negative barrier will repel electrons from the immediate vicinity of the junction and will prevent the diffusion of any more electrons from the N side over into the P side of the crystal. Similarly on the N side of the junction there is a barrier of the positive ions which will repel holes away from the immediate vicinity of the P side of the junction and prevent diffusion of any additional holes across the junction from the P material into the N material.

The two layers of ionized atoms form a barrier to any further diffusion across the junction. Because the charges at the junction force the majority carriers away from the junction, the barrier is known as the *depletion layer*. It is also known as the barrier layer, or barrier potential.

The charge on the impurity atoms is distributed across the PN junction as shown in Fig. 11.41. In the P region the ionized acceptors have a negative charge, and in the N region the ionized donor atoms have a positive charge. At the junction, the charge is zero.

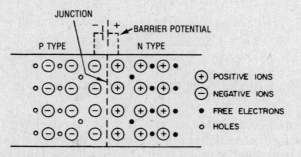
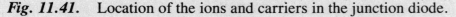

Fig. 11.41. Location of the ions and carriers in the junction diode.

However, in the P region there are holes which have a positive charge, and in the N region there are free electrons which have a negative charge. The distribution of holes and free electrons is shown in the illustration.

The potentials at the junction have driven the holes away from the junction in the P region and the electrons away from the junction in the N region so that the charges in the P region and the N region are moved farther apart. The charge at the junction is zero. The net charges on the crystal in the P region are equal to the difference between the charge on the ionized acceptor atoms and the electrons. These charges cancel except in the immediate region of the junction.

In the area near the junction there is a negative charge in the P region and a positive charge in the N region. As stated previously, they act as a barrier to prevent further diffusion of holes from the P region into the N region and the diffusion of electrons from the N region into the P region. This potential barrier is a potential difference, or voltage, across the junction and is in the order of a few tenths of a volt. It may be represented as a dotted battery with the negative terminal connected to the P material and with the positive terminal connected to the N material.

This barrier potential is like the plate-cathode voltage of a diode. If the plate is made positive and the cathode is made negative, the diode can be made to conduct a current. If the plate is negative with respect to the cathode, the diode will block the flow of current. Thus, the diode tube is a rectifier. The semiconductor diode also is a rectifier.

The Point Contact Diode   There are a number of diodes. They are designed for special applications in some cases. The point contact diode is a very small, physically speaking, unit that is used for rectifying signals. The junction diode is used for rectifying power line frequencies and higher currents.

Unlike the junction diode, the point contact (Fig. 11.42) type depends on the pressure or contact between a point and a semiconductor crystal for its operation. One section consists of a small rectangular crystal of N material (either germanium or silicon) and a fine beryllium-

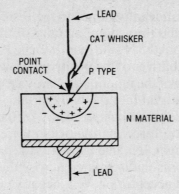

Fig. 11.42. A point contact diode.

Fig. 11.43. Symbol for a diode. Note the (+) end is the cathode.

copper, phosphor-bronze, or tungsten wire called the *cat whisker.* The cat whisker presses against the semiconductor material and forms the other part of the diode. The reason for using a fine-pointed wire instead of a flat metal plate is to produce a high-density electric field at the point of contact without using too large an external voltage source. The opposite end of the cat whisker is used as the diode terminal for connection purposes.

Both contacts with the external circuit are low-resistance connections. During the manufacturing process of the point contact diode, a relatively large current is passed through the cat whicser to the silicon crystal. The result of this large current is the formation of a small region of P material around the crystal in the vicinity of the point contact. Thus, there is a PN junction formed which behaves in the same way as the PN junction described in the junction diode operation.

This very small contact area has a reduced capacitance effect (over the junction type with two pieces of material actually touching along a wide surface) that can be used for rectifying higher frequencies than the junction diode. However, since the size of the cat whicser is limited, the amount of current the diode can handle is also limited.

Tunnel Diodes   Tunnel diodes can be used in extremely small spaces such as part of an integrated circuit (IC) or chip. They can switch at very high rates (2 to 10 GH$_z$). A gigahertz (GH$_z$) is 1000 (MH$_z$). A megahertz is *1 million times per second,* and a gigahertz is *1000 times faster than that.*

Tunnel diodes are doped by using gallium arsenide, gallium antimonide, and indium antimonide.

The Silicon Controlled Rectifier (SCR)

Another type of specialized rectifier or diode is the silicon controlled rectifier (SCR). It has another name, but the SCR was coined by General Electric (GE) and has persisted. It was originally the *thyrister.* Inasmuch as GE dominated the marketplace, it soon became known by GE's abbreviated version.

The SCR is a four-layer device. That is, it has either an NPNP or PNPN arrangement for the semiconductor materials. It is a specialized type of device used for the control of current through its cathode-to-anode path. A gate is used to control the resistance between the cathode and anode. By applying a small voltage between the gate and the cathode, it is possible to control that resistance and, as a result, the amount of current flow through the device. An SCR conducts current in the *forward* direction only. The symbol for the device is shown in Fig. 11.44.

Fig. 11.45 shows a circuit with an SCR. The function of an SCR is current control. Examples of this are the light dimmer or the speed control for a small hand drill or other hand tool that is electrically powered. The resistor is a rheostat. This adjustable resistor is used to control the amount of voltage delivered to the gate of the SCR. The greater the voltage, the less the anode-to-cathode resistance and the more current is allowed to flow through the cathode-anode connection. By adjusting the rheostat, it is possible to control the amount of current flow through the device. As the current increases, the load—if a lamp—will get brighter. As the current increases, the load—if a drill or electric motor—speeds up. Thus, the SCR can be used to control either type of circuit. Other control circuits also use the SCR for their main operating device. Fig. 11.46 shows two of the design packages for SCRs.

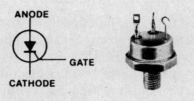

Fig. 11.44.   Symbol for SCR, or thyrister.

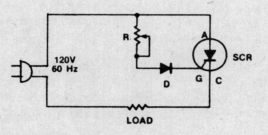

Fig. 11.45.   A circuit with the SCR as a control device.

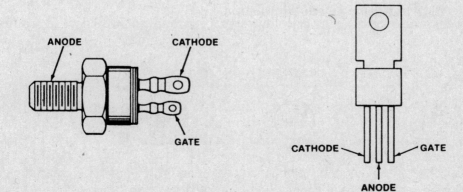

Fig. 11.46.   Two packages used for SCRs.

Transistors

The word *transistor* comes from two other words: **trans**fer and re**sistor.** Thus, it is a transfer resistor or a device that has more impedance (resistance) in the input than in the output, or the other way around depending on its use. By having a difference in impedance between the input and output, it is able to amplify.

There are two ways in which transistors are used. One is switching, and the other is amplifying a signal. The switching ability of a semiconductor has previously been discussed under the diode section of this chapter. However, we will mention it briefly here in the study of transistors. Main emphasis will be on the ability of the transistor to amplify and thereby serve as a replacement for the vacuum tube.

Transistors are made from N and P materials, such as the semiconductor diode. Once they are joined, they resemble two diodes back to back (see Fig. 11.47).

Transistors have an emitter, a base, and a collector. These are the connections to the N and P materials that make up the device. We will look at two types of transistors here: the point contact and the junction transistor.

The point contact was developed first. The junction transistor followed later. Transistors are classified as PNP or NPN according to the arrangement of the impurities in the crystal. Symbols used for transistors are shown in Fig. 11.48.

The point contact transistor is similar to the point contact diode except that it has two cat whiskers instead of one. The two cat whiskers are placed with their point contacts very close together (about 0.002 in.). The diameter of the contacts is about 0.005 in. The contacts are arranged to provide a springlike pressure on the flat surface of the crystal (see Fig. 11.49). The crystal may be either N or P germanium.

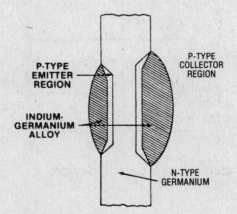

Fig. 11.47.   PNP transistor junction formation.

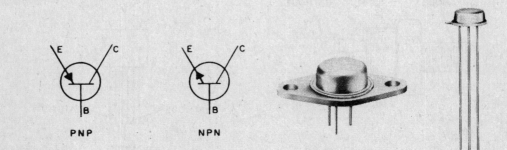

Fig. 11.48.   Transistor symbols.

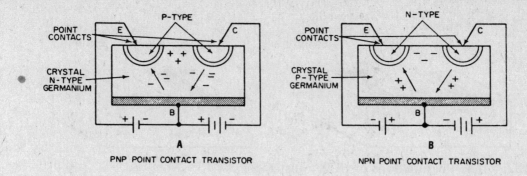

Fig. 11.49.   Point contact transistors.

A wide variety of types of transistors have evolved during the short period of time that they have been available. In addition to the point contact transistor you should be aware of three or four other main types in your study of electronics.

Junction Transistors   Fig. 11.50, shows the current flow in the external circuit of a PNP junction transistor. The junction transistor uses the same semiconductor materials as the point contact transistor but is arranged in the form of a sandwich. There are also transistors with NPN or the opposite configuration. This means that the polarity of the power source is opposite to that of the PNP transistor. The silicon transistor is usually NPN. A few are made with the PNP, but in most instances the PNP is the germanium.

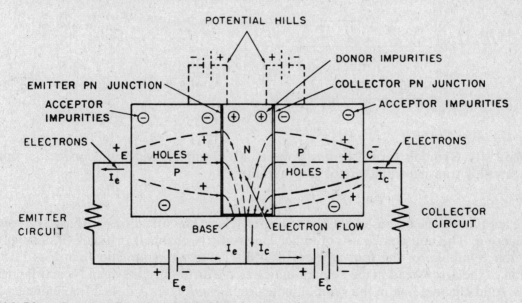

Fig. 11.50.   Current flow in a PNP junction transistor.

Other types of transistors are alloy transistors, grown-junction transistors, microalloy transistors, germanium mesa and silicon planar transistors, and field-effect transistors. Field-effect transistors, or FETs, as they are called, are small in size and are mechanically rugged. They have low power consumption and high input impedance similar to a vacuum tube.

The term MOS means *metal-oxide semiconductor.* The metal control gate is separated from the semiconductor channel. An FET is not affected by the polarity of the bias on the control gate. Changes in temperature affect the FET. They are used in voltage amplifiers, RF amplifiers, and voltage-controlled attenuators. To attenuate means to *reduce.*

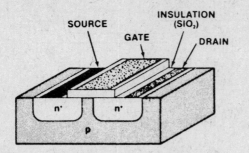
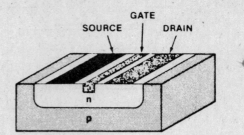

Fig. 11.51.   The PN junctions of FET transistors.

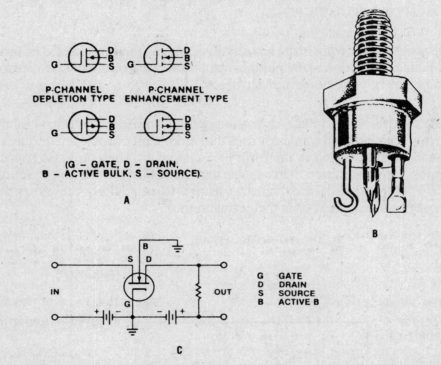

Fig. 11.52   A. Symbols for FET transistors. B. MOS (metal-oxide semiconductor) transistor. C. An FET transistor in a circuit configuration.

There are four distinct types of MOS transistors. These classifications are based on sources of conduction. The units make use of either electrons (N channel) or holes (P channel) for conduction. Symbols for the four types of MOSFET transistors are shown in Fig. 11.52A. Direction of the arrowhead in the symbol indicates the difference between N- and P-channel types. A solid channel line in the symbol indicates *normally on.* A dotted line indicates *normally off.*

MOS field-effect transistors (MOSFETs) are used in broadcast band receivers in low-power circuits. Their use can be seen in RF amplifiers and converters. They are also used in IF stages and the first audio. In other words, they are used in almost all the circuits in a broadcast receiver except the output stage that drives the speaker.

Fig. 11.52C consists of a circuit with a MOSFET transistor. Note the parts and how they are connected in the circuit. They can be used in FM receivers as well as AM receivers. The FM receiver uses FETs in the RF amplifier, conversion stages, IF stages, and limiter stages. They are as versatile as the vacuum tube and substitute almost directly in the circuits designed for tubes. However, the voltages are different, and there is no need for a filament in an FET.

Amplitude-Modulated Receivers

In this discussion we will limit our study to a six-transistor AM receiver that is most often purchased in a discount store for less than $10. Communications receivers have some special circuits that are not important to the basics of AM reception at this time.

The block diagram of an AM receiver will give us some idea of how the entire unit operates, then we will take it stage by stage to obtain the circuit functions. See Fig. 11.53 for a block diagram of the AM receiver.

Note how the signal is injected from the antenna into the RF amplifier. This is the case in most communications and more expensive sets. If you have a standard six-transistor type, there will be no RF amplifier. The mixer will be the first stage to view. However, in the interest of getting a better look at the receiver, we will take a closer look at the RF amplifier when we analyze the circuit functions later in the chapter.

The RF amplifier takes the antenna signal and selects it. The broadcast AM band covers a wideband of frequencies (535 to 1605 kHz). This wideband of frequencies has to be beaten down to one in order for selectivity to be improved. This is where the principle of heterodyning comes in.

Heterodyning takes place in the mixer stage. This is where two frequencies (in this case the incoming frequency from the antenna, which is selected by the first tuning circuit) are mixed or beaten against a local oscillator frequency. The local oscillator puts out nonmodulated frequency. However, the incoming frequency is modulated. The beating of the two frequencies produces the sum and difference frequencies, and the original two are also present. All four frequencies are now modulated in the collector tank circuit which is the output of the mixer stage. Once the proper frequency [455kHz is the usual *intermediate frequency* (IF) selected for AM] is selected, it is passed on to the IF amplifier because of the signal loss during the previous processing. There may be a minimum of two IF amplifiers to amplify the signal, each time there is a tuned circuit tuned to only 455 kHz with ± 5 kHz for sidebands.

After the IF with the sidebands or modulation is amplified to the desired level, it is put through the detector stage where the modulation is taken from the RF carrier and passed on to the audio amplifiers. This audio amplification causes the signal to be of the proper level to drive a speaker.

The automatic volume control (AVC) or automatic gain control (AGC) is part of the detector stage and feeds back a strong bias voltage when the signal is too strong and cuts down on the amplification of the signal before it can be heard by the human ear as being too loud. The power supply is needed to furnish the proper voltages for the operation of the various stages.

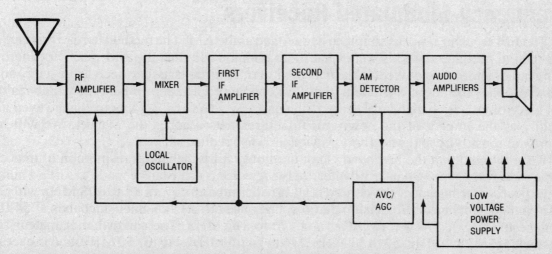

Fig. 11.53.   Block diagram of an AM receiver with an RF stage.

The first stage in a AM receiver is the RF amplifier. The major assignment of the RF amplifier is to amplify the incoming signals from the antenna after a particular one has been selected. Four characteristics of the RF stage are very important in any receiver. It should have the proper ability to amplify or produce the required gain; it should have a low noise output since the signal itself will have a certain amount of noise depending on the signal-to-noise ratio of the received signal; it will need to be selective since it has the entire band to select from; it will also need to have a linear characteristic throughout the entire band of AM frequencies.

Keep in mind that the RF amplifier stage is not a common stage for less expensive, portable radios used for local reception. It is used in military equipment, ham radios, or advanced communications receivers and in the more demanding situations where special equipment is needed for receiving weak signals.

The oscillator stage is needed whenever heterodyning is used to improve the selectivity of a receiver. It produces the beat frequency which is used to beat against the incoming frequency to produce the IF.

The purpose of combining a RF with an oscillator frequency to produce an IF is called *mixing,* or *frequency conversion.*

There is usually a minimum of two IF amplifiers. The major function of the IF amplifier is to give the signal good linear amplification through the range of frequencies it will be handling. The main objective of the amplifier after its use as an amplifier is to provide selectivity. By using a couple of additional tuned circuits tuned to the same frequency, it is possible to become very selective. That is one of the reasons for using superheterodynes rather than some earlier type of receiver. The 455-kHz signal has been chosen as the input to the first IF, and the output of that stage is also tuned. The 455-kHz signal is fed to the second IF and amplified further so that it is sufficient to be rectified by the detector to provide an audio signal that is not too noisy.

In most AM receivers the bandwidth is about 3 kHz. this severely limits the quality of music heard from the speakers. That means the IF cans have to be tuned to 455 kHz $\pm$ 3 kHz.

Now, let us back up for a minute and look at the automatic gain control, or as it is sometimes called the *automatic volume control.* This stage is used to adjust the amplification of the RF and IF stages. The strength of the input signal determines the loudness of the speaker. Therefore controls must be placed on the RF and IF stages if we want to control the volume. If the signals that reach the antenna are weak, the signal amplitude reaching the detector will also be weak, producing a low output volume. If strong signals are received, they will create overload signal conditions in the amplifiers and cause distortion. To correct this, a feedback signal is used to adjust bias on the first IF amplifier.

Frequency-Modulated Receivers

The FM receiver is not as simple to understand as the AM. The method used to produce FM and then to produce stereo is somewhat more complicated than the AM receiver. There are some rather interesting devices in the way of integrated circuits used to decode the stereo signal and to produce the output sufficient to drive a couple of speakers. In fact, the whole realm of FM electronics has changed markedly in the past few years and is going to change even more rapidly as the impact of the newly manufactured sets reaches the market. We will have improved sensitivity and selectivity as well as noise reduction.

Keep in mind that the FM band is not used only for wideband transmission of music for home receivers. Narrowband FM where only the voice is used can be made to serve a number of purposes. For instance, the commercial broadcast band covers 88 to 108 MHz with 200-kHz channel sidebands. Television audio signals use 50-kHz channel sidebands at 54 to 88 megahertz (MHz), 174 to 216 MHz, and 470 to 890 MHz. The narrowband amateur radio channels are at 29.6 MHz, 52 to 53 MHz, 146 to 147.5 MHz, 440 to 450 MHz, and in excess of 890 MHz for experimental purposes.

There is a reason for not using FM on frequencies lower than 30 MHz. The earth's iono-sphere introduces phase distortion to FM signals at frequencies below the 30-MHz point. The line-of-sight method of transmission is used for those signals above 30 MHz because of nat-ure's way of not reflecting these signals and allowing them to continue through the ionosphere. Since the earth curves, it limits the communications range of FM to about 80 mi maximum. This is especially true of the narrowband public service channels that operate on 108 to 175 MHz, right in between channels 6 and 7 on TV. The narrowband is also assigned to frequencies in excess of 890 MHz. Output power from a TV FM transmitter is about 50 kilowatts (kW), while the amateurs use some walkie-talkies with only 100 milliwatts (mW) of power.

Of course, one of the main advantages of FM over AM is its ability to transmit music with very little noise, or static, being heard in the receiver. This was one of the selling points in its favor when it was introduced and then dropped and introduced once again.

Fig. 11.54 shows a block diagram of the FM receiver with the stages needed for reception of the standard monaural signal.

The antenna is usually a piece of wire where the signal is very strong, but a folded dipole is needed if any type of signal strength is desired at the front end of the receiver. The first two stages are called the front end of the receiver, which usually includes the RF amplifier and the mixer.

The RF amplifier, or preselector, performs the same function in the FM receiver as it does in the AM receiver, that is, it increases the sensitivity of the receiver. Such an increase in sensitivity is often a practical necessity in fringe areas. However, the gain of the IF stages is relatively much greater, perhaps 100 times that of the preselector, since the chief advantage of the superheterodyne lies in the uniformity of response and gain of the IF stages within the receiver band. The principal functions of the RF stage are to discriminate against undesired signals and to increase the amplitude of weak signals so that the signal-to-noise ratio will be improved.

Mixing the incoming FM signal with the set's oscillator frequency is basically the same in principle, but the frequencies are changed. FM for home use employs the 10.7-MHz IF. The beating together of the incoming frequency and the oscillator frequency produces the 10.7-MHz IF. This signal is passed on the IF strip where it is amplified. The IFs are important here since they take the signal from the mixer and amplify it sufficiently for detection. They also increase the selectivity of the set since the heterodyning principle produces the IF for the purpose of allowing it to be amplified by stages which are tuned slightly off their normal 10.7-MHz. This detuning produces a wide enough bandwidth to allow the modulation (up to 200 kHz) to pass through the IF cans.

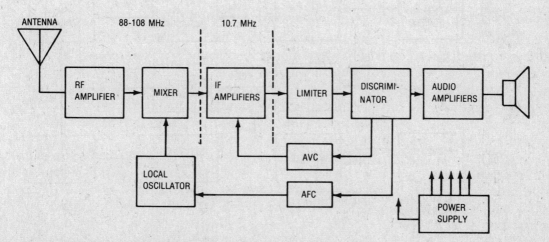

Fig. 11.54. Block diagram of a basic FM receiver.

The IF cans in the IF stages are stagger-tuned to produce a wide enough bandpass for the music to pass through. This means that there are usually three IF stages in an FM receiver.

A limiter puts out a signal with a constant amplitude. This eliminates any noise that may be riding on the incoming signal. A good limiter is essential to the proper operation of an FM receiver. The limiter stage also provides automatic gain control (AGC) since its signals are from minimum value up to a maximum value constant in amplitude. This provides a constant input level to the discriminator. Limiters require an input signal voltage of at least 1 V. This is why the IFs are used to boost the signal from the antenna (which may be about 1.5 μV) to this level. The sensitivity of an FM set refers to how much input signal is required to produce a specific level of quieting. This is normally 30 decibels (dB). A good-quality receiver will have a sensitivity of 1.5 μV with a background noise 30 dB down from the input signal level of 1.5 μV. Most IF stages in today's receivers are made in integrated circuits that have built-in limiting action.

The translation of the FM variations into audio is the function of the discriminator, ratio detector, or slope detector. The detection takes place at the 10.7-MHz level of the IF. The IF has the modulation ($\pm$75 kHz) on it and must be separated to obtain good audio for the audio stages.

In order for the receiver to operate properly, the local oscillator that beats against the incoming frequency must be stable in its output frequency to produce the 10.7-MHz needed for the IFs. One way of keeping an oscillator frequency stable is to keep the voltages applied to the transistor (or vacuum tube) constant. This source of voltage correction can be obtained from the output of the audio stage. Take this dc produced by the audio signal and feed it back to the local oscillator to keep it on frequency.

The AFC may cause the receiver to miss some weak stations when tuning. That is why the *defeat switch* is used. FM and AFC are the switch labels used to designate this condition. The FM or defeat position means weaker stations can be tuned in and then the AFC turned on to capture or hold the stations.

Newer receivers do not use the AFC system of control since the problem of keeping an oscillator over 100 MHz from drifting is no longer the problem it once was. The newer chips and phase-locked loops have automatic correction for frequency drift.

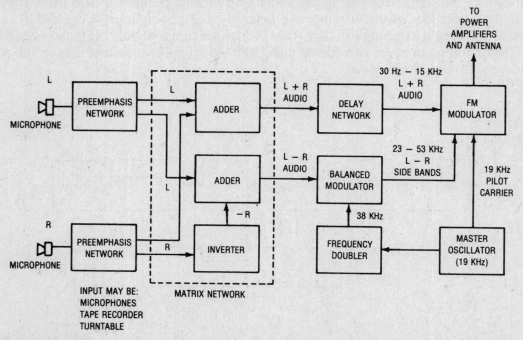

Fig. 11.55 FM stereo transmitter.

Once the signals have been detected, the audio is coupled to the audio amplifiers. In the AM-FM sets the same audio section takes care of both the AM and FM outputs. However, they are switched with an external source usually mounted so that the AM, FM, and stereo are marked on the switch. FM stereo calls for two speakers and two amplifiers for the audio.

FM Stereo

Most of today's FM receivers are made with stereo. For the receiver to receive and decode this stereo signal, several stages have to be added to the regular monaural FM receiver.

Fig. 11.55 shows a typical block diagram for such a receiver. The FCC authorized FM stereo in 1961. This made it possible for home receivers to obtain the complete information on records and tapes which were already available. Stereo uses two separate signals to produce a spatial dimension to the music or speech. This also called for another channel to be added to the FM single-channel transmissions. Stereo high fidelity requires two channels of 30-Hz to 15-kHz signals to modulate the carrier frequency in such a way that the receiver can separate them and reproduce the outputs in a left and right speaker.

More efficient use of the 200-kHz bandwidth was the answer to the stereo problem. This was done by the process of multiplexing. *Multiplexing* is the simultaneous transmission of two different signals on one carrier. It is also possible to broadcast more than two under the right conditions. The FCC approved a compatible system for stereo broadcasts. This means that the

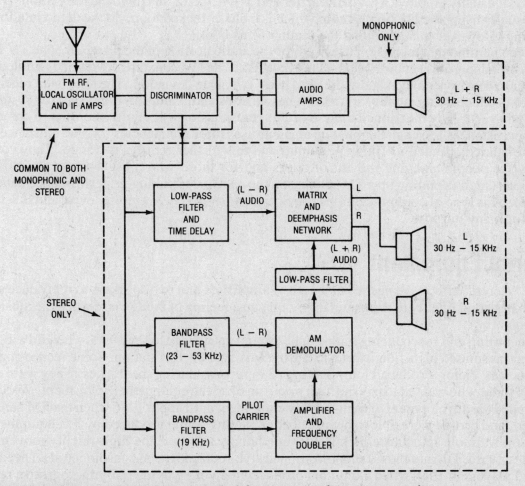

Fig. 11.56 Comparison of stages needed for mono and stereo reception.

stereo and the FM monaural signals can be received on receivers that normally receive the monaural. Or, the stereo receiver can receive the monaural signal and reproduce it properly.

The FM receiver and the FM stereo receiver are the same up to the discriminator stage. At this point the stereo signal must be detected and processed properly to add the missing channel.

Take a look at Fig. 11.56 to see the common stages and those needed for obtaining the extra channel. The output of the discriminator is 30 Hz to 15 kHz, or the audio frequencies normally transmitted by the monaural transmitter, but there is also the 19-kHz subcarrier and the 23-kHz to 53-kHz (L − R) signal. The 30- to 15-kHz signal is called the L + R signal. Keep in mind that the 19 kHz is above the human hearing range and the audio amplifiers are not capable in most instances of amplifying it.

The standard monaural receiver reproduces the 30-Hz to 15-kHz (L + R) signal and is not aware of the other frequencies. That makes it compatible with stereo signals; since it does not have the stages to reproduce it, the other channel is ignored, and the L + R signal is sufficient to broadcast what is normally heard through one channel or speaker.

Other FM Users

There are other users of FM. The FCC allows some stations to multiplex music on a channel with no commercials, and the station owner can charge customers for the music they use as background for workers in plants, on elevators, and in offices.

This multiplexing system is referred to as the subsidiary communication authorization (SCA). It usually employs a 67-kHz carrier and a ±7.5-kHz (narrowband) deviation. Decoders, usually using the NE 565 IC chip which is a phase-locked loop, do the demodulation and filtering. However this is beyond the realm of this book.

Keep in mind that television uses FM for the audio portion of the program. The TV FM is not as broadband as regular FM on 88 to 108 MHz. The FM standard deviation is limited to ± 25 kHz to conserve on the bandwidth. FM uses ±75-kHz deviation. The television receiver is able to produce better-quality sound if it has a better audio amplifier and speaker system.

We have already mentioned the use of FM transmission by people who wish to communicate for distances less than 80 mi. The amateur uses these frequencies for short distances; the walkie-talkie is limited to 100-mW output, and this further reduces its range. They come in handy for people enjoying the out of doors and for those who must work in two different locations (such as putting up a TV antenna on the roof and checking its performance inside the house). This type of communications provides comparatively low noise levels and is satisfactory for many purposes.

Stereo Equipment

For a "stereo" effect, we needed at least two amplifiers and two speakers to reproduce sound which has good fidelity to the original, giving you a feeling of *being there* when the music was recorded.

Recording and reproducing high-quality sound dates back to the 1930s when Edwin Armstrong transmitted high-fidelity musical programs over his FM station. Some record companies, such as Victor, produced long-playing 33⅓ records during the thirties. They were available to those who wanted to pay the high prices and had the equipment to play them. World War II stopped the development of high-fidelity equipment until about 1946 when the FM band was shifted, and people were able to hear the better-fidelity sound produced by FM equipment. In 1947 the variable reluctance pickup for the phonograph gave the high-fidelity movement a boost forward. Diamond- and sapphire-tipped styli replaced the old-fashioned steel needle for record players in 1948 when Columbia produced the long-playing (LP) microgroove record, and plastic records replaced the shellac. The development of the Williamson amplifier and the use of two-speaker systems launched the movement toward today's high-quality sound.

The word *stereo* is derived from the Greek meaning "solid," or "three-dimensional," space. When properly reproduced, stereophonic sound creates an aural perspective and produces a feeling of presence and an illusion of depth. It causes the ear to reject distortion and helps it to hear a wider range of frequencies. A primitive attempt to demonstrate stereo sound reproduction was made at the Paris Exposition of 1881 when engineers used two telephone circuits for the transmission of programs from the stage of the Paris Opera.

There are a number of types of microphones — carbon, dynamic, velocity, ribbon, and crystal. Turntables and record changers are used to produce music from recorded disks. Turntables can produce a higher-quality sound than a record changer. There are at least six types of record pickups or styli. The first magnetic recorder was produced in Denmark in 1898 by Valdemar Poulsen. Recording tapes today are available in $1/4$-, $1/2$-, $3/4$-, 1-, and 2-in widths. Everything is recorded on tape from music to television pictures and sound to computer data. Preamplifiers are usually needed to amplify the inputs to stereo power amplifiers. The vacuum tube push-pull amplifier was one of the standbys of olden days for power amplification.

Today the transistor and integrated circuit (IC) have replaced the vacuum tube in most applications.

The permanent magnet (PM) speaker is the most popular today and comes in a wide variety of diameters and shapes. The size of voice coil wire limits the amount of current a speaker can handle. Crossover networks control which speaker reproduces the various frequencies. There are a number of different speaker enclosures. One of them is the bass-reflex type which has a ducted port or hole in the front. Other types include the infinite baffle and the plane baffle.

Transducers

Transducers are devices that convert pressure, light, heat, and sound to electrical energy. A microphone is a good example. It uses the pressure waves of sound to produce a varying electrical current. This varying current is then amplified and fed to a speaker so it can be heard, or it is recorded on tape, disc or wire. The oil pressure gage in an automobile has a transducer causing it to operate. The transducer operates by pressure of the oil on a diaphram that causes a change in resistance in the circuit therefore causing the meter or gage to read the pressure of the oil. The same is true with the temperature gage in a car. The heat causes the resistance of the transducer to change. This change in resistance causes a change in current in the circuit which is indicated by the movement of the meter needle. The meter is calibrated in degrees Fahrenheit instead of milliamperes.

Transducers take many forms and are used in any number of electronic devices. Without transducers, the electrical control and operation of devices would be extremely limited.

Television

A number of basic elements must be considered in setting up any television system:
- Camera and scanning
- Sync signals
- Video amplifiers
- Audio amplifiers
- FM transmitter for audio
- AM transmitter for video

Camera Tubes   A number of different camera tubes were tried before the ones available today, which can work in low levels of light, were produced. The oldest was the iconoscope developed in 1933 by Zworykin. The iconoscope tube had an electron gun with a magnetic beam deflection yoke located in the handle (see Fig. 11.57). The photosensitive mosaic consisted of silver globules, sensitized with cesium and deposited on one side of a mica sheet, the other side had a metallic backing. The mica was the dielectric of the capacitor formed by the silver deposit and the metal plate. When light struck the silver surface, it produced photoemission at each of the silver globules. An electron beam scanned the surface and struck each globule that was charged by the light striking it. The electrons from the scan replaced the electrons lost by photoemission. This caused a proportionate current pulse to flow in the signal plate. The amplitudes of the pulses from the signal plate current would then represent the relative brightnesses of the mosaic elements as the beam scanned across them.

The iconoscope had some very strong light requirements and was replaced by the image orthicon (see Fig. 11.58). That tube worked basically the same with some improvement in light levels. It was bulky, temperamental, and costly. It was the standard tube used in television studios for a number of years. However, another type of camera tube was the vidicon. It was smaller, simpler, and more rugged than the image orthicon. Its operation is somewhat different also since its target depends on photoconductivity rather than photoemission.

The vidicon works by having an image focused through a transparent conductive film. The film acts as the signal electrode. The image is impressed on the photoconductive target. The target is biased slightly positive. When the layer is not exposed to light, such as in darkness, it acts as an insulator. The electron gun provides a beam. The beam is slowed by the wall coating and screen to a moderate velocity and deflected magnetically. Once the scanning beam strikes the back of the target, it neutralizes the charge on the target. This causes the target to give up just enough electrons to make up for those that leaked through the partially conductive coatings since the last scan. As the brightness of the target area increases, so does the conductivity of the target. This produces a larger leakage current and a greater number of electrons taken from the beam. This action produces a burst of current at the signal electrode in proportion to the brightness of the spot being scanned.

More sensitive tubes are being developed. It is now possible to make color television programs at night using available light. The tubes have become more rugged for use in portable home cameras. They also use less light to obtain an acceptable picture.

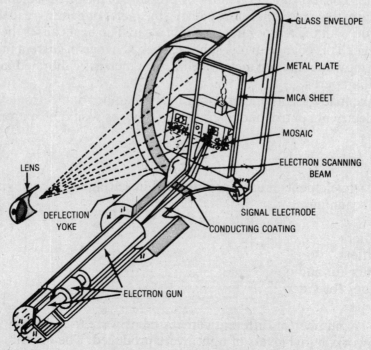

Fig. 11.57. The iconoscope.

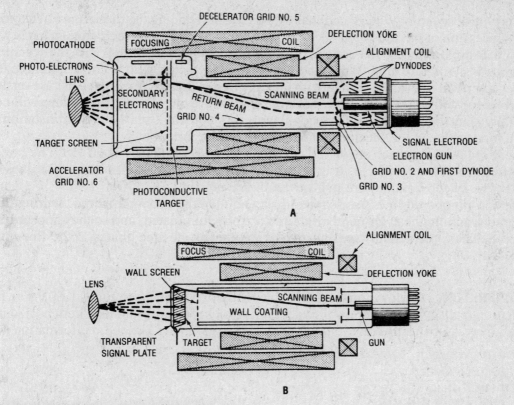

Fig. 11.58 A. Image orthicon. B. Vidicon.

Scanning   In order to have the camera tube operate, it has to be scanned. The beam of light which scans the target area is swept back and forth and up and down. The rate at which it is moved from left to right and from top to bottom of the area will determine what type of picture is reproduced at the receiver.

The Electronics Industries Association standard for the United States is 525 lines horizontally (see Fig. 11.59). The 525 lines are produced as the beam scans from top to bottom of the image area. This scanning is done in one-thirtieth of a second. This scan from top to bottom is called *one frame.* However, in the interlaced method, the sweep is from top to bottom in one-sixtieth of a second. This means that the odd-numbered lines are swept from top to bottom, and then the beam returns to sweep the even-numbered lines from top to bottom. The two fields make up a frame.

Fig. 11.59.   The 525 scan lines for a TV picture.

This type of scanning, interlaced, has a tendency of reducing the flickering effect produced by the succession of pictures. The receiver uses the same scanning technique. That is why the sync signals are produced: to keep the transmitter scanning rate in step with the scanning rate of the receiver's picture tube. If they are not in step, the picture will become scrambled. If the receiver's vertical scan is out of step with the transmitter's vertical scan, the picture on the tube at the receiver will roll slowly. If the horizontal scans are out of sync, the picture will become diagonally slanted and will not be recognizable. As you can see, the synchronization of the camera tube scan and the receiver tube scan is very important.

There are 60 fields each second. The vertical sweep frequency is 60 Hz. The horizontal sweep frequency is 15,750 Hz. It is based on the fact that 30 frames times 525 lines equals 15,750. The sweep voltages are in a sawtooth waveform.

The odd-numbered lines are scanned first and then the even-numbered. During the odd-numbered scanning the even-numbered lines are not illuminated, and so they appear black on the screen. Thus, you actually see only half of the lines at one time, that is, 262.5 lines make up a field.

TV Transmitter   A television transmitter is really two in one (see Fig. 11.60). The picture information (called video) is transmitted with its synchronization signals, both horizontal and vertical, by way of an amplitude-modulated (AM) transmitter. The audio information is trans-

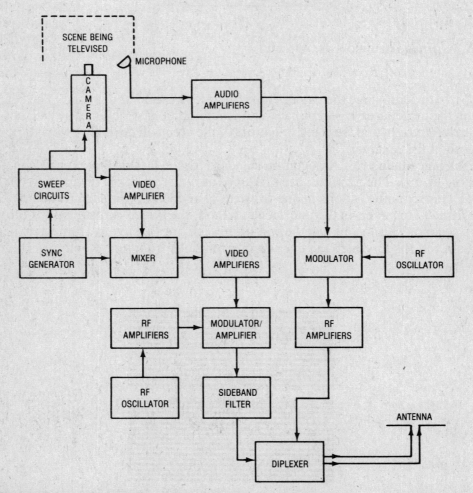

Fig. 11.60   Black and white TV transmitter block diagram.

mitted by a frequency-modulated (FM) transmitter. They both use the same antenna. The band of frequencies which contain both picture and audio is 6-megahertz (MHz) wide.

The critical part of the video transmitter is the sync generator. It provides all the critical timing functions to both the local camera's sweep circuits and to the mixer for transmission to the receiver's sync circuits. The output of the camera is amplified and mixed, with the sync signals forming the composite video signal. The rest of the video transmitter is like any other AM transmitter, except that it operates in the TV frequency band and has a sideband filter to suppress the lower video sidebands.

Color Television

The monocolor, or black-and-white (B/W), television was first on the scene. Once it was developed, people were looking for better pictures and with color. Thus, the millions of TV sets that were purchased for B/W reception also had to be able to receive the color-transmitted programs in black and white. This produced a problem or two since the bandwidth had already been assigned and filled with information for black and white and the sound. There simply was not any space to add color signals. However, a few people had ideas that would make color and black and white compatible.

Color television relies on the principle that any visible color may be reproduced by using the proper combinations of the three primary or chromatic colors: red, blue, and green. All systems of transmitting color television signals use some method of analyzing the colors of the scene being scanned in terms of these three colors and of converting the information into electric signals. Fig. 11.6 shows how color separators work to produce the color TV picture. Three monochrome cameras look at each scene through the same lens. The color of the scene is then divided into red, green, and blue light by the dichroic mirrors. A mirror of this type is a plate of glass coated with a thin, metallic layer. It will then reflect one of the primary colors while allowing the others to pass through. The camera has three outputs corresponding to the three primary colors. The picture is transmitted by converting these signals into other signals that correspond to the brightness, hue, and saturation of the scene.

In color television the brightness signal, called the *luminance signal*, is represented by the letter Y. Keep this in mind since the Y signal shows up again in the discussion of color receivers. Signals that correspond to the hue and saturation are called the *chrominance signals*. The process of combining the outputs of the cameras to form chrominance signals is called *encoding* and is accomplished in a circuit called a *matrix*.

There is no difference between the luminance, or Y signal, and the monochrome camera signal. It is all that is needed to produce a B/W picture. The luminance signal is made up of 30 percent of the output of the red camera, 59 percent of the output of the green camera, and 11 percent of the output of the blue camera. These are roughly the rates or percentages that the human eye responds to the various colors.

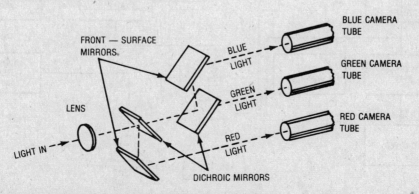

Fig. 11.61.   Color separator system for a color camera.

The Television Receiver   There is no difference between the television receiver and the AM and FM receivers. For now, we will take a look at the color receiver to see how it works in principle.

Fig. 11.62 shows the B/W television set in block diagram form. The audio is separated at the video detector and sent to an FM section which demodulates the signal and produces the sound. The picture information is sent to the cathode ray tube where it is displayed as the signal dictates. In order to keep the picture synchronized properly, sync signals are picked from the incoming signal and fed to the deflection coils around the neck of the tube. These signals cause the beam of electrons in the picture tube to be moved back and forth and up and down by the sawtooth waveform fed into them. The scanning of the phosphorous coating on the picture tube causes it to glow and not glow according to the intensity of the beam. If the beam is not too bright, it will show as a gray. This produces a white-and-gray more so than a black-and-white picture.

Now that you have taken a quick look at the B/W television receiver, we shall modify the receiver slightly to enable it to receive the color signal and produce a picture and sound. Keep

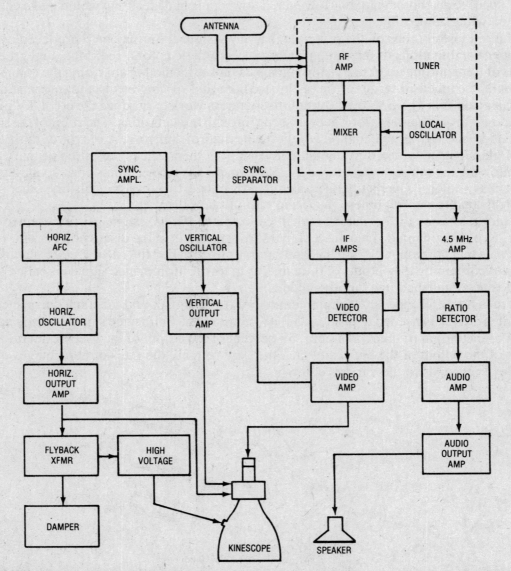

Fig. 11.62.   Block diagram of a black-and-white TV receiver.

in mind that the color and the B/W technology had to be compatible in order for the Federal Communications Commission to approve the system back in the 1940s and early 1950s.

In order to understand clearly how the color picture is produced, we had better back up and take a look at some information on color and how the eye perceives it. In order for color television to be developed, there were three things about color that had to be understood and incorporated into the signal to be broadcast: (1) color has hue, or chroma, (2) color has saturation, or purity, and (3) color has brightness. *Hue* is the basic characteristic that gives color its name, such as orange or purple. *Saturation* tells you how much the color is diluted with white. For instance, red can be seen in tomatoes and blood, while the less saturated color would appear as pink in strawberries or anything with a lower intensity of red. *Brightness* refers to the brilliance of the color. Brilliance is a whole range of colors from white to dark grays to black. These three characteristics of color have to be taken into consideration for the purposes of reproducing a color television picture.

Now, take a look at the other colors that will have to be understood before a device can be designed to reproduce all the colors known today. White, of course, is not a color, it is the *presence* of *all* the colors. Therefore, it can be reproduced if all the colors are mixed together. Black is not a color either: It is the *absence* of *light*. Gray is a weak white. Browns are reds, oranges, and yellows of low brightness. When a beam of light is broken up by a prism, there are six colors that emerge: red, orange, yellow, green, blue, and violet. They are called the spectral colors. By mixing the red and the violet, purple and the magentas can be formed from the various proportions of red and violet. These are called the nonspectral colors.

When you take three colors — red, green, and blue — and project them until they overlap, some interesting combinations result. The overlap of the red and green produces a yellow area. The red and blue-violet mix to form a magenta. The blue-violet with green combinations produce an aqua color which is called cyan in the printing business. By adjusting the brightness of the various lamps, you can obtain any color. This is the additive process of producing color. Keep in mind that the chrominance signals that are produced by the camera and transmitted by the color TV station are called orange-cyan and bluegreen-magenta.

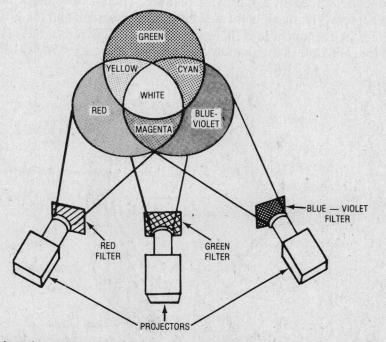

Fig. 11.63. Mixing the primary colors in an additive mode.

Phase Modulation The subcarrier generated at the studio and modulated with the various outputs from three sources of color is filtered out before the TV signal is broadcast. It must be regenerated at the receiver by an oscillator. The oscillator has a tendency to drift if not kept at a perfectly stable temperature. This is why the 3.58-MHz burst is transmitted from the transmitter to keep the oscillator operating properly in the receiver. The two chrominance signals are blended with the subcarrier but they are 90° out of phase with one another. Once the subcarrier is removed at the transmitter, it leaves only these two sidebands with the chrominance signals 90° apart. These become part of the sidebands of the regular carrier frequency assigned to the channel. They are placed on the regular carrier frequency by the process of phase modulation. Thus, the B/W receiver will ignore them completely since it has no way of recognizing their existence.

The amplitude of the combined chrominance signal carries the saturation information, and the phase angle carries the hue. The sync signals and the luminance signal along with the picture information are broadcast over the assigned frequency for the channel. The receiver picks them up and starts the process of demodulation and of putting the information where it will be used to produce a color picture.

The Color Picture Tube The color picture tube has three guns which emit electrons in the end of the tube. There are three cathodes and three filament windings. The filaments heat up the tube (this is the red glow at the base of the tube) and boil off the electrons. A series of plates properly placed inside the neck of the picture tube called a kinescope accelerate the electrons toward the phosphorous coating on the front of the tube. Two coils are used to do the horizontal deflecting of the beam of electrons, and two vertical deflecting coils are used to deflect the beam up and down Fig. 11.64.

Another name for the picture tube is the *kinescope*. The kinescope made for the reproduction of color pictures is a rather complex device which needs some explanation before you can understand how it reproduces all the colors needed for any picture. Fig. 11.65 shows the way the phosphors are placed on the inside of the tube. The inside face of the screen is coated with three different phosphors. A phosphor glows when struck with an electron beam. The phosphors are put onto the screen in a three-dot pattern. The shadow mask is placed near the phosphor-coated screen. The mask is located between the screen and the guns. The mask has about 250,000 holes in it. Each hole is there for a purpose. There is a red, a blue, and a green dot on the screen for each hole in the shadow mask. Thus, there are 750,000 dots on the screen.

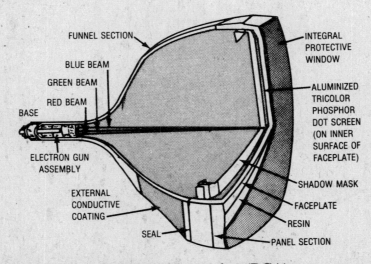

Fig. 11.64. Cutaway view of the color picture tube. (RCA)

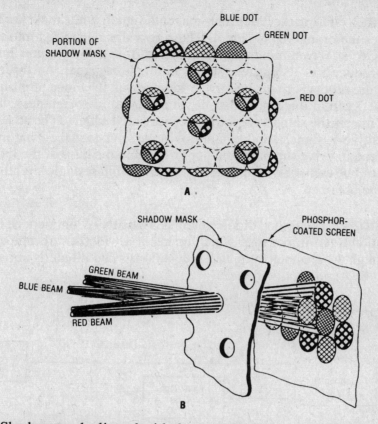

Fig. 11.65.   A. Shadow mask aligned with the color dot pattern. B. The three beams passing through the shadow mask.

A convergence electrode is operated at about 11,000 volts (V) to cause the red, the blue, and the green beams to go through the same shadow mask hole. Once the beams are through the shadow mask, the blue hits the blue dot, the red hits the red dot, and the green hits the green dot in any given pattern. Now, how does this produce color?

The dots are too small to be seen by the human eye. If the same intensity of beams hits all three dots, they produce a white dot. However, if the red and green are the only ones hitting their dots within the pattern of that hole, a yellow is produced. This goes on for all the various combinations of colors that were discussed earlier in the production of the color signal. The color signal then is displayed on the phosphors of the tube in accordance with what they were in the studio or where the camera saw them.

Receiver Stages   Fig. 11.66 shows the block diagram of the color TV receiver. In it you will notice some differences from that of the B/W receiver.

All the stages shown in Fig. 11.66 are utilized to produce the color picture. The radio frequency (RF), intermediate frequency (IF), and video stages that are normally found in a B/W receiver are located here also. However, from there the signal is taken into different stages to be processed for color components and sync signals. The sync signals are taken off, and the 3.58-MHz bursts that appear during the horizontal retrace time are used by the automatic frequency control (AFC) circuit to check and compare with the receiver's 3.58-MHz crystal oscillator and to keep it in phase with that which is broadcast with the color information. The subcarrier (3.58 MHz) is again added to the sidebands that contain the color information. This allows the color information to be extracted. The subcarrier oscillator stage puts out two signals for the two modulators, and the signals are 90° out of phase with one another. A low-pass filter of 0.5 MHz then puts out the bluegreen-magenta signal, while the other low-pass filter of 1.5 MHz produces the orange-cyan signal. These two signals are fed into the matrix. After demodulation, the R − Y (red minus luminance) and B − Y (blue minus luminance) signals are matrixed to produce a G − Y (green minus luminance) signal. All three signals are then applied to the picture tube where the positive Y signal from the video amplifier cancels all the − Y components. Keep in mind now that the third signal, or brightness, is added after the matrix. From the matrix the signals are fed to the individual adders. The adders add the brightness signal (a positive Y signal), and this removes the − Y signals. That in turn produces a blue, green, and red to drive the individual color guns in the base of the kinescope.

When the tint or hue control is adjusted, it changes the phase angle slightly so that the exact color match can be obtained.

Receiver Antennas   The folded dipole antenna is usually recommended for outside reception. It has a 300-ohm (Ω) impedance which makes it a wideband receptor, wide enough to handle the 2 through 13 channel frequency allocations. The dipole is about one-half wave-

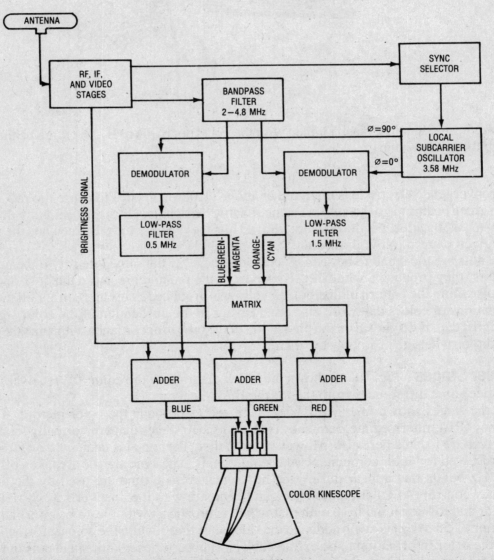

Fig. 11.66.   Color TV receiver, simplified block diagram.

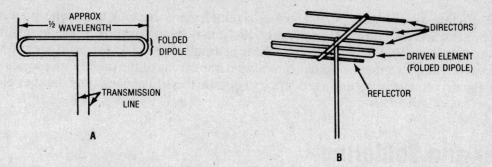

Fig. 11.67.   A. Basic folded dipole. B. Typical single-bay yagi with five elements.

length (see Fig. 11.67). The folded dipole is bidirectional, the major lobes are at right angles to the elements. Dipoles may be stacked for higher gain in areas of weak signals. Outside antennas usually have directors in front of the dipole and reflectors in the back of it. The directors make the antenna a little more directional, and the reflector rejects the unwanted waves from the back of the antenna. The directors are shorter than the dipole or driven element, while the

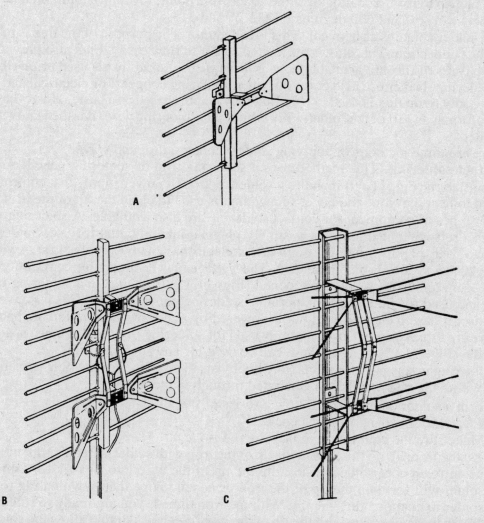

Fig. 11.68.   Bow-tie UHF antenna with a sheet reflector. B. Stacked bow-tie with sheet reflector. C. A two-bay UHF antenna using a sheet reflector.

reflectors are longer in physical size than the driven element. In some cases where a weak UHF signal is present and the color information is lost, it may be to your advantage to obtain a bow-tie UHF antenna (see Fig. 11.68). These antennas usually have a screen wire backup with two to four bow-tie-shaped antenna elements mounted one on top of the other with proper spacing. Stacking the driven elements has a tendency to double the signal each time another element is added.

Solder and Soldering

The most common technique for joining wires, lugs and terminals in electrical and electronics circuits is soldering.

Solder is an alloy metal. It is made from tin and lead. There are three standard alloy mixtures for solder. These mixtures are given as percentages. The tin percentage is always stated first. Thus, a 40/60 solder contains 40 percent tin, 60 percent lead. There are also 50/50 and 60/40 solders. In general, the more tin contained in solder, the higher the quality. In industry, 60/40 solder is used by quality manufacturers.

Soldering is the technique of joining electrical or electronic connections. In soldering, solder is melted to form a coating over the connection point, forming a joint. Standard solders melt at between 450 and 600 degrees F [232.2° and 315.5° C].

Most solder contains a chemical. This is called *flux*. The purpose of the flux is to clean the area of the connection. This allows the melted solder to flow easily. Flux also prevents oxidation. Two types of flux are available. One is an acid core. Acid flux is used primarily in sheet metal soldering. Never use acid core flux when soldering copper. For electrical and electronics work, only rosin flux is used. Rosin flux may be purchased as a paste. However, the most common form is as part of the solder. Flux is built into soldering wire. It is then known as rosin-core solder.

There are three methods of applying solder: contact, dip, and wave.

Contact soldering. This method uses a soldering iron or soldering pencil. A complete soldering station (Fig. 11.69) includes a soldering iron, a power supply that controls the current used to heat the iron, and a wet sponge that is used to clean the tip of the iron.

Other types of equipment for contact soldering are also available. A soldering iron (Fig. 11.70) is a self-contained unit that is simply plugged into an outlet for use. Soldering irons come in a variety of power ratings. For work on electronics, a low-wattage iron — with a rating between 20W and 30W is recommended. The wattage may be higher for heavy duty electrical devices — up to 500W. A soldering pencil (Fig. 11.71) is similar to a soldering iron but is smaller and used for finer work. A portable soldering pencil (Fig. 11.72) is convenient and easy to use: it has no electric cord but is powered by a rechargeable cell in the handle.

There are three types of tips commonly used for soldering irons and pencils: spade, chisel, and needle (Fig. 11.73). Any of these can be used for any soldering job.

A soldering gun is popular with many hobbyists. The trigger of the gun activates a transformer within the unit and heat is generated through induction.

To form a solder connection, follow a series of steps:
1. Clean the soldering iron or pencil.
2. Make sure the connection to be soldered is *clean*.
3. *Tin* the iron. To do this, touch the tip of the iron with solder wire. This assumes you are using rosin-core solder. If not, dip the tip of the wire into flux first. A small spot of solder will form on the tip of the iron or pencil. Wipe the tip with a rag to cause the solder to coat or "tin" the tip. With the iron tinned, you are ready to solder.
4. Touch the connection with the tip of the iron or pencil. Simply allow the solder to flow into the connection. The flowing solder makes the connection.

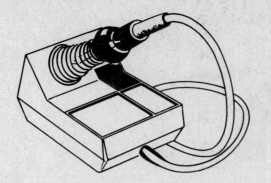

Fig. 11.69.

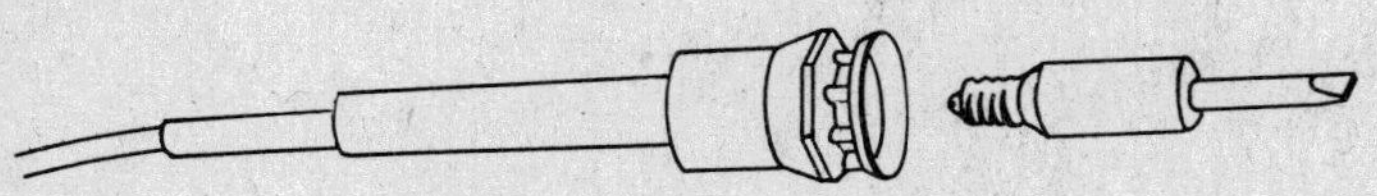

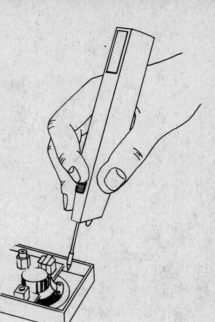

Fig. 11.72.

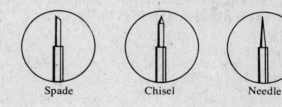

Fig. 11.70.

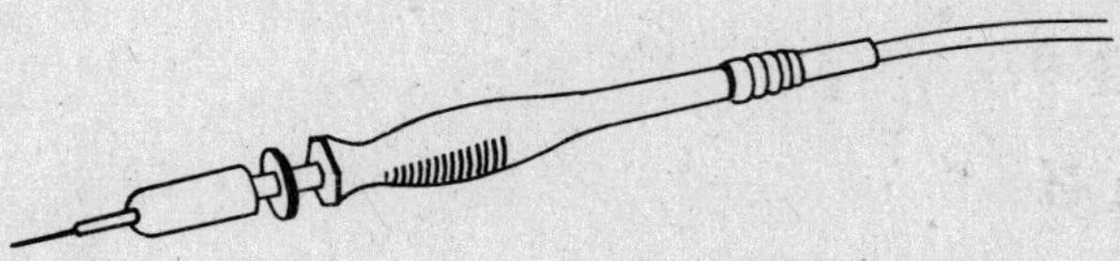

Fig. 11.71.

Spade   Chisel   Needle

Fig. 11.73.

5. Check the quality of your work. A good solder connection should be clean and shiny. There should be no cracks. If the solder is cracked or dull, this indicates a cold solder connection. A cold solder connection is unsatisfactory. The connection should be reheated. Also, be careful that the solder does not bridge. *Bridging* occurs when solder runs across copper strips along a printed circuit board. This causes a short circuit.

Dip Soldering. For mass production, it is possible to solder a number of connections in one operation. This is done to secure components into printed circuit boards. All of the components are put into position first. Then the bottom of the board is lowered into liquid solder contained in a pot. The leads of the connecting wires pick up solder. When the board is removed from the pot, the solder cools and components are held in place.

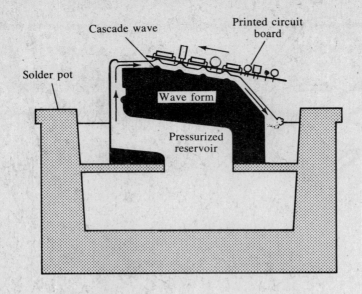

Fig. 11.74.

Wave Soldering. Wave soldering is a faster, more advanced, mass-production technique. Boards are prepared in the same way as described above for dip soldering. However, there is a pressure mechanism in the pot. This causes the hot solder to flow upward in waves. Circuit boards with components in position are placed just above the level of the hot solder. The waves cause the solder to touch the connection. Soldering is clean and fast. The wave soldering process is illustrated in Fig. 11.74.

TEST YOURSELF

12 MODEL EXAMINATION TWO

PART 7 AUTO & SHOP INFORMATION

1. Ⓐ Ⓑ Ⓒ Ⓓ	6. Ⓐ Ⓑ Ⓒ Ⓓ	11. Ⓐ Ⓑ Ⓒ Ⓓ	16. Ⓐ Ⓑ Ⓒ Ⓓ	21. Ⓐ Ⓑ Ⓒ Ⓓ
2. Ⓐ Ⓑ Ⓒ Ⓓ	7. Ⓐ Ⓑ Ⓒ Ⓓ	12. Ⓐ Ⓑ Ⓒ Ⓓ	17. Ⓐ Ⓑ Ⓒ Ⓓ	22. Ⓐ Ⓑ Ⓒ Ⓓ
3. Ⓐ Ⓑ Ⓒ Ⓓ	8. Ⓐ Ⓑ Ⓒ Ⓓ	13. Ⓐ Ⓑ Ⓒ Ⓓ	18. Ⓐ Ⓑ Ⓒ Ⓓ	23. Ⓐ Ⓑ Ⓒ Ⓓ
4. Ⓐ Ⓑ Ⓒ Ⓓ	9. Ⓐ Ⓑ Ⓒ Ⓓ	14. Ⓐ Ⓑ Ⓒ Ⓓ	19. Ⓐ Ⓑ Ⓒ Ⓓ	24. Ⓐ Ⓑ Ⓒ Ⓓ
5. Ⓐ Ⓑ Ⓒ Ⓓ	10. Ⓐ Ⓑ Ⓒ Ⓓ	15. Ⓐ Ⓑ Ⓒ Ⓓ	20. Ⓐ Ⓑ Ⓒ Ⓓ	25. Ⓐ Ⓑ Ⓒ Ⓓ

PART 8 MATHEMATICS KNOWLEDGE

1. Ⓐ Ⓑ Ⓒ Ⓓ	6. Ⓐ Ⓑ Ⓒ Ⓓ	11. Ⓐ Ⓑ Ⓒ Ⓓ	16. Ⓐ Ⓑ Ⓒ Ⓓ	21. Ⓐ Ⓑ Ⓒ Ⓓ
2. Ⓐ Ⓑ Ⓒ Ⓓ	7. Ⓐ Ⓑ Ⓒ Ⓓ	12. Ⓐ Ⓑ Ⓒ Ⓓ	17. Ⓐ Ⓑ Ⓒ Ⓓ	22. Ⓐ Ⓑ Ⓒ Ⓓ
3. Ⓐ Ⓑ Ⓒ Ⓓ	8. Ⓐ Ⓑ Ⓒ Ⓓ	13. Ⓐ Ⓑ Ⓒ Ⓓ	18. Ⓐ Ⓑ Ⓒ Ⓓ	23. Ⓐ Ⓑ Ⓒ Ⓓ
4. Ⓐ Ⓑ Ⓒ Ⓓ	9. Ⓐ Ⓑ Ⓒ Ⓓ	14. Ⓐ Ⓑ Ⓒ Ⓓ	19. Ⓐ Ⓑ Ⓒ Ⓓ	24. Ⓐ Ⓑ Ⓒ Ⓓ
5. Ⓐ Ⓑ Ⓒ Ⓓ	10. Ⓐ Ⓑ Ⓒ Ⓓ	15. Ⓐ Ⓑ Ⓒ Ⓓ	20. Ⓐ Ⓑ Ⓒ Ⓓ	25. Ⓐ Ⓑ Ⓒ Ⓓ

PART 9 MECHANICAL COMPREHENSION

1. Ⓐ Ⓑ Ⓒ Ⓓ	6. Ⓐ Ⓑ Ⓒ Ⓓ	11. Ⓐ Ⓑ Ⓒ Ⓓ	16. Ⓐ Ⓑ Ⓒ Ⓓ	21. Ⓐ Ⓑ Ⓒ Ⓓ
2. Ⓐ Ⓑ Ⓒ Ⓓ	7. Ⓐ Ⓑ Ⓒ Ⓓ	12. Ⓐ Ⓑ Ⓒ Ⓓ	17. Ⓐ Ⓑ Ⓒ Ⓓ	22. Ⓐ Ⓑ Ⓒ Ⓓ
3. Ⓐ Ⓑ Ⓒ Ⓓ	8. Ⓐ Ⓑ Ⓒ Ⓓ	13. Ⓐ Ⓑ Ⓒ Ⓓ	18. Ⓐ Ⓑ Ⓒ Ⓓ	23. Ⓐ Ⓑ Ⓒ Ⓓ
4. Ⓐ Ⓑ Ⓒ Ⓓ	9. Ⓐ Ⓑ Ⓒ Ⓓ	14. Ⓐ Ⓑ Ⓒ Ⓓ	19. Ⓐ Ⓑ Ⓒ Ⓓ	24. Ⓐ Ⓑ Ⓒ Ⓓ
5. Ⓐ Ⓑ Ⓒ Ⓓ	10. Ⓐ Ⓑ Ⓒ Ⓓ	15. Ⓐ Ⓑ Ⓒ Ⓓ	20. Ⓐ Ⓑ Ⓒ Ⓓ	25. Ⓐ Ⓑ Ⓒ Ⓓ

PART 10 ELECTRONICS INFORMATION

1. Ⓐ Ⓑ Ⓒ Ⓓ	6. Ⓐ Ⓑ Ⓒ Ⓓ	11. Ⓐ Ⓑ Ⓒ Ⓓ	16. Ⓐ Ⓑ Ⓒ Ⓓ
2. Ⓐ Ⓑ Ⓒ Ⓓ	7. Ⓐ Ⓑ Ⓒ Ⓓ	12. Ⓐ Ⓑ Ⓒ Ⓓ	17. Ⓐ Ⓑ Ⓒ Ⓓ
3. Ⓐ Ⓑ Ⓒ Ⓓ	8. Ⓐ Ⓑ Ⓒ Ⓓ	13. Ⓐ Ⓑ Ⓒ Ⓓ	18. Ⓐ Ⓑ Ⓒ Ⓓ
4. Ⓐ Ⓑ Ⓒ Ⓓ	9. Ⓐ Ⓑ Ⓒ Ⓓ	14. Ⓐ Ⓑ Ⓒ Ⓓ	19. Ⓐ Ⓑ Ⓒ Ⓓ
5. Ⓐ Ⓑ Ⓒ Ⓓ	10. Ⓐ Ⓑ Ⓒ Ⓓ	15. Ⓐ Ⓑ Ⓒ Ⓓ	20. Ⓐ Ⓑ Ⓒ Ⓓ

1

GENERAL SCIENCE

Directions

This test has questions about science. Pick the best answer for each question, then blacken the space on your separate answer form which has the same number and letter as your choice.

Here is a sample question.

1. The planet nearest to the sun is

   1-A   Venus.
   1-B   Mars.
   1-C   Earth.
   1-D   Mercury.

Mercury is the correct answer, so you would blacken the space for 1-D on your answer form.

Your score on this test will be based on the number of questions you answer correctly. You should try to answer every question. Do not spend too much time on any one question.

When you begin, be sure to start with question number 1 in Part 1, and number 1 in Part 1 on your answer form.

Do not turn this page until told to do so.

GENERAL SCIENCE

Time: 11 minutes; 25 questions

1. Sound travels fastest through

   1-A   air.
   1-B   steel.
   1-C   water.
   1-D   a vacuum.

2. In order to use sea water on board ship for boilers, the water must first be

   2-A   distilled.
   2-B   aerated.
   2-C   chlorinated.
   2-D   refined.

3. The most abundant metal in a free state in the earth's crust is

   3-A   nitrogen.
   3-B   aluminum.
   3-C   copper.
   3-D   iron.

4. An object will most effectively absorb the sun's rays if it is

   4-A   polished, and dark in color.
   4-B   polished, and light in color.
   4-C   rough, and light in color.
   4-D   rough, and dark in color.

5. The most effective farming method for returning minerals to the soil is

   5-A   crop rotation.
   5-B   strip farming.
   5-C   contour plowing.
   5-D   furrowing.

6. An example of a lever is the

   6-A   wedge.
   6-B   crowbar.
   6-C   saw.
   6-D   escalator.

7. A lunar eclipse occurs when the

   7-A   earth casts its shadow on the sun.
   7-B   sun casts its shadow on the moon.
   7-C   earth casts its shadow on the moon.
   7-D   moon casts its shadow on the earth.

8. The part of the body that would suffer most from a diet deficient in calcium is the

   8-A   pancreas.
   8-B   stomach.
   8-C   skeleton.
   8-D   skin.

9. Which of the following is found in the greatest quantities in automobile exhaust gases?

   9-A   sulfur dioxide
   9-B   sulfur trioxide
   9-C   carbon monoxide
   9-D   water

10. Which common electrical device contains an electric magnet?

    10-A   flatiron
    10-B   lamp
    10-C   telephone
    10-D   toaster

11. In a vacuum, radio waves and visible light waves must have the same

    11-A   intensity.
    11-B   frequency.
    11-C   wavelength.
    11-D   speed.

12. The most accurate description of the earth's atmosphere is that it consists

    12-A   mostly of oxygen, argon, carbon dioxide, and water vapor.
    12-B   entirely of ozone, nitrogen, and water vapor.
    12-C   of a mixture of gases, liquid droplets, and minute solid particles.
    12-D   of gases which cannot be compressed.

13. Object A with a mass of 2 kilograms and object B with a mass of 4 kilograms are dropped simultaneously from rest near the surface of the earth. Neglecting air resistance, at the end of 3 seconds, what is the ratio of the speed of object A to the speed of object B?

    13-A   1:4
    13-B   1:2
    13-C   1:1
    13-D   2:1

14. In June, a weather station in a New England city reports a falling barometer and southeast winds. The best weather forecast is probably

14-A fair and warmer.
14-B fair and colder.
14-C rain and warmer.
14-D rain and colder.

15. Which substance can be removed from water by filtration?

15-A sand
15-B ink
15-C alcohol
15-D sugar

16. As a balloon rises, the gas within it

16-A solidifies.
16-B freezes.
16-C condenses.
16-D expands.

17. The best estimate of the age of the earth comes from the study of

17-A the salt content of the oceans.
17-B the thickness of sedimentary rock.
17-C radioactive material.
17-D the rate of erosion of the land.

18. The presence of coal deposits in Alaska shows that, at one time, Alaska

18-A was covered with ice.
18-B was connected to Asia.
18-C was connected to Europe.
18-D had a tropical climate.

19. When an airplane is in flight, the air pressure on the top surface of the wing is

19-A less than on the bottom surface.
19-B the same as on the bottom surface.
19-C slightly more than on the bottom surface.
19-D more or less than on the bottom surface, depending on the shape of the wing.

20. In the human eye, which structure is like the film in a camera?

20-A pupil
20-B retina
20-C lens
20-D cornea

21. When water is taken apart by electricity, what two substances are formed?

21-A carbon and oxygen
21-B hydrogen and oxygen
21-C oxygen and nitrogen
21-D hydrogen and nitrogen

22. Which of the following statements is true for the right side of this equation?

$$Fe + H_2SO_4 \rightarrow FeSO_4 + H_2 \uparrow$$

22-A There are two elements on the right side.
22-B There are two compounds on the right side.
22-C There are an element and a gas on the right side.
22-D There are a compound and an element on the right side.

23. The three elements found most commonly in commercial fertilizers are

23-A calcium, phosphorus, iron.
23-B phosphorus, nitrogen, sulfur.
23-C nitrogen, phosphorus, potassium.
23-D magnesium, iron, calcium.

24. Two non-porous rocks seem to lose the same weight when a string is attached to each and they are submerged in water. These two rocks must have the same

24-A weight in air.
24-B weight in water.
24-C volume.
24-D chemical and physical properties.

25. The thermos bottle is most similar in principle to

25-A storm windows.
25-B the freezing unit in an electric refrigerator.
25-C solar heating systems.
25-D radiant heaters.

ARITHMETIC REASONING

Directions

This test has questions about arithmetic. Each question is followed by four possible answers. Decide which answer is correct. Then, on your answer form, blacken the space which has the same number and letter as your choice. Use your scratch paper for any figuring you wish to do.

Here is a sample question.

1. If 10 pounds of sugar cost $2.00, what is the cost of one pound?

    1-A   90 cents
    1-B   80 cents
    1-C   50 cents
    1-D   20 cents

The cost of one pound is 20 cents; therefore, the answer 1-D is correct.

Your score on this test will be based on the number of questions you answer correctly. You should try to answer every question. Do not spend too much time on any one question.

Notice that Part 2 begins with question number 1. When you begin, be sure to mark your first answer next to number 1 on your answer form.

Do not turn the page until told to do so.

ARITHMETIC REASONING

Time: 36 minutes; 30 questions

1. You need 8 barrels of water to sprinkle ½ mile of roadway. How many barrels of water do you need, to sprinkle 3½ miles of roadway?

   1-A 7
   1-B 15
   1-C 50
   1-D 56

2. A snapshot 8 inches long and 6 inches wide is to be enlarged so that its length will be 12 inches. How many inches wide will the enlarged snapshot be?

   2-A 8
   2-B 6
   2-C 9
   2-D 10

3. Lee Robinson has an ordinary life insurance policy with a face value of $10,000. At her age, the annual premium is $24.00 per thousand. What is the total premium paid for this policy every six months?

   3-A $100
   3-B $120
   3-C $240
   3-D $400

4. If two pounds of cottage cheese cost $3.20, what is the cost of a 3-ounce portion of cottage cheese?

   4-A $0.30
   4-B $0.20
   4-C $0.25
   4-D $0.15

5. Mr. Green drove for 12 hours at a speed of 55 miles per hour. If his car covered 22 miles for each gallon of gas used, how many gallons of gas did he use?

   5-A 32 gallons
   5-B 34 gallons
   5-C 36 gallons
   5-D 30 gallons

6. Matty Smith earns $7.50 per hour. If he works from 8:45 A.M. until 5:15 P.M., with one hour off for lunch, how much does he earn in one day?

   6-A $58.50
   6-B $56.25
   6-C $55.00
   6-D $53.75

7. If 5 shirts and 3 ties cost $52 and each tie costs $4, what is the cost of a shirt?

   7-A $6
   7-B $8
   7-C $10
   7-D $7.50

8. What is the fifth term in the series: 5; 2; 9; 6; ____?

   8-A 16
   8-B 15
   8-C 14
   8-D 13

9. In a theater audience of 500 people, 80% were adults. How many children were in the audience?

   9-A 20
   9-B 50
   9-C 100
   9-D 125

10. A table usually sells for $240, but because it is slightly shopworn, the store manager lets it go for $210. What is the percent of reduction?

    10-A 12½%
    10-B 14²⁄₇%
    10-C 16⅔%
    10-D 18¾%

11. Mr. and Mrs. Turner bought a home for $55,000. It was assessed at 80% of the purchase price. If the real estate tax was $4.74 per $100, how much realty tax did the Turners pay?

    11-A $2,085.60
    11-B $1,985.60
    11-C $2,607
    11-D $285.60

12. A scale on a map is 1 inch to 50 miles. On the map, two cities are 2½ inches apart. What is the actual distance between the two cities?

12-A   75 miles
12-B   100 miles
12-C   225 miles
12-D   125 miles

13. A shipment of 2,200 pounds of fertilizer is packed in 40-ounce bags. How many bags are needed for the shipment?

13-A   800
13-B   880
13-C   780
13-D   640

14. A television set priced at $400 was reduced 25% during a weekend sale. In addition, there was a 10% discount for cash. What was the cash price of the set during the sale?

14-A $130
14-B $260
14-C $270
14-D $320

15. In a store, four clerks each receive $255 per week, while two part-timers each earn $120. What is the average weekly salary paid these six workers?

15-A $200
15-B $210
15-C $187.50
15-D $190

16. The perimeter of a rectangle is 40 feet. If the length is 15 feet, 6 inches, what is the width of the rectangle?

16-A   4 feet, 6 inches
16-B   9 feet, 6 inches
16-C   5 feet, 6 inches
16-D   5 feet

17. What is the result of dividing 0.675 by 0.9?

17-A   7.5
17-B   0.075
17-C   75
17-D   0.75

18. Two planes leave the same airport, traveling in opposite directions. One is flying at the rate of 340 miles per hour, the other at 260 miles per hour. In how many hours will the two planes be 3,000 miles apart?

18-A   5
18-B   4
18-C   6
18-D   10

19. What is the cost of 5 feet, 3 inches of plastic slipcover material that sells for $8 per foot?

19-A $14
19-B $42
19-C $23
19-D $21.12

20. If one gallon of milk costs $3.84, what is the cost of 3 pints?

20-A $1.44
20-B $2.82
20-C $2.04
20-D $1.96

21. A man left $72,000 to his wife and son. The ratio of the wife's share to the son's share was 5:3. How much did his wife receive?

21-A $27,000
21-B $14,000
21-C $45,000
21-D $54,000

22. A recipe calls for 2½ ounces of chocolate and ½ cup of corn syrup. If only 2 ounces of chocolate are available, how much corn syrup should be used?

22-A   ½ cup
22-B   ⅓ cup
22-C   ⅖ cup
22-D   ³⁄₁₀ cup

23. A ship sails x miles the first day, y miles the second day, and z miles the third day. What was the average distance covered per day?

23-A $\dfrac{xyz}{3}$

23-B $\dfrac{x + y + z}{3}$

23-C   3xyz
23-D   none of these

24. A man invests $6,000 at 5% annual interest. How much more must he invest at 6% annual interest so that his annual income from both investments is $900?

    24-A $3,000
    24-B $5,000
    24-C $8,000
    24-D $10,000

25. Which of these is an example of similar figures?

    25-A a plane and a scale model of that plane
    25-B a pen and a pencil
    25-C a motorcycle and a car
    25-D an equilateral triangle and a right triangle

26. Find the numerical value of $5a^2b - 3ab^2$ if $a = 7$ and $b = 4$.

    26-A 846
    26-B 644
    26-C 488
    26-D 224

27. If the circumference of a circle is divided by the length of its diameter, what is the result?

    27-A 2
    27-B 27
    27-C Pi
    27-D 7

28. A businesswoman spends $\frac{1}{5}$ of her income for rent, and $\frac{3}{8}$ of the remainder of her income for salaries. What part of her income does she spend for salaries?

    28-A $\frac{23}{40}$
    28-B $\frac{3}{10}$
    28-C $\frac{1}{2}$
    28-D $\frac{3}{4}$

29. Using the following formula, find the value of C when F = 50.

    $$C = \frac{5}{9}(F - 32)$$

    29-A 10
    29-B 18
    29-C 90
    29-D 40

30. What is the average of these temperature readings, taken on a cold day last winter?

    6:00 A.M.   −12 degrees
    7:00 A.M.   −7 degrees
    8:00 A.M.   −2 degrees
    9:00 A.M.   0 degrees
    10:00 A.M. +6 degrees

    30-A 0 degrees
    30-B 2 degrees
    30-C −1 degree
    30-D −3 degrees

ANSWER SHEET— SECOND MODEL EXAM

PART 1 GENERAL SCIENCE

1. Ⓐ Ⓑ Ⓒ Ⓓ	6. Ⓐ Ⓑ Ⓒ Ⓓ	11. Ⓐ Ⓑ Ⓒ Ⓓ	16. Ⓐ Ⓑ Ⓒ Ⓓ	21. Ⓐ Ⓑ Ⓒ Ⓓ
2. Ⓐ Ⓑ Ⓒ Ⓓ	7 Ⓐ Ⓑ Ⓒ Ⓓ	12. Ⓐ Ⓑ Ⓒ Ⓓ	17. Ⓐ Ⓑ Ⓒ Ⓓ	22. Ⓐ Ⓑ Ⓒ Ⓓ
3. Ⓐ Ⓑ Ⓒ Ⓓ	8. Ⓐ Ⓑ Ⓒ Ⓓ	13. Ⓐ Ⓑ Ⓒ Ⓓ	18. Ⓐ Ⓑ Ⓒ Ⓓ	23. Ⓐ Ⓑ Ⓒ Ⓓ
4. Ⓐ Ⓑ Ⓒ Ⓓ	9. Ⓐ Ⓑ Ⓒ Ⓓ	14. Ⓐ Ⓑ Ⓒ Ⓓ	19. Ⓐ Ⓑ Ⓒ Ⓓ	24. Ⓐ Ⓑ Ⓒ Ⓓ
5. Ⓐ Ⓑ Ⓒ Ⓓ	10. Ⓐ Ⓑ Ⓒ Ⓓ	15. Ⓐ Ⓑ Ⓒ Ⓓ	20. Ⓐ Ⓑ Ⓒ Ⓓ	25. Ⓐ Ⓑ Ⓒ Ⓓ

PART 2 ARITHMETIC REASONING

1. Ⓐ Ⓑ Ⓒ Ⓓ	7. Ⓐ Ⓑ Ⓒ Ⓓ	13. Ⓐ Ⓑ Ⓒ Ⓓ	19. Ⓐ Ⓑ Ⓒ Ⓓ	25. Ⓐ Ⓑ Ⓒ Ⓓ
2. Ⓐ Ⓑ Ⓒ Ⓓ	8. Ⓐ Ⓑ Ⓒ Ⓓ	14. Ⓐ Ⓑ Ⓒ Ⓓ	20. Ⓐ Ⓑ Ⓒ Ⓓ	26. Ⓐ Ⓑ Ⓒ Ⓓ
3. Ⓐ Ⓑ Ⓒ Ⓓ	9. Ⓐ Ⓑ Ⓒ Ⓓ	15. Ⓐ Ⓑ Ⓒ Ⓓ	21. Ⓐ Ⓑ Ⓒ Ⓓ	27. Ⓐ Ⓑ Ⓒ Ⓓ
4. Ⓐ Ⓑ Ⓒ Ⓓ	10. Ⓐ Ⓑ Ⓒ Ⓓ	16. Ⓐ Ⓑ Ⓒ Ⓓ	22. Ⓐ Ⓑ Ⓒ Ⓓ	28. Ⓐ Ⓑ Ⓒ Ⓓ
5. Ⓐ Ⓑ Ⓒ Ⓓ	11. Ⓐ Ⓑ Ⓒ Ⓓ	17. Ⓐ Ⓑ Ⓒ Ⓓ	23. Ⓐ Ⓑ Ⓒ Ⓓ	29. Ⓐ Ⓑ Ⓒ Ⓓ
6. Ⓐ Ⓑ Ⓒ Ⓓ	12. Ⓐ Ⓑ Ⓒ Ⓓ	18. Ⓐ Ⓑ Ⓒ Ⓓ	24. Ⓐ Ⓑ Ⓒ Ⓓ	30. Ⓐ Ⓑ Ⓒ Ⓓ

PART 3 WORD KNOWLEDGE

1. Ⓐ Ⓑ Ⓒ Ⓓ	8. Ⓐ Ⓑ Ⓒ Ⓓ	15. Ⓐ Ⓑ Ⓒ Ⓓ	22. Ⓐ Ⓑ Ⓒ Ⓓ	29. Ⓐ Ⓑ Ⓒ Ⓓ
2. Ⓐ Ⓑ Ⓒ Ⓓ	9. Ⓐ Ⓑ Ⓒ Ⓓ	16. Ⓐ Ⓑ Ⓒ Ⓓ	23. Ⓐ Ⓑ Ⓒ Ⓓ	30. Ⓐ Ⓑ Ⓒ Ⓓ
3. Ⓐ Ⓑ Ⓒ Ⓓ	10. Ⓐ Ⓑ Ⓒ Ⓓ	17. Ⓐ Ⓑ Ⓒ Ⓓ	24. Ⓐ Ⓑ Ⓒ Ⓓ	31. Ⓐ Ⓑ Ⓒ Ⓓ
4. Ⓐ Ⓑ Ⓒ Ⓓ	11. Ⓐ Ⓑ Ⓒ Ⓓ	18. Ⓐ Ⓑ Ⓒ Ⓓ	25. Ⓐ Ⓑ Ⓒ Ⓓ	32. Ⓐ Ⓑ Ⓒ Ⓓ
5. Ⓐ Ⓑ Ⓒ Ⓓ	12. Ⓐ Ⓑ Ⓒ Ⓓ	19. Ⓐ Ⓑ Ⓒ Ⓓ	26. Ⓐ Ⓑ Ⓒ Ⓓ	33. Ⓐ Ⓑ Ⓒ Ⓓ
6. Ⓐ Ⓑ Ⓒ Ⓓ	13. Ⓐ Ⓑ Ⓒ Ⓓ	20. Ⓐ Ⓑ Ⓒ Ⓓ	27. Ⓐ Ⓑ Ⓒ Ⓓ	34. Ⓐ Ⓑ Ⓒ Ⓓ
7. Ⓐ Ⓑ Ⓒ Ⓓ	14. Ⓐ Ⓑ Ⓒ Ⓓ	21. Ⓐ Ⓑ Ⓒ Ⓓ	28. Ⓐ Ⓑ Ⓒ Ⓓ	35. Ⓐ Ⓑ Ⓒ Ⓓ

PART 4 PARAGRAPH COMPREHENSION

1. Ⓐ Ⓑ Ⓒ Ⓓ	5. Ⓐ Ⓑ Ⓒ Ⓓ	9. Ⓐ Ⓑ Ⓒ Ⓓ	13. Ⓐ Ⓑ Ⓒ Ⓓ
2. Ⓐ Ⓑ Ⓒ Ⓓ	6. Ⓐ Ⓑ Ⓒ Ⓓ	10. Ⓐ Ⓑ Ⓒ Ⓓ	14. Ⓐ Ⓑ Ⓒ Ⓓ
3. Ⓐ Ⓑ Ⓒ Ⓓ	7. Ⓐ Ⓑ Ⓒ Ⓓ	11. Ⓐ Ⓑ Ⓒ Ⓓ	15. Ⓐ Ⓑ Ⓒ Ⓓ
4. Ⓐ Ⓑ Ⓒ Ⓓ	8. Ⓐ Ⓑ Ⓒ Ⓓ	12. Ⓐ Ⓑ Ⓒ Ⓓ	

PART 5 NUMERICAL OPERATIONS

1. Ⓐ Ⓑ Ⓒ Ⓓ	11. Ⓐ Ⓑ Ⓒ Ⓓ	21. Ⓐ Ⓑ Ⓒ Ⓓ	31. Ⓐ Ⓑ Ⓒ Ⓓ	41. Ⓐ Ⓑ Ⓒ Ⓓ
2. Ⓐ Ⓑ Ⓒ Ⓓ	12. Ⓐ Ⓑ Ⓒ Ⓓ	22. Ⓐ Ⓑ Ⓒ Ⓓ	32. Ⓐ Ⓑ Ⓒ Ⓓ	42. Ⓐ Ⓑ Ⓒ Ⓓ
3. Ⓐ Ⓑ Ⓒ Ⓓ	13. Ⓐ Ⓑ Ⓒ Ⓓ	23. Ⓐ Ⓑ Ⓒ Ⓓ	33. Ⓐ Ⓑ Ⓒ Ⓓ	43. Ⓐ Ⓑ Ⓒ Ⓓ
4. Ⓐ Ⓑ Ⓒ Ⓓ	14. Ⓐ Ⓑ Ⓒ Ⓓ	24. Ⓐ Ⓑ Ⓒ Ⓓ	34. Ⓐ Ⓑ Ⓒ Ⓓ	44. Ⓐ Ⓑ Ⓒ Ⓓ
5. Ⓐ Ⓑ Ⓒ Ⓓ	15. Ⓐ Ⓑ Ⓒ Ⓓ	25. Ⓐ Ⓑ Ⓒ Ⓓ	35. Ⓐ Ⓑ Ⓒ Ⓓ	45. Ⓐ Ⓑ Ⓒ Ⓓ
6. Ⓐ Ⓑ Ⓒ Ⓓ	16. Ⓐ Ⓑ Ⓒ Ⓓ	26. Ⓐ Ⓑ Ⓒ Ⓓ	36. Ⓐ Ⓑ Ⓒ Ⓓ	46. Ⓐ Ⓑ Ⓒ Ⓓ
7. Ⓐ Ⓑ Ⓒ Ⓓ	17. Ⓐ Ⓑ Ⓒ Ⓓ	27. Ⓐ Ⓑ Ⓒ Ⓓ	37. Ⓐ Ⓑ Ⓒ Ⓓ	47. Ⓐ Ⓑ Ⓒ Ⓓ
8. Ⓐ Ⓑ Ⓒ Ⓓ	18. Ⓐ Ⓑ Ⓒ Ⓓ	28. Ⓐ Ⓑ Ⓒ Ⓓ	38. Ⓐ Ⓑ Ⓒ Ⓓ	48. Ⓐ Ⓑ Ⓒ Ⓓ
9. Ⓐ Ⓑ Ⓒ Ⓓ	19. Ⓐ Ⓑ Ⓒ Ⓓ	29. Ⓐ Ⓑ Ⓒ Ⓓ	39. Ⓐ Ⓑ Ⓒ Ⓓ	49. Ⓐ Ⓑ Ⓒ Ⓓ
10. Ⓐ Ⓑ Ⓒ Ⓓ	20. Ⓐ Ⓑ Ⓒ Ⓓ	30. Ⓐ Ⓑ Ⓒ Ⓓ	40. Ⓐ Ⓑ Ⓒ Ⓓ	50. Ⓐ Ⓑ Ⓒ Ⓓ

PART 6 CODING SPEED

1. Ⓐ Ⓑ Ⓒ Ⓓ Ⓔ	15. Ⓐ Ⓑ Ⓒ Ⓓ Ⓔ	29. Ⓐ Ⓑ Ⓒ Ⓓ Ⓔ	43. Ⓐ Ⓑ Ⓒ Ⓓ Ⓔ	57. Ⓐ Ⓑ Ⓒ Ⓓ Ⓔ	71. Ⓐ Ⓑ Ⓒ Ⓓ Ⓔ
2. Ⓐ Ⓑ Ⓒ Ⓓ Ⓔ	16. Ⓐ Ⓑ Ⓒ Ⓓ Ⓔ	30. Ⓐ Ⓑ Ⓒ Ⓓ Ⓔ	44. Ⓐ Ⓑ Ⓒ Ⓓ Ⓔ	58. Ⓐ Ⓑ Ⓒ Ⓓ Ⓔ	72. Ⓐ Ⓑ Ⓒ Ⓓ Ⓔ
3. Ⓐ Ⓑ Ⓒ Ⓓ Ⓔ	17. Ⓐ Ⓑ Ⓒ Ⓓ Ⓔ	31. Ⓐ Ⓑ Ⓒ Ⓓ Ⓔ	45. Ⓐ Ⓑ Ⓒ Ⓓ Ⓔ	59. Ⓐ Ⓑ Ⓒ Ⓓ Ⓔ	73. Ⓐ Ⓑ Ⓒ Ⓓ Ⓔ
4. Ⓐ Ⓑ Ⓒ Ⓓ Ⓔ	18. Ⓐ Ⓑ Ⓒ Ⓓ Ⓔ	32. Ⓐ Ⓑ Ⓒ Ⓓ Ⓔ	46. Ⓐ Ⓑ Ⓒ Ⓓ Ⓔ	60. Ⓐ Ⓑ Ⓒ Ⓓ Ⓔ	74. Ⓐ Ⓑ Ⓒ Ⓓ Ⓔ
5. Ⓐ Ⓑ Ⓒ Ⓓ Ⓔ	19. Ⓐ Ⓑ Ⓒ Ⓓ Ⓔ	33. Ⓐ Ⓑ Ⓒ Ⓓ Ⓔ	47. Ⓐ Ⓑ Ⓒ Ⓓ Ⓔ	61. Ⓐ Ⓑ Ⓒ Ⓓ Ⓔ	75. Ⓐ Ⓑ Ⓒ Ⓓ Ⓔ
6. Ⓐ Ⓑ Ⓒ Ⓓ Ⓔ	20. Ⓐ Ⓑ Ⓒ Ⓓ Ⓔ	34. Ⓐ Ⓑ Ⓒ Ⓓ Ⓔ	48. Ⓐ Ⓑ Ⓒ Ⓓ Ⓔ	62. Ⓐ Ⓑ Ⓒ Ⓓ Ⓔ	76. Ⓐ Ⓑ Ⓒ Ⓓ Ⓔ
7. Ⓐ Ⓑ Ⓒ Ⓓ Ⓔ	21. Ⓐ Ⓑ Ⓒ Ⓓ Ⓔ	35. Ⓐ Ⓑ Ⓒ Ⓓ Ⓔ	49. Ⓐ Ⓑ Ⓒ Ⓓ Ⓔ	63. Ⓐ Ⓑ Ⓒ Ⓓ Ⓔ	77. Ⓐ Ⓑ Ⓒ Ⓓ Ⓔ
8. Ⓐ Ⓑ Ⓒ Ⓓ Ⓔ	22. Ⓐ Ⓑ Ⓒ Ⓓ Ⓔ	36. Ⓐ Ⓑ Ⓒ Ⓓ Ⓔ	50. Ⓐ Ⓑ Ⓒ Ⓓ Ⓔ	64. Ⓐ Ⓑ Ⓒ Ⓓ Ⓔ	78. Ⓐ Ⓑ Ⓒ Ⓓ Ⓔ
9. Ⓐ Ⓑ Ⓒ Ⓓ Ⓔ	23. Ⓐ Ⓑ Ⓒ Ⓓ Ⓔ	37. Ⓐ Ⓑ Ⓒ Ⓓ Ⓔ	51. Ⓐ Ⓑ Ⓒ Ⓓ Ⓔ	65. Ⓐ Ⓑ Ⓒ Ⓓ Ⓔ	79. Ⓐ Ⓑ Ⓒ Ⓓ Ⓔ
10. Ⓐ Ⓑ Ⓒ Ⓓ Ⓔ	24. Ⓐ Ⓑ Ⓒ Ⓓ Ⓔ	38. Ⓐ Ⓑ Ⓒ Ⓓ Ⓔ	52. Ⓐ Ⓑ Ⓒ Ⓓ Ⓔ	66. Ⓐ Ⓑ Ⓒ Ⓓ Ⓔ	80. Ⓐ Ⓑ Ⓒ Ⓓ Ⓔ
11. Ⓐ Ⓑ Ⓒ Ⓓ Ⓔ	25. Ⓐ Ⓑ Ⓒ Ⓓ Ⓔ	39. Ⓐ Ⓑ Ⓒ Ⓓ Ⓔ	53. Ⓐ Ⓑ Ⓒ Ⓓ Ⓔ	67. Ⓐ Ⓑ Ⓒ Ⓓ Ⓔ	81. Ⓐ Ⓑ Ⓒ Ⓓ Ⓔ
12. Ⓐ Ⓑ Ⓒ Ⓓ Ⓔ	26. Ⓐ Ⓑ Ⓒ Ⓓ Ⓔ	40. Ⓐ Ⓑ Ⓒ Ⓓ Ⓔ	54. Ⓐ Ⓑ Ⓒ Ⓓ Ⓔ	68. Ⓐ Ⓑ Ⓒ Ⓓ Ⓔ	82. Ⓐ Ⓑ Ⓒ Ⓓ Ⓔ
13. Ⓐ Ⓑ Ⓒ Ⓓ Ⓔ	27. Ⓐ Ⓑ Ⓒ Ⓓ Ⓔ	41. Ⓐ Ⓑ Ⓒ Ⓓ Ⓔ	55. Ⓐ Ⓑ Ⓒ Ⓓ Ⓔ	69. Ⓐ Ⓑ Ⓒ Ⓓ Ⓔ	83. Ⓐ Ⓑ Ⓒ Ⓓ Ⓔ
14. Ⓐ Ⓑ Ⓒ Ⓓ Ⓔ	28. Ⓐ Ⓑ Ⓒ Ⓓ Ⓔ	42. Ⓐ Ⓑ Ⓒ Ⓓ Ⓔ	56. Ⓐ Ⓑ Ⓒ Ⓓ Ⓔ	70. Ⓐ Ⓑ Ⓒ Ⓓ Ⓔ	84. Ⓐ Ⓑ Ⓒ Ⓓ Ⓔ

WORD KNOWLEDGE

Directions

This test has questions about the meanings of words. Each question has an underlined boldface word. You are to decide which one of the four words in the choices most nearly means the same as the underlined boldface word, then mark the space on your answer form which has the same number and letter as your choice.

Now look at the sample question below.

1. It was a **small** table.

    1-A   sturdy
    1-B   round
    1-C   cheap
    1-D   little

The question is which of the four words means the same as the boldface word—the word **small.**

Little means the same as small so the D answer is the best one.

Your score on this test will be based on the number of questions you answer correctly. You should try to answer every question. Do not spend too much time on any one question.

When you begin, be sure to start with question number 1 in Part 3 of your test booklet and number 1 in Part 3 on your answer form.

Do not turn this page until told to do so.

WORD KNOWLEDGE

Time: 11 minutes; 35 questions

1. **Opulence** means most nearly

   1-A affluence
   1-B generosity
   1-C poverty
   1-D luxury

2. **Mimesis** means most nearly

   2-A impersonation
   2-B pretense
   2-C cartoon
   2-D imitation

3. **Languid** means most nearly

   3-A sad
   3-B energetic
   3-C healthy
   3-D listless

4. **Inherence** means most nearly

   4-A essential
   4-B intrinsic
   4-C accidental
   4-D necessity

5. **Anomie** means most nearly

   5-A essential
   5-B vacuum
   5-C control
   5-D anonym

6. **Tenuous** means most nearly

   6-A tensile
   6-B tentative
   6-C ethereal
   6-D substantial

7. **Salutation** means most nearly

   7-A offering
   7-B greeting
   7-C discussion
   7-D appeasement

8. **Mesmerize** means most nearly

   8-A hypnotize
   8-B hypostatize
   8-C metabolize
   8-D change

9. **Panoply** means most nearly

   9-A pansophy
   9-B display
   9-C resistance
   9-D parry

10. **Syntactic** means most nearly

    10-A morphological
    10-B grammatical
    10-C standard
    10-D inflexional

11. **Umbrage** means most nearly

    11-A resentment
    11-B umbo
    11-C impertinence
    11-D pleasure

12. **Raucous** means most nearly

    12-A ravenous
    12-B harsh
    12-C pleasing
    12-D rankling

13. **Prosecution** means most nearly

    13-A protection
    13-B imprisonment
    13-C trial
    13-D punishment

14. **Miasma** means most nearly

    14-A pollution
    14-B fumes
    14-C exhalations
    14-D stench

15. **Paragon** means most nearly

    15-A paradox
    15-B model
    15-C prototype
    15-D ideal

16. **Innate** means most nearly

    16-A eternal
    16-B well-developed
    16-C temporary
    16-D native

17. **Urbanity** means most nearly

17-A loyalty
17-B refinement
17-C weakness
17-D barbarism

18. To **encounter** means most nearly

18-A to recall
18-B to overcome
18-C to retreat
18-D to meet

19. **Banal** means most nearly

19-A commonplace
19-B forceful
19-C tranquil
19-D indifferent

20. **Small** most nearly means

20-A sturdy.
20-B round.
20-C cheap.
20-D little.

21. The accountant **discovered** an error.

21-A searched
21-B found
21-C enlarged
21-D entered

22. **Inform** most nearly means

22-A ask.
22-B turn.
22-C tell.
22-D ignore.

23. The wind is **variable** today.
23-A shifting
23-B chilling
23-C steady
23-D mild

24. **Cease** most nearly means

24-A start.
24-B change.
24-C continue.
24-D stop.

25. **Impair** most nearly means

25-A direct.
25-B improve.
25-C weaken.
25-D stimulate.

26. **Rudiments** most nearly means

26-A basic methods and procedures.

26-B politics.
26-C promotion opportunities.
26-D minute details.

27. **Imprudent** most nearly means

27-A reckless
27-B unexcitable
27-C poor
27-D domineering

28. **Dissension** most nearly means

28-A friction
28-B analysis
28-C injury
28-D slyness

29. **Disconnect** most nearly means

29-A separate
29-B cripple
29-C lesson
29-D dismiss

30. **Rudimentary** most nearly means

30-A discourteous
30-B brutal
30-C displeasing
30-D elementary

31. **Autonomous** most nearly means

31-A self-important
31-B self-educated
31-C self-explanatory
31-D self-governing

32. **Meander** most nearly means

32-A grumble
32-B wander aimlessly
32-C come between
32-D weigh carefully

33. **Destitution** most nearly means

33-A fate
33-B lack of practice
33-C extreme poverty
33-D recovery

34. **Malign** most nearly means

34-A slander
34-B prophesy
34-C entreat
34-D praise

35. **Impotent** most nearly means

35-A unwise
35-B lacking strength
35-C free of sin
35-D commanding

4

PARAGRAPH COMPREHENSION

Directions

This is a test of your ability to understand what you read. In this section you will find one or more paragraphs of reading material followed by incomplete statements or questions. You are to read the paragraph and select one of four lettered choices which best completes the statement or answers the question. When you have selected your answer, blacken in the correct numbered letter on your answer sheet.

Now look at the sample question below.

In certain areas water is so scarce that every attempt is made to conserve it. For instance, on one oasis in the Sahara Desert the amount of water necessary for each date palm tree has been carefully determined.

2. How much water is each tree given?

2-A   no water at all
2-B   exactly the amount required
2-C   water only if it is healthy
2-D   water on alternate days

The amount of water each tree requires has been carefully determined so the answer 2-B is correct.

Your score on this test will be based on the number of questions you answer correctly. You should try to answer every question. Do not spend too much time on any one question.

When you begin, be sure to start with question number 1 in Part 4 of your test booklet and number 1 in Part 4 on your answer form.

Do not turn this page until told to do so.

PARAGRAPH COMPREHENSION

Time: 13 minutes; 15 questions

1. The duty of the lighthouse keeper is to keep the light burning no matter what happens, so that ships will be warned of the presence of dangerous rocks. If a shipwreck should occur near the lighthouse, even though he would like to aid in the rescue of its crew and passengers, the lighthouse keeper must

   1-A stay at his light.
   1-B rush to their aid.
   1-C turn out the light.
   1-D quickly sound the siren.

In certain areas water is so scarce that every attempt is made to conserve it. For instance, on one oasis in the Sahara Desert the amount of water necessary for each date palm tree has been carefully determined.

2. How much water is each tree given?

   2-A no water at all
   2-B exactly the amount required
   2-C water only if it is healthy
   2-D water on alternate days

Plants should be gradually "hardened," or toughened, for 2 weeks before being moved outdoors. This is done by withholding water and lowering the temperature. Hardening slows down the plants' rate of growth to prepare them to withstand such conditions as chilling, drying winds, or high temperatures.

3. You toughen a seedling

   3-A by putting it in a cooler environment.
   3-B by putting it in a six-inch pot.
   3-C by watering it thoroughly.
   3-D by using ready-made peat pellets.

At depths of several miles inside the earth, the weight of rocks causes great pressure. This rock pressure, as well as other forces, sometimes causes rocks to break and slip. Faults (great cracks) form. When slippage occurs, shock waves are felt and can be detected with seismographs thousands of miles away.

4. The most frequent cause of major earthquakes is

   4-A faulting
   4-B folding
   4-C landslides
   4-D submarine currents

The leaf can catch sunlight and turn this energy into food which is stored in the tree or plant. To run this factory the leaf must have air, water, and sunlight. By a chemical process called *photosynthesis,* the leaf combines the air and water with the energy of the sun.

5. The process of *photosynthesis:*

   5-A combines air, water, and sun to make food
   5-B makes leaves grow in fancy shapes
   5-C causes water to form in clouds
   5-D is a physical process

Most telephone sales are made by *reputable* persons, who try to sell in an honest manner. These persons use the telephone as an aid to business and they know they depend upon being fair and reasonable. The opposite of the reputable salesmen are the *over-aggressive* talkers who try to force you to make up your mind quickly.

6. The word *reputable* is closest in meaning to:

   6-A reasonable
   6-B trusted
   6-C friendly
   6-D aggressive

When someone in your family suffers a minor burn, reach for an ice cube fast. Place it directly over the burn until the sting is gone when the cube is removed. Ice is a great first aid for burns and kills the pain. Afterwards you'll be amazed to discover there is very little swelling, blisters probably won't appear, and healing will be much faster.

7. The topic sentence or key idea in this paragraph is that

   7-A ice prevents burn blisters.
   7-B ice cubes remove the pain.
   7-C ice is great first aid for burns.
   7-D ice reduces swelling.

A stranger meets you and shows you some cash he has just "found." He wants to divide it with you. He says that you must show your "good faith" and put up some of your own money. When you agree to give your money, the stranger finds some reason to leave for a while. Do you see him again? Not likely; you have just been cheated or swindled.

8. The main theme of this passage is:

8-A   Do not speak to strangers
8-B   Be careful of "get-rich-quick" plans
8-C   How to make money
8-D   Do not believe strangers

Statistically, by far the most common types of home accidents are falls. Each year over 10,500 Americans meet death in this way, within the four walls of their home, or in yards around the house. Nine out of 10 of the victims are over 65, but people of all ages experience serious injuries as a result of home falls.

9. Falls most frequently result in death for

9-A   children
9-B   adults under 35
9-C   all age groups
9-D   adults over 65

"Gray water" is slightly used water—the water you have collected at the bottom of the tub after you have showered or the rinse water from the washing machine. It is still useful, and we cannot afford to let it go down the drain.

10. Which of the following is an example of gray water?

10-A   carbonated water
10-B   rain water
10-C   soapy water
10-D   tap water

Glaciers are frozen masses of snow and ice. As the weight of snow increases each year, the lower layers become hard-packed like ice. The weight also causes the glacier to move slowly down hill. Speeds of glaciers are usually figured in inches per day rather than miles per hour.

11. The glacier moves as a result of its:

11-A   speed
11-B   weight
11-C   temperature
11-D   layers

It is time to get this country moving again. No American wants to stand by and see this country go the other way. The men who have been elected are no longer in touch. A fresh point of view, new ideas, and more action are needed. The voters should finally wake up and give power to those who will make changes.

12. This passage tries to make you believe that

12-A   changes are needed.
12-B   no changes are needed.
12-C   changes wil never happen.
12-D   no action is needed.

Up until a few years ago most parents, teachers, baby doctors, and coaches felt that right was right. There was even an old wives' tale that left-handed people did not learn as well. But, I'm happy to report, this right-thinking is gone. Today parents and teachers understand left-handedness, and our number is rising.

13. The main idea of this passage is that the feelings about left-handedness:

13-A   have not changed at all
13-B   have completely changed
13-C   have changed partly
13-D   will not change

According to Newton's Third Law, to each action there is an equal and opposite reaction. You can illustrate the principle by blowing up a rubber balloon, and then allowing the air to escape. Notice that the balloon moves forward as the air escapes in the opposite direction.

14. Which of the following describes Newton's Third Law?

14-A   an object at rest
14-B   gravitational force
14-C   falling bodies
14-D   action equals reaction

Water is a good conductor of sound waves. If you were swimming under water while someone struck two rocks together under water ten feet away, you would be surprised at how loud the sound was. The U.S. Navy makes use of this knowledge in detecting enemy submarines.

15. Of the following, which can best be concluded from this selection?

15-A   Fish cannot hear ordinary sounds.
15-B   Sound waves become compressed in very deep water.
15-C   Water is a good conductor of sound waves.
15-D   Submarines cannot detect sound waves.

NUMERICAL OPERATIONS

Directions

This is a test to see how rapidly and accurately you can do arithmetic problems. Each problem is followed by four answers, only one of which is correct. Decide which answer is correct, then blacken the space on your answer form which has the same number and letter as your choice.

Now look at the sample problem below.

1. 5 − 2 =

    1-A   10
    1-B   7
    1-C   0
    1-D   3

The answer to the problem is 3, so you would blacken the space for 1-D on your answer form.

This is a speed test, so work as fast as you can without making mistakes. Do each problem as it comes. If you finish before time is up, go back and check your work. Part 5 of this model test begins with question 1. Thus, your first answer should be recorded next to 1 on your answer form.

Do not turn this page until told to do so.

NUMERICAL OPERATIONS

Time: 3 minutes; 50 questions

1. 7 + 2 =

    1-A   5
    1-B   14
    1-C   9
    1-D   10

2. 2 − 0 =

    2-A   2
    2-B   0
    2-C   1
    2-D   20

3. 8 × 3 =

    3-A   28
    3-B   26
    3-C   24
    3-D   22

4. 6 + 1 =

    4-A   5
    4-B   6
    4-C   8
    4-D   7

5. 9 − 3 =

    5-A   27
    5-B   3
    5-C   12
    5-D   6

6. 4 ÷ 1 =

    6-A   0
    6-B   4
    6-C   5
    6-D   1

7. 10 − 6 =

    7-A   7
    7-B   6
    7-C   5
    7-D   4

8. 3 × 9 =

    8-A   12
    8-B   21
    8-C   27
    8-D   30

9. 5 × 6 =

    9-A   30
    9-B   25
    9-C   20
    9-D   15

10. 1 + 8 =

    10-A   1
    10-B   7
    10-C   9
    10-D   11

11. 4 + 7 =

    11-A   13
    11-B   11
    11-C   9
    11-D   15

12. 0 ÷ 6 =

    12-A   0
    12-B   6
    12-C   1
    12-D   3

13. 7 + 6 =

    13-A   16
    13-B   15
    13-C   13
    13-D   11

14. 10 ÷ 1 =

    14-A   8
    14-B   9
    14-C   11
    14-D   10

15. 9 + 5 =

    15-A   14
    15-B   13
    15-C   16
    15-D   15

16. 3 + 7 =

    16-A   10
    16-B   4
    16-C   21
    16-D   9

17. $15 \div 5 =$

   17-A   5
   17-B   0
   17-C   3
   17-D   10

18. $13 - 9 =$

   18-A   7
   18-B   6
   18-C   5
   18-D   4

19. $2 + 5 =$

   19-A   3
   19-B   10
   19-C   8
   19-D   7

20. $8 + 4 =$

   20-A   12
   20-B   13
   20-C   14
   20-D   15

21. $5 \times 2 =$

   21-A   3
   21-B   7
   21-C   10
   21-D   15

22. $5 - 0 =$

   22-A   5
   22-B   1
   22-C   0
   22-D   4

23. $19 - 1 =$

   23-A   19
   23-B   20
   23-C   18
   23-D   21

24. $7 + 8 =$

   24-A   15
   24-B   16
   24-C   17
   24-D   18

25. $1 \times 0 =$

   25-A   0
   25-B   1
   25-C   2
   25-D   10

26. $2 \times 4 =$

   26-A   6
   26-B   2
   26-C   8
   26-D   10

27. $6 - 4 =$

   27-A   3
   27-B   4
   27-C   5
   27-D   2

28. $9 \times 2 =$

   28-A   11
   28-B   18
   28-C   21
   28-D   7

29. $8 \div 1 =$

   29-A   9
   29-B   8
   29-C   1
   29-D   0

30. $4 + 3 =$

   30-A   7
   30-B   12
   30-C   9
   30-D   6

31. $12 \div 3 =$

   31-A   9
   31-B   6
   31-C   4
   31-D   3

32. $17 - 6 =$

   32-A   15
   32-B   13
   32-C   11
   32-D   9

33. $8 - 6 =$

   33-A   5
   33-B   4
   33-C   3
   33-D   2

34. $6 \times 3 =$

   34-A   9
   34-B   12
   34-C   15
   34-D   18

35. 3 − 0 =

    35-A 3
    35-B 0
    35-C 1
    35-D 2

36. 11 + 3 =

    36-A 12
    36-B 13
    36-C 14
    36-D 15

37. 21 ÷ 3 =

    37-A 18
    37-B 9
    37-C 7
    37-D 6

38. 10 + 1 =

    38-A 11
    38-B 9
    38-C 10
    38-D 1

39. 7 − 1 =

    39-A 8
    39-B 7
    39-C 6
    39-D 1

40. 0 ÷ 5 =

    40-A 0
    40-B 5
    40-C 1
    40-D 6

41. 4 − 2 =

    41-A 0
    41-B 1
    41-C 2
    41-D 3

42. 5 × 7 =

    42-A 35
    42-B 28
    42-C 25
    42-D 21

43. 4 − 1 =

    43-A 4
    43-B 3
    43-C 1
    43-D 2

44. 8 + 2 =

    44-A 16
    44-B 14
    44-C 12
    44-D 10

45. 6 ÷ 6 =

    45-A 36
    45-B 1
    45-C 12
    45-D 0

46. 9 + 2 =

    46-A 7
    46-B 11
    46-C 18
    46-D 15

47. 11 − 5 =

    47-A 16
    47-B 14
    47-C 6
    47-D 4

48. 20 + 1 =

    48-A 21
    48-B 19
    48-C 1
    48-D 20

49. 8 ÷ 4 =

    49-A 12
    49-B 4
    49-C 2
    49-D 32

50. 4 × 4 =

    50-A 8
    50-B 1
    50-C 12
    50-D 16

CODING SPEED

Directions

This is a test to see how quickly and accurately you can assign code numbers. At the top of each set of questions there is a code number "key." The key is a group of words with a code number for each word.

Each question in the test is a word taken from the key at the top. From among the possible answers listed for each question, you are to find the one which is the correct code number for that word. Then blacken the square for that answer on your answer sheet.

The sample questions below have already been answered for you. Make sure you understand them. Then try to answer the 84 questions following them as best you can.

Sample Question

Key

green .. 2715	man ... 3451	salt 4586
hat 1413	room... 2864	tree 5972

Answers

	A	B	C	D	E
room	1413	2715	2864	3451	4586
green	2715	2864	3451	4586	5972
tree	2715	2864	3451	4596	5972
hat	1413	2715	2864	3451	4586
room	1413	2864	3451	4586	5972

Notice that each of the questions is one of the words in the key. To the right of each question are possible answers listed under the letters A, B, C, D, and E. By looking at the key you see that the code number for the first word, "room," is 2864. 2864 is listed under the letter C so C is the correct answer. The correct answers for the other four questions are A, E, A, and B.

Do not turn this page until told to do so.

CODING SPEED

Time: 7 minutes; 84 questions

Key

book . . . 7285	mail . . 2857	room . . 8217
captain . 6749	motel . . 9512	sofa . . 8703
house . . 4465	pistol . . . 7120	speed . . 1133
	table . . . 9038	

Answers

		A	B	C	D	E
1.	mail	1133	2857	6749	7120	9038
2.	table	1133	2857	4465	6749	9038
3.	speed	1133	4465	6749	8217	9038
4.	book	6749	7120	7285	8217	8703
5.	pistol	2857	4465	6749	7109	7120
6.	motel	1133	4465	7120	7285	9512
7.	room	2857	6749	7120	8217	9038
8.	table	1133	6749	8703	9038	9512
9.	house	2857	4465	6749	9038	9512
10.	captain	4465	6749	7285	8217	9512
11.	speed	1133	7120	7285	8217	9038
12.	house	2857	4465	6749	8217	9512

Key

admit . . 5927	fire 7986	plant . . . 1228
circle . . 5430	fox 8721	red . . . 1005
column . 5272	glass . . . 4789	street . . 6634
	sunshine 9137	

Answers

		A	B	C	D	E
13.	plant	1228	4789	5430	8721	9137
14.	circle	1005	5272	5430	6634	9137
15.	red	1005	5272	5927	6634	7986
16.	fox	1228	4789	5430	6634	8721
17.	street	4789	5430	5927	6634	9138
18.	sunshine	1005	5272	5927	7986	9137
19.	glass	1228	4789	5927	6749	8721
20.	street	1005	1228	6634	7986	8721
21.	column	4789	5272	6634	8721	9512
22.	fire	1005	1228	5430	5927	7986
23.	admit	1228	5927	7986	8721	9137
24.	red	1005	4789	5430	7986	9137

Key

answer . 3569	flower . . 2665	marry . . 2939
boy 7780	green . . 7218	nation . . 1812
cat 5540	hat 9224	pair 4325
	salt . . . 1932	

Answers

		A	B	C	D	E
25.	cat	1812	1932	2939	3569	5540
26.	flower	1812	2665	4325	5540	7218
27.	green	1932	3569	7218	7780	9224
28.	hat	2665	3569	4325	7218	9224
29.	cat	1812	1932	4325	5540	7780
30.	marry	2665	2939	3569	7780	9224
31.	salt	1932	4325	7218	7780	9224
32.	answer	1812	3569	5540	7218	7780
33.	green	1932	2665	2939	4325	7218
34.	nation	1812	2939	4325	5540	7780
35.	flower	2665	2939	5540	7218	7780
36.	boy	1812	2939	3569	7780	9224

Key

absent . 3917	debt . . . 1037	rent 4200
beet . . . 6138	insect . . 5559	sick 2451
brick . . . 8626	one 9674	tailor . . . 8507
	wages . 3892	

Answers

		A	B	C	D	E
37.	beet	4200	6138	8507	8626	9674
38.	wages	3892	3917	6138	8507	8626
39.	sick	1037	2451	3892	6138	9674
40.	insect	3892	3917	4200	5559	9674
41.	debt	1037	3892	4200	6138	8507
42.	brick	2451	3917	5559	8507	8626
43.	absent	1037	3917	6138	8507	8626
44.	rent	2451	4200	6138	8507	9674
45.	debt	1037	3917	5559	6138	8626
46.	one	2451	3892	4200	8507	9674
47.	tailor	2451	3892	3917	5559	8507
48.	absent	1037	3917	4200	6138	8507

Key

able . . . 1279	juice . . . 7543	sea . . . 4096
ill 4903	oil 5691	sew 6837
iron 9976	pepper . 8104	size 7744
	yellow . . 3624	

Answers

		A	B	C	D	E
49.	sew	4096	4903	5961	6837	8104
50.	juice	1279	3624	5691	7543	8104
51.	ill	4096	4903	7543	7744	9976

		A	B	C	D	E
52.	yellow	1279	3624	5691	8104	9976
53.	able	1279	3624	4096	6837	8104
54.	size	3624	4096	4903	7543	7744
55.	oil	4096	4903	5691	8104	9976
56.	ill	1279	3624	4903	7543	8104
57.	iron	1279	5691	7543	7744	9976
58.	pepper	3624	4096	4903	5691	8104
59.	sea	3624	4096	6839	7543	9976
60.	able	1279	3624	4096	7744	8104

Key

cancel . 7384	heat ... 4679	spare . 3574
credit .. 9277	odor ... 1984	taste ... 3695
girl 2253	office .. 8860	twin 1215
	week... 6218	

Answers

		A	B	C	D	E
61.	girl	2253	3574	3695	4679	6218
62.	week	1215	1984	3574	6218	8860
63.	cancel	2243	3574	3695	6218	7384
64.	heat	1984	4679	6218	8860	9277
65.	credit	1215	1984	3574	8860	9277
66.	odor	1984	2253	3574	3695	8860
67.	office	3695	4679	7384	8860	9277
68.	spare	1215	3574	3695	4679	6218

		A	B	C	D	E
69.	heat	1984	2253	3695	4679	8860
70.	twin	1215	3574	7384	8860	9277
71.	taste	1984	3574	3695	6218	8860
72.	odor	1984	2253	3574	4679	7384

Key

art 8598	dog 9362	flag 4400
body ... 4186	enforce. 1273	purple.. 3857
candle . 8930	exit 6529	road ... 5271
	yield ... 6049	

Answers

		A	B	C	D	E
73.	body	1273	4186	4400	5271	8598
74.	road	3857	5271	6049	8930	9362
75.	candle	3857	4400	5271	8598	8930
76.	flag	1273	4400	5271	6049	9362
77.	enforce	1273	3857	4186	5271	6049
78.	dog	3857	4400	8598	8930	9362
79.	exit	1273	3857	4400	4186	6049
80.	exit	3857	4186	5271	6049	6529
81.	art	5271	6049	8598	8930	9362
82.	yield	3857	6049	6529	8598	9362
83.	purple	1273	4186	4400	5271	6529
84.	flag	1273	3857	4400	6529	8930

7

AUTO AND SHOP INFORMATION

Directions

This test has questions about automobiles. Pick the best answer for each question, then blacken the space on your separate answer form which has the same number and letter as your choice.

Here is a sample question.

1. The most commonly used fuel for running autombile engines is

    1-A   kerosene.
    1-B   benzine.
    1-C   crude oil.
    1-D   gasoline.

Gasoline is the most commonly used fuel, so 1-D is the correct answer.

Your score on this test will be based on the number of questions you answer correctly. You should try to answer every question. Do not spend too much time on any one question.

When you are told to begin, be sure to start with question number 1 in Part 7 of your test booklet and number 1 in Part 7 on your separate answer form.

Do not turn this page until told to do so.

AUTO AND SHOP INFORMATION

Time: 11 minutes; 25 questions

1. Which is the right side of an engine?

   1-A The right side when you stand in front and look at the engine.
   1-B The side that the distributor is on.
   1-C It depends on the manufacturer.
   1-D The right side when you stand in back and look at the engine.

2. The letter and numbers, G 78-14, printed on a tire refer to

   2-A load, width, diameter.
   2-B diameter and air pressure.
   2-C cubic inch displacement.
   2-D price code.

3. "Tracking," in terms of front-end alignment, means that

   3-A each wheel travels independently of the other.
   3-B the wheels follow well on ice or in snow.
   3-C the front tires leave stronger tracks than the rear tires.
   3-D the rear wheels follow the front wheels correctly.

4. A car with worn-out shock absorbers

   4-A cannot carry a heavy load.
   4-B will bounce a lot on a rough road.
   4-C sags very low to the ground.
   4-D will have no traction on a wet road.

5. In a three-speed transmission, the cluster gear is supported by the

   5-A pinion shaft.
   5-B countershaft.
   5-C main shaft.
   5-D output shaft.

6. A clutch release bearing

   6-A rotates whenever the engine is turning.
   6-B rotates when only the clutch is engaged.
   6-C rotates whenever the clutch pedal is depressed.
   6-D holds the clutch shaft in alignment.

7. The general procedure to follow when adjusting a band on an automatic transmission is

   7-A loosen, tighten to a specified torque, loosen a specified number of turns, and lock.
   7-B tighten to a specified torque with a torque wrench and lock.
   7-C tighten to a specified torque, loosen 5 turns, and lock.
   7-D loosen, tighten to a specified torque, and lock.

8. The purpose of the drive shaft is to connect the

   8-A piston to the transmission.
   8-B differential to the transmission.
   8-C flywheel to the crankshaft.
   8-D camshaft to the crankshaft.

9. The order in which the spark plugs in the engine fire is established by the order in which the

   9-A plugs are mounted in the engine.
   9-B plug leads are connected to the distributor cap.
   9-C condenser is connected.
   9-D contact points are opened.

10. The terminals exposed on the ignition induction coil are

    10-A two secondary and one primary.
    10-B one secondary and one primary.
    10-C one secondary and two primary.
    10-D two secondary and two primary.

11. Battery electrolyte is a mixture of distilled water and

    11-A baking soda.
    11-B sulphuric acid.
    11-C lead peroxide.
    11-D carbon particles.

12. The brushes in an alternator ride on

    12-A the commutator.
    12-B the stator.
    12-C slip rings.
    12-D the heat sink.

13. When all other lights show normal illumination but one headlight is dim, it is a good indication that the

    13-A   battery is weak.
    13-B   headlight switch is defective.
    13-C   headlight unit needs adjustment.
    13-D   headlight has a poor ground connection.

14. Should air get into the hydraulic brake system,

    14-A   brake application will be hard.
    14-B   it will have no effect.
    14-C   brake pedal action will be spongy.
    14-D   the brake pedal will stick.

15. The proportioning valve in a hydraulic brake system

    15-A   reduces pressure to the front brakes.
    15-B   controls the brake warning switch.
    15-C   is used only on a drum type brake system.
    15-D   reduces pressure to the rear brakes.

16. The coping saw blade is placed in the saw

    16-A   with the teeth pointing upward.
    16-B   with the teeth pointing toward the handle.
    16-C   so it cuts with the wood grain.
    16-D   so it cuts across the wood grain.

17. Carpenters use

    17-A   ball peen hammers.
    17-B   chisel point hammers.
    17-C   claw hammers.
    17-D   planishing hammers.

18. The term penny is used

    18-A   to designate the cost of a nail.
    18-B   to designate the size of a nail.
    18-C   to indicate a rosin coated nail.
    18-D   to indicate a galvanized nail.

19. A tool used to cut sheet metal is

    19-A   the bar folder.
    19-B   the box and pan brake.
    19-C   the slip roll.
    19-D   the squaring shear.

20. One of the most common ways to fasten sheet metal today is

    20-A   to solder it.
    20-B   to braze it.
    20-C   to spot weld it.
    20-D   to glue it.

21. A welding torch can also be used as

    21-A   a light source.
    21-B   a burning tool.
    21-C   a cutting torch.
    21-D   a pipe wrench.

22. Tubing cutters are smaller versions of

    22-A   pipe cutters.
    22-B   ring cutters.
    22-C   hole cutters.
    22-D   glass cutters.

23. If you "overwork" concrete, it will cause

    23-A   loss of a smooth surface.
    23-B   separation and create a less durable surface.
    23-C   loss of strength throughout the slab.
    23-D   puddles in the middle of the slab.

24. Concrete reaches 98% of its strength in

    24-A   3 days.
    24-B   50 days.
    24-C   28 days.
    24-D   10 days.

25. Deciduous trees produce

    25-A   soft wood.
    25-B   dead wood.
    25-C   hard wood.
    25-D   conifers.

MATHEMATICS KNOWLEDGE

Directions

This is a test of your ability to solve general mathematical problems. Each problem is followed by four answer choices. Select the correct response from the choices given. Then mark the space on your answer form that has the same number and letter as your choice. Use scratch paper to do any figuring that you wish.

Now look at this sample problem.

1. $10 + 1 =$

    1-A   11
    1-B   10
    1-C   9
    1-D   8

The correct answer is 11, so 1-A is the correct response.

Your score on this test will be based on the number of questions you answer correctly. You should try to answer every question. Do not spend too much time on any one question.

Start with question number 1 in Part 8. Mark your answer for this question next to number 1, Part 8, on your answer form.

Do not turn this page until told to do so.

MATHEMATICS KNOWLEDGE

Time: 24 minutes: 25 questions

1. If $b - 3 = 7$, then b is equal to

   1-A   10
   1-B   4
   1-C   21
   1-D   8

2. What is the product of $(z + 2)(2z - 3)$?

   2-A $3z - 6$
   2-B $z + 4z - 3$
   2-C $z^2 + 4z - 6$
   2-D $2z^2 + z - 6$

3. Smith Township has a public pool in the shape of a quadrilateral. If the town wants to put a lifeguard on each side of the pool, how many lifeguards are needed?

   3-A   8
   3-B   6
   3-C   4
   3-D   3

4. If the largest possible circular tabletop is cut from a square whose side is 2 feet, how much wood is wasted? (Use 3.14 for Pi.)

   4-A   1 square foot
   4-B   1.86 square feet
   4-C   5.86 square feet
   4-D   0.86 square feet

5. Solve for x: $3x + 2 = -13$

   5-A $x = 13$
   5-B $x = -4\frac{1}{3}$
   5-C $x = 8$
   5-D $x = -5$

6. An artist sold 4 of his paintings. These represented 0.05 of all the artwork he had done. How many paintings had he made?

   6-A   100
   6-B   80
   6-C   50
   6-D   20

7. One of the equal angles of an isosceles triangle is 40 degrees. What is the angle opposite the unequal side?

   7-A   40 degrees
   7-B   90 degrees
   7-C   100 degrees
   7-D   140 degrees

8. If you divide $24x^3 + 16x^2 - 8x$ by $8x$, how many x's will there be in the quotient?

   8-A   0
   8-B   5
   8-C   2
   8-D -1

9. A room is 19 feet long, 10 feet wide, and 8 feet high. If you want to paint the walls and ceiling, how many square feet of surface would you cover with paint?

   9-A   232 square feet
   9-B   422 square feet
   9-C   464 square feet
   9-D   654 square feet

10. If a car traveled 200 miles at an average rate of speed of r miles per hour, the time it took for the trip could be written as

    10-A $200/r$
    10-B $r/200$
    10-C $200r$
    10-D $r/60$

11. An equilateral triangle has the same perimeter as a square whose side is 12". What is the length of a side of the triangle?

    11-A   9"
    11-B   12"
    11-C   18"
    11-D   16"

12. What is the value of $(0.1)^3$?

    12-A   0.3
    12-B   0.003
    12-C   0.1
    12-D   0.001

13. How many inches are contained in f feet and i inches?

    13-A $f \times i$
    13-B $f + i$
    13-C $f + 12i$
    13-D $12f + i$

14. A good rule of thumb is that a house should cost no more than 2½ times its owner's income. How much should you be earning to afford a $64,000 home?

    14-A $20,500
    14-B $25,600
    14-C $32,000
    14-D $160,000

15. What is the value of $(+2)(-5)(+3)(-3)$?

    15-A +90
    15-B +60
    15-C −13
    15-D −3

16. Solve for x: $x^2 = 3x + 10$

    16-A $x = 3$, $x = 10$
    16-B $x = -3, x = -10$
    16-C $x = -2, x = 5$
    16-D $x = 2$, $x = -5$

17. Which of these is a cylinder?

    17-A a stick of butter
    17-B an orange
    17-C a stereo album
    17-D a frozen-juice can

18. Solve the following formula for R.

    $$N = \frac{CR}{C + R}$$

    18-A $R = \dfrac{C}{C + N}$

    18-B $R = \dfrac{NC}{C - N}$

    18-C $R = \dfrac{N}{C - R}$

    18-D $R = \dfrac{C - N}{R}$

19. What is the reciprocal of ⅗?

    19-A 0.6
    19-B 1⅔
    19-C 2
    19-D 1

20. What is the value of $(\sqrt{13})^2$?

    20-A 26
    20-B 13
    20-C 87
    20-D 169

21. Mr. Larson drove his car steadily at 40 mph for 120 miles. He then increased his speed and drove the next 120 miles at 60 mph. What was his average speed?

    21-A 48 miles per hour
    21-B 52 miles per hour
    21-C 50 miles per hour
    21-D 46 miles per hour

22. An architect designs two walls of a museum to meet at an angle of 120 degrees. What is an angle of this size called?

    22-A acute
    22-B obtuse
    22-C right
    22-D straight

23. Solve the following equations for x.

    $$5x + 4y = 27$$
    $$x - 2y = 11$$

    23-A $x = 3$
    23-B $x = 9$
    23-C $x = 4.5$
    23-D $x = 7$

24. If a is a negative number, and ab is a positive number, then which of the following must be true?

    24-A b is positive.
    24-B a is greater than b.
    24-C b is negative.
    24-D b is greater than a.

25. Solve the following inequality.

    $$x + 5 > 7$$

    25-A $x = 2$
    25-B $x > 2$
    25-C $x - 7 > 5$
    25-D $x - 5 > 7$

MECHANICAL COMPREHENSION

Directions

This test has questions about general mechanical and physical principles. Pick the best answer for each question, then blacken the space on your separate answer form which has the same number and letter as your choice.

Here is a sample question.

17. The follower is at its highest position between points

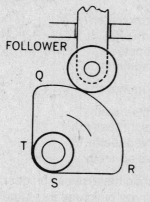

17-A   Q and R.
17-B   R and S.
17-C   S and T.
17-D   T and Q.

The correct answer is between Q and R, so you would blacken the space for 17-A on your answer form.

Your score on this test will be based on the number of questions you answer correctly. You should try to answer every question. Do not spend too much time on any one question.

When you are told to begin, be sure to start with question number 1 in Part 9 of your test booklet and number 1 in Part 9 of your separate answer form.

Do not turn this page until told to do so.

MECHANICAL COMPREHENSION

Time: 19 minutes; 25 questions

1. Cap screws are ordered by

    1-A   wrench size.
    1-B   diameter and wrench size.
    1-C   diameter and number of threads.
    1-D   wrench size and kind of threads.

2. A round piece of stock having a different type of thread at each end is called a

    2-A   head bolt.
    2-B   stud.
    2-C   screw.
    2-D   cap screw.

3. The measurement across the flats of a cap screw head determines the

    3-A   wrench size.
    3-B   bolt size.
    3-C   thread size.
    3-D   diameter.

4. Ring and pinion backlash is checked with

    4-A   a micrometer.
    4-B   a round feeler gauge.
    4-C   Prussian blue.
    4-D   a dial indicator.

5. The clutch aligning arbor is used to align the clutch disc to the

    5-A   transmission.
    5-B   pilot bearing.
    5-C   pressure plate.
    5-D   main drive gear.

6. An oscilloscope is used to diagnose problems in which automotive system?

    6-A   charging
    6-B   starting
    6-C   fuel
    6-D   ignition

7. Which tool is used to adjust the preload on a front wheel bearing?

    7-A   pliers
    7-B   torque wrench
    7-C   dial indicator
    7-D   bearing cup driver

8. Which device measures electrical resistance?

    8-A   an ammeter
    8-B   a voltmeter
    8-C   an ohmmeter
    8-D   a hydrometer

9. The tool used to tighten a cylinder head bolt is a

    9-A   box wrench.
    9-B   breaker bar.
    9-C   ratchet.
    9-D   torque wrench.

10. The strength of the antifreeze solution is tested with a

    10-A   thermometer.
    10-B   thermostat.
    10-C   voltmeter.
    10-D   hydrometer.

11. Helical gears have

    11-A   slanted teeth.
    11-B   straight teeth.
    11-C   curved teeth.
    11-D   beveled teeth.

12. The gear train that uses a sun gear, internal gear and three pinion gears is known as

    12-A   bevel spiral pinion.
    12-B   worm and sector.
    12-C   planetary gears.
    12-D   differential gears.

13. Reciprocating motion is changed into rotary motion by which one of the following engine parts?

    13-A   camshaft
    13-B   connecting rod bearings
    13-C   pistons
    13-D   crankshaft

14. Moisture forming on the inner surface of a windshield on a cold day is an example of

    14-A   vaporization.
    14-B   evaporation.
    14-C   distillation.
    14-D   condensation.

15. Which of the following statements concerning the poles of a magnet is correct?

   15-A   South repels north.
   15-B   Like poles attract.
   15-C   North attracts north.
   15-D   Unlike poles attract.

16. Torque means

   16-A   number of cylinders.
   16-B   turning effort.
   16-C   ratio of drive shaft to rear axle.
   16-D   drive shaft.

17. Water in an automobile engine may cause damage in cold weather because

   17-A   ice is a poor conductor of heat.
   17-B   water expands as it freezes.
   17-C   cold water is compressible.
   17-D   ice is denser than water.

18. What is the rear axle ratio in a standard differential with eleven teeth on the pinion gear and forty-three teeth on the ring gear?

   18-A   4.10 to 1
   18-B   3.90 to 1
   18-C   3.73 to 1
   18-D   3.54 to 1

19. Gear B is intended to mesh with

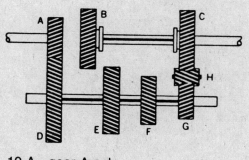

   19-A   gear A only.
   19-B   gear D only.
   19-C   gear E only.
   19-D   all of the above gears.

20. As cam A makes one complete turn, the setscrew will hit the contact point

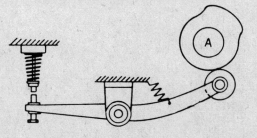

   20-A   once.
   20-B   twice.
   20-C   three times.
   20-D   not at all.

21. If gear A makes 14 revolutions, gear B will make

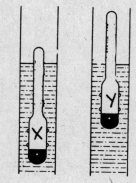

15 TEETH   10 TEETH

   21-A   21.
   21-B   17.
   21-C   14.
   21-D   9.

22. Which of the other gears is moving in the same direction as gear 2?

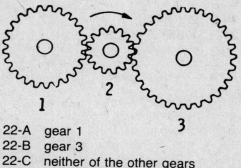

   22-A   gear 1
   22-B   gear 3
   22-C   neither of the other gears
   22-D   both of the other gears

23. Floats X and Y are measuring the specific gravity of two different liquids. Which float indicates the liquid with the highest specific gravity?

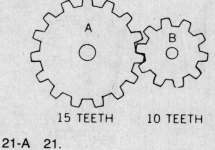

   23-A   Y
   23-B   X
   23-C   neither X nor Y
   23-D   both X and Y are the same

24. Which vacuum gauge will indicate the highest vacuum as air passes through the carburetor bore?

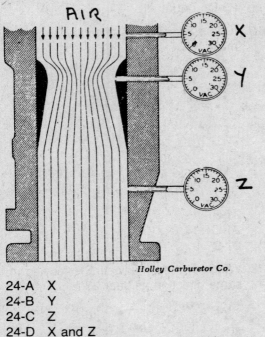

Holley Carburetor Co.

24-A X
24-B Y
24-C Z
24-D X and Z

25. The wheelbarrel is an example of a

25-A first class lever.
25-B second class lever.
25-C third class lever.
25-D first and third class lever.

10

ELECTRONICS INFORMATION

Directions

This is a test of your knowledge of electrical, radio, and electronics information. You are to select the correct response from the choices given. Then mark the space on your answer form which has the same number and letter as your choice.

Now look at the sample question below.

1. What does the abbreviation AC stand for?

   1-A   additional charge
   1-B   alternating coil
   1-C   alternating current
   1-D   ampere current

The correct answer is alternating current, so 1-C is the correct response.

Your score on this test will be based on the number of questions you answer correctly. You should try to answer every question. Do not spend too much time on any one question.

When you are told to begin, be sure to start with question number 1 in Part 10 of your test booklet and number 1 in Part 10 on your separate answer form.

Do not turn this page until told to do so.

ELECTRONICS INFORMATION

Time: 9 minutes; 20 questions

1. A 9-volt transistor battery contains how many cells?

   1-A   1
   1-B   4
   1-C   6
   1-D   9

2. Compared to a number 12 wire a number 22 wire is

   2-A   longer.
   2-B   shorter.
   2-C   larger in diameter.
   2-D   smaller in diameter.

3. A resistor marked 1.5K Ω would have a value of

   3-A   1.5 ohms.
   3-B   105 ohms.
   3-C   1,500 ohms.
   3-D   1,500 watts.

4. An equivalent term for "electromotive force" is

   4-A   voltage.
   4-B   current.
   4-C   resistance.
   4-D   reactance.

5. The property of a circuit that opposes any change in voltage is

   5-A   conductance.
   5-B   capacitance.
   5-C   resistance.
   5-D   inductance.

6. The composition of 60/40 rosin core solder is

   6-A   60% lead, 40% tin.
   6-B   60% tin, 40% lead.
   6-C   60% silver, 40% rosin.
   6-D   60% lead, 40% silver.

7. A hair dryer is rated at 1200 watts. Assuming it is operated at 120 volts, how much current will this appliance draw?

   7-A   10 amps
   7-B   100 amps
   7-C   1000 amps
   7-D   144,000 amps

8. Another term for "cycles per second" is

   8-A   hertz.
   8-B   henry.
   8-C   kilo.
   8-D   mega.

9. A crystal microphone is an example of what electrical phenomenon?

   9-A   thermoionic emission
   9-B   piezoelectric effect
   9-C   inductance
   9-D   hysteresis

10. The process of transmitting voice by varying the height of a carrier wave is known as

    10-A   frequency modulation.
    10-B   amplitude modulation.
    10-C   demodulation.
    10-D   detection.

11. The primary of a transformer is connected to 120 volts. The voltage across the secondary is 40 volts. This transformer has a turns ratio of

    11-A   1:1.
    11-B   1:4.
    11-C   1:3.
    11-D   3:1.

12. A carbon resistor marked with the color bands of red, red, red, gold is of what value and tolerance?

    12-A   2,000 ohms ± 5%
    12-B   222 ohms ± 5%
    12-C   2,200 ohms ± 5%
    12-D   6 ohms ± 5%

13. Which is the correct schematic symbol of a tetrode tube?

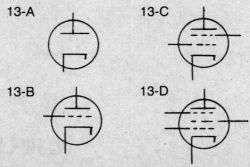

13-A

13-C

13-B

13-D

14. What is the total resistance in this circuit?

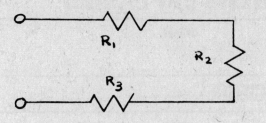

14-A   1,500 watts
14-B   1,500 ohms
14-C   1.5 ohms
14-D   500 ohms

15.

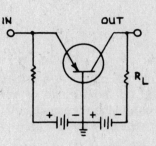

The above schematic represents which transistor configuration?

15-A   common gate
15-B   common collector
15-C   common base
15-D   common emitter

16. Which choice correctly identifies the waveform pictured?

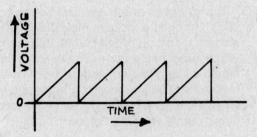

16-A   sine wave
16-B   square wave
16-C   sawtooth wave
16-D   pure DC

17. Of the choices illustrated, which is the correct schematic symbol for a potentiometer?

17-A

17-B

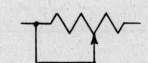

17-C

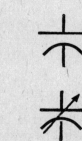

17-D

18. A component on a parts list has the following specifications, "1μFd., 50 wvdc." The component specified is a

18-A   potentiometer.
18-B   coil.
18-C   transistor.
18-D   capacitor.

19.

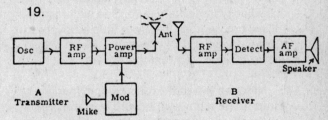

The illustration is a block diagram of a transmitter and receiver. What is the purpose of the oscillator?

19-A   to generate a radio frequency
19-B   to produce a carrier wave for the intelligence
19-C   to produce a high frequency alternating current
19-D   all of the above choices

20. Referring to the schematic in question 19, what is the purpose of the detector stage?

20-A   to amplify the audio signal
20-B   to tune in the carrier wave
20-C   to separate the audio from the radio wave
20-D   to amplify the radio frequency.

ANSWERS AND ANSWERS EXPLAINED

1

GENERAL SCIENCE

Answers

1-B	5-A	9-D	13-C	17-C	20-B	23-C
2-A	6-B	10-C	14-C	18-D	21-B	24-C
3-C	7-C	11-D	15-A	19-A	22-D	25-A
4-D	8-C	12-C	16-D			

Answers Explained

1-B Sound travels fastest in the densest, or heaviest materials. The molecules in heavy materials are closer together and transmit sound vibrations more rapidly than the molecules in light materials. Sound does not travel through a vacuum.

2-A In the process of distillation, a liquid is evaporated by heat and then condensed by cooling. When sea water is distilled, the salts remain behind as a residue, and the distilled water is very pure. Sea water is distilled before it is used in a ship's boilers in order to get rid of the salts, which would form a scale and ruin the boilers.

3-C Nitrogen is a gas. Iron is seldom found in a free state, aluminum occurs in combination with other elements in the earth's crust. Copper is found in combination with other elements and also in a free state.

4-D When the sun's rays strike a surface that is smooth, shiny, or light in color, the rays are reflected. When the sun's rays strike a surface that is rough and dark, the rays are absorbed.

5-A In crop rotation, plants such as legumes are planted periodically to add nitrogen to the soil, after other crops have exhausted it. None of the other methods returns minerals to the soil.

6-B The crowbar is a form of lever. By placing a crowbar over a support, you can exert pressure on one end and overcome resistance at the other. A crowbar could be balanced on the surface of one rock, for example, and then pressed hard to dislodge another rock on top.

7-C The lunar surface is darkened when the earth comes between the sun and the moon. This is caused by the fact that the shadow of the earth falls on the moon's surface.

8-C Calcium is a very important constituent of bone. Without it, the bones in our skeleton become brittle.

9-D The oxidation of the gasoline, which contains hydrogen, produces moisture. There is also an oxidation of the carbon in gasoline, which produces carbon dioxide (not mentioned in the question) and traces of carbon monoxide. These traces can be dangerous when the engine of a car is running in a confined, poorly ventilated place.

10-C The telephone receiver has an electromagnet with a metal diaphragm mounted close to it. The metal diaphragm vibrates (moves back and forth) and reproduces the sounds spoken into the transmitter. The sound waves produced by the speaker's voice cause the transmitter to make the current in the wires weaker and stronger. These changes occur thousands of times per second.

These changes in current affect the electromagnet in the receiver at the other end of the phone call. The receiving electromagnet affects its diaphragm strongly or weakly as the current changes. This in turn reproduces the sound waves made originally by the speaker's voice.

11-D   Radio and light waves are two forms of electromagnetic radiation. In a vacuum, all electromagnetic waves have the same speed—that is, the speed of light.

12-C   The earth's atmosphere consists of a mixture of nitrogen (about 78% by volume); oxygen (about 21%); carbon dioxide (about 0.03%); small amounts of rare gases such as neon, xenon, krypton, and helium; and some water vapor and dust particles.

13-C   All freely falling objects, regardless of their masses near the earth, fall toward the earth with equal acceleration. Any two objects at rest that begin to fall at the same instant will have equal velocities at the end of 3 seconds, or at any other time interval. Thus the ratio of their speeds will be 1:1.

14-C   A falling barometer indicates the approach of low pressure and rising air. The rising of warm, moist air usually results in precipitation. We have reason to assume that the air is warm since we know that the southeast winds come from lower latitudes where the air was warmed, picking up moisture when it passed over the Atlantic Ocean.

15-A   Sand particles are visible and comparatively large. They can be caught in the small holes of a filter. Sugar, alcohol, and most inks form true solutions in which the particles are of molecular size. These will pass through filters.

16-D   Barometric pressure decreases one inch for every 900 feet of altitude. The gas in the balloon expands because it enters regions of lower and lower pressure. Balloons being prepared for ascent are only partially filled with helium. The balloonist knows that the gas will expand and fill the balloon completely at higher altitudes.

17-C   The analysis of radioactive material has given scientists an accurate estimate of the age of the earth.

18-D   Coal deposits were formed when layers of giant ferns as well as other vegetation were compressed into layers of coal by the earth's movement. Its coal deposits tell us that Alaska must have had a tropical climate.

19-A   The curve in the top of an airplane wing forces the air to flow faster over the top of the wing than below it. This faster flowing air results in less pressure above the wing. The principle behind this was first described by Bernoulli. In any flowing liquid, the pressure becomes less as the speed of the flowing liquid becomes greater.

20-B   The lens focuses the light on the retina, which "records the image," sending impulses along the optic nerve to the brain. The cornea is the transparent tissue covering the eyeball. The pupil is the opening through which light enters the eye.

21-B   When water is decomposed by electrolysis, the water breaks up into hydrogen and oxygen. The ratio is two volumes of hydrogen to one of oxygen.
$$2H_2O \rightarrow 2H_2 \uparrow + O_2 \uparrow$$

22-D $FeSO_4$ is a compound of three different elements—iron (Fe), sulfur (S), and oxygen (O). Hydrogen (H) is a separate element.

23-C   Nitrogen is needed most by plants. They also have some need for phosphorus and potassium. Only traces of the other elements are needed by plants; they are not a major concern for companies that produce fertilizers.

24-C   When an object is placed in water, it loses the exact same weight as the weight of the water it displaces. If two objects that are placed in water appear to lose the same weight, then they must have both displaced the same amount of water. That means that they are equal in size, or "volume."

25-A   A thermos is made with a vacuum between its double walls. In this vacuum, there are no molecules to receive the transfer of heat energy from the wall near the contents of the thermos. Thus, the vacuum prevents the loss of heat. Even though a storm window allows some air between it and the "year-round" window, it is the closest match to a thermos, among the choices given.

2

ARITHMETIC REASONING

Answers

1-D	6-B	11-A	15-B	19-B	23-B	27-C
2-C	7-B	12-D	16-A	20-A	24-D	28-B
3-B	8-D	13-B	17-D	21-C	25-A	29-A
4-A	9-C	14-C	18-A	22-C	26-B	30-D
5-D	10-A					

Answers Explained

1-D You need 8 barrels of water to sprinkle ½ mile.
You need 16 barrels of water to sprinkle 1 mile.
You need 3 × 16 (or 48 barrels) to sprinkle 3 miles.
You need 48 + 8 (or 56) barrels to sprinkle 3½ miles.

2-C Since the picture and its enlargement are similar, the lengths have the same ratio as the widths.

$$\frac{\text{length of picture}}{\text{length of enlargement}} = \frac{\text{width of picture}}{\text{width of enlargement}}$$

$$\frac{8}{12} = \frac{6}{\text{width of enlargement}\,(x)}$$

To solve this, cross-multiply the measurements, using x for the one you don't know.

$$8 \times x = 12 \times 6 = 72$$
$$x = {}^{72}\!/_8 = 9 \quad \text{(width)}$$

3-B There are ten units of $1,000 in $10,000. Thus, Lee Robinson pays 10 × $24 (or $240) each year in premiums. That means that every 6 months, Lee Robinson pays ½ of $240, or $120.

4-A There are 16 ounces in 1 pound. Therefore, if
2 pounds of cottage cheese cost $3.20, then
1 pound of cottage cheese costs $1.60
1 ounce costs $1.60 ÷ 16 (or $0.10)
3 ounces cost 3 × $0.10, (or $0.30)

5-D To find the distance Mr. Green drove, multiply the hours by the miles per hour. Thus
12 × 55 = 660 (distance covered)

To find the number of gallons he used, divide the distance by the miles for each gallon. Thus
660 ÷ 22 = 30 (gallons used)

6-B From 8:45 A.M. to 4:45 P.M. is 8 hours.
From 4:45 P.M. to 5:15 P.M. is ½ hour.
Subtract Matty's lunch hour.
8½ − 1 = 7½ (or 7.5 hours)
Multiply his work hours by his hourly rate.
7.5 × $7.50 = $56.25 (day's salary)

7-B Find the cost of 3 ties: 3 × $4 = $12
Find the cost of the shirts alone:
$52 − $12 = $40
Find the cost of 1 shirt: $40 ÷ 5 = $8

8-D Find the relationship between each pair of numbers in the series. Thus
(5; 2) 5 − 3 = 2
(2; 9) 2 + 7 = 9
(9; 6) 9 − 3 = 6
The pattern so far is: −3, +7, −3
To continue the series, add 7 to the fourth number in the series: 6 + 7 = 13

9-C If 80% of the audience were adults, then the percentage of children was
100% − 80% = 20% (or 0.2)
To find the number of children, multiply
500 × 0.2 = 100.0 = 100 children

10-A Find the amount of reduction by subtracting.
$240 − $210 = $30
To find the percentage of reduction, divide it by the original price.
$$\frac{\text{(reduction) } \$30}{\text{(original price) } \$240} = \frac{1}{8} = 12\tfrac{1}{2}\%$$

11-A Multiply the cost of the home by the assessment rate.

$$\$55{,}000 \times 80\% =$$
$$\$55{,}000 \times 0.8 = \$44{,}000$$

The realty tax is \$4.74 for each \$100 in \$44,000.

$$\$44{,}000 \div 100 = 440 \text{ (hundreds)}$$
$$\$4.74 \times 440 = \$2{,}085.60 \text{ (tax)}$$

12-D If 1 inch equals 50 miles, then 2½ inches equal 2½ times 50.

$$\frac{50}{1} \times \frac{5}{2} = 125 \text{ (miles)}$$

13-B One pound equals 16 ounces. Find the number of ounces in 2,200 pounds by multiplying.

$$2{,}200 \times 16 = 35{,}200 \text{ (ounces)}$$

Find the number of 40-ounce bags needed to pack 35,200 ounces by dividing.

$$35{,}200 \div 40 = 880 \text{ (bags)}$$

14-C Find the first reduction and the weekend sale price. (25% = ¼)

$$\$400 \times \tfrac{1}{4} = \$100 \text{ (first reduction)}$$
$$\$400 - \$100 = \$300 \text{ (weekend sale price)}$$

Use this weekend sale price to find the reduction for paying cash and the final price. (10% = 0.1)

$$\$300 \times 0.1 = \$30 \text{ (second reduction)}$$
$$\$300 - \$30 = \$270 \text{ (cash price)}$$

15-B Find the combined salaries of the 4 clerks.

$$\$255 \times 4 = \$1{,}020$$

Find the combined salaries of the part-timers.

$$\$120 \times 2 = \$240$$

Add both totals and divide by 6 for the average.

$$\$1{,}020 + \$240 = \$1{,}260$$
$$\$1{,}260 \div 6 = \$210 \text{ (average salary)}$$

16-A The perimeter of a rectangle is equal to the sum of two lengths and two widths. If 15 feet, 6 inches (15½ feet) equal 1 length, then

$$2 \times 15\tfrac{1}{2} = 31 \text{ feet (2 lengths)}$$
$$40 - 31 = 9 \text{ feet (both widths)}$$
$$9 \div 2 = 4\tfrac{1}{2} \text{ feet (1 width)}$$

17-D Before dividing by a decimal, clear the decimal point in both the divisor and the dividend.

$$\frac{0.675}{0.9} = \frac{6.75}{9} = 0.75$$

18-A In the first hour, the two planes will be a combined distance of 340 plus 260 miles apart. Thus

$$340 + 260 = 600 \text{ miles apart in 1 hour}$$

Find how many hours it will take them to be 3,000 miles apart by dividing.

$$3{,}000 \div 600 = 5 \text{ (hours)}$$

19-B Multiply the cost per foot by the length of the material.

12 inches equal 1 foot
3 inches equal ¼ foot
5 feet, 3 inches equal 5¼ feet (or 5.25 feet)

$$\$8 \times 5.25 = \$42$$

20-A Find the cost of 1 pint. (There are 8 pints in 1 gallon.)

$$\$3.84 \div 8 = \$0.48$$

Find the cost of 3 pints.

$$\$0.48 \times 3 = \$1.44$$

21-C Begin by letting x equal 1 share of the inheritance. According to the ratio, the widow received 5 shares ($5x$), and the son received 3 shares ($3x$). Together, they inherited \$72,000. This can be written as an equation

$$5x + 3x = \$72{,}000$$

Solve for x by combining similar terms.

$$8x = \$72{,}000$$
$$x = \$9{,}000 \text{ (one share)}$$

Multiply the value of 1 share by the number of shares the mother received.

$$5x = \$45{,}000 \text{ (mother's share)}$$

22-C Begin by setting up a statement of proportion.

$$\frac{\text{chocolate}}{\text{chocolate}} = \frac{\text{corn syrup}}{\text{corn syrup}} \begin{array}{l}\text{(recipe)}\\ \text{(amount available)}\end{array}$$

$$\frac{2\tfrac{1}{2} \text{ cups}}{2 \text{ cups}} = \frac{\tfrac{1}{2} \text{ cup}}{x \text{ cup}} \text{ (or) } \frac{\tfrac{5}{2}}{2} = \frac{\tfrac{1}{2}}{x}$$

Simplify each side of the proportion.

(a) $\dfrac{5}{2} \div \dfrac{2}{1} = \dfrac{5}{2} \times \dfrac{1}{2} = \dfrac{5}{4}$

(b) $\dfrac{1}{2} \div \dfrac{x}{1} = \dfrac{1}{2} \times \dfrac{1}{x} = \dfrac{1}{2x}$

Then solve the proportion by cross-multiplying.

$$\frac{5}{4} = \frac{1}{2x} \text{ (or) } 10x = 4$$

Divide each side of the equation by 10, to find the value of x.

$$10x = 4$$
$$x = \tfrac{4}{10}$$
$$x = \tfrac{2}{5} \text{ cup of corn syrup}$$

23-B   To find the average of three numbers, divide their sum by 3.
$x + y + z$ (sum of three numbers)
$\dfrac{x + y + z}{3}$ (sum of numbers, divided by 3)

24-D   First find the income he gets on the $6,000 at 5% annual interest.
$6,000 × 0.05 = $300.00 (income)
Next find how much more interest he wants to earn in a year.
$900 − $300 = $600 (additional interest)
This $600 will equal 6% of the amount (x) he has to invest. Write this as an equation.
$600 = 0.06 times x
$600 = 0.06$x$
To solve for x, divide each side of the equation by 0.06.
(Clear the decimal in the divisor) $\dfrac{$600.00}{0.06} = \left(\dfrac{0.06}{0.06}\right)x$
$10,000 = x$
(new amount needed) $x = $10,000

25-A   Two figures are similar if they have the same shape. They may or may not have the same size. A plane and a scale model of that plane have the same shape and are therefore similar.

26-B   Solve by substituting number values for letters and then doing the arithmetic operations.
$5a^2b − 3ab^2 =$
$(5 × a^2 × b) − (3 × a × b^2) =$
$(5 × 7^2 × 4) − (3 × 7 × 4^2) =$
$(5 × 49 × 4) − (3 × 7 × 16) =$
$980 − 336 \qquad = 644$

27-C   The formula for the circumference (C) of a circle can be written in terms of its radius (R) or its diameter (D).
C = 2 × R × Pi (or) C = D × Pi
Thus, if you divide the circumference of a circle by its diameter, you are left with Pi.
$\dfrac{C}{D} = \dfrac{D × Pi}{D}$
$\dfrac{C}{D} = Pi$

28-B   If the businesswoman spends ⅕ of her income for rent, she has ⅘ of her income left.
$\dfrac{5}{5} − \dfrac{1}{5} = \dfrac{4}{5}$ (remainder)
She then spends ⅜ of the remainder on salaries.
$\dfrac{4}{5} × \dfrac{3}{8} = \dfrac{12}{40} = \dfrac{3}{10}$ (salaries)

29-A   Solve by substituting the number value for F, and then doing the arithmetic operations.
$C = \dfrac{5}{9}(F − 32)$
$C = \dfrac{5}{9}(50 − 32)$
$C = \dfrac{5}{9} × (18)$
$C = 10$

30-D   To obtain the average, add the five temperatures and divide the total by 5.
Add: $−12 + (−7) + (−2) + 0 + 6$
$= −21 + 6$
$= −15$
Divide: $\dfrac{−15}{5} = −3$ (average temperature)

3

WORD KNOWLEDGE

Answers

1-A	6-C	11-A	16-D	21-B	26-A	31-D
2-D	7-B	12-B	17-B	22-C	27-A	32-B
3-D	8-A	13-C	18-D	23-A	28-A	33-C
4-B	9-B	14-A	19-A	24-D	29-A	34-A
5-B	10-B	15-B	20-D	25-C	30-D	35-B

Answers Explained

1-A Luxury, like **opulence** (from the Latin "rich, wealthy"), is conducive to sumptuous living.

2-D **Mimesis** (from the Greek, "imitation") means reproduction of the supposed words of another, usually in order to represent his or her character.

3-D **Languid** means weak, indifferent, weary, or exhausted, implying a languid person.

4-B **Inherence** (from the Latin, "sticking in or to") means the state or fact of existing in something as a permanent and inseparable element, quality, or attribute, and thus, like intrinsic, implies belonging to the nature of a thing itself.

5-B **Anomie** (from the Greek, "lawlessness") describes a social condition marked by the absence of social norms or values, and therefore, like vacuum, implies the absence of components from an area.

6-C Ethereal describes something which is light and airy, and thus may be unsubstantial, as implied by **tenuous** (from the Latin, "thin").

7-B Like **salutation,** greeting means to address with some expression of pleasure.

8-A Hypnotize, like mesmerize, means to put in the condition or state allied to sleep.

9-B Display, similar to **panoply,** means an impressive array of assembled persons or things.

10-B Like **syntactic** (from the Greek, "arrangement"), which pertains to patterns of formation of sentences and phrases in a particular language, grammatical pertains to sounds, words, formation and arrangement of words.

11-A Resentment, like **umbrage,** describes the feeling of indignation at something regarded as an injury or insult.

12-B Harsh means rough to any of the senses, while **raucous** denotes hoarse, or harsh of voice or sound.

13-C Trial, like **prosecution,** means determining a person's guilt or innocence by due process of law.

14-A Pollution, which means defiling, rendering impure, making foul, unclean, dirty, is closely related to **miasma** (from the Greek, "pollution").

15-B Model, like **paragon,** is a pattern of excellence for exact imitation.

16-D **Innate,** like native, means belonging by birth.

17-B **Urbanity** indicates elegant courtesy or politeness, hence refinement.

18-D To **encounter** means to come upon, hence to meet.

19-A **Banal,** like commonplace, characterizes as lifeless and uninteresting.

20-D **Little,** like small, means not much in comparison to other things.

21-B **Found,** like discover, means to unearth something hidden or lost.

22-C **Tell,** like inform, means to communicate knowledge or give information.

23-A **Shifting,** like variable, means subject to change.

24-D **Stop,** like cease, means to end.

25-C **Weaken,** like impair, means to worsen or to damage.

26-A Rudiments are fundamental skills or basic principles, like basic methods and procedures.

27-A **Reckless,** like imprudent, means lacking discretion.

28-A **Friction,** like dissension, both refer to quarreling.

29-A **Separate,** like disconnect, means to become detached.

30-D **Elementary,** like rudimentary, refers to something fundamental or imperfectly developed.

31-D **Self-governing,** like autonomous, means governing without control.

32-B **Wander aimlessly,** like meander, means to follow a winding course without a definite destination.

33-C **Extreme poverty,** like destitution, characterizes the state of lacking resources and possessions.

34-A **Slander,** like malign, means to speak misleading or false reports about someone.

35-B **Lacking strength,** like impotent, means lacking power or vigor.

4

PARAGRAPH COMPREHENSION

Answers

1-A	4-A	6-B	8-B	10-C	12-A	14-D
2-B	5-A	7-C	9-D	11-B	13-C	15-C
3-A						

Answers Explained

1-A The first sentence states that the duty of the lighthouse keeper is to keep the light burning no matter what happens.

2-B The second sentence mentions that the exact amount of water needed has been carefully determined.

3-A "Hardening" or toughening seedlings is done by reducing the water the seedlings obtain and lowering the temperature.

4-A Earthquakes occur when rock layers break and slip, forming cracks or faults.

5-A Photosynthesis combines air, water and energy from the sun to make food.

6-B In this selection reputable means honest, or trusted.

7-C The main idea of the selection is that ice can relieve many of the effects of a burn and is therefore great first aid.

8-B The main idea of the selection is to warn you to be careful of "get-rich-quick" plans.

9-D The third sentence mentions that 9 out of 10 victims of fatal falls are over 65.

10-C "Gray water" is defined as slightly used water. The only choice which represents used water is soapy water.

11-B The third sentence specifies that a glacier moves because of its weight.

12-A Every sentence of the selection expresses disapproval of the present state of things and implies that changes are needed.

13-C The selection states that some categories of people have changed, but the fact that the "number is growing" implies not everyone has changed.

14-D According to the first sentence, Newton's Third Law is that to each action there is an equal and opposite reaction, or action equals reaction.

15-C The first sentence states that water is a good conductor of sound waves.

5

NUMERICAL OPERATIONS

Answers

1-C	9-A	16-A	23-C	30-A	37-C	44-D
2-A	10-C	17-C	24-A	31-C	38-A	45-B
3-C	11-B	18-D	25-A	32-C	39-C	46-B
4-D	12-A	19-D	26-C	33-D	40-A	47-C
5-D	13-C	20-A	27-D	34-D	41-C	48-A
6-B	14-D	21-C	28-B	35-A	42-A	49-C
7-D	15-A	22-A	29-B	36-C	43-B	50-D
8-C						

Answers Explained

There is no analysis of the answers for this part of the test. See Review Section on Mathematical Knowledge for general information.

6

CODING SPEED

Answers

1. B	13. A	25. E	37. B	49. D	61. A	73. B
2. E	14. C	26. B	38. A	50. D	62. D	74. B
3. A	15. A	27. C	39. B	51. B	63. E	75. E
4. C	16. E	28. E	40. D	52. B	64. B	76. B
5. E	17. D	29. D	41. A	53. A	65. E	77. A
6. E	18. E	30. B	42. E	54. E	66. A	78. E
7. D	19. B	31. A	43. B	55. C	67. D	79. E
8. D	20. C	32. B	44. B	56. C	68. B	80. E
9. B	21. B	33. E	45. A	57. E	69. D	81. C
10. B	22. E	34. A	46. E	58. E	70. A	82. A
11. A	23. B	35. A	47. E	59. B	71. C	83. E
12. B	24. A	36. D	48. B	60. A	72. A	84. C

7

AUTO AND SHOP INFORMATION

Answers

1-D	5-B	9-B	13-D	17-C	20-C	23-B
2-A	6-C	10-C	14-C	18-B	21-C	24-C
3-D	7-A	11-B	15-D	19-D	22-A	25-C
4-B	8-B	12-C	16-B			

Answers Explained

1-D   When viewed from the rear, the side to your right is the right side of an engine. This method is used by all manufacturers.

2-A   "G" indicates the load carrying capacity of a tire. "78" is the aspect ratio. The aspect ratio is the relationship between the tire height and width. When a tire is marked 78, the height is 78% of the width. "14" indicates that the tire will fit a 14 inch rim.

3-D   Tracking is correct when both rear wheels are parallel to, and the same distance from, the vehicle center line (an imaginary line drawn through the center of the vehicle). A bent frame or twisted body structure will cause improper tracking.

4-B   Shock absorbers control spring oscillation. Original equipment shocks that do not use air or spring assist are not designed to control vehicle height.

5-B   The countershaft is pressed into the transmission case and supports the cluster gear. The main shaft or output shaft is splined with the driveshaft.

6-C   When a clutch pedal is depressed, the release bearing comes in contact with the fingers of the clutch pressure plate and rotates.

7-A   To properly adjust an automatic transmission band, loosen the adjusting screw locknut. Then tighten the adjusting screw to the specified torque with a torque wrench. Next, loosen the adjusting screw the specified number of turns. Complete the job by holding the adjusting screw and tightening the locknut.

8-B   On a rear-wheel drive vehicle, the driveshaft transmits power from the transmission to the differential. The flywheel is bolted directly to the crankshaft.

9-B   The spark plug leads must be installed in the correct tower of the cap to insure the proper firing order. The firing order is the order that the spark plugs ignite the air/fuel mixture in the combustion chamber. A typical firing order for a six-cylinder engine is 1-5-3-6-2-4.

10-C   On a conventional ignition coil the center tower is the secondary or high voltage terminal. The two small studs at the top of the coil are primary or low voltage terminals.

11-B   Battery electrolyte is a mixture of approximately 60% distilled water and 40% sulphuric acid.

12-C   Two slip rings are mounted on the rotor shaft. Two brushes ride on the slip rings and deliver electrical energy to the rotor windings.

13-D   A loose or corroded headlight ground connection will cause a dim light. If the headlight switch is faulty, all lights will be affected, not just one headlight.

14-C   Air is compressible and will cause a spongy or soft brake pedal action.

15-D   A proportioning valve is commonly used on a vehicle equipped with front disc and rear drum type brakes. The valve reduces hydraulic pressure to the rear drum brakes to prevent rear wheel lockup and skidding during heavy brake pedal application.

16-B   The coping saw blade is placed in the saw with the teeth of the blade facing the handle. That means you cut with a coping saw on the downward stroke. That also calls for a special type of vise to hold whatever it is you are cutting.

17-C   Carpenters use claw hammers so they can remove nails if they don't go where they belong or are bent on the way into the wood. Machinists use ball peen hammers. Planishing hammers are used by people trying to flatten or shape sheet metal. There is no such thing as a chisel point hammer.

18-B   The term penny is an old English way to designate the size of a nail. It has no definite bearing to today's measuring units. You can, however, keep in mind that the larger the number, the larger the nail.

19-D   The squaring shear is used to shear or cut sheet metal.

20-C   One of the most common ways to fasten sheet metal today is by spot welding it. This is done with the bodies of automobiles to make them sturdier.

21-C   A welding torch can be used as a cutting torch when the proper amount of oxygen is used.

22-A   Tubing cutters are nothing more than a smaller version of a pipe cutter.

23-B   If you overwork concrete, it brings up all the water to the surface and the cement comes to the surface also. The heavier particles settle farther down into the slab and you wind up with separation and create a less durable surface when it is dry.

24-C   Concrete reaches 98% of its strength in 28 days.

25-C   Deciduous trees are those that produce leaves that drop off in the fall. The wood produced by this type of tree is usually hard when properly dried.

8

MATHEMATICS KNOWLEDGE

Answers

1-A	5-D	9-D	13-D	17-D	20-B	23-D
2-D	6-B	10-A	14-B	18-B	21-A	24-C
3-C	7-C	11-D	15-A	19-A	22-B	25-B
4-D	8-C	12-D	16-C			

Answers Explained

1-A This equation means "a number, decreased by 3, is equal to 7."

$$b - 3 = 7$$

To arrive at a true statement for b, we want to eliminate -3 on the left side of the equation. We do this by adding 3. (This is undoing the subtraction.) We then add 3 to the other side, so that the statement remains an equation.

$$(b - 3) + 3 = 7 + 3$$

By simplifying both sides, we isolate b, and thus find the solution.

$$b = 10$$

2-D An easy way to perform the multiplication is to do four separate multiplications. Then the procedure looks like ordinary multiplication in arithmetic.

$$
\begin{array}{l}
2z - 3 \\
\underline{z + 2} \\
4z - 6 \quad \text{Multiply } (2z - 3) \text{ by } 2 \\
\underline{2z^2 - 3z} \quad \text{Multiply } (2z - 3) \text{ by } z \\
2z^2 + \ z - 6 \quad \text{Add the partial products as}
\end{array}
$$
you do in arithmetic.

3-C Since a quadrilateral is a four-sided figure, the township will need four lifeguards. (If the sides of a quadrilateral are parallel, it is also called a parallelogram. If all four sides are equal and all four angles are right angles, it is called a square.)

4-D Step 1. Find the area of the square.

$$2' \times 2' = 4 \text{ square feet}$$

Step 2. Find the area of the circle, using the formula, $A = Pi \times R^2$. (The radius equals one-half the diameter; the diameter of this circle is 2 feet—the same length as one side of the square.)

$$3.14 \times 1^2 = 3.14 \text{ square feet}$$

Step 3. Subtract 3.14 square feet from 4 square feet to find the wood that is wasted, 0.86 square feet.

5-D Step 1. Subtract 2 from each side of the equation in order to eliminate $+ 2$ from the left side. (You are undoing the addition.)

$$3x + 2 - 2 = - 13 - 2$$
$$3x = - 15$$

Step 2. Now divide each side by 3 to find x. (You are undoing the multiplication.)

$$\frac{3x}{3} = \frac{-15}{3}$$
$$x = - 5$$

6-B Let p stand for the number of paintings the artist made. The 4 paintings he sold are equal to 0.05 of all his paintings. This can be expressed as an equation.

$$0.05p = 4$$

To solve for p, divide both sides by 0.05. You are undoing the multiplication of 0.05 and p.

$$\frac{0.05p}{0.05} = \frac{4}{0.05} \quad \text{(Clear the decimal in the divisor.)}$$

$$\frac{1p}{1} = \frac{400}{5}$$
$$p = 80 \quad \text{(paintings made)}$$

7-C In an isosceles triangle, two of the sides are equal. This means that the angles opposite them are equal, too. If one is 40 degrees, then so is the other. To find the angle opposite the unequal side, begin by adding the equal angles.

$$40 + 40 = 80 \text{ degrees}$$

To find the third angle, subtract this amount from 180 (the number of degrees in any triangle).

$$180 - 80 = 100 \text{ degrees (third angle)}$$

8-C An easy way to do this example is to break it into three examples, dividing each term by $8x$. Divide the numbers first, and then the letters. However, to divide the exponents of x, just find the difference between them. (Thus, $x^3 \div x = x^{(3-1)} = x^2$).

$$\frac{24x^3}{8x} + \frac{16x^2}{8x} - \frac{8x}{8x} =$$
$$3x^2 + 2x - 1$$

Since the question asks only how many x's there are in the quotient (not how many x^2's), the answer is 2.

9-D First, find the area (surface) of the ceiling. Since it is opposite the floor, it has the same length and width. ($A = l \times w$)

$19' \times 10' = 190$ square feet (ceiling)

Next find the combined area of two matching (opposite) walls. Start with the walls formed by the length and height of the room.

$19' \times 8' = 152$ square feet (first wall)
$152' \times 2 = 304$ square feet (matching walls)

Then find the area of the walls formed by the width and height of the room.

$10' \times 8' = 80$ square feet (second wall)
$80' \times 2 = 160$ square feet (matching walls)

Finally, combine all surfaces to be painted.

$190 + 304 + 160 = 654$ square feet

10-A The basic formula for travel is "distance equals rate multiplied by time," or $D = rt$. The car traveled 200 miles (D); therefore

$$200 = rt$$

To solve for t (time), divide both sides of the equation by r. (You are undoing the multiplication.)

$$\frac{200}{r} = \frac{rt}{r}$$
$$\frac{200}{r} = t \text{ (time it took for trip)}$$

11-D The perimeter of a square is 4 times a side. Therefore, the perimeter of this square is $4 \times 12'$ or $48'$. The equilateral triangle has the same perimeter as the square. Since the 3 sides of an equilateral triangle are equal, divide by 3 to find the length of one side.

$48' \div 3 = 16'$ (length of one side)

12-D The exponent in $(0.1)^3$ means you use 0.1 as a multiplier three times.

$$(0.1)^3 =$$
$$(0.1)(0.1)(0.1) = 0.001$$

When multiplying decimals, count off one decimal place in the answer for each decimal place in the numbers you multiply.

13-D In 1 foot, there are 12 inches (12×1). In 2 feet, there are 24 inches (12×2). Therefore, in f feet, there are $12 \times f$, or $12f$ inches. Add $12f$ inches to i inches to obtain the total of $12f + i$.

14-B Use m as the owner's income. According to the rule of thumb, a house costing $64,000 should be no more than 2½ times an owner's income, or $2\frac{1}{2}m$ ($2.5m$). This can be stated as an equation.

$$2.5m = \$64,000$$

To solve for m, divide both sides by 2.5. You are undoing the multiplication.

$$\frac{2.5m}{2.5} = \frac{\$64,000}{2.5m} \quad \text{(Clear the decimal in the divisor.)}$$
$$m = \frac{\$640,000}{25} = \$25,600 \text{ (owner's income)}$$

15-A To find the product of more than two numbers, work on only two numbers at a time. If both of these numbers have plus signs ($+$), their product has a plus sign. If both have minus signs ($-$), their product has a plus (not a minus) sign. But if their signs are different, the product has a minus sign.

$$(+2)(-5)(+3)(-3)$$
$$= (-10)(+3)(-3)$$
$$= (-30)(-3)$$
$$= +90$$

16-C To solve the equation $x^2 = 3x + 10$, turn it into an equation equal to 0, find the two factors of the new equation, and then set each factor equal to 0, to solve for x.

Step 1. Move all expressions to one side of the equal sign. Change the signs of terms that are moved.

$$x^2 - 3x - 10 = 0$$

Step 2. Find the two factors that you would multiply to produce this polynomial. Do this one expression at a time. What gives you x^2? The answer is x times x. Therefore place an x at the beginning of each factor.

$$(x \quad)(x \quad)$$

Next find the two numbers you would multiply to get 10. They could be 10 and 1, or 5 and 2, but remember that the two numbers also have to produce 3, the middle term in the polynomial. The difference between 5

384 Test Yourself

and 2 is 3. Therefore 5 and 2 are the numbers that complete the factors.

$$(x \quad 5)(x \quad 2)$$

Now decide the signs that belong in each factor. The appearance of -10 in the polynomial means that 5 and 2 have different signs. The $-3x$ in the polynomial indicates that 5 (the larger number) has the minus sign, and that 2 has a plus sign. Thus

$$(x - 5)(x + 2)$$

Step 3. Set each factor equal to zero and solve the equations.

$$x - 5 = 0 \quad x + 2 = 0$$
$$x = 5 \quad x = -2$$

CHECK. Substitute each answer in the original equation.

$$x^2 = 3x + 10 \qquad x^2 = 3x + 10$$
$$(-2)^2 = 3(-2) + 10 \quad (5)^2 = 3(5) + 10$$
$$4 = -6 + 10 \qquad 25 = 15 + 10$$
$$4 = 4 \qquad 25 = 25$$

This proves that x is equal to -2 and 5.

17-D A cylinder is a solid figure, whose upper and lower bases are circles. A small can of frozen-juice concentrate is an example of a cylinder. (An orange is a sphere. A stick of butter is a rectangular solid. A stereo album is a combination of different objects.)

18-B Your goal is to find the value of R in terms of the other letters in the equation.

$$N = \frac{CR}{C + R}$$

Begin by multiplying both sides of the equation by $(C + R)$. You are undoing the division.

$$N(C + R) = \frac{CR}{(C + R)} \times (C + R)$$
$$N(C + R) = CR$$
$$NC + NR = CR \text{ (isolate terms with R)}$$

Next, gather all terms with R on one side of the equation. To do this, subtract NR from both sides. You are undoing the addition.

$$NC + NR - NR = CR - NR$$
$$NC = CR - NR$$
$$NC = R(C - N) \text{ (simplify for R)}$$

Finally, divide both sides of the equation by $(C - N)$. You are undoing the multiplication.

$$\frac{NC}{(C - N)} = \frac{R(C - N)}{(C - N)}$$
$$\frac{NC}{(C - N)} = R \text{ (transpose the statement)}$$
$$R = \frac{NC}{(C - N)}$$

19-A When the product of two numbers is 1, each number is the reciprocal of the other. In the following equation, r is the reciprocal you want to find.

$$r \times \tfrac{5}{3} = 1$$

To isolate r, divide each side by $\tfrac{5}{3}$. This is undoing the multiplication.

$$r \times \frac{5}{3} \div \frac{5}{3} = 1 \div \frac{5}{3}$$
$$r \times \frac{5}{3} \times \frac{3}{5} = 1 \times \frac{3}{5}$$
$$r = \frac{3}{5} \text{ (reciprocal of } \tfrac{5}{3})$$

Written as a decimal, $\tfrac{3}{5}$ equals 0.6.

20-B This problem does not have to be computed, because the two symbols cancel each other. The radical sign ($\sqrt{}$) in $(\sqrt{13})^2$ tells you to find the square root of 13. But the exponent (^{2}) tells you to square the answer—that is, to multiply the square root of 13 by itself. This would get you back to 13.

21-A To find the average rate of speed (mph), divide the distance he covered by the time he spent traveling ($R = D/T$). In this example, begin by finding the distance traveled.

$$120 + 120 = 240 \text{ miles (distance)}$$

Next find the length of time he traveled. At the beginning of his trip, he drove 120 miles at 40 mph.

$$\frac{120}{40} = 3 \text{ hours (first part of trip)}$$

Later, he increased his speed.

$$\frac{120}{60} = 2 \text{ hours (second part of trip)}$$

Altogether, he traveled for 5 hours. Now apply the formula for finding his average rate of speed.

$$\frac{D}{T} = \frac{240}{5} = 48 \text{ mph (Rate of speed)}$$

22-B An angle of 180 degrees is a straight angle.
An angle of 90 degrees is a right angle.
An angle greater than 90 degrees, but less than 180 degrees is an obtuse angle.
An angle less than 90 degrees is an acute angle.

23-D To solve these equations for x, begin by finding a way to eliminate y. Multiply both sides of the second equation by 2.

$$2(x - 2y) = 2 \times 11$$
$$2x - 4y = 22$$

Add the new form of the second equation to the first equation, and solve for x.

$$5x + 4y = 27$$
$$\underline{2x - 4y = 22} \text{ (+ 4 cancels − 4)}$$
$$7x \qquad = 49$$
$$x = 7$$

24-C The product of a negative number and a positive number is always negative. The product of two negative numbers is always a positive number. Since ab is positive, and a is negative, b must be negative, too.

25-B The expression $(x + 5 > 7)$ is a statement of inequality. It means that x plus 5 is greater than 7—not equal to it. To solve this inequality, subtract 5 from both sides of the statement.

$$x + 5 > 7$$
$$x + 5 - 5 > 7 - 5$$
$$x > 2$$

Thus the statement of inequality is true for any value of x that is greater than 2. Try it with 3, for example.

$$3 + 5 > 7$$
$$8 > 7, \text{ a true statement}$$

9

MECHANICAL COMPREHENSION

Answers

1-C	5-B	9-D	13-D	17-B	20-A	23-A
2-B	6-D	10-D	14-D	18-B	21-A	24-B
3-A	7-B	11-A	15-D	19-C	22-C	25-B
4-D	8-C	12-C	16-B			

Answers Explained

1-C Cap screws are identified by diameter, pitch (threads per inch), material, hardness and length. Two common types of thread are National Coarse (NC) and National Fine (NF).

2-B A stud is a headless bolt that has threads on both ends. Usually one side will have NF threads and the other side, NC threads.

3-A To find the wrench size of a cap screw, etc., measure across the flats of its hexagon head.

4-D The dial indicator uses a gauge to register movement. It is used to measure variations in dimensions and backlash (clearance) between two meshed gears.

5-B A pilot bearing is pressed into a hole at the end of the engine crankshaft. The purpose of the bearing is to support the tip of the transmission input (clutch) shaft. During the installation of a new clutch assembly, it is necessary to line up the clutch disc with the pilot bearing. If these parts are not aligned, the transmission will not slide into place on the engine.

6-D The oscilloscope, or scope, is a special type of voltmeter that displays traces and oscillations on a TV type picture tube. The scope has the capability of showing the rapid changes in voltage that occur in the ignition system. This is helpful in diagnosing problems in the circuit.

7-B A torque wrench is a special type of turning tool that is equipped with a gauge. It is used to tighten nuts and bolts to a specified torque or tightness.

8-C An ohmmeter is a test instrument that measures the resistance in an electrical circuit. Resistance is the opposition to the flow of current through a circuit.

9-D A cylinder head must be tightened in a specific sequence using a torque wrench. Failure to tighten the head properly can result in a blown head gasket. Note: see the answer to question 7 for additional information.

10-D The specific gravity of antifreeze solution is tested with a special hydrometer. It compares the weight of the antifreeze solution to water.

11-A Spur gears have straight teeth. Hypoid and spiral gears have curved or beveled teeth.

12-C Planetary gears are used in an automatic transmission. The three members are in constant mesh and provide gear reduction and reverse without shifting. To obtain a gear reduction or reverse, one member must be held stationary by a band or clutch assembly.

  Worm and sector gears are used in some types of steering gear assemblies. Differential or spider gears are used in a rear end assembly.

13-D The crankshaft changes the reciprocating (up and down) motion of the piston to rotary motion.

14-D Condensation takes place when a gas or vapor changes to a liquid. Moisture on the windshield is the result of water vapor in the air changing back to liquid.

15-D   Unlike poles attract, like poles repel.

16-B   The differential, which connects the driveshaft to the rear axle, increases engine torque through gear reduction. Engine torque is increased because the driveshaft turns faster than the rear axles.

17-B   Water expands as it freezes. Water is not compressible.

18-B   To calculate the gear ratio of a rear axle assembly, divide the number of teeth on the pinion gear into the number of teeth on the ring gear. 43 divided by 11 = 3.90.

19-C   A and D are in constant mesh and F is too small.

20-A   When the lobe (high spot) on cam A makes contact with the follower (roller) on the contact arm, the contacts will close. Since cam A has only one lobe, the contacts will close one time per revolution.

21-A   To calculate the revolutions of gear B, use this formula: r = D × R divided by d.
D = number of teeth on gear A
R = revolutions of gear A
d = number of teeth on gear B
r = revolutions of gear B
r = D × R divided by d
$$r = \frac{15 \times 14}{10}$$
$$r = \frac{210}{10}$$
r = 21

22-C   Gears that are meshed turn in opposite directions. Gear 2 is turning clockwise; 1 and 3 are turning counterclockwise.

23-A   Hydrometers use floats to measure specific gravity. Specific gravity is the weight of a liquid compared to the weight of water. The liquid with the highest specific gravity will cause the float to rise higher in the glass tube.

24-B   Vacuum is greatest at the narrow or restricted area of an air passage. The narrow area is called a venturi. Gauge Z will also indicate a vacuum, but it will read lower than Y.

25-B   On a second class lever, the fulcrum is at one end, the effort is at the other end and the load is between.

10

ELECTRONICS INFORMATION

Answers

Answers Explained

1-C A cell has a voltage of approximately 1.5 volts. A nine volt battery would therefore contain 6 cells or 1.5v × 6 = 9v.

2-D The higher the gage number of a wire, the smaller its diameter.

3-C The symbol "K" represents "kilo" or one thousand. A 1.5 K ohm resistor would therefore have a value of 1.5 × 1000 or 1,500 ohms. Choice D is incorrect because the unit of measurement for resistance is the ohm. Watts is a unit of measurement for power.

4-A The interchangeable terms for voltage are, electrical pressure, electromotive force, potential difference, difference of potential and electrical force. The other choices are incorrect because they represent other circuit properties that may not be substituted for the property of voltage.

5-B Capacitance can be defined as the circuit property that opposes any change in voltage. Inductance is the circuit property that opposes any change in current. Resistance is the circuit property that opposes the flow of electrons and reactance is the opposition to the flow of an alternating current as a result of inductance or capacitance present in a circuit.

6-B Choice A has the quantities reversed and choices C & D are incorrect because the amount of silver present in solder is minute, and rosin is a substance in the center of solder added to aid in the soldering process.

7-A To calculate the current requirement of an appliance the power law may be applied.

Power = Current × Voltage

$$P = I \times E$$

$$I = \frac{P}{E}$$

$$I = \frac{1200 \text{ watts}}{120 \text{ volts}}$$

$$I = 10 \text{ amperes.}$$

8-A Henry is the unit of measurement for inductance. Kilo represents a quantity of one thousand and mega represents a quantity of a million.

9-B The piezoelectric effect is the property of certain crystalline substances to change shape when a voltage is impressed upon them as in the crystal microphone. Thermoionic emission is the escape of electrons from a surface due to the presence of heat. Inductance is the circuit property that opposes any change in current and hysteresis is the property of a magnetic substance that causes magnetization to lag behind the force that produces it.

10-B The height of a wave is known as the wave's amplitude. Varying the height of a carrier wave is known as AM or amplitude modulation. Frequency modulation would transmit intelligence by varying the frequency of the carrier wave. Demodulation is the process of separating the intelligence from the carrier wave. Another term for this process is detection.

11-D The primary of this transformer has three times the voltage of its secondary. Therefore, the primary must have three times as many turns of wire as the secondary, or a turns ratio of 3:1. If its turns ratio was 1:1 the primary and secondary would have the same voltage. In choice B, a turns ratio of 1:4 would result in an output voltage of 480v. In choice C a turns ratio of 1:3 would result in a secondary voltage of 360v.

12-C   Reading the resistor color code, the first two bands indicate numbers; the third band is the multiplier or the number of zeros to write after the first two numbers. The fourth band indicates the tolerance of the resistor. Following the color code, the value of this resistor is 2,200 ohms ± 5%. Red, representing a number value of 2 and a multiplier value of 100 (or two zeros to write after the first two numbers) would indicate a resistor coded as follows:

2	2
Band 1- red	Band 2- red
00	± 5%
band 3- red	band 4- gold

The tolerance of a fixed carbon resistor is a set value. Gold represents 5% tolerance.

13-C   Choice A = diode, choice B = triode, choice D = pentode.

14-C   In a series circuit, the total resistance is equal to the sum of the individual resistors, or $R_T = R_1 + R_2 + R_3 \ldots R_n$. As all resistors have a value of 500 ohms, the total resistance in this circuit is equal to:
$R_T = R_1 + R_2 + R_3$ or
$R_T = 500 + 500 + 500$
$R_T = 1,500$ ohms

Choice A is incorrect because watts is a unit of power, not a unit of resistance.

15-C   The base element is common or shared by both circuits. Choice A is not a transistor circuit configuration as there is no gate element in a transistor.

16-C   The waveforms corresponding to the other choices are given in the review section on waveforms.

17-B   A potentiometer is a variable resistor. Choice A is the symbol for a fixed resistor and choice B is the symbol for a variable resistor; note the arrow connected to the fixed symbol. Choice C is a fixed capacitor and choice D is the symbol for a variable capacitor.

18-D   The unit of measurement for capacitance is the FARAD, abbreviated Fd. A potentiometer would be specified in ohms, a coil in henrys, and a transistor by its type or generic number.

19-D   The purpose of the local oscillator is to generate a high alternating frequency also known as a radio or carrier wave.

20-C   A detector demodulates a signal. This is the process of separating the audio or intelligence from the radio wave. The AF amp is used to amplify the audio signal and the RF amp is used to amplify the radio frequency. A tuner would be used to tune in a frequency, making choices A, B and D incorrect.

13 MODEL EXAMINATION THREE

ANSWER SHEET—THIRD MODEL EXAM

PART 1 GENERAL SCIENCE

1. Ⓐ Ⓑ Ⓒ Ⓓ	6. Ⓐ Ⓑ Ⓒ Ⓓ	11. Ⓐ Ⓑ Ⓒ Ⓓ	16. Ⓐ Ⓑ Ⓒ Ⓓ	21. Ⓐ Ⓑ Ⓒ Ⓓ
2. Ⓐ Ⓑ Ⓒ Ⓓ	7. Ⓐ Ⓑ Ⓒ Ⓓ	12. Ⓐ Ⓑ Ⓒ Ⓓ	17. Ⓐ Ⓑ Ⓒ Ⓓ	22. Ⓐ Ⓑ Ⓒ Ⓓ
3. Ⓐ Ⓑ Ⓒ Ⓓ	8. Ⓐ Ⓑ Ⓒ Ⓓ	13. Ⓐ Ⓑ Ⓒ Ⓓ	18. Ⓐ Ⓑ Ⓒ Ⓓ	23. Ⓐ Ⓑ Ⓒ Ⓓ
4. Ⓐ Ⓑ Ⓒ Ⓓ	9. Ⓐ Ⓑ Ⓒ Ⓓ	14. Ⓐ Ⓑ Ⓒ Ⓓ	19. Ⓐ Ⓑ Ⓒ Ⓓ	24. Ⓐ Ⓑ Ⓒ Ⓓ
5. Ⓐ Ⓑ Ⓒ Ⓓ	10. Ⓐ Ⓑ Ⓒ Ⓓ	15. Ⓐ Ⓑ Ⓒ Ⓓ	20. Ⓐ Ⓑ Ⓒ Ⓓ	25. Ⓐ Ⓑ Ⓒ Ⓓ

PART 2 ARITHMETIC REASONING

1. Ⓐ Ⓑ Ⓒ Ⓓ	7. Ⓐ Ⓑ Ⓒ Ⓓ	13. Ⓐ Ⓑ Ⓒ Ⓓ	19. Ⓐ Ⓑ Ⓒ Ⓓ	25. Ⓐ Ⓑ Ⓒ Ⓓ
2. Ⓐ Ⓑ Ⓒ Ⓓ	8. Ⓐ Ⓑ Ⓒ Ⓓ	14. Ⓐ Ⓑ Ⓒ Ⓓ	20. Ⓐ Ⓑ Ⓒ Ⓓ	26. Ⓐ Ⓑ Ⓒ Ⓓ
3. Ⓐ Ⓑ Ⓒ Ⓓ	9. Ⓐ Ⓑ Ⓒ Ⓓ	15. Ⓐ Ⓑ Ⓒ Ⓓ	21. Ⓐ Ⓑ Ⓒ Ⓓ	27. Ⓐ Ⓑ Ⓒ Ⓓ
4. Ⓐ Ⓑ Ⓒ Ⓓ	10. Ⓐ Ⓑ Ⓒ Ⓓ	16. Ⓐ Ⓑ Ⓒ Ⓓ	22. Ⓐ Ⓑ Ⓒ Ⓓ	28. Ⓐ Ⓑ Ⓒ Ⓓ
5. Ⓐ Ⓑ Ⓒ Ⓓ	11. Ⓐ Ⓑ Ⓒ Ⓓ	17. Ⓐ Ⓑ Ⓒ Ⓓ	23. Ⓐ Ⓑ Ⓒ Ⓓ	29. Ⓐ Ⓑ Ⓒ Ⓓ
6. Ⓐ Ⓑ Ⓒ Ⓓ	12. Ⓐ Ⓑ Ⓒ Ⓓ	18. Ⓐ Ⓑ Ⓒ Ⓓ	24. Ⓐ Ⓑ Ⓒ Ⓓ	30. Ⓐ Ⓑ Ⓒ Ⓓ

PART 3 WORD KNOWLEDGE

1. Ⓐ Ⓑ Ⓒ Ⓓ	8. Ⓐ Ⓑ Ⓒ Ⓓ	15. Ⓐ Ⓑ Ⓒ Ⓓ	22. Ⓐ Ⓑ Ⓒ Ⓓ	29. Ⓐ Ⓑ Ⓒ Ⓓ
2. Ⓐ Ⓑ Ⓒ Ⓓ	9. Ⓐ Ⓑ Ⓒ Ⓓ	16. Ⓐ Ⓑ Ⓒ Ⓓ	23. Ⓐ Ⓑ Ⓒ Ⓓ	30. Ⓐ Ⓑ Ⓒ Ⓓ
3. Ⓐ Ⓑ Ⓒ Ⓓ	10. Ⓐ Ⓑ Ⓒ Ⓓ	17. Ⓐ Ⓑ Ⓒ Ⓓ	24. Ⓐ Ⓑ Ⓒ Ⓓ	31. Ⓐ Ⓑ Ⓒ Ⓓ
4. Ⓐ Ⓑ Ⓒ Ⓓ	11. Ⓐ Ⓑ Ⓒ Ⓓ	18. Ⓐ Ⓑ Ⓒ Ⓓ	25. Ⓐ Ⓑ Ⓒ Ⓓ	32. Ⓐ Ⓑ Ⓒ Ⓓ
5. Ⓐ Ⓑ Ⓒ Ⓓ	12. Ⓐ Ⓑ Ⓒ Ⓓ	19. Ⓐ Ⓑ Ⓒ Ⓓ	26. Ⓐ Ⓑ Ⓒ Ⓓ	33. Ⓐ Ⓑ Ⓒ Ⓓ
6. Ⓐ Ⓑ Ⓒ Ⓓ	13. Ⓐ Ⓑ Ⓒ Ⓓ	20. Ⓐ Ⓑ Ⓒ Ⓓ	27. Ⓐ Ⓑ Ⓒ Ⓓ	34. Ⓐ Ⓑ Ⓒ Ⓓ
7. Ⓐ Ⓑ Ⓒ Ⓓ	14. Ⓐ Ⓑ Ⓒ Ⓓ	21. Ⓐ Ⓑ Ⓒ Ⓓ	28. Ⓐ Ⓑ Ⓒ Ⓓ	35. Ⓐ Ⓑ Ⓒ Ⓓ

PART 4 PARAGRAPH COMPREHENSION

1. Ⓐ Ⓑ Ⓒ Ⓓ	5. Ⓐ Ⓑ Ⓒ Ⓓ	9. Ⓐ Ⓑ Ⓒ Ⓓ	13. Ⓐ Ⓑ Ⓒ Ⓓ
2. Ⓐ Ⓑ Ⓒ Ⓓ	6. Ⓐ Ⓑ Ⓒ Ⓓ	10. Ⓐ Ⓑ Ⓒ Ⓓ	14. Ⓐ Ⓑ Ⓒ Ⓓ
3. Ⓐ Ⓑ Ⓒ Ⓓ	7. Ⓐ Ⓑ Ⓒ Ⓓ	11. Ⓐ Ⓑ Ⓒ Ⓓ	15. Ⓐ Ⓑ Ⓒ Ⓓ
4. Ⓐ Ⓑ Ⓒ Ⓓ	8. Ⓐ Ⓑ Ⓒ Ⓓ	12. Ⓐ Ⓑ Ⓒ Ⓓ	

PART 5 NUMERICAL OPERATIONS

1. Ⓐ Ⓑ Ⓒ Ⓓ	11. Ⓐ Ⓑ Ⓒ Ⓓ	21. Ⓐ Ⓑ Ⓒ Ⓓ	31. Ⓐ Ⓑ Ⓒ Ⓓ	41. Ⓐ Ⓑ Ⓒ Ⓓ
2. Ⓐ Ⓑ Ⓒ Ⓓ	12. Ⓐ Ⓑ Ⓒ Ⓓ	22. Ⓐ Ⓑ Ⓒ Ⓓ	32. Ⓐ Ⓑ Ⓒ Ⓓ	42. Ⓐ Ⓑ Ⓒ Ⓓ
3. Ⓐ Ⓑ Ⓒ Ⓓ	13. Ⓐ Ⓑ Ⓒ Ⓓ	23. Ⓐ Ⓑ Ⓒ Ⓓ	33. Ⓐ Ⓑ Ⓒ Ⓓ	43. Ⓐ Ⓑ Ⓒ Ⓓ
4. Ⓐ Ⓑ Ⓒ Ⓓ	14. Ⓐ Ⓑ Ⓒ Ⓓ	24. Ⓐ Ⓑ Ⓒ Ⓓ	34. Ⓐ Ⓑ Ⓒ Ⓓ	44. Ⓐ Ⓑ Ⓒ Ⓓ
5. Ⓐ Ⓑ Ⓒ Ⓓ	15. Ⓐ Ⓑ Ⓒ Ⓓ	25. Ⓐ Ⓑ Ⓒ Ⓓ	35. Ⓐ Ⓑ Ⓒ Ⓓ	45. Ⓐ Ⓑ Ⓒ Ⓓ
6. Ⓐ Ⓑ Ⓒ Ⓓ	16. Ⓐ Ⓑ Ⓒ Ⓓ	26. Ⓐ Ⓑ Ⓒ Ⓓ	36. Ⓐ Ⓑ Ⓒ Ⓓ	46. Ⓐ Ⓑ Ⓒ Ⓓ
7. Ⓐ Ⓑ Ⓒ Ⓓ	17. Ⓐ Ⓑ Ⓒ Ⓓ	27. Ⓐ Ⓑ Ⓒ Ⓓ	37. Ⓐ Ⓑ Ⓒ Ⓓ	47. Ⓐ Ⓑ Ⓒ Ⓓ
8. Ⓐ Ⓑ Ⓒ Ⓓ	18. Ⓐ Ⓑ Ⓒ Ⓓ	28. Ⓐ Ⓑ Ⓒ Ⓓ	38. Ⓐ Ⓑ Ⓒ Ⓓ	48. Ⓐ Ⓑ Ⓒ Ⓓ
9. Ⓐ Ⓑ Ⓒ Ⓓ	19. Ⓐ Ⓑ Ⓒ Ⓓ	29. Ⓐ Ⓑ Ⓒ Ⓓ	39. Ⓐ Ⓑ Ⓒ Ⓓ	49. Ⓐ Ⓑ Ⓒ Ⓓ
10. Ⓐ Ⓑ Ⓒ Ⓓ	20. Ⓐ Ⓑ Ⓒ Ⓓ	30. Ⓐ Ⓑ Ⓒ Ⓓ	40. Ⓐ Ⓑ Ⓒ Ⓓ	50. Ⓐ Ⓑ Ⓒ Ⓓ

PART 6 CODING SPEED

1. Ⓐ Ⓑ Ⓒ Ⓓ Ⓔ	15. Ⓐ Ⓑ Ⓒ Ⓓ Ⓔ	29. Ⓐ Ⓑ Ⓒ Ⓓ Ⓔ	43. Ⓐ Ⓑ Ⓒ Ⓓ Ⓔ	57. Ⓐ Ⓑ Ⓒ Ⓓ Ⓔ	71. Ⓐ Ⓑ Ⓒ Ⓓ Ⓔ
2. Ⓐ Ⓑ Ⓒ Ⓓ Ⓔ	16. Ⓐ Ⓑ Ⓒ Ⓓ Ⓔ	30. Ⓐ Ⓑ Ⓒ Ⓓ Ⓔ	44. Ⓐ Ⓑ Ⓒ Ⓓ Ⓔ	58. Ⓐ Ⓑ Ⓒ Ⓓ Ⓔ	72. Ⓐ Ⓑ Ⓒ Ⓓ Ⓔ
3. Ⓐ Ⓑ Ⓒ Ⓓ Ⓔ	17. Ⓐ Ⓑ Ⓒ Ⓓ Ⓔ	31. Ⓐ Ⓑ Ⓒ Ⓓ Ⓔ	45. Ⓐ Ⓑ Ⓒ Ⓓ Ⓔ	59. Ⓐ Ⓑ Ⓒ Ⓓ Ⓔ	73. Ⓐ Ⓑ Ⓒ Ⓓ Ⓔ
4. Ⓐ Ⓑ Ⓒ Ⓓ Ⓔ	18. Ⓐ Ⓑ Ⓒ Ⓓ Ⓔ	32. Ⓐ Ⓑ Ⓒ Ⓓ Ⓔ	46. Ⓐ Ⓑ Ⓒ Ⓓ Ⓔ	60. Ⓐ Ⓑ Ⓒ Ⓓ Ⓔ	74. Ⓐ Ⓑ Ⓒ Ⓓ Ⓔ
5. Ⓐ Ⓑ Ⓒ Ⓓ Ⓔ	19. Ⓐ Ⓑ Ⓒ Ⓓ Ⓔ	33. Ⓐ Ⓑ Ⓒ Ⓓ Ⓔ	47. Ⓐ Ⓑ Ⓒ Ⓓ Ⓔ	61. Ⓐ Ⓑ Ⓒ Ⓓ Ⓔ	75. Ⓐ Ⓑ Ⓒ Ⓓ Ⓔ
6. Ⓐ Ⓑ Ⓒ Ⓓ Ⓔ	20. Ⓐ Ⓑ Ⓒ Ⓓ Ⓔ	34. Ⓐ Ⓑ Ⓒ Ⓓ Ⓔ	48. Ⓐ Ⓑ Ⓒ Ⓓ Ⓔ	62. Ⓐ Ⓑ Ⓒ Ⓓ Ⓔ	76. Ⓐ Ⓑ Ⓒ Ⓓ Ⓔ
7. Ⓐ Ⓑ Ⓒ Ⓓ Ⓔ	21. Ⓐ Ⓑ Ⓒ Ⓓ Ⓔ	35. Ⓐ Ⓑ Ⓒ Ⓓ Ⓔ	49. Ⓐ Ⓑ Ⓒ Ⓓ Ⓔ	63. Ⓐ Ⓑ Ⓒ Ⓓ Ⓔ	77. Ⓐ Ⓑ Ⓒ Ⓓ Ⓔ
8. Ⓐ Ⓑ Ⓒ Ⓓ Ⓔ	22. Ⓐ Ⓑ Ⓒ Ⓓ Ⓔ	36. Ⓐ Ⓑ Ⓒ Ⓓ Ⓔ	50. Ⓐ Ⓑ Ⓒ Ⓓ Ⓔ	64. Ⓐ Ⓑ Ⓒ Ⓓ Ⓔ	78. Ⓐ Ⓑ Ⓒ Ⓓ Ⓔ
9. Ⓐ Ⓑ Ⓒ Ⓓ Ⓔ	23. Ⓐ Ⓑ Ⓒ Ⓓ Ⓔ	37. Ⓐ Ⓑ Ⓒ Ⓓ Ⓔ	51. Ⓐ Ⓑ Ⓒ Ⓓ Ⓔ	65. Ⓐ Ⓑ Ⓒ Ⓓ Ⓔ	79. Ⓐ Ⓑ Ⓒ Ⓓ Ⓔ
10. Ⓐ Ⓑ Ⓒ Ⓓ Ⓔ	24. Ⓐ Ⓑ Ⓒ Ⓓ Ⓔ	38. Ⓐ Ⓑ Ⓒ Ⓓ Ⓔ	52. Ⓐ Ⓑ Ⓒ Ⓓ Ⓔ	66. Ⓐ Ⓑ Ⓒ Ⓓ Ⓔ	80. Ⓐ Ⓑ Ⓒ Ⓓ Ⓔ
11. Ⓐ Ⓑ Ⓒ Ⓓ Ⓔ	25. Ⓐ Ⓑ Ⓒ Ⓓ Ⓔ	39. Ⓐ Ⓑ Ⓒ Ⓓ Ⓔ	53. Ⓐ Ⓑ Ⓒ Ⓓ Ⓔ	67. Ⓐ Ⓑ Ⓒ Ⓓ Ⓔ	81. Ⓐ Ⓑ Ⓒ Ⓓ Ⓔ
12. Ⓐ Ⓑ Ⓒ Ⓓ Ⓔ	26. Ⓐ Ⓑ Ⓒ Ⓓ Ⓔ	40. Ⓐ Ⓑ Ⓒ Ⓓ Ⓔ	54. Ⓐ Ⓑ Ⓒ Ⓓ Ⓔ	68. Ⓐ Ⓑ Ⓒ Ⓓ Ⓔ	82. Ⓐ Ⓑ Ⓒ Ⓓ Ⓔ
13. Ⓐ Ⓑ Ⓒ Ⓓ Ⓔ	27. Ⓐ Ⓑ Ⓒ Ⓓ Ⓔ	41. Ⓐ Ⓑ Ⓒ Ⓓ Ⓔ	55. Ⓐ Ⓑ Ⓒ Ⓓ Ⓔ	69. Ⓐ Ⓑ Ⓒ Ⓓ Ⓔ	83. Ⓐ Ⓑ Ⓒ Ⓓ Ⓔ
14. Ⓐ Ⓑ Ⓒ Ⓓ Ⓔ	28. Ⓐ Ⓑ Ⓒ Ⓓ Ⓔ	42. Ⓐ Ⓑ Ⓒ Ⓓ Ⓔ	56. Ⓐ Ⓑ Ⓒ Ⓓ Ⓔ	70. Ⓐ Ⓑ Ⓒ Ⓓ Ⓔ	84. Ⓐ Ⓑ Ⓒ Ⓓ Ⓔ

PART 7 AUTO & SHOP INFORMATION

1. Ⓐ Ⓑ Ⓒ Ⓓ	6. Ⓐ Ⓑ Ⓒ Ⓓ	11. Ⓐ Ⓑ Ⓒ Ⓓ	16. Ⓐ Ⓑ Ⓒ Ⓓ	21. Ⓐ Ⓑ Ⓒ Ⓓ
2. Ⓐ Ⓑ Ⓒ Ⓓ	7. Ⓐ Ⓑ Ⓒ Ⓓ	12. Ⓐ Ⓑ Ⓒ Ⓓ	17. Ⓐ Ⓑ Ⓒ Ⓓ	22. Ⓐ Ⓑ Ⓒ Ⓓ
3. Ⓐ Ⓑ Ⓒ Ⓓ	8. Ⓐ Ⓑ Ⓒ Ⓓ	13. Ⓐ Ⓑ Ⓒ Ⓓ	18. Ⓐ Ⓑ Ⓒ Ⓓ	23. Ⓐ Ⓑ Ⓒ Ⓓ
4. Ⓐ Ⓑ Ⓒ Ⓓ	9. Ⓐ Ⓑ Ⓒ Ⓓ	14. Ⓐ Ⓑ Ⓒ Ⓓ	19. Ⓐ Ⓑ Ⓒ Ⓓ	24. Ⓐ Ⓑ Ⓒ Ⓓ
5. Ⓐ Ⓑ Ⓒ Ⓓ	10. Ⓐ Ⓑ Ⓒ Ⓓ	15. Ⓐ Ⓑ Ⓒ Ⓓ	20. Ⓐ Ⓑ Ⓒ Ⓓ	25. Ⓐ Ⓑ Ⓒ Ⓓ

PART 8 MATHEMATICS KNOWLEDGE

1. Ⓐ Ⓑ Ⓒ Ⓓ	6. Ⓐ Ⓑ Ⓒ Ⓓ	11. Ⓐ Ⓑ Ⓒ Ⓓ	16. Ⓐ Ⓑ Ⓒ Ⓓ	21. Ⓐ Ⓑ Ⓒ Ⓓ
2. Ⓐ Ⓑ Ⓒ Ⓓ	7. Ⓐ Ⓑ Ⓒ Ⓓ	12. Ⓐ Ⓑ Ⓒ Ⓓ	17. Ⓐ Ⓑ Ⓒ Ⓓ	22. Ⓐ Ⓑ Ⓒ Ⓓ
3. Ⓐ Ⓑ Ⓒ Ⓓ	8. Ⓐ Ⓑ Ⓒ Ⓓ	13. Ⓐ Ⓑ Ⓒ Ⓓ	18. Ⓐ Ⓑ Ⓒ Ⓓ	23. Ⓐ Ⓑ Ⓒ Ⓓ
4. Ⓐ Ⓑ Ⓒ Ⓓ	9. Ⓐ Ⓑ Ⓒ Ⓓ	14. Ⓐ Ⓑ Ⓒ Ⓓ	19. Ⓐ Ⓑ Ⓒ Ⓓ	24. Ⓐ Ⓑ Ⓒ Ⓓ
5. Ⓐ Ⓑ Ⓒ Ⓓ	10. Ⓐ Ⓑ Ⓒ Ⓓ	15. Ⓐ Ⓑ Ⓒ Ⓓ	20. Ⓐ Ⓑ Ⓒ Ⓓ	25. Ⓐ Ⓑ Ⓒ Ⓓ

PART 9 MECHANICAL COMPREHENSION

1. Ⓐ Ⓑ Ⓒ Ⓓ	6. Ⓐ Ⓑ Ⓒ Ⓓ	11. Ⓐ Ⓑ Ⓒ Ⓓ	16. Ⓐ Ⓑ Ⓒ Ⓓ	21. Ⓐ Ⓑ Ⓒ Ⓓ
2. Ⓐ Ⓑ Ⓒ Ⓓ	7. Ⓐ Ⓑ Ⓒ Ⓓ	12. Ⓐ Ⓑ Ⓒ Ⓓ	17. Ⓐ Ⓑ Ⓒ Ⓓ	22. Ⓐ Ⓑ Ⓒ Ⓓ
3. Ⓐ Ⓑ Ⓒ Ⓓ	8. Ⓐ Ⓑ Ⓒ Ⓓ	13. Ⓐ Ⓑ Ⓒ Ⓓ	18. Ⓐ Ⓑ Ⓒ Ⓓ	23. Ⓐ Ⓑ Ⓒ Ⓓ
4. Ⓐ Ⓑ Ⓒ Ⓓ	9. Ⓐ Ⓑ Ⓒ Ⓓ	14. Ⓐ Ⓑ Ⓒ Ⓓ	19. Ⓐ Ⓑ Ⓒ Ⓓ	24. Ⓐ Ⓑ Ⓒ Ⓓ
5. Ⓐ Ⓑ Ⓒ Ⓓ	10. Ⓐ Ⓑ Ⓒ Ⓓ	15. Ⓐ Ⓑ Ⓒ Ⓓ	20. Ⓐ Ⓑ Ⓒ Ⓓ	25. Ⓐ Ⓑ Ⓒ Ⓓ

PART 10 ELECTRONICS INFORMATION

1. Ⓐ Ⓑ Ⓒ Ⓓ	6. Ⓐ Ⓑ Ⓒ Ⓓ	11. Ⓐ Ⓑ Ⓒ Ⓓ	16. Ⓐ Ⓑ Ⓒ Ⓓ
2. Ⓐ Ⓑ Ⓒ Ⓓ	7. Ⓐ Ⓑ Ⓒ Ⓓ	12. Ⓐ Ⓑ Ⓒ Ⓓ	17. Ⓐ Ⓑ Ⓒ Ⓓ
3. Ⓐ Ⓑ Ⓒ Ⓓ	8. Ⓐ Ⓑ Ⓒ Ⓓ	13. Ⓐ Ⓑ Ⓒ Ⓓ	18. Ⓐ Ⓑ Ⓒ Ⓓ
4. Ⓐ Ⓑ Ⓒ Ⓓ	9. Ⓐ Ⓑ Ⓒ Ⓓ	14. Ⓐ Ⓑ Ⓒ Ⓓ	19. Ⓐ Ⓑ Ⓒ Ⓓ
5. Ⓐ Ⓑ Ⓒ Ⓓ	10. Ⓐ Ⓑ Ⓒ Ⓓ	15. Ⓐ Ⓑ Ⓒ Ⓓ	20. Ⓐ Ⓑ Ⓒ Ⓓ

1

GENERAL SCIENCE

Directions

This test has questions about science. Pick the best answer for each question, then blacken the space on your separate answer form which has the same number and letter as your choice.

Here is a sample question.

1. An example of a chemical change is

　1-A　melting ice.
　1-B　breaking glass.
　1-C　rusting metal.
　1-D　making sawdust from wood.

The correct answer is rusting metal, so you would blacken the space for 1-C on your answer form.

Your score on this test will be based on the number of questions you answer correctly. You should try to answer every question. Do not spend too much time on any one question.

When you begin, be sure to start with question number 1 in Part 1, and number 1 in Part 1 on your answer form.

Do not turn this page until told to do so.

GENERAL SCIENCE

Time: 11 minutes; 25 questions

1. Which of the following determines the sex of a human offspring?

   1-A   egg cell
   1-B   polar body
   1-C   egg nucleus
   1-D   sperm

2. Rocks are frequently split apart by

   2-A   running water
   2-B   wind
   2-C   sudden changes in temperature
   2-D   meteorites

3. Sand is made up of colorless crystals of

   3-A   iron
   3-B   mica
   3-C   shale
   3-D   quartz

4. Which material is an acid?

   4-A   ammonia water
   4-B   baking soda
   4-C   vinegar
   4-D   rain water

5. Isotopes of the same element have the same number of

   5-A   protons only
   5-B   electrons and protons only
   5-C   neutrons only
   5-D   neutrons and protons only

6. As heat is applied to boiling water, the temperature remains the same. The best explanation for this is that

   6-A   convection increases at the boiling point of water
   6-B   radiation increases at the boiling point of water
   6-C   escaping vapor is taking away energy
   6-D   the applied heat is absorbed quickly by the surroundings

7. Which of the following is outside the solar system?

   7-A   Mars
   7-B   nebulae
   7-C   satellites
   7-D   asteroids

8. Solar energy is transmitted through space by

   8-A   convection
   8-B   radiation
   8-C   reflection
   8-D   absorption

9. Which is an example of a sex-linked trait?

   9-A   eye color
   9-B   anemia
   9-C   height
   9-D   hemophilia

10. The fact that supports the position that viruses are living is that viruses

   10-A   are made of common chemicals
   10-B   cause disease
   10-C   duplicate themselves
   10-D   are protein molecules

11. A thermometer which indicates the freezing point of water at zero degrees and the boiling point of water at 100 degrees is called the

   11-A   Centigrade thermometer
   11-B   Fahrenheit thermometer
   11-C   Kelvin thermometer
   11-D   Reaumur thermometer

12. Vegetation should be kept on slopes because

   12-A   plants aid weathering
   12-B   runoff increases
   12-C   plant roots hold the soil
   12-D   plants enrich the soil

13. A 25-pound force has two components which are at right angles to each other. If one component is 15 pounds, the other component is

   13-A   10 pounds
   13-B   20 pounds
   13-C   40 pounds
   13-D   25 pounds

14. What device is used to test the solution in a storage battery?

   14-A   voltameter
   14-B   hydrometer
   14-C   ammeter
   14-D   anemometer

15. Fluorides are added to drinking water in order to

   15-A   improve taste
   15-B   increase metabolism
   15-C   prevent caries
   15-D   prevent typhoid fever

16. Blinking in response to bright light is an example of a (an)

   16-A   phototropism
   16-B   habit
   16-C   reflex
   16-D   instinct

17. The Rh factor is important in the study of

   17-A   fingerprinting
   17-B   the blood
   17-C   the acidity of a solution
   17-D   the determination of sex

18. What mineral element is part of hemoglobin?

   18-A   calcium
   18-B   fluorine
   18-C   carbon
   18-D   iron

19. In the winter the coldest areas are usually

   19-A   island coasts
   19-B   continental interiors
   19-C   oceans
   19-D   hilltops

20. If the mass of an object were doubled, its acceleration due to gravity would be

   20-A   halved
   20-B   doubled
   20-C   unchanged
   20-D   quadrupled

21. Respiration in plants takes place

   21-A   only during the day
   21-B   only in the presence of carbon dioxide
   21-C   both day and night
   21-D   only at night

22. Wind is mainly the result of

   22-A   clouds
   22-B   storms
   22-C   high humidity
   22-D   unequal heating of air

23. Which appeared most recently on the earth?

   23-A   reptiles
   23-B   mammals
   23-C   amphibians
   23-D   insects

24. When all the colors of the spectrum are mixed, the light is

   24-A   yellow
   24-B   black
   24-C   white
   24-D   blue

25. A solution that has a high ratio of solute to solvent is said to be

   25-A   unsaturated
   25-B   saturated
   25-C   dilute
   25-D   concentrated

ARITHMETIC REASONING

Directions

This test has questions about arithmetic. Each question is followed by four possible answers. Decide which answer is correct. Then, on your answer form, blacken the space which has the same number and letter as your choice. Use your scratch paper for any figuring you wish to do.

Here is a sample question.

1. If 1 quart of milk costs $0.80, what is the cost of 2 quarts?

    1-A $2.00
    1-B $1.60
    1-C $1.20
    1-D $1.00

The cost of 2 quarts is $1.60; therefore, the answer 1-B is correct.

Your score on this test will be based on the number of questions you answer correctly. You should try to answer every question. Do not spend too much time on any one question.

Notice that Part 2 begins with question number 1. When you begin, be sure to mark your first answer next to number 1 on your answer form.

Do not turn this page until told to do so.

ARITHMETIC REASONING

Time: 36 minutes; 30 questions

1. Mr. Winter bought a $500 TV set that was marked at a 15% discount. He made a down payment of $65 and agreed to pay the balance in 12 equal monthly installments. How much was each installment?

   - 1-A $25
   - 1-B $30
   - 1-C $42.50
   - 1-D $360

2. A farmer uses 2 gallons of insecticide concentrate to spray each $\frac{1}{4}$ acre of his land. How many gallons of the concentrate will he need to spray $10\frac{1}{2}$ acres?

   - 2-A   80
   - 2-B $80\frac{1}{4}$
   - 2-C   82
   - 2-D   84

3. An engineering drawing on a sheet of paper that measures 12 inches by 18 inches is to be enlarged so that the length is 45 inches. How many inches wide will the enlarged drawing be?

   - 3-A   30
   - 3-B   39
   - 3-C   66
   - 3-D   33

4. In a quality control test at a factory, of 280 products inspected at random, 266 were found to be acceptable. What percent of the items inspected were found acceptable?

   - 4-A   66%
   - 4-B   95%
   - 4-C   5%
   - 4-D   86%

5. A candy store sells 3 pounds of a candy mix for $4.80. What is the price of a 5 ounce bag of this mix?

   - 5-A $1.00
   - 5-B $2.40
   - 5-C $0.25
   - 5-D $0.50

6. The perimeter of a square is 13 feet, 8 inches. What is the length of one side of the square?

   - 6-A   3 feet, 2 inches
   - 6-B   3 feet, 5 inches
   - 6-C   3 feet, 3 inches
   - 6-D   3 feet, 6 inches

7. A military unit has 360 members. 20% are officers. How many members of the unit are enlisted personnel?

   - 7-A   90
   - 7-B   270
   - 7-C   72
   - 7-D   288

8. Marcella Jones earns $8.50 per hour with time and a half paid for overtime in excess of 8 hours on any one day. One day she worked 10 hours. How much did she earn on that day?

   - 8-A $85.00
   - 8-B $117.50
   - 8-C $97.75
   - 8-D $93.50

9. What is the next term in the series:

   $2\frac{1}{4}; 3\frac{3}{4}; 3\frac{1}{4}; 4\frac{3}{4};$ ____?

   - 9-A $4\frac{1}{4}$
   - 9-B $6\frac{1}{4}$
   - 9-C $5\frac{1}{4}$
   - 9-D $3\frac{1}{4}$

10. Tickets for movie admissions for adults are $4.00 each, but half price is charged for children. If 265 adult tickets were sold and the box office collected $1,200, how many children's tickets were sold?

    - 10-A   70
    - 10-B   35
    - 10-C   280
    - 10-D   140

11. A woman budgets her income so that she spends $\frac{1}{4}$ of it for rent and $\frac{2}{5}$ of the remainder for food. What part of the total income does she budget for food?

    - 11-A $\frac{1}{10}$
    - 11-B $\frac{1}{5}$

11-C $\frac{3}{20}$

11-D $\frac{3}{10}$

12. A survey of a small group of people found that 3 of them each watched 2 hours of TV per day. 2 of them watched 1 hour per day, and 1 watched 4 hours per day. What is the average number of hours of TV watched by members of this group?

12-A $1\frac{1}{3}$

12-B $2\frac{2}{3}$

12-C 2

12-D 3

13. What is the cost of 3 yards, 2 feet of an upholstery edging material that costs $9 per yard?

13-A $30

13-B $36

13-C $29

13-D $33

14. A partnership agreement calls for the two partners to share the profits of their business in the ratio 4:5. If the profit for the year is $63,000, what is the share paid to the partner who gets the smaller portion?

14-A $28,000

14-B $7,000

14-C $35,000

14-D $15,750

15. A courier leaves an office driving at the average rate of 30 miles per hour, but forgets part of the material he was supposed to take with him. An hour later, a second courier is dispatched with the missing material and is instructed to overtake the first courier in 2 hours more. How fast must the second courier travel?

15-A 90 miles per hour

15-B 60 miles per hour

15-C 45 miles per hour

15-D 40 miles per hour

16. A merchant buys radios listed wholesale for $60 apiece at a 25% discount. He sells these radios at a 20% markup above the original wholesale price. What is his profit on each radio?

16-A $9.00

16-B $27.00

16-C $12.00

16-D $18.00

17. An airplane travels a distance of x miles in y hours. What is its average rate of speed in miles per hour?

17-A $\frac{xy}{y}$

17-B $\frac{yx}{x}$

17-C $\frac{y}{x}$

17-D $\frac{x+y}{2}$

18. The cost of sending a telegram is $1.50 for the first 10 words and $0.05 for each additional word. How many words can be sent by telegram for $4.00?

18-A 51

18-B 60

18-C 81

18-D 90

19. A mapmaker is told to prepare a map with a scale of 1 inch to 40 miles. If the actual distance between two points is 110 miles, how far apart should the mapmaker show them on the map?

19-A 7 inches

19-B $3\frac{1}{2}$ inches

19-C $2\frac{1}{2}$ inches

19-D $2\frac{3}{4}$ inches

20. In the Town of Hampshire, houses are assessed at 75% of their purchase price. If Mr. Johnson buys a house in Hampshire for $80,000 and real estate taxes are $4.83 per $100 of assessed valuation, how much realty tax must he pay?

20-A $2,898

20-B $3,864

20-C $600

20-D $604.83

21. The ingredients in a cake recipe include $4\frac{1}{2}$ cups of flour and $\frac{3}{4}$ cup of sugar. It is desired to make a cake that will require only $\frac{1}{4}$ cup of sugar. How much flour should be used?

21-A $1\frac{1}{4}$ cups

21-B $1\frac{1}{2}$ cups

21-C 4 cups

21-D $1\frac{3}{4}$ cups

22. When the tolls on a bridge were increased in price, the traffic declined from 1,200

cars crossing per day to 1,044. What is the percent of the decline in traffic?

22-A 87%
22-B 156%
22-C 13%
22-D 15%

23. If a 2 gallon bucket of liquid floor polish costs $19.20, how much should a one quart can cost?

23-A $4.80
23-B $2.40
23-C $1.20
23-D $0.60

24. A man takes a trip in which he first drives for 3 hours at 50 miles per hour. He then drives for 2 hours more at 55 miles per hour. If his car gets 20 miles per gallon, how many gallons of gas did he use for the trip?

24-A 10
24-B 9.5
24-C 26
24-D 13

25. A woman has $5,000 invested at 8% annual interest. At what rate must she invest an additional $10,000 so that her annual income from both investments is equivalent to 9% of her total investment?

25-A 10%
25-B $10\frac{1}{2}$%
25-C 9%
25-D $9\frac{1}{2}$%

26. The fuel tank of a gasoline generator contains a sufficient capacity to operate the generator for 1 hour and 20 minutes. How many times must the fuel tank be filled to run the generator from 9:15 A.M. to 3:55 P.M.?

26-A 5
26-B 6
26-C $4\frac{1}{2}$
26-D 4

27. A nurseryman mixes 10 pounds of hardy grass seed worth $1.20 per pound with 8 pounds of premium grass seed worth $3.00 per pound. At what price per pound should he sell the mixture?

27-A $2.10
27-B $2.00
27-C $1.90
27-D $2.50

28. What is the value of $\frac{0.02 \times 3}{0.001}$

28-A 60
28-B 6
28-C 0.6
28-D 0.06

29. Find the numerical value of $1 + 5xy^2 - 3x^2y$ if $x = 3$ and $y = 2$.

29-A 25
29-B 18
29-C 739
29-D 7

30. Using the formula $I = \sqrt{\frac{P}{R}}$, find the value of I when $P = 48$ and $R = 3$.

30-A 12
30-B 8
30-C 4
30-D $\frac{4}{3}$

WORD KNOWLEDGE

Directions

This test has questions about the meanings of words. Each question has an underlined boldface word. You are to decide which one of the four words in the choices most nearly means the same as the underlined boldface word, then mark the space on your answer form which has the same number and letter as your choice.

Now look at the sample question below.

1. It was a **small** table.

    1-A   sturdy
    1-B   round
    1-C   cheap
    1-D   little

The question is which of the four words means the same as the boldface word—the word **small.**

Little means the same as small so the D answer is the best one.

Your score on this test will be based on the number of questions you answer correctly. You should try to answer every question. Do not spend too much time on any one question.

When you begin, be sure to start with question number 1 in Part 3 of your test booklet and number 1 in Part 3 on your answer form.

Do not turn this page until told to do so.

WORD KNOWLEDGE

Time: 11 minutes; 35 questions

1. **Inform** most nearly means

   1-A   Ask.
   1-B   Heed.
   1-C   Tell.
   1-D   Ignore.

2. **Crimson** most nearly means

   2-A   Crisp.
   2-B   Neatly Pressed.
   2-C   Reddish.
   2-D   Colorful.

3. **Caution** most nearly means

   3-A   Signals.
   3-B   Care.
   3-C   Traffic.
   3-D   Haste.

4. **Intermittently** most nearly means

   4-A   Constantly.
   4-B   Annually.
   4-C   Using intermediaries (to stay).
   4-D   At irregular intervals.

5. **Occurrence** most nearly means

   5-A   Event.
   5-B   Place.
   5-C   Occupation.
   5-D   Opinion.

6. **Deception** most nearly means

   6-A   Secrets.
   6-B   Fraud.
   6-C   Mistrust.
   6-D   Hatred.

7. **Cease** most nearly means

   7-A   Start.
   7-B   Change.
   7-C   Continue.
   7-D   Stop.

8. **Acclaim** most nearly means

   8-A   Amazement.
   8-B   Laughter.
   8-C   Booing.
   8-D   Applause.

9. **Erect** most nearly means

   9-A   Paint.
   9-B   Design.
   9-C   Destroy.
   9-D   Construct.

10. **Relish** most nearly means

    10-A   Care.
    10-B   Speed.
    10-C   Amusement.
    10-D   Enjoy.

11. **Sufficient** most nearly means

    11-A   Durable.
    11-B   Substitution.
    11-C   Expendable.
    11-D   Appropriate.

12. **Fortnight** most nearly means

    12-A   Two weeks.
    12-B   One week.
    12-C   Two months.
    12-D   One month.

13. **Blemish** most nearly means

    13-A   Defect.
    13-B   Mixture.
    13-C   Accusation.
    13-D   Decoration.

14. **Impose** most nearly means

    14-A   Disguise.
    14-B   Escape.
    14-C   Require.
    14-D   Purchase.

15. **Jeer** most nearly means

    15-A   Peek.
    15-B   Scoff.
    15-C   Turn.
    15-D   Judge.

16. **Alias** most nearly means

    16-A   Enemy.
    16-B   Sidekick.
    16-C   Hero.
    16-D   Other name.

17. **Impair** most nearly means

    17-A   Direct.
    17-B   Improve.
    17-C   Weaken.
    17-D   Stimulate.

18. **Itinerant** most nearly means

    18-A   Traveling.
    18-B   Shrewd.
    18-C   Insurance.
    18-D   Aggressive.

19. **Abandon** most nearly means

    19-A   Relinquish.
    19-B   Encompass.
    19-C   Infiltrate.
    19-D   Quarantine.

20. **Resolve** most nearly means

    20-A   End.
    20-B   Understand.
    20-C   Recall.
    20-D   Forget.

21. **Ample** means

    21-A   Plentiful.
    21-B   Enthusiastic.
    21-C   Well shaped.
    21-D   Fat.

22. **Stench** most nearly means

    22-A   Puddle of slimy water.
    22-B   Pile of debris.
    22-C   Foul odor.
    22-D   Dead animal.

23. **Sullen** most nearly means

    23-A   Grayish yellow.
    23-B   Soaking wet.
    23-C   Very dirty.
    23-D   Angrily silent.

24. **Rudiments** most nearly means

    24-A   Basic methods and procedures.
    24-B   Politics.
    24-C   Promotion opportunities.
    24-D   Minute details.

25. **Clash** most nearly means

    25-A   Applaud.
    25-B   Fasten.
    25-C   Conflict.
    25-D   Punish.

26. **Camaraderie** most nearly means

    26-A   Interest in photography.
    26-B   Close friendship
    26-C   Petty jealousies.
    26-D   Arts and crafts projects.

27. **Superficial** most nearly means

    27-A   Excellent.
    27-B   Official.
    27-C   Profound.
    27-D   Cursory.

28. **Tapestry** most nearly means

    28-A   Fabric of woven designs.
    28-B   Tent
    28-C   Piece of elaborate jewelry.
    28-D   Exquisite painting.

29/ **Terse** most nearly means

    29-A   Pointed.
    29-B   Trivial.
    29-C   Oral.
    29-D   Lengthy.

30. **Concoction** most nearly means

    30-A   Combination of ingredients.
    30-B   Appetizer.
    30-C   Drink made of wine and spices.
    30-D   Relish tray.

31. **Brevity** most nearly means

    31-A   Boldness.
    31-B   Shortness.
    31-C   Nearness.
    31-D   Length.

32. **Clemency** most nearly means

    32-A   Justice.
    32-B   Punishment.
    32-C   Mercy.
    32-D   Dismissal.

33. **Insubordination** most nearly means

    33-A   Humiliation.
    33-B   Rejection.
    33-C   Disobedience.
    33-D   Carelessness.

34. **Preferential** most nearly means.

    34-A Weekly.
    34-B Constant.
    34-C Unlimited.
    34-D Special.

35. **Doldrums** most nearly means.

    35-A Fearful.
    35-B Diseased.
    35-C Low spirits.
    35-D Embarrassment

4

PARAGRAPH COMPREHENSION

Directions

This is a test of your ability to understand what you read. In this section you will find one or more paragraphs of reading material followed by incomplete statements or questions. You are to read the paragraph and select one of four lettered choices which best completes the statement or answers the question. When you have selected your answer, blacken in the correct numbered letter on your answer sheet.

Now look at the sample question below.

In certain areas water is so scarce that every attempt is made to conserve it. For instance, on one oasis in the Sahara Desert the amount of water necessary for each date palm tree has been carefully determined.

2. How much water is each tree given?

    2-A   no water at all
    2-B   exactly the amount required
    2-C   water only if it is healthy
    2-D   water on alternate days

The amount of water each tree requires has been carefully determined so the answer 2-B is correct.

Your score on this test will be based on the number of questions you answer correctly. You should try to answer every question. Do not spend too much time on any one question.

When you begin, be sure to start with question number 1 in Part 4 of your test booklet and number 1 in Part 4 on your answer form.

Do not turn this page until told to do so.

PARAGRAPH COMPREHENSION

Time: 13 minutes; 15 questions

Professional drivers, the people who drive trucks and buses for a living, have a low opinion of the average motorist. They complain that the average driver does not maintain proper speed, changes lanes without signaling, and stops without warning.

1. The topic sentence or key idea in this paragraph is that

   1-A professional drivers do not think much of the average driver
   1-B people who drive trucks are professional drivers
   1-C the average driver is not a good driver
   1-D the average driver does not like professional drivers

The trees stood quietly under the dark gray clouds. Their bare branches shuddered as the cold wind slipped around them. Sailing along on the wind a few birds flew to shelter. No other animals were to be seen.

2. In this paragraph the word *shuddered* means:

   2-A fell
   2-B shook
   2-C cracked
   2-D remained still

Many think of the log cabin as a New England invention. Others feel it was first made by the pioneers who crossed the Appalachian Mountains. According to one authority, the log cabin was introduced to America by the Swedes. The area around the Delaware River was settled by Swedes and Finns. These two European peoples were first to use the log cabin.

3. According to this passage, the log cabin was introduced to this country by

   3-A New England colonists
   3-B Swedes and Finns
   3-C Appalachian Mountain pioneers
   3-D the English

Down the gently drifting stream, the boat glided softly. Soft breezes and warm sun bathed him. The fishing pole lay unused. The floppy hat shaded his half-closed eyes and much of his face. Only his lower features, framed in a pleasant smile, could be seen.

4. This passage describes a man who is

   4-A sad
   4-B active
   4-C contented
   4-D exhilarated

Would you like to be good at a trade? Would you like to know a skill that pays well? One sure way to skill, good pay, and regular work is to train on the job. This is called apprentice training. While it is not the only way to learn, apprentice training has good points. You can earn while you learn, can learn the skill "from the ground up," and can advance on the job.

5. Apprentice training is described in this paragraph by

   5-A discussing both sides
   5-B discussing the good side only
   5-C discussing the bad side only
   5-D by comparing it to other types of training

Move into a house with six closets and all of them will be jammed in a short time. Move into a house with 15 closets — and the same thing will happen. In short, we never have enough closets no matter how many closets we have. But there's one thing we can do. We can make better use of the space within a closet.

6. The author of this paragraph suggests that we:

   6-A should build more closets in houses
   6-B never have enough things to fill the closets
   6-C usually fill every closet in the house
   6-D make the best use of space within a closet

There is a big difference between a liberal and a reactionary. The person who favors new ideas, tries to change, and looks for new ways is more free or liberated. On the other hand, a person may look back or want to return to the way things used to be. This person does not like progress and resents change.

7.   The word *reactionary* can be used to describe a person who:

7-A   looks ahead to the future
7-B   looks back to the past
7-C   favors new ideas
7-D   likes change

This forest must be preserved. These trees have stood against natural forces for over a hundred years. Within the area wildlife flourishes and the streams are clear and sparkling. Thousands of people can find pleasure through camping or walking in a spot of unspoiled nature. The beauty and peace of this forest can renew the spirit of many a person.

8.   This passage was probably written by a:

8-A   lumber company spokesperson
8-B   religious society
8-C   house-building company
8-D   conservation group

There has been enough talk. The problem has been studied from every viewpoint. The figures add up to the need for the bridge. When the bonds are approved their cost will be met by future tolls. All groups favor this and no property-owners will be hurt by it. The time for action has come.

9.   According to this paragraph, the next logical step would be to:

9-A   build the bridge
9-B   pass a law to raise the money
9-C   decide how to collect the tolls
9-D   have a meeting of property-owners

Lightning is a gigantic spark, a tremendous release of energy between earth and cloud. The shorter the gap between earth and cloud, the greater the chances of discharge. Thus, lightning tends to favor objects that thrust above the surrounding terrain. This might mean you sitting in a boat or the lone tree on the golf course.

10.   Lightning is described as:

10-A   man-made energy
10-B   a bolt from heaven
10-C   a release of electrical energy
10-D   a poorly understood phenomenon

Every large city has problems of traffic and people trying to use transportation. The problem is at its worst in the two hours before 9 a.m. and the two hours after 4 p.m. So many businesses, stores and companies start work and end work at the same time. This becomes a very great problem in the downtown business centers with their many-storied skyscrapers and their thousands of workers.

11.   The morning transportation rush starts at:

11-A   9 a.m.
11-B   7 a.m.
11-C   8 a.m.
11-D   6 a.m.

A vision care technician assists the patient in frame selection and fitting and provides instruction in the use of contact lenses. Such a technician works with children in visual training programs and assists with testing for corneal curvature, visual acuity, and eye pressure.

12.   The word *acuity* means:

12-A   cuteness
12-B   strength
12-C   sharpness
12-D   pressure

An agricultural research scientist wishes to test the germination power of a particular strain of wheat. That is, he wants to know what proportion of the seeds will grow to maturity. He picks one seed at random from a bunch of wheat and that particular grain of wheat produces a strong and healthy stalk of wheat.

13.   We can conclude from this experiment that:

13-A   the rest of the seeds are the same
13-B   this seed is the only healthy one
13-C   more seeds must be tested
13-D   it was an accident that this seed was good

Most breads and cereals are well-liked, fit easily into meal plans, and cost little per serving. These foods, with whole-grain or enriched bread as examples, provide good food value. Mostly they give food energy, but they also supply vitamins and minerals. According to a recent survey, bread and cereal products provided 40% of the thiamine (a B vitamin) and 30% of the iron needed daily by a person.

14.   What percent of the daily needs of a B vitamin come from bread and cereals?

14-A   30%
14-B   more than half
14-C   40%
14-D   70%

In the many years before 1800 there was a great fear of plague and other illnesses. Most of the problem came from poor medical knowledge and no scientific way to fight the diseases. People knew the results of plague would be suffering and death. Naturally they tried to stay away from infection or they tried to keep the danger away from them.

15.   The main reason for the fear of plague before 1800 was

15-A   crowded cities and seaports
15-B   little medical or scientific knowledge
15-C   long time needed for quarantine
15-D   difficulty in avoiding infection

NUMERICAL OPERATIONS

Directions

This is a test to see how rapidly and accurately you can do arithmetic problems. Each problem is followed by four answers, only one of which is correct. Decide which answer is correct, then blacken the space on your answer form which has the same number and letter as your choice.

Now look at the sample problem below.

1. 4 + 3 =

 1-A 1
 1-B 12
 1-C 7
 1-D 2

The answer to the problem is 7, so you would blacken the space for 1-C on your answer form.

This is a speed test, so work as fast as you can without making mistakes. Do each problem as it comes. If you finish before time is up, go back and check your work. Part 5 of this model test begins with question 1. Thus, the first answer should be recorded next to 1 on your answer form.

Do not turn this page until told to do so.

NUMERICAL OPERATIONS

Time: 3 minutes; 50 questions

1. 8 − 5 =

    1-A   40
    1-B   13
    1-C   3
    1-D   2

2. 4 × 6 =

    2-A   10
    2-B   24
    2-C   12
    2-D   26

3. 8 − 1 =

    3-A   9
    3-B   8
    3-C   7
    3-D   6

4. 6 ÷ 3 =

    4-A   0
    4-B   1
    4-C   2
    4-D   3

5. 6 + 1 =

    5-A   7
    5-B   8
    5-C   5
    5-D   1

6. 9 × 0 =

    6-A   10
    6-B   9
    6-C   1
    6-D   0

7. 3 + 6 =

    7-A   8
    7-B   9
    7-C   10
    7-D   11

8. 5 + 1 =

    8-A   6
    8-B   7
    8-C   4
    8-D   5

9. 3 − 2 =

    9-A   0
    9-B   1
    9-C   2
    9-D   3

10. 8 − 3 =

    10-A   3
    10-B   6
    10-C   5
    10-D   4

11. 5 + 8 =

    11-A   13
    11-B   14
    11-C   12
    11-D   11

12. 0 ÷ 9 =

    12-A   9
    12-B   8
    12-C   0
    12-D   1

13. 5 + 7 =

    13-A   14
    13-B   11
    13-C   13
    13-D   12

14. 11 ÷ 1 =

    14-A   10
    14-B   11
    14-C   12
    14-D   1

15. 9 + 7 =

    15-A   16
    15-B   63
    15-C   2
    15-D   15

16. 4 + 6 =

    16-A   10
    16-B   2
    16-C   11
    16-D   9

17. 16 ÷ 4 =

    17-A 12
    17-B 5
    17-C 4
    17-D 8

18. 17 − 9 =

    18-A 6
    18-B 7
    18-C 9
    18-D 8

19. 3 + 6 =

    19-A 8
    19-B 9
    19-C 10
    19-D 3

20. 7 + 6 =

    20-A 12
    20-B 13
    20-C 14
    20-D 11

21. 8 − 0 =

    21-A 0
    21-B 7
    21-C 8
    21-D 9

22. 6 × 0 =

    22-A 0
    22-B 5
    22-C 6
    22-D 7

23. 7 ÷ 7 =

    23-A 0
    23-B 1
    23-C 7
    23-D 14

24. 10 ÷ 2 =

    24-A 7
    24-B 8
    24-C 12
    24-D 5

25. 8 + 7 =

    25-A 13
    25-B 14
    25-C 15
    25-D 16

26. 6 × 6 =

    26-A 36
    26-B 12
    26-C 24
    26-D 26

27. 10 ÷ 5 =

    27-A 10
    27-B 7
    27-C 5
    27-D 2

28. 8 × 1 =

    28-A 9
    28-B 8
    28-C 7
    28-D 6

29. 7 ÷ 1 =

    29-A 1
    29-B 6
    29-C 7
    29-D 8

30. 6 + 5 =

    30-A 11
    30-B 12
    30-C 13
    30-D 10

31. 1 + 9 =

    31-A 8
    31-B 9
    31-C 10
    31-D 11

32. 18 − 1 =

    31-A 1
    32-B 17
    32-C 18
    32-D 19

33. 16 ÷ 2 =

    33-A 4
    33-B 8
    33-C 14
    33-D 18

34. 3 + 8 =

    34-A 5
    34-B 12
    34-C 10
    34-D 11

35. 7 − 3 =

   35-A 4
   35-B 5
   35-C 2
   35-D 10

36. 9 ÷ 3 =

   36-A 12
   36-B 6
   36-C 3
   36-D 2

37. 4 × 5 =

   37-A 20
   37-B 25
   37-C 9
   37-D 30

38. 9 − 5 =

   38-A 3
   38-B 4
   38-C 6
   38-D 2

39. 4 + 11 =

   39-A 7
   39-B 14
   39-C 15
   39-D 16

40. 3 × 6 =

   40-A 3
   40-B 9
   40-C 12
   40-D 18

41. 6 − 4 =

   41-A 1
   41-B 2
   41-C 3
   41-D 10

42. 7 × 5 =

   42-A 35
   42-B 28
   42-C 25
   42-D 21

43. 7 − 1 =

   43-A 7
   43-B 6
   43-C 5
   43-D 8

44. 7 + 3 =

   44-A 12
   44-B 11
   44-C 10
   44-D 9

45. 4 ÷ 4 =

   45-A 16
   45-B 1
   45-C 8
   45-D 0

46. 12 − 7 =

   46-A 19
   46-B 6
   46-C 5
   46-D 4

47. 17 + 1 =

   47-A 17
   47-B 1
   47-C 16
   47-D 18

48. 0 ÷ 7 =

   48-A 0
   48-B 1
   48-C 7
   48-D 6

49. 3 + 4 =

   49-A 9
   49-B 7
   49-C 1
   49-D 12

50. 7 × 7 =

   50-A 36
   50-B 45
   50-C 49
   50-D 63

CODING SPEED

Directions

This is a test to see how quickly and accurately you can assign code numbers. At the top of each set of questions there is a code number "key." The key is a group of words with a code number for each word.

Each question in the test is a word taken from the key at the top. From among the possible answers listed for each question, you are to find the one which is the correct code number for that word. Then blacken the square for that answer on your answer sheet.

The sample questions below have already been answered for you. Make sure you understand them. Then try to answer the 84 questions following them as best you can.

Sample Question

Key

green .. 2715	man ... 3451	salt 4586
hat 1413	room ... 2864	tree 5972

Answers

	A	B	C	D	E
room	1413	2715	2864	3451	4586
green	2715	2864	3451	4586	5972
tree	2715	2864	3451	4596	5972
hat	1413	2715	2864	3451	4586
room	1413	2864	3451	4586	5972

Notice that each of the questions is one of the words in the key. To the right of each question are possible answers listed under the letters A, B, C, D, and E. By looking at the key you see that the code number for the first word, "room," is 2864. 2864 is listed under the letter C so C is the correct answer. The correct answers for the other four questions are A, E, A, and B.

Do not turn this page until told to do so.

CODING SPEED

Time: 7 minutes; 84 questions

Key

forward ..7861	square...2980	president.1962
goal.....3287	show 5933	honor....2935
red......9154	true 8791	elbow....8841
	cover 3245	

Answers

		A	B	C	D	E
1.	true	3287	3245	8791	1962	5933
2.	goal	3287	8791	8841	1962	9154
3.	elbow	2980	8841	8791	2935	9154
4.	president	2935	8841	8791	1962	3287
5.	forward	2980	7861	2935	1962	8791
6.	show	3287	5933	2935	7861	5933
7.	honor	5933	9154	2935	3245	8841
8.	red	9154	1962	3287	8791	7861
9.	cover	7861	8791	3245	2935	3287
10.	square	3245	1962	2935	2980	3287
11.	red	3287	2980	2935	9154	8791
12.	honor	2980	2935	5933	3245	8791

Key

circle 1568	green....2992	mayor ...6102
aim 5670	berry 7041	film 3113
butter....7912	rear 4427	public ...9520
	mud.....8855	

Answers

		A	B	C	D	E
13.	film	7041	3113	9520	2992	6102
14.	butter	7041	3113	7912	6102	2992
15.	aim	7912	3113	7041	5670	2992
16.	mud	7912	8855	1568	5670	9520
17.	berry	7041	5670	1568	3113	6102
18.	mayor	3113	7912	3113	2992	6102
19.	film	4427	3113	7912	2992	1568
20.	green	8855	7041	5670	2992	6102
21.	public	1568	2992	6102	9520	4427
22.	circle	4427	7041	1568	5670	7912
23.	rear	2992	4427	6102	5670	9520
24.	berry	6102	3113	9520	7041	7912

Key

meat ...5563	summer..4207	desk.....7039
purple ...1117	rain 9088	cry 8868
boy 7191	study 6440	package..3206
	pocket ...4159	

Answers

		A	B	C	D	E
25.	meat	4159	9088	5563	8868	6440
26.	package	4159	9088	3206	7039	1117
27.	desk	7039	4207	3206	8868	6440
28.	study	4207	6440	4159	8868	5563
29.	summer	4207	6440	4159	7191	5563
30.	cry	3206	1117	9088	8868	7191
31.	purple	3206	1117	9088	8868	7039
32.	boy	1117	7191	4207	5563	9088
33.	desk	7039	9088	7191	5563	6440
34.	pocket	8868	9088	4159	1117	5563
35.	rain	3206	7039	4207	9088	7191
36.	purple	6440	4159	1117	7039	7191

Key

house ...6629	grass 9095	guitar....9009
woman...7189	train.....4038	winter ...2163
orange...1114	nylon 9876	knee 5047
	poor.....8091	

Answers

		A	B	C	D	E
37.	woman	9876	9095	2163	7189	5047
38.	winter	9876	8091	2163	9009	6629
39.	train	5047	8091	4038	1114	6629
40.	orange	1114	9876	9095	9009	2163
41.	knee	1114	5047	9095	6629	4038
42.	nylon	9876	5047	7189	6629	4038
43.	house	8091	6629	7189	5047	1114
44.	poor	9009	6629	2163	7189	8091
45.	grass	9095	8091	9876	9009	7189
46.	orange	9876	1114	6629	9009	5047
47.	guitar	9876	1114	9009	7189	4038
48.	nylon	9009	2163	6629	9876	4038

Key

write 7028	neck 5428	sweater ..6680
black 4762	ice 2763	plant 2446
bread....8721	learn 7650	false.....1161
	paper....5553	

Answers

		A	B	C	D	E
49.	learn	2763	2446	6680	7650	4762
50.	plant	2763	4762	2446	1161	7028
51.	bread	5428	8721	2446	7650	7028
52.	write	8721	5553	7028	4762	1161
53.	false	2446	1161	4762	5553	7028
54.	ice	2763	1161	6680	7650	4762
55.	learn	5428	6680	2446	7028	7650
56.	neck	2446	6680	5428	1161	7028
57.	black	8721	2763	4762	8721	1161
58.	sweater	6680	7650	7028	4762	5428
59.	paper	7028	8721	5553	5428	4762
60.	black	8721	7028	5553	1161	4762

Key

tree 7760	table 7620	flesh 5711
man.....2332	brown ...4407	envelope .6901
wool.....3497	spring ...1874	soil......3313
	stand 6290	

Answers

		A	B	C	D	E
61.	tree	7620	1874	6901	7760	1874
62.	spring	1874	7760	5711	2332	3497

63.	soil	1874	6901	5711	3313	7760
64.	flesh	4407	5711	3313	2332	7760
65.	wool	4407	1874	7620	3497	6901
66.	brown	3313	6901	4407	5711	2332
67.	stand	6290	6901	4407	7620	7760
68.	envelope	6290	6901	1874	7760	7620
69.	spring	2332	1874	3313	7760	3497
70.	man	2332	1874	7760	6901	4407
71.	table	4407	7620	3497	3313	1874
72.	flesh	1874	3313	6901	2332	5711

Key

skin 1659	bacon ...7055	drink 7994
print.....9080	bottle....9997	night 6646
card.....7822	grow 7152	bad 3702
	conceal ..2229	

Answers

		A	B	C	D	E
73.	conceal	7152	7055	7994	6646	2229
74.	grow	9997	9080	7152	3702	7994
75.	skin	9080	3702	1659	6646	7055
76.	card	9997	7152	7822	3702	1659
77.	drink	7055	2229	7994	6646	9080
78.	bad	3702	6646	9080	7055	9997
79.	conceal	7152	3702	2229	1659	7994
80.	bottle	9997	9080	3702	7822	6646
81.	print	7152	7055	9080	3702	7994
82.	night	2229	6646	7055	1659	7994
83.	card	9997	7055	1659	6646	7822
84.	bacon	7822	2229	7055	9080	1659

7

AUTO AND SHOP INFORMATION

Directions

This test has questions about automobile tools, and shop practices. Pick the best answer for each question, then blacken the space on your separate answer form which has the same number and letter as your choice.

1. The most commonly used fuel for running automobile engines is

   1-A   kerosene.
   1-B   benzine.
   1-C   crude oil.
   1-D   gasoline.

Gasoline is the most commonly used fuel, so 1-D is the correct answer.

Your score on this test will be based on the number of questions you answer correctly. You should try to answer every question. Do not spend too much time on any one question.

When you are told to begin, be sure to start with question number 1 in Part 7 of your test booklet and number 1 in Part 7 on your separate answer form.

Do not turn this page until told to do so.

AUTO AND SHOP INFORMATION

Time: 11 minutes; 25 questions

1. The universal joint is needed to

   1-A   allow the drive shaft to flex.
   1-B   hold the drive shaft rigid.
   1-C   make the transmission shift.
   1-D   make the differential turn corners.

2. Three major pollutants emitted by a gasoline engine are

   2-A   carbon dioxide, carbon monoxide and oxygen.
   2-B   hydrocarbons, nitric acid and nitrogen.
   2-C   hydrocarbons, carbon monoxide and oxides of nitrogen.
   2-D   nitrogen, oxygen and carbon monixide.

3. The catalytic converter

   3-A   converts gasoline to the air/fuel ratio needed.
   3-B   reduces the input pressure of exhaust gases to the muffler.
   3-C   converts intake manifold pressure to a lower value.
   3-D   converts exhaust gases to better quality emissions.

4. The differential is

   4-A   located in the transmission.
   4-B   located in the clutch housing.
   4-C   consists of three small bevel gears on the ends of the axle shafts.
   4-D   consists of two small bevel gears on the ends of the axle shafts.

5. PCV is the abbreviation for

   5-A   Pollution Control Valve.
   5-B   Pollution Valve Control.
   5-C   Positive Crankcase Ventilation.
   5-D   Pollution Control Ventilator.

6. The formation of NO_x in an engine is minimized by

   6-A   diluting the fuel/air mixture entering the combustion chamber.
   6-B   burning more fuel.
   6-C   using an alcohol enriched fuel.
   6-D   not using a muffler.

7. With any two gears the gear with the greater number of teeth will

   7-A   turn slower than the smaller gear and produce less torque.
   7-B   always turn slower and produce greater torque.
   7-C   never produce much torque.
   7-D   always turn faster and produce less torque.

8. The clutch is used to

   8-A   change compression ratios.
   8-B   stop the car.
   8-C   make it possible to change gears.
   8-D   drive the transmission.

9. First gear in a car is used

   9-A   at high speeds.
   9-B   at the start of the car from a standstill.
   9-C   when the car is moving faster than 35 mph.
   9-D   at speeds above 55 mph.

10. The torque converter is found in

    10-A   the differential housing.
    10-B   the manual transmission housing.
    10-C   the engine compartment.
    10-D   in an automatic transmission.

11. Disc brakes are made with

    11-A   two pads and a rotating drum.
    11-B   two pads and a rotating disc.
    11-C   two brake shoes that slide along the inside drum mounted on the rear wheels.
    11-D   all-steel pads to stop the car quickly.

12. In a front-wheel drive car the transmission

    12-A   is located in the rear of the car.
    12-B   is located in the engine compartment.
    12-C   has a long propeller shaft.
    12-D   has a short propeller shaft.

13. L₀ or L on the automatic transmission is the same as

    13-A   1st gear in the manual transmission.

    13-B   2nd gear in the manual transmission.

    13-C   3rd gear in the manual transmission.

    13-D   4th gear in the manual transmission.

14. Park (P) position on an automatic transmission indicator means the transmission

    14-A   is in idle and can be towed.

    14-B   is in a locked position that prevents the car from moving.

    14-C   is in its highest speed position.

    14-D   is ready for pulling heavy loads.

15. The internal combustion engine can be best described as

    15-A   a high torque engine even at low speeds.

    15-B   a low torque engine even at low speeds.

    15-C   a low speed engine.

    15-D   a high speed engine.

16. In a four-wheel drive car the

    16-A   transfer case puts power to the front wheels.

    16-B   transmission is placed in the rear.

    16-C   transmission has to be of the automatic type.

    16-D   transmission has to be of the manual type.

17. Which of these tools breaks easily when twisted?

    17-A   Folding rule

    17-B   Ruler

    17-C   Yard Stick

    17-D   Hand saw

18. Which type of saw is mounted in a mitre box?

    18-A   Rip Saw

    18-B   Hack Saw

    18-C   Cross-Cut Saw

    18-D   Back Saw

19. In order to shape concrete it is placed in a

    19-A   lake.

    19-B   form.

    19-C   hole.

    19-D   large round object.

20. In concrete work a "darby" is

    20-A   a metal pole.

    20-B   a metal trowel.

    20-C   a type of wooden float.

    20-D   a stake to hold a form.

21. Nail sets are used for

    21-A   driving tacks.

    21-B   setting nails below the surface of the wood.

    21-C   setting nails above the surface of the wood.

    21-D   setting carpet tacks.

22. A tool used for marking wood is called a

    22-A   saw.

    22-B   plane.

    22-C   screwdriver.

    22-D   scratch awl.

23. In selecting the proper grinding wheel it is important to

    23-A   choose the proper grain size for the job to be done.

    23-B   choose the proper manufacturer.

    23-C   choose the proper priced wheel.

    23-D   choose the proper concrete binder.

24. Which of these metals can be made thinner than a coat of paint?

    24-A   Copper

    24-B   Aluminum

    24-C   Gold

    24-D   Silver

25. When making a hole in sheet metal, it is safer to

    25-A   drill it.

    25-B   punch it.

    25-C   cut it.

    25-D   burn it.

MATHEMATICS KNOWLEDGE

Directions

This is a test of your ability to solve general mathematical problems. Each problem is followed by four answer choices. Select the correct response from the choices given. Then mark the space on your answer form that has the same number and letter as your choice. Use scratch paper to do any figuring that you wish.

Now look at this sample problem.

1. $4 \times 2 =$

    1-A   10
    1-B   8
    1-C   6
    1-D   4

The correct answer is 8, so 1-B is the correct response.

Your score on this test will be based on the number of questions you answer correctly. You should try to answer every question. Do not spend too much time on any one question.

Start with question number 1 in Part 8. Mark your answer for this question next to number 1, Part 8, on your answer form.

Do not turn this page until told to do so.

MATHEMATICS KNOWLEDGE

Time: 24 minutes; 25 questions

1. Solve for x: $2x + 6 = 12 - x$.

   1-A 6
   1-B 9
   1-C 2
   1-D 3

2. From $8x^2 - 7x$ subtract $2x - 3x^2$.

   2-A $11x^2 - 9x$
   2-B $5x^2 - 5x$
   2-C $6x^2 - 4x$
   2-D $10x^2 - 10x$

3. What is the product of $2x^3y$ and $(3x^2y - 4)$?

   3-A $6x^5y^2 - 4$
   3-B $6x^5y^2 - 8x^3y$
   3-C $6x^6y^2 - 8x^3y$
   3-D $6x^6y - 8x^3y$

4. A worker can do $\frac{1}{3}$ of a job by himself in one day, and his helper can do $\frac{1}{5}$ of the job by himself in one day. What portion of the job can they do if they work together for one day?

   4-A $\frac{1}{4}$
   4-B $\frac{8}{15}$
   4-C $\frac{1}{8}$
   4-D $\frac{2}{15}$

5. A length of chain is 5 feet, 3 inches long. If a piece 3 feet, 9 inches in length is cut from the chain, what is the length of the remaining piece?

   5-A 2 feet, 6 inches
   5-B 1 foot, 1 inch
   5-C 1 foot, 4 inches
   5-D 1 foot, 6 inches

6. In a regular hexagon, all the angles are equal and one of them is 120°. What is the sum of all the angles of the regular hexagon?

   6-A 240°
   6-B 480°
   6-C 720°
   6-D 360°

7. What is the product of $(3a - 2)$ and $(a + 3)$?

   7-A $4a + 1$
   7-B $3a^2 - 6$
   7-C $3a^2 - 2a - 6$
   7-D $3a^2 + 7a - 6$

8. If $x = 3$, what is the value of $|x - 7|$?

   8-A 4
   8-B -4
   8-C 10
   8-D -10

9. Solve the following system of equations for x: $3x + y = 13$
   $x - 2y = 2$

   9-A 18
   9-B 4
   9-C 3
   9-D 6

10. How many feet are there in a length of y yards and i inches?

    10-A $3y + i$
    10-B $3y + 12i$
    10-C $\dfrac{y + 12i}{3}$
    10-D $\dfrac{36y + i}{12}$

11. Solve the following formula for F: $C = \frac{5}{9}(F - 32)$.

    11-A $F = \frac{9}{5}C + 32$
    11-B $F = \frac{5}{9}C + 32$
    11-C $F = \dfrac{9C + 32}{5}$
    11-D $F = \frac{9}{5}C + 288$

12. A woman travels 3 miles directly east and then travels 4 miles directly north. How many miles is she from her starting point?

    12-A 7
    12-B 5
    12-C 25
    12-D $3\frac{1}{2}$

13. A line is drawn perpendicular to the base of an equilateral triangle at one of the vertices of the triangle. Find the number of degrees in the angle made by this perpendicular and the other side of the triangle that contains this vertex.

13-A 30°
13-B 45°
13-C 60°
13-D 90°

14. Solve the following inequality: $x - 6 \leq 5$

14-A $x \leq 1$
14-B $x \leq 11$
14-C $x \geq 11$
14-D $x < 11$

15. A fence which had been installed around a rectangular field 40 feet long and 36 feet wide is torn down. The entire fence is then reused to completely enclose a square field. What is the length in feet of a side of the square field?

15-A 76
15-B 19
15-C 42
15-D 38

16. A cereal manufacturer packages breakfast cereal in individual-sized boxes measuring 2 inches by 3 inches by 4 inches. The same product is also packaged in large family-sized boxes measuring 3 inches by 8 inches by 12 inches. The contents of how many of the individual-sized boxes would be required to fill one family-sized box?

16-A 6
16-B 12
16-C 10
16-D 8

17. A wheel has a diameter of 14 inches. How many inches will the wheel roll along the ground during one rotation? (Use $\frac{22}{7}$ as the value of pi)

17-A 44
17-B 22
17-C 14
17-D 28

18. In a right triangle whose hypotenuse has a length of 21 feet, the sine of one of the angles is $\frac{3}{7}$. What is the length in feet of the side opposite this angle?

18-A 6
18-B 14
18-C 9
18-D 10

19. Find the value of $-x^4$ if $x = -0.1$.

19-A -0.1
19-B 0.0001
19-C -0.0001
19-D -0.4

20. Under the terms of a Federal subsidy, a real estate developer is required to rent at least 30% of the apartments he builds to low-income families. If he plans on having 108 low-income apartments, what is the maximum number of apartments of all types that he may build?

20-A 360
20-B 252
20-C 324
20-D 396

21. A student has grades of 60% on each of two tests and a grade of 70% on a third test. What grade must he get on a fourth test to raise his average to 75%?

21-A 95%
21-B 85%
21-C 100%
21-D He cannot achieve a 75% average

22. A motorist travels for 3 hours at 40 miles per hour and then travels for 2 more hours at 50 miles per hour. What is her average rate of speed in miles per hour for the entire trip?

22-A 45
22-B 44
22-C 43
22-D 90

23. A radar device is capable of detecting objects within the area around it up to a radius of 10 miles. If it is used to cover a 36° angular portion of this area, how many square miles of area will it cover? (Use 3.14 as the value of pi)

23-A 360
23-B 6.28
23-C 31.4
23-D 3.6

24. Solve for x: $x^2 + 2x = 15$.

    24-A $x = 3, x = 5$
    24-B $x = -3, x = 5$
    24-C $x = -5, x = 3$
    24-D $x = -15, x = 1$

25. 12 quarts of a radiator coolant contains 25% antifreeze and 75% water. How many quarts of water must be added to change the mixture to one containing 20% antifreeze?

    25-A 1
    25-B 2
    25-C 3
    25-D 4

MECHANICAL COMPREHENSION

Directions

This test has questions about general mechanical and physical principles. Pick the best answer for each question, then blacken the space on your separate answer form which has the same number and letter as your choice.

Here is a sample question.

17. The follower is at its highest position between points

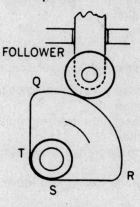

FOLLOWER

Q

T

R

S

    17-A   Q and R.
    17-B   R and S.
    17-C   S and T.
    17-D   T and Q.

The correct answer is between Q and R, so you would blacken the space for 17-A on your answer form.

Your score on this test will be based on the number of questions you answer correctly. You should try to answer every question. Do not spend too much time on any one question.

When you are told to begin, be sure to start with question number 1 in Part 9 of your test booklet and number 1 in Part 9 of your separate answer form.

Do not turn this page until told to do so.

MECHANICAL COMPREHENSION

Time: 19 minutes; 25 questions

1. Most of the lift on an aircraft's wings is because of

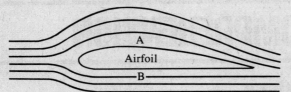

Airfoil

  1-A   a decrease in pressure on the upper side, A.
  1-B   a decrease in pressure on the bottom side, B.
  1-C   a vacuum created under the wing at point A.
  1-D   none of the above.

2. It is well known that oil rises in lamp wicks, melted wax rises in the wick of a candle, and water rises in a narrow tube. This phenomenon is called

  2-A   wicking.
  2-B   erosion.
  2-C   capillarity.
  2-D   osmosis.

3. Two strips of metal, one iron and one brass, are welded or riveted together to form a

  3-A   heating element.
  3-B   thermal bridge.
  3-C   heat switch.
  3-D   thermostat.

4. Which of the following metals expands the most when heated?

  4-A   Steel
  4-B   Aluminum
  4-C   Iron
  4-D   Tungsten

5. Clocks with pendulums tend to run faster when cold. This is caused by

  5-A   the pendulum becoming longer when cold.
  5-B   the pendulum becoming shorter when cold.
  5-C   the air expands and slows the pendulum.
  5-D   the air contracts and speeds up the pendulum.

6. Heat is a form of

  6-A   energy.
  6-B   motion.
  6-C   thermals.
  6-D   calories.

7. Which of the metals listed below is the best conductor of heat?

  7-A   Aluminum
  7-B   Copper
  7-C   Iron
  7-D   Silver

8. Heat is transferred from one place to another by conduction, convection and

  8-A   condensation.
  8-B   evaporation.
  8-C   radiation.
  8-D   cooling.

9. When a salt is dissolved in water it causes

  9-A   an increase in the freezing point of the solution.
  9-B   a decrease in the freezing point of the solution.
  9-C   little or no difference in the freezing point.
  9-D   the water to freeze and leave the salt.

10. When a liquid is changed to a vapor the process is called

  10-A   evaporation.
  10-B   dehydration.
  10-C   pressurization.
  10-D   condensation.

11. When water is heated and confined to a closed container so the steam cannot escape, the pressure inside increases and the temperature of the boiling water becomes

  11-A   lower.
  11-B   higher.
  11-C   stays the same.
  11-D   none of the above.

12. Crude petroleum is a mixture of many substances with different boiling points. The process of refining to obtain gasoline is called

12-A   condensation.
12-B   pressurization.
12-C   dehydration.
12-D   fractional distillation.

13.   The speed of sound at 0°C has been found to be

13-A   1492 meters per second.
13-B   3500 meters per second.
13-C   1086 feet per second.
13-D   186,000 miles per second.

14.   The meter used to measure extremely high resistances is called a

14-A   ohmmeter.
14-B   megger.
14-C   resistance meter.
14-D   ammeter.

15.   In the figure below a hole is being drilled in 1. What is taking place in 2?

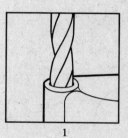
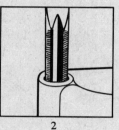

1   2

15-A   The hole is being reamed.
15-B   The hole is being drilled.
15-C   The hole is being tapped.
15-D   The hole is being plugged.

16.   The units shown are used on small gasoline engines as

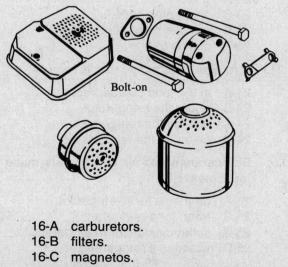

Bolt-on

16-A   carburetors.
16-B   filters.
16-C   magnetos.
16-D   mufflers.

17.   The outboard engine shown is water-cooled and gets its cooling water from

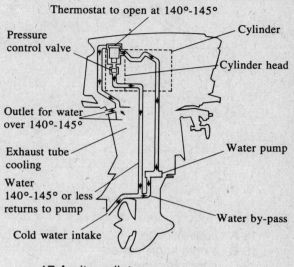

Thermostat to open at 140°-145°
Pressure control valve
Cylinder
Cylinder head
Outlet for water over 140°-145°
Exhaust tube cooling
Water pump
Water 140°-145° or less returns to pump
Water by-pass
Cold water intake

17-A   its radiator.
17-B   its oil cooler.
17-C   the lake or river.
17-D   its water holding tank.

18.   In a small gasoline engine's fuel tank, the ball drops when suction stops. This prevents

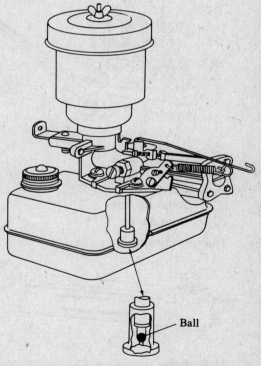

Ball

18-A   the engine from running any more.
18-B   the gasoline from running back into the tank.
18-C   back firing.
18-D   the engine from exploding.

19.   The type of cutter shown is called a

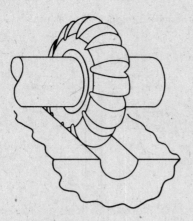

19-A   convex cutter.
19-B   single angle cutter.
19-C   concave cutter.
19-D   corner rounding cutter.

20.   In the figure shown the set-up is being used to

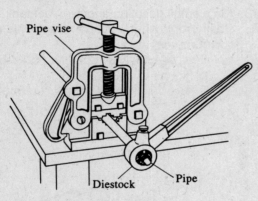

20-A   ream a pipe.
20-B   cut a pipe.
20-C   thread a pipe.
20-D   bore a pipe.

21.   The tool shown is used in a

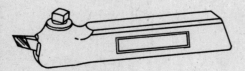

21-A   lathe.
21-B   grinder.
21-C   shaper.
21-D   drill press.

22.   The thickness gage shown in the figure is used most often in

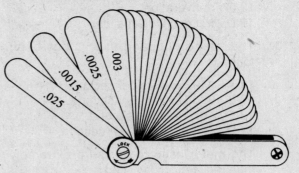

22-A   woodworking shops.
22-B   automotive work.
22-C   plastics work.
22-D   ceramics work.

23.   The gage shown is used to measure the size of

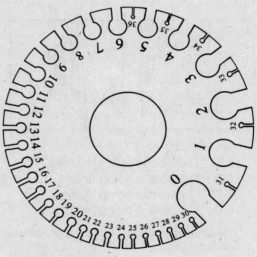

23-A   wire.
23-B   spark plug gaps.
23-C   breaker point gaps.
23-D   plastic rods.

24.   A refrigerator's evaporator is located

24-A   in the food compartment.
24-B   under the refrigerator.
24-C   outside the refrigerator.
24-D   on top of the refrigerator.

25.   Refrigerators and air conditioners made for homes use

25-A   ammonia for a refrigerant.
25-B   freon for a refrigerant.
25-C   sulfur dioxide for a refrigerant.
25-D   water as a refrigerant.

ELECTRONICS INFORMATION

Directions

This is a test of your knowledge of electrical, radio, and electronics information. You are to select the correct response from the choices given. Then mark the space on your answer form which has the same number and letter as your choice.

Now look at the sample question below.

1. What does the abbreviation AC stand for?

    1-A   additional charge
    1-B   alternating coil
    1-C   alternating current
    1-D   ampere current

The correct answer is alternating current, so 1-C is the correct response.

Your score on this test will be based on the number of questions you answer correctly. You should try to answer every question. Do not spend too much time on any one question.

When you are told to begin, be sure to start with question number 1 in Part 10 of your test booklet and number 1 in Part 10 on your separate answer form.

Do not turn this page until told to do so.

ELECTRONICS INFORMATION

Time: 9 minutes; 20 questions

1. Which of the following causes the inductance of a coil to decrease?

    1-A   A Copper Core
    1-B   An Iron Core
    1-C   More Turns of Wire
    1-D   Shortening the Length of the Coil

2. Permeability is

    2-A   a unit of measurement of magnetism.
    2-B   a force field intensity measurement.
    2-C   the ease with which magnetic lines of force distribute themselves throughout a material.
    2-D   a property of a permanent magnet.

3. Which of the following is not a factor in determining capacitance of a capacitor?

    3-A   Area of the Plates
    3-B   Distance Between the Plates
    3-C   Material Used as a Dielectric
    3-D   Voltage Applied to the Plates

4. Capacitors placed in series produce

    4-A   less capacitance.
    4-B   a lower WVDC rating.
    4-C   more capacitance.
    4-D   higher reliability.

5. X_c is equal to:

    5-A $\frac{1}{2} \pi FC$
    5-B $\frac{1}{2} \pi FL$
    5-C $2 \pi FL$
    5-D $2 \pi FC$

6. Capacitors connected in parallel produce

    6-A   more capacitance.
    6-B   less capacitance.
    6-C   higher WVDC rating.
    6-D   handle more voltage.

7. Impedance (Z) of a series RL circuit can be found by using

    7-A $Z = \sqrt{R^2 + X_c^2}$
    7-B $Z = \sqrt{R^2 + X_L^2}$
    7-C $Z = \sqrt{R + X_L}$
    7-D $Z = \sqrt{R + X_L^2}$

8. Parallel resonance occurs in a circuit when

    8-A $Z = X_L$
    8-B $Z = X_c$
    8-C $X_c = 2 \pi FC$
    8-D $X_L = X_c$

9. A filter is used in a power supply to

    9-A   change AC to DC.
    9-B   change DC to AC.
    9-C   smooth out voltage variations.
    9-D   smooth out power surges.

10. Another name for a transistor is

    10-A   diode.
    10-B   semiconductor.
    10-C   crystal amplifier.
    10-D   integrated circuit.

11. Radio frequency amplifiers are used in

    11-A   audio amplifiers.
    11-B   differential amplifiers.
    11-C   operational amplifiers.
    11-D   receivers and transmitters.

12. A crystal microphone uses

    12-A   the piezoelectrical effect.
    12-B   the pressure pack effect.
    12-C   magnetic waves to operate.
    12-D   a permanent magnet to operate.

13. The voice coil of a speaker has an impedance that is

    13-A   high.
    13-B   low.
    13-C   made of ceramic materials.
    13-D   made of ferrite materials.

14. A crossover network is used to

    14-A   direct the proper frequency range to the right speaker.
    14-B   eliminate noise.
    14-C   filter out high frequencies.
    14-D   filter out low frequencies.

15. The klystron is used in

    15-A   low frequency transmitters.
    15-B   radar units.
    15-C   audio frequency amplifiers.
    15-D   frequency detectors.

16. There are two basic types of oscillators used for microwave generation. They are the magnetron and the

    16-A   klystron.
    16-B   op amp.
    16-C   Clapp oscillator.
    16-D   multivibrator.

17. There are two types of diodes used in electronics work. They are the semiconductor diode and the

    17-A   vacuum tube diode.
    17-B   full-wave diode.
    17-C   half-wave diode.
    17-D   Zener diode.

18. Color television relies upon three colors to produce the full color range needed for a good picture. These colors are red, blue and

    18-A   gray.
    18-B   orange.
    18-C   yellow.
    18-D   green.

19. The folded dipole antenna has an impedance of

    19-A   72 ohms.
    19-B   300 ohms.
    19-C   600 ohms.
    19-D   75 ohms.

20. Television sets in the USA use a horizontal frequency of

    20-A   525 Hz.
    20-B   60 Hz.
    20-C   15,750 Hz.
    20-D   15,625 Hz.

ANSWERS AND ANSWERS EXPLAINED

1

GENERAL SCIENCE

Answers

1-D	6-C	11-A	16-C	21-C
2-C	7-B	12-C	17-B	22-D
3-D	8-B	13-B	18-D	23-B
4-C	9-D	14-B	19-B	24-C
5-B	10-C	15-C	20-C	25-D

1-D   The sperm carries an X or Y chromosome, while all eggs normally have one X chromosome. The union of XX results in a female, while the union of an X chromosome with a Y chromosome results in a male.

2-C   Rocks do not conduct heat very quickly. If a rock becomes cold during the night but is rapidly heated during the day, the expansion and contraction may cause the outer layer to peel off. If water gets into a crack in the rock, the freezing and thawing may cause the rock to split.

3-D   Sand results from the weathering of igneous rock which contains quartz crystals. Because of the relative hardness and insolubility of quartz the crystals of quartz remain after other portions of the eroded rock have been dissolved or carried away.

4-C   Vinegar contains acetic acid.

5-B   All atoms of the same element have the same number of protons. In the neutral atom the number of electrons is the same as the number of protons. (Protons are inside the nucleus of an atom; electrons are outside it.) Atoms of the same element may differ in the number of neutrons.

6-C   When heat is applied to a liquid at its boiling point the added energy is used to separate the molecules from their neighbors, but no increase in the temperature of the liquid occurs. The molecules of vapor that leave the surface of the liquid possess increased potential energy because of the work done to overcome the forces acting on them.

7-B   Nebulae are large clouds of gas and dust located between the stars. Our solar system is made up of the sun, the planets and their satellites, and asteroids.

8-B   Space is a nearly perfect vacuum. The process by which solar energy (in the form of ultraviolet rays) is transmitted through space is called radiation.

9-D   The gene for hemophilia lies on the X chromosome; this disorder is therefore inherited as a sex-linked disorder.

10-C   Only living things can duplicate themselves.

11-A   The thermometer that indicates the freezing point of water at zero and the boiling point of water at 100 degrees is known as the Centigrade, or Celsius, thermometer.

12-C   A steep surface will increase runoff since the water will flow rapidly, giving it little time to be absorbed by the soil. Vegetation will make the surface more porous, decreasing the runoff and thereby decreasing the erosion of the soil.

13-B   The 25-pound force is the resultant of two forces acting at right angles to each other. The resultant can be represented as the hypotenuse of a right triangle, with one side representing the 15-pound force and the other side the unknown (x)

force. Then, applying the Pythagorean Theorem

$$(\text{hypotenuse})^2 = (\text{side})^2 + (\text{side})^2$$
$$(25)^2 = (15)^2 + x^2$$
$$625 = 225 + x^2$$
$$400 = x^2$$
$$20 = x$$

14-B   The hydrometer is used to test the specific gravity of the acid in the storage battery. The specific gravity is an index of the extent of charge of the battery.

15-C   Fluorides are added to drinking water to reduce the incidence of dental caries (cavities).

16-C   A *reflex* is a simple inborn response. An *instinct* involves a series of reflexes. A *habit* is an acquired trait. *Phototropism* is a response in plants.

17-B   The Rh factor is an inherited condition of the blood.

18-D   Iron is part of hemoglobin, the pigment of red blood cells.

19-B   Land heats up rapidly in summer and cools off rapidly in winter. The result is the climate found in continental interiors where the winters are extremely cold and the summers extremely hot.

20-C   All freely falling objects, regardless of their masses near the earth, fall towards the earth with equal acceleration. Any two objects at rest that begin to fall at the same instant will have equal velocities at the end of 3 seconds or any other time interval.

21-C   Living things carry on respiration at all times. Respiration in plants goes on independently of photosynthesis, which only occurs in the presence of sunlight.

22-D   Where a place is heated, the warm air rises and overflows, far above the earth, toward a colder region. Meanwhile other unheated air flows in to take its place. This causes a horizontal air current which, when close to the earth's surface, is called wind.

23-B   Mammals appeared most recently on earth.

24-C   White light is a mixture of all of the colors of the spectrum. With the aid of a prism it may be separated into the individual colors.

25-D   A solution has a high ratio of solute to solvent if there is a large amount of solute dissolved in a small amount of solvent. Such a solution, by definition, is a concentrated solution.

2

ARITHMETIC REASONING

Answers

1-B	7-D	13-D	19-D	25-D
2-D	8-D	14-A	20-A	26-A
3-A	9-A	15-C	21-B	27-B
4-B	10-A	16-B	22-C	28-A
5-D	11-D	17-B	23-B	29-D
6-B	12-C	18-B	24-D	30-C

Answers Explained

1-B   The discount is 15% (or 0.15) of the marked price.

$$\$500 \times .15 = \$75$$

The cost is $\$500 - \$75 = \$425$.

Subtract the down payment to find the balance due.

$$\$425 - \$65 = \$360$$

Each installment is $\frac{1}{12}$ of $360.

$$\frac{\$360}{12} = \$30$$

2-D   2 gallons will cover $\frac{1}{4}$ acre.

4×2 gallons, or 8 gallons, will cover 1 acre.

10×8 gallons, or 80 gallons, will cover 10 acres.

Since 2 gallons cover $\frac{1}{4}$ acre, 2×2 gallons, or 4 gallons, cover $\frac{1}{2}$ acre.

80 gallons + 4 gallons, or 84 gallons, will cover $10\frac{1}{2}$ acres.

3-A   The drawing and its enlargement will be similar. Therefore the lengths and widths will be in proportion.

$$\frac{\text{length of original}}{\text{length of enlargement}} = \frac{\text{width of original}}{\text{width of enlargement}}$$

$$\frac{18}{45} = \frac{12}{\text{width of enlargement } (x)}$$

Reduce $\frac{18}{45}$ by dividing numerator and denominator by 9.

$$\frac{2}{5} = \frac{12}{x}$$

To solve, cross-multiply the measurements.

$$2 \times x = 5 \times 12 = 60$$
$$x = \frac{60}{2}$$
$$x = 30$$

4-B   Divide the number of acceptable products by the total number inspected. Then change your answer to a percent.

$$\frac{266}{280} = \frac{133}{140} = \frac{19}{20}$$
$$\frac{19}{20} = \frac{95}{100} = 0.95 = 95\%$$

5-D   If 3 pounds of candy costs $4.80, then 1 pound costs $\$4.80 \div 3$, or $1.60. There are 16 ounces in 1 pound.

1 ounce of the mix costs $\frac{\$1.60}{16} = \$0.10$

5 ounces cost $5 \times \$0.10 = \$0.50$

6-B   The perimeter of a square is the sum of the lengths of all four sides. But the four sides of a square are all equal in length.

The length of one side = 13 feet, 8 inches ÷ 4

Change 1 foot to 12 inches so that 13 feet, 8 inches becomes 12 feet, 20 inches.

12 feet, 20 inches ÷ 4 = 3 feet, 5 inches

7-D   If 20% of the unit are officers, then the percent of enlisted men is
$$100\% - 20\% = 80\%.$$
To find the number of enlisted men, multiply the total number by 80%.

$$360 \times 0.80 = 288.00$$
$$= 288 \text{ enlisted men.}$$

8-D   Her overtime is 10 hours − 8 hours regular work = 2 hours.

2 hours at "time and a half" is paid as $2 \times 1\frac{1}{2}$ hours, or $2 \times \frac{3}{2}$ hours, or $\frac{6}{2}$ hours, or 3 hours.

8 hours + 3 hours = 11 hours of pay.
11 × $8.50 = $93.50

9-A   Find the relationship between each pair of numbers in the series. Thus

$$(2\frac{1}{4}; 3\frac{3}{4}) \quad 2\frac{1}{4} + 1\frac{1}{2} = 3\frac{3}{4}$$

$$(3\frac{3}{4}; 3\frac{1}{4}) \quad 3\frac{3}{4} - 2\frac{1}{2} = 3\frac{1}{4}$$

$$(3\frac{1}{4}; 4\frac{3}{4}) \quad 3\frac{1}{4} + 1\frac{1}{2} = 4\frac{3}{4}$$

The patterns so far is: $+ 1\frac{1}{2} - \frac{1}{2}, + 1\frac{1}{2}$.
To continue the series, subtract $\frac{1}{2}$ from the fourth member of the series.

$$4\frac{3}{4} - \frac{1}{2} = 4\frac{1}{4}$$

10-A   Find the amount collected for adult tickets.

$$265 \times \$4 = \$1,060$$

Out of the $1,200 in receipts, the remainder came from the sale of children's tickets.

$$\$1,200 - \$1,060 = \$140$$

Divide $140 by the price of a child's ticket.

$$\$140 \div \$2 = 70 \text{ tickets}$$

11-D   If she budgets $\frac{1}{4}$ of her income for rent, she has $\frac{3}{4}$ of her income left.

$$\frac{4}{4} - \frac{1}{4} = \frac{3}{4} \text{ (remainder)}$$

She then budgets 5 of this remainder for food.

$$\frac{2}{5} \times \frac{3}{4} = \frac{6}{20} = \frac{3}{10} \text{ (food)}$$

12-C   The 3 who watched 2 hours each watched a total of 3 × 2 hours, or 6 hours. The 2 who watched 1 hour each watched a total of 2 × 1 hours, or 2 hours. 1 watched for 4 hours.
Add the numbers of hours watched.

$$6 + 2 + 4 = 12 \text{ hours (total time spent)}$$

Add the number of people.

3 + 2 + 1 = 6 persons were in the group

Divide the total time spent by the number of persons in the group to find the average number of hours one person watches.

12 hours ÷ 6 persons = 2 hours per person average

13-D   Multiply the cost per yard by the length of the material in yards.

3 feet = 1 yard, so 2 feet = $\frac{2}{3}$ yard.

3 yards, 2 feet = $3\frac{2}{3}$ yards.

$$\$9 \times 3\frac{2}{3} = \frac{9}{1} \times \frac{11}{3} = \$33$$

14-A   Let x represent one of the 9 shares into which the profit must be divided. According to the ratio agreed on, the smaller partner's share is $4x$ and the larger partner's share is $5x$. Together, the shares must add up to the $63,000 profit. This can be written as an equation.

$$4x + 5x = 63,000$$

Solve by combining similar terms.

$$9x = 63,000$$
$$x = 7,000 \text{ (one share)}$$

Multiply the value of 1 share by the number of shares the smaller partner is to get.

$$4x = 4 \times 7,000 = \$28,000$$

15-C   The first courier will travel for 1 hour + 2 hours, or a total of 3 hours, before he is overtaken. Traveling 30 m.p.h. for 3 hours will take the first courier 30 × 3 or 90 miles away.

The second courier must travel the 90 miles in 2 hours. Therefore, he must travel at a rate of 90 ÷ 2 or 45 miles per hour.

16-B   Find the discounted price paid by the merchant.

$60 × 25% = $60 × 0.25
= $15 (discount)
$60 − $15 = $45 (price paid by the merchant)

Next find the merchant's selling price, based on an increase of 20% over the original wholesale price.

$60 × 20% = $60 × 0.20 or
$60 × 5 = $12
(increase over wholesale price)
$60 + $12 = $72 (merchant's selling price)
Finally, find the merchant's profit.

$$\$72 - \$45 = \$27$$

17-B To find the rate of speed when the distance and the time are known, divide the distance, x, by the time, y. x divided by y is expressed as $\frac{x}{y}$.

18-B Since the first 10 words cost $1.50, the balance is left for the cost of the remaining words.

$$\$4.00 - \$1.50 = \$2.50$$

To find the number of words $2.50 will pay for at $0.05 per word, divide $2.50 by $0.05.

$$\$2.50 \div \$0.05 = 250 \div 5 \text{ (clearing decimals)}$$

$$250 \div 5 = 50 \text{ words}$$

50 words added to the first 10 words makes a total of 60 words.

19-D Since 1 inch represents 40 miles, divide 110 miles by 40 miles to find the number of inches required to represent it.

$$110 \div 40 = \frac{110}{40} = \frac{11}{4} = 2\frac{3}{4} \text{ inches}$$

20-A Multiply the purchase price of the home by the assessment rate to find the assessed value.

$$\$80,000 \times 75\% = \$80,000 \times \frac{3}{4} =$$
$$\frac{80,000}{1} \times \frac{3}{4} = \frac{20,000}{1} \times \frac{3}{1} =$$
$$\$60,000 \text{ (assessed value)}$$

find the number of hundreds in the assessed value.

$$60,000 \div 100 = 600 \text{ (hundreds)}$$

Multiply the number of hundreds by the tax rate.

$$600 \times \$4.83 = \$2,898.00 \text{ (tax)}$$

21-B Set up a proportion.

$$\frac{\text{recipe sugar}}{\text{sugar actually used}} = \frac{\text{recipe flour}}{\text{flour actually used}}$$

$$\frac{\frac{3}{4}\text{ cup}}{\frac{1}{4}\text{ cup}} = \frac{4\frac{1}{2}\text{ cups}}{x\text{ cups}} \text{ or } \frac{\frac{3}{4}}{\frac{1}{4}} = \frac{\frac{9}{2}}{x}$$

Simplify each side of the proportion.

$$\frac{3}{4} \div \frac{1}{4} = \frac{3}{4} \times \frac{4}{1} = \frac{3}{1}$$
$$\frac{9}{2} \div \frac{x}{1} = \frac{9}{2} \times \frac{1}{x} = \frac{9}{2x}$$

The proportion becomes $\frac{3}{1} = \frac{9}{2x}$

Solve the proportion by cross-multiplying.

$$6x = 9$$

Divide each side of the equation by 6 to find the value of x.

$$x = \frac{9}{6} = 1\frac{1}{2} \text{ cups of flour}$$

22-C Find the amount of the decline by subtracting.

$$1,200 - 1,044 = 156$$

To find the percent of decline, divide the amount of the decline by the original number of cars crossing the bridge.

$$156 \div 1,200 = \frac{156}{1,200} = \frac{13}{100} = 13\%$$

23-B First find the cost of one gallon. If 2 gallons cost $19.20, 1 gallon will cost $19.20 ÷ 2 or $9.60.
There are 4 quarts in one gallon. Divide the cost of 1 gallon by 4 to find the cost of 1 quart.

$$\$9.60 \div 4 = \$2.40$$

24-D Find the distance he drove on each leg of the trip by multiplying the rate in miles per hour by the time in hours.

$$50 \times 3 = 150 \text{ miles}$$
$$55 \times 2 = 110 \text{ miles}$$

Add the two distances to get the total distance he traveled.

$$150 + 110 \text{ miles} = 260 \text{ miles}$$

Divide the total distance traveled by the number of miles per gallon of gas to get the amount of gas used.

$$260 \div 20 = 13 \text{ gallons}$$

25-D First find the income from the $5,000 invested at 8%.

$$\$5,000 \times 0.08 = \$400.00$$

Next find the income desired from the total investment of $15,000.

$15,000 × 0.09 = $1,350.00

Subtract the income from the first investment to find out how much income she
must get from the second.

$1,350 − $400 = $950

Divide the income, $950, by the invest-
ment, $10,000, to find the rate of interest.

$$\$950 \div \$10,000 = \frac{950}{10,000} = \frac{95}{1,000} =$$

.095 or $9\frac{1}{2}$%

26-A Find the number of hours the generator
operates.
From 9:15 A.M. to 3:15 P.M. is 6 hours
From 3:15 P.M. to 3:55 P.M. is 40
minutes (or $\frac{2}{3}$ of an hour)

6 hours + 40 minutes = $6\frac{2}{3}$ hours

Divide the total time run by the time
provided by one fuel tank filling (1 hour,
20 minutes or $1\frac{1}{3}$ hours).

$$6\frac{2}{3} \div 1\frac{1}{3} = \frac{20}{3} \div \frac{4}{3} = \frac{20}{3} \times \frac{3}{4} = 5 \text{ fillings}$$

27-B Find the total value of each kind of seed
in the mixture.

10 pounds @ $1.20 per pound is worth
10 × $1.20 or $12.00
8 pounds @ $3.00 per pound is worth
8 × $3.00 or $24.00
Add the values of each kind to get the
total value of the mixture.

$12.00 + $24.00 = $36.00

Divide the total value of the mixture by
the total number of pounds, 18, to get the
price per pound.

$36.00 ÷ 18 = $2.00 per pound

28-A First multiply out the numerator.

$$\frac{0.02 \times 3}{0.001} = \frac{0.06}{0.001}$$

Clear the decimal in the divider by
moving the decimal point in both numerator and denominator 3 places to the
right.

$$\frac{0.06}{0.001} = \frac{60}{1} = 60$$

29-D Substitute the number values for the
letters and then do the arithmetic operations.

$$1 + 5xy^2 - 3x^2y \qquad =$$
$$1 + (5 \times x \times y^2) - (3 \times x^2 \times y) =$$
$$1 + (5 \times 3 \times 2^2) - (3 \times 3^2 \times 2) \qquad =$$
$$1 + (5 \times 3 \times 3 \times 4) - (3 \times 9 \times 2) =$$
$$1 + 60 - 54 \qquad = 7$$

30-C Substitute the number values for P and
R.

$$I = \sqrt{\frac{P}{R}}$$

$$I = \sqrt{\frac{48}{3}}$$

$$I = \sqrt{16}$$

The square root of 16 is the number that
when multiplied by itself is 16; therefore
$\sqrt{16}$ = 4.

$$I = 4$$

3

WORD KNOWLEDGE

Answers

1-C	8-D	15-B	22-C	29-A
2-C	9-D	16-D	23-D	30-A
3-B	10-D	17-C	24-A	31-B
4-D	11-D	18-A	25-C	32-C
5-A	12-A	19-A	26-B	33-C
6-B	13-A	20-A	27-D	34-D
7-D	14-C	21-A	28-A	35-C

Answers Explained

1-C Tell, like **inform**, means to communicate knowledge or give information.

2-C **Crimson** is a vivid red or purplish red.

3-B **Caution** means forethought to avoid danger or harm; carefulness.

4-D **Intermittently** means starting and stopping, as in rain starting and stopping at irregular intervals.

5-A Event, like **occurrence**, means a happening or incident.

6-B Fraud, like **deception**, means the use of deceit.

7-D Stop, like **cease**, means to end.

8-D Applause, like **acclaim**, means enthusiastic approval.

9-D Construct, like **erect**, means to raise upright, as to erect or construct a building.

10-D Enjoy, like **relish**, means to take pleasure in.

11-D **Sufficient** means enough, adequate. Of the words given, sufficient most nearly means appropriate, as in a sufficient or appropriate amount.

12-A **Fortnight** means two weeks.

13-A A defect, like a **blemish**, is an imperfection, or fault.

14-C To **impose** or require means to make compulsory.

15-B Scoff, like **jeer**, means to mock or poke fun at.

16-D An assumed name is an **alias**.

17-C Weaken, like **impair**, means to worsen or to damage.

18-A **Itinerant** means traveling, as in an itinerant salesman.

19-A **Relinquish**, like abandon, means to give up possession.

20-A **Resolve** means to bring to a conclusion or end.

21-A Plentiful, like **ample**, means existing in great quantity.

22-C A **stench** is a foul odor; a stink.

23-D Angrily silent, like **sullen**, means resentful.

24-A **Rudiments** are fundamental skills or basic principles, like basic methods and procedures.

25-C To **conflict**, or clash, means to disagree or to be in opposition.

26-B **Camaraderie** means good will and rapport among friends.

27-D Cursory, like **superficial**, means hasty, not thorough.

28-A A **tapestry** is a fabric with multicolored woven designs.

29-A **Terse**, or pointed, as in a terse or pointed

comment, means brief but expressing a great deal.

30-A   A combination of ingredients, as in cookery, is a **concoction**.

31-B   Shortness, or **brevity**, means briefness of duration.

32-C   Mercy, like **clemency**, means leniency, especially toward an offender or enemy.

33-C   Disobedience, like **insubordination**, means failure to recognize authority or to accept the authority of a superior.

34-D   **Preferential** means having or obtaining an advantage, as in receiving special or preferential treatment.

35-C   Low spirits, like **doldrums**, are marked by listlessness, inactivity, or depression.

4

PARAGRAPH COMPREHENSION

Answers

1-A	4-C	7-B	10-C	13-C
2-B	5-B	8-D	11-B	14-C
3-B	6-C	9-B	12-C	15-B

Answers Explained

1-A The main idea of this paragraph is given in the first sentence, which states that professional drivers have a low opinion of the average motorist.

2-B In this selection the word shuddered means shook.

3-B The paragraph clearly states that the Swedes and Finns (these two European peoples) were the first to use the log cabin.

4-C The tone or mood of this passage is one of contentment. The man is described at rest with a smile on his face.

5-B This paragraph points out the favorable or good points about apprentice training. It does not discuss any negative or bad points and it does not compare it to any other type of training.

6-C The paragraph states "we never have enough closets no matter how many closets we have."

7-B A reactionary person looks to the past. The paragraph describes a liberal, using the key word liberal or free. The words "on the other hand" tell you that the description was shifting from one way to another.

8-D You can infer from the passage that a conservation group wrote it. A lumber company or house-building company would more likely want to cut the forest to use the lumber in its businesses.

There is no reason to think that a religious group wrote the paragraph.

9-B The time for action suggests that the bridge should be built but the paragraph makes it clear that official action — approval of bonds — must be taken first.

10-C The paragraph describes lightning as a "spark" and as a "release of energy."

11-B The paragraph clearly states that the morning rush hour starts two hours before 9 a.m.

12-C Acuity means sharpness. If you do not know the meaning of the word you can figure it out from the context. You can immediately eliminate A; you can eliminate D because pressure is referred to in the phrase "eye pressure." You must then choose between strength and sharpness and in terms of the subject of this passage — vision — sharpness is more accurate.

13-C More than one seed of wheat has to be tested to form a conclusion.

14-C The last sentence states that bread and cereal provide 40% of the daily needs of thiamine, one of the B vitamins.

15-B The second sentence states that most problems came from poor medical knowledge and lack of ways to fight disease.

5

NUMERICAL OPERATIONS

Answers

1-C	11-A	21-C	31-C	41-B
2-B	12-C	22-A	32-B	42-A
3-C	13-D	23-B	33-B	43-B
4-C	14-B	24-D	34-D	44-C
5-A	15-A	25-C	35-A	45-B
6-D	16-A	26-A	36-C	46-C
7-B	17-C	27-D	37-A	47-D
8-A	18-D	28-B	38-B	48-A
9-B	19-B	29-C	39-C	49-B
10-C	20-B	30-A	40-D	50-C

Answers Explained

There is no analysis of the answers for this part of the test. See Review Section on Mathematical Knowledge for general information.

6

CODING SPEED

Answers

1. C	13. B	25. C	37. D	49. D	61. D	73. E
2. A	14. C	26. C	38. C	50. C	62. A	74. C
3. B	15. D	27. A	39. C	51. B	63. D	75. C
4. D	16. B	28. B	40. A	52. C	64. B	76. C
5. B	17. A	29. A	41. B	53. B	65. D	77. C
6. B	18. E	30. D	42. A	54. A	66. C	78. A
7. C	19. B	31. B	43. B	55. E	67. A	79. C
8. A	20. D	32. B	44. E	56. C	68. B	80. A
9. C	21. D	33. A	45. A	57. C	69. B	81. C
10. D	22. C	34. C	46. B	58. A	70. A	82. B
11. D	23. B	35. D	47. C	59. C	71. B	83. E
12. B	24. D	36. C	48. D	60. E	72. E	84. C

7

AUTO AND SHOP INFORMATION

Answers

1-A	6-A	11-B	16-A	21-B
2-C	7-B	12-B	17-A	22-D
3-D	8-C	13-A	18-D	23-A
4-D	9-B	14-B	19-B	24-C
5-C	10-D	15-D	20-C	25-B

Answers Explained

1-A The universal joint allows the drive shaft to move up and down as the road surface changes. At least one, and in most instances two, are needed for rear wheel drive cars and trucks.

2-C Much attention has been given to the pollutants emitted from today's cars. Nitrous oxides (NO_x) are of particular concern and the air pump and the catalytic converter have been added to reduce these emissions. Hydrocarbons, carbon monoxide and the oxides of nitrogen are of concern since they can contaminate the air and kill trees, plants, and small animals as well as damage the lungs of humans.

3-D The catalytic converter eliminates some pollutants and reduces other pollutants. It reaches high temperatures and needs to be shielded from the body of the car by a heat deflector. An air pump is used on most late model cars to add to the combustion that takes place inside the converter and helps to reduce the amount of NO_x emitted from the exhaust pipe.

4-D The differential is located in the rear of the car when it is a rear wheel drive. It is located in front of the car on a front wheel drive vehicle. It consists of two small bevel gears on the ends of the axle shafts that are mounted in the differential frame. These bevel gears mesh with others to allow one wheel to turn faster than the other whenever the car makes a turn around a curve.

5-C The PCV valve is used to recirculate the fumes that would normally be exhausted to the atmosphere from the crankcase. By recirculating these fumes it is possible to cut down on the hydrocarbon contents of auto exhaust. This valve provides positive crankcase ventilation from the valve cover through the carburetor for recirculation.

6-A One of the ways to reduce the NO_x produced by the combustion of the internal combustion engine is to dilute the air/fuel mixture as it enters the combustion chamber.

7-B The number of teeth in a gear determines its speed when meshed with a second gear with similar teeth. The number of teeth in one gear is compared to the number of teeth in the one it meshes with. The number of teeth in the first gear as compared to the second is the gear ratio. If, for instance, one gear has 16 teeth and the one it meshes with has only 8 the gear ratio is 2:1 or 2 to 1. The gear with the greater number of teeth always turns slower and produces greater torque than the gear with the smaller number of teeth.

8-C The clutch is used to disconnect the engine from the wheels while the car is in neutral or when gears are being shifted.

9-B The first gear is used because of its ability to produce the starting torque needed to get the car moving from a stand-still. The internal combustion engine is known as a fast engine. It must be revving up pretty fast to develop the torque needed to start the car rolling.

10-D The torque converter is located in the automatic transmission. It produces the torque needed to get the car started and to change speeds. Most torque converter transmissions also provide an intermediate and low gear range that can aid in braking the car when coming down steep hills and in hard pulling.

11-B Disc brakes use two pads to grasp the rotor that is attached to the wheel. The pads press against the rotor (disc) from both sides to make a faster and surer stop with little fading on hot days and with heavy braking.

12-B The transmission on front wheel cars is located in the front engine compartment. It must be small enough to fit into the space allowed for the engine and the accessories. It took a few years to design a transmission to fit in front with the engine and leave space for the accessories needed to cause the engine to function properly.

13-A L_o or L on older automatic transmissions were the same as 1st gear in manual transmissions. In most recent cars the L has been replaced by a 1 to indicate 1st gear and 2 to represent 2nd gear instead of D_1, S, or L_2.

14-B Park (P) position on the automatic transmission gear selector indicator represents the position that locks up the transmission and prevents the wheels from rolling. The car is in neutral when placed in park and can be started only when in Park or Neutral.

15-D The internal combustion engine is best described as a high speed engine. We cannot run an internal combustion engine at slow speed and get enough torque to get the vehicle moving. A higher speed engine is needed to produce the torque. That is where the transmission plays an important role in allowing the engine to speed up and still not have a very fast moving drive shaft connected to the wheels. The transmission's gear ratio plays a role in producing the torque needed to get the car moving from a resting position.

16-A In a four-wheel drive vehicle the transfer case is used to drive the front wheels while the conventional transmission drives the rear wheels. The case has a set of three gears meshing together in series and extending outside to one side of the transmission.

17-A The folding rule is well known for breaking easily when it is twisted the least bit.

18-D The mitre box uses the back saw — the one with the metal band across the top of it — to cut angles as needed or provided by the type of mitre box being used.

19-B In order to shape concrete it is placed in a *form*.

20-C In concrete work the "darby" is made of wood and is used to float the concrete after it has set for the proper length of time.

21-B Nail sets are used to set nails just below the surface of the wood. Then a filler is added before painting or finishing so that there is a smooth surface.

22-D A scratch awl is used to do many things, one of which is to mark wood where you want to cut it. A saw is used to cut wood. A plane is used to smooth wood. A screwdriver is used to drive screws.

23-A In selecting the proper grinding wheel there are a number of things to be considered, one of the important being the proper grain size for the job to be done.

24-C Gold can be hammered into leaves so thin that it takes a fine camel haired brush to pick them up. This is usually the way gold is placed on the domes of state capitol buildings. Once placed on the surface it is burnished or rubbed with a piece of smooth metal to make the extremely thin foil stick to the surface being coated.

25-B When making a hole in sheet metal it is safer for the person performing the work to punch the hole rather than drill it. If the piece of sheet metal is not properly secured the drill bit will catch and cause it to be whirled, possibly cutting the operator who may not be quick enough to get out of the way of the spinning object.

8

MATHEMATICS KNOWLEDGE

Answers

1-C	6-C	11-A	16-B	21-D
2-A	7-D	12-B	17-A	22-B
3-B	8-A	13-A	18-C	23-C
4-B	9-B	14-B	19-C	24-C
5-D	10-D	15-D	20-A	25-C

Answers Explained

1-C First isolate all terms containing x on one side of the equation and all terms not containing x on the other side. To do this, add x to both sides of the equation and also subtract 6 from both sides of the equation. Remember to change the sign of any term when it is moved from one side of the equation to the other.

$$2x + x + 6 - 6 = 12 - 6 - x + x$$
$$3x = 6$$

Divide each side of the equation by 3 to undo the multiplication of 3 by x.

$$\frac{3x}{3} = \frac{6}{3}$$
$$x = 2$$

2-A Write the binomial to be subtracted underneath the binomial from which it is to be subtracted, placing similar terms in the same columns.

$$\text{From} \qquad 8x^2 - 7x$$
$$\text{Subtract} \quad -3x^2 + 2x$$

Change the signs of the terms in the bottom row (the subtrahend) and combine the similar terms in each column.

$$8x^2 - 7x$$
$$3x^2 - 2x$$
$$\overline{11x^2 - 9x}$$

3-B Multiply $3x^2y$ by $2x^3y$ and also multiply -4 by $2x^3y$. To multiply $3x^2y$ by $2x^3y$, first multiply their numerical factors.

$$3 \times 2 = 6$$

To multiply powers of the same letter, add the exponents. Remember that y stands for y^1. Thus, $x^2 \times x^3 = x^5$ and $y \times y = y^2$.

$$2x^3y \times (3x^2y - 4) = 6x^5y^2 - 8x^3y$$

4-B Add the portions that each one does.

$$\frac{1}{3} + \frac{1}{5}$$

To add fractions, they must have a common denominator. The least common denominator for 3 and 5 is 15, the smallest number into which they both divide evenly. Change $\frac{1}{3}$ and $\frac{1}{5}$ to equivalent fractions having 15 as their denominator. Fractions with the same denominator may be added by adding their numerators.

$$\frac{5}{15} + \frac{3}{15} = \frac{8}{15}$$

5-D Subtract the length of the piece to be cut off.

$$5 \text{ feet,} \quad 3 \text{ inches}$$
$$- 3 \text{ feet,} \quad 9 \text{ inches}$$

Since we cannot subtract 9 inches from 3 inches, we borrow 1 foot from the 5 feet and convert it to 12 inches; thus 5 feet, 3 inches becomes 4 feet, 15 inches.

$$4 \text{ feet, 15 inches}$$
$$- 3 \text{ feet,} \quad 9 \text{ inches}$$
$$\overline{1 \text{ foot,} \quad 6 \text{ inches}}$$

6-C A hexagon is a polygon having 6 sides. If it has 6 sides, it must also have 6 angles. The sum of the 6 equal angles is 6 times the size of one of them.

$$6 \times 120° = 720°$$

7-D Set up the product like a multiplication example in arithmetic. Multiply each term of $(3a - 2)$ by a and write the results as the first line of partial products. Remember that the product of a positive number and a negative number is negative. Next multiply each term of $(3a - 2)$ by $+3$ and write the results as the second line of partial products. Add the partial products as you do in arithmetic to get the final answer.

$$
\begin{array}{r}
3a - 2 \\
a + 3 \\
\hline
3a^2 - 2a \\
+ 9a - 6 \\
\hline
3a^2 + 7a - 6
\end{array}
$$

8-A   Substitute 3 for x in the given expression.

$|x - 7|$ becomes $|3 - 7|$ or $|-4|$

$|-4|$ stands for the absolute value of -4. The absolute value of a number is its value without regard to sign. Thus, $|+4|$ equals 4, and $|-4|$ also equals 4.

9-B   To solve these equations for x, we must eliminate y. First multiply both sides of the first equation by 2.

$$2 \times (3x + y) = 2 \times 13$$
$$6x + 2y = 26$$

Adding the original second equation to the new form of the first equation will eliminate y.

$$
\begin{array}{r}
6x + 2y = 26 \\
x - 2y = 2 \\
\hline
7x = 28
\end{array}
$$

Divide both sides of the equation by 7 to undo the multiplication of x by 7.

$$\frac{7x}{7} = \frac{28}{7}$$

$$x = 4$$

10-D   Convert all units of measure to inches.

In 1 yard, there are 36 inches, so in y yards there are y times as many, or $36y$. The total length of y yards and i inches, expressed in inches, is $36y + i$ inches.

There are 12 inches in 1 foot. To find the number of feet in $36y + i$ inches, divide $36y + i$ by 12.

$$(36y + i) \div 12 = \frac{36y + i}{12}$$

11-A   The goal is to find an equation with F alone on one side and all other letters and numbers on the other side.

Begin by multiplying both sides of the formula by 9 to get rid of the fraction.

$$9 \times C = 9 \times \frac{5}{9}(F - 32)$$

$$9C = 5(F - 32)$$

Next remove the parentheses by multiplying each term inside them by 5.

$$9C = 5 \times F - 5 \times 32$$
$$9C = 5F - 160$$

To isolate the term containing F on one side of the equation, add 160 to both sides of the equation.

$$9C + 160 = 5F - 160 + 160$$
$$9C + 160 = 5F$$

To get an expression for F alone, divide both sides of the equation by 5.

$$\frac{9C + 160}{5} = \frac{5F}{5}$$

$$\frac{9}{5}C + 32 = F$$

The equation may be transposed to read

$$F = \frac{9}{5}C + 32.$$

12-B   The path directly east forms a right angle with the path directly north. The distance from the starting point is measured on the third side (or hypotenuse) of the right triangle which contains the paths to the east and to the north.

The Pythagorean Theorem states that in any right triangle, the square of the hypotenuse (c^2) equals the sum of the square of the other two sides, $a^2 + b^2$.

$$\text{Thus, } c^2 = a^2 + b^2$$
$$c^2 = 3^2 + 4^2$$

Perform the arithmetic operations.

$$c^2 = 9 + 16$$
$$c^2 = 25$$

To find c, take the square root of both sides of the equation. The square root of a number is another number which, when multiplied by itself, equals the original number. Thus, the square root of 25 is 5, and the square root of c^2 is c.

$$c = 5$$

13-A   The line perpendicular to the base of the triangle makes a right angle with the base; a right angle contains 90°.

An equilateral triangle has 3 equal sides and 3 equal angles. Since the sum of all 3 angles of any triangle is 180°, each angle of an equilateral triangle is $\frac{180°}{3}$ or 60°.

The 60° angle must be subtracted from the 90° angle to find the angle formed by the perpendicular and the other side of the triangle.

$$90° - 60° = 30°$$

14-B   The inequality, $x - 5 \leq 5$, is a statement that x minus 6 is less than or equal to 5.

To solve this inequality, isolate x on one side of it by adding 6 to both sides.

$$x - 6 + 6 \leq 5 + 6$$
$$x \leq 11$$

The solution states that the inequality is true if x has any value less than or equal to 11. For example, suppose $x = 9$. Substitute 9 for x in the original inequality:

$$9 - 6 \leq 5$$
$$3 \leq 5, \text{ which is a true statement.}$$

15-D   If the same fence fits around the rectangle and the square field, then their perimeters are equal. The perimeter of a rectangle is the sum of the lengths of its four sides.

$$P = 40 + 36 + 40 + 36$$
$$P = 152 \text{ feet}$$

The perimeter of a square is the sum of its four equal sides. Therefore, the length of one side is the perimeter divided by 4.

$$152 \div 4 = 38 \text{ feet}$$

16-B   The volume of a rectangular box is equal to the length times the width times the height.

The volume of one individual-sized box $= 3 \times 2 \times 4 = 24$ cubic inches.

The volume of one family-sized box $= 8 \times 3 \times 12 = 8 \times 36 = 288$ cubic inches.

Divide the volume of the larger box by the volume of the smaller box.

$$288 \div 24 = 12$$

17-A   Rotation of a wheel as it rolls on the ground has the effect of "laying out" its circumference along the ground. One rotation will move the wheel along by a distance equal to the circumference. The circumference, C, of a circle is given by the formula, $C = 2 \times Pi \times R$, where R is the radius, or by the formula, $C = Pi \times D$, where D is the diameter. If the first formula is used, R can be computed since the radius is one-half the diameter. However, it is easier in this case to use the second formula since we are given the diameter.

$$C = \frac{22}{7} \times 14 = \frac{22}{7} \times \frac{14}{1} = \frac{22}{1} \times \frac{2}{1} =$$
44 inches

18-C   The sine of an angle in a right triangle is the ratio of the length of the side opposite the angle to the length of the hypotenuse. If the unknown length is x, the ratio of x to the length of the hypotenuse must be the same as the ratio, $\frac{3}{7}$.

$$\frac{x}{21} = \frac{3}{7}$$

To solve for x in this proportion, cross-multiply.

$$7 \times x = 3 \times 21$$
$$7x = 63$$

To undo the multiplication of 7 by x, divide both sides of the equation by 7.

$$\frac{7x}{7} = \frac{63}{7}$$
$$x = 9$$

19-C $- x^4$ means $- (x)(x)(x)(x)$.
Substitute 0.1 for x.
$$- x^4 = - (0.1)(0.1)(0.1)(0.1)$$
To multiply $(0.1)(0.1)(0.1)(0.1)$, remember that the number of decimal places in the product is the total of the number of decimal places in the numbers being multiplied together.

$$- x^4 = - 0.0001$$

20-A   Change 30% to a decimal and let x represent the total number of apartments. 30% of x is 108.

$$.30x = 108 \text{ or } .3x = 108$$

Clear the decimals by multiplying both sides of the equation by 10.

$$10 \times .3x = 10 \times 108$$
$$3x = 1080$$

Undo the multiplication of 3 by x by dividing both sides of the equation by 3.

$$\frac{3x}{3} = \frac{1080}{3}$$
$$x = 360$$

21-D   Let x equal the mark on the fourth test. The average is obtained by dividing the sum of the four marks by 4.

$$\frac{60 + 60 + 70 + x}{4} = 75$$

To remove the fraction, multiply both sides of the equation by 4.

$$4 \times \frac{60 + 60 + 70 + x}{4} = 4 \times 75$$

$$60 + 60 + 70 + x = 300$$

$$190 + x = 300$$

To isolate x on one side, subtract 190 from both sides of the equation.

$$190 - 190 + x = 300 - 190$$

$$x = 110$$

He would need 110% on the fourth test, which is impossible.

22-B   First find the distance traveled. Distance traveled is found by multiplying rate of speed by time.

3 hours × 40 miles per hour = 120 miles

2 hours × 50 miles per hour = 100 miles

The entire trip was 120 miles + 100 miles, or 220 miles.

The total time was 3 hours + 2 hours, or 5 hours.

The average rate of speed is obtained by dividing the total distance by the total time.

220 miles ÷ 5 hours = 44 miles per hour

23-C   The radar is capable of covering a complete circle whose radius is 10 miles. First find the area of this circle, using the formual, $A = Pi, \times R^2$, where R is the radius.

$A = 3.14 \times 10^2 = 3.14 \times 100 = 314$ square miles

There are 360° of rotation in the complete circle. If the radar is used to cover portion of this, it covers $\frac{36}{360}$ or $\frac{1}{10}$ of the complete circle.

$$\frac{1}{10} \times 314 = 31.4 \text{ square miles}$$

24-C   To solve a quadratic equation like $x^2 + 2x = 15$, first move all terms to the same side of the equation so that they equal 0 on the other side.

$$x^2 + 2x - 15 = 0$$

Find the two binomial factors that would multiply to produce the polynomial on the left side. The factors of the first term, x^2, are x and x. Use them as the first term in each of the binomial factors.

$$(x \quad)(x \quad) = 0$$

Now find the two numbers that would multiply together to give 15. They could be 15 and 1 or 5 and 3. Remember that when multiplying the two binomials together, $+2x$ must result for the middle term. This suggests that $+5x$ and $-3x$ were added to give $+2x$. Therefore, $+5$ and -3 are the factors to choose for -15.

$$(x + 5)(x - 3) = 0$$

The equation is now in a form in which the product of two factors equals 0. This is possible if either one or both of the factors equals 0.

$$x + 5 = 0 \qquad x - 3 = 0$$

$$x = -5 \qquad x = 3$$

These results may be checked by substituting them in the original equation.

$$x^2 + 2x = 15 \qquad\qquad x^2 + 2x = 15$$

$$(-5)^2 + 2(-5) = 15 \qquad (3)^2 + 2(3) = 15$$

$$25 - 10 = 15 \qquad\qquad 9 + 6 = 15$$

$$15 = 15 \checkmark \qquad\qquad 15 = 15 \checkmark$$

25-C   First find the number of quarts of antifreeze in the original mixture.

$.25 \times 12$ or $\frac{1}{4} \times 12 = 3$ quarts of antifreeze

Let x equal the number of quarts of water to be added. The total mixture will now be $12 + x$ quarts. 20% of the new total mixture will be the 3 quarts of antifreeze still present in the mixture.

$.20(12 + x) = 3$ or $.2(12 + x) = 3$

Remove the parentheses by multiplying each term inside by .2.

$$2.4 + .2x = 3$$

Clear decimals by multiplying each term in the equation by 10.

$$10 \times 2.4 + 10 \times .2x = 10 \times 3$$

$$24 + 2x = 30$$

Isolate the term containing x by subtracting 24 from both sides of the equation.

$$24 - 24 + 2x = 30 - 24$$

$$2x = 6$$

Undo the multiplication of 2 by x by dividing both sides of the equation by 2.

$$\frac{2x}{2} = \frac{6}{2}$$

$$x = 3$$

9

MECHANICAL COMPREHENSION

Answers

1-A	6-A	11-B	16-D	21-A
2-C	7-D	12-D	17-C	22-B
3-D	8-C	13-C	18-B	23-A
4-B	9-B	14-B	19-A	24-A
5-B	10-A	15-C	20-C	25-B

Answers Explained

1-A   Air flowing over the top of the wing creates a vacuum and the air underneath remains relatively the same. That means the upward push of the air under the wing into the vacuum above is rather easy. So, most of the lift on an aircraft's wing is because of a decrease in pressure on the upper side.

2-C   *Capillary* action is responsible for the wax creeping up the wick and the water remaining on the sides of the small tube once the major portion of the water is back in a lower level. *Osmosis* is the gradual penetration of a shell or membrane. Erosion is the wearing away by wind or water or some gradual process.

3-D   Two dissimilar metals put together expand at different rates so they can be used to form a thermostat — to move a switch and turn a furnace or other object on or off as the temperature makes the metals expand or contract.

4-B   Aluminum is the metal that expands the most of those listed. Tungsten expands very little even at high temperatures and is used for incandescent lamp filaments.

5-B   As the cold causes the pendulum to contract it is shortened. This shortened pendulum causes the clock to run faster since it moves back and forth more quickly.

6-A   Heat is a form of energy. The calorie is one unit of measurement of heat. Thermals are usually upward movements of columns of air caused by heat rising.

7-D   The best conductor of heat of the metals listed is silver. Aluminum expands rapidly but it does not conduct heat as readily as does silver since it does not have its atoms as closely packed as silver.

8-C   There are three ways of transferring heat from one place to another: conduction, convection and radiation.

9-B   Putting salt into water increases the specific gravity of the solution and lowers its freezing point.

10-A   Changing a liquid to a gas or vapor is called evaporation. Boiling is one method of accomplishing the process.

11-B   Adding heat to a container of boiling water that is totally enclosed increases the pressure of the steam inside the compartment or container and increases the temperature of the water. This can be very dangerous if the container is not capable of handling the pressure.

12-D   Fractional distillation is the process used to produce gasoline, kerosene, tar and heating oil as well as other products from petroleum.

13-C   Sound travels at 1086 feet per second at 0°C. It travels at 1492 meters per second in sea water and at 3500 meters per second in copper. The speed of light is 186,000 miles per second.

14-B   The meter used to measure extremely high resistances is called a *megger* since the units of measurement will be in the millions, or megs.

15-C   The hole is being tapped with a tap. This tool is used to make threads in the drilled hole.

16-D The units shown are a few of the many types of devices used to muffle the noise made by small gasoline engines.

17-C Outboard engines use the lake, river, or water that they are placed in to obtain cooling water. The water pump pulls the water into the engine and circulates it to the areas that need cooling.

18-B The drop of the ball prevents all the gasoline from draining from the carburetor so it can be easily started again if the need arises quickly after the loss of suction or a few days later.

19-A The shape of the cutter tells you its type. This type of cutter cuts a rounded groove. The groove cut is the opposite of the shape of the cutter itself. A concave shaped cutter cuts a convex groove and the convex cutter makes a concave shaped groove.

20-C The die is mounted in the tool that fits over the end of the pipe. The die is then rotated to cut threads on the pipe.

21-A The tool holder shown here is made for use in a tool post on a lathe. The tool bit is shaped to do whatever job is desired.

22-B The thickness gage shown here is used most often in automotive work to set points, check clearances of valves, and check other tolerances.

23-A This is the American Standard Wire Gage. It can also be used to check the gage of sheet metal and small diameter rods.

24-A The evaporator of the refrigerator is located inside the refrigerator in the food compartment or freezer, depending on the model. The evaporator allows the freon to vaporize and take the heat inside the food compartment or freezer to the outside to be dissipated into the room.

25-B Freon is used as the refrigerant for all home equipment and air conditioners for cars. Sulfur dioxide is rarely used today. It was once used in ship cooling and freezing units. Water is used as a refrigerant in some large commercial and industrial processes. Ammonia is used in large freezer plants for making ice or freezing on a commercial scale.

10

ELECTRONICS INFORMATION

Answers

1-A	5-A	9-C	13-B	17-A
2-C	6-A	10-C	14-A	18-D
3-D	7-B	11-D	15-B	19-B
4-A	8-D	12-A	16-A	20-C

Answers Explained

1-A   When copper is inserted inside a coil, it makes the inductance decrease.

2-C   Permeability is the ease with which magnetic lines of force distribute themselves throughout a material.

3-D   The area of the plates, distance between the plates, and the material of the dielectric all have a direct relationship on the capacitance of a capacitor. The voltage on the capacitor does not have an effect on its capacitance.

4-A   When capacitors are placed in series it is the same as placing the plates farther apart. This causes a decrease in the amount of capacitance for the series combination.

5-A   Capacitive reactance is equal to the reciprocal of the product of 2π FC.

6-A   Capacitors connected in parallel effectively increase the plate area. That allows for more storage of electrons and more capacity or capacitance.

7-B   Impedance of a series RL circuit can be found by taking the square root of the sum of the squares of the resistance and inductance. Inductance is in henrys and the resistance is in ohms.

8-D   Resonance occurs in any circuit when the inductive reactance and the capacitive reactance are equal.

9-C   A filter is placed in the power supply to smooth out the voltage variations. In some cases a choke is used in the filter to smooth out the current variations.

10-C   Another name for the transistor is the crystal amplifier. It has also been called the transfer resistor from which it takes its name *trans-istor*.

11-D   Radio frequency amplifiers are used in receivers and transmitters to amplify frequencies above the human hearing range.

12-A   A crystal microphone relies upon the piezoelectrical effect where a pressure on a crystal produces an electric current.

13-B   The voice coil of a speaker usually has a very low impedance. Some specially made speakers have higher impedances to match the system.

14-A   A crossover network is designed to make sure that the right frequencies get to a speaker so it can reproduce them better.

15-B   The klystron is used as a frequency source in microwave units — whether it be a microwave range for the kitchen or a radar unit for an aircraft.

16-A   The two basic types of oscillators used in microwave installations are the klystron and magnetron.

17-A   The two general types of diodes are the semiconductor and the vacuum tube diode. Both types have particular applications and advantages.

18-D   Color television uses red, blue and green guns to direct electron streams toward the phosphors in the front of the picture tube. They produce the full color spectrum when combined properly.

19-B   The folded dipole antenna has an impedance of 300 ohms. It is the one most commonly used for home television reception. The dipole has an impedance of 72 ohms.

20-C   Television sets in the USA use a horizontal frequency of 15,750 Hz while those in Europe use 15,625 Hz. There are 525 lines that make up the television picture in the USA but 625 in Europe. The vertical oscillator frequency is 60 Hz in the USA but 50 in Europe.

14   ANALYZING YOUR TESTS

After you take the first Model Test, record your scores on the Progress Chart. Find out the subjects in which you have the lowest scores and study those topics. Then take Model Test Two and Three and see your progress as your scores rise.

PROGRESS CHART

Subtest	Number of Questions	Your Number Correct			Scale
		TEST ONE	**TEST TWO**	**TEST THREE**	
1. General Science	25				23-25 right— excellent 22 right— good 21 right— fair under 21 right— poor
2. Arithmetic Reasoning	30				28-30 right— excellent 27 right— good 26 right— fair under 26 right— poor
3. Word Knowledge	35				32-35 right— excellent 31 right— good 30 right— fair under 30 right— poor
4. Paragraph Comprehension	15				15 right— excellent 14 right— good 13 right— fair under 13 right— poor
5. Numerical Operations	50				46-50 right— excellent 43-45 right— good 42 right— fair under 42 right— poor
6. Coding Speed	84				76-80 right— excellent 73-75 right— good 72 right— fair under 72 right— poor
7. Auto and Shop Information	25				23-25 right— excellent 22 right— good 21 right— fair under 21 right— poor
8. Mathematics Knowledge	25				
9. Mechanical Comprehension	25				
10. Electronics Information	20				19-20 right— excellent 18 right— good 17 right— fair under 17 right— poor

Study Guide

After you finish each test, determine your score, and record it on the Progress Chart. You should plan how and what to study to improve your scores.

• If you are weak in Subtest 1 then concentrate on Chapter 4 — General Science Review.

• If you are weak in Subtests 2, 5, and 8, then concentrate on Chapter 5 — Mathematics Review.

• If you are weak in Subtests 3 and 4, then concentrate on Chapter 6 — Paragraph Comprehension and Word Knowledge Review.

• If you are weak in Subtest 6, then concentrate on Chapter 7 — Coding Speed Skills.

• If you are weak in Subtest 7 then concentrate on Chapters 8 and 9 — Auto and Shop Information Reviews.

• If you are weak in Subtest 9, then concentrate on Chapter 10 — Basic Mechanics Review.

• If you are weak in Subtest 10, then concentrate on Chapter 11 — Electronics Review.

Note: Consider yourself weak in a section if you receive other than an excellent rating in it.

15 Analyzing Your Job Opportunities

The ASVAB test, first administered on July 1, 1984, is designed to evaluate your potential for further formal education, as well as your aptitude in vocational-technical career fields. It does this by providing two types of composites: *academic* and *occupational*. Each type contributes to understanding your ASVAB results and their relation to career exploration and decision-making. An explanation of each composite follows.

Academic Composites

The *academic composites* report your potential for further formal education and indicate performance in general areas requiring verbal and mathematical skills. The three *academic composites* are listed and defined below.

Composite	Potential ✓	Subtest Composition	Purpose
VERBAL	___ ___	(Word Knowledge + Paragraph Comprehension) + General Science	Measures capacity for verbal activities
MATH	___ ___	Mathematics Knowledge + Arithmetic Reasoning	Measures capacity for mathematical activities
ACADEMIC ABILITY	___ ___	(Word Knowledge + Paragraph Comprehension)* + Arithmetic Reasoning	Measures potential for further formal education

*Subtests in brackets are weighted as one unit.

Occupational Composites

The *occupational composites* report your aptitude in four career areas and can be used to make predictions about future occupational performance. The *occupational composites*, determined empirically as effective predictors of performance in military jobs, are listed below, along with the subtests which make them up, and examples of civilian counterparts of military jobs associated with each composite.

Composite	Potential ✓	Subtest Composition	Sample Occupational Groupings
MECHANICAL & CRAFTS	___ ___ ___ ___	Arithmetic Reasoning + Mechanical Comprehension + Auto and Shop Information + Electronics Information	Machinist Auto Mechanic Diesel Mechanic Sheet Metal Worker Carpenter
BUSINESS & CLERICAL	___ ___ ___	(Word Knowledge + Paragraph Comprehension)* + Mathematics Knowledge + Coding Speed	Clerk Typist Personnel Clerk Transport. Agent Data Entry Oper. Paralegal Assist.

Composite	Potential ✓	Subtest Composition	Sample Occupational Groupings
ELECTRONICS & ELECTRICAL	____ ____ ____ ____	Arithmetic Reasoning + Mathematics Knowledge + Electronics Information + General Science	TV and Radio Repair, Automatic Equipment Technician, Line Installer-Repairer, Electrician
HEALTH, SOCIAL, & TECHNOLOGY	____ ____	(Word Knowledge + Paragraph Comprehension)* + Arithmetic Reasoning + Mechanical Comprehension	Medical Service Technician, Computer Operator, Police Officer, Dental Technician, Fire Fighter

*Subtests in brackets are weighted as one unit.

You can determine your areas of greatest potential by analyzing your test scores on the Model Exams, and then determining how these scores relate to the composites above. In order to do this, turn to the Progress Chart on page 455 and note the areas in which you did well on each test by putting a "✓" mark in the table below. (Note: Consider that you did well in a section only if you received an excellent rating in it. You will probably find that your scores have some consistency, and you will see check marks for the same subtests on each examination.)

Finding Your Best Test Areas

Subtests	Model Exam One	Model Exam Two	Model Exam Three
1. General Science	____	____	____
2. Arithmetic Reasoning	____	____	____
3. Word Knowledge	____	____	____
4. Paragraph Comprehension	____	____	____
5. Numerical Operations	____	____	____
6. Coding Speed	____	____	____
7. Auto and Shop Information	____	____	____
8. Mathematics Knowledge	____	____	____
9. Mechanical Comprehension	____	____	____
10. Electronics Information	____	____	____

Then, for all subtests for which you have placed a "check" mark, place another check mark in the tables labeled "Academic Composites" and "Occupational Composites." This will help you pinpoint your areas of greatest strength.

If you did better in the Academic Composites, seriously consider furthering your formal education. If you did better in the Occupational Composites, consider which occupation you might like. *In any event, remember that a test* **cannot** *tell everything about your abilities.* Don't think that a low score must mean a lack of aptitude. Many factors that have nothing to do with aptitude could have influenced your score, such as a lack of experience with the subject matter tested or the lack of school courses on the information tested. Nevertheless, the ASVAB can give you some ideas about careers and can show you a general pattern of occupational interest.